Employee Benefits Glossary

13th Edition

Employee Benefits Glossary

13th Edition

Edited by Patricia A. Bonner, Ph.D., CEBS

International Foundation
OF EMPLOYEE BENEFIT PLANS
Education | Research | Leadership

Copies of this book may be obtained from:
    Publications Department
    International Foundation of Employee Benefit Plans
    18700 West Bluemound Road
    Brookfield, WI 53045

Payment must accompany order.

Call (888) 334-3327, option 4, for price information, or see www.ifebp.org/bookstore.

Published in 2016 by the International Foundation of Employee Benefit Plans, Inc.
©2016 International Foundation of Employee Benefit Plans, Inc.
All rights reserved.
Library of Congress Control Number: 2016931764
ISBN 978-0-89154-7570
Printed in the United States of America

CONTENTS

Foreword vii

Acknowledgments ix

Glossary 1

Appendix A: Affordable Care Act of 2010 (ACA) 249

Appendix B: Acronyms and Abbreviations 255

FOREWORD

Four decades have passed since the International Foundation of Employee Benefit Plans first compiled this glossary to bring together, in one volume, the diverse terminology used by those in the employee benefits field. With this updated 13th edition, the International Foundation continues its commitment to providing a practical, easy-to-use guide to benefit and compensation terms that will be a valuable resource for benefit plan trustees, administrators and other benefits stakeholders.

This new version of the glossary defines a record 4,000-plus terms. More than 700 of these terms are new. Many other terms have been revised to reflect changing public policies and the evolving interests of those in the benefits arena. Definitions for the terms in this book have been derived from current Canadian and U.S. sources covering the following:

- Compensation
- Employee benefits design, funding and administration
- Government programs, regulations and legislation
- Health care and health care cost-containment strategies
- Human resources
- Insurance
- Investments
- Labor relations
- Taxes.

Special features of this publication include:

- A 6-page section devoted to the Affordable Care Act of 2010—providing explanations of key terms and summarizing some of the most important changes that are part of this landmark health care reform package

- At the back of the book, a list of over 1,100 acronyms and abbreviations covering a wide range of benefit-related topics.

Please keep in mind that this glossary has been created to provide you with a starting point when you are seeking information on a particular employee benefits topic; it should not be viewed as a definitive source. Every effort has been made to present accurate and up-to-date information, but employee benefits is a complex and rapidly changing arena. Use this glossary as a resource, not an authority. Refer to standard texts and reference works for more details and the most current information on the terms presented. Seek professional assistance in making decisions regarding benefit planning and administration.

The International Foundation welcomes feedback for future updates of this glossary. Contact the Publications Department directly with any suggestions.

ACKNOWLEDGMENTS

The editor extends sincere appreciation to all the dedicated employees at the International Foundation who contributed to this endeavor from the start to when it rolled off the press. Special thanks to Suzy Aschoff, Kathy Bergstrom, Barb Pamperin, Rose Plewa and Chris Vogel for their assistance identifying many of the terms that have been added to this edition of the glossary. Special thanks also to those who helped to ensure the accuracy of definitions: Kelli Kolsrud, Lois Gleason, Robbie Hartman, Sharon Olecheck, Jenny Lucey and Amanda Wilke.

x

1% owner—Internal Revenue Code (IRC) reference to an employee who owns more than 1% of the fair market value of a corporate employer's outstanding stock or possesses more than 1% of the total combined voting power of all stock. If the employer is not a corporation, a 1% owner is any employee who owns more than 1% of the capital or profit interest in the employer. See also *key employee* and *top-heavy plan*.

3% rule—upon separation from service, an employee's accrued benefit must be at least equal to 3% of the projected normal retirement benefit to which he or she would be entitled if he or she began participation at the earliest possible entry age under the plan and worked continuously until the earlier of the age of 65 or the normal retirement age specified in the plan multiplied by the number of years (not in excess of 33½) of his or her participation in the plan. See also *accrued benefit* and *fractional rule*.

5% owner—for Internal Revenue Service (IRS) purposes, an employee who owns more than 5% of the fair value of a corporate employer's outstanding stock or possesses more than 5% of the total combined voting power of all stock. If the employer is not a corporation, a 5% owner is any employee who owns more than 5% of the capital or profit interest in the employer. See also *key employee* and *top-heavy plan*.

12b-1 fee—also known as a level load fee, the annual fee charged by some mutual funds to cover distribution, marketing and, on occasion, shareholder service expenses. This charge is typically a percentage of a share's value; federal law in the U.S. caps the amount. Named for the section of the Securities and Exchange Commission (SEC) rule that permits them, these fees come out of a fund's assets along with other operating costs, collectively known as a fund's expense ratio.

24-hour coverage—single insurance plan that combines workers' compensation with disability and health care insurance to cover both work- and non-work-related injuries and illnesses. See also *integrated disability management (IDM)*.

30 and out—option that permits retirement after 30 years of credited service, regardless of age.

133⅓% rule—IRS rule that an employee's accrued retirement benefit on any given date be no greater than 133⅓% of the employee's accruals in any prior year. See also *accrued benefit* and *fractional rule*.

360-degree feedback—system or process in which employees receive confidential, anonymous comments from the people who work around them. This typically includes the employee's manager, peers and direct reports.

401(h) account—established under provisions of IRC Section 401(h), a separate fund within a defined benefit retirement plan that can be used (within limits) to pay for the medical expenses of retired employees, their spouses and their dependents.

401(k) plan—deferred compensation option established by an employer that allows employees to contribute a portion of their earnings to a retirement account on a pretax basis. Some employers make matching contributions to these accounts. Contributions and earnings are not taxable until the money is withdrawn. With an exception for financial hardship, funds removed from an account before an employee reaches retirement age as defined by the plan are generally subject to an early distribution penalty. Federal rules govern when plan participants must start withdrawals and the minimum amount that must be withdrawn. When an employee leaves a job, the 401(k) account generally stays active for the rest of the employee's life. The IRS considers 401(k) plans to be defined contribution plans. See also *KSOP, Section 401(k)* and *solo 401(k) plan*.

401(k) wraparound plan—unfunded plan established and controlled by an employer that allows highly compensated employees to defer compensation through pretax contributions beyond those made to a 401(k) plan. Participants have the same preferential tax treatment in a wraparound as they do in a qualified 401(k); however, employers do not. Funds set aside by the employer cannot be expensed until payout is made; and, if the funds are invested in taxable vehicles, the accumulated interest is taxed. As a nonqualified plan, the account is not subject to or protected by the provisions of ERISA. Payout to the employee is more flexible as the IRS requires only that the payout be specified in advance and that it occur after a substantial passage of time.

403(b) plan—deferred compensation plan established by public schools and other not-for-profit organizations that gives employees opportunities for retirement savings and tax deferment similar to those that for-profit employees receive through a 401(k) plan. Plan accounts may be an annuity contract or investments such as a mutual fund. 403(b) plans are considered by the IRS to be defined contribution plans. See also *Section 403(b)*.

404(c) plan—individual account plan (generally a money purchase, profit-sharing, 401(k) or 403(b) plan) for which a participant or beneficiary exercises control over the assets and is given the opportunity to choose from a broad range of investment options with varying levels of risk and return. Plan fiduciaries are not held liable for losses resulting from participant control. See also *Section 404(c)* and *self-directed retirement plan*.

412(i) plan—defined benefit plan that allows the owner of a small business to purchase annuities or life insurance for a retirement fund. Due to the large premium required, the business must typically be established and quite profitable with a large, steady cash flow. Premiums paid are tax-deductible. Plans that meet IRS criteria under Section 412 are exempt from the complex funding rules applicable to all other defined benefit plans. See also *Section 412*.

414(k) transfer—the transfer of some or all of an individual's retirement funds from a defined contribution plan to an affiliated defined benefit plan that has the same sponsor under Internal Revenue Code Section 414(k). The money from the defined contribution plan is converted to an annuity payable from the defined benefit plan.

415 limits—see *Section 415*.

419A trust—health or welfare benefit plan to which unrelated employers contribute. Considered nonqualified multiemployer plans, 419A trusts do not require IRS approval and have fewer restrictions on employers than 501(c)(9) trusts. Investment earnings in these trusts are usually subject to corporate tax rates, but it is possible to avoid taxation by using tax-exempt securities. See also *self-funding* and *voluntary employees' beneficiary association (VEBA)*.

419(e) plan—type of employer-sponsored employee welfare benefit plan that qualifies under Section 419(e) of the Internal Revenue Code. Among the benefits that may be provided employees under a 419(e) plan are life, health, disability, long-term care and postretirement medical coverage; all are intended to provide additional financial security for employees during their retirement years. A single company pays for all of the benefits of the plan and does not pool benefits among employees of other companies. Irrevocable cash contributions are made on behalf of the employees on a periodic basis. The assets in these plans are usually held by an independent trustee and are exempt from seizure by any creditors a company may have.

457 plan—deferred compensation plan for employees of state and local governments, as well as those employed by 501(c)(3) nonprofits, that provides opportunities for retirement savings and tax deferment similar to those that for-profit employees receive through a 401(k) plan. See also *Section 457*.

501(c) organization—nonprofit group exempt from some federal income taxes under IRC Section 501. Retirement trusts, labor organizations, state-chartered credit unions, veterans organizations, recreational clubs and mutual insurance companies are just a few of the more than two dozen types of organizations that may be classified as a 501(c) organization if they meet the requirements listed in Sections 503 through 505. Many states reference Section 501(c) for definitions of organizations exempt from state taxation as well.

501(c)3 organization—specific type of nonprofit 501(c) organization whose purpose is religious, educational, charitable, scientific, literary, testing for public safety, fostering national or international amateur sports competition, or the prevention of cruelty to children or animals.

501(c)(9) trust—see *voluntary employees' beneficiary association (VEBA)*.

529 plan—state-administered tuition program established under IRC Section 529. Developed by state legislatures to encourage saving for postsecondary education, there are two specific types of 529 plans: savings plans and prepaid tuition plans. Both allow tax-free earnings on investments for a child's education. The plans differ from state to state in the flexibility and degree of risk they impose on participants. See also *Coverdell Education Savings Account (ESA)*.

A

absence management—employer efforts to reduce unscheduled employee absenteeism and, in turn, lower the associated costs such as health care expenses and lost productivity. Among the approaches used to reduce absenteeism are paid-time-off (PTO) programs, case management, integrated disability management (IDM), wellness programs and safety training.

absenteeism—an employee's frequent failure to physically appear for work.

absolute return—appreciation or depreciation in the value of an investment (usually a stock or mutual fund) over a certain period of time expressed as a percentage. See also *relative return*.

absolute return strategy—approach to investing that seeks a positive return using nontraditional techniques and unconventional assets. Investment managers seeking an absolute return use techniques such as short selling, futures contracts, options, derivatives, arbitrage and leverage. Hence, hedge funds are focused on absolute return. In contrast, "traditional" managers are concerned with relative return—how the return on assets compares with similar assets or the market as a whole. See also *absolute return, arbitrage, derivative, futures contract, option agreement, and short selling.*

academic detailing—see *detailing.*

academic medical center (AMC)—health care organization whose mission is teaching and training medical students. AMCs are typically hospitals affiliated with or part of a medical school or other health-related university program.

accelerated death benefit (ADB)—see *viatical settlement.*

acceleration clause—provision in a loan contract (e.g., bond, mortgage) that gives the lender the right to demand immediate payment of the unpaid balance of the debt if the borrower fails to make a payment.

access
—ability to obtain health care services from providers, which includes factors such as patient affordability, facility location and hours of operation, appointment availability and time spent in waiting rooms prior to an appointment.
—ability to read, write, modify or communicate data/information or otherwise use a system resource.

Access Board—independent federal agency in the U.S. devoted to accessibility for people with disabilities. Also referred to as the Architectural and Transportation Barriers Compliance Board, the Access Board developed the accessibility guidelines for the Americans with Disabilities Act and provides technical assistance and training on these guidelines.

accessible—as defined by the Americans with Disabilities Act, a site, facility, work environment, service or program that is easy to approach, enter, operate, participate in and/or use safely and with dignity by a person with a disability.

accidental death and dismemberment (AD&D) benefit—lump-sum payment provided by an insurance policy if there is a loss of life, limb or eyesight as the result of an accident.

accidental death benefit (ADB)—provision added to an insurance policy that pays an additional benefit in case of death by accidental means.

accident insurance—form of health insurance that protects against loss by accidental bodily injury. See also *insurance.*

accommodation—changes made by an employer to assist an individual with a disability in the performance of a job. See also *Americans with Disabilities Act of 1990 (ADA).*

accountability—obligation to periodically disclose appropriate information in adequate detail and consistent form to all involved parties in a benefit plan.

accountable care organization (ACO)—sometimes referred to as an accountable health plan, a network of health care providers coordinating and providing a full spectrum of health care services and managing the funds required to pay for the services rendered. An ACO is "accountable" for the quality and cost of care. Members in the network include primary care physicians, specialists, hospital, home health care providers, etc. An ACO may be a *group practice,* a *managed care organization (MCO),* an *integrated delivery system* or another joint venture between care providers. Similarities exist between *health maintenance organizations (HMOs)* and ACOs, but ACOs do not require patients to stay within their network of care providers. The *Affordable Care Act of 2010 (ACA)* proposes pilot programs in Medicare and Medicaid that offer financial incentives for ACOs to improve quality and reduce costs by allowing them to share in any savings achieved as a result of these efforts.

accountable health plan—see *accountable care organization (ACO).*

account-based plan—usually a high-deductible health plan with an employee-directed, tax-advantaged health care account—either a health reimbursement arrangement or health savings account. See also *consumer-driven health care (CDHC) plan, high-deductible health plan (HDHP), health reimbursement arrangement (HRA)* and *health savings account (HSA).*

account fee—monetary charge that some mutual funds impose on investors for maintenance of accounts.

Accounting Principles Board (APB)—predecessor organization to the Financial Accounting Standards Board (FASB). Opinions published as APB releases are applicable today unless superseded or revoked by FASB opinions.

account limit—for tax purposes, the maximum dollars that an employer may contribute to a qualified fund for a welfare benefit. This amount equals the sum of (1) what is reasonably and actuarially necessary to fund benefit claims incurred but unpaid at the end of the taxable year, (2) administrative costs and (3) certain contributions to an additional reserve for postretirement medical or life insurance benefits.

accreditation—formal recognition by an agency or organization that evaluates and recognizes a program of study or an institution as meeting predetermined standards. Accreditation may be for a specified period of time or permanent. See also *Accreditation Canada, certification, Joint Commission, licensure* and *National Committee for Quality Assurance (NCQA)*.

Accreditation Canada—nonprofit, independent organization that provides national and international health care organizations with an external peer review process to assess and improve the services they provide to patients based on standards of excellence. See also *accreditation* and *Joint Commission*.

accrual of benefits
—in the case of a defined benefit retirement plan, the process of accumulating benefit credits for years of service with an employer. Credits are expressed in the form of an annual benefit to begin payment at a specified retirement age.
—in the case of a defined contribution or money purchase retirement plan, the process of accumulating funds in an employee's personal retirement account.

accrue—dollar amount that is accumulating periodically over time. Interest accrues on savings accounts. A pension plan sponsor accrues liability for future payments due to plan participants.

accrued benefit
—in the case of a defined benefit pension plan, a participant's accumulated pension credits. The number of credits is generally based on an employee's years of service and earnings.
—for any retirement plan that is not a defined benefit pension plan, the balance in a participant's account regardless of whether it is vested. See also *133⅓% rule, backloading* and *fractional rule.*

accrued future service benefit—portion of a participant's retirement benefit that relates to his or her period of credited service after the effective date of the plan and before a specified future date.

accrued interest—accumulated interest earned on a savings vehicle that is due and payable. Accrued interest for investment securities is calculated from the issue date or the last payment date up to but not including the settlement date. When a buyer purchases a bond, the buyer owes the seller the accrued interest in addition to the market price of the security purchased.

accrued liability—see *actuarial accrued liability.*

accrued pension—amount of pension credited to a plan member according to service, earnings, etc., up to a specified date.

accumulated benefit obligation (ABO)—present value measure of pension plan liability if the plan was terminated on the date the calculation was performed. Liability is based on employee service and compensation up to the date of termination. Both vested and nonvested benefits are included. For plans with flat benefit or non-pay-related pension benefit formulas, the accumulated benefit obligation is the same as the projected benefit obligation. See also *projected benefit obligation (PBO)* and *unfunded accumulated benefit obligation.*

accumulated earnings—see *retained earnings.*

accumulated eligibility credits (AEC)—estimate of a benefit plan's obligation to provide benefits to participants and their dependents following the termination of the participant's employment. When such coverage is provided, it is usually extended for a period of time—typically 30 to 90 days following termination or a period where sufficient hours have not been worked to achieve full benefits.

accumulated funding deficiency—when a qualified pension plan fund fails to meet the minimum funding level established by ERISA. Plans with an accumulated funding deficiency are subject to penalties and other legal actions designed to correct the situation before participants are hurt by the underfunding. After the Pension Protection Act of 2006, only multiemployer pension plans are subject to the rules pertaining to an accumulated funding deficiency. See also *funding standard account (FSA).*

accumulation—with respect to saving and investing, the act of purchasing or otherwise amassing assets. Accumulation is essentially the opposite of *decumulation.*

accumulation fund—account from which an investor receives benefits based on his or her contributions to the fund in addition to the earnings on the money in the account. The earnings are lessened by any taxes and/or fees deducted from the fund.

accumulation period
—phase when an investor builds up value in savings, investments or a deferred annuity for a future goal such as retirement.
—when used in a major medical or comprehensive medical policy, the period during which the insured person must incur eligible medical expenses equal to the deductible before claims may be made.

acid test ratio—measure used to estimate the capacity of a company to quickly convert assets to sufficient cash to pay its liabilities. Also known as the quick ratio or liquid ratio, the acid test ratio is quick assets (i.e., current assets less inventories) divided by current liabilities. See also *current ratio*.

acquired fund fees and expenses (AFFE)—line item in a fund of funds prospectus that shows the operating expenses of the underlying funds. Reporting this information is required by the SEC. See also *fund of funds*.

active account—bank, brokerage or credit account that has regular or frequent transactions.

actively-at-work provision—group health insurance policy provision that requires an employee to be at work (versus sick or on leave) on the day the employee's coverage takes effect. If the employee is not actively at work on the specified day, coverage does not become effective until the next day that the employee is actively at work.

active management—style of investing that seeks to attain above-average returns. When compared with passive managers, active managers tend to buy and sell frequently in an effort to exploit short-term investment trends. See also *passive management*.

active member—see *active participant*.

active market—market where securities are heavily traded and the volume of sales is above normal.

active participant—individual who is a benefit plan participant and for whom benefits are accrued under the plan on his or her behalf at any time during the taxable year. A participant is also considered active if his or her employer (1) is obligated to contribute on the employee's behalf or (2) would have been obligated to contribute on the employee's behalf if any contributions were made. See also *plan participant*.

activities of daily living (ADL)—activities such as bathing, dressing and toileting that are needed for self-care. Activities of daily living are used to evaluate the continued feasibility of self-care and to determine eligibility for long-term care benefits.

actual acquisition cost (AAC)—true cost paid by a pharmacy for a drug after all discounts, rebates and price concessions are taken into account.

actual contribution percentage (ACP) test—calculation used by the IRS to determine whether a qualified defined contribution retirement plan gives favorable treatment to highly compensated employees over those who are not highly compensated. To determine ACP and whether discrimination is occurring, the actual contribution ratios for employees in the two groups are averaged separately and compared. If certain limits are exceeded in this nondiscrimination test, corrective action is required. See also *actual contribution ratio (ACR)*, *actual deferral percentage (ADP) test*, *alternative limitation*, *excess aggregate contribution* and *nondiscrimination rule*.

actual contribution ratio (ACR)—sum of an employee's after-tax contributions and employer matching contributions to the employee's retirement account for a plan year divided by the employee's compensation for the year. If an eligible employee makes no contributions and there are no matching funds, the ratio is zero.

actual deferral percentage (ADP) test—calculation used by the IRS to determine whether the deferred compensation for non-highly compensated employees is being treated unfavorably compared with the deferred compensation for highly compensated employees. To determine ADP and whether there is discrimination, the average of the actual deferral ratios for employees in the two groups is determined separately and compared. If certain limits are exceeded in this nondiscrimination test, corrective action is required. See also *actual contribution percentage (ACP) test*, *actual deferral ratio (ADR)*, *alternative limitation* and *nondiscrimination rule*.

actual deferral ratio (ADR)—ratio of an employee's elective retirement contributions to compensation for a plan year.

actuarial accrued liability—amount that is owed but for which payment has not yet been made. The accrued liability for a pension plan is the excess of the present value of total anticipated future benefits owed (plus administrative expenses if included in the normal cost) over the present value of future normal cost accruals. Accrued liability should be accompanied by a reference as to the actuarial cost method used to establish the amount stated. See also *liability*.

actuarial adjustment—change in values to reflect actual loss experience, expenses and expected benefits to be paid. When a pension plan participant retires before or after the normal retirement age, an actuarial adjustment is made to reflect the change in the number of years that the participant is expected to receive benefits.

actuarial asset value—see *actuarial value of assets (AVA)*.

actuarial assumptions—factors used to forecast uncertain future benefits and costs associated with a fund. Among these factors may be investment return, salary increases, employee turnover, retirement ages and mortality.

actuarial cost—present value of future benefits payable to plan participants and fund administration expenses.

actuarial cost method—technique used to determine the periodic contributions to a pension benefit plan needed to cover future benefit payments and administrative costs. This approach also may be used to determine the level of benefits if contributions are fixed. In addition to forecasts of mortality, interest and expenses, some methods involve estimates regarding future wages, employee turnover and retirement rates. See also *actuarial assumptions*.

actuarial equivalent
—two or more payment streams that have the same present value based on the appropriate actuarial assumptions. For example, a lifetime monthly benefit of $67.60 beginning at the age of 60 can be said to be the actuarial equivalent of $100 a month beginning at the age of 65. The actual benefit amounts are different, but the present value of the two benefits, considering mortality and interest, are the same.
—two or more health benefit plans that provide similar coverage. Plans that are actuarially equivalent do not necessarily have the same premiums, cost-sharing requirements or benefits; however, the spending by the insurer(s) is the same.

actuarial funding method—see *actuarial cost method*.

actuarial gain/loss—difference between what was predicted and what actually occurs. A gain results when the actual experience is more favorable than the estimate, while a loss reflects an adverse deviation.

actuarial justification—demonstration by an insurer that premiums collected are reasonable given the benefits provided under the plan or that the distribution of premiums among policyholders is proportional to the distribution of expected costs, subject to limitations of state and federal law. The Affordable Care Act of 2010 (ACA) requires insurers to publicly disclose the actuarial justifications behind unreasonable premium increases.

actuarial present value (APV)—current value of an amount or series of amounts receivable over a set period of time that is determined using a set of actuarial assumptions.

actuarial reduction—decrease in the normal retirement benefit that offsets the cost increase to the plan when a participant retires ahead of schedule.

actuarial report—statement prepared by an actuary that describes the financial position of a benefits fund and recommends the level of contributions needed to provide promised benefits. Plan sponsors use this information to determine whether changes in fund contributions are required.

actuarial risk—loss an insurance company is willing to cover in exchange for premiums.

actuarial valuation—assessment of a pension plan's worth to determine whether contributions are being accumulated at a rate sufficient to provide future benefits. The value is determined by examining the fund's normal cost, actuarial accrued liability, actuarial value of assets, and other relevant costs and values.

actuarial value—mathematical calculation to determine the monetary value of benefits. Under the Affordable Care Act of 2010 (ACA), actuarial value is the percentage of the total average cost of covered benefits covered by a health plan. If a plan has an actuarial value of 70%, the average person covered by the plan is responsible for 30% of the cost of all covered benefits. For specific individuals covered by this plan, the amount they are responsible for will likely be a higher or lower percentage depending on their actual health care needs and the terms of the insurance policy. Placing an average value on health plan benefits allows different health plans to be compared.

actuarial value of assets (AVA)—value of cash, investments and other property belonging to a benefit plan. A statement of assumptions should be provided that identifies the process used to establish the amount stated.

actuary—person professionally trained in the technical and mathematical aspects of insurance, pensions and related fields. An actuary is used by a pension fund to estimate how much money must be contributed to the fund each year in order to provide the promised benefits. Insurance companies use actuaries to determine policy rates, required reserves and dividends as well as for other statistical tasks. See also *Enrolled Actuary (EA)*.

acupuncture—form of complementary and alternative medicine of Asian origin used to treat pain or disease. Fine needles are inserted into specific points on the body, manipulated and removed.

acute care—short-term medical treatment for a person who has a severe illness or injury. Acute care may include surgery, a hospital stay and/or visits with skilled professionals (e.g., doctors).

additional drug benefit list—see *maintenance drug list*.

additional voluntary contribution (AVC)—money an employee puts into a pension plan that is beyond any required contributions. In Canada, an AVC is distinguished from other types of optional contributions in that there is no corresponding contribution made by the employer. Thus, AVCs are not subject to locking-in rules.

adequate consideration—fair value of an asset as determined in good faith. In the case of a security for which there is a national securities exchange, the fair value is the market price of the security. If the security is not traded on an exchange, the value is established by an independent party based on current bid and ask prices. For assets other than a security, adequate consideration means the value as determined in good faith by a trustee or named fiduciary.

adherence—see *compliance*.

ad hoc adjustment—in contrast to an indexed adjustment, an amount added to a pension after retirement on an irregular basis that is not the result of a prior commitment or contract.

adjudication—legal process by which an arbiter or judge reviews the arguments and evidence of opposing parties in order to make a decision regarding the rights and obligations of the litigants. Adjudication is an involuntary, adversarial process. Arguments are presented to prove one side right and one side wrong, resulting in win-lose outcomes.

adjustable interest rate—interest rate that fluctuates with changes in an established index, such as the prime rate. An adjustable interest rate is also called a floating or variable interest rate. See also *adjustable rate mortgage (ARM)* and *index*.

adjustable rate mortgage (ARM)—also referred to as a variable rate mortgage, a loan for the purchase of real property in which the interest rate and the buyer's monthly payment fluctuate, depending on interest rates in the economy. When rates decline, homeowners benefit. When rates go up, however, the monthly payment will go up. In some cases, the amount or length of the mortgage adjusts instead of the monthly payment. See also *fixed rate mortgage*.

adjusted community rating—modification of an insurance premium initially based on the average claims experience of a group to recognize specific factors of those in the group such as age, gender, family status and geographic composition of those covered. For example, the Affordable Care Act of 2010 (ACA) permits health insurance premium adjustments in the individual market and small group market for age, family size, geographic location and tobacco usage. It does not, however, allow premiums to vary by an individual's health status.

adjusted gross income (AGI)—total of annual income (e.g., wages, interest and dividends) minus certain federal income tax deductions (e.g., contributions to a 401(k) account). This figure is used to determine taxable income. See also *gross income* and *net income (NI)*.

administration—process of running a business, organization, etc.

Administration on Aging—part of the U.S. Department of Health and Human Services, this agency provides home- and community-based services to older persons through programs funded under the Older Americans Act. Some of the services provided include home-delivered meals, nutrition services in congregate settings, transportation, adult day care, legal assistance and health promotion programs. The agency also monitors the care and conditions in long-term care facilities.

administrative agent—see *third-party administrator (TPA)*.

administrative cost—expense incurred for management of a benefit plan such as maintenance of eligibility records, claims review, claims adjudication and benefit payments. Administrative costs do not include the actual cost of benefits.

administrative manager—individual or firm providing professional services to an employee benefit plan such as maintenance or eligibility records, claims review, claims adjudication and benefit payments. Compensation for services may be made through a salary or contract arrangement.

Administrative Policy Regarding Self-Correction (APRSC)—see *Employee Plans Compliance Resolution System (EPCRS)*.

administrative safeguards—as defined by HIPAA privacy legislation, the administrative policies and procedures for (1) managing the selection, development, implementation and maintenance of security measures that safeguard protected health information (PHI) and (2) managing the conduct of the covered entity's workforce in relation to the protection of PHI. See also *physical safeguards* and *technical safeguards*.

administrative services only (ASO)—arrangement in which a benefit plan hires a third party, often an insurance company, to provide services such as account management, claims processing, customer service and fee negotiations. The plan bears the risk for claims. Such an arrangement is common in self-funded health care plans. See also *self-funding* and *third-party administrator (TPA)*.

administrative services organization (ASO)—type of professional employer organization (PEO) that provides outsourcing of human resources tasks but does not create a coemployment relationship. Employees remain solely under the control of the client company. Tax and insurance filings are done by the PEO but under the client company's Employer Identification Number. See also *professional employer organization (PEO)*.

administrator—person or entity managing a benefit plan. A plan administrator is usually an employer sponsoring the plan, a board of trustees for a multi-employer plan, or a plan committee.
—under ERISA, a plan administrator is a person designated by the documents under which the plan is operated. If an administrator has not been designated, the administrator is the plan sponsor. If the administrator has not been designated and the plan sponsor cannot be identified, the administrator is a person prescribed by U.S. Department of Labor regulation. See also *third-party administrator (TPA)*.

admission certification—form of utilization review in which an assessment is made concerning the need to admit a patient to a hospital or other inpatient institution. The assessment considers the patient's health status (both physical and psychological) and treatment needs.

admission rate—measure of how frequently persons are admitted to a hospital for care. The measure can be used to assess performance of a health plan or provider in managing care.

admitted carrier—insurance company allowed to operate in a particular area. In the United States, insurers generally are licensed by a state's insurance department. The company is obligated to comply with the regulations of that state.

adoption assistance program—benefit program created for employees who legally adopt a child. Common benefits include information resources; leave; reimbursement of costs such as adoption agency and legal fees; the pregnancy and hospital expenses of the natural mother; and immigration and naturalization expenses.

adult day care—provision of a range of services to a disabled or elderly person in the home or at a center that may include medical, psychological, social, nutritional and educational services. Such care is often used when a primary caregiver is at work or otherwise unavailable.

advance directive—see *durable power of attorney* and *living will*.

advanced premium tax credit (APTC)—see the "Premium tax credit" in the *Appendix A: Affordable Care Act of 2010 (ACA)*.

Advanced Trust Management Standards (ATMS™)—assessment-based certificate program for Canadian pension and benefit plan trustees who have completed the *Foundations of Trust Management Standards (FTMS™)* program. Both programs are sponsored by the International Foundation of Employee Benefit Plans.

advance funding—approach to funding retirement or other benefits whereby the employer sets aside money for each employee or for a group of employees on some systematic basis during the employees' working years.

adverse benefit determination (ABD)—see *adverse determination*.

adverse determination—denial of or failure to provide a benefit payment. See also "Claims and appeals" in the *Appendix A: Affordable Care Act of 2010 (ACA)*.

adverse drug reaction (ADR)—undesirable patient response to a medication that compromises therapeutic efficacy, enhances toxicity or both. ADRs range from mild to severe. See also *drug misadventure*.

adverse event—undesirable consequence associated with the medical treatment of a patient.

adverse impact—in the context of employment, an action such as hiring or promotion that may appear neutral but has a discriminatory effect on a protected group. The impact may be unintentional.

adverse opinion—conclusion by an independent auditor that financial statements inaccurately characterize a company's or benefit plan's financial standing. See also *disclaimer of opinion, qualified opinion, unmodified opinion* and *unqualified opinion*.

adverse selection—tendency of individuals to consider their health status when selecting an insurance plan and making choices most favorable to them but more costly to the plan. For example, a person with poor health is more likely to purchase health insurance and select a plan with higher levels of coverage to the detriment of the insurance company. Adverse selection is also known as antiselection and negative selection.

advisory opinion—decision written by a regulatory agency or court regarding the legality of an action or situation.

affidavit—sworn written statement made before a notary or other authorized official.

affiliated service group—group of businesses with some common ownership that work together to provide services for clients.

affinity fraud—investment scam that targets members of a group based on a factor such as race, age or religion. The scam artist either is or pretends to be a member of the group, and the trust of the group is exploited. For example, a church leader may be asked to help spread the word regarding an opportunity that allegedly will financially benefit members of the congregation. Affinity fraud is often used in combination with a pyramid or Ponzi scheme. See also *Ponzi scheme* and *pyramid scheme*.

affinity health plan (AHP)—see *association health plan (AHP)*.

affirmative action—regulations, programs and other endeavors to eliminate discrimination (both overt and subtle) and to compensate for discriminatory practices of the past. Affirmative action includes outreach, recruitment, mentoring, training, management development and other programs designed to help employers hire, retain and advance qualified minorities, women and members of other protected groups.

affirmative action program (AAP)—written, results-oriented plan in which an employer or contractor details the steps it will take to ensure equal employment opportunities and, where appropriate, remedy existing discrimination. While some programs are voluntary, others are required by law or a court order.

Affordable Care Act of 2010 (ACA)—see the Appendix A for a short summary of key provisions and terms from this landmark health care reform legislation.

affordable coverage—see "Employer Shared Responsibility" in the *Appendix A: Affordable Care Act of 2010 (ACA)*.

aftercare—continued contact to support and increase gains made as the result of health treatment and to prevent relapse.

after-tax contribution—contribution to a benefits plan that is subject to federal income tax. After-tax contributions are not as financially advantageous to a plan participant as pretax contributions. See also *pretax contribution*.

after-tax savings plan—benefit plan to which employees and/or employers can contribute for retirement or another purpose. The contributions are considered taxable income for the employee in the year they are made. Examples of these plans include the *Roth IRA* in the U.S. and the *Tax-Free Savings Account (TFSA)* in Canada.

age 50 catch-up contribution—see *catch-up contribution*.

age-based fund—see *target-date fund*.

Age Discrimination in Employment Act of 1967 (ADEA)—federal legislation and amendments in the United States that protect job applicants and employees aged 40 and over from discrimination on the basis of age in hiring, promotion, discharge, layoffs and other elements of employment. Employers are subject to ADEA if they engage in an industry affecting interstate commerce and have 20 or more employees in each working day of 20 or more weeks for the current or preceding calendar year. ADEA is enforced by the Equal Employment Opportunity Commission. See also *Older Workers Benefit Protection Act (OWBPA)*.

agency bond—debt instrument issued by one of the private organizations (e.g., Sallie Mae, Fannie Mae) chartered by Congress to increase the supply of funds available for student loans and mortgages. The agency purchases these loans from the financial institutions that make the loans, then groups the loans into pools. Unit shares in the pools are sold to investors. Agency bonds are considered just one step below Treasury issues in terms of risk, due to their government affiliation. The low risk results in relatively low return compared with other private bonds. Agency bonds tend to have lower capital requirements and high liquidity. They are usually exempt from state and local taxes, but not federal tax. See also *Federal Agricultural Mortgage Corporation (FAMC or Farmer Mac)*, *Federal Home Loan Mortgage Corporation (FHLMC or Freddie Mac)*, *Federal National Mortgage Association (FNMA or Fannie Mae)* and *Student Loan Marketing Association (SLM or Sallie Mae)*.

Agency for Healthcare Research and Quality (AHRQ)—lead federal agency for research on health care quality, costs, outcomes and patient safety in the United States. Part of the U.S. Department of Health and Human Services, AHRQ is a major source of funding and technical support for research that helps people make more informed health decisions and improves the quality of health care services. The agency works with the public and private sector to identify what works—and what does not work—with respect to health care.

agency risk—potential loss when an entity delegates decisions to another who may not act in the entity's best interest.

agent—person or firm authorized to act on behalf of or represent another. Agents, sometimes referred to as brokers, are frequently used to buy and sell financial products and services. For example, insurance agents sell insurance policies and recommend which policies should be purchased. Licensed at the state and/or federal level, agents typically get a payment (commission) for each sale/transaction. Some agents are only allowed to sell products from specific companies. See also *durable power of attorney*.

age-weighted profit-sharing plan—retirement plan that combines the simplicity and flexibility of a profit-sharing plan with the ability of a pension plan to skew benefits in favor of older employees. An age factor is used in the allocation formula of the profit-sharing plan, and each participant receives a contribution based on age as well as compensation. Maximum contributions to the plan by the employer and employee are based on percentages of the employee's compensation. There are no required minimum contributions. See also *hybrid pension plan*.

aggregate excess-loss insurance—see *stop-loss insurance*.

aggregate funding method—strategy for determining the contributions required for future pension plan payments. An actuary determines the present value of all future benefit payments, deducts from this value whatever funds may be on hand with the trustee or insurance company, and distributes the cost of the balance over the future on a reasonable basis. The aggregate funding method is less expensive to use than performing individual calculations.

aggregate stop-loss insurance—see *stop-loss insurance*.

aggregation—treatment of a group of individuals or other entities as one. Under ERISA and IRC, separate plans or companies must sometimes be considered as one when determining whether certain requirements are met.

aggressive growth fund—mutual fund that invests in new or undervalued companies to maximize long-term growth. These funds are the most volatile and speculative of the capital appreciation funds. There is a risk of above-average losses. See also *mutual fund*.

aggressive portfolio—investment almost entirely in equities that are expected to appreciate in value over the long term. See also *defensive portfolio*.

algorithm—process or set of rules designed to direct decision making (e.g., flow chart, decision tree or decision grid).

alienation of benefits—see *assignment of benefits*.

Alien Registration Receipt Card—see *green card*.

Aligning Forces for Quality (AF4Q)—initiative of the Robert Wood Johnson Foundation to help improve the quality of health care in 16 targeted geographically, economically and racially diverse communities. AF4Q operates on the premise that no single person, group or profession can improve the quality of care without the support of others. The program seeks to align health care providers (physicians/physician groups, nurses and clinics), health care purchasers (employers and insurers) and health care consumers (patients).

Alliance of Specialty Medicine (ASM)—nonpartisan coalition of 11 national medical societies representing specialty physicians in the United States. ASM is dedicated to developing federal health care policy fostering patient access to the highest quality specialty care. See also *specialist*.

allied health professional—health care practitioner with formal education and clinical training but no medical degree. He or she may be credentialed through certification, registration and/or licensure. Allied health professionals include speech and language therapists, radiographers, occupational therapists, dietitians, paramedics, physician's assistants, certified nurse midwives, phlebotomists, social workers, nurse practitioners and others who perform tasks that supplement physician services.

allocated funding instrument—see *funding instrument*.

allowable amount/charge—maximum dollar amount paid by a health plan, insurance company or other third-party payer to a health care provider. If a provider charges more than the allowable amount, the patient may have to pay the difference. The allowed amount may also be subject to a patient deductible or other cost sharing. Terms used interchangeably with allowable amount are allowed amount (or charge), eligible expense, maximum allowable amount, payment allowance and negotiated rate.

Allowance for the Survivor—federal benefit available to persons aged 60 to 64:
- Who are a Canadian citizen or a legal resident
- Who reside in Canada and have resided in Canada for at least 10 years since the age of 18
- Have had their spouse or common-law partner die
- Have not remarried or entered into a common-law relationship
- Have an income that falls below the maximum annual income threshold.

allowed amount—see *allowable amount.*

allowed charge—see *allowable amount.*

all-payers system—health insurance term that indicates both public and private third-party payers are subject to the same rules and rates when paying for health care services. The term is most commonly used in reference to hospital rate-setting programs.

all-risk insurance—contract with an insurer covering any risk the contract does not specifically omit.

all-salaried workforce—pay policy that makes exempt/nonexempt status (with respect to overtime) invisible to workers. All employees are paid on a salaried basis and all pay is defined in the same terms, such as a monthly or annual salary. In the United States, the Fair Labor Standards Act requirements for overtime and minimum wage must still be met, but exempt status is not made a basis for differentials in the organization. See also *exempt employee* and *nonexempt employee.*

all-weather fund—mutual fund that tends to perform well despite economic and market conditions. This result is typically accomplished through diversification of asset classes and/or the use of hedging strategies. There are no funds titled all-weather funds. The term is used to describe the nature of a fund's investing strategy. See also *fair-weather fund, foul-weather fund, hedge* and *mutual fund.*

alpha—risk-adjusted performance measure for a stock or mutual fund. Alpha for the specific security is compared with the risk-adjusted performance of a benchmark index. A positive alpha of 1.0 means the security has outperformed its benchmark index by 1%. A similar negative alpha would indicate an underperformance of 1%.

alter ego—separate business created to commit fraud or to provide a shield from liability.

alternate benefit provision (ABP)—element of a contract that states the benefit payable will be based on the least expensive professionally acceptable procedure necessary to treat a given problem. ABP is most common in dental plans due to the many procedural and materials options available for care. When the ABP is applied, the beneficiary is responsible for the difference in fees between the procedure performed and the alternate treatment.

alternate payee—spouse, former spouse, child or other dependent who is recognized by a domestic relations order as having a right to receive all, or a portion of, a participant's plan benefits. See also *qualified domestic relations order (QDRO).*

alternate ranking method—appraisal of employee performance in which employees are ranked from best to worst. First, the employee who is highest and lowest are chosen. The appraiser continues to select the remaining employees in the same fashion until all employees have been ranked. Alternate ranking is a variation on the *straight ranking method.*

alternate recipient—reference to a child in a *qualified medical child support order (QMCSO)* who has the right to receive benefits under a noncustodial parent's group health plan.

alternative delivery system (ADS)—arrangement for the provision of dental or health care services in a way that is not the traditional fee-for-service approach. See also *exclusive provider organization (EPO), health maintenance organization (HMO)* and *preferred provider organization (PPO).*

alternative dispute resolution (ADR)—variety of methods used to resolve disagreements out of court. These methods include negotiation, conciliation, mediation and arbitration. ADR tends to be faster, less formal and less expensive than litigation. The process may be voluntary or involuntary and binding or nonbinding. See also *arbitration, conciliation, fact finding* and *mediation.*

alternative investment—financial product that is not one of the three traditional asset types (i.e., stocks, bonds and cash) or the mutual funds and managed accounts that invest in these assets. Art, commodities, derivatives, hedge funds, limited partnerships, precious metals, private equity, real estate and venture capital are all examples of alternative investments. Because the returns on these investments have a low correlation with those of standard asset classes, many large institutional funds such as pension funds allocate a small portion of their portfolios to these products. Socially responsible investments are another example of an alternative investment. See also *commodity, derivative, hedge fund, limited partnership, private equity, real property, socially responsible investment* and *venture capital.*

alternative limitation—substitute nondiscrimination test for highly and nonhighly compensated employees established by the IRS for retirement plans. The actual contribution percentage (ACP) and actual deferral percentage (ADP) of highly compensated employees cannot be more than double the ACP and ADP of non-highly compensated employees. In addition, the difference cannot exceed two percentage points. See also *actual contribution percentage (ACP) test* and *actual deferral percentage (ADP) test*.

alternative medicine—see *complementary and alternative medicine (CAM)*.

alternative minimum tax (AMT)
—tax calculation created by the IRS to ensure that high-income taxpayers pay at least a minimum amount of federal income tax. The calculation puts certain items such as passive losses from tax shelters back into adjusted gross income. If the AMT is higher than the regular tax liability for a year, the regular tax and the amount by which the AMT exceeds the regular tax must be paid. See also *adjusted gross income (AGI)*.
—in Canada, a tax payable in addition to regular income tax, or the minimum tax payable on adjusted income greater than a certain dollar amount.

amalgamation—in Canada, a merger or combining of two or more companies or corporations.

ambulatory care—see *outpatient service* and *outpatient surgery*.

ambulatory care facility—freestanding or hospital-based center that provides medical services that do not require overnight admission. See also *ambulatory surgery center (ASC)* and *freestanding ambulatory facility*.

Ambulatory Care Quality Alliance (AQA)—broad-based coalition of organizations that includes physicians, health insurance plans, consumers and others seeking to improve health care quality and patient safety through a collaborative process. Key stakeholders agree on and promote strategies to (1) measure performance at the physician, other clinician or group level; (2) collect and aggregate data in an appropriate way; and (3) report meaningful information to inform care choices and improve outcomes.

ambulatory care-sensitive conditions—medical issues that do not require hospitalization if patient care is provided to prevent complications or the onset of more severe forms of an illness. Asthma, diabetes and hypertension are examples of such conditions.

ambulatory surgery—see *outpatient surgery*.

ambulatory surgery center (ASC)—also called a same-day surgery center, a freestanding or hospital-based establishment that performs surgery of an uncomplicated nature that has traditionally been done in an inpatient setting but now can be done with equal efficiency without hospital admission.

amendment—addition, deletion or change in a legal document. A change in the terms of an insurance policy or benefit plan is often called an amendment. Usually, a document is prepared stating the changes that must be signed by the parties or representatives of those affected by change.

American Academy of Actuaries (the Academy)—organization assisting public policy makers by providing leadership, objective expertise and advice on risk and financial security issues. The Academy also sets qualification, practice and professional standards for actuaries credentialed by any of the five U.S.-based actuarial organizations. See also *Society of Actuaries (SOA), American Society of Pension Professionals and Actuaries College of Pension Actuaries (ACOPA), Casualty Actuarial Society (CAS)* and *Conference of Consulting Actuaries (CCA)*.

American Academy of Family Physicians (AAFP)—one of the nation's largest medical organizations, AAFP represents family physicians, residents and medical students. The organization's mission is to (1) shape health care policy, (2) enhance the ability of members to fulfill their practice/career goals, (3) promote high-quality, innovative education for its members and (4) assume a leadership role in health promotion, disease prevention and chronic disease management.

American Depositary Receipt (ADR)—dollar-denominated certificate issued by a U.S. bank that represents one or more shares in a foreign stock. The ADRs, not the stock shares, are bought and sold on a U.S. exchange. The underlying shares, referred to as American Depositary Shares, are held by a U.S. financial institution overseas. ADRs eliminate the need to ship stock certificates between the United States and other countries, which expedites transactions in foreign securities and reduces transaction costs. See also *Global Depositary Receipt (GDR)* and *International Depository Receipt (IDR)*.

American Depositary Share (ADS)—see *American Depositary Receipt (ADR)*.

American Federation of Labor (AFL)—formed in 1881 as a national federation of local unions, the AFL was originally organized for trade and crafts persons. Today it also grants charters to industrial unions. Each local retains the right to govern its own affairs. In 1955, the AFL and the Congress of Industrial Organizations merged to form the AFL-CIO. See also *Congress of Industrial Organizations (CIO)*.

American Federation of Labor and Congress of Industrial Organizations (AFL-CIO)—formed in 1955, the largest federation of North American labor unions. As the name suggests, the organization was a merger of the American Federation of Labor (AFL) and the Congress of Industrial Organizations (CIO).

American Health Quality Association (AHQA)—educational, not-for-profit national association of community-based Quality Improvement Organizations and other professionals dedicated to improving health care quality and patient safety in the United States. See also *Quality Improvement Organization (QIO)*.

American Hospital Association (AHA)—national organization representing and serving hospitals, health systems and related organizations. AHA provides education for health care leaders and is a source of information on health care issues and trends. Through its advocacy activities, AHA ensures member perspectives and needs are heard in national health policy development and on judicial matters.

American Jobs Creation Act of 2004 (AJCA)—U.S. law that established a new Section 409A to the IRC that applies to most nonqualified deferred compensation plans and many equity-based awards. Amounts deferred in 2005 and beyond are affected. The new rules limit the flexibility employers have in structuring deferrals, timing distributions, accelerations and securing benefits. Special rules apply to performance-based compensation. In general, initial elections to defer compensation must be made in the tax year before the year the compensation is earned. New participants have up to 30 days to make an election to defer compensation for future services. Distributions are payable only upon an employee's separation from service, death or disability, a change in control of the company, an unforeseeable emergency or a specific date in the future. The timing and schedule of payments cannot be accelerated (unless in accordance with certain regulatory exceptions). Technical corrections affecting the nonqualified compensation provision of this act were made as part of the Gulf Opportunity Zone Act of 2005.

American Medical Association (AMA)—professional association for doctors that promotes the art and science of medicine and the betterment of public health. Among the issues addressed by AMA are the cost and quality of health care, improving access to care, prevention and wellness.

American Nurses Association (ANA)—professional organization representing the nation's registered nurses (RNs) through its constituent member associations and organizational affiliates. ANA advances the nursing profession by fostering high standards, promoting the rights of nurses in the workplace, projecting a positive and realistic view of nursing, and lobbying on health care issues affecting nurses and the public.

American Recovery and Reinvestment Act of 2009 (ARRA)—legislation providing appropriations to jumpstart the U.S. economy, create and preserve jobs, invest in infrastructure, encourage energy efficiency, assist the unemployed, and help stabilize state and local economies.

American Society of Pension Professionals and Actuaries College of Pension Actuaries (ACOPA)—pension-oriented group responsible for identifying and addressing the professional development needs of members of the American Society of Pension Professionals and Actuaries (ASPPA).

American Stock Exchange (AMEX)—now known as the NYSE MKT LLC, a mutual stock trading organization located in New York.

Americans with Disabilities Act Amendments Act of 2008—effective January 1, 2009, this law made several significant changes, including a broadened definition of the term disability.

Americans with Disabilities Act of 1990 (ADA)—U.S. law and amendments that protect qualified applicants and employees with disabilities from discrimination in hiring, promotion, pay, job training, fringe benefits and other aspects of employment on the basis of disability. Employers are required to make reasonable accommodations to enable employees with disabilities to perform the essential parts of a job. ADA is enforced by the Equal Employment Opportunity Commission. See also *Americans with Disabilities Act Amendments Act of 2008, auxiliary aids and services, mitigating measures, reasonable accommodation* and *Rehabilitation Act of 1973*.

America's Health Insurance Plans (AHIP)—national trade association representing companies offering medical expense, long-term care, disability income, dental, supplemental and stop-loss insurance through employer-sponsored coverage, the individual insurance market, and public programs such as Medicare and Medicaid. Among AHIP's goals are providing a unified voice for the health care financing industry; expanding access to high-quality, cost-effective health care to all Americans; and consumer choice.

amortization

—systematic write-off of an asset over a period of time by expensing the item over the period for which the asset is used. Intangible assets such as copyrights, patents and product development costs are commonly amortized. See also *depreciation*.

—on the liability side, amortization is the process used for installment loans and mortgages paid over a specified period of time. Amortized loan payments must be sufficient to cover both the amount borrowed (principal) and the interest. Amortization of a liability is also used to defer revenue when payments are received in advance of delivery of goods or services and must be recognized as income distributed over some future period.

amortized value—financial worth of an item at a given point in time.

ancillary benefit—secondary or supplementary benefit that accompanies a major benefit. In addition to regular retirement benefits, a pension plan might provide benefits in the event of termination, death, disability or early retirement that may be referred to as ancillary benefits. Miscellaneous medical expenses associated with a hospital stay and covered by health insurance such as ambulance service, blood, medicines, bandages, x-rays, diagnostic tests and anesthetics are also referred to as ancillary benefits. In its broadest sense, ancillary benefit refers to any benefit other than health and retirement benefits. Life and disability insurance, vision coverage and any work/life benefit would all fit within this broad definition. See also *flexible pension plan, supplemental unemployment benefit (SUB)* and *voluntary benefit*.

ancillary services—supplemental services beyond the hospital room, medical procedures and nursing provided to a patient in the course of care. Such services include lab work, radiology, pharmacy and physical therapy.

anniversary date—month and day when an individual began his/her employment or when an insurance policy was issued.

annual addition—yearly contribution made to a participant's defined contribution account. The annual addition includes employer and employee (participant) contributions.

annual addition limit—maximum dollar amount that may be contributed to a qualified retirement plan by, or on behalf of, a participant during a one-year period. The limit applies to the combination of employee contributions, employer contributions and forfeitures allocated to the individual participant's account. Also referred to as the annual contribution limit or contribution limit. IRC Section 415 established this limit as the lesser of (1) 100% of the participant's compensation for the year or (2) the dollar limit that is in effect for the year.

annual benefit limit—maximum dollar amount that a beneficiary may receive each year from a qualified defined benefit pension plan under IRC Section 415. The limit is the lesser of (1) 100% of the participant's average compensation (generally the highest three consecutive years of service) or (2) the dollar limit that is in effect for the year. See also *annual compensation limit*.

annual benefits statement—individualized report issued to plan participants that provides information on their plan status, account balance and projected retirement income. Some statements include a description of the value and cost of health and welfare benefits. The statement is often distributed to employees to promote awareness and appreciation of benefits.

annual bonus—additional pay in cash or stock beyond an employee's normal pay for a fiscal or calendar year based on individual, business unit and/or company performance. It is usually a lump-sum payment.

annual compensation limit—maximum employee payment amount established by IRC Section 401(a)(17) that is used to calculate the annual benefit limit on qualified retirement plan contributions. See also *annual benefit limit*.

annual contribution limit—see *annual addition limit*.

annual deductible combined—usually in *health savings account (HSA)* eligible plans, the total amount family members on a plan must pay out-of-pocket for health care or prescription drugs before the health plan begins to pay.

annual funding notice—document providing funding and other information concerning a defined benefit retirement plan that ERISA requires must be provided each year to the Pension Benefit and Guaranty Corporation, plan participants and beneficiaries, the labor organization representing the participants and beneficiaries, and each employer with an obligation to contribute to the plan.

annual incentive—see *annual bonus*.

annual information return (AIR)—pursuant to Canada's Pension Benefits Standards Act, pension plans must file financial and other information each year with the Canada Revenue Agency and the appropriate provincial government.

annualize—to express a rate of return for a period greater than one year or less than one year in terms of 12 months.

annualized linked-median return—rate of return calculated by compounding annual median returns and annualizing the result.

annual leave—see *vacation*.

annual limit
—maximum benefits a person may get from a health benefit plan in a plan year. After the limit is reached, the plan no longer pays for covered services. See also "Benefit mandates" in the *Appendix A: Affordable Care Act of 2010 (ACA)*.
—for retirement plans, see also *annual benefit limit* and *annual compensation limit*.

annual percentage rate (APR)—interest rate that allows a borrower to compare the actual financial cost of different loans. When calculated, the APR includes interest, points, origination fees and any other costs that are considered a finance charge. The APR is disclosed as part of the truth-in-lending statement required by the U.S. Truth in Lending Act. Generally, the lower the APR the better, provided that the loan is not paid off early.

annual percentage yield (APY)—rate of return on savings over a one-year period. The APY takes into account the effect of compounding. For example, if money in a savings account earns interest at an annual percentage rate of 6% compounded yearly, the APY will be 6%. But if the 6% interest is compounded monthly, the APY will be 6.17%.

annual report
—formal financial statement issued annually by public corporations that details assets, liabilities, earnings and other information of interest to shareholders. In the U.S., the annual corporate report helps companies comply with the SEC requirement that public companies keep stockholders regularly informed on the state of business. See also *asset* and *liability*.
—generally, pension and welfare benefit plans in the U.S. are also required to file an annual report regarding their financial condition, investments and operations. The reporting requirement is satisfied by filing Form 5500 and any required attachments. The U.S. Department of Labor, IRS and Pension Benefit Guaranty Corporation jointly developed the Form 5500 series so benefit plans can use one process to satisfy various reporting requirements under ERISA and the IRC. The form is used to determine whether a plan is in compliance with federal requirements.

annual statement—yearly report providing financial data such as assets, liabilities, receipts and disbursements.

annual yield—dollar value of interest and dividends received from an investment over a one-year period. See also *yield*.

annuitant—person on whose life an annuity contract is based. The annuitant receives the payments due on the contract.

annuitization—conversion of a lump sum of money to a stream of periodic income payments. Annuitization for a plan participant's life or the lifetimes of the participant and participant's spouse is an option offered by many retirement plans.

annuity
—when referring to defined benefit pension plans, periodic payments (usually monthly) provided for the lifetime of an individual (the *annuitant*). The payments may be fixed or a varying amount, and may continue for a period after the annuitant's death.
—insurance contract purchased with a lump sum of money or a series of premium payments in which an insurance company agrees to provide a series of payments at regular intervals over a period of more than one full year to an individual (the *annuitant*). Annuities can provide a source of retirement income with payments starting at or after retirement. Payments may be promised for a specific number of years, the life of the annuitant or even the life of the annuitant and the annuitant's spouse. The purchase of an annuity is a means of transferring mortality risk and investment risk to an insurance company. In the U.S., if an annuity is purchased as part of a retirement plan with funds that were not taxed, the annuity payments are taxable. However, if an annuity is purchased with after-tax dollars, the annuity benefits are not taxable. Annuity contracts are also called allocated contracts. See also *annuity certain, automatic survivor coverage, contingent annuity option, deferred annuity, equity-index annuity, exclusion ratio, fixed annuity, fixed period annuity, group annuity, guaranteed annuity, hybrid annuity, immediate annuity, individual retirement account (IRA), joint and survivor benefit, lifetime annuity, market value adjusted annuity, qualified annuity, refund annuity, reversionary annuity, single life annuity, single premium deferred annuity, tax-sheltered annuity (TSA)* and *variable annuity*.

annuity certain—insurance contract in which an insurance company agrees to make payments to a person for a specified number of years, regardless of whether the person is living or deceased. If the person dies, his or her designated beneficiary will receive payments for the years remaining in the contract. An annuity certain is also referred to as a period certain annuity, term certain annuity or years certain annuity.

annuity consideration—lump-sum payment or series of payments made to purchase an annuity.

annuity rate—price charged by an insurance company to provide one dollar of annuity payments (usually per month) to an individual based on the person's age, interest rates and other specified conditions.

annuity starting date—first day of the first period for which an annuity payment is paid to an annuitant.

antialienation rule—regulation that generally prohibits the transfer or assignment of ERISA-qualified pension benefits to a third party. Creditors are not allowed to garnish pension benefits as payment on a defaulted loan. This provision, however, is not intended to interfere with the practice of using vested benefits as collateral for reasonable loans from a plan. One exception to this rule is a qualified domestic relations order, which permits the attachment of an employee's account to pay for child support and alimony. Because individual retirement accounts (IRAs) are not considered ERISA-qualified plans, they do not enjoy the same protection. See also *qualified domestic relations order (QDRO)*.

antiassignment rule—see *antialienation rule*.

anticutback rules—provisions in IRC Section 401(d)(6) that prohibit plan sponsors from reducing or eliminating benefits in a qualified retirement plan by plan amendment, other than an amendment that has been approved by the U.S. secretary of labor freezing benefit accruals for the most recent plan years. These rules protect a participant's accrued benefits, early retirement benefits, retirement-type subsidies and optional forms of benefits offered under qualified retirement plans subject to ERISA.

antikickback rule—ERISA Section 406(b)(3) prohibits a fiduciary from receiving gifts, gratuities or any consideration in connection with a plan transaction.

antiselection—see *adverse selection*.

antistacking provision—clause in an insurance contract used to avoid the application of multiple sets of deductibles or limits to a single loss event. Such clauses are sometimes included in insurance policies covering exposures that may occur over long periods and trigger coverage under multiple policies. A clause stipulates that, in such an event, only one policy limit or one deductible (rather than the limit or deductible under each policy) applies to the occurrence.

any willing provider law—law in some states that prohibits health insurers from excluding participation of willing and qualified health care providers who agree to abide by the same contractual terms and payment levels as other providers. Most laws are limited to pharmacies and pharmacists, but several states have adopted broad provisions that also apply to hospitals, physicians, chiropractors, therapists and nurses. The intent of these laws is to preserve the patient's freedom of choice. However, the laws directly affect managed care organizations that attempt to control health care costs and quality by selecting the most efficient providers. See also *closed panel* and *IPA model HMO*.

appeal—request for an insurer or benefit plan to review a benefit decision.

appraisal—estimate of quantity, quality or market value of property by an expert.

appreciation—increase in asset value. A stock advancing from $70 to $80 is said to have appreciated ten points.

apprenticeship agreement—generally, a written agreement between an apprentice program sponsor and an apprentice setting forth the terms and conditions for the employment and training of the apprentice. In the United States, the Department of Labor specifies the contents of the agreement.

apprenticeship and training fund—see *training and education fund*.

approved plan—pension, deferred profit-sharing or stock bonus plan that meets the requirements of the applicable Revenue Canada regulations. Such approval qualifies the plan for favorable tax treatment. Approval of a pension plan, however, does not indicate any judgment regarding the plan's actuarial soundness.

arbitrage—technique employed to take advantage of price differences for identical or similar securities in separate markets. This is accomplished by purchasing in one market for immediate sale in another at a better price. Technology has made it increasingly difficult to find instances where such differences occur.

arbitrage fund—hedge fund that seeks to exploit differences in the price or rate of the same or similar securities. A relative value fund manager will take long positions on securities considered undervalued, while taking short positions on securities considered overvalued. Also known as relative value fund.

arbitrary and capricious standard—guide employed by courts to determine whether a plan's decision to deny benefits should be upheld or overruled. A benefits decision is considered arbitrary and capricious if no rational connection can be found between the facts and the choice made.

arbitration—process of resolving a dispute using an impartial individual (or group of people) appointed by mutual consent or statutory provision. The arbitrator listens to the facts of a dispute, then provides a judgment. Arbitration is often used to settle disputes between labor and management. It is also a common strategy for resolving disagreements between insurance companies and claimants. Arbitration may be voluntary or involuntary, and binding or nonbinding. See also *alternative dispute resolution (ADR)*, *fact finding* and *mediation*.

Archer medical savings account (MSA)—account used in conjunction with a qualified high-deductible health plan that can be used by employees to pay medical expenses not covered by insurance. Funds may accumulate in the account from year to year. These accounts, established by Congress in 1997, are specifically for employees of small businesses, and self-employed persons and their spouses. If the employer pays for the entire cost of the plan, the payments are not taxable to the employee. If the employee contributes to the account, the contribution is tax-deductible. The employer and the employee are not allowed to both contribute money in the same year. Money drawn from an MSA is also not taxed if it is used to pay for qualifying medical expenses of the employee, the employee's spouse or dependents. At age 65 or upon disability, the accountholder may make withdrawals from an MSA for any reason without a penalty; however, the withdrawals will be taxed as ordinary income. See also *Medicare Advantage MSA*.

Architectural and Transportation Barriers Compliance Board—see *Access Board*.

Architectural Barrier Removal Tax Deduction—expense a business can subtract from income for the removal of "qualified" barriers to make a facility or public transportation vehicle owned or leased in connection with a trade or business more accessible to, and usable by, individuals who have a disability.

arm's length transaction—agreement made by two or more parties freely and independent of each other, with no special relationship. Certain individuals connected by a blood relationship, marriage, common-law partnership or adoption are examples of related persons that may be deemed under the law as to not be dealing at arm's length. Persons who have some level of control over a business may also be considered to not be dealing at arm's length.

ASC 965 liability—present value of a plan's long-term cost of retiree health care coverage for current active and retired participants plus their dependents. The value to be paid in the future assumes the plan remains in effect indefinitely. Retiree health benefits include dental, vision and life benefits as well as medical, prescription drug and other health-related coverages. The costs are adjusted for inflation and may be offset by the expected value of retiree contributions for coverage, medical claim refunds and subrogation recoveries, prescription drug rebates and Medicare Part D subsidies.

asking price—lowest price that any potential seller declares acceptable for a given security. For mutual funds, the asking price is the net asset value plus any sales charges. Asking price is also referred to as ask price, asked price and offering price.

assessed value—worth of real estate or other property assigned by a public tax assessor for tax purposes.

asset—resource, property right or property owned by an individual or organization. Specific examples of assets include cash, securities, materials and inventory. See also *capital asset, current asset, intangible asset* and *tangible asset*.

asset allocation—strategy that apportions a portfolio's investments according to an investor's goals, risk tolerance and investment horizon. Asset allocation typically involves selecting investments representing different asset classes. The assets in each class have different levels of risk and return, and may behave differently over time. See also *asset allocation fund* and *asset class*.

asset allocation fund—mutual fund that invests mainly in a mix of stocks, bonds and cash equivalents. Some asset allocation funds maintain a fixed proportion of these asset classes over time, while others adjust the proportion of each as economic and investment circumstances change. The objective of an asset allocation fund is to provide investors with a diversified portfolio without purchasing a large number of different funds. *Balanced funds, target-date funds* and *target-risk funds* can all be categorized as asset allocation funds.

asset-backed security (ABS)—pool of consumer debt such as auto loans, revolving credit accounts, home-equity loans and home-equity lines of credit. Loan payments are passed through to ABS investors.

asset class—category of investment securities that share common financial traits. Stocks, bonds and cash (including cash equivalents) are major asset classes. Other classes include real estate, derivatives, futures contracts and precious metals. See also *asset allocation*.

asset liability matching—investment strategy that attempts to time future asset sales and income streams to correspond with future expenses. Pension fund managers use this technique in an effort to minimize a portfolio's liquidation risk—trying to match asset sales, interest and dividend payments with expected benefit payments to plan beneficiaries. Also known as liability matching and liability-driven investing (LDI).

asset/liability modeling—projection of a benefit plan's financial situation using assumptions concerning the future such as demographic trends, effects of inflation and anticipated return on investments. The projections are used by plan sponsors in an effort to make better choices in the present and avoid future problems. Modeling is especially useful when plan changes, such as mergers, are contemplated. See also *asset* and *liability*.

asset mix—see *asset allocation*.

asset reversion—termination of a pension plan by a plan sponsor in order to reclaim assets in excess of the amounts needed to pay accrued fund benefits.

asset smoothing—method by which the actuarial value of assets is determined. Fluctuations in market values are "smoothed" by gradual recognition of investment return.

assigned payment—see *assignment of benefits.*

assignment—transfer of rights from one party (the assigner) to another (the assignee).

assignment of benefits
—also referred to as alienation of benefits or assigned payment, an arrangement by which benefit payments are transferred (assigned) by a beneficiary to a third party. For example, a patient may request that health benefit payments be made directly to a health care provider. With the exception of a qualified domestic relations order, the assignment of tax-qualified pension plan benefits to a party other than the plan participant is generally prohibited under ERISA. See also *antialienation rule* and *qualified domestic relations order (QDRO).*
—in Canada, assignment of group life insurance normally is not allowed under most plan provisions. Hospital and dental benefits, however, may be assigned to most providers.

assisted living facility—shared and supervised housing for persons who cannot function independently. Various types of homes exist, ranging from those that serve persons who need minimal support to those that house the more severely impaired. An assisted living facility (also referred to as a residential care facility) offers less skilled service than a nursing home. See also *extended care facility (ECF)* and *nursing home.*

association group insurance—individual insurance offered to a group of persons who share a common interest (an association). Most professions and trades have associations. The self-employed, small businesses and religious organizations also have associations. Individuals within the association have the option of purchasing insurance (typically health insurance). See also *association health plan (AHP), insurance* and *group insurance.*

association health plan (AHP)—health insurance offered to those in a similar industry or trade group. Members of the association may be self-employed or work for companies such as subcontractors that do not typically offer health insurance to their employees. Associations are also formed by franchise owners who work for a larger corporation. Insurance companies typically use the same underwriting guidelines that apply to individual/family health plans. These plans are not considered group health insurance plans. How these plans are structured, whom they sell to and whether an association is state-based or national determines whether they are subject to state or federal regulation, or both, or are largely exempt from regulations. AHPs may also be referred to as affinity health plans.

assurance—synonymous with insurance in Canada and Great Britain.

attachment point—in self-funded plans, the dollar amount at which stop-loss coverage is triggered. Similar to a deductible, once the attachment point is reached, the stop-loss insurance carrier is responsible for additional claims. A *specific attachment point* is the point at which the stop-loss coverage protects a plan against a high claim for any one individual or family unit. An *aggregate attachment point* sets the maximum total dollar amount of claims a plan must pay in a specific period.

attained age—individual's age at his or her last birthday.

attainment rate—when used with dental plans, the percentage of eligible beneficiaries who saw a dentist and reached or exceeded their annual maximum limit during the plan year. Attainment rates help a group gauge whether its maximum is too high or too low.

attending dentist's statement—dental claim form.

attest—agreeing that information provided is correct, true or genuine. For example, when a person applies for individual health coverage, the applicant is required to attest to the truth of the information provided in the application

attestation—affirmation that something is correct, true or genuine.

at the market—see *market order.*

at the money—condition in which the strike price (i.e., the amount per share to be paid) of an option is equal to the price of the underlying stock. See also *exercise price.*

attitude survey—questions designed to elicit feelings, concerns, expectations and/or preferences on issues.

attorney-client privilege—legal right that keeps communication between a lawyer and his/her client confidential.

attorney-in-fact—see *durable power of attorney.*

attribution—assigning pension benefits or costs to periods of employee service.

audit—systematic investigation of procedures, operations, records or financial accounts. The purpose of an audit is typically to determine whether practices conform with prescribed criteria and/or to verify accuracy. See also *claims audit, compliance audit, comprehensive audit, eligibility audit, hospital audit, operational audit, participant audit, payroll audit, performance guarantee audit, rebate audit, repricing audit* and *retail network audit.*

Audit Closing Agreement Program (Audit CAP)—one of three EPCRS programs established by the IRS that allow a benefit plan sponsor to correct operational and plan document errors affecting a tax-qualified plan. An Audit CAP allows a plan sponsor, at any time before an audit, to pay a limited fee and receive approval for a correction. There are special procedures for anonymous submissions. See also *Employee Plans Compliance Resolution System (EPCRS), Self-Correction Program (SCP)* and *Voluntary Correction Program (VCP).*

audit finding—conclusion about a monetary or nonmonetary matter resulting from an investigation of procedures, financial records, etc. A finding typically identifies a problem (e.g., a weakness in internal controls or noncompliance with applicable laws) and provides recommendations for corrective action. Findings are ordinarily presented together with a statement from management that concurs or disagrees with the finding and any plan for corrective action.

audit of provider treatment/charges—review of services and/or fees rendered or proposed by a health care provider. The audit may be a comparison of patient records and claim form information, a patient questionnaire, a review of hospital and practitioner records, an examination of pre- or postoperative radiographs or a pre- or posttreatment clinical examination of a patient.

audit trail—availability of records containing evidence of activities such as transactions or communications by individual people, systems, accounts, etc.

authentication—process by which a person's identity or fact is confirmed. Authentication can be as simple as looking at a person's driver's license or using a password, to using new technologies such as smart cards and retina scans.

automatic benefit election—see *automatic enrollment.*

automatic contribution arrangement—retirement plan feature that allows an employer to automatically reduce an employee's pay by a default percentage stated in the plan and contribute this amount to the employee's retirement account, unless the employee chooses not to contribute or to contribute a different amount. The IRS allows the following plans to have such an arrangement: 401(k) plans, 403(b) plans, 457(b) plans, simplified employee pensions and SIMPLE IRAs. See also *automatic enrollment, default investment, eligible automatic contribution arrangement (EACA), qualified automatic contribution arrangement (QACA)* and *qualified default investment alternative (QDIA).*

automatic deferral—see *automatic enrollment.*

automatic enrollment—process by which an employer signs up all eligible employees for a benefit plan pursuant to a salary reduction agreement such as a cafeteria plan or defined contribution retirement plan unless the employee informs the employer otherwise during the applicable enrollment period. When the employee is hired, the employer provides the employee with a notice explaining the automatic enrollment process and the employee's right to decline participation. A notice describing existing coverage, if any, is also given to each current employee before the beginning of each plan year. Plan design specifies the amount of earnings to be contributed and how these deferrals will be used or invested. Generally, participants can also change the size of the salary reduction and allocations in the plan. Automatic enrollment is also referred to as automatic deferral, negative election and negative enrollment. See also *automatic contribution arrangement.*

automatic escalation—in a defined contribution retirement plan, the process of automatically increasing participant contributions at a specified rate over time to overcome a participant's tendency to remain at the default contribution rate. Participants may choose to opt out.

automatic premium loan—agreement between an insurer and the insured that the payment for a life insurance policy will be lent to the insured from the cash value of the policy if the insured (or other policyholder) does not pay on time.

automatic rebalancing—investment design feature that automatically redistributes portfolio assets to realign them with the original asset allocation. Automatic rebalancing offsets changes to asset allocation that result from market price fluctuations.

automatic reliance—IRS provision that a standardized retirement plan is qualified if certain conditions are met. An employer establishing such a plan must have a determination letter that the standard plan is qualified and that no modifications have been made to the plan. See also *qualified retirement plan* and *standardized plan*.

automatic retirement—see *compulsory retirement*.

automatic rollover—transfer of funds from a retirement plan cashout to an individual retirement account without the participant's consent that occurs when a participant has not responded to plan notifications.

automatic survivor coverage—under the Retirement Equity Act of 1984, defined benefit plans and money purchase plans in the United States are required to provide automatic survivor benefits to the surviving spouse of a participant. In the case of a vested participant who retires under the plan, the coverage must be in the form of a qualified joint and survivor annuity. In the case of a vested participant who dies before retirement, the coverage must be in the form of a qualified preretirement survivor annuity. A participant may, with his or her spouse's consent, opt out of the joint and survivor annuity option or preretirement survivor annuity coverage. The automatic survivor coverage rule also applies to a profit-sharing or stock bonus plan unless (1) the participant's full vested account balance will be paid to the surviving spouse (or to another beneficiary if the spouse consents), (2) the participant does not elect payment of benefits in the form of an annuity and (3) with respect to the participant, the funds in the plan were not transferred from a plan required to provide automatic survivor benefits. See also *qualified joint and survivor annuity (QJSA)*, *qualified optional survivor annuity (QOSA)* and *qualified preretirement survivor annuity (QPSA)*.

auxiliary aids and services—under Titles II and III of the Americans with Disabilities Act, a wide range of services and devices that promote effective communication or allow access to goods and services. Examples for individuals who are hearing-impaired include qualified interpreters, note takers, computer-aided transcription services, written materials, telephone handset amplifiers, assistive listening systems, telephones compatible with hearing aids, closed caption decoders, open and closed captioning, telecommunications devices for deaf persons (TDDs), videotext displays and exchange of written notes. Examples for individuals with vision impairments include qualified readers, taped texts, audio recordings, Braille materials, large print materials and assistance in locating items. Examples for individuals with speech impairments include TDDs, computer terminals, speech synthesizers and communication boards.

auxiliary fund—see *conversion fund*.

average age at entry—average age of members when they enter a retirement plan. This average age is frequently used to estimate the cost of plan benefits.

average annual compensation—employee's yearly pay averaged over a specified number of years.

average benefit test—one of three standards that can be used to determine whether a qualified retirement plan satisfies the IRS minimum coverage requirement. The average of the benefit percentages for the group of employees who are not highly compensated must be at least equal to 70% of the average of the benefit percentages for highly compensated employees. The alternative tests are the *percentage test* and *ratio test*.

average daily census—average number of inpatients (other than newborns) in a hospital or other health facility each day throughout a given period. The census is calculated by dividing the number of patient days during a period by the number of calendar days in the period.

average indexed monthly earnings (AIME)—calculation used to determine a worker's Social Security benefits. A worker's earnings are adjusted (indexed) to reflect changes in general wage levels that have occurred during the worker's years of employment. The highest 35 years of indexed earnings are added together, then divided by 420—the number of months in 35 years. The result (the average indexed monthly earnings) is rounded down to the nearest dollar amount.

average length of stay (ALOS)—measure of the use of a health care facility, often used for health planning services. One approach for calculating ALOS is to divide total inpatient days of care (excluding newborns) by total admissions. An alternative method is to divide the total discharge days by the total discharges. The figure varies depending on factors such as patient diagnosis and hospital efficiency.

average life—length of time that will pass before half of the principal on a debt obligation has been paid. Average life is an artificial number used when determining the yield to maturity for a bond, mortgage or other debt obligation. It is only an estimate, as it depends on borrower prepayments and other factors. When used to compare bonds of different maturities and different repayment schedules, the term *average maturity* is sometimes used. Weighted average life is used for mortgage-backed securities.

average manufacturer price (AMP)—what a drug manufacturer lists as the cost of a drug sold to wholesalers after prompt pay discounts. AMP is the basis for Medicaid drug reimbursement. It is reported monthly and published on the U.S. Centers for Medicare and Medicaid Services (CMS) website.

average maturity—see *average life*.

average price—also referred to as the mean price, the sum of the dollar amounts paid for an item divided by the number of prices. Calculating the average price is a common method used when calculating taxes owed on mutual funds. The average price (or cost per share) for a mutual fund is found by determining the total cost of the fund shares and dividing it by the number of shares owed.

average sales price (ASP)—submitted quarterly by drug manufacturers to the U.S. Centers for Medicare and Medicaid Services (CMS). ASP is the weighted average cost of nonfederal sales by manufacturers to wholesale, including incentives to the wholesaler or retailer. ASP is currently used to price Medicare Part B drugs administered in physician offices.

average up/down—to purchase more shares of a stock that one already owns. If the price of the new shares is higher, the average cost of the stock increases, so the buyer has averaged up. If the new shares have a lower price than those already owned, the average cost of the shares declines and the buyer has averaged down.

average wholesale price (AWP)—term used by the prescription drug industry that refers to the average price at which wholesalers sell a drug to physicians, pharmacies and other customers. Throughout the health care industry, drug payments are typically based on AWP minus some percentage. In reality, what is reported as AWP is a price derived from self-reported manufacturer data collected by commercial publishers. There are no requirements that the AWP reflect the price of any actual sale of drugs by a manufacturer or that it be updated at established intervals. AWP is also criticized for failing to take into account the deep discounts available to various large purchasers such as the federal government and health maintenance organizations. See also *list price*.

B

baby bonus—financial payment used by some nations to encourage the decision to have more children and to help lighten the financial costs of raising children.

baby boomer—individual born between 1946 and 1964.

back-end load—fee charged an investor upon the sale of mutual fund shares. The fee is a percentage of the value of the shares being sold. The percentage is highest in the first year and decreases yearly until a specified holding period ends, at which time the percentage drops to zero. The time frame and size of the fee varies among funds. Also referred to as a back-end sales load, a contingent deferred sales charge or load, a deferred sales charge or load, an exit fee and a redemption fee. See also *front-end load*.

backloading—providing a faster rate of benefit accrual after an employee has attained a specified age or has completed a specified number of years of service. For example, backloading occurs in a plan that provides a benefit of 1.5% of compensation for each year of service before age 50 and 2% per year thereafter. The practice is limited under ERISA through the satisfaction of one of two accrual rules: the fractional rule or the 133 1/3% rule. See also *accrued benefit*.

backpay—salary and wages from a prior pay period to which an employee is entitled. A retroactive pay increase is provided in the form of backpay. Backpay may also be ordered by a court as the result of an employment practice (e.g., dismissal, treatment of overtime hours) that is deemed illegal.

bad boy clause—contract provision that withholds benefits or compensation if an employee engages in an activity that is detrimental to the employer. There is great variation as to what behavior is considered harmful, so circumstances considered detrimental must be clearly defined.

balance billing—charging patients for health care fees that exceed the amount approved by a plan or third-party insurer. Some locales and insurers have placed limits on or prohibit balance billing.

Balanced Budget Act of 1997 (BBA)—in addition to committing to balance the federal budget by 2002, this legislation included significant changes in health and welfare programs. New dollars were devoted to providing health insurance coverage for children, states were given unprecedented flexibility in administering their Medicaid programs and new coverage options for Medicare beneficiaries were made possible including the establishment of the Medicare+ Choice plan and high-deductible medigap policies. To further mental health coverage parity, the act required annual payments and lifetime caps associated with Medicaid and the new children's health initiative to be equal for mental health and physical health benefits. Special rules were also approved for medical savings accounts. See also *Medicare Advantage* and *medigap*.

balanced fund—mutual fund that combines stocks, bonds and sometimes a money market component into one investment portfolio to provide current income and long-term growth. The mix of fund types tends to be relatively fixed, typically 60% stocks and 40% bonds. See also *asset allocation fund, growth and income fund, hybrid fund* and *mutual fund*.

balance sheet—condensed financial statement showing the nature and amount of an organization's assets and liabilities on a given date. See also *asset* and *liability*.

balance sheet approach—technique used by companies to ensure that expatriates operating in other nations are not at a financial disadvantage when compared with home country peers with respect to the purchase of goods and services, and payment of taxes. Purchasing power in the home country is matched to that abroad. The company pays any additional costs that result from expatriation. This approach does not include incentives that may be necessary to induce employees to accept expatriate assignments.

balloon maturity—repayment schedule for an issue of bonds that has a large number of the bonds coming due at the same time, typically the final maturity date. A company's cash flow can be at risk if adequate preparation has not been made for the date when many bond payments come due.

balloon mortgage—short-term debt obligation for a house in which small periodic payments are made until a specific point in time when the borrower is required to pay the balance owed or arrange new financing.

bank draft—check drawn by one bank that authorizes a second bank to make payment to the person named on the draft. Since the check is guaranteed by the first bank, the second bank usually treats the draft as cash and clears it instantly. A bank draft is most often used when a payee is not certain that a check will clear or when rapid settlement is necessary. A bank draft may also be called a bank check, cashier's check, demand draft, official check, teller's check or treasurer's check.

bankers acceptance (BA)—order to a bank to pay a sum of money at a future date, typically within one to six months. When the bank endorses the order as "accepted," it assumes responsibility for ultimate payment to the holder of the acceptance. At this point, the acceptance may be traded in secondary markets much like any other claim on the bank. BAs are often used in importing and exporting, where the creditworthiness of one trader is unknown to the other trader.

bank investment contract (BIC)—contract issued by a bank to an investor that guarantees a rate of return on an investment for a specific period of time. Popular for the investment of pension funds, a BIC is similar to a guaranteed investment contract. An advantage of a BIC is protection of the principal available through federal deposit insurance. See also *guaranteed investment contract (GIC)* and *stable value fund*.

Bank of Canada—central bank of Canada, similar to the Federal Reserve System in the United States. Founded in 1934, the Bank of Canada is responsible for managing the nation's banking system, including issuing currency and administering monetary policy. The governor and senior deputy governor are appointed by the bank's board of directors (with the approval of the cabinet). The deputy minister of finance sits on the board of directors but has no vote. See also *monetary policy*.

bank of hours—see *hour bank*.

bankruptcy—inability to repay debts in full because liabilities exceed assets. In the U.S., The Bankruptcy Act provides procedures for various forms of bankruptcy: Chapter 7 refers to a business entity that must be liquidated due to insolvency, Chapter 11 applies to a business that is reorganizing, Chapter 12 applies to family farms and Chapter 13 allows for consumer debt adjustments. See also *receivership*.

Bankruptcy Abuse Prevention and Consumer Protection Act of 2005 (BAPCPA)—enacted April 20, 2005 and effective October 17, 2005, this U.S. legislation protects retirement plan assets from creditors during bankruptcy proceedings by exempting the assets from the debtor's bankruptcy estate. Funds that are in a qualified retirement plan, SEP plan, SIMPLE plan, Section 457 plan, TSA, individual retirement account (IRA) or Roth IRA are protected. Generally, the amount of IRA assets that is protected is limited to $1 million; amounts attributable to rollovers from protected plans do not count toward the $1 million limit.

barbell strategy—bond portfolio that is invested only in short- and long-term bonds. There are no investments in intermediate bonds.

bare-bones health plan—no-frills health plan or insurance policy that typically offers a reduced set of benefits for a lower premium. Features of the plan include limited coverage, large deductibles and copayments, and low policy limits. The plan may cover basic and preventive care. Many terms are used for this type of plan, including limited benefit health plan, mandate-light plan, mandate-free plan, minimum benefit plan, mini med coverage and mini med plan.

bargaining unit—group of employees authorized to negotiate working terms and conditions on behalf of all the employees of an employer or an industry.

barriers to care—obstacles (e.g., cost, availability, health literacy, behavioral) that prevent persons from getting quality health care and/or complying with recommended treatment guidelines.

barter—trade in which goods or services are directly exchanged for other goods or services, without the use of money. Also referred to as a swap.

base benefit percentage—rate at which employer-provided benefits are determined under a defined benefit plan with respect to an employee's average annual compensation at or below the integration level. See also *excess rate method, integration, integration level* and *permitted disparity.*

base capitation—specific amount per person per period (e.g., month, year) paid to a provider to cover health care costs that typically excludes pharmacy and administrative costs. Coverage for mental health and substance abuse services is also commonly excluded.

base contribution percentage—proportion of an employee's compensation for the year at or below the integration level rate that is allocated to an employee's defined contribution account. See also *excess rate method, integration, integration level* and *permitted disparity.*

base country—nation on which an expatriate's compensation is based. The base country is usually the expatriate's home country, but it may also be the country of original employment. See also *home country.*

base rate—interest rate used by banks as the basis for setting the interest rates charged borrowers. See also *base wage rate.*

base wage rate—dollars paid per hour for a job excluding bonuses, incentive premiums, shift differentials and overtime. Also referred to as base rate.

basic earning power—operating income divided by total assets. See also *earning power.*

basic market value—worth of an asset at a particular point in time.

basic medical insurance—form of health care coverage that pays for a limited set of hospital services and supplies regardless of whether the care is performed in or out of a hospital. Typically, some doctor visits are also covered. The limits of basic medical insurance can be quickly reached if a person has a serious accident or illness; major medical insurance plans are designed to take over where basic medical plans stop. See also *insurance* and *major medical insurance.*

basis—purchase price of a security after commissions and other related expenses are deducted. Also known as cost basis or tax basis, this figure is used to calculate capital gains and losses when a security is sold.

basis book—see *bond basis book.*

basis point (BP)—one-hundredth of a percent. Basis points are used to measure very small changes or differences between yields on fixed income securities. If the yield on a bond increases from 4% to 4.5%, it has increased by 50 basis points. A change of 0.01% in a bond's yield would be 1 basis point. Basis points are also used to state investment fees.

Bay Street—street in Toronto housing the headquarters of many financial institutions; similar to Wall Street in the United States.

bear—someone who believes the price of a particular security (i.e., stock, bond) or prices in a market are going to drop. A bear is the opposite of a bull.

bearer bond—debt obligation payable to the holder of a debt instrument (the bearer), not necessarily the owner whose name is registered on the books of the issuing company. Coupon bonds fall into this classification. See also *coupon bond* and *registered bond.*

bear market—generally considered a period in which investment prices fall sharply (20% or more) against a background of widespread pessimism. Bear markets usually occur when the economy is in recession and unemployment is high, or when inflation is rising quickly. The most famous bear market in U.S. history was the Great Depression of the 1930s. A bear market is the opposite of a bull market.

bed days—number of inpatient hospital days per 1,000 persons covered by a plan for a year or other period.

behavioral economics or finance—relatively new field of study that combines psychology and human behavior to explain monetary decisions and why people make irrational choices.

behavioral health—emotions, behaviors and biology relating to people's mental well-being, their ability to cope with the everyday challenges of life and their concept of self. A person struggling with his or her behavioral health may face stress, depression, anxiety, relationship problems, grief, addiction, ADHD, learning disabilities, mood disorders or other psychological concerns. Professionals help individuals manage behavioral health concerns with treatments such as therapy, counseling and/or medication. Behavioral health is sometimes used interchangeably with mental health. Others differentiate mental health as only the biological components of behavioral health issues. See also *mental health*.

behavioral intervention—treatment to modify what a person does or how he or she reacts using strategies such as positive and negative reinforcement, behavior modification and behavioral therapy.

behavior-based appraisal—performance evaluation that considers what a person does versus what he or she produces. Performance is rated using a behavior expectation or observation scale. This method is in contrast to those that focus on results, such as management by objective.

benchmark—standard by which something can be measured or judged. For example, a company may benchmark its compensation or benefit package in order to determine how it compares with others in an industry or geographic locale. The process of benchmarking can be very helpful when an employer wants to improve its ability to attract quality employees. Investors benchmark the performance of their investments with major market indices such as the S&P 500 to quantify how far they are from investment goals.

benchmark job—job for which specifications and pay data are available and used as a reference point for making comparisons. Published surveys are often available that provide pay data for benchmark jobs.

benchmark price—dollar amount paid for the purchase of a pharmaceutical. For example, a state may set its Medicaid reimbursement rate at a benchmark price such as the wholesale acquisition cost (WAC).

bend point percentage—see *primary insurance amount (PIA)*.

beneficiary—person or group that receives benefits, profits or advantages. In the benefits arena, a beneficiary is typically someone who receives a benefit from a plan or insurance policy. A beneficiary may be a plan participant or a person eligible for benefits through the plan participant. An example of the latter is a person who receives benefits upon the death of a spouse.

benefit—right of a participant or beneficiary to cash, goods or services after meeting the eligibility requirements of a benefit plan.

benefit accrual—see *accrual of benefits*.

benefit booklet—publication for employees that contains a general explanation of benefits.

benefit design—process used to determine which benefits and the level of benefits that will be offered to plan participants, the extent to which participants are expected to share the cost of these benefits and how a participant can access these benefits.

benefit differential—plan design feature that offers greater benefits when participants use a network provider.

benefit formula—mathematical equation used to calculate life insurance and retirement benefits to which an employee is entitled. Pension benefit formulas usually include an employee's years of service, compensation or both.

benefit fund—money set aside for the payment of benefits.

benefit in kind—see *employee benefit*.

benefit multiplier—percentage multiplied by a participant's salary or wages, which is commonly used to determine the monthly benefit paid by a defined benefit pension plan. The multiplier typically reflects an employee's years of service; the more years of service, the higher the percentage.

benefit package—specific goods, services and/or payments provided by a benefit plan or insurance contract.

benefit payment schedule—see *table of allowances*.

benefit period—in an insurance plan, a specified number of days or visits relating to coverage. Benefit periods and how they are applied vary greatly from one insurance plan to another. Medicare defines a benefit period as starting the day a beneficiary is admitted to the hospital or skilled nursing facility and ending when 60 days go by without hospital or skilled nursing care. With commercial health insurance policies, the benefit period is frequently a calendar year; at the beginning of each benefit period (January), the beneficiary is required to satisfy deductibles before health care expenses are covered by the policy. The benefit period for long-term care policies is how long the benefits will last, typically stated in terms of a maximum number of days, years or visits.

benefit plan—see *employee benefit plan*.

benefit plan summary—see *summary plan description (SPD)*.

benefit specialist—individual in an organization who is responsibile for administering an employee benefits program.

bereavement leave—paid time off for employees, usually following the death of a relative. Bereavement policies typically specify the relatives whose death qualifies an employee for leave. Also known as funeral leave.

best practice—method, process or technique that is most effective at delivering the desired results.

best price—lowest dollar charge available for a good or service that is available to any buyer including wholesalers, retailers and government. Best price reflects any discounts, rebates and free goods provided with the purchase.

beta—measure of how an investment's price moves in relation to a financial market as a whole. Beta is the average change in the value of a security corresponding to a 1% change in the market. For example, a beta of 0.5 means the security is only half as volatile as the average security, while a beta of 2.0 means the security is twice as risky. An asset with a beta of 0 means that its price is independent of the market. The higher the beta, the higher the return required and vice versa. Whether the beta is positive or negative is also important. A positive beta means the value of the asset generally follows the market, while a negative beta indicates the value of the asset is inversely related to the market; the value of the asset generally decreases when the value of the market goes up and vice versa. See also *capital asset pricing model (CAPM)*, *market risk* and *volatility*.

bid-ask spread—also known simply as the spread, the difference between a security's bid price (the price offered for a security) and its ask price (the price sellers will accept for a security). If the bid price is $20 and the ask price is $21, then the bid-ask spread is $1. On a trading floor, there may be several bid prices and several ask prices for a security at any point in time. Only the highest bid and the lowest ask are used to calculate the bid-ask spread.

big board—nickname for the New York Stock Exchange.

bid price—the dollar amount a buyer offers to pay for securities; the price at which sellers are willing to sell.

bioavailability—rate and extent of a medication's absorption in the human body.

bioequivalent—medication that has the same active ingredients, strength, dosage and delivery form as a drug approved by the FDA. Bioequivalent are also referred to as biological equivalent drugs.

biologic—biology-based drug that structurally mimics compounds found in the body. Biologics include a wide range of products such as vaccines, blood and blood components, allergenics, gene therapy, tissues and therapeutic proteins created by biological process in contrast to traditional medications created through chemistry. Biologics are also referred to as biopharmaceuticals.

biological equivalent drug—see *bioequivalent*.

biometric screening—examination of a person's physical characteristics to determine his or her risk level for certain diseases and medical conditions. Common elements in biometric screening are measurement of height, weight, blood cholesterol, blood glucose, blood pressure, heart rate, body mass index (BMI) and bone density. In the value-based approach to health care, incentives may be provided to employees based upon positive changes made in their individual biometrics such as weight loss, lower cholesterol levels or better management of blood sugar levels.

biopharmaceutical—see *biologic*.

biosimilar—biology-based drug (biologic) similar to a brand-name biologic that is available once the patent on the brand-name product has expired.

biotech drug—medication that is produced using living organisms such as yeast, bacteria or human cells. See also *specialty drug*.

birthday rule—method used to determine primary and secondary insurance coverage for a child covered by both parents' health plans. Primary coverage falls to the parent who has the earlier birthday (month and day, not year). In the event that the birthdays occur on the same day, the employer-provided health insurance plan that has covered a parent the longest pays first. See also *coordination-of-benefits (COB) provision*.

birth rate—number of live births per 1,000 people in a specific geographic locale. The birth rate is calculated by dividing the total population into the number of live births and multiplying by 1,000.

biweekly pay systems—schedule by which employees receive salary or wages every two weeks.

black box trading—computerized trading system that automatically buys and sells stock shares according to pre-programmed rules or algorithms. The benefits of a black box trading system is that a computer isn't subject to human error. In addition, a computer can do millions of calculations per minute, which a human being is just not capable of doing.

black knight—individual or company that makes an acquisition bid deemed unwelcome by the target firm. The threatened management may then ask a white knight to rescue it. See also *white knight*.

blacklist—collection of people or entities to be shunned, banned or in some other way penalized. Blacklists have been used to deny persons employment, credit, entrance to social clubs, service in restaurants, etc. The legality of blacklisting varies depending on the situation; in some cases, it is perfectly acceptable, whereas, in other instances, it is viewed as discrimination. Insurers have been known to blacklist (refuse to insure) high-risk industries, professions or individuals (especially those who might inherit diseases). Many states and federal law now bar large health insurers from using genetic testing to discriminate against individuals because of the potential for developing a disease in the future.

Black Monday—October 19, 1987, when the Dow Jones Industrial Average plummeted a record-shattering 508 points, almost 23% in a single day. The event marked the beginning of a global stock market decline; and, by the end of the month, most of the major exchanges had dropped over 20%. While there are many theories as to what caused the crash, no agreement has been reached beyond the fact that panic caused the crash to escalate. Since Black Monday, there have been multiple mechanisms built into the market to prevent panic selling, such as trading curbs and circuit breakers that temporarily halt trading under extreme circumstances. See also *circuit breaker*, *panic selling* and *trading curb*.

blackout period—this term can be defined in two ways with respect to retirement plans. It is sometimes used to describe the period during which a surviving spouse no longer receives survivor benefits and before he or she is eligible for retirement benefits. It can also refer to a period of time during which employees are not allowed to adjust investments contained in their retirement plans. Such a period occurs when a plan is undergoing significant changes such as a switch in plan recordkeepers, trustees, vendors and valuation systems. It may also occur during a company merger or acquisition. This latter type of blackout period is also known as a lockdown. One purpose of such a period is to prevent insider trading. Since an employee's investments may also be jeopardized during a blackout period, federal regulations in the United States stipulate that administrators provide employees with a minimum of 30 days' (maximum of 60 days) notice before a blackout period takes effect. See also *Sarbanes-Oxley Act of 2002 (SOX)*.

Black-Scholes model—formula used to calculate the value of a call option. The model considers the current option's value, the strike price and expiration date, the price of the underlying security, stock-price volatility, the time to the option's maturity, the risk-free rate of return and the standard deviation of the annualized continuously compounded rate of return on the stock. A modified version of this model is used for valuing stock options when completing an FAS123R. See also *option agreement* and *exercise price*.

block—large quantity of the same security bought or sold by a large investor. While there is no official quantity considered a block, 10,000 equity shares or more than $200,000 of debt securities is commonly considered the threshold.

blue chip—nickname for large, well-established, financially sound corporations that are known for stable growth and consistent profitability. The price of blue chip stocks are usually less volatile than stocks that have not been given blue-chip status. Coca-Cola, Gillette, ExxonMobil and Wal-Mart are all blue-chip companies.

Blue Cross and Blue Shield Association (BCBSA)—nonprofit federation of community-based and locally operated Blue Cross and Blue Shield companies in the United States. BCBSA licenses the Blue Cross and Blue Shield brand names, giving members the franchise right to sell Blue-branded health plans within defined regions. The association coordinates the BlueCard program, which allows members covered by a local BCBS company to have coverage by BCBS companies in other service areas. The association also coordinates the Federal Employees Health Benefit Plan, which covers more than half of federal government employees, retirees and their dependents.

Blue Cross and Blue Shield plan—independent insurance company that offers health insurance within a defined region of the United States. These plans also act as Medicare administrators in many parts of the country. Historically, Blue Cross plans provided hospital coverage, while Blue Shield plans were used for medical (e.g., physician) expenses. This split has almost disappeared today. While some plans are administered by not-for-profit organizations, others are for-profit companies.

blue-sky laws—state statutes governing the sale of securities that attempt to protect investors from fraud. Blue-sky laws require corporations advertising and selling shares to the public to get approval from a state regulatory commission and/or SEC after providing details on financing and management. The term developed from the desire to prevent the existence of corporations that have nothing behind them but "blue sky."

board certified—physician or other health professional who has passed an examination given by a medical board and has been certified by that board as a specialist in a specific type of care.

board eligible—physician or other health professional who has completed the requirements to practice a specialty (e.g., medical school and residency) but has not taken and passed the required examination.

body mass index (BMI)—measure of body fat that equals the weight of an individual in kilograms divided by the square of the person's height in meters. For an adult, a BMI of 25 to 29.9 is considered overweight, while 30 or more indicates obesity.

bona fide occupational qualification (BFOQ)—requirement which, when viewed on the surface, seems biased but actually is reasonably necessary for the performance of the job. When permitted, job requirements such as gender, religion and national origin are considered exceptions to Title VII of the Civil Rights Act of 1964. For example, religion could be considered a bona fide occupational qualification when membership in a certain religion is reasonably necessary to the performance of a job. A company selling religious books might be allowed to insist on hiring salespeople of the particular religion involved. An employer, however, cannot refuse to hire a janitor because of his religion, as it is not reasonably necessary to the operation of the business.

bona fide purchaser—one who buys an asset for a stated and fair value, unaware of any claims or rights that might be made by a third party. The legal importance of this concept occurs if a true owner shows up to claim the property. The bona fide purchaser is allowed to keep the asset, and the real owner must pursue reimbursement from the fraudulent seller. See also *holder in due course*.

bond—certificate of debt similar to an IOU issued by a company or government entity. An investor lends money to the issuer and, in exchange, the issuer promises to repay the loan at a future date (the bond's maturity date). Depending on the type of bond, the issuer may be required to make periodic interest payments to the bondholder (owner) between the date of issuance and maturity. When comparing the return on bonds, an investor uses one of these yields, depending on the type of bond and its maturity date: coupon yield, current yield, tax-equivalent yield or yield to maturity. See also *Canada Note, Canada Premium Bond (CBP), Canada Savings Bond (CSB), coupon bond, discount bond, income bond, municipal bond, note, registered bond, savings bond, straight bond, Treasury bill, Treasury bond, Treasury note* and *zero-coupon bond*.

bond basis book—collection of tables used to convert bond yields of different maturities and coupon rates to equivalent dollar prices. Also called a basis book. See also *yield*.

bond fund—mutual fund that invests in corporate, municipal and/or g bonds. Bond funds generally aim for an income stream and protection of capital. Depending on the securities held, the fund may be taxable or tax-free. See also *municipal bond fund* and *mutual fund*.

bond immunization—see *immunization*.

bonding—insurance contract in which an insurance company promises to reimburse a benefit plan (the insured) for losses caused by acts of theft or misappropriation by plan fiduciaries and any other persons who handle plan assets. See also *surety bond*.

bond premium—amount by which the issue price of a bond exceeds its face value. A premium occurs when the coupon rate of interest on a bond is higher than the market interest rate at the time a bond is issued.

bond ratings—system for measuring the quality and safety of a bond, based on the financial condition of the issuer. Among the better known rating services are Standard & Poor's, Moody's and Fitch. Rating systems vary but usually use a combination of letters, numbers or plus (+) and minus (-) signs that indicate where a bond falls in a range from highest quality (low risk) to lowest quality (high risk). Standard & Poor's uses an "A" to indicate the best quality bonds, a "B" for highly speculative bonds and "C" or "D" when a bond is in or near default.

bond swap—sale of a bond and the purchase of another bond of similar value. Reasons this might be done include to establish a tax loss, upgrade credit quality and to extend or shorten maturity.

bonus—payment in addition to normal salary and wages typically given at a manager's discretion to recognize work performance. Payment is usually made as one lump sum. Unlike a salary or wage increase, a bonus is not a permanent increase in compensation.

book reserve—method for recognizing pension liabilities on an employer's balance sheet. Money set aside for future pension liabilities (on reserve) may or may not be segregated from other assets of the employer.

book value—dollar amount at which an asset is carried on a balance sheet. Book value may be more or less than market value. The value of a capital asset is its cost plus any additions, minus depreciation. A corporation's book value is its assets minus liabilities. See also *asset* and *liability*.

boomerang employee—employee who leaves an employer, for whatever reason, then returns to work for the same employer at a later point.

bottom-up manager—investor who looks for stocks company by company, seeking favorable individual companies regardless of the industry. See also *top-down manager*.

brand-name drug—medication marketed under a specific trade name. A brand-name drug is a proprietary or patent-protected pharmaceutical available from only one manufacturer. Production of the drug by other companies is prohibited as long as the patent remains in effect. See also *generic drug*.

brand-name interchange—substitution of a brand-name drug that is the chemical or therapeutic equivalent of another brand-name drug. See also *brand-name drug*, *chemical equivalent* and *therapeutic equivalent*.

brand-name medication—see *brand-name drug*.

breach of fiduciary duty—conduct that falls short of the standard expected. In the United States, a benefit plan trustee who fails to manage plan assets prudently may be charged with a breach of the ERISA-mandated fiduciary duties.

breach of trust—act that (1) violates the duties of a trustee or (2) breaks a promise or confidence. A breach of trust does not need to be intentional or done with malice. It can be the result of negligence.

break in service (BIS)—under ERISA, a calendar year, plan year or other 12-consecutive-month period designated by a plan during which a plan participant does not complete more than 500 hours of service. This general rule has been modified for certain industries, particularly those characterized by seasonal employment patterns. Special rules also apply to prevent certain maternity and paternity leaves of absence from being treated as breaks in service. After a break in service occurs, the participant must again meet the plan's eligibility requirements to participate. A plan is allowed to require an employee to complete one year of service upon return before recognizing any pre-break service for eligibility or vesting purposes. Once the year (referred to as a one-year holdout period) has been met, the plan must retroactively apply credit for the year. See also *rule of parity*.

breakpoint—dollar threshold at which a mutual fund purchaser qualifies for a reduction in sales charges on a volume order.

Bretton Woods Conference—officially known as the United Nations Monetary and Financial Conference, a gathering of delegates from 44 nations that met during July 1944 in Bretton Woods, New Hampshire. At the meeting, delegates agreed upon a series of new rules for the post-war international monetary system including an agreement for each nation to maintain a currency exchange rate within a fixed value—plus or minus 1%. One of the most significant accomplishments was the creation of the International Monetary Fund. See also *fixed exchange rate*, *flexible exchange rate* and *International Monetary Fund*.

bridging benefit—temporary, supplemental pension benefit payable from the date of early retirement until death or the age of entitlement for government pensions in Canada.

bridging supplement—payment in addition to regular pension plan benefits provided an employee who retires before becoming eligible for Canadian government benefits. Payment of this supplement ceases when Old Age Security (OAS) and Canada Pension Plan (CPP)/Québec Pension Plan (QPP) benefits are payable (or offset by those benefits).

broadbanding—strategy for salary structures that consolidates a large number of pay grades into a few broad categories (bands). Broadbanding attempts to overcome a rigid, hierarchical pay structure.

broker—person or business that buys or sells for another in exchange for a commission. Insurance brokers bring together clients who are seeking insurance coverage and insurance companies. The broker represents the buyer rather than the company, even though he or she receives a commission from the company. Those who handle orders to buy and sell securities, commodities and other property are also referred to as brokers. How the commission is paid in these transactions varies depending on what is being sold, who the buyer and seller are and the amount of the transaction. See also *discount broker, insurance broker, real estate broker, securities broker* and *traditional broker.*

broker-dealer—person or business that buys and sells securities for others (as a broker) as well as itself (as a dealer). See also *blue-sky laws* and *Securities Exchange Act of 1934.*

brokerage account—account established with a brokerage firm that allows an investor to buy and sell securities. A professional broker at the brokerage firm is instructed by the investor as to what securities to buy and sell. The brokerage firm is paid a commission for making the transaction. See also *broker fee.*

broker fee—dollar charge by a broker for the execution of a securities transaction. The size of the fee is usually an amount per transaction or a percentage of the total value of the transaction. This fee can range from as little as $5 to several hundred dollars depending on the number of transactions, the dollar value of the transactions and whether a discount or traditional broker handles the exchange. Broker fees are often negotiable. See also *commission, discount broker* and *traditional broker.*

bronze plan—see "Qualified health plans" in the *Appendix A: Affordable Care Act of 2010 (ACA).*

bubble—rise in the price of an asset or group of assets to a level that is considered unsustainable. The prices are based on the expectation that prices will continue to rise. When these expectations cease to exist, the bubble bursts and there is a rapid decline in prices. The speculation in, and rapid price growth of, Internet stocks in the 1990s is commonly referred to as the dot-com bubble.

bubble economy—situation in which there are one or more bubbles in asset markets. In the late 1980s, Japan was said to have a bubble economy.

builder's lien—see *mechanic's lien.*

bull—someone who believes the price of a particular security (i.e., stock, bond) or prices in a market are going to rise. A bull is the opposite of a bear.

bullion—precious metal such as gold or silver in the form of bars or ingots that are sold by weight. Some central banks use bullion for settlement of international debt, and some investors purchase bullion as a hedge against inflation.

bull market—generally considered a period in which investment prices rise 20% or more. Bull markets can happen as a result of an economic recovery, an economic boom or investor psychology. A bull market is the opposite of a bear market.

bundled payment—reimbursement for a package of related goods and services for a single price from a contractor. Plan sponsors sometimes contract for multiple services (e.g., investment management and administration) from the same vendor. A bundled payment arrangement can also be used by a health plan to pay for the services a patient needs for a specific medical condition or disease (e.g., delivery of a baby, or an occurrence of cancer or coronary artery disease). Bundled payments can motivate a provider to control the unit cost and utilization of services—yielding efficiencies and cost savings passed on to the purchaser that would not be possible if the services had been contracted separately. See also *unbundling.*

bundled sales/services—packaging of different types of related goods or services for a single price that is less than the price if the items were purchased separately. See also *bundled payment* and *unbundling.*

Bureau of Labor Statistics (BLS)—unit within the U.S. Department of Labor that collects and reports labor statistics, including data on pay, employee benefits, productivity and unemployment.

business associate—for purposes of HIPAA privacy legislation, an individual or entity that, on behalf of a covered entity, performs or assists with a function or activity involving protected health information. Examples include lawyers, consultants, third-party administrators, doctors and health care clearinghouses. See also *Health Insurance Portability and Accountability Act of 1996 (HIPAA).*

business continuation insurance—contract issued by an insurance company that promises protection to business partners if a partner dies or is disabled. The remaining partners are provided with the funds to purchase that partner's interest in the firm. See also *insurance* and *key employee insurance.*

business cycle—pattern of historically observed economic behavior comprised of economic growth and decline. Business cycles generally consist of four stages: expansion, peak, recession and trough. During expansion, the economy strengthens and business activity accelerates. The point at which the economy overheats, causing inflation and interest rates to rise, is referred to as a peak. Higher interest rates lead to waning business activity and a contracting economy called a recession. A trough occurs when the lower inflation and interest rates spark the beginnings of an economic rebound, or expansion. See also *depression* and *recession*.

business judgment rule—legal doctrine that shields corporate officers and directors from personal liability for their actions, as long as the actions were taken in good faith and with reasonable care.

business life insurance—see *business continuation insurance* and *key employee insurance*.

business representative (BR)—official who represents union workers on a paid, full-time basis. Also referred to as a business agent.

business risk—chance the value of a company will drop due to something specific to the company. For example, a belief among investors that the business is poorly managed, a news story that the business is not going to earn as much profit as expected or the introduction of a competing product that is better or less expensive.

business travel accident insurance—financial protection by an insurance company for the death or injury of an employee while traveling on company business. An employer can customize this insurance to meet specific needs such as travel on a company plane, war and terrorism. Coverage can also be expanded to include additional family members and personnel as well as business-related travel.

buy-back provision—pension plan provision that allows a terminated employee who has received a plan distribution to repay the withdrawn amount and buy back the forfeited benefits.

buying on margin—borrowing money from a broker to purchase stocks or other securities. The investor establishes a margin account, which is like a credit line for securities purchases. The investor must deposit and maintain a minimum amount of cash or securities as collateral, usually a percentage of the current value of the securities. The minimum amount required in the account changes as the values of the securities fluctuate. Buying on margin also requires the investor to make interest payments on the borrowed money. While there is the potential for greater profit, there is also the potential for greater losses. Hence, buying on margin is extremely risky. See also *margin, margin account* and *margin call*.

bylaws—rules and regulations adopted by an association or corporation that govern its activities. Bylaws must not be contrary to the laws where the organization is located. They affect only the members of the given organization; they do not apply to third parties.

by report—written narrative submitted with a claim form by a health or dental care provider to (1) describe a service that does not have a code or (2) more fully explain a procedure specified in the code set as a "by report" procedure.

C

Cadillac Tax—see "Fees/Taxes" in the *Appendix A: Affordable Care Act of 2010 (ACA)*.

cafeteria plan—benefit plan maintained by an employer that offers employees the choice between a taxable benefit (e.g., cash) and one or more nontaxable benefits. This choice can be offered through a premium payment plan, a salary reduction plan or a more elaborate flexible benefit plan. To qualify for special tax treatment in the United States, the plan must comply with IRC Section 125. The benefits that may be offered through a Section 125 cafeteria plan include accident and health benefits, adoption assistance, dependent care assistance, group term life insurance, contributions to a health savings account and a cash-or-deferred-savings feature in the form of a 401(k) plan. See also *flexible benefit plan, flexible spending arrangement (FSA), health savings account (HSA), premium-only plan (POP)* and *Section 125*.

calendar-year deductible—portion of expenses that an insured must pay before an insurer will begin benefit payments. See also *deductible*.

call—process of redeeming a bond or preferred stock before its scheduled maturity.

callable—when a bond or other security may be redeemed by the issuer. Terms for the redemption are designated at the time of issuance. Callable bonds may be redeemed by the issuer at a specified date and price prior to maturity. The term also applies to preferred shares of stock that may be redeemed by the issuing company. Callable and redeemable are used interchangeably. See also *call date* and *call price.*

call center—facility equipped to handle telephone requests. Benefit plan sponsors and service providers call the center for activities such as handling enrollment, processing claims and responding to employee benefit questions. See also *employee self-service (ESS), interactive benefits communication* and *interactive voice response (IVR).*

call date—date on which a callable bond may be redeemed before its maturity.

called bond—debt security redeemed by its issuer before maturity.

call option—see *option agreement.*

call price—price at which an issuer may redeem (1) a callable bond prior to maturity or (2) a preferred stock that has a call provision. The call price (also known as the redemption price) is usually at or above the bond's face value.

call risk—chance that the holder of a bond or other security will redeem the security prior to maturity.

CalPERS (California Public Employees' Retirement System)—as the nation's largest pension fund, CalPERS provides retirement benefits for current and retired California state government employees.

Canada Health Act—federal legislation that requires each Canadian province to provide legal residents with health care coverage for hospital and medical services. Unofficially, the program is referred to as medicare.

Canada Industrial Relations Board (CIRB)—administrative tribunal whose functions and powers are established by the Canada Labour Code. Among other things, CIRB is empowered to adjudicate labor relations disputes arising under the code. CIRB was formerly the Canada Labour Relations Board.

Canada Labour Code—federal legislation that mandates minimum wage and overtime standards in Canada similar to the standards established by the Fair Labor Standards Act in the United States.

Canada Note—debt issued by the Government of Canada that is usually denominated in U.S. dollars of $1,000 and integral multiples thereof. Canada Notes can be issued for terms of nine months or longer and can be issued at a fixed or floating rate. Purchase is through select dealers and directly from the government.

Canada Pension Plan (CPP)/Québec Pension Plan (QPP)—the Canada Pension Plan is a social insurance program that ensures a measure of protection to contributors and their families against the loss of income due to retirement, disability or death. The plan operates throughout Canada. The Québec Pension Plan, a virtually identical plan, operates in the province of Québec. Mandatory government programs, both are funded by employee and employer contributions over a person's working life on a partial pay-as-you-go basis. The maximum benefit under CPP/QPP is 25% of career average earnings up to the average industrial wage set annually. Unlike OAS and GIS, the CPP/QPP is not income tested. Spouses receive 60% of their partner's benefit if they do not receive other CPP benefits. Given the initial intent of CPP/QPP was to help people without a workplace plan, many pension plans integrate their benefit formulae and target income replacement payouts with CPP/QPP benefits. To keep pace with inflation, benefits from these plans are indexed to the Consumer Price Index and adjusted annually. See also *children's benefits, Old Age Security (OAS)* and *Guaranteed Income Supplement (GIS).*

Canada Premium Bond (CPB)—debt issued by the Government of Canada that is available for purchase at most financial institutions in Canada. CPBs offer a higher rate of interest at the time of issue compared to a Canada Savings Bond available at the same time. They are redeemable only once a year on the anniversary date of issue and during the 30 days that follow without a penalty. Once the issue date has passed, the announced interest rate for the posted period does not change. Available in both regular interest and compound interest forms. Regular interest bonds are available starting at $300, while compound interest bonds are available for as little as $100. See also *Canada Savings Bond (CSB).*

Canada Revenue Agency (CRA)—administrator of tax laws for the Government of Canada as well as most provinces and territories. CRA also administers various social and economic incentive programs delivered through the tax system; it was formerly known as Revenue Canada and as the Canada Customs and Revenue Agency.

Canada Savings Bond (CSB)—debt issued by the Government of Canada and offered for sale by most financial institutions in Canada. With limited exceptions, CSBs may only be registered in the name of a Canadian resident. They are available in denominations ranging from $100 to $10,000. They are non-callable and, in most cases, also non-transferable. See also *Canada Premium Bond (CPB)*.

Canadian Association of Pension Supervisory Authorities (CAPSA)—senior government officials (federal and provincial) responsible for the administration of pension legislation in each jurisdiction.

Canadian Council of Superintendents of Insurance—formerly the Association of Superintendents of Insurance of the Provinces of Canada, this group promotes uniformity in the regulation of insurance matters and provides a forum for consultation. Members include superintendents of insurance in the non-common-law provinces of Canada (except Québec).

Canadian Human Rights Act—federal legislation that prohibits decisions and actions that treat a person or a group negatively for reasons on the grounds of race, national or ethnic origin, color, religion, age, sex, sexual orientation, marital status, family status, disability and a conviction for which a pardon has been granted or a record suspended. Practices considered discriminatory and prohibited when based on one or more of the grounds just listed are:
- Denying someone goods, services, facilities or accommodation
- Providing someone goods, services, facilities or accommodation in a way that treats them adversely and differently
- Refusing to employ or continue to employ someone, or treating them unfairly in the workplace
- Following policies or practices that deprive people of employment opportunities
- Paying men and women differently when they are doing work of the same value
- Retaliating against a person who has filed a complaint with the Commission or against someone who has filed a complaint for them
- Harassing someone.

The Canadian Institute of Actuaries (CIA)—professional body that regulates the actuarial profession in Canada. The CIA is responsible for ensuring the appropriate level of education, skill and expertise exists among its members and requires actuaries to comply its prescribed qualification criteria and Rules of Professional Conduct.

cancelable—term in an individual insurance policy that indicates the policy can be terminated at any time by the insurer. See also *conditionally renewable, guaranteed renewable, noncancelable and guaranteed renewable* and *optionally renewable*.

cap—upper limit on what is allowed; for example, the maximum dollar amount that will be paid or the maximum number of years of service for which a benefit credit will be given.

capital—cash and other assets owned by an individual or business. Capital is required to establish and operate a business.

capital accumulation—gathering of wealth; for example, defined contribution plans provide an opportunity for employees to accumulate capital that will be used upon retirement. See also *salary reduction plan*.

capital accumulation plan (CAP)—tax-assisted savings or investment plan that permits members to make investment decisions among two or more options offered within the plan. In Canada, such plans may be established by an employer, trade union, association or any combination of these entities for the benefit of employees or members. CAPs are subject to the *Capital Accumulation Plan (CAP) Guidelines*.

Capital Accumulation Plan (CAP) Guidelines—standards published by the Canadian Association of Pension Supervisory Authorities (CAPSA). While the CAP Guidelines do not have the force of law, they may be used as a benchmark by the courts and/or regulators to assess whether a plan administrator has fulfilled its fiduciary obligations. See also *capital accumulation plan (CAP)*.

capital appreciation—increase in the price of an asset.

capital appreciation fund—see *growth fund*.

capital asset—tangible property such as a building or equipment that is usually held for a long period of time and that is not easily converted into cash.

capital asset pricing model (CAPM)—method for assessing the relationship between risk (measured by a beta coefficient) and expected return. A CAPM is used in the pricing of risky securities with the expected return of the security or portfolio equal to the rate on a risk-free security plus a risk premium. If CAPM does not meet or beat the required return, then the investment should not be undertaken. See also *beta*.

capital expenditure—money spent to purchase or improve capital assets. Also referred to as capital spending or capital expense.

capital gain distribution—payment to mutual fund shareholders of profits from assets sold by the fund. These gains are usually paid near the end of a calendar year.

capital gain/loss—increase or decrease in the value of a capital asset. A capital gain occurs when the value is higher than the purchase price. If the value is lower, a capital loss has occurred. Capital gains and losses are not realized until an asset is sold. See also *long-term gain/loss, paper profit/loss, realized profit/loss* and *short-term gain/loss*.

capitalization—total value of securities (i.e., bonds, stocks) issued by a corporation.

capital market—market where securities (i.e., bonds, stocks) are bought and sold.

capital stock—shares issued by a corporation that represent ownership, including both *preferred stock* and *common stock*.

capital structure—mix of debt and equity used by a business to purchase assets and finance operations. Debt includes bonds and accounts payable while equity includes preferred stock, common stock and retained earnings. Some analysts exclude accounts payable and short-term debts, preferring to include these only in a broader term referred to as financial structure. The capital structure of a company is an indicator of risk. A company that is more heavily financed by debt is considered to pose a greater investment risk.

capital sum—see *principal sum*.

capitation—payment of a fixed amount to a service provider per plan member, regardless of the number or type of services used by the member. With capitation, the payment is typically expressed as "per member per month" or "per member per year." The actual payment is known as a capitation fee. Capitation is commonly used by health maintenance organizations and primary care providers. This approach shifts some risk to the providers, who assume the increased number of patients will level out the risk.

captive insurance company—insurer that is a subsidiary of a noninsurance corporation. The captive company's primary purpose is to underwrite some or all of the risk of its parent and parent's other subsidiaries, although nonrelated business may be solicited. While the form and structure of captive insurance companies continue to evolve, most can be categorized as either a *group captive, pure captive* or *rent-a-captive*.

card program—see *prescription drug card program*.

Care Continuum Alliance—formerly the Disease Management Association of America (DMAA), a nonprofit organization of corporations and individuals promoting strategies to raise care quality, improve health outcomes and reduce preventable health care costs for individuals with or at risk of chronic disease. The Alliance accomplishes these goals through advocacy, research and the promotion of best practices. The care continuum is described by the organization as including wellness and health promotion, prevention, care coordination and patient advocacy, condition management and complex case management.

career average (earnings) plan—defined benefit retirement plan that calculates benefits by using a percentage of an employee's compensation over the entire period of service with the employer. See also *accrued benefit* and *backloading*.

career pay plan—retirement plan that considers an employee's pay each year when calculating the dollar benefit that will be paid, in contrast to a final pay plan that considers the employee's pay for a period just prior to retirement. Unless an employer makes adjustments, a disadvantage of a career pay plan is that it does not take into account inflation. A defined contribution plan is essentially a career pay plan; however, the type of investments selected for the plan can provide some inflation protection. See also *career average (earnings) plan* and *final earnings plan*.

care pathway—see *clinical pathway*.

carrier—see *insurer*.

carry forward—portion of a Registered Retirement Savings Plan (RRSP) deduction entitlement not used in one year that may be used in the following seven years. The amount carried forward is in addition to the regular RRSP contribution for that current year.

carryover deductible—deductible amount satisfied within a specified time period (usually the last three months of a plan year), which can also be applied to the deductible of the following year. Under COBRA, amounts paid as deductibles before a qualifying event are credited (carried over) to the continuing coverage deductible. See also *deductible*.

carryover provision—employer policy that lets employees take unused vacation or other leave in a subsequent calendar or fiscal year. Some health insurance plans also permit expenses arising out of claims during the last three months of a year to be carried over to the next year without requiring the insured to pay new deductibles or coinsurance.

carve-in—inclusion of a prescription drug or other benefit program as part of a total health care package. Such packages are sometimes referred to as unified benefits or a unified program.

carve-out—also referred to as a standalone plan, a program separate from a primary group health plan designed to provide a specialized type of care (e.g., mental health care and chemical dependency services or prescription drugs). Carve-out is also used in reference to the coordination of employer-sponsored benefits with other benefits. See also *Medicare carve-out* and *spousal carve-out*.

case management—patient care model that focuses on coordinating the health care and disability services needed by individual patients. Type of services rendered and who functions as a case manager vary by where the services are provided but can include checking benefits available, negotiating provider fees, arranging for special services, coordinating referrals, coordinating claims among benefit plans, providing post-care follow-up, health education, etc. Case management by an insurance provider or benefit plan is a type of utilization management. See also *large case management* and *utilization management (UM)*.

case manager—doctor, nurse or social worker who works with patients, care providers and third-party payers to coordinate the services considered necessary and appropriate for a patient.

case mix—classifications or categories of patients treated by a hospital.

case rate—method of paying for health care services in which a benefit plan negotiates with a hospital a flat amount the plan will pay for a specific type of service (e.g., the birth of a baby or outpatient surgery). The hospital absorbs any costs in excess of this fixed amount. See also *bundled payment*.

cash balance plan—defined benefit plan that simulates a defined contribution plan. Hypothetical individual accounts are maintained for each employee. Each year, the employee's account is given a pay credit (usually a percentage of compensation) along with an interest credit (either a fixed rate or variable rate linked to an index such as a Treasury bill rate). The benefit for a cash balance plan is the stated account balance that the participant is generally permitted to take as a lump sum upon retirement. Increases and decreases in the value of investments do not directly affect the benefit amounts promised to participants. Investment risks and rewards on plan assets are borne solely by the employer. See also *hybrid pension plan*.

cash equivalents—short-term and, typically, very safe savings places to put money such as savings accounts, money market accounts and certificates of deposit (CDs). Offered by banks, credit unions and other financial organizations, cash equivalents tend to have no maturity date or mature in a very short period of time. They are called cash equivalents since they are easy to buy and sell.

cash flow—net income of a business or specific project during a defined period of time. Cash flow excludes bookkeeping deductions not paid out in actual dollars (e.g., depreciation and amortization).

cashier's check—see *bank draft*.

cashing out—surrendering a life insurance policy in exchange for its cash value.

cash management bill—see *Treasury bill*.

cash or deferred arrangement (CODA)—usually part of a profit sharing or stock bonus plan, a feature that gives an employee the option to contribute some of his or her salary to a qualified retirement plan (e.g., 401(k), 403(b) or 457(b) plan).

cash out—see *cash surrender*.

cash profit-sharing plan—see *current profit-sharing plan*.

cash refund annuity—see *refund annuity*.

cash surrender—receipt of the accumulated monetary value of an insurance policy when the policy is cashed in or canceled before maturity. Cash surrender is sometimes referred to as cashing out.

cash surrender value—see *surrender value*.

cash value life insurance—life insurance policy that combines insurance with a savings or investment plan. If the insured dies before the policy matures (usually in a specified number of years or when the insured reaches a certain age) and the policy has been kept in force, the beneficiary receives the face value of the policy. Some cash value policyholders who do not need insurance protection in their later years claim the policy's cash surrender value (which grows tax-free) and purchase an annuity to supplement their retirement income. Premiums on cash value life insurance policies are higher than those on a term life policy because the insured must pay for the insurance coverage as well as the savings component of the plan. See also *endowment insurance, insurance, life insurance, surrender value, term life insurance* and *whole life insurance*.

Casualty Actuarial Society (CAS)—organization focused on property, casualty and similar risk exposures.

catastrophic case management—see *large case management.*

catastrophic health insurance—see *high-deductible health plan (HDHP), major medical insurance* and "Qualified health plans" in the *Appendix A: Affordable Care Act of 2010 (ACA).*

catchment area—area served by an organization; for example, the geographic area defined by a local EMS agency in its trauma care system plan as the area served by a designated trauma center.

catch-up contribution—for years beginning after 2001, eligible employees aged 50 or older can make higher tax-deferred annual contributions to their individual retirement accounts, 401(k) plans, 403(b) plans, 457 plans and federal Thrift Savings Plan. As the name implies, this option allows individuals to catch up, or expand, on retirement savings. The catch-up contribution provision was created by the Economic Growth and Tax Relief Reconciliation Act of 2001. The Pension Protection Act of 2006 made these contributions and other pension-related provisions permanent.

categorically needy—groups of persons for which the U.S. government gives the option of providing Medicaid coverage. These optional groups share characteristics of the mandatory groups, but the eligibility criteria are somewhat more liberally defined. Examples of persons who may be covered include children under the age of 21; pregnant women; aged, blind, disabled, and/or institutionalized individuals (or eligible for institutionalization); tuberculosis-infected persons; and women with breast or cervical cancer. See also *Medicaid* and *medically needy.*

C corporation—most common corporate structure in the United States. Also referred to as a C corp. or general corporation, the C corporation may have an unlimited number of stockholders. It is considered a taxpaying entity unto itself under Subchapter C of the IRC. Individual shareholders must also pay tax on capital gains and dividends they receive from the corporation. See also *corporation* and *S corporation.*

Center for Health Care Strategies (CHCS)—nonprofit health policy resource center dedicated to improving the quality and cost-effectiveness of health care services for low-income persons and people with chronic illnesses and disabilities. CHCS works with states, federal agencies, health plans and health care providers to develop innovative programs that better serve people with complex and high-cost health care needs.

Center for Health Improvement (CHI)—national, independent, nonprofit health policy and technical assistance organization dedicated to improving population health and encouraging healthy behaviors at the community level in the United States.

Center for Studying Health System Change (HSC)—nonpartisan organization that conducts health policy research focused on U.S. health care and the market forces driving changes in the nation's health system. HSC does not take policy positions; instead, it is a resource providing data and objective analysis for decision makers on all sides of issues.

Centers for Disease Control and Prevention (CDC)—agency within the U.S. Department of Health and Human Services that researches and investigates causes of diseases, provides educational and prevention programs, and issues definitions of diseases and the conditions used in determining eligibility for state, federal and private benefit programs.

Centers for Medicare and Medicaid Services (CMS)—agency within the U.S. Department of Health and Human Services that administers Medicare, Medicaid and other federal programs established by the Social Security Act of 1935.

centers of excellence—network of designated, nationally recognized medical facilities that perform select, highly sophisticated, high-cost procedures such as organ transplants, open-heart surgery and the treatment of advanced forms of cancer.

CERES Principles—ten-point environmental reporting and accountability code previously called the Valdez Principles and now named after the Coalition for Environmentally Responsible Economies. Companies are asked to publicly endorse the ten principles as an environmental mission statement or ethic. Embedded in the code of conduct is the mandate to report periodically on environmental management structures and results.

certificate holder—typically, the primary individual covered by a benefit plan. In the U.S., this person is also referred to as participant. Member is a term frequently used in Canada.

certificate of creditable coverage—document provided by an insurance company or health care plan that provides evidence of previous health care coverage. With the passage of the Affordable Care Act of 2010 and its prohibition on preexisting condition exclusions, certificates of creditable coverage are no longer needed. The requirement for plans (both grandfathered and non-grandfathered) to provide certificates has been eliminated for all individuals as of January 1, 2015.

certificate of deposit (CD)—money deposited in an interest-bearing account at a bank, thrift institution or credit union. The financial institution offers a written certification that the dollar amount has been deposited for a certain period of time at a fixed rate of interest. The length of time may be anywhere from a week to several years. Upon maturity, the accountholder receives the principal and interest as agreed upon when the account was established. Early withdrawal of the money is penalized. Some but not all CDs are FDIC or NCUA insured. See also *negotiable certificate of deposit (NCD)*.

certificate of insurance (COI)—document issued by an insurance company that is used to verify the existence of insurance coverage. The certificate usually lists the effective date, type and dollar amount of coverage. In life and health insurance, a COI is issued to members of a group insurance plan as evidence of their participation. Also called an insurance certificate.

certificate of need (CON)—legal document issued by a government agency to an individual or organization proposing to construct or modify a health facility, purchase new medical equipment or offer a new service. A CON states that the facility, service and/or equipment in the proposed location is warranted. The CON is intended to prevent excessive expansion or duplication.

certification—confirmation of certain characteristics of an object, person or organization. Various government and nongovernment organizations recognize service providers as qualified to perform a job or task. Typically there are predetermined actions or standards that must be met in order to be granted certification. Physicians can be certified by the American Board of Medical Specialties. Hospices that meet conditions for program participation are certified by Medicaid and Medicare. Some health care plans require certification of patients for an extended stay in a hospital.

certified applicant counselor—person affiliated with a designated organization who has been trained and has the ability to help consumers, small businesses and the employees of small businesses who are seeking health coverage through the *health insurance marketplace*. Assistance may include helping applicants complete eligibility and enrollment forms. See also "Navigators" in the *Appenxix A: Affordable Care Act of 2010 (ACA)*.

Certified Employee Benefit Specialist (CEBS)—designation granted jointly by the International Foundation of Employee Benefit Plans and the Wharton School of the University of Pennsylvania to individuals who complete eight college-level courses and examinations in the areas of compensation and employee benefit plans. Persons who receive this designation pledge to a code of ethical standards and continuing education. In Canada, the program is presented jointly by the International Foundation of Employee Benefit Plans and Dalhousie University of Halifax. See also *Compensation Management Specialist (CMS), Group Benefits Associate (GBA)* and *Retirement Plans Associate (RPA)*.

Certified Financial Planner (CFP)—individual who has met the education, examination and experience requirements set by the Certified Financial Planner Board of Standards that show the person is able to manage a client's banking, estate, insurance, investment and tax affairs. CFPs must agree to ethical standards of conduct and meet continuing education requirements. See also *financial planner*.

certified health plan—managed care program that has been certified by a state's health services organization or office of the insurance commissioner to provide a uniform health benefits package to state residents. States vary in terms of which managed care organizations (MCOs) must be certified. Some states require health maintenance organizations be certified but exempt other MCOs such as preferred provider organizations and independent practice associations. See also *health maintenance organization (HMO), independent practice association (IPA), managed care organization (MCO)* and *preferred provider organization (PPO)*.

certified length of stay—period of time determined necessary and appropriate for inpatient care in a hospital. If a patient stays in a hospital beyond the time established via utilization review, the hospital or patient may have to absorb the cost of the extended care. Certified length of stay is a utilization management technique. See also *utilization management (UM)* and *utilization review (UR)*.

Certified Public Accountant (CPA)—professional license granted to persons meeting certain educational, experience and examination requirements. Standards vary from state to state, but typically include a college degree with accounting and auditing course work, and qualifying experience. A CPA must pass the Uniform CPA Examination, which covers accounting theory and practice, auditing and business law.

change-in-control (CIC) agreement—see *parachute*.

change in status—life-changing event that may permit a participant to make midyear changes in a benefit plan. These events may include a change in marital status, number of dependents, dependent eligibility for a benefit, employment, residence or the beginning or termination of adoption proceedings/assistance.

channeling—practice in which a plan or medical provider directs patients or workload away from one source to another, such as to a different plan, physician or hospital.

charge-back—money returned to a wholesaler by a manufacturer to compensate the wholesaler for the difference between a drug's acquisition cost and the contracted price agreed upon in advance by the wholesaler and wholesaler's retail customers.

charge limit—see *limiting charge*.

charitable corporations—organization with philanthropic purposes. Nonprofit charitable organizations that meet the requirements of Section 501(c)(3) of the IRC are exempt from federal taxation, and their employees may participate in tax-deferred retirement plans under Sections 403(b) and 457 of the IRC. See also *403(b) plan, 457 plan, Section 403(b)* and *Section 457*.

charitable pooled income fund—see *charitable remainder trust (CRT)*.

charitable remainder trust (CRT)—arrangement in which a donor sets aside assets in a trust that provides income for a specific period of time to beneficiaries named by the donor. Once this time expires, the remainder of the assets are transferred to a philanthropic organization. The arrangement makes it possible for a donor to get an income tax deduction for the fair value of the donation and avoid taxes on capital gains. In addition, the asset is removed from the estate, which may reduce subsequent estate taxes. While the donor cannot reclaim the contribution, the grantor may have some control over how the assets are invested, and may even switch from one charity to another (as long as it's still an IRS qualified charitable organization). CRTs come in three types: (1) a charitable remainder annuity trust pays a fixed dollar amount annually, (2) a charitable remainder unit trust pays a fixed percentage of the trust's value annually and (3) a charitable pooled income fund is set up by the charity, making it possible for many donors to contribute.

Chartered Financial Analyst (CFA)—designation held by financial analysts, money managers, investment advisors and other financial professionals who have completed a graduate-level, self-study curriculum and examination program covering a broad range of investment topics. CFA charter holders are required to affirm their commitment to high ethical standards and voluntarily submit to the authority of the CFA Institute.

Chartered Financial Consultant® (ChFC)®—title used by accountants, attorneys, bankers, insurance agents, brokers and securities representatives who have completed The American College's eight-course education program, met experience requirements and agreed to uphold a code of ethics. See also *financial planner*.

Chartered Life Underwriter (CLU)—designation conferred on individuals by The American College recognizing the attainment of certain standards of education pertaining to personal risk management, life insurance and estate planning issues.

chemical equivalent—medication that contains the same active ingredient as another. See also *generic drug* and *therapeutic equivalent*.

chemotherapy—use of drugs to treat or control disease; typical uses are the treatment of cancer and select mental illnesses.

child and dependent care credit—reduction in U.S. income tax for expenses incurred caring for a child under the age of 13, a qualifying spouse or a dependent that makes it possible for an individual to work or look for work. A spouse or dependent must be physically or mentally incapable of self-care. The credit is a percentage of expenses paid to a qualified care provider and depends on household income. The federal government has also established an annual dollar limit per household. The amount claimed must be reduced by any dependent care benefits provided by an employer that are not reported as income. See also *child care* and *family allowance*.

child benefit—see *family allowance*.

child care—provision of a range of services that may include health, medical, psychological, social, nutritional and educational services for a child by someone other than the child's parents or legal guardian. Such care may be provided at home or in a center. It is often used when a child's primary caretaker is at work or otherwise unavailable.

children's benefit—dependent children of disabled or deceased contributors to either the *Canada Pension Plan (CPP)* or *Québec Pension Plan (QPP)* are eligible to receive a fixed monthly payment. The child must be:
- Under the age of 18, or between the ages of 18 and 25 and in full-time attendance at a recognized school or university
- A natural or an adopted child, or a child that is/was in the care and control of the contributor who is disabled/diseased.

Children's Health Insurance Program (CHIP)—federal program established in 1997 to help states provide free and low-cost health insurance for needy infants, children and teens who are not covered by health insurance (including Medicaid). Typical children in this target group have parents who earn too much to qualify for Medicaid, but not enough to afford private health insurance.

child tax benefit—tax-free, monthly payment from the Canadian government for low- and middle-income families with children. See also *family allowance*.

chiropractic care—medical treatment based on the theory that illness is caused by a malfunction of the nervous system and that normal function can be achieved by manipulation of the body structure, primarily the spinal column. A practitioner is a doctor of chiropractic. Chiropractic care is categorized as a form of complementary and alternative medicine.

chronic care management—coordination of health care and other services to improve the health status of patients with chronic conditions such as diabetes and asthma. In addition to providing care specific to the problem, chronic care management may also include efforts to promote health, encourage self-care, reduce costs etc.

Chronic Care Model (CCM)—based on a synthesis of scientific literature in the early 1990s by the MacCall Center for Health Care Innovation at the Group Health Research Institute, then further refined and launched in 1998, CCM calls for a structural change in the care of people with illnesses. The model requires collaboration among health care providers, community resource persons and patients themselves. Six elements have been identified that must be coordinated to provide high-quality care: community resources, health systems, self-management support, delivery system design, decision support and clinical information systems.

chronic condition—health state that tends to develop slowly and is long-lasting or recurrent. Chronic illnesses generally are not life-threatening nor do they require hospitalization, but they do require managed care on a long-term basis. For purposes of viatical settlements, HIPAA defines "chronically ill" as being permanently and severely disabled by illness.

chronic illness—see *chronic condition*.

chronic obstructive pulmonary disease (COPD)—illness that makes it increasingly difficult to breathe. Causes of COPD include cigarette smoking and long-term exposure to other lung irritants such as air pollution, chemical fumes and dust. Two major types of COPD are emphysema and chronic bronchitis.

church plan—under ERISA and the IRC, a Section 403(b) or Section 457 plan that has been established by a church-controlled organization or association of churches that is tax-exempt under Section 501(c)(3). The following are not considered church plans: (1) a plan that is primarily for the benefit of employees of an unrelated business (as described in IRC Section 513) and (2) a multiemployer plan that includes one or more employers that are not tax-exempt churches or conventions of churches. Although exempt, a church plan can make an irrevocable election to be covered by the participation, vesting and funding requirements of ERISA. See also *403(b) plan, 457 plan, Section 403(b)* and *Section 457*.

churning—unethical and frequently illegal practice that involves the excessive provision of services. In health care, churning occurs when a service provider bills for the same medical procedure more than once or sees a patient more than is medically necessary. Churning also occurs in the buying and selling of investment securities; for example, a broker who trades excessively to increase commissions rather than pursue a client's objectives and interests.

circuit breaker—procedure established by the major securities and futures exchanges for coordinated cross-market trading halts if a severe market price decline reaches levels that may exhaust market liquidity. A circuit breaker may halt trading temporarily or, under extreme circumstances, close a market before the end of the trading session's normal close. See also *Black Monday, trading curb* and *trading halt*.

civil action—lawsuit brought before a court in which the party filing the suit (the plaintiff) seeks to enforce or protect individual rights. The suit may be between private parties or filed by a private party against a government entity. Those who have been sued (the defendants) are required to respond to the plaintiff's complaint. If the plaintiff is successful, a court may order a range of remedies including the enforcement of a right, an order to stop or compel an act, and the payment of damages. Civil actions can also be described as any action that is not a criminal action.

Civilian Health and Medical Program of the Uniformed Services (CHAMPUS)—see *TRICARE*.

Civil Rights Act of 1964—see *discrimination* and *Title VII of the Civil Rights Act of 1964*.

Civil Service Retirement System (CSRS)—defined benefit retirement program for certain federal employees in the U.S. established by the Civil Service Retirement Act, which became effective on August 1, 1920. Employees share in the cost of the annuities to which they become entitled. While CSRS-covered employees generally pay no Social Security tax, they must pay the Medicare tax. The employing government agency matches the employee's CSRS contributions. For federal employees who first entered covered service on or after January 1, 1987, CSRS has been replaced by the Federal Employees Retirement System (FERS). See also *Federal Employees Retirement System (FERS)*.

claim—request for the return of property, payment or reimbursement. Benefit claims are typically submitted to a plan administrator or insurer. Health service claims include an itemized statement of health services rendered by a provider for a given patient. See also *claimant*.

claim adjudication—processing a request for payment submitted to a benefit plan or insurance company.

claim administrator—individual or organization that determines whether to make a payment on behalf of a benefit plan or insurance company. The administrator may be an employee of the plan, a third-party administrator or another private contractor.

claimant—individual or organization that files a claim, generally a service provider, plan participant or plan beneficiary.

claim form—document used to request payment from a benefit plan or insurance company.

claim review—examination of a request for payment by a professional to determine the amount of payment due from a benefit plan or insurance company for goods and services rendered. A claim review may also involve determining the eligibility of the claimant, whether a service is covered and is necessary, whether the claim is covered by another insurance policy and whether the dollar amount of the claim is reasonable.

claims audit—examination of a health provider's records to assess whether services provided were necessary, properly administered and correctly billed.

claims cost control—efforts both inside and outside an organization to restrain and direct claim payments so benefit dollars are used as efficiently as possible.

claims charged—payment requests submitted and paid by an insurance policy. If pooling or claim averaging is used to stabilize a group's experience during a contract period, the claim expense "charged" to the group's premium in that period may be more or less than the group's actual incurred claims.

claims experience—frequency, cost and type of claims that are being filed by a group over time. Insurance companies use this information when calculating insurance premiums for individual and group insurance plans.

claims fluctuation reserve (CFR)—also known as the premium stabilization fund (PSF), a surplus held by an insurer of a group benefit plan when the premium paid exceeds the claims incurred. This money is used to offset deficits the group plan experiences in the future. Upon termination of a contract, any funds remaining are usually refunded to the policyholder.

claims incurred—see *incurred claims*.

claims-made extension—clause added to a claims-made liability insurance contract after the policy period has begun when the insured becomes aware of a wrongful act that could later lead to a claim. Upon learning of the act, the insured must notify the insurance company and request the additional coverage. If a claim is later made related to the act, coverage is provided as if the claim was first made during the policy period even though the policy may no longer be in effect (i.e., canceled or not renewed). See also *claims-made policy*.

claims-made and reported policy—type of liability insurance contract that requires a claim must both be made against the insured and reported to the insurer during the policy period for coverage to apply. Claims-made and reported policies are unfavorable from the insured's standpoint because it is sometimes difficult to report a claim to an insurer during a policy period if the claim is made late in that policy period. However, more liberal versions of claims-made and reported policies provide a postpolicy "window" that allow the insureds to report claims to the insurer within 30 to 60 days following policy expiration. See also *claims-made policy*.

claims-made policy—type of liability insurance contract that covers only "claims made" against the insured and reported to the insurer during the policy period. The timing of fiduciary liability claims is different from liability claims for a home or car. The latter are triggered by the date a loss or injury occurs (e.g., the day of an accident or bad weather). With fiduciary liability coverage, the policy that provides coverage is the one in force when a claim is made—not the policy in force when it is claimed a wrongdoing occurred. See also *claims-made and reported policy, claims-made extension, interrelated claim provision, occurrence policy* and *prior acts coverage*.

claims procedure
—process to be followed by plan participants and other beneficiaries when filing an insurance or benefit claim. Under ERISA, employers are required to give employees information on the claims process for health and disability benefits as part of the summary plan document and to have a fair process for handling benefit claims. The claims procedure must explain how to file a benefit claim, notification of benefit determinations and appeal of benefit claim denials. Using its authority under ERISA, the U.S. Department of Labor has also outlined requirements for insurers' appeals processes and established time lines for insurers in their response to claims and appeals. See also *summary plan description (SPD)*.
—process to be followed by those handling claims submitted to an insurer or benefit plan.

claims reserve—money set aside by an insurance company or benefit plan to meet claims incurred but not yet settled. An example is a workers' compensation case where benefits are payable for several years.

claims services only (CSO)—administration contract designed for fully self-insured employers that need very little administrative assistance. Under a CSO arrangement, an insurer administers only the claims portion of the plan.

classification method—when used in employment evaluation, jobs organized into a structure or hierarchy that considers factors such as job duties and responsibilities, knowledge, skills and abilities, education and experience requirements, etc.

class rating—approach to determining insurance premiums (rates). Similar insureds are placed in the same group (class) and charged the same rate. For example, people in a particular age range or buildings with a certain type of construction might be put into the same rate class. The insurer uses its own past experience and sometimes the experience of other insurers to estimate the group's expected claims. Those that do not qualify for a class rating, usually persons or properties with high risk, may be rated separately via a physical examination. In some situations, rate classes are given names such as preferred plus, preferred, standard plus, standard and substandard. Those rated preferred plus are charged premium rates lower than preferred, which are lower than standard plus, and so on. See also *community rating, declined risk class, experience rating, manual rate, preferred risk class, qualified impairment insurance, rated policy, retrospective experience rating, standard risk class* and *substandard risk class*.

clawback—taking back of money given to people in another way. The Medicare Part D drug benefit is considered a clawback because each state must pay the federal Medicare program an amount roughly equal to the expenditures the state would have had if it had continued to pay for outpatient Medicaid prescriptions for persons enrolled in both Medicare and Medicaid. In the pension field, clawback is used interchangeably with integration. See also *integration*.

cliff vesting—granting plan participants their full and nonforfeitable rights to employer contributions in a pension plan after a specific number of years of service. If the participant chooses to change employers or is terminated prior to the vesting date, no partial benefits are received. Vesting occurs in full at a specified time rather than gradually. See also *full vesting, graded vesting, immediate vesting* and *vesting*.

clinical indication—generally accepted use of a drug to treat a medical condition. Regulatory confirmation of the drug's appropriate use is provided by the FDA.

clinical outcome—end result of medical treatment. Clinical outcomes are measured in a multitude of ways, including the level to which a disease exists in a specific locale, death rates, the functional ability of patients, patient symptoms and satisfaction with care.

clinical outlier—patient with atypical characteristics relative to other patients in a diagnosis-related group; for example, a patient who has a very rare condition or who has a unique combination of diagnoses and surgeries. See also *diagnosis-related group (DRG)*.

clinical pathway—tool used to manage the quality of health care that standardizes care processes. Clinical pathways are essentially "maps" for treatment based on research or common practice for a specific disease or event. Treatment is defined and may be sequenced by the hour, day or visit. Such pathways are typically a single all-encompassing document that indicates patient care and progress as the pathway is taken. Such design is an attempt to identify and prompt actions most commonly representing best practice for most patients. Also referred to as care pathway, critical pathway and integrated care pathway.

clinical practice guideline—see *practice guideline*.

clinical practice management—see *practice guideline*.

closed-end fund—legally known as a closed-end company, a closed-end investment fund generally does not continuously offer shares for sale. Rather, a fixed number of shares are sold to the public as an initial public offering (IPO), after which the shares trade via a secondary market such as a stock exchange. The price of the shares after the IPO is determined by market demand; shares may sell above or below their net asset value. Closed-end funds are not required to redeem shares from investors, though some do offer to repurchase their shares at specified intervals. The investment portfolios of closed-end funds tend to invest in a greater amount of illiquid securities than mutual funds. Also referred to as a publicly traded fund. See also *illiquid* and *open-end fund*.

closed formulary—also called a restrictive or proprietary formulary, a list of the medications reimbursed by a patient's benefit plan. Medications typically include brand-name and generic drugs, with several choices available in each category. The process for adding new drugs is very selective. Drugs not on the list are not covered, and the patient must incur the entire cost of the prescription unless the patient's doctor is able to get authorization to prescribe a medication outside the formulary. See also *drug formulary, incentive formulary, limited formulary, open formulary, partially closed formulary* and *unlimited formulary*.

closed network—select group of health or health-related service providers that contract to provide goods and services to plan participants at a discounted rate. Providers within the group are referred to as preferred providers. Financial incentives may be used to encourage plan participants to use these providers. See also *open network, open access network, pharmacy network* and *preferred provider*.

closed panel—requirement that plan participants use only professionals and facilities that have signed on with the participants' benefit plan to provide goods and services. Health care, dental care and legal services plans often have this provision. For example, health maintenance organizations (HMOs) mandate service by a closed panel. Physicians are either employees of the HMO or belong to a group of physicians who have contracted with the HMO. See also *any willing provider law* and *IPA model HMO*.

closed plan—health benefit program that requires plan participants to use participating providers. See also *closed network* and *closed panel*.

closed shop—company or place of business that hires only members of a labor union (often one union and no other). Closely allied with the closed shop is the union shop where employees do not have to belong to the union when they are hired, but they are required to join within a specified period of time in order to keep their jobs. In 1947, the Taft-Hartley Act declared the closed shop illegal. The act did allow a collectively bargained agreement for a union shop if certain safeguards were met. Many states, through "right to work" legislation or court decision, have banned closed shops. See also *open shop*.

closely held corporation—firm in which a small number of stockholders own and control operations. Some definitions of closely held corporations limit them to those that are not publicly traded on any stock exchange. Most, but not all, closely held firms are family businesses that have no interest in selling their stock.

closing—conclusion of a real estate transaction where all documents are signed.

closing cost—fee paid at the conclusion of a transaction in addition to the sales price. Closing costs are commonly paid at the conclusion (settlement) of a real estate or mortgage transaction. These fees may include expenses related to a property appraisal, title search and insurance, land survey, taxes, mortgage points, property insurance, realtors, recording of the deed, a credit report charge, etc. See also *Real Estate Settlement Procedures Act (RESPA)*.

closing price—amount of money at which a security is traded on a particular day.

coalition—see *health care coalition*.

COBRA—see *Consolidated Omnibus Budget Reconciliation Act of 1985 (COBRA)*.

code
—set of rules, principles or laws. Codes are usually recorded in a written format. See also *Internal Revenue Code (IRC)*.
—system of symbols, numbers or signals that conveys information to a computer. Such abbreviations are frequently used for tracking health care services and benefit payments. See also *coding*.

code gaming—use of incorrect billing codes to increase provider income or to enable a patient to receive reimbursement for a treatment that otherwise would not be reimbursable. See also *code* and *coding*.

code set—under HIPAA, any set of codes used for encoding data elements such as tables of terms, medical concepts, medical diagnosis codes or medical procedure codes. See also *code*.

coding—process of converting information into coded values for the purpose of data storage. Coding is frequently used by health care providers and insurers to identify, track and bill for services. See also *code*.

coercion—forcing another party to do something by using threats, intimidation, trickery or some other form of pressure or force.

co-fiduciary liability—see *fiduciary responsibility*.

coinsurance—occasionally, referred to as a percentage participation clause, a form of cost sharing between an insurance company and the insured. In major medical insurance, the cost of coverage is shared at a specified ratio. Very typical is payment of 80% by the insurer and 20% by the insured after the deductible is met. In property insurance, a coinsurance clause requires the insured to share in losses to the extent that the property was underinsured at the time of loss. See also *copayment/copay* and *deductible*.

COLA—see *cost-of-living adjustment (COLA)*.

collateral—in a lending agreement, property (e.g., house, car, stocks) pledged if a borrower is unable to pay back the loan and interest on the money borrowed.

collateralized mortgage obligation (CMO)—legal entity that owns a set of mortgages that have been grouped together and called a pool. CMO investors buy bonds issued by the entity and receive payment according to an established set of rules referred to as the "structure." The mortgages are called collateral, while the bonds are referred to as tranches or classes. Institutional investors are those most likely to invest in this type of investment vehicle. A CMO is a specific type of legal entity, but investors sometimes refer to other entities such as REMICs as CMOs. See also *commercial mortgage-backed security (CMBS)*, *mortgage-backed security (MBS)*, *real estate mortgage investment conduit (REMIC)* and *tranche*.

collectible—property that is rare, popular and readily marketable. Common collectibles include antiques, toys, coins, comic books and stamps. Items that have been mass-produced and, thus, are not rare are sometimes marketed as collectibles to drive consumer demand.

collective bargaining—negotiation between an employer (or group of employers) and a union on behalf of employees regarding wages, benefits and other conditions of employment. See also *concession bargaining*.

collective bargaining agreement (CBA)—legal contract that results from negotiations between one or more employers and one or more unions on behalf of employees. Elements of the written agreement typically include wages, benefits, work hours and other conditions of employment.

collective bargaining contract—see *collective bargaining agreement (CBA)*.

collective investment fund—pooling of investment funds with those of other investors, which allows greater diversification than an individual investor could do alone. Collective investment funds are promoted with a wide range of investment aims and may target a specific geographic region. A collective fund may have a different name depending on the nation where it has been issued, including investment fund, managed fund or mutual fund. In the United States, mutual fund has a more specific meaning.

collectively bargained plan—benefit program established as part of negotiations between an employer and a union on behalf of employees. Retirement and health care benefits are commonly part of a collective bargaining process. See also *unilateral plan*.

collective trust fund (CTF)—see *common trust fund*.

combination drug—two or more medications combined in a single dose.

combination plan—use of two or more plans to provide a benefit. A life insurance policy might have elements of both term and whole life coverage. A pension plan might combine an insurance policy with some type of auxiliary fund. A money purchase plan might be combined with a defined benefit pension plan or another defined contribution plan, such as a profit-sharing plan.

commercial bank
—traditionally, the main business of a commercial bank was accepting deposits for savings and checking accounts, and using this money to make loans. Banks also provided money market accounts and accepted time deposits. Since the passage of the Gramm-Leach-Bliley Act in 1999, commercial banks have been able to take on many of the functions previously limited to investment banks, brokerage firms and insurance companies.
—alternatively, a bank or a division of a bank that deals primarily with deposits and loans from corporations or large businesses, in contrast to a retail bank that deals directly with consumers.

commercial mortgage-backed security (CMBS)—pool of loans financing the purchase of income-producing properties such as office buildings, multifamily residences, shopping centers, industrial properties and hospitals. The income generated by a CMBS provides the cash flow to investors.

commercial paper (CP)—short-term unsecured debt issued by large banks and companies to get funds for short-term needs. Since it is not backed by collateral, only those with excellent credit ratings are able to sell CP at a reasonable price. Commercial paper usually has a face value of $100,000 or more, sells at a discount and has a repayment period ranging from two days to nine months, which is shorter than the repayment period for bonds. Interest rates fluctuate with the market but are usually better than what is available from banks. Commercial paper is a major component of many money market mutual funds.

commingled fund—investment vehicle similar to a mutual fund that pools money from several clients into one portfolio that is managed using a particular strategy. Clients benefit from professional money management, reduced management expenses and diversification. Small pension funds unable to meet the requirements for a separately managed account find a commingled fund, also known as a pooled fund, attractive. See also *separately managed account (SMA)*.

commission—form of payment to a salesperson or agent for services rendered, often a percentage of the money in the transaction. A broker fee is a form of commission. See also *broker fee*.

commodity—basic good used in commerce that is interchangeable with other goods of the same type. Commodities are most often used as inputs in the production of other goods or services. The quality of a given commodity may differ slightly but is essentially uniform across producers. Agricultural goods such as beans, cocoa, coffee, sugar, corn, wheat, chickens and hogs are all considered commodities. So are natural resources and energy products (e.g., aluminum, copper, crude oil, electricity, natural gas and gold).

commodity exchange—market for buying and selling contracts for commodities and derivatives. The New York Mercantile Exchange (NYMEX) is the world's largest physical commodity futures exchange. See also *commodity, Commodity Futures Trading Commission (CFTC)* and *derivative*.

Commodity Futures Trading Commission (CFTC)—independent U.S. government agency established in 1974 to administer the Commodity Exchange Act. CFTC monitors the futures markets to detect and prevent market manipulation and to protect those who use the markets for either commercial or investment purposes.

common control—when one entity owns 80% of the stock or capital interest in a business, or when five or fewer people own a controlling interest. See also *controlled group*.

common law—legal principles that have been established over the years via court decisions as opposed to legislative statutes and executive action.

common law employee—individual who performs services for an employer that controls what will be done and how it is done. This is true even if the employer gives the employee the freedom to make these decisions. The facts used by the IRS to determine the degree of control (and whether an individual is an independent contractor or common law employee) fall into three categories: behavioral control, financial control and the type of relationship between the parties. While there are some exceptions, employers in general must withhold and pay income, Social Security and Medicare taxes for common law employees. See also *independent contractor*.

common-law marriage—treatment of two persons as legally married without the couple having formally registered their relationship through a marriage ceremony or the acquisition of a marriage license. Not all jurisdictions recognize common-law marriages. Where they are acknowledged, criteria used to determine common-law marriage status often include that the couple live together for a specific period of time and hold themselves out as a married couple (e.g., refer to a partner as husband or wife).

controlled businesses—see *common control*.

common stock—fraction of ownership in a public corporation represented by a certificate or book entry. Owners usually have voting rights on important issues concerning the company and are entitled to a share of the company's success through dividends and/or capital gains. Should the company be forced to liquidate, corporate assets are distributed to creditors and preferred stockholders, then common stockholders. Common stockholders assume greater risk than preferred stockholders, but generally have greater control and may gain greater reward in the form of dividends and capital appreciation. The terms *common stock* and *capital stock* are often used interchangeably when the company has no preferred stock. See also *capital stock, guaranteed stock* and *preferred stock*.

common stock fund—mutual fund that primarily invests its assets in common stocks. Common stock funds generally bring higher returns than bond funds in the long term, but they also have higher risk. See also *common stock* and *mutual fund*.

common trust fund (CTF)—pooled investment vehicle that is comprised of multiple trusts exempt from federal income tax. Retirement funds, profit sharing and stock bonuses are frequently the sources of the money in these trust funds. A CTF is managed by a bank trust department and is similar to an open-end mutual fund, but participation is limited to those with trust accounts. Also referred to as collective trust funds, CTFs have been around since 1927. Interest waned with the availability of mutual funds but is resurging as the result of lower fees when compared with mutual funds.

community health center (CHC)—facility that provides care for the needy at the local level. An emphasis is placed on prevention, early intervention, rehabilitation and education as well as direct care. Services are provided on a sliding scale based on income. Grants (federal or private) may be used to fund some endeavors.

community health information network (CHIN)—integrated computer and telecommunication systems that permit multiple health service providers, plan sponsors, payers and others within a geographic area to share and communicate information concerning patients, patient care and payment. Also referred to as a community health management information system.

community health management information system—see *community health information network (CHIN)*.

community rating—process of determining the premium for a group risk on the basis of the average claims experience for the general population instead of a particular employer. This is especially helpful for small groups, whose claims experience over two or three years may not be typical. Community ratings are used by most health maintenance organizations (HMOs), which use the plan's entire client population to set premiums. See also *class rating, experience rating* and *retrospective experience rating*.

commuted value—present value of a future series of payments that will fulfill a pension obligation. The higher the interest rate and the further into the future the money is paid out, the lower the commuted value.

comorbidity—presence of one or more illnesses in addition to a primary illness.

company match—see *matching contribution*.

company pharmacy—see *in-house pharmacy*.

comparability plan—profit-sharing or money purchase pension plan that allows contributions to be higher for one group than for another. While these plans are considered defined contribution plans, they are tested as though they were defined pension plans under the cross-testing rules of IRC Section 401(a)(4) to satisfy nondiscrimination requirements. For this reason, comparability plans are also referred to as cross-tested plans. They are generally used by small businesses that want to maximize contributions for owners and higher-paid employees while minimizing those for all other employees. See also *hybrid pension plan*.

comparable worth—principle that compensation should be based on the value of the work performed, taking into consideration such factors as education, training, skills, experience, effort, responsibility and working conditions. The issue of comparable worth is frequently raised when comparing salaries in traditionally female occupations to traditionally male occupations. In contrast, equal pay is more likely to be used to refer to situations in which men and women do the same jobs. See also *Equal Pay Act of 1963 (EPA)*.

compa-ratio—percentage used to analyze how close actual pay compares to the midpoint of a salary range. A compa-ratio is calculated by dividing an employee's actual pay (or the average actual pay for a group of employees) by the midpoint of the applicable salary range. For example, if the range is $50,000 to $75,000 and the salary is $60,000, the range midpoint is $62,500. The compa-ratio is .96, or 96%. See also *market index ratio*.

comparative effectiveness research—analysis of the impact of different options for treating a given condition in a particular group of patients. The analysis may focus only on the medical risks and benefits of each treatment or may also consider the costs and benefits of particular treatment options.

Comparative Clinical Effectiveness Research Fee—see "Fee/Taxes" in the *Appendix A: Affordable Care Act of 2010 (ACA)*.

compassionate care leave and benefits—in Canada, the amended Employment Insurance Act (EI) provides an insurance benefit payable for a maximum period of 26 weeks to those who have to be absent from work to provide care or support to a gravely ill family member at risk of dying within 26 weeks. Unemployed persons on EI can also ask for this type of benefit. The eligibility requirements and benefit amounts are similar to those for EI maternity, parental and sickness benefits. See also *family and medical leave*.

compensable factor—criteria used to evaluate the value of jobs or to establish a job hierarchy. Each criterion (factor) is normally assigned a weight of importance. There are typically between five and 12 compensable factors. The Equal Pay Act of 1963 defines four generic compensable factors: skill, effort, responsibility and working conditions.

compensable hours—any activity required by an employer and performed for the employer's benefit. At minimum, compensable hours include all of the time an employee is required to be on the employer's premises, on duty or at a prescribed workplace. Under the Fair Labor Standards Act, an employee who is required to remain on call on an employer's premises is considered working compensable hours. In contrast, an employee who is required to remain on call at home, or who is allowed to leave a message where he or she can be reached, is usually not working while on call. Additional constraints on an employee's freedom, however, could require this time to be compensated.

compensation
—money or something else given as payment for the provision of a good or service. Employees are given compensation in exchange for their work. Cash compensation may include wages, salary, base pay, overtime pay, profit sharing and other monetary payments. Total compensation is a broader term that includes cash and benefits, and sometimes perquisites. Total compensation may also include nonfinancial elements such as job satisfaction and status.
—alternatively, reparation as the result of a loss or injury.

compensation committee—group of individuals responsible for reviewing pay proposals and recommending action to the board of directors. Publicly traded companies are required to have such a committee to set the pay of executives named in the proxy.

Compensation Management Specialist (CMS)—specialty designation granted jointly by the International Foundation of Employee Benefit Plans and the Wharton School of the University of Pennsylvania to persons who complete three college-level courses and examinations focused on compensation and human resources topics. In Canada, the program is presented jointly by the International Foundation of Employee Benefit Plans and Dalhousie University of Canada. See also *Certified Employee Benefit Specialist (CEBS), Group Benefits Associate (GBA)* and *Retirement Plans Associate (RPA)*.

compensatory time—see *comp time*.

competence—ability to do something successfully or efficiently.

competency-based pay—monetary compensation given on the basis of an employee acquiring the knowledge, skills and abilities needed to perform a job.

competitive bidding—process that requires vendors (e.g., health care providers, accountants) to submit payment rates in advance to a potential buyer. In exchange for providing a lower rate, the vendor may obtain a contract from the buyer.

complementary and alternative medicine (CAM)—diverse health care systems and practices that are not generally considered part of conventional medicine. Examples include acupuncture, chiropractic care, herbal medicine, homeopathy, massage therapy and yoga.

complete withdrawal—as defined under ERISA, when an employer (including all controlled group members) permanently ceases to have an obligation to contribute to a multiemployer plan or permanently ceases all covered operations under the plan. If the plan has unfunded vested benefits allocable to the employer, the plan determines the amount of withdrawal liability, notifies the employer of the amount and collects it from the employer. See also *mass withdrawal* and *partial withdrawal*.

compliance—the extent to which an entity follows guidelines or rules. For example, the extent to which a benefit plan follows laws and regulations concerning reporting and disclosure, privacy protection, etc. Also, the extent to which a patient takes a prescribed medication or follows other medical advice. Compliance and adherence are often used interchangeably.

compliance audit—inspection of financial reports or other records to assess whether an entity is following the terms of a legal agreement, government rules and regulations, medical guidelines, etc. See also *payroll audit*.

complication—medical condition that occurs during medical treatment that makes care more difficult, negatively affects the outcome for the patient and/or increases the amount of care required.

composite index—combining of equities, indexes or other factors in a standardized way to provide a measure of the overall investment performance of a sector or market. See also *NASDAQ Composite Index, New York Stock Exchange Composite Index* and *stock market index*.

compound annual growth rate (CAGR)—interest rate that, if compounded annually, would take an investment from its initial value to the final value.

compound interest—interest calculated on both the principal and the accrued interest in a savings account. Interest may be compounded daily, monthly, quarterly, semiannually or annually. For example, a $100 savings account earning 5% interest compounded annually would earn $5 and be worth $105 ($100 + $5) at the end of the first year. At the end of the second year, $5.25 (5% x $105) would be earned, increasing the account balance to $110.25 ($105 + $5.25). In year three, the account would earn $5.51 (5% x $110.25), which increases the balance to $115.76 ($110.25 + $5.51). See also *interest*.

comprehensive audit—with respect to pharmacy benefit managers (PBMs), an examination of performance that takes into account factors such as whether persons were eligible for benefits received, products dispensed were covered under plan design, discounts were applied according to the contract, dispensing fees were accurate, copays were applied correctly, etc. Clinical services of a PBM may also be included in the scope of the audit. See also *audit*.

comprehensive major medical insurance—health care policy that combines basic and major medical coverage in one plan. Two types of plans exist. Those with first dollar coverage begin to pay benefits as soon as covered medical expenses are incurred; in effect, these plans have no deductible. Plans without first dollar coverage require the insured to pay a deductible before benefits begin. See also *basic medical insurance* and *major medical insurance*.

comprehensive medical care—complete package of health care services and benefits, including prevention, early detection and early treatment of conditions.

compressed work week—employee work schedule that involves fewer than the traditional five days in one week or ten days in two weeks. This arrangement usually involves working more hours per day.

compression—see *pay compression*.

comp time—overtime hours that are worked and then taken later as paid time off. Comp time is short for compensatory time and is also known as time off in lieu.

compensatory time—see *comp time*.

comptroller—chief accountant of a company or government entity. A comptroller, also referred to as a controller or financial controller, oversees the accounts, supervises financial reporting and has responsibility over implementing and monitoring internal financial controls.

compulsory retirement—when an employee must retire upon reaching a certain age or under other specified conditions. The Age Discrimination in Employment Act of 1967 prohibits mandatory retirement in the United States if it is based solely on age, though there are exceptions for certain executives or where public safety outweighs individual protection (e.g., airline pilots). Mandatory retirement is also known as automatic or mandatory retirement.

computerized axial tomography (CAT or CT) scan—complex x-ray technique used to produce detailed cross-sectional internal images of a body part. See also *magnetic resonance imaging (MRI)* and *positron emission tomography (PET)*.

concession bargaining—negotiation between an employer and a union in which employees are asked to give back previously gained improvements in wages, benefits or working conditions. Workers generally agree to such concessions in exchange for some form of job security, such as protection against layoffs.

concierge benefit—convenience services offered by an employer to employees. Benefits may be in the form of errands (e.g., dry-cleaning pickup, shopping) or on-site services (e.g., banking, medical care, package pickup and delivery). Concierge benefits are designed to help employees balance work and personal needs, improve morale and increase productivity.

conciliation—process in which two opposing sides are brought together in an attempt to reach a compromise that avoids taking a case to trial. Conciliation is used in labor disputes before arbitration and may also take place in several areas of the law. A court of conciliation is one that suggests the manner in which two opposing parties may avoid trial by proposing mutually acceptable terms. See also *alternative dispute resolution (ADR)*.

concurrent review—process to determine if a medical treatment and/or continued care are necessary. Typically initiated by a health care provider (i.e., doctor or hospital), the review may be conducted internally or through an outside party. In certain situations, such as an extended hospital stay, a health plan may require such a review. A concurrent review focused specifically on extending a patient's hospital stay is sometimes called a continued stay review or recertification. See also *precertification, prospective review, retrospective review* and *utilization review (UR)*.

conditionally renewable—feature in an insurance policy that grants an insurer the right to refuse to renew the policy for reasons specified in the policy at the end of a premium payment period. See also *cancelable, guaranteed renewable, noncancelable and guaranteed renewable* and *optionally renewable*.

conditional vesting—under a contributory pension plan, limitation of an employee's right to receive vested benefits. The employee can withdraw contributions to the pension plan only according to stated conditions. See also *unconditional vesting* and *vesting*.

conduit IRA—see *rollover IRA*.

Conference of Consulting Actuaries (CCA)—association of consulting actuaries in all practice areas and many nations.

confidentiality—protecting the privacy of information concerning a plan participant or patient.

conflict of interest—situation in which an individual or organization has competing concerns that might compromise its ability to act objectively and in the best interests of another. For example, a plan trustee has a fiduciary duty to act solely in the interest of plan participants and their beneficiaries. A conflict of interest occurs if the trustee might benefit personally from a construction project financed by the plan the trustee represents.

conglomerate—group of different businesses that have common ownership and are run as a single organization. The businesses may appear to be unrelated.

Congress of Industrial Organizations (CIO)—established in 1935, the CIO was initially the Committee for Industrial Organization within the American Federation of Labor. Comprised primarily of industrial unions, the CIO became an independent body in 1937 and, eventually, the Congress of Industrial Organizations. The CIO merged with the AFL to form the AFL-CIO in 1955. See also *American Federation of Labor and Congress of Industrial Organizations (AFL-CIO)*.

consideration—contractual element that each party to a contract has received or been promised something of value (e.g., money, property or a promise to perform an act) from the other party.

connected person—for the purposes of registered pension plans (RPPs), a person who does not deal at arm's length with an employer, is a specified shareholder of the employer or holds (alone or in combination with someone he or she does not deal with at arm's length) 10% or more of the issued shares of any class of shares of the employer or related employer. Subsection 8500(3) of Canada's Income Tax Regulations provides a more precise definition.

Consolidated Omnibus Budget Reconciliation Act of 1985 (COBRA)—U.S. legislation that gives workers and their families who lose health benefits the right to choose to continue group health coverage for limited periods of time under certain circumstances, including voluntary or involuntary job loss, reduction in hours worked, transition between jobs, death, divorce and other life events. Qualified individuals may be required to pay the entire premium for coverage plus administrative expenses, up to a limit of 102% of the plan's cost to the employer. COBRA generally requires that group health plans sponsored by employers with 20 or more employees in the prior year offer employees and their families the opportunity for this continuation coverage. A qualified beneficiary must be given an election period with a minimum of 60 days to decide whether to continue coverage, which begins with the date coverage terminates. Notice of this period must be provided in person or by first-class mail within 14 days after the plan administrator receives notice that a qualifying event has occurred. Other elements of the act:
- Prohibit employer-provided medical plans from requiring Medicare to be the primary payer for participants aged 70 and over
- Extend Medicare coverage to state and local government employees
- Restrict the definition of *insured termination* as it relates to coverage by the Pension Benefit Guaranty Corporation. See also *qualified beneficiary* and *qualifying event*.

construction lien—see *mechanic's lien*.

constructive discharge—situation in which an employee is forced to quit a job because the employer has made working conditions intolerable; for example, the employee is discriminated against or harassed, or suffers a negative change in pay, benefits or workload for reasons that are not performance-related. In most cases, an employee who voluntarily leaves a company, as opposed to one whose employment is terminated by the company against his or her will, is not entitled to unemployment benefits and loses the right to sue the company for wrongful termination. However, the law recognizes constructive discharge as an exception to this rule. See also *wrongful discharge*.

constructive receipt—as defined by the IRS, the first date when a taxpayer has the right to claim wages, dividends or other income, regardless of whether a claim was actually exercised. A taxpayer is subject to tax on income in the year when constructive receipt occurred. Unlike actual receipt, constructive receipt does not require physical possession of the income in question. See also *economic benefit*.

consultant—person or firm offering expert business, professional or technical advice. Compensation is provided through commission, on a fee-for-service basis or a combination thereof.

Consumer Assessment of Healthcare Providers and Systems (CAHPS)—program administered by the U.S. Agency for Healthcare Research and Quality within the U.S. Department of Health and Human Services, CAHPS develops and supports the use of comprehensive standardized surveys asking consumers/patients to report on and evaluate their experiences with health care. These surveys cover topics that are important to consumers, such as the communication skills of providers and the accessibility of services.

consumer-driven health care (CDHC)—there is no single definition for consumer-driven health care, but it generally refers to a health insurance plan that gives members more choice with respect to health care decisions and provides incentives for seeking out the most cost-effective care. CDHCs often combine a high-deductible health insurance policy providing protection from catastrophic medical expenses with a prefunded and consumer-controlled account that is used to directly pay for routine health care expenses not covered by the insurance policy. Also referred to as defined contribution care and self-directed health care. See also *Archer medical savings account (MSA), flexible spending arrangement (FSA), health reimbursement arrangement (HRA)* and *health savings account (HSA)*.

Consumer Financial Protection Bureau (CFPB)—government agency established in January 2012 by the Dodd-Frank Wall Street Reform and Consumer Protection Act of 2010 (Dodd-Frank Act) to protect consumers by carrying out federal consumer financial laws. Among other things, the CFPB:
- Writes rules, supervises companies and enforces federal consumer financial protection laws
- Restricts unfair, deceptive or abusive acts or practices
- Takes consumer complaints
- Promotes financial education
- Researches consumer behavior
- Monitors financial markets for new risks to consumers.

consumerism—see *health consumerism*.

Consumer Operated and Oriented Plan (CO-OP) program—see "Consumer Operated and Oriented Plan (CO-OP) program" in the *Appendix A: Affordable Care Act of 2010 (ACA)*.

Consumer Price Index (CPI)—measure of price changes for a basket of goods and services purchased by urban households. The CPI makes it possible to compare the relative cost of living over time. Considered a key indicator of inflation and deflation in the economy, the index is used by the U.S. government to make annual adjustments in Social Security benefits and tax rates. Published monthly by the U.S. Bureau of Labor Statistics, the CPI is also known as the cost-of-living index. See also *deflation, inflation* and *purchasing power*.

Consumer-Purchaser Disclosure Project (CPDP)—group of leading employer, consumer and labor organizations working to ensure that all persons have access to publicly reported health care performance information that will help people better select hospitals, physicians and treatments based on nationally standardized measures for clinical quality, consumer experience, equity and efficiency.

contingency reserve—also referred to as a contingency fund, money set aside for use in case of an emergency or unforeseen event (e.g., a decline in investment values, higher benefit claims or natural disaster that affects operations).

contingent annuity option—feature in an annuity contract that allows payments to begin when a named event (contingency) occurs. For example, payments may begin upon the death of a spouse. See also *annuity*.

contingent beneficiary—person or entity identified to receive insurance, retirement or other benefits if the first person named to receive the benefits is deceased. See also *primary beneficiary, secondary beneficiary* and *tertiary beneficiary*.

contingent deferred sales charge or load—see *back-end load*.

contingent employee—any worker employed on less than a permanent full-time basis and who has no explicit or implicit expectation for continued employment.

continuation coverage—temporary continuation of health insurance benefits paid for by a qualified beneficiary following the occurrence of a qualifying event as mandated by COBRA. See also *Consolidated Omnibus Budget Reconciliation Act of 1985 (COBRA)*.

continued stay review—examination of a patient's case to determine whether the current place of care is still the most appropriate.

continuation of benefits—extension of an employee benefit after the employment relationship ceases. For health care insurance provided by many U.S. employers, temporary continuation is mandated by COBRA following the occurrence of a qualifying event. See also *Consolidated Omnibus Budget Reconciliation Act of 1985 (COBRA)*.

continued stay review (CSR)—see *concurrent review*.

continuing care retirement community (CCRC)—long-term care arrangement in which all housing and nursing care required for the lifetime of an individual is provided in exchange for an entrance fee and monthly charge. Facilities for independent living, assisted living, nursing care and hospitalization are available, with residents moving from one option to another as their needs change. CCRCs are sometimes called life care communities.

continuity of care—coordination of the care received by a patient over time and across multiple health care providers.

continuous quality improvement (CQI)—management process that involves ongoing internal assessment and action to improve and maintain quality. CQI is similar to total quality management.

continuous service—uninterrupted period of employment by the same employer. The definition of such service may be established by pension plan or law to include certain periods of absence and service with an associated or predecessor employer. In contrast, see *credited service*.

contract—oral or written agreement between two or more parties to do, or refrain from doing, an act, which is enforceable in a court of law.

contract administrator—see *third-party administrator (TPA)*.

contracted fee—dollar amount a health care provider agrees in advance to accept for a specific service rendered. Contracted fees are usually specified in a fee schedule that lists various procedures and the amount to be charged for each procedure.

contracted provider—see *preferred provider*.

contract group—see *enrolled group*.

contract in/out—agreement to take part/stop taking part in an official plan or system.

contract worker—see *independent contractor*.

contrarian—investor who goes against the prevailing wisdom of other investors. When others are buying, a contrarian is likely to sell.

contraindication—patient condition or fact that makes a particular medical treatment harmful and generally not useful in managing a patient's health issue.

contribution—money or property placed into a fund or given to a charity.

contribution base unit (CBU)—for the purposes of multiemployer benefit plans, a unit by which an employer's contribution to a plan is measured (e.g., hours worked, tons of coal mined, containers handled). See also *multiemployer plan* and *partial withdrawal*.

contribution carryover—money placed in a benefit fund in excess of the maximum that may be deducted for the year. This carryover can be deducted in future years when contribution payments are less than the maximum.

contribution holiday—reducing or eliminating current deposits in a pension fund by drawing on surplus assets in the fund.

contribution integration—reducing of required payments to a pension plan based on payments prescribed in the Canada Pension Plan or Québec Pension Plan. See also *step-rate integration*.

contribution limit—see *annual addition limit*.

contribution rate—a factor (e.g., a percentage of compensation) used to determine payments to a retirement plan by an employee or employer.

contributory plan—retirement benefit program that requires employees to make contributions to qualify for plan benefits.

controlled account—see *discretionary account*.

controlled group—two or more businesses, each of which is at least 80% owned by the same parent corporation or a group of five or fewer individuals, estates or trusts. Ownership may be direct or through one or more subsidiary corporations. In the United States, a controlled group is usually treated as one company for benefit plan purposes. See also *common control*.

controller—see *comptroller*.

conventional loan—mortgage that is neither insured nor guaranteed by a government agency (e.g., FHA, VA loans). Conventional loans are the most prevalent type of mortgages. They may be insured by a private mortgage insurer. See also *private mortgage insurance (PMI)*.

conversion—process of making a change. For example, persons who are insured through a group policy may be given the option to convert to an individual policy without evidence of insurability. Investors who own convertible bonds or preferred stock may be able to make an exchange for common stock, usually at a predetermined price on or before a predetermined date. In a third scenario, an employer may make a conversion from one type of retirement plan to another, such as from a defined benefit to a defined contribution plan. See also *conversion premium, convertible bond or debenture* and *convertible preferred stock*.

conversion fund—account in which unallocated employer contributions are held for the later purchase of individual annuity contracts. Also referred to as an auxiliary or side fund.

conversion premium—amount by which the price of a convertible security (i.e., bond, preferred stock) exceeds the market price of the common stock for which it can be exchanged at a given point in time. Most convertible securities trade at a price above their conversion value.

conversion price—price per share at which a convertible security (i.e., bond, preferred stock) may be exchanged for common stock. The conversion price is determined when the convertible security is issued. This price is usually set at an amount that is substantially higher than the current price of the common stock, so that conversion is desirable only if there is a substantial increase in the value of the common shares.

conversion privilege—see *conversion* and *convertible term insurance*.

conversion ratio—number of shares of common stock received when one bond or one share of preferred stock is converted.

convertible (CV)—see *convertible bond or debenture* and *convertible preferred stock*.

convertible bond or debenture—corporate debt instrument that the owner (holder) can exchange for shares of the corporation's common stock at a predetermined price or ratio. If the stock value increases substantially, the conversion option gives the creditor the opportunity to profit over and above the bond's coupon rate. Convertible debt instruments tend to offer a lower rate of return in exchange for the option to make the conversion.

convertible mortgage—property loan that allows the borrower to switch to another type of mortgage during a predetermined time period. For example, a borrower might be allowed to switch from an adjustable rate mortgage to a fixed rate mortgage to lock in a favorable interest rate and avoid prepayment penalties. A convertible option usually comes with additional fees.

convertible preferred stock—preferred stock in a company that the shareholder is allowed to exchange for a specified number of the company's common stock. Most convertible preferred stock is exchanged at the request of the shareholder, but sometimes there is a provision that allows the company to force conversion. See also *cumulative preferred stock, noncumulative preferred stock, participating preferred stock* and *preferred stock*.

convertible term insurance—term insurance policy that gives the policyholder the right to switch to another form of insurance without penalties and regardless of physical condition. This option, sometimes referred to as a conversion privilege, usually allows conversion of the term policy to a cash value policy that combines a saving or investing element with the insurance protection. See also *cash value life insurance* and *term life insurance*.

convexity—measure of the curvature in the relationship between bond prices and bond yields that shows how the duration of a bond changes as the interest rate changes. Convexity is a risk-management tool that helps measure and manage the amount of market risk to which a portfolio of bonds is exposed. As convexity increases, the systemic risk to which a portfolio is exposed increases. As convexity decreases, the exposure to market interest rates decreases and the bond portfolio can be considered hedged. In general, the higher the coupon rate, the lower the convexity (or market risk) of a bond.

coordination-of-benefits (COB) provision—provision in health benefit plans and health insurance policies designed to eliminate duplicate payments. A sequence is established as to which coverage will apply (primary and secondary) when a person is insured under two contracts. See also *birthday rule, duplication of benefits, primary payer* and *secondary payer*.

copayment/copay—flat fee paid by an insured beneficiary each time a medical service or prescription drug is provided. See also *coinsurance, cost sharing, deductible, differential copayment* and *reverse copayment*.

copayment relief—reduction or elimination of a copayment by a benefit plan. Copayment relief can be used as an incentive to encourage a specific behavior on the part of plan participants such as using a generic drug or adhering to drug therapy. Also referred to as a copayment waiver.

copayment waiver—see *copayment relief*.

core alternative—minimum of three diverse investment options that must be offered to participants and beneficiaries by a participant-directed retirement plan to satisfy the broad range of investment alternatives requirement in Section 404(c) of ERISA. See also *404(c) plan* and *Section 404(c)*.

core benefit
—employee benefit received by all employees regardless of position.
—when applied to health insurance, the central components of the plan. Major medical and hospitalization benefits are core benefits, while dental and vision benefits are noncore benefits.

core measures—set of standards developed by the Joint Commission to minimize data collection efforts while improving the quality of care for specific health conditions. The measures were derived largely from a set of quality indicators defined by the Centers for Medicare and Medicaid Services and have been shown to reduce the risk of complications and recurrences for hospital patients. Core measure sets currently exist for conditions such as stroke, pneumonia, perinatal care, children's asthma, heart failure and hospital-based inpatient psychiatric services. See also *Joint Commission*.

core-plus-options plan—flexible benefit plan that groups benefits providing a minimum level of economic security with a wide array of other benefit options that employees can add to the core. Under these plans, employees receive benefit credits that entitle them to purchase additional benefits.

core real estate—broad category of real estate that includes fully-leased office, retail, residential, industrial and hotel properties. Core real estate generally has lower price volatility and potential return than other categories of real estate. The return is more likely to be in the form of income than price appreciation. See also *opportunistic real estate* and *real property*.

core stock—stock in the middle zone between value stocks and growth stocks. See also *growth stock* and *value stock*.

corporate bond—see *bond*.

corporate governance—set of processes, customs, policies, laws and institutions that affect how a corporation is directed, administered and controlled. Corporate governance also includes the relationships among the various stakeholders, including shareholders, board of directors and committees, management, employees, customers, creditors, suppliers, regulators and the community at large. An important element of corporate governance is the accountability of individuals within the organization.

corporate-owned life insurance (COLI)—also referred to as company-owned life insurance or employer-owned life insurance, a contract with an insurance company that provides financial protection if a key employee dies. The insurance is purchased by the employer. If the covered employee dies, the employer receives the cash stated in the insurance policy. See also *life insurance* and *split dollar life insurance*.

corporate trustee—independent custodian of assets who is expected to act in the best interests of those who own the assets. The prime responsibility is that of a prudential supervisor, not a hands-on manager.

corporation—legal entity established under state or federal law to conduct business or another activity. A corporation is separate and distinct from its owners. It is treated by the courts as an artificial person that can own property, incur debts, sue or be sued. Corporations organized for business purposes typically issue stock, are centrally managed and have an unlimited life. Owner liability for corporate actions is limited to the amount the owners have invested in the corporation. See also *C corporation* and *S corporation*.

corrective distribution—mechanism for handling excess additions made by employees and employers to qualified defined contribution plans such as 401(k) and profit-sharing plans in order to satisfy IRC Section 415(c) limits and tests for ADP and ACP. See also a*ctual contribution percentage (ACP) test, actual deferral percentage (ADP) test, alternative limitation* and *Section 415*.

correlation—extent to which two economic or statistical variables move together, normalized so that its value ranges from -1 to +1. If two variables move in the same direction, there is positive correlation; if they move in opposite directions, the correlation is negative. Investors can combine investments that have high negative correlations to reduce risk.

corridor deductible—fixed dollar amount per loss often paid by the insured after benefits from a basic medical policy are paid and before benefits from a major medical policy are paid. Benefits paid under the basic plan do not apply toward this deductible. See also *basic medical insurance, deductible* and *major medical insurance*.

cost basis—see *basis*.

cost-avoidance analysis (CAA)—measuring the cost of treatment against future costs that might be prevented such as paying for additional medications, office visits, hospitalizations, surgery, long-term care and lost productivity. See also *cost-consequence analysis (CCA)*.

cost-benefit analysis (CBA)—comparison of the gains and losses associated with different choices during a decision process. For example, the cost of a worksite flu vaccination program might be compared with the total cost of medical care and lost productivity of workers if the program is not offered.

cost-benefit evaluation—see *cost-benefit analysis (CBA)*.

cost certificate—signed document provided by an actuary to justify the funding of benefits provided under a defined benefit provision plan.

cost-consequence analysis (CCA)—variation of cost-avoidance analysis that measures multiple costs and outcomes but does not aggregate them as is done with cost-benefit analysis and cost-effectiveness analysis. See also *cost-avoidance analysis (CAA)*, *cost-benefit analysis (CBA)* and *cost-effectiveness analysis (CEA)*.

cost containment—benefit plan strategies used to reduce or eliminate benefit payments.

cost-effectiveness analysis (CEA)—determination of which therapy achieves its goal with the least cost. Typically CEA is expressed as a C/E ratio—the denominator is a gain in health from a measure (e.g., years of life, premature births averted, sight-years gained), and the numerator is the cost associated with the health gain. The most commonly used measure is quality-adjusted life year (QALY). It is possible for a more expensive treatment to be considered more cost-effective, if the less expensive treatment has a greater risk such as a patient relapse.

cost-minimization analysis (CMA)—determining the lowest cost option among equally acceptable medical alternatives with respect to effectiveness and safety. CMA is the most common type of analysis used in pharmacy benefit management.

cost of illness analysis (COA)—assessment of the cost of an illness or condition, including treatment.

cost of living—average cost of the goods and services required by a person or family to maintain a given level of living. In the United States, the consumer price index is used to measure changes in the cost of living. See also *Consumer Price Index (CPI)*.

cost-of-living adjustment (COLA)—across-the-board increase (or decrease) in payments according to the rise (or fall) in the cost of living as measured by some index. Social Security benefits in the United States are pegged to changes in the Consumer Price Index (CPI). Changes in wages and pension benefits are also frequently connected to the CPI. See also *Consumer Price Index (CPI)*.

cost-of-living allowance (COLA)—adjustment in compensation for cost of living differences that exist between an employee's host country and home country. A COLA can also offer protection against exchange rate fluctuations. See also *equalization component*.

cost of living index—see *Consumer Price Index (CPI)*.

cost-of-living rider—provision added to a life insurance policy that increases a death benefit when inflation occurs. In these situations, benefits are usually tied to changes in the Consumer Price Index (CPI).

cost-plus arrangement—insurance agreement in which the monthly premium is based on the claims paid by the insurance company during the preceding month plus a preset retention charge for the policy period. Many insurance companies place a maximum limit on the monthly premium so premiums paid do not exceed the cost of the premiums that would have been paid without the cost-plus arrangement. Such arrangements are primarily used by large employers to provide life insurance. They may also be referred to as flexible funding.

cost sharing—arrangement in which some benefit costs are paid by benefit plan participants. In addition to paying a portion of a insurance plan premium, cost-sharing techniques include *coinsurance, copayments, deductibles* and *exclusions*.

cost shifting
—charging one group of patients more in order to make up for underpayment by others. For example, hospitals charge some privately insured patients more to make up for underpayments by Medicaid and Medicare.
—also used to describe situations when there is a change in the relative proportion of health care costs between an employer and employee.

cost-utility analysis—measurement of therapeutic outcomes in quantitative and qualitative terms. A quantitative factor might be the cost per day of therapy multiplied by the average number of days that therapy is required, while a qualitative factor might be the number of quality-adjusted life years (QALYs) made possible by a cancer drug.

countercyclical stock—stock that tends to rise in value when the economy is trending downward or in recession. For example, the stock of discount retail stores, fast-food restaurants and the manufacturers of antidepressants are often countercyclical because they do better when the economy is in turmoil. See also *cyclical stock* and *defensive stock*.

counter detailing—see *detailing*.

country risk—chance that a nation will not be able to honor its financial commitments.

coupon—see *coupon bond*.

coupon bond—debt security with interest and principal payable to the holder, regardless of to whom the bond was originally issued. Tickets, called coupons, are attached to the bond, with each coupon representing one interest payment. The holder clips the coupons and presents them to the issuer or paying agent to receive payment. Upon maturity, the holder (bearer) is paid the face value of the bond. A coupon bond, also called a bearer bond, is unregistered and the opposite of a registered bond. See also *coupon yield*.

coupon rate—see *coupon yield*.

coupon stripping—separating the coupons from coupon bonds to create zero-coupon bonds. The bond principal and coupon amounts can then be traded separately.

coupon value—dollar amount payable upon surrendering a bond coupon to a bond issuer.

coupon yield—interest rate stated on the face of a bond, note or other fixed income security, expressed as a percentage of the par (face) value. The coupon rate on a bond is the same as the bond's yield. Also referred to as the coupon rate or nominal yield. See also *par value* and *yield*.

covariance—degree to which two variables (e.g., the price of two stocks) move together. See also *correlation*.

coverage—extent to which someone or something is included or protected. For example, coverage is used to describe the number or percentage of employees eligible for participation under an employee benefit plan. Coverage is also used to describe the scope of protection provided by an insurance policy.

coverage testing—rules used to determine that a retirement plan's coverage of eligible, active participants does not prohibitively favor highly compensated employees.

Coverdell Education Savings Account (ESA)—trust or custodial account that can be used to pay for qualified K-12 and college education expenses for a designated beneficiary. ESAs were established by the federal government to help parents fund their children's education. When an account is established, the designated beneficiary must be under age 18 or meet the requirements for a special needs beneficiary. The accounts are transferable among family members, and contributions can be made by anyone on behalf of the beneficiary. Contributions to the accounts are taxed, but the accounts grow tax-free. In some circumstances, the funds can also be withdrawn tax-free. The Coverdell Education Savings Account was introduced in 2002 to replace the education IRA. See also *529 plan*.

covered charge—fee for services or supplies that qualify for payment under a benefit plan. The covered charge may be different from an allowable fee, which takes into account any contractually-based discounts on the provider's usual fee. Actual payment may be in whole, in part or none depending on plan design provisions such as deductibles, coinsurance, annual and lifetime maximums, and limitations.

covered compensation—average wage ceiling for U.S. Social Security taxes (a.k.a. taxable wage base) for the 35 years up to and including the calendar year in which an employee reaches Social Security retirement age.

covered entity—for the purposes of HIPAA, any health plan that provides, bills or pays the costs of medical care; any health care provider that furnishes, bills or is paid for health care; and any health care clearinghouse that processes or facilitates the processing of health information. See also *Health Insurance Portability and Accountability Act of 1996 (HIPAA)*.

covered expense—cost incurred by an insured that will be paid or reimbursed through an insurance policy. Hospital care is an example of a covered expense in most health insurance policies. The precise expenses covered by insurance can vary greatly from one policy to another.

covered option—situation in which the writer (seller) of an option owns the underlying stock. See also *call option, option* and *put option*.

covered person—individual in whose name a health plan or policy is issued. In the case of family coverage, covered persons also include the enrollee's dependents.

covered service
—service to which an insurance policyholder is entitled under the terms of an insurance contract or benefit plan. For example, covered services under a health insurance policy are typically surgery, lab work and nursing care.
—may also refer to the period of employment during which an employee is a participant in an employee benefit plan.

CPT code—see *current procedural terminology (CPT)*.

credentialing—obtaining and reviewing the documentation (e.g., license, certification, evidence of malpractice insurance) of a health care provider. Typically, the credentialing process includes verifying that the information is correct and complete.

credit—entitlement to a pension or welfare benefit that is payable sometime in the future.

creditable coverage—for the purposes of Medicare Part D, prescription drug coverage that meets or exceeds Part D coverage. Health plans are required to notify participants if their drug coverage is creditable so that they may choose to opt out of Medicare Part D coverage.

credit default swap—see *swap*.

credited earnings—maximum taxable income for each year that forms the basis for Social Security benefits in the United States.

credited projected benefit—see *projected benefit*.

credited service—years of employment counted toward seniority or used to determine benefit amounts and entitlement to benefits—sometimes referred to as pensionable service.

credit rating—assessment by a credit bureau or agency of a person's or organization's ability to fulfill financial obligations. Among the factors that are usually taken into consideration as part of the assessment are current assets, income, debt and payment history.

credit risk—see *default risk*.

credit splitting—provision in a pension plan or legislation entitling a spouse, on divorce or breakup, to a share of pension credits earned by the other during the marriage or thereafter. Also referred to as division of pension credits.

criminal action—legal proceeding in which the government charges a party with violating the law. A key part of the action is a trial in which the guilt of the accused is determined. If the accused (the defendant) is found to be guilty, a punishment is imposed according to the statute under which the party was prosecuted. Punishment may be a fine, imprisonment or, in some locales, even death.

critical and declining status—new funding status created by the Multiemployer Pension Reform Act of 2014 (MPRA) for multiemployer benefit plans in the U.S. that are projected to become insolvent:
- During the current plan year or in the next 14 plan years OR
- In the next 19 plan years and (1) the ratio between *inactive participants* and *active participants* exceeds 2:1 or (2) the plan is less than 80 percent funded.

Sponsors of plans meeting one of these two criteria are permitted to decrease accrued benefits regardless of whether a participant is eligible to receive or is receiving benefits. See also *green zone, critical status, endangered status, Multiemployer Pension Reform Act of 2014 (MPRA)* and *seriously endangered status*.

critical care—medical treatment provided to acutely ill patients during a health crisis. Critical care is usually provided in a specialized unit. The name for this unit may be intensive care unit, coronary care unit, trauma center or, simply, critical care unit.

critical illness covereage—limited form of health insurance in which an insurer agrees to pay if the policyholder is diagnosed with a specific condition such as cancer, heart attack, stroke, Alzheimer's disease, kidney failure, organ transplant, disability, etc. Some policies require that the policyholder survive a specified number of days from when the illness was first diagnosed. Payment is typically a lump-sum cash amount stated in the policy. Critical illness insurance is also referred to as a dread disease policy.

critical pathway—see *clinical pathway*.

critical status—designation specified by the Pension Protection Act of 2006 for multiemployer pension plans when any of these situations exist:
- The plan has an accumulated funding deficiency in the current plan year or a projected deficiency in the next three years (four years if funded at less than 65%), without regard to PPA amortization extensions
- The plan's funded percentage is less than 65% and the plan fails a seven-year solvency test
- Expected contributions for the current plan year do not cover the plan's normal cost plus interest on unfunded liability, the present value of the plan's inactive liability exceeds the present value of the plan's active liability, and there is a projected accumulated funding deficiency in the current or next four years.
- The plan fails the five-year solvency test.

If a plan actuary certifies that a plan is in critical status (a.k.a. the red zone), the plan must notify the U.S. Department of Labor, the Pension Benefit Guaranty Corporation, beneficiaries, unions and employers of the designation. A rehabilitation plan must be prepared and implemented. See also *accumulated funding deficiency, critical and declining status, endangered status, green zone, rehabilitation plan* and *seriously endangered status*.

cross-testing—checking for nondiscrimination based on either current contributions or future benefits. Cross-testing provides greater flexibility in plan design. See also *nondiscrimination rule*.

cross-trading—transaction in which an investment manager sells securities for one client and buys the same securities for another client. The trade is not recorded on an exchange and is prohibited by most major exchanges. The Pension Protection Act of 2006 provides an exemption for cross-trading between ERISA accounts if certain conditions are satisfied, including the adoption of written cross-trading policies and procedures.

Crown corporation—government-controlled company or enterprise in Canada. Examples include the Canadian Broadcasting Corporation and Canada Post.

culture of health—environment that values, supports and promotes health and safety. To foster this culture in the workplace, plan sponsors and employers use a variety of strategies (e.g., health risk assessments, disease management counseling, stress-reduction activities, smoking-cessation programs, healthy eating initiatives, physical fitness facilities and workplace safety programs) to encourage employees to take charge of their own health, manage chronic conditions and adopt healthier behaviors.

Cumulative Bulletin (CB)—IRS publication containing revenue rulings and other pertinent pronouncements. The CB is a semiannual, indexed consolidation of information published in the weekly Internal Revenue Bulletin.

cumulative preferred stock—preferred stock with a provision that gives the stockholder priority over common stock in the payment of dividends. If one or more dividends due to preferred owners are not paid as promised, the dividends in arrears must be paid before any dividends may be paid to common stock owners. In other words, the preferred stockholders' unpaid dividends accumulate until they can be paid. See also *convertible preferred stock, noncumulative preferred stock, participating preferred stock* and *preferred stock*.

cumulative rate of return—compounded percentage of the money gained or lost (both realized and unrealized) on an investment covering more than one period or year. For example, a $100 investment that grows to $200 in ten years has a cumulative return of 100%.

cumulative trauma disorder (CTD)—broad category of injuries to soft body tissues that result from repeated overuse or shock to a body part. Ergonomic hazards at work are one cause of this disorder, which is also referred to as repetitive stress injury. Examples of the condition include carpal tunnel syndrome, low back pain and eyestrain.

currency depreciation—reduction in the value of a nation's money relative to the money issued by other nations. In contrast to currency devaluation, currency depreciation occurs automatically and is determined by the supply and demand for various currencies. See also *currency exchange rate* and *floating exchange rate*.

currency devaluation—official reduction in the value of a nation's money within a fixed exchange rate system. Currency devaluation occurs when the monetary authority within a nation sets a new fixed rate for its currency relative to the currency of another nation, a basket of foreign currencies or a precious metal. See also *fixed exchange rate*.

currency exchange rate—value of one nation's money stated in terms of another nation's money. Also referred to as the exchange rate or rate of exchange. See also *fixed exchange rate* and *floating exchange rate*.

currency risk—also called exchange rate risk, the chance that a change in the value of one nation's money relative to the money of other nations could affect the value of an investment.

current asset—cash or another resource that can be quickly converted to cash, usually within one year. Besides cash, current assets include bonds, accounts receivable and product inventory.

current capital—see *working capital*.

Current Dental Terminology (CDT)—alphanumeric coding system for dental services developed by the American Dental Association that involves a set of five digits beginning with the letter "D" that is used to identify each specific dental procedure. The coding is accompanied by a name and description for each procedure. The system is used to submit claims for payment and to report services rendered.

current distribution profit-sharing plan—program established and maintained by an employer that allows employees and their beneficiaries to benefit from the money remaining after all costs of operating a business are paid. A current distributions plan pays profits directly to employees in the form of cash, check or stock as soon as profits are determined. See also *incentive pay plan* and *profit-sharing plan*.

current income return—see *rate of return (ROR)*.

current liability—cash obligations due within the current business cycle or one year. Examples include accounts payable, interest on debt obligations, short-term notes and accrued expenses.

currently insured—as used for Social Security eligibility in the U.S., a worker who has earned a minimum of six quarters of coverage in the most recent 13-quarter period.

Current Procedural Terminology (CPT)—coding system developed by the American Medical Association to categorize medical procedures for billing.

current profit-sharing plan—
program established and maintained by an employer that allows employees to benefit from corporate profits. Distribution is at the discretion of the employer. Proceeds are given directly to employees in the form of cash or stock. See also *incentive pay plan* and *profit-sharing plan*.

In Canada, these plans are also referred to as *cash profit-sharing plans*. See also *deferred profit-sharing plan (DPSP)*, *employee's profit-sharing plan (EPSP)*, *profit-sharing plan* and *registered profit-sharing pension plan*.

current ratio—also known as the working capital ratio, a financial measure used to determine whether a business has enough liquid resources to pay its short-term and long-term debt obligations. The current ratio considers the total assets of the business (both liquid and illiquid) relative to the total liabilities of the business. It is called "current" because, unlike some other liquidity rations, it includes all current assets and liabilities. A ratio under 1 indicates the liabilities of a business are greater than its assets and suggests the business would be unable to pay off its debt if the debt were due. A ratio of 2 is considered a healthy condition for most businesses. Depending on how a company's assets are allocated, a current ratio greater than 3 may suggest a company is not using its current assets efficiently, not doing a good job of securing financing or managing its working capital poorly. See also *acid test ratio*.

current service benefit—portion of future retirement benefits that relates to a plan participant's present year of service.

current service cost—cost of benefits credited to members of a plan in a given year.

current value—amount of money that would be realized from the sale of property at the present time.

current yield—dollar interest (coupon value) paid on a bond divided by the present market price of the bond. Because current yield does not take into account any premium or discount an investor incurs when purchasing a bond, this measure is not a good indicator of actual return on investment. See also *coupon bond* and *yield*.

curtailment—reduction in future pension benefits or the raising of pension eligibility requirements leading to a partial termination of the plan. See also *settlement* and *termination*.

custodial arrangement—warehousing of securities by a bank, trust company or other entity for safekeeping. This entity may also collect income and do simple reporting on the value of the assets.

custodial care—assistance with daily living activities (e.g., bathing, dressing, eating, taking medicine) that a person is unable to do on his or her own. Custodial care may be provided in a person's home or through a special facility such as a nursing home.

custodian—individual or organization entrusted with the care of someone or something. Banks, brokerage firms and mutual fund companies function as custodians when they hold the cash and securities of a retirement plan; they may collect income and do simple reporting on the value of the assets.

customary charge—fee most commonly charged for a service by health care providers within a defined geographic region. The customary charge is sometimes the maximum amount a health insurance plan will allow for covered expenses. See also *reasonable and customary (R&C) charge* and *usual, customary and reasonable (UCR) fee*.

cyber liability—risk posed by conducting business over the Internet and other networks, and using electronic storage technology. "First-party" cyber liability refers to occasions when an organization's own information is breached; for example, a hack threatens to expose trade secrets that would affect an organization's competitiveness. "Third-party" cyber liability occurs when the information of a customer or patient is breached; for example, a hack that accesses customer Social Security numbers, which could lead to lawsuits and trigger statutory fines.

cyclical stock—share in a corporation that is particularly sensitive to changes in the business cycle and economic conditions. When the economy is doing well, cyclical stocks tend to do well. But when there is an economic decline, these stocks and the companies they represent tend to decline as well. Automobile, steel, chemical and machinery stocks tend to be cyclical. To reduce this sensitivity, many companies try to diversify their operations among other fields and products. See also *countercyclical stock* and *defensive stock*.

D

daily benefit—flat dollar amount an insurance company pays under specific circumstances stated in an insurance policy. A daily benefit is frequently a feature of long-term care insurance policies. The benefit is the amount the insurer will pay for each day of care the insured receives in a care facility or at home.

daily valuation—market value of a fund's underlying assets that is determined and available to accountholders every business day. This contrasts with quarterly valuation in which a fund administrator calculates and reports the value of an individual's account every three months. With daily valuation, mutual fund investors and retirement accountholders can know the value of their holdings on almost any day.

damages—amount claimed or paid as compensation for injuries and losses caused by the wrongful acts or negligence of another.

danger pay—compensation provided over and above hardship pay for employees living and working in a foreign country subject to civil war, revolution, terrorism, etc. The rate of increased compensation typically varies with the locale and assessed level of danger. See also *hardship allowance/pay*.

data analytics—process of inspecting, cleaning, transforming, interpreting and modeling data to discover trends, patterns and other information to make benefit plan decisions and changes.

data collection—planning for and obtaining information for analysis. Patient characteristics such as age, gender, race, illness or injury, medical therapies used in treatment, outcome of treatment and cost of treatment are all examples of health care data that are collected. Such information helps providers, insurers, plan sponsors and other stakeholders identify what is working and where improvement is needed.

data mining—sifting through dozens of fields in large relational databases using artificial intelligence and advanced statistical tools (e.g., cluster and regression analyses) to identify trends, patterns and relationships. Data mining attempts to discover information that can be used to increase revenue, cut costs, etc.

Davis-Bacon Act of 1931—U.S. law that requires projects receiving financial assistance from the federal government to pay wages and benefits prevailing in the area where the work is performed. Wage determinations are the responsibility of the Wage and Hour Division of the U.S. Department of Labor.

day care—provision of a range of services that may include health, medical, psychological, social, nutritional and educational services for children, the disabled or elderly persons. Such care is often used when a primary caregiver is at work or otherwise unavailable.

days per thousand—number of hospital days in a period (e.g., year) per thousand plan participants. Days per thousand is a standard measure used to assess the impact of care-management strategies.

day surgery—see *outpatient surgery*.

DB(k) plan—also known as an eligible combined plan, a hybrid pension plan created by the Pension Protection Act of 2006. The plan, which consists of a defined benefit plan and a 401(k) plan held in a single trust, is available to employers with 500 or fewer employees. If the DB(k) plan includes the required design specifications, it is exempt from top-heavy rules and satisfies the nondiscrimination tests. The plan uses one plan document, one summary plan description, one Form 5500 report and one audit (if an audit is required). The 401(k) component must provide automatic enrollment and a fully vested 50% match on the first 4% of deferred pay. The defined benefit component is either a 1% of final average pay formula for up to 20 years of service or a cash balance formula that increases with the participant's age; it is this element that promises a source of income, regardless of the performance of the 401(k) portion of the plan.

dealer—person or firm acting as a principal in buying and selling securities.

death benefit—payment to a beneficiary upon the death of a plan participant. See also *nonoccupational death benefit* and *occupational death benefit*.

death rate—proportion of persons who die within a year, usually expressed per 1,000.

debenture—debt backed only by the integrity of the borrower, not by an asset or other collateral. An unsecured bond is an example of a debenture.

debit card—plastic card resembling a credit card that lets the holder make purchases using funds drawn directly from a bank or other account. Debit cards are now being provided to those participating in a flexible spending arrangement (FSA), health reimbursement arrangement (HRA) or health savings account (HSA). Debit cards are also used for employer-sponsored transportation reimbursement plans.

debt—something that is owed.

debt limit/ceiling—maximum dollar amount that can be borrowed. A debt limit is common on credit cards.

debt service—payments of principal and interest owed to a lender.

debt-to-equity ratio—comparison of liabilities to assets. The long-term debt-to-equity ratio for a company is calculated by dividing the company's long-term liabilities by its equity. In contrast, the total debt-to-equity ratio is the company's long-term and current liabilities (debt that will be paid off within one year) divided by its equity. The higher the ratio, the more important it is for a company to have positive earnings and steady cash flow to pay off the debt. These ratios are also helpful in comparing companies within the same industry.

declined risk class—group of life insurance applicants who have medical histories or conditions with the potential for claims so great that an insurer cannot provide coverage to them at an affordable cost. Also known as an uninsurable class. See also *class rating, preferred risk class, qualified impairment insurance, rated policy* and *standard risk class*.

decreasing term life—annual renewable life insurance that provides a death benefit that declines at a predetermined rate over the life of the policy. Premiums throughout the contract are usually constant, but the benefit is usually reduced monthly or annually. Most decreasing term insurance is in the form of mortgage life insurance, which pegs the term of coverage and benefit to the remaining amount owed on the home being purchased. See also *life insurance* and *term life insurance*.

decumulation—drawing down of retirement assets that have been accumulated during an employee's working life. Decumulation is essentially the reverse of *accumulation*.

dedicated bond portfolio—collection of debt securities selected to meet a specific set of future benefit payments with the cash flow. The most common use of such a portfolio is to provide benefits when due to retired employees. Ideally, the cash flow from the portfolio exactly matches each future payment, both in amount and timing. If this exact matching is achieved, the funding of future payments will not depend on the level of future interest rates.

dedication strategy—method by which the anticipated returns on an investment portfolio are matched with estimated future liabilities. This strategy is frequently used in pension funds and insurance company portfolios to ensure future liabilities can be met.

deductible—amount of expenses (loss) that an insured must pay before an insurer begins payment. The deductible is usually a flat amount and is common to health, property and liability insurance contracts. See also *calendar year deductible, carryover deductible, coinsurance, copayment/copay, corridor deductible, family deductible* and *first dollar coverage.*

deductible carryover—see *carryover deductible.*

deed—legal document by which ownership of real estate is transferred from one owner to another.

deed of trust—legal document, also referred to as a trust deed, that is sometimes used instead of a mortgage to transfer property to a neutral third party (trustee) as a security for a debt. If the borrower defaults on the loan, the lender has the right to foreclose on a property. See also *trust agreement.*

deemed dependency—in the U.S., a Social Security requirement for spousal benefits that requires a spouse be financially dependent on the retiree. A spouse is a deemed dependent if his or her own full retirement benefit is less than half of the other spouse's full retirement benefit.

deemed IRA—traditional or Roth individual retirement account (IRA) that employees with a qualified 401(a) pension, a profit-sharing or stock bonus plan, a qualified 403(a) employee annuity plan, a 403(b) tax-sheltered annuity plan or a 457 governmental deferred compensation plan can use for additional retirement savings. Set up by an employer, contributions to the account are voluntary on the part of employees. Deemed IRAs, also known as sidecar IRAs, are part of the Economic Growth and Tax Relief Reconciliation Act of 2001. The same rules that apply to IRAs apply to deemed IRAs. For example, contributions to a deemed Roth IRA are after-tax. The accounts are also subject to the exclusive benefit and fiduciary rules of ERISA, but not ERISA's reporting and disclosure, participation, vesting, funding and enforcement requirements that apply to qualified retirement plans. See also *individual retirement account (IRA)* and *Roth IRA.*

deep value stock—ownership share of a corporation that has a very low price/earnings (P/E) ratio (i.e., the current share price of the stock divided by its current or estimated future earnings per share). A corporation with deep value stock is often a very distressed business for which any sign of a turnaround will be rewarded. See also *value stock.*

default—failure to meet the obligations of a contract (e.g., repaying a loan).

default investment—fund option into which retirement contributions are invested when a retirement plan participant has not chosen specific investment options. Default investments are often needed when a defined contribution plan has an automatic enrollment feature, since participants are enrolled without any action on their part. See also *automatic contribution arrangement* and *qualified default investment alternative (QDIA).*

default risk—also known as credit risk or financial risk, the chance that the issuer of a bond or another debtor will not pay a debt obligation in the time frame established.

defendant—individual, company or other entity accused or sued in a court of law. Defendants must "defend" their innocence. See also *plaintiff.*

Defense of Marriage Act (DOMA)—enacted September 21, 1996, a U.S. federal law that defined marriage to be the union of one man and one woman for federal purposes such as insurance benefits for government employees, Social Security survivors' benefits, immigration and the filing of joint tax returns. The act also allowed states to refuse to recognize same-sex marriages granted under the laws of other states. In 2013, these provisions of the DOMA were declared unconstitutional by the U.S. Supreme Court in *United States v. Windsor.*

defensive medicine—unnecessary medical procedures, tests and other practices carried out primarily to reduce the chance of a malpractice suit.

defensive portfolio—collection of financial instruments (e.g., short-term bonds, preferred stocks) that are unlikely to fluctuate much in value. See also *aggressive portfolio.*

defensive stock—equity shares in a business that are relatively unaffected by business cycles, such as the food or utility industry. See also *countercyclical stock* and *cyclical stock.*

deferred annuity—insurance contract in which the insurer agrees to provide payments that will begin at some future date, frequently the point at which a person anticipates retiring. This is in contrast to an immediate annuity, which starts making income payments within a short period (e.g., one month, one year) after purchase. See also *annuity* and *single premium deferred annuity (SPDA)*.

deferred benefits—noncash compensation to which an employee may be entitled at a future date, assuming he or she has met the eligibility requirements for the benefits. Pensions plans, 401(k) savings plans and stock options plans are examples of programs providing deferred benefits.

deferred compensation—arrangement in which a portion of an employee's income is paid out at a date after which the income is actually earned. Examples of deferred compensation include pensions, retirement plans and stock options. A primary benefit of most deferred compensation is the deferral of tax.

deferred group annuity—see *group deferred annuity*.

deferred income—monetary payments received after the period in which they were earned. Retirement plans are a way employers help employees defer income for postemployment years.

deferred load—see *back-end load*.

deferred payment—money to be paid at a future date.

deferred pensioner—terminated employee who is entitled to a retirement benefit at some future date.

deferred premium arrangement—also referred to as a premium-delay arrangement, an agreement between an insurance company and a group policyholder that extends the grace period for premiums, usually by one to three months. The arrangement, which is used for the payment of health, disability and life insurance premiums, allows the business purchasing the policy to invest the funds that would otherwise held by the insurer, hence, increasing a company's cash flow and year-end earnings. If the contract is terminated at some future date, the deferred premiums must be paid to the insurance company. These agreements are usually granted only to companies with excellent credit ratings.

deferred profit-sharing plan (DPSP)—program established and maintained by an employer that allows employees and their beneficiaries to benefit from the money remaining after all costs of operating a business are paid. In contrast to a current profit-sharing plan, which pays profits directly to employees as soon as profits are determined, a DPSP places profits in individual savings accounts.
—in the United States, DPSPs must have a predetermined formula for allocating contributions among the participants and for distributing the funds accumulated after a fixed number of years, attainment of a stated age or upon the prior occurrence of some event such as a layoff, illness, disability, retirement, death or severance of employment. DPSPs are subject to the participation, vesting, reporting and disclosure, and fiduciary rules of ERISA but excluded from the funding and plan termination provisions. If a DPSP is a qualified plan according to the IRS, employer contributions are tax-deductible as a business expense. Benefits are taxed at the time of distribution. See also *incentive pay plan* and *profit-sharing plan*.
—in Canada, a DPSP provides an alternative to a registered pension plan (RPP) and can be set up for an individual or group of individuals. Defined in Section 147 of the Income Tax Act, only employers may contribute to a DPSP, and the funds put in an account must be paid out of profits (which includes retained earnings from prior years). Employer and employee contributions to this and other non-defined benefit plans are combined and tax-deductible to the extent total contributions do not exceed 18% of earned income up to the federal maximum established per annum. Interest and other returns accumulated on the funds in a plan are also not taxed but withdrawals are subject to income tax. The money in a DPSP is paid out at retirement or upon termination of employment. Withdrawal from a DPSP is also permitted while a person is still employed. See also *current distribution profit-sharing plan, employee profit-sharing plan (EPSP), profit-sharing plan* and *registered profit-sharing pension plan*.

deferred retirement—when an employee works beyond normal retirement. Also referred to as delayed, late and postponed retirement.

deferred retirement option plan (DROP)—arrangement permitting an employee who is eligible to retire to continue working, but retire from a retirement plan. Pension benefits that would have been paid to the employee are deposited into a special account during the period of time the employee continues to work. This account earns interest at a rate stated in the plan or based on the earnings of the underlying retirement plan trust. When the employee actually retires, the money in the separate account is paid to the employee in addition to the benefit the employee acquired under the defined benefit plan. An advantage of a DROP plan is that it enables employees who may have "maxed out" on the benefit payable under a defined benefit plan to continue to accrue benefits. Even for those who have not maxed out, the rate of accrual is often more favorable than continued accrual under the defined benefit arrangement. In many instances, the DROP benefit is payable as a lump sum, while the defined benefit is available only as a lifetime annuity.

deferred sales load—see *back-end load*.

deferred stock—equity share in a company that does not pay a dividend until a specified date or event. Deferred stock is usually issued to company founders and certain members of management to restrict their access to dividends until dividends have been distributed to all other shareholders. The point at which dividends on deferred stock are paid may be when the corporation reaches a certain level of profitability or the shareholder is no longer employed by the company. Holders of deferred stock are usually granted voting rights only after a specified date has passed. If the company goes into bankruptcy, those holding deferred stock do not have any rights to the assets of the company until all preferred and common stockholders have been paid. See also *equity compensation*.

deferred vested pension—determination of retirement benefits when a person's employment has ended or the plan has been terminated, but the employee is not yet retired. Payments are not made until a later date, usually normal retirement age.

deferred vesting—requirement that an employee must work a minimum number of service years before his or her retirement benefits are vested. See also *vesting*.

deficit—when an entity (e.g., a business or government) spends more money than it takes in.

Deficit Reduction Act of 1984 (DEFRA)—in combination with the Tax Reform Act of 1984, this legislation:
- Provided new discrimination guidelines for welfare benefit plans similar to those for qualified retirement plans and placed limits on their funding
- Provided clarification as to which benefits may be included in a Section 125 plan and instituted plan reporting requirements
- Established the use-it-or-lose-it rule for flexible spending arrangements (FSAs)
- Required companies to give employee spouses over the age of 65 the opportunity to enroll under employer group health plans
- Granted a specific tax exemption for many fringe benefits
- Modified top-heavy plan provisions, definition of key employees and rules on distribution limits from qualified plans that were part of the Tax Equity and Fiscal Responsibility Act of 1982
- Exempted government retirement plans from top-heavy requirements
- Changed the nondiscrimination test for 401(k) plans
- Established more tax incentives to encourage the formation of employee stock option plans
- Allowed contributions to be made to an individual retirement account (IRA) no later than April 15 after the tax year for which an IRA benefit is sought; the previous cutoff was the following October 15
- Allowed partial distributions from a pension plan to be rolled over into an IRA
- Applied restrictive distribution rules to 5% owners only
- Made Medicare the secondary payer for covered health expenses of workers ages 65 to 69
- Restricted golden parachute payments to executives by eliminating the corporate tax-deductibility of these payments and subjecting them to a nondeductible 20% excise tax
- Repealed the estate tax exclusion for death benefits from a pension plan or IRA
- Imposed a tax on employer-provided group term life insurance in excess of $5,000 for retirees
- Imposed a tax penalty on early distribution of universal life insurance annuities.

Employee Benefits Glossary

Deficit Reduction Act of 2005—U.S. legislation to slow the growth of spending for Medicare and Medicaid, as well as change student loan formulas and other measures. Benefit provisions include:
- Extending the Medicaid look-back period for the transfer of assets from three to five years
- Making any individual with home equity above $500,000 ineligible for Medicaid nursing home care, although states may raise the threshold to as high as $750,000
- Increasing the flat rate premiums paid by plans to the Pension Benefit Guaranty Corporation.

deficit reduction contribution—total amount of unfunded liability owed by a pension plan that is less than 100% funded. This total must include (1) the expected increase in current liability that is attributable to benefits accruing during the plan year and (2) the amount needed to amortize increased current liability that is attributable to future changes in the required mortality tables. Unfunded old liabilities are amortized over 18 years, beginning with the first plan year after 1988. The unfunded new liability is generally the amount by which the plan's current liability exceeds the actuarial value of plan assets, determined without regard to certain liabilities such as the unfunded old liability and unpredictable contingent event benefits.

defined benefit formula—method used for calculating a participant's retirement benefits from a pension plan. See also *flat benefit plan*.

defined benefit health plan—employer-determined package of health benefits provided through a group benefit or insurance plan typically provided by an employer or group of employers. A defined benefit plan is the traditional way employees have provided health benefits. See also *defined contribution health plan*.

defined benefit limit
—in the U.S., the maximum annual benefit allowed by the IRC that a participant may receive from a qualified retirement plan.
—in Canada, amount equal to one-ninth of the money purchase limit for a specific calendar year and one of the limits on the maximum amount of pension that may be paid out of a defined benefit pension plan for a year of pensionable service.

defined benefit (DB) plan—employee retirement plan established and maintained by an employer that uses a predetermined formula to calculate the amount of an employee's retirement benefit. Early DB plans (referred to as flat benefit plans) were commonly a set dollar amount that was the same for all employees, regardless of their actual compensation, or a fixed percentage of an employee's compensation. Any employee who worked for the company a minimum number of years received the same dollar amount or fixed percentage upon retirement. Today, DB plans and their formulas are more likely to take into consideration an employee's years of service; such plans are called unit benefit plans. Employer contributions to DB plans are determined actuarially. No individual accounts are maintained, as is done for defined contribution plans. In the United States, ERISA and the IRC consider any plan that is not an individual account plan to be a defined benefit pension plan. See also *flat benefit plan, qualified retirement plan* and *variable benefit plan*.

defined benefit provision—provision providing a certain level of retirement income at retirement according to a predetermined formula.
—Canada's Income Tax Act defines it as any plan provision under which benefits are determined in a way other than under a money purchase provision.

defined contribution health plan—arrangement in which a predetermined dollar amount is provided annually by an employer to employees who use this money to select from multiple health plan options for themselves and their dependents. A defined contribution plan makes it possible for an employer to cap its health care exposure. See also *consumer-driven health care (CDHC)*.

defined contribution limit—maximum dollar contribution an employer may make on behalf of a plan participant to a defined contribution pension plan.

defined contribution (DC) plan—benefit program in which a specific amount or percentage of money is set aside each year for the benefit of an employee. With a DC retirement plan, an individual retirement account is established with benefits based solely on (1) the amount contributed to the employee's personal account plus (2) any income, expenses, gains, losses and forfeitures from other participants. Contributions to an account may be made by the employee, the employer or both.
—in the U.S., defined contribution plans include 401(k), 403(b) and 457 plans. See also *401(k) plan, 403(b) plan, 457 plan, defined contribution health plan* and *qualified retirement plan*.
—in Canada, the terms money purchase plan and defined contribution plan are used interchangeably. Such a plan is also referred to as defined contribution pension plan (DCPP).

deflation—phase of the business cycle during which consumer spending is seriously curtailed, bank loans contract and the amount of money in circulation is reduced. Deflation is the opposite of inflation. See also *inflation, purchasing power* and *reflation*.

de-identified patient data—health information that has had all elements removed that might allow identification of an individual. HIPAA privacy protections specifically state what information must be removed before data is considered de-identified. Examples of information that must be removed are names, phone numbers, e-mail addresses, Social Security numbers and health plan account numbers. De-identified health data is used for various purposes including public health and research. See also *Health Insurance Portability and Accountability Act of 1996 (HIPAA)*.

delayed retirement—see *deferred retirement*.

delinquent contributions—failure by a participating employer to make promised payments to a multiemployer benefit fund.

Delinquent Filer Voluntary Compliance Program (DFVCP)—program established by the U.S. Department of Labor to encourage delinquent benefit plan administrators to meet the annual reporting requirements under ERISA. The program gives late filers a way to avoid higher civil penalties by paying a reduced penalty amount.

demand management—efforts to help patients make wise health care decisions concerning their personal health care and, as a result, reduce the need for services by improving health. Emphasis is placed on wellness, risk reduction, prevention and early detection. Demand management includes education and the provision of tools such as telephone advice lines that can help health care consumers make choices. See also *self-care*.

de minimis—Latin expression meaning minimal or trivial.

de minimis **benefit**
—when the value of any property or service that an employer provides to an employee is so minimal that accounting for it would be unreasonable or administratively impractical. As a result, the employee is not required to report it to the IRS as income. Examples of *de minimis* benefits are occasional use of an employer's copy machine for personal business, cups of coffee, a holiday gift (other than cash) with a low market value and occasional parties or picnics for employees and their guests. Cash is not excludable, regardless of the amount.
—when a retirement plan is terminated or merged with another plan, Section 4209 of ERISA allows the reduction or elimination of small amounts of multiemployer withdrawal liability.
—under tax rules, if a bond is purchased with a discount equal to less than 0.25% of the bond's face value times the number of complete years between the bond's acquisition date and its maturity date, the market discount is considered to be zero.

demographics—basic statistical data on the characteristics of a population such as age, race, gender, marital status, employment, income and geographical location.

dental capitation plan—dental benefit plan that provides services via a closed panel of dentists for a fixed fee per person.

dental care benefits—care and treatment of teeth, gums and the mouth. Dental care benefits are sometimes considered a part of health care benefits.

dental health maintenance organization (DHMO)—system for the delivery of comprehensive dental services for a fixed, prepaid, periodic payment. See also *health maintenance organization (HMO)*.

deoxyribonucleic acid (DNA)—self-replicating material present in nearly all living organisms as the main constituent of chromosomes. DNA is the carrier of genetic information.

dependent—person who relies on, or obtains benefit coverage through, a covered individual. Dependents are most commonly a spouse, domestic partner and/or minor children, but they could also be a sibling or parent. A benefit contract typically defines who is considered a dependent. See also *Working Families Tax Relief Act of 2004*.

dependent care assistance program (DCAP)—benefit provided by an employer that directly or indirectly funds care for an employee's dependent(s). Within limits, the employee is not required to include the cost of this benefit as taxable income if (1) the services are provided to a dependent who is considered qualified by the IRS and (2) the care makes it possible for the employee to work.

dependent care flexible spending account (DCFSA)—see *dependent care reimbursement account (DCRA)*.

dependent care reimbursement account (DCRA)—employer-sponsored fund that permits employees to use pretax dollars to pay for the care of a child or other dependent (e.g., spouse, sibling or elderly parent incapable of self-care) that is not reimbursed by another source. The IRS has very specific guidelines as to who is considered a dependent and the services that are covered. See also *flexible spending arrangement (FSA)* and *Section 125*.

dependent child's benefit—see *children's benefit and family allowance*.

dependent life insurance—life insurance policy that covers dependents of the person who is the primary insured. See also *juvenile insurance* and *life insurance*.

deposit administration—contract with an insurance company to administer a pension plan. The employer remains responsible for solvency until funds are used to purchase annuities from the insurer, usually at the time of retirement.

deposition—questioning of a party or witness in a court proceeding before trial, usually in an attorney's office. The questions and answers are recorded by a court reporter. Depositions give attorneys an opportunity to test the strength of a case and, more specifically, test the ability of witnesses (and any documents the witnesses provide) to tell the story leading to the lawsuit.

depreciation—accounting technique used to expense the cost of a tangible asset over its estimated useful life. Depreciation does not represent any cash outlay, nor are any funds earmarked for this purpose. See also *amortization*.

depreciation reserve
—total value of the expired portion of the useful life of an asset.
—fund into which the probable replacement cost of equipment or other asset is accumulated each year.

depression—prolonged period of sharply reduced business activity characterized by widespread unemployment, low production, a contraction of credit and a drop in consumer buying. See also *business cycle* and *recession*.

deregulation—when government rules for an industry are ended or relaxed. For example, in the 1970s, deregulation of the securities industry allowed brokerage firms to set their own commissions rather than charge a rate set by the federal government. In 1999, the Gramm-Leach-Bliley Act repealed the Glass Steagall Act of 1933, removing the legal barriers that existed between banks, insurance companies and investment firms, making it possible for one firm to function as all three.

derisking—activity or series of activities that are taken to lower risk. Managers of defined benefit retirement plans may select certain investments in an attempt to derisk (reduce the volatility of) the plan's funded ratio.

derivative—financial contract with a value derived from the value of an underlying asset (e.g., bonds, commodities, stocks, residential mortgages, commercial real estate, loans), an index (e.g., interest rates, exchange rates, stock market index, price index) or other item (e.g., weather conditions) to pay or receive money in the future based on the performance of some underlying asset such as a currency of a portfolio of stocks or bonds. Derivatives are used to reduce the chance of loss from changes in the value of the underlying element. This strategy is called hedging. Alternatively, derivatives can be used to increase profit if the value of the underlying element moves in the direction anticipated. This strategy is referred to as speculation. The main types of derivatives are futures, options and swaps. See also *futures contract, option agreement* and *swap*.

designated factor—factor used in Canada to determine the minimum payment required from a defined contribution pension plan after retirement. This factor is the same as the one used to determine the minimum payment under a Registered Retirement Income Fund (RRIF).

designated plan—in Canada, a defined benefit registered retirement plan (RRP) which, through a calendar year, is not maintained pursuant to a collective bargaining agreement and for which the total of the pension credits for specified individuals exceeds 50% of the total of the pension credits for all plan members.

designated Roth account—separate account created under a qualified Roth contribution program to which employees may elect to put part or all of their elective deferrals to a 401(k) or 403(b) plan designated. Elective deferrals that are designated as Roth contributions are treated as taxable income. However, qualified distributions are not taxed. See also *Roth IRA*.

detailing—process used by drug manufacturers and others to persuade prescribers to change their prescribing behaviors. Strategies that may be part of the process include one-on-one visits, e-mails, faxes, letters, promotional brochures and free samples. Manufacturers use detailing to encourage use of products manufactured by the firm. A pharmacy benefit management company, health plan or other organization may use detailing to promote adherence with formulary guidelines or better patient care. In this scenario, the terms academic detailing, educational detailing and counterdetailing are often used.

determination letter—communication issued by the IRS that indicates whether a benefit plan meets the requirements for qualification.

determination period—with respect to COBRA, any 12-month period selected by a health plan. This period must be applied consistently from year to year. The premium to be charged for continuation coverage under COBRA must be calculated and fixed in advance before the determination period begins.

diagnosis-related group (DRG)—classification of patients by illness or procedure (and sometimes gender and/or age) for determining payment of hospital charges. This claims reimbursement system was first implemented by Medicare to encourage health care providers to reduce costs. DRG is based on the premise that treatment of similar diagnoses will have similar costs. Also called a diagnostic-related group. See also *major diagnostic categories (MDC)*.

Diagnostic and Statistical Manual of Mental Disorders—published by the American Psychiatric Association, standard classification of mental disorders used by mental health professionals in the United States. It is intended to be applicable in a wide array of contexts and used by clinicians and researchers of many different orientations.

dialysis—process of removing waste from the body when kidneys are no longer functioning adequately.

diagnosis criteria—illnesses or types of patients for which a drug or other medical treatment is appropriate. See also *drug-specific criteria*.

differential copayment—application of a higher copayment for some drugs than others; for example, plan participants might pay a higher copayment for brand-name versus generic drugs. See also *copayment/copay*.

direct billing—when a health care provider directly bills a patient for services rendered. The patient must pay the bill then submit a claim form to the plan administrator for reimbursement of covered expenses.

direct contracting—strategy for controlling costs in which an employer or group of employers contract directly with health care providers (e.g., physicians, hospitals) to obtain reduced prices. The cost savings come through bypassing an insurer or other third party.

directed trust—trust in which one of the trustees does not have full managerial authority. Someone else, who is not a trustee, has the power to control specific actions. ERISA identifies three situations in which a plan may shift authority over assets from a trustee. The power may be given to (1) plan participants or beneficiaries allocating their own individual accounts, (2) a named fiduciary who is not a trustee or (3) an investment manager.

director—person who has been appointed or elected to serve on a board of directors. Jointly, the directors establish policies and oversee activities of the company or organization. Directors are responsible for selecting the president, vice president and other operating officers. Corporate directors decide if and when dividends are paid.

direct placement—see *private placement*.

direct price (DP)—amount a manufacturer charges for a drug sold directly to pharmacists and other non-wholesalers. The DP does not have the discounts, rebates and other reductions provided to wholesalers.

direct reimbursement (DR)—method of providing financial assistance for dental services that permits the beneficiary to use the dentist of his or her choice, pay the bill, turn in proof of payment to the plan and get paid, or the benefit payment is assigned to the dental office. The benefit is a maximum dollar amount per year per individual or percentage thereof.

direct rollover—movement of money between two retirement plans without the owner taking receipt of the funds. Rollovers frequently occur when a person changes jobs. No taxes or penalties are incurred.

direct-to-consumer (DTC) advertisements—promotion of prescription drugs through newspaper, magazine, television and Internet marketing. DTC ads also include a range of other materials, including brochures and videos available in doctors' offices and distributed to medical professionals and patient groups.

disability
—for disability benefits and insurance programs, definitions can vary substantially depending on who uses the term. Disability may be defined as a condition that renders a person incapable of performing one or more duties of his or her own occupation while others encompass any job.
—the U.S. Social Security program provides benefits only for a total disability which means the recipient:
- Cannot do work that was done before
- Cannot adjust to other work because of the medical condition(s)
- Has a disability that lasted or is expected to last for at least one year or will result in death.

For the purposes of the Americans with Disabilities Act, a physical or mental impairment that substantially limits one or more major life activities. An impairment need not prevent, or significantly or severely restrict performance of this activity in order to be considered substantially limiting. See also *Americans with Disabilities Act of 1990 (ADA)*, *reasonable accommodation* and the *Rehabilitation Act of 1973*.
—in respect to a member of a registered pension plan (RPP) in Canada, a physical or mental impairment that prevents a member from performing the duties of employment in which the individual was engaged before the commencement of the impairment.

disability benefit—periodic payments (usually monthly) when a person is unable to perform the duties of his or her occupation. Disability benefits may be paid through a life, disability or workers' compensation plan. They may also be provided as part of a retirement plan if a plan participant is totally and permanently disabled prior to the normal retirement date. See also *disability*, *employment insurance (EI)*, *nonoccupational disability benefit* and *occupational disability benefit*.

disability freeze—see *Social Security disability freeze*.

disability income rider—provision added to a life insurance policy that pays income replacement benefits in the case of disability. See also *disability*.

disability insurance—contract in which an insurance company (the insurer) agrees to provide a person (the insured) with periodic payments to replace a certain percentage of income lost when the insured is unable to work as a result of illness, injury or disease. In exchange, the insured pays the insurer money (the premium) for the transfer of the risk. Other names for disability insurance are disability income, income protection, wage loss and weekly indemnity insurance. Substantial variances exist in how insurance companies define disability. See also *partial disability*, *permanent disability*, *temporary disability* and *total disability*.

disability insured—for the purposes of Social Security, a worker is eligible to receive disability benefits if that person has earned at least 20 quarters of coverage during the last ten years and is fully insured. Exceptions apply for those under the age of 31 and in certain other cases. See also *fully insured* and *Social Security*.

disability management—steps taken to reduce the likelihood of work-related injury and disease, and if a worker is unable to work, the efforts to help the employee return to work. The process often requires a partnership among labor, management, insurance carriers, health care providers and vocational rehabilitation professionals.

disability pension—regular payments from a retirement plan to a worker who is unable to work because of injury or illness before the age of normal retirement.

disability retirement—termination of employment as a result of an illness or injury occurring before a participant is eligible for normal retirement.

disbursed self-funded plan—self-insured plan in which employee benefit claims are paid directly out of the company's cash flow as part of the expense of doing business. The plan sponsor sets aside no reserves. Most sponsors that employ this type of plan buy stop-loss insurance, usually in the range of 120% of expected claims, in order to protect themselves against a significantly poorer-than-expected experience. See also *self-funding*.

discharge planning—preparation for the transfer of a patient to an alternate and less-costly setting for care (e.g., skilled nursing facility, rehabilitation center, home health care) based on an evaluation of the follow-up care and services the patient will need. See also *case management* and *utilization management (UM)*.

disclaimer—statement denying legal responsibility for the accuracy or correctness of the presented facts.

disclaimer of opinion—statement issued when an auditor is unable to obtain sufficient information to give an opinion on an entity's financial statements. Auditors also issue a disclaimer when they have a conflict of interest. See also *adverse opinion*, *qualified opinion*, *unmodified opinion* and *unqualified opinion*.

disclosure—release or provision of information. Disclosure of information is required by law in a variety of scenarios. For example, benefit plan administrators are required by ERISA to provide summary plan descriptions and annual reports to plan participants and beneficiaries. The SEC requires issuers of corporate stock to publicly disclose financial statements and other material information that may influence the value of the security. The Real Estate Settlement Procedures Act (RESPA) requires lenders to give written disclosures to those applying for residential mortgage loans. See also *release of information (ROI)*.

discount—reduction in price. See also *discount bond* and *discount factor*.

discount bond—bond purchased for an amount below its par (face) value, such as a zero-coupon bond. Discount bonds usually accumulate interest through the life of the bond, paying both principal (the original purchase price) and accumulated interest at maturity. See also *coupon bond*.

discount broker—investment broker who tailors services to more self-directed investors. Discount brokers usually don't offer investment advice; they simply make the transaction as directed by the investor. The fees for using a discount broker tend to be much lower than the fees charged by a traditional broker, who provides advice and a wider range of services. See also *traditional broker*.

discounted fee-for-service plan—reimbursement system in which a health care provider charges separately each time services for care are rendered. The provider agrees in advance to provide the service at a fee that is lower than those usually charged by the provider. See also *fee-for-service (FFS) plan*.

discount factor—see *discount rate*.

discount rate
—often used interchangeably with discount factor, a multiplier greater than zero and less than one used to calculate the present value of future dollars or a reduction in price (discount).
—interest charged to commercial banks and other depository institutions on short-term loans they receive from their regional Federal Reserve Bank. See also *Federal Reserve System* and *monetary policy*.

discount stock option—see *stock option*.

discovery—in legal cases, the compulsory disclosure of relevant documents by a party to the action.

discretionary account—sometimes referred to as a managed account or controlled account, an arrangement in which an individual client gives a broker or other professional the authority to buy and sell securities without prior consent. When the arrangement is first established, the client does give the broker written authorization to act on the client's behalf. Guidelines may also be established regarding trading, such as the type of securities, timing, amount and price to be paid or received.

discretionary contribution formula—retirement plan arrangement in which the employer decides each year whether to place money in the plan and the amount to put in the plan. If the employer elects to make a contribution in a given year, the contributions must be allocated among employees using the plan's predetermined formula. Plans that may have this type of arrangement include simplified employee pension and profit-sharing plans. The alternative to a discretionary formula is a fixed formula with a set amount mandated by the plan. See also *fixed contribution formula*.

discrimination
—unfair treatment of a person or group on the basis of race, sex, religion, national origin, age, disability or other such classification. Many such actions by employers are prohibited by federal law. See also *Age Discrimination in Employment Act of 1967 (ADEA), Americans with Disabilities Act of 1990 (ADA), disparate impact, Equal Pay Act of 1963 (EPA), Rehabilitation Act of 1973, Title VII of the Civil Rights Act of 1964* and *Title IX of the Education Amendments of 1972*.
—to retain qualified status, benefit plans may not discriminate in favor of highly compensated employees, officers or stockholders. It is permissible to discriminate by employee group definition, such as salaried only, union employees only or hourly workers only.

discrimination testing—to meet IRS guidelines, qualified retirement plans must use a series of numerical measurements to determine whether contributions and benefits are being provided fairly to a wide range of employees; specifically, whether a plan favors highly compensated employees. See also *actual contribution percentage (ACP) test* and *actual deferral percentage (ADP) test*.

disease-centered care—model of care in which physicians make almost all treatment decisions based on clinical experience and data from medical tests. Health care is moving away from this model and toward patient-centered care.

disease management (DM)—also known as disease state management (DSM), a coordinated health care approach focused on reducing costs and/or improving the quality of life for individuals who have (or are at risk of having) a chronic condition. DM integrates preventive, diagnostic and therapeutic measures. It may also focus on monitoring patient compliance with a prescribed therapy.

Disease Management Association of America (DMAA)—see *Care Continuum Alliance.*

disease registry—database with information on patients with a specific diagnosis or condition. Most disease registries are used to manage and log data on chronic illnesses and diseases for a hospital or population. The reasons for establishing a registry are diverse but may include maintaining an accurate record of trends, identifying patient or provider needs, providing support to patients and their families, and offering assistance to those researching the particular condition being tracked.

disease state management (DSM)—see *disease management (DM).*

disenrollment—termination of an individual's participation in a health plan. Disenrollment may be voluntary or involuntary.

dismemberment—loss of an appendage, limb, sight, hearing or speech.

disparate impact—when an employer action or policy does not appear unfair or unlawful, but it adversely affects one class of employees more than others. Title VII of the Civil Rights Act of 1964 prohibits such practices. See also *discrimination* and *Title VII of the Civil Rights Act of 1964.*

dispense as written (DAW)—directive to pharmacists to dispense only the medication ordered by the prescribed. Generic substitution is prohibited.

dispensing fee—flat dollar amount paid to a pharmacy for distributing a prescription in addition to the cost of the drug. The dispensing fee covers administrative and labor costs incurred by the pharmacy.

disposable income—income an individual has available for saving and spending after taxes are paid.

disqualification—determination that a person or entity is ineligible. For example, a decision by the IRS that a benefit plan is not qualified for tax-favored status.

disqualified benefit—in a welfare benefit fund context, the IRS considers the following as disqualified benefits: (1) any postretirement medical or life insurance benefit provided to a key employee that requires a separate account to be established for the employee under Section 419A(d) of the IRC and payment is not from the primary welfare benefit fund account; (2) any postretirement medical or life insurance benefit provided to an individual in whose favor discrimination is prohibited unless the plan meets the requirements of Section 505 (b); and (3) any portion of a welfare benefit fund reverting to the benefit of the employer. Employers are subject to an excise tax equal to 100% for a disqualified benefit.

distress termination—see *plan termination.*

distribution—process of spreading or apportioning a payment or other benefit. Corporations distribute income to shareholders in the form of stock dividends. Mutual funds distribute earnings in the form of capital gains and dividends. Distribution is also used to describe payments from some retirement plans.

distributive services—medication delivery-related services performed by pharmacists that include acquiring, storing, handling, repackaging, dispensing and administering medications.

diversification—strategy of mixing securities in a portfolio to reduce investment risk. Diversification may involve different types of securities (i.e., stocks, bonds, mutual funds), issuers, maturity dates, geographical regions, etc. The investor hopes the positive performance of some securities will neutralize the negative performance of others. Individuals with small portfolios use mutual funds as an inexpensive way to diversify. See also *mutual fund.*

diversifiable risk—see *nonmarket risk.*

divestiture—disposal of an asset by sale, liquidation or other means. Some divestitures are voluntary, such as investor decisions to purge specific portfolio holdings to put economic pressure on a business or nation. For example, divestiture has also been used to encourage nations to change human rights policies. In other cases, a divestiture may be mandated. Forcing a company to divest itself of a part of its operations has been used by the U.S. government to remedy antitrust violations. A divestiture is sometimes referred to as a spin-off.

dividend—share of profits paid to corporate shareholders or participating insurance policyholders. Dividends are usually paid in cash at the end of a fiscal quarter. See also *participating insurance* and *stock dividend.*

dividend equivalent—part of incentive stock options, the right to additional shares equal to the value of the dividends a corporation is paying on its shares.

dividend fund—see *income fund*.

dividend reinvestment plan (DRIP)—program offered by a corporation that allows investors to reinvest their dividends to purchase additional shares of stock in the company. In the case of mutual funds, capital gains may also be reinvested.

dividend yield—annual return from stock dividends expressed as a percentage of the stock's current market price. Dividend yield is calculated by dividing the total dividends paid on a share of stock by its current price. See also *yield*.

divisible surplus—portion of an insurance company's end-of-year surplus that is distributed as a dividend to those who are participating insurance policyholders. See also *participating insurance*.

division of pension credits—see *credit splitting*.

Dodd-Frank Wall Street Reform and Consumer Protection Act of 2010—federal legislation passed by the U.S. Congress in an attempt to prevent the recurrence of events that caused the 2008 financial crisis. The most comprehensive financial regulatory reform effort since the Great Depression, the act does the following, among other things:
- Affects the oversight and supervision of financial institutions
- Implements a new agency responsible for implementing and enforcing compliance with consumer financial laws
- Reforms the regulation of credit rating agencies
- Implements changes to corporate governance and compensation practices
- Requires registration of advisors to certain private funds
- Effects changes in the securitization market.

See also *Consumer Financial Protection Bureau (CFPB)* and *say on pay*.

dollar cost averaging—investment strategy of buying the same dollar amount of a specific investment on a regular schedule, regardless of price. The investor is able to average the purchase price of the shares over many years, which reduces the risk of buying the shares when prices are high. Using dollar cost averaging to purchase mutual fund shares over the long term is a common strategy for reducing risk when saving for retirement.

dollar temporary annuity—see *annuity certain*.

dollar-weighted rate of return—also called the internal rate of return, a measure of a fund's rate of growth that takes into consideration the amount and timing of cash flows (e.g., deposits) into the fund's investment portfolio during a given time period. The dollar-weighted return makes the present value of the cash flows plus the ending market value of the portfolio equal to the initial market value of the portfolio. While this measure is helpful in assessing what happened to all the money in a fund during a given period, it is not particularly useful in evaluating the success of an investment manager, as a manager has no control over the timing and amount of cash flows. Compare with *time-weighted rate of return*.

domestic partnership—definitions of this term vary from state to state. In addition, employers sometimes have their own definitions when considering the implementation of a benefits program for domestic partners. Generally, domestic partners are not joined by either marriage or civil union. Common elements of domestic partnership are that the persons: (1) have reached a minimum age, usually 18; (2) are not related by blood closer than what is permitted by state law for marriage; (3) share a committed, exclusive relationship and (4) are financially interdependent. The couple may be of the same sex or opposite sex. Proof of a relationship may be required such as a written agreement or proof of a financial relationship such as a joint lease or mortgage. The IRS has addressed the issue of domestic partner coverage in several private letter rulings for tax purposes. Employment-based health benefits for domestic partners or nonspouse cohabitants are excludable from taxable income only if the recipients are legal spouses or legal dependents. Domestic partners are also referred to as cohabitants, life partners or spousal equivalents. See also *common-law marriage*.

domestic relations order (DRO)—see *qualified domestic relations order (QDRO)*.

domicile—location legally regarded as the main place of residence for a person or business entity.

donee—recipient of a gift.

donor—person or other entity that makes a gift.

donut hole—gap in Medicare Part D prescription drug coverage where the participant pays the full cost of medications. With the passage of the Affordable Care Act of 2010, the donut hole is being phased out.

double-dipping—most commonly, receiving two incomes from the same source such as holding a government job while receiving a pension from the same government. Double-dipping can also refer to receiving pension benefits from two or more plans or receiving pension benefits from one employer's plan while working for another employer.

double indemnity—insurance provision that doubles a payment for specific events or circumstances. For example, the face amount payable on a life insurance policy may be doubled if the insured person dies as the result of using public transportation.

double taxation—when income taxes are paid twice on the same source of income. For example, the U.S. government requires corporations to pay corporate income taxes on profits. Any remaining profits distributed as dividends to shareholders are taxed again by the U.S. government as the personal income of the shareholders.

Dow Jones Industrial Average (DJIA)—price-weighted average of 30 actively traded stocks (primarily large, high-quality industrial stocks) on the New York Stock Exchange. Started in 1896, the Dow is the oldest and one of the most widely used stock indexes. The stocks in the Dow have changed over the years as industry evolved and companies have merged. The DJIA is most often used to track the performance of large cap stocks in the United States. See also *Dow theory, large cap* and *stock market index*.

Dow Jones Transportation Average (DJTA)—price-weighted average of 20 transportation stocks traded in the United States. Started in 1884, the index includes airlines, railways, trucking and delivery companies. See also *Dow theory*.

downcoding—practice by third-party payers in which the codes for medical procedures are changed to a less complex and/or lower cost procedure than was reported. See also *upcoding*.

downsizing—from an employment perspective, a reduction in the number of workers.

Dow theory—approach to analyzing markets based on Dow Jones indexes. If there is an upward trend in either the Dow Jones Industrial or Transportation Average above a previous important high, a similar increase occurs in the other. When both averages dip below a previous important low, this is an indicator of a basic downward trend. The theory does not attempt to predict how long either trend will continue, although it is widely misinterpreted as a method of forecasting future action. See also *Dow Jones Industrial Average (DJIA)* and *Dow Jones Transportation Average (DJTA)*.

dread disease policy—see *critical illness insurance*.

DRG payment method—see *diagnosis-related group (DRG)*.

drop-out months—under the Canada Pension Plan, certain low earnings months not counted when calculating the average contributory earnings on which a contributor's pension is based.

drug assistance program—free or reduced-price medications provided by pharmaceutical companies and nonprofit groups for persons who do not have prescription drug coverage and cannot afford a medication. Also referred to as a prescription assistance program or pharmaceutical assistance program. The Partnership for Prescription Assistance (PPA) is a national effort to link persons to programs that will provide assistance.

drug card program—see *pharmacy card program*.

Drug Efficacy Study Implementation (DESI)—project mandated by the 1962 Kefauver-Harris amendments to the Food, Drug, and Cosmetic Act, which required manufacturers to prove that their products were effective. The amendments were applied to all new drugs and, retroactively, to those approved by the FDA between 1938 and 1962. Drugs found to be ineffective were taken off the market, while other drugs were relabeled to remove questionable claims. A few remaining products are still undergoing DESI reviews, and a final determination regarding efficacy has not yet been made.

drug formulary—list of prescription medications that will be covered by a health insurance plan. Criteria for placing a drug on a formulary are often based on what is deemed to be the most effective and economical. Drugs not on the formulary may not be available, may carry a higher cost-share amount or may be accessible only with prior authorization (PA). A formulary can have a single tier, where all drugs have the same cost to patients, or multiple tiers, where cost varies. Many formularies are three-tiered: generic drugs have the lowest copay (tier one), preferred brand name medications have a higher copay (tier two) and non-formulary drugs have the highest copay (tier three) to encourage the use of lower cost drugs. See also *closed formulary, generic drug, incentive formulary, limited formulary open formulary, partially closed formulary* and *unlimited formulary*.

drug formulary committee—see *pharmacy* and *therapeutics (P&T) committee*.

Drug-Free Workplace Act of 1988—U.S. law that requires employers with $25,000 or more in government contracts and all federal grantees to provide a drug-free workplace.

drug misadventure—error in ordering, transcribing, dispensing or administering a medication. A misadventure may also refer to an adverse drug reaction (ADR).

drug regimen review (DRR)—examination of medical records to identify cases where (1) patient drug regimens do not fit medical conditions and (2) duplicative therapy may exist. Under the Omnibus Budget Reconciliation Act (OBRA) of 1987, DRR is required in nursing homes with any irregularities documented plus recommendations for changes made to the medical staff.

drug reimportation—shipping a prescription drug back to the nation where it was originally manufactured and exported for sale in another country. Persons residing in the United States sometimes reimport drugs for personal use by filling prescriptions in Canadian or Mexican pharmacies. Current U.S. law forbids reimportation with the exception of drugs manufactured in the U.S. that are reimported by the original manufacturer and those drugs required for "emergency medical care."

drug-specific criteria—appropriate dose, duration and other characteristics specific to the use of a drug. In a drug utilization review (DUR) program, a dosage outside the drug-specific criteria requires specific action. See also *diagnosis criteria* and *drug utilization review (DUR)*.

drug test—examination of urine, hair, blood, sweat or oral fluid samples to determine the presence of specific chemical substances in the body. A test may be administered on a pre-employment basis, for probable cause (after an accident) or at random. A combination of these approaches is used to comply with the Drug-Free Workplace Act of 1988 and to facilitate drug-free workforces.

drug use evaluation (DUE)—examination of the process for prescribing, dispensing, administering and monitoring drugs; and in some cases, assessing treatment outcomes for the purpose of improving patient outcomes. DUE is founded on the belief that improved systems and processes will reduce the number of undesirable outcomes.

drug utilization management (DUM)—efforts to ensure a prescribed drug therapy is cost-effective and appropriate for a patient. DUM tools include prior authorization for select drugs and placing limits on the type and amount of drugs covered by a health care plan. See also *generic substitution, precertification, step therapy* and *utilization management (UM)*.

drug utilization review (DUR)—monitoring of prescription drugs used by a patient to identify one or a combination of the following: medical errors, potential drug interactions, unnecessary or duplicate drugs and cost-effective alternatives. Some health care plans conduct a review each time a patient fills a prescription. Though the terms have different meanings, DUR is often used interchangeably with *drug regimen review (DRR)* and *drug use evaluation (DUE)*. See also *concurrent review, prospective review* and *retrospective review.*

dual choice—permitting eligible members of a group the choice between health plans, usually the employer's primary insurer and an HMO.

dual eligible—individual who is eligible for both Medicare and some Medicaid benefits. Most dual eligibles qualify for full Medicaid benefits including nursing home services; then Medicaid pays their Medicare premiums and cost sharing. For other dual eligibles, Medicaid provides enrollees with financial help for Medicare premiums, deductibles and other cost sharing requirements through Medicare Savings Programs.

due diligence—careful investigation and analysis of information that is material to a decision, such as choosing an investment or hiring an employee.

due process—administration of justice according to established rules and principles. The U.S. Constitution adopted the due process phrase in the Fifth Amendment, ratified in 1791. When a person is charged with a criminal violation, due process includes an individual's right to (1) legal counsel; (2) receive written notice of alleged violations; (3) personally appear at any hearings; (4) cross-examine witnesses; (5) present witnesses, testimony and documentary evidence and (6) a written decision by an impartial body.

duplication of benefits—overlapping or identical coverage of a person by two or more health plans (usually insurance companies). Duplication of benefits is synonymous with multiple coverage. See also *coordination-of-benefits (COB) provision* and *proration of coverage*.

durable medical equipment (DME)—apparatus used to provide health care that is not disposable (i.e., used repeatedly). Examples of DME include hospital beds, wheelchairs, oxygen tanks and glucose monitors. Medicare permits the supplies used with glucose monitors (e.g., blood testing strips for diabetes) to also be covered as a DME expense.

durable power of attorney—legal document in which an individual designates another person to act as his or her representative in the event the individual becomes incompetent and unable to handle certain responsibilities on his or her own. The document may specify who will handle financial transactions, health decisions or both. The person authorized to act may be referred to as an agent, attorney-in-fact, health care proxy or even, simply, the attorney. See also *living will* and *power of attorney (PIA)*.

duration
—weighted average time until receipt of all of a bond's cash flows.
—expressed as a number of years, a measure of the sensitivity of a bond's price to a change in interest rates. Calculation of duration is relatively complicated, involving present value, yield, coupon, maturity and call features. This indicator of interest rate risk is part of the standard information provided on bonds and bond mutual funds. The bigger the duration number, the greater the interest rate risk or reward for bond prices. See also *interest rate risk*.

duty-to-defend coverage—provision of a liability insurance policy that grants the insurance company both the right and obligation to defend a claim—even if it is groundless.

duty-to-reimburse coverage—liability insurance that states it is the responsibility of the insured—not the insurance company—to defend a claim. The insured controls the defense but submits expenses to the insurance company for reimbursement. The insurance company retains the right to approve the defense counsel selected, but consent cannot be "unreasonably withheld."

E

early and periodic screening, diagnosis and treatment (EPSDT)—child health component of Medicaid. Required in every state, the goal of EPSDT is to improve the health of low-income children by financing appropriate and necessary pediatric services. Targeting those under the age of 21, the program includes screening and diagnostic services for detecting physical and mental problems, as well as the provision of health care and treatment. See also *Medicaid*.

early distribution—see *early withdrawal*.

early retirement—termination of employment before a participant has met a plan's usual criteria for retirement, such as a specific age and number of service years. Benefits payable in the event of early retirement are often lower than those that would be paid with a normal retirement.

early retirement age—age established by the terms of an employee retirement plan that is earlier than the plan's normal retirement age. The participant is allowed to retire and receive benefits at the earlier retirement age, but plan benefits are typically reduced.

early retirement incentive program (ERIP)—employer-sponsored plan designed to encourage employees to decide to retire sooner than they had otherwise planned. ERIPs are voluntary and are often used to get employees at the top of the pay scale to retire sooner. The program may be offered to an entire company, or it may be limited to particular employees within the company, such as those in a certain department or those doing specific jobs. Common incentives are subsidies and a waiver of early retirement penalties. Also referred to as an early retirement window plan.

early retirement window plan—see *early retirement incentive program (ERIP)*.

early withdrawal—taking funds from an account before the agreed-upon date for removal.

early withdrawal penalty—money forfeited when funds are taken out of an account prior to an agreed-upon date. For example, an early withdrawal penalty is imposed by issuers of certificates of deposit when these savings vehicles are cashed in before their date of maturation. To discourage the use of funds from a qualified retirement plan before a participant reaches the age of 59½, the IRS imposes a 10% penalty on the money withdrawn in addition to any income tax owed on funds. Under special circumstances, such as the disability or death of the plan participant, the penalty for withdrawal of retirement funds is waived.

earmarked account—separate account established for each participant in a retirement plan trust, with the specific investments for each account selected and controlled by the participant.

earned income—under U.S. income tax laws, the money (usually salary and wages) an individual is paid for services performed as an employee or through self-employment. Earned income includes wages, salaries, tips, union strike benefits, long-term disability benefits received prior to minimum retirement age and net earnings from self-employment. It does not include money received as interest, profit on the sale of property or rent.

earned income tax credit (EITC)—special tax treatment for workers with low earned incomes. Calculated using a worksheet provided by the IRS, each dollar of credit results in a dollar reduction in income tax paid to the U.S. government. The tax credit is indexed and can change annually. See also *earned income*.

earned premium (EP)—portion of an insurance policy's premium that applies to the expired portion of the policy. For example, at the end of nine months for a one-year policy, the insurance company has earned 75% of an annual premium.

earned surplus—see *retained earnings*.

earning power—company's ability to earn a profit on invested capital. Loan officers consider earning power when analyzing the risk associated with approving a loan application. See also *basic earning power*.

earnings—money income from employment or self-employment. Rent and other investment income is usually excluded. In some situations, bonuses, sick pay, etc., may also be excluded.

earnings equivalency method—one of three equivalency approaches that U.S. employers may use when tracking an employee's hours-of-service credit for a qualified retirement plan. The employee's earnings are divided by his or her hourly rate to calculate the number of hours. If an hourly employee's hours total 870 or more, the employee receives 1,000 hours of service credit. For salaried employees, 750 hours are equivalent to 1,000 hours of credit service. See also *hours of service* and *year of service*.

earnings multiple—see *price/earnings (P/E) ratio*.

earnings per share (EPS)—corporation's income minus expenses, taxes and dividends paid to preferred stockholders, which is then divided by the number of shares of common stock outstanding.

earnings record—information maintained by the U.S. Social Security Administration on each individual's Social Security and Medicare covered wages and self-employment income, which is used to calculate Social Security benefits.

earnings-related plan—benefit program that bases benefits on earnings as opposed to a flat benefit plan.

earnings report—see *income statement*.

earnings yield—corporate earnings per share for the most recent 12-month period divided by the current market price per share. The earnings yield (which is the inverse of the price/earnings ratio) shows the percentage of each dollar invested in the stock that was earned by the company. Money managers often compare the earnings yield of a broad market index (such as the S&P 500) to prevailing interest rates, such as the current ten-year Treasury yield. If the earnings yield is less than the rate of the ten-year Treasury yield, a corporation's stocks as a whole may be considered overvalued. If the earnings yield is higher, stocks may be considered undervalued relative to bonds.

econometrics—use of computers, modeling techniques and economic data for analyzing the relationship among key economic forces such as consumer spending, employment rates, interest rates and government policies.

economically targeted investment (ETI)—selection of securities for the economic benefits they create apart from investment return. For example, investments that create jobs, improve the stock of affordable housing, or improve the infrastructure in a particular geographic locale might be given preference over other investments. The U.S. Department of Labor issued an advisory for ETIs in 2008 that states the circumstances in which benefit plan fiduciaries may consider factors other than the economic interest of the plan are "very limited." See also *socially responsible investment*.

economic benefit—IRS doctrine used to determine tax liability when there is no constructive receipt. A taxpayer must include as current taxable income any financial or economic benefit derived from property promised in the future that has irrevocably been set aside for the taxpayer in a trust or fund. Generally, this includes amounts an employer transfers into an irrevocable trust for the exclusive future benefit of an employee. The doctrine has also been applied to prize winnings when they are irrevocably placed in a fund to be paid to the winner at a later date. See also *constructive receipt*.

Economic Growth and Tax Relief Reconciliation Act of 2001 (EGTRRA)—federal legislation that made significant changes in several areas of the IRC, including lower income tax rates and exclusions for estate and gift taxes. Benefit-specific provisions:
- Increased the limits on individual retirement accounts and 401(k), 403(b) and 457 plans
- Allowed employers to amend 401(k) and 403(b) plans to enable them to offer a Roth IRA
- Permitted catch-up contributions for persons aged 50 and older
- Created tax credits to help small businesses start retirement plans
- Liberalized portability and vesting rules.

economic indicators—statistics that provide evidence as to whether an economy is growing or contracting. Among these indicators are housing starts, retail sales, unemployment, inflation and the balance of trade.

economic obsolescence—loss in the desirability or value of real property due to external events or conditions. Possible causes include a decline in a local economy, encroachment of objectionable enterprises, loss of material or labor source, lack of efficient transportation or passage of new legislation.

Economic Recovery Tax Act of 1981 (ERTA)—federal legislation that included reductions in income tax rates, reductions in estate and gift taxes, indexing of income tax brackets to the inflation rate and incentives for business. Provisions of the bill relating to benefits included the expansion of individual retirement accounts to all working persons and nonworking spouses, increasing the amount self-employed people can contribute to a Keogh plan, permitting 401(k) plans for tax-exempt organizations, providing alternative methods of meeting nondiscrimination requirements, establishing a simple retirement account matching plan for employees of small businesses, and permitting multiple salary reduction agreements.

economics—study of how the forces of supply and demand allocate scarce resources. Economics is subdivided into (1) microeconomics, which examines the behavior of firms, consumers and the role of government and (2) macroeconomics, which looks at inflation, unemployment, industrial production and the role of government.

economic value added (EVA)—measure of a company's financial performance calculated by deducting the cost of capital from its operating profit (adjusted for taxes). Also referred to as economic profit.

economies of scale—reduction in the per unit cost of an item as more units are produced. As production increases, a business is able to spread fixed production costs over more units and institute procedures that increase the output per input.

edit—message or warning sent online, in real time, from a PBM to a pharmacist. Edits are one of the services that may be part of a *point-of-sale (POS) network*.

educational assistance plan—employer-sponsored program that partially or fully reimburses an employee for education and training expenses. The IRS allows an employee to exclude some of this money from taxable income. The IRS has established guidelines on the types of expenses that may be reimbursed and a maximum dollar amount per year.

educational detailing—see *detailing*.

education IRA—tax-deferred investment vehicle set up for future education-related expenses that has now been replaced by the Coverdell Education Savings Account. The term is misleading—an education IRA is not actually an individual retirement account and is not related to retirement in any way. Contributions are not tax-deductible, but all deposits and earnings can be withdrawn tax-free. See also *Coverdell Education Savings Account (ESA)*.

effective care—health services that are of proven value and have no significant trade-offs. The benefits of these therapies outweigh the risks.

effective date—date on which a change in benefit status occurs; for example, the day when insurance coverage begins, a retirement officially starts or a pay increase goes into effect.

efficient frontier—curved line that graphically represents the maximum expected investment return for different amounts of risk. Investment portfolios below the efficient frontier curve are not "efficient" because investors can achieve greater return for the same risk. Portfolios that cluster to the right of the efficient frontier are also suboptimal because they have a higher level of risk for the defined rate of return. No investment portfolios exist above the curve.

efficient market hypothesis (EMH)—theory that it is impossible to outperform the overall stock market because relevant information regarding individual stocks and the market as a whole is incorporated into the price of securities very quickly. Stock share prices trade at their fair value, which makes it pointless to use fundamental analysis to find undervalued stocks or technical analysis to predict future prices. The only way an investor can possibly obtain higher returns is by purchasing riskier investments. Widely accepted for many years, EMH is controversial today. Critics point to investors who have been able to consistently beat the market and the fact that, during a stock market crash, stock prices can dramatically deviate from their fair market values. See also *fundamental analysis, random walk theory* and *technical analysis*.

efficient portfolio—collection of investments that provides the greatest return for a given level of risk or the lowest risk for a given level of return. Efficient portfolio is synonymous with *optimal portfolio*.

elapsed time method—alternative approach to the time-tracking methods that employers may use when recording an employee's hours-of-service credit for a qualified retirement plan. The elapsed time method is designed to lessen the administrative burden of counting hours of service or converting wages or periods of payment into hours. An employee receives credit for the period of time that elapses while he or she is employed, regardless of the number of hours the employee works. The period of service begins when the employee first performs an hour of service and continues until the termination of service. See also *hours of service* and *year of service*.

elder care—provision of services addressing the special needs and requirements of senior citizens. See also *Administration on Aging* and *adult day care*.

election period—time frame in which an employee may choose to enroll in a benefit program or change options within a program. The period may be a specific number of days after an event (e.g., employment, marriage, birth of a child) or particular dates during the calendar year. Election periods are commonly used with health and retirement plans.

elective-deferred contribution—amount of pretax compensation an employee chooses to set aside for participation in an employer-sponsored retirement plan. Elective-deferred contributions are not taxed until the money is distributed, typically as a benefit after retirement. These contributions are also referred to as salary deferrals or salary reduction contributions. See also *salary reduction plan*.

electronic data interchange (EDI)—transmission of information via computer-based networks. For example, health care claims are processed using EDI, and data can be gathered for analysis on improving cost efficiency.

electronic health record—digital collection of a patient's medical history including medical conditions, prescribed medications, vital signs, immunizations, lab results and personal characteristics such as age and weight.

electronic media—computers, personal digital assistants and other devices capable of storing information. Removable/transportable hard drives, magnetic tapes and disks, optical disks and digital memory cards are all considered electronic media.

electronic prescribing—see *e-prescribing*.

electronic protected health information (EPHI or ePHI)—individually identifiable data that is stored and/or transmitted digitally via a computer or other electronic technology that relates to the past, present or future health of a person. As part of HIPAA, standards have been established for protecting the privacy and security of ePHI. See also *protected health information (PHI)*.

Electronic Signatures in Global and National Commerce Act (E-Sign)—U.S. law providing that, notwithstanding any other law or regulation, a contract, signature or other record "may not be denied legal effect, validity, or enforceability solely because it is in electronic form."

eligible expense—see *allowed amount*.

eligible period of reduced pay—in Canada, a time of employment in which compensation is less than what the person normally would receive, provided the person was not connected with the employer and had been employed by the employer for at least 36 months previously. Examples of periods of reduced pay include a temporary reduction in hours or phased-in retirement. A period of disability is not included.

eligible period of temporary absence—employment episode in Canada when an individual does not render services to his or her employer but remains employed. Such periods of temporary absence include a leave of absence, layoff, strike and lockout. A period of disability is not included.

eligibility audit—verification that a plan participants and their dependents meet the criteria for receiving benefits.

eligibility date—day an individual is entitled to participate in a benefit plan or receive benefits from the plan.

eligibility period—frame of time, usually 31 days, when potential members of a group life or health insurance plan can enroll without evidence of insurability.

eligibility requirements—conditions that an employee must satisfy to participate in a plan or obtain a benefit.

eligible automatic contribution arrangement (EACA)—automatic contribution arrangement that may allow employees to withdraw automatic enrollment contributions, up to 90 days from the date the contributions first start, without incurring the 10% early withdrawal tax. See also *automatic contribution arrangement*.

eligible combined plan—see *DB(k) plan*.

eligible employee—member of a group who has met the requirements for participation in a benefit plan.

eligible expense—charge for which an insurance policy will provide coverage.

elimination period—see *waiting period*.

emergency child care service—provision of (or financial support for) last-minute care for an employee's child so the employee is able to be at work. Types of care include reserved slots at a local child care center, a sick child infirmary and a caregiver who goes to the employee's home.

emergency department—section of a hospital or other health care facility providing rapid treatment to victims of sudden injury or illness. An emergency department may use a system that screens and classifies patients to determine those with priority needs that will be treated first.

emergency medical condition—sudden, unexpected, acute medical condition that, without medical care, could result in death or cause serious impairment of bodily functions. See also *prudent layperson standard*.

emergency medical service (EMS)—provision of care and/or transport for persons with a sudden and severe illness or injury.

emergency room care—health care services in a hospital or other primary care facility provided for a broad spectrum of illnesses and injuries, some of which may be life-threatening and require immediate attention.

emerging market fund—mutual fund that invests in less developed markets in places such as Africa, Latin America, Asia and Eastern Europe that are undergoing dramatic economic changes such as making the transition from a state-run to free-market economy. While they offer the potential for high returns, they also have more risk given the uncertainty that comes with the changes that are occurring.

eminent domain—right of a government to take private property for public use. Eminent domain is typically used to obtain real property that cannot be purchased from owners in a voluntary transaction.

emphasis of matter—paragraph by an auditor that draws user attention to a matter or matters other than those presented or disclosed in the financial statements that are relevant to understanding the audit, the auditor's responsibilities or the auditor's report. See also *unqualified opinion*.

employee—individual who is compensated for services performed and whose duties are under the control of an employer.

employee appraisal—see *performance appraisal*.

employee assistance program (EAP)—employment-based program designed to assist in the identification and resolution of a broad range of employee personal concerns that may affect job performance. These programs deal with situations such as substance abuse, marital problems, stress and domestic violence, financial difficulties, health education and disease prevention. The assistance may be provided within the organization or by referral to outside resources. Also called an employee assistance plan.

employee benefit—nonwage compensation provided to workers by an employer in addition to normal wages and salaries. Benefits may include retirement income, group insurance (e.g., health, dental, disability, life), vision care, housing, child care, cafeteria meals, education assistance, training, sick leave, vacation, counseling, legal advice, shopping discounts and wellness programs, among others. Fringe benefits and benefits in kind are often used interchangeably with employee benefits, though the IRS has established a specific definition for the former. Some employee benefits (e.g., life insurance up to a limit, health insurance, health savings accounts) are not subject to federal income tax. Others (e.g., Section 125 spending arrangements, 401(k) and 403(b) retirement plans) provide an opportunity for employees to defer compensation (and taxes on this compensation). Employers provide benefits to attract and retain workers as well as to increase the economic security of workers. Many employee benefits are tax-deductible for employers. See also *fringe benefit* and *perquisite*.

employee benefit liability insurance—contract from an insurance company that covers the insured in the event a claim arises out of errors and/or omissions in the administration of a benefit plan.

employee benefit plan—under ERISA, any plan, fund or program established by an employer, employee organization or both that provides retirement income, the deferral of income for use after termination of employment, medical, sickness, accident, unemployment, vacation, disability, day care, scholarships, training programs, prepaid legal services or other benefits to employees. ERISA covers every employee benefit plan unless there is a specific exemption. Benefits may be paid for through an employer, the employees or a combination of both. Money contributed to a plan is typically used to establish a trust fund or to purchase insurance coverage. Some employers self-fund benefits. See also *cafeteria plan, employee benefit, employee benefit trust, Employee Benefits Security Administration (EBSA), plan sponsor* and *self-funding*.

Employee Benefits Security Administration (EBSA)—agency of the U.S. Department of Labor that provides information and assistance on private sector, employer-sponsored retirement and health benefit plans. Formerly known as the Pension and Welfare Benefits Administration, EBSA oversees ERISA compliance on employee benefit matters.

employee benefit trust—assets placed in a fund and managed to provide benefits to employees and retirees. ERISA sets minimum standards for most voluntarily established pension, health and welfare plans in private industry. See also *fiduciary* and *prudent person rule.*

employee contribution—money that a worker contributes (voluntarily or involuntarily) to participate in an employer-sponsored benefit plan. See also *contributory plan, salary reduction plan* and *voluntary contribution.*

employee-directed plan—see *consumer-driven health care (CDHC), self-directed investment* and *self-directed retirement plan.*

employee engagement—also referred to as worker engagement, the degree to which an employee is fully involved and enthusiastic regarding his or her employer, his or her job or a particular program (e.g., wellness). Engagement influences a worker's attitudes and behaviors.

employee health and welfare benefit plan—see *employee welfare benefit plan.*

employee health and welfare fund—synonymous with an employee welfare fund, a pool of money to which employers, employees or a combination of both contribute to fund an employee health and welfare benefit plan.

employee health benefit plan—employer-sponsored program for providing medical and health care benefits to workers. See also *employee benefit plan.*

employee organization—labor union, association, agency, committee or group in which employees participate that exists, in whole or in part, to deal with employers regarding an employee benefit plan or other matters incidental to employment relationships. This term also includes any employees' beneficiary organization formed to establish a benefit plan.

employee-pay-all plan—benefit program for which employees pay all costs; the employer makes no financial contributions to the plan.

Employee Plans Compliance Resolution System (EPCRS)—IRS-created system that allows a sponsor to correct operational and plan document errors affecting a tax-qualified plan. EPCRS is comprised of three programs; see *Audit Closing Agreement Program (Audit CAP), Self-Correction Program (SCP)* and *Voluntary Correction Program (VCP).*

Employee Retirement Income Security Act of 1974 (ERISA)—U.S. law that sets minimum standards for the protection of individuals in most voluntarily established pension, health and welfare plans within private industry. ERISA requires plans to (1) provide participants with information about plan features and funding, (2) provides fiduciary responsibilities for those who manage and control plan assets, (3) requires plans to establish a grievance and appeals process by which participants can get benefits, and (4) gives participants the right to sue for benefits and breaches of fiduciary duty. ERISA established the Pension Benefit Guaranty Corporation—the insurance program designed to guarantee workers receipt of pension benefits if their defined benefit pension plan should terminate. There have been a number of amendments to ERISA, including the Newborns' and Mothers' Health Protection Act of 1996, the Mental Health Parity Act of 1996 (MHPA), the Women's Health and Cancer Rights Act of 1998 (WHCRA) and the Consolidated Omnibus Budget Reconciliation Act of 1985 (COBRA). See also *excluded plans, exclusive benefit rule, fiduciary, preemption, prudent person rule* and *Retirement Equity Act of 1984 (REA).*

employee retirement plan—fund or program that provides retirement income or that makes it possible to defer income until termination of covered employment or beyond. These plans may be established and maintained by an employer, an employee organization (such as a union) or both. Employee retirement plans fall into two categories: defined benefit plans and defined contribution plans. See also *defined benefit (DB) plan, defined contribution (DC) plan* and *employee benefit plan.*
—Requirements for qualified plans in the United States, which offer favorable tax treatment for employers and employees, are found in Sections 401 through 419 of the IRC. Section 457 contains provisions pertaining to the deferred compensation plans that may be offered by government and tax-exempt organizations. Most voluntarily established pension plans in private industry are covered by ERISA. The Employee Benefits Security Administration of the U.S. Department of Labor is responsible for administering and enforcing the provisions of ERISA. See also *Employee Benefits Security Administration (EBSA)* and *Employee Retirement Income Security Act of 1974 (ERISA).*
—In Canada, employee retirement (and pension) plans must comply with the minimum standards of the federal Pension Benefits Standards Act and provincial pension protections. Maximum benefit provisions permitted are set by the nation's Income Tax Act and Canada Revenue Agency (CRA) guidelines.

employee self-service (ESS)—web-based application that gives workers access to their personal data, payroll details and/or benefit records. Activities that ESS may allow employees to do include updating home address information and next of kin, tracking hours worked and leave used, enrolling in and making benefit plan changes, and accessing a company's personnel handbook. ESS can operate as a feature on an employer's intranet or via other web-based tools. See also *call center, interactive benefits communication, interactive voice response (IVR)* and *kiosk*.

employee profit-sharing plan (EPSP)—Canadian benefit program that permits employers to share corporate profits with employees. Employers make tax-deductible contributions to a trustee to be held and invested for the benefit of the employees who are beneficiaries of the plan. Funds are allocated to employees in proportion to each employee's earnings, length of service or other formula. Vesting of an employer's contributions can vary from immediate to vesting only on death, termination of employment or retirement. Each year, the trustee is required to allocate to beneficiaries all employer contributions, profits from trust property, capital gains and losses, and certain amounts in respect to forfeitures. The allocated amounts, with some exceptions, are included as taxable income in the year they are allocated and are not subject to tax when actually received. See also *current distribution profit-sharing plan, deferred profit-sharing plan (DPSP), profit-sharing plans* and *registered profit-sharing pension plan*.

employee stock option plan (ESOP)—mechanism by which a company gives employees the right to buy a specific number of company shares at a fixed price within a certain period of time. If the price of the stock increases, an employee exercises the option to buy. The difference between the market price and the option price is profit. If the market price of the stock never rises above the option price, the employee simply never exercises the option. See also *swap*.

employee stock ownership plan (ESOP)—qualified retirement program that has most or all plan assets invested in ownership shares of the employer's company. Employees do not actually buy shares in an ESOP. Instead, the company contributes its own shares to the plan, contributes cash to buy its own stock (often from an existing owner) or, most commonly, has the plan borrow money to buy stock with the company repaying the loan. ESOPs have significant tax benefits for the company, the employees and the sellers. Employees gradually vest in their accounts and receive their benefits when they leave the company (although there may be distributions prior to that). ESOPs are often used in closely held companies to buy part or all of the shares of existing owners, but they also are used in public companies. See also *employee stock ownership trust (ESOT), KSOP* and *leveraged ESOP*.

employee stock ownership trust (ESOT)—generally, the account created to hold the assets of an employee stock ownership plan. An ESOT can also be established to simply facilitate the acquisition and distribution of a company's shares to employees. See also *employee stock ownership plan (ESOP)*.

employee stock purchase plan (ESPP)—mechanism that allows employees to buy company stock, usually at a discount. A typical plan gives employees the option to purchase stock at the end of an offering period at a price of between 85% and 100% of the stock's fair market value. If the employee chooses to participate, he or she indicates a percentage or dollar amount of compensation to be deducted from his or her pay to be used to purchase stock at the preestablished price. The amount that may be set aside is usually limited by the plan.

employee welfare benefit plan—as defined by ERISA, a benefit program for workers that provides benefits other than retirement, including health, disability, death, apprenticeship and training, prepaid legal services, vacation benefits, day-care centers and scholarship funds. Discounts on employer services, holiday and severance benefits, and housing assistance benefits may also qualify depending on the facts and circumstances. See also *employee benefit plan*.

employer—person or organization that contracts with workers (employees) providing compensation in exchange for the workers' services.

employer group waiver plan (EGWP)—Medicare Part D prescription drug plan in which an employer partners with a pharmacy benefit manager (PBM) that contracts directly with Medicare to be a Part D provider. The EGWP provides standard Medicare Part D prescription drug coverage only to Medicare-eligible retirees and covered Medicare-eligible dependents of the sponsoring employer. An EGWP is not open to the individual market.

Employer Identification Number (EIN)—unique nine-digit number assigned by the IRS to sole proprietors, corporations, partnerships and other entities with paid employees. An organization may have one or several EINs, and an EIN may cover one or several locations. Also referred to as a Federal Employee Identification Number (FEIN).

employer-owned life insurance—see *corporate-owned life insurance (COLI)*.

employer real property—land, anything permanently affixed to the land (e.g., buildings) and anything leased to an organization or its affiliates that contracts with workers. With some exceptions, ERISA does not permit a benefit plan to invest more than 10% of its assets in qualifying employer real property and qualifying employer securities.

Employer Shared Responsibility Payment (ESRP)—see "Employer shared responsibility" in the *Appendix A: Affordable Care Act of 2010 (ACA)*.

employer-sponsored IRA—an arrangement available in the United States where an employer establishes a personal account (or annuity) for the retirement savings of workers. The employer can choose to make contributions into an IRA or Roth IRA. The employer has complete flexibility over which employees will receive an IRA contribution and the amount that will be contributed in a particular year. Deemed, simplified employee pension and SIMPLE IRAs are other types of employer-sponsored IRAs that an employer may establish; these accounts permit employees to save for their own retirement. See also *deemed IRA, individual retirement account (IRA), SIMPLE IRA* and *simplified employee pension (SEP) plan*.

employer-sponsored medical center—facility (often on site) funded by an employer to provide health care to employees.

Employment and Training Administration (ETA)—housed within the U.S. Department of Labor, ETA manages federal government job training and worker dislocation programs, dispenses federal grants to states for public employment service programs, and administers unemployment insurance benefits. These services are primarily provided through state and local workforce development systems.

employment at will—legal doctrine that maintains it is the right of either the employer or employee to terminate the employment relationship with no liability, provided there was no express contract or definite term governing the relationship. There are several exceptions to the doctrine, particularly with respect to termination connected to illegal discrimination. See also *discrimination*.

Employment Cost Index (ECI)—quarterly measure of the growth in civilian labor expenses comprised of wage and salary payments, employee benefits, and payroll taxes for insurance programs such as Social Security. ECI is essentially a price index for workers' compensation and benefits. See also *price index*.

employment discrimination—see *discrimination*.

Employment Insurance (EI)—Canadian program that provides temporary income support to those who are between jobs; cannot work for reasons of sickness, childbirth or parenting; or who are providing care or support to a family member who is gravely ill with a significant risk of death.

employment law—see *labor law*.

employment practices—any policies, procedures, systems, programs or actions by an employer that have a direct impact on the terms and conditions of the employer-employee relationship.

Employment Standards Administration (ESA)—unit of the U.S. Department of Labor that has been given responsibility for enhancing the welfare and protecting the rights of the nation's workers. As an enforcement and benefit delivery agency, ESA is composed of four major programs that enforce and administer laws governing legally mandated wages and working conditions. See also *Office of Federal Contract Compliance Programs, Office of Labor-Management Standards (OLMS), Office of Workers' Compensation Programs (OWCP)* and *Wage and Hour Division (WHD)*.

encryption—algorithmic transformation of text into code to make the information unreadable to anyone except those possessing special knowledge, usually referred to as a key. Encryption is used to keep health and financial records confidential.

endangered status—under the Pension Protection Act (PPA) of 2006, a designation for multiemployer pension plans that are not in critical status but:
- Have a funded percentage less than 80%, or
- Are expected to have an accumulated funding deficiency in the current plan year or any of the next six plan years (taking into account PPA amortization and extensions).

Upon receiving certification of this endangered status (a.k.a. yellow zone), plan trustees must notify the U.S. Department of Labor, the Pension Benefit Guaranty Corporation, beneficiaries, unions and employers of the designation. A funding improvement plan must be prepared and implemented. See also *accumulated funding deficiency, critical status, funding improvement plan (FIP), green zone* and *seriously endangered status*.

endodontics—branch of dentistry dealing with the diagnosis, prevention and treatment of diseases and injuries of the pulp and surrounding tissues.

endorsement
—with respect to insurance, a written agreement added to the end of an insurance policy that modifies coverage. Endorsements (also called riders) supersede the original terms of the policy. Endorsements are used to cover items such as jewelry, art, camera equipment, coin and stamp collections, and computer equipment.
—in banking, an endorsement is the signature of the payee on a check or similar negotiable instrument required for cashing.

endowment insurance—form of life insurance that provides a policy benefit payable either (1) when the insured dies or (2) on a stated date if the insured is still alive (e.g., the day the person reaches 120 years). See also *cash value life insurance*.

end-stage renal disease (ESRD)—final phase of kidney disease when the body retains fluid and harmful wastes build up. A patient with ESRD needs dialysis or a transplant to replace the failed kidneys.

Enrolled Actuary (EA)—person professionally trained in the technical and mathematical aspects of insurance, pensions and related fields who has been approved by the Joint Board for the Enrollment of Actuaries to perform actuarial services required under ERISA. An EA must meet knowledge and experience requirements, which include passing an examination.

enrolled group—persons enrolled in a health plan through the same employer or member organization. Stipulations sometimes exist regarding the minimum size of the group and the minimum percentage of the group that must enroll before coverage is available. Also referred to as a contract group.

Enrolled Retirement Plan Agent (ERPA)—person who has been approved to represent taxpayers and others before the IRS on certain retirement plan issues including the Employee Plans Determination Letter program, Employee Plans Compliance Resolution System, and Employee Plans Master and Prototype and Volume Submitter programs. In addition, ERPAs are generally permitted to represent taxpayers with respect to IRS forms of the 5300 and 5500 series that are filed by retirement plans and plan sponsors, but not with respect to actuarial forms or schedules. To obtain the ERPA designation, an individual must demonstrate special competence on specific tax matters and pass an examination administered by the IRS.

enrollee—person who has applied to be or has become a member/participant of an organization or plan.

enrollment—process by which an individual becomes a member/participant of an organization or plan. Enrollment in a benefit plan may be done through the actual signing up of the individual, by virtue of a collective bargaining agreement or by conditions of employment.

entitlement—right to something that may be established by law or simply perceived by an individual or group.

entry age normal—actuarial cost method that projects the benefit costs of each person from entry age into a plan to the assumed exit age from the plan. Relative to other actuarial cost methods, entry age normal tends to produce more stable, predictable contribution rates and makes it easier to budget benefit costs and establish the premium for an insured group.

entry date—day an individual is entitled to participate or be covered by a benefit plan.

epidemiology—branch of medicine that deals with the treatment, transmission and control of disease.

episode-based payment—see *bundled payment*.

episode of care—treatment for a diagnosis rendered within a defined time frame; for example, the time between admission and discharge from a hospital.

e-prescribing—abbreviation for electronic prescribing referring to the use of technology such as a computer or wireless device to write and transmit a prescription directly to a pharmacy. In addition to the transfer of a prescription, e-prescribing may provide the prescriber and pharmacists access to clinical and cost information on drug therapy options, a patient's medical history, safety alerts and options for reducing a participant's out-of-pocket costs.

equal employment opportunity (EEO)—system of employment practices under which no individuals are excluded from consideration, participation, promotion or benefits because of their race, color, religion, gender, national origin, age, disability or other classification.

Equal Employment Opportunity Commission (EEOC)—independent U.S. government agency that promotes equal opportunity in employment. EEOC enforces federal civil rights laws including Title VII of the Civil Rights Act of 1964, the Age Discrimination in Employment Act of 1967, Americans with Disabilities Act of 1990, Equal Pay Act of 1963 and other fair employment practices legislation.

equalization component—adjustment in compensation for taxes and cost-of-living differences that an employee operating outside his or her base country incurs. See also *cost-of-living allowance (COLA)*.

Equal Pay Act of 1963 (EPA)—amendment to the Fair Labor Standards Act that requires men and women be given equal pay for equal work in the same establishment. Employers may not pay unequal wages to men and women who perform jobs that require substantially the same skill, effort and responsibility and that are performed under similar working conditions within the same establishment. Pay differentials are permitted when they are based on seniority, merit, quantity or quality of production, or a factor other than gender. These are known as affirmative defenses, and it is the employer's burden to prove that they apply. See also *comparable worth*.

equity
—investment by an owner or owners in a property or business. Equity (or equity shares) is often used to refer to stockholder shares in a corporation. More specifically, equity equals assets minus liabilities. A homeowner's equity in a home is the property's market value minus the amount of any loans and liens owed on the property.
—for employment and tax purposes, equity refers to a principle of fairness. Compensation for work is not equal but it can be fair (equitable) if it reflects the differences that exist in the knowledge, skills and responsibilities of each job. Taking a larger proportion of income from high-income taxpayers is a way government attempts to achieve equity in tax policy.

equity compensation—provision of stock options, deferred stock, restricted stock, stock bonuses and other stock awards instead of cash. See also *deferred stock, employee stock option plan (ESOP), employee stock purchase plan (ESPP), incentive stock option (ISO), restricted stock* and *stock bonus plan.*

equity-index annuity—type of fixed annuity that looks like a hybrid. An equity-indexed annuity credits a minimum rate of interest just as a fixed annuity does, but the value of the annuity is also based on the performance of a specified stock index, usually calculated as a fraction of that index's total return. See also *annuity, fixed annuity* and *hybrid annuity.*

equity securities—see *stock.*

equity theory—in an employment relationship, the idea that job satisfaction occurs when an employee perceives his or her ratio of input to outcome is equal or similar to that of a comparable person or group.

equivalency method—in calculating credited hours and years of service for qualified retirement plans, the U.S. Department of Labor allows employers the option of using alternative approaches referred to as equivalency methods. See also *earnings equivalency method, period-of-service equivalency method* and *working time equivalency method.*

equivalent—that which is equal or essentially equal. Many brand-name drugs have generic equivalents. See also *generic drug.*

equivalent position—for purposes of the Family and Medical Leave Act (FMLA), a job that is virtually identical to an employee's former job in terms of pay, benefits and working conditions, including privileges, perquisites and status. The job must involve the same or substantially similar duties and responsibilities, which must entail substantially equivalent skill, effort, responsibility and authority.

ergonomics—study of how to adapt equipment, tools and the work environment to accommodate human needs, especially to reduce operator fatigue, discomfort and injury.

ERISA—see *Employee Retirement Income Security Act of 1974 (ERISA).*

errors and omissions (E&O) insurance—protection against financial losses that result from negligent acts or mistakes. E&O insurance may be purchased by an employee benefit plan, a plan administrator or trustees as well as professionals in such fields as accounting, insurance, law and real estate. See also *fiduciary liability insurance.*

escrow—deed or something of value delivered to a third person to hold until the fulfillment or performance of some act or condition.

escrow account—fund set up by a lender into which the borrower must makes periodic payments, usually monthly, for taxes, hazard insurance, assessments and mortgage insurance premiums. The funds are held in trust by the lender who pays the sums as they become due.

essential health benefits—see "Benefit mandates" in the *Appendix A: Affordable Care Act of 2010 (ACA).*

essential job functions—fundamental, crucial job duties performed in an employment position. Essential functions do not include marginal functions that are extra or incidental duties. See also *marginal job functions.*

estate—assets and liabilities of a deceased person including land, personal belongings and debts.

estate plan—strategy established for the management and disposition of a person's property during his or her lifetime and at death. An estate plan takes into consideration minimizing the impact of estate taxes.

estate tax—tax that a government imposes on the assets of a person at the time of death.

estimated acquisition cost—discount on a drug's average wholesale price paid to a pharmacy for a prescription. See also *average wholesale price (AWP).*

ethnic group—persons identified on the basis of religion, color or national origin.

euro—introduced in 1999, the monetary unit of a subset of European Union members that replaces member country currencies including the French franc, German mark, Irish pound and Italian lira.

eurodollars—interest-bearing time deposits, denominated in U.S. dollars, at banks and other financial institutions outside the United States.

European Depositary Receipt (EDR)—see *Global Depositary Receipt (GDR)*.

European Union (EU)—economic and political alliance established by the Treaty of Maastricht in 1993 based upon the foundation of the preexisting European Economic Community. The EU has developed a single market with standardized laws that apply in all 28 member states, guaranteeing the freedom of movement of people, goods, services and capital. Important institutions and bodies of the EU include the European Commission, European Parliament, Council of the European Union, European Council, European Court of Justice and European Central Bank.

Europe, Australasia and Far East (EAFE) Index—created by Morgan Stanley Capital International, the EAFE Index includes prices for international equities from the three regions considered to represent the most developed areas outside of North America. The most widely used international stock index, EAFE is often used as a benchmark for the performance of international equity investments. See also *stock market index*.

evaluative mediation—see *mediation*.

event-driven fund—hedge fund that invests in securities of corporations involved in special situations such as bankruptcy, spinoffs, mergers, acquisitions and other restructuring events.

evergreening—process by which pharmaceutical manufacturers and producers of other medical products prolong patent protection by filing a patent for a marginally different or improved form of a product. Specific strategies that have been used include an extended release version, a different dosage requiring fewer pills, a liquid capsule form and a transdermal patch for an established brand-name drug.

E-Verify—program run by the U.S. Department of Homeland Security that seeks to reduce the hiring of illegal immigrants. Government databases are used to check the names, dates of birth and Social Security numbers of new hires to determine whether they are eligible to work in the United States. While the program is voluntary at the federal level, a few states have passed laws requiring businesses or public employers to participate.

evidence-based case rate—see *bundled payment*.

evidence-based guidelines—health care recommendations developed through the analysis of the best available scientific findings concerning the risks and benefits of diagnostic tests and treatments.

evidence-based medicine (EBM)—integration of clinical expertise, patient values and preferences, and the best research evidence into clinical decisions regarding the care of a patient.

evidence-based practice—see *evidence-based medicine* and *evidence-based guidelines*.

evidence of insurability—proof of a person's physical condition, occupation or other factor that affects enrollment in an insurance or benefit plan. Individual life insurance policies frequently require applicants to respond to a medical history questionnaire or provide a doctor's report after a medical examination. Requiring such evidence for health insurance is prohibited under the Affordable Care Act of 2010.

excepted benefit—see "Excepted benefits" in the *Appendix A: Affordable Care Act of 2010 (ACA)*.

exception—see *exclusion*.

excess accumulation—also called an underdistribution, the amount of a required distribution that a retirement account owner or beneficiary failed to remove from his or her account during a calendar year. In the U.S., this amount is subject to an IRS tax penalty of 50%.

excess aggregate contribution—amount of employee elective contributions and employer matching contributions made to a qualified retirement plan on behalf of highly compensated employees in a plan year that is in excess of the maximum amount permitted under the ACP test. See also *actual contribution percentage (ACP) test*.

excess benefit percentage—percentage of compensation at which employer-derived benefits are accrued with respect to compensation of participants above the integration level.

excess benefit plan—nonqualified plan maintained by an employer solely for the purpose of providing select employees with benefits in excess of those that can be provided by the employer's qualified plan under IRC Section 415.

excess compensation—for the purposes of pension plan integration with Social Security in the United States, the portion of employee compensation above the breakpoint in compensation (referred to as the integration level) specified using the excess rate method. See also *excess rate method, integration, integration level* and *permitted disparity*.

excess contribution—dollar amount by which contributions to a qualified retirement plan exceed the allowable tax-deductible limits and on which an IRS penalty applies.

excess deferral—pretax participant contribution amount to a qualified retirement plan that exceeds the maximum limit for the taxable year.

excess earnings—return from investments that exceed an assumed or expected rate of return.

excess loss insurance—see *stop-loss insurance*.

excess parachute payment—when a contractual agreement provides payments or benefits to an officer, director or highly compensated person upon a change in corporate control (e.g., merger, acquisition), the portion of the total value of the package that equals or exceeds three times the individual's average annual compensation during the five tax years immediately preceding the change in control. The IRS does not allow a corporation to deduct the part of a payment that constitutes the excess parachute payment.

excess rate method—also referred to as a step rate method, an integration method that calculates benefits at different income replacement rates for employees whose earnings are above and below a certain breakpoint. A common breakpoint in the United States is the maximum taxable earnings base for Social Security. Those retirees who have an income above the maximum receive a higher percentage of their earnings from the employer plan. This adjustment reflects the fact that the replacement of income above the maximum by Social Security is zero. See also *integration, integration level* and *permitted disparity*.

excess return—money derived from a security that is greater than what would have been received if an investor had put the money into a riskless security (e.g., short-term government obligation) or a market measure (e.g., index fund) during a given period of time.

exchange fee—monetary charge that some mutual funds impose on shareholders if they transfer to another fund within the same fund group.

exchange fund—mutual fund that allows an investor to swap large holdings in a single stock for shares in a portfolio. Exchange funds provide an investor the opportunity to diversify holdings and defer the payment of capital gains taxes. Also referred to as a swap fund, an exchange fund can be private or public. Private funds are not publicly traded; they invest in privately held equity. In contrast, public funds invest in publicly traded firms. See also *mutual fund*.

exchange rate
—see *currency exchange rate*.
—from a compensation perspective, the rate of pay at which labor demand and labor supply intersect in the external market—in other words, the wage rate that employers are willing to pay and labor is willing to accept.

exchange rate risk—see *currency risk*.

exchange-traded fund (ETF)—marketable security that seeks to achieve the same return as a particular market in a fashion similar to an index mutual fund. The index may be focused on a specific type of security, for example, the international marketplace, a specific sector or a particular asset category (e.g., bonds, commodities, small cap stocks, gold). Unlike a mutual fund, an ETF trades like a common stock on a stock exchange with price changes throughout the day as the ETF is bought and sold. Most ETFs offer the ability to sell short and buy on margin. Expense ratios are lower than those of many mutual funds. See also *index fund* and *mutual fund*.

excise tax
—tax levied on the production or sale of a specific good or service. Excise taxes are common on tobacco, alcohol, air transportation services and luxuries.
—tax imposed as a penalty for failing to perform a required action. A number of these taxes deal with the administration of benefit programs (e.g., failure to meet minimum funding standards, excess contributions, excess distributions, prohibited transactions).

Excise Tax on High-Cost Health Plans—see "Fees/Taxes" in the *Appendix A: Affordable Care Act of 2010 (ACA)*.

excludable employees—employees who do not need to be considered when conducting a nondiscrimination test on a pension plan. Examples include employees who do not meet age and length-of-service requirements, nonresident aliens with no U.S. source of income and employees whose retirement benefits are covered under a collective bargaining agreement.

excluded plans—benefit programs exempt from the regulatory provisions of ERISA. These plans include the following: (1) government plans; (2) church plans for which no election has been made for coverage under the IRC; (3) plans maintained solely for the purpose of complying with applicable workers' compensation, unemployment or disability laws; (4) plans maintained outside of the United States primarily for the benefit of nonresident aliens; and (5) unfunded plans maintained solely to provide benefits in excess of the limitations imposed on contributions and benefits for tax purposes. See also *Employee Retirement Income Security Act of 1974 (ERISA)*.

excluded service—see *exclusion*.

exclusion—contractual provision in an insurance policy that denies coverage for a certain peril, person, property, treatment, etc. Damage caused by floods, earthquakes and acts of war are excluded from nearly all homeowner insurance policies. Homeowner policies also contain coverage exclusions (or limitations) on some types of personal property that are particularly susceptible to loss, such as jewelry and antiques. See also *endorsement*.

exclusion ratio—portion of the return on an annuity payment that is not taxed because it represents a return of the initial investment. See also *annuity*.

exclusive benefit rule—under ERISA, plan fiduciaries must discharge their duties solely in the interest of participants and beneficiaries for the exclusive purpose of providing benefits to participants and beneficiaries and paying administration expenses. Any transaction that compromises this requirement jeopardizes the plan's tax qualification.

exclusive provider organization (EPO)—network of health care providers or dental professionals who discount their services to plan participants. EPOs are similar to PPOs in organization; however, they function more like an HMO with a primary care physician acting as a gatekeeper to the network of other providers. There is an authorization system and, if a patient goes outside the network, he or she must pay the full cost of the services received. There are some exceptions for emergency and out-of-area services. See also *health maintenance organization (HMO)* and *preferred provider organization (PPO)*.

executive—chief executive officer, chief financial officer, company president or other upper level manager.

executive compensation—salary, bonuses, benefits, perquisites, stock, stock options, etc., provided to officers and other upper level managers.

executive perk/perquisite—see *perquisite*.

executor—person named in a will to manage the estate of a deceased person. The executor's duties include identifying the assets of the deceased, paying any debts and distributing the property of the deceased according to the will. See also *probate*.

exempt—free from an obligation (e.g., tax liability, laws) to which others are subject. See also *exempt employee* and *tax-exempt*.

exempt employee—positions of employment in an organization that are exempt from government regulations. For example, salaried employees in the U.S. are typically not covered by the overtime provisions in the Fair Labor Standards Act.

exemption—special privilege or freedom from a requirement imposed on others. See also *tax exemption*.

exercise price—also known as the strike price, the price per share to be paid to exercise a derivative security such as a stock option. See also *stock option*.

exit fee—see *back-end load*.

expatriate—person temporarily or permanently residing outside his or her home country or legal residence. See also *inpatriate*.

expected claims—forecasted payout an insurance company will make for an insured person or a group of insured persons. Expected claims are one of the factors considered when an insurance company establishes the premium for insurance coverage.

expected rate of return (ERR)—weighted average of the possible outcomes for an asset or investment portfolio. To calculate it, an investor first lists all of the possible rates of return that an investment could have and subjectively assigns a probability to each outcome. ERR equals the sum of each possible return multiplied by the probability it will occur.

expense ratio—percentage of total investment that shareholders pay annually for mutual fund management fees and operating expenses. The expense ratio is derived by dividing a fund's operating expenses by its net asset value.

experience—loss record of an insured or a class of coverage over a specific period of time used to calculate insurance renewal rates.

experience deficiency—unfunded liability revealed in the actuarial review of a pension plan. The experience deficiency is the difference between actual experience (investment earnings, salary levels, etc.) and assumptions made at the time of a previous valuation.

experience-rated premium—amount of money an insurer charges to provide coverage based on anticipated claims that takes into consideration age, gender and any other attributes of the group that may affect the number and size of claims. Such a premium is subject to periodic adjustment in line with actual claims or utilization experience.

experience rating—process of determining the insurance premium for a group, wholly or partially on the basis of the group's actual claims. The insurer compares the actual claims with the claims experience that is normally expected in the insured's rating class. The premium is modified to reflect this difference. If the experience rating is better than that of the insured's rating class, the result may be a lower premium. Of course, if the opposite is the case, the premium may be higher. See also *class rating, community rating, prospective experience rating* and *retrospective experience rating.*

experience refund—premium amount returned by an insurer to a group policyholder when the financial experience of the group (or class to which the group belongs) has been more favorable than anticipated when the premium was set. See also *risk charge.*

experience study—actuarial analysis of insurance claims (e.g., health, long-term care) as they relate to attributes of the insured, such as age, gender, salary, employment turnover, etc.

experimental drug—also known as an investigational drug, a substance in the process of being tested for safety and effectiveness that the FDA has not yet approved for marketing or a new use. A drug may be approved for use in treating one disease or condition but be considered experimental for other diseases and conditions.

experimental medical procedure—health care service or treatment that is not widely accepted as medically effective or that has not been scientifically proved to be effective.

expiration date—termination date such as when insurance coverage ends or the last day a stock option may be exercised.

explanation of benefits (EOB)—statement from an insurance company that reports the services and amounts paid on behalf of the insured. The EOB summarizes the charges submitted, the dollar amount allowed by the insurer for each service, the amount paid and the balance owed by the insured, if any. If any services were not paid, reasons are given for the denial of coverage.

extended benefit—continuation of insurance coverage past the stated termination date. During times of high unemployment, the period that an individual may receive unemployment payments is sometimes lengthened by government. A government mandate in COBRA makes it possible for employees to purchase extended group health insurance under special circumstances. A provision in a private health insurance policy may also extend benefits under certain circumstances, such as the insured is hospitalized or disabled on the policy termination date. If a dental plan is terminated after a tooth was prepared for a crown but before the crown was cemented, an extended benefit provision would permit coverage to continue long enough for the rest of the procedure to be completed. Also known as continuation of coverage and extension of benefits.

extended care facility (ECF)—institution providing medical, nursing or custodial care over a prolonged period, such as during the course of a chronic disease or the rehabilitation phase after an acute illness. Types of extended care facilities are intermediate care facilities, nursing homes and skilled nursing facilities.

extended coverage—additional insurance at an extra premium for coverage not generally found in the normal insurance contract. For example, a provision in certain health policies allows the insured to receive benefits for specific losses sustained after termination of coverage (e.g., maternity benefits for a pregnancy in progress at the time a health insurance plan is terminated). In some property insurance policies, the insurer agrees to provide protection for specified risks that aren't covered by a typical policy (e.g., smoke damage, windstorm, vehicle damage and civil disorders).

extended health care (EHC) plan—supplemental insurance that picks up where a basic health plan leaves off. It may boost some benefits in a basic plan and provide additional benefits not covered otherwise. Benefits provided in an EHC plan vary greatly. Examples of what may be included are a higher lifetime maximum, complementary and alternative medicine, ambulance and paramedic services, a semiprivate or private hospital room, private duty nursing, home care, prescription drugs, vision and hearing care, and dental care such as major restoration and orthodontics. See also *complementary and alternative medicine (CAM).*

extended medical expense—medical plan that has a deductible and/or reimburses covered expenses at some percentage less than 100%. In Canada, extended medical expense plans offer coverage beyond provincial medical coverage and are sometimes referred to as major medical plans.

extension of benefits—see *extended benefit*.

extra risk policy—see *rated policy*.

F

face amount—amount indicated on the face of a life insurance policy that will be paid in the event of death or when the contract matures. Excluded are dividend additions and amounts payable under accidental death or other special provisions.

face value
—the stated death benefit of a life insurance policy.
—for investment face value, see *par value*.

facilitative mediation—see *mediation*.

facility—for the purposes of HIPAA privacy legislation, physical premises including the interior and exterior of a building.

fact finding—alternative dispute resolution procedure in which opposing parties present the arguments and issues in a dispute to a neutral party (a fact finder or fact-finding panel). Following the hearing of the issues, the neutral party recommends a nonbinding solution, usually in writing. See also *alternative dispute resolution (ADR), arbitration* and *mediation*.

facts and circumstances test—measure or set of standards that are used to determine whether a particular circumstance exists or a designation may be made. The U.S. government has established tests for determining when a partial benefit plan termination exists, whether financial need warrants a hardship withdrawal from a retirement plan, what organizations are tax-exempt, etc.

fail-first requirement—see *step therapy*.

Fair Labor Standards Act of 1938 (FLSA)—U.S. law (with amendments) that governs minimum wage, maximum weekly hours, overtime pay, child labor, and equal pay for men and women in the same types of jobs. FLSA requires that most employees in the U.S. be paid at least the federal minimum wage for all hours worked, and overtime pay at one and one-half times the regular rate of pay for all hours worked over 40 in a workweek. FLSA does have exemptions from both minimum wage and overtime pay for executive, administrative, professional and outside sales employees. See also *Equal Pay Act of 1963 (EPA)* and *fair pay overtime initiative*.

fair market value—price that a property would garner in an open market assuming the prospective buyer and seller are (1) reasonably knowledgeable regarding the property for sale, (2) acting in their individual best interests and (3) not subject to pressure to trade.

fair pay overtime initiative—regulations published by the U.S. Department of Labor that clarify, update and strengthen overtime protections (particularly for executive, administrative, professional, outside sales and computer employees) under the Fair Labor Standards Act.

fair rate of return—rate of return that a government entity allows on an investment. A fair rate of return is one of the factors that public utility regulators consider when approving the utility prices that consumers will be charged. The return (profit) is used by the utility to pay investors and provide service upgrades. See also *rate of return (ROR)*.

fair value accounting—method for establishing the worth of investments based on the dollar amount at which the asset (or liability) could be bought or sold (settled) in a current transaction between a willing buyer and a willing seller. Fair value accounting assumes the transaction was not a liquidation and that both parties to the transaction had reasonable knowledge of the relevant facts. In the past, most financial reporting was based on historical cost, which is the original price paid for an asset. Fair value accounting, sometimes referred to as mark-to-market accounting, has been adopted in an effort to make investment information more transparent.

fair-weather fund—mutual fund that tends to outperform the market when the market is doing well but tends to do worse than the market when the market is doing poorly. Funds are not formally given the name fair-weather fund; this language is used primarily to describe the performance of a fund. See also *all-weather fund, foul-weather fund* and *mutual fund*.

family allowance—government cash payment or tax reduction to parents or guardians based on the presence and number of children in a family. In some nations, the benefit is means-tested. While Norway and Denmark use the term *family allowance,* the payment is referred to as a "child benefit" in the United Kingdom and Ireland. In Australia, it is referred to as a "family tax benefit." See also *child and dependent care credit, earned income tax credit (EITC)* and *tax exemption*.

family and medical leave—general term to describe the time an employee may take off from work for personal illness, for the arrival and care of a child and to care for an ill family member. Employers may offer leave that is paid or unpaid in addition to that which is legally required. See also *compassionate care leave and benefits, Family and Medical Leave Act of 1993 (FMLA), maternity leave, military caregiver leave* and *parental leave*.

Family and Medical Leave Act of 1993 (FMLA)—federal legislation that requires employers with more than 50 employees to provide eligible workers with up to 12 weeks of unpaid leave during any 12-month period if the employee is unable to work because of a serious health condition. The same unpaid leave is available for the birth of a child and newborn care, adoption, foster care placement, and care of an immediate family member (spouse, child or parent) with a serious health condition. See also *equivalent position* and *military caregiver leave*.

family deductible—deductible that is satisfied by the combined expenses of all covered family members. For example, a program with a $100 deductible per covered individual may limit its application to a maximum of $300 for the family. This aggregate family deductible may be met by one or more family members. See also *deductible*.

family of funds—see *fund family*.

family practice—medical specialty that provides health care for people of all ages. Family practice physicians are generalists in the provision of health care services.

family tax benefit—see *family allowance*.

Fannie Mae—see *Federal National Mortgage Association (FNMA or Fannie Mae)*.

Federal Agricultural Mortgage Corporation (FAMC or Farmer Mac)—publicly traded, shareholder-owned corporation chartered by the U.S. Congress in 1988. Farmer Mac's mission is to establish a secondary market for agricultural real estate and rural housing mortgage loans as well as to increase the availability of long-term credit at affordable, stable interest rates. Farmer Mac purchases loans from lenders and issues long-term standby commitments to purchase agricultural mortgage loans. The loans that FAMC purchases are packaged as mortgage-backed securities. Farmer Mac's mission and programs are very similar to those of Fannie Mae and Freddie Mac, which focus on traditional residential mortgages. See also *agency bond* and *mortgage-backed security (MBS)*.

Federal Deposit Insurance Corporation (FDIC)—independent agency of the federal government created in 1933 in response to the bank failures that occurred in the 1920s and early 1930s. The FDIC maintains stability and promotes public confidence in the nation's financial system by insuring deposits in banks and thrift institutions, examining and supervising these institutions, and intervening when a bank or thrift institution fails.

Federal Employee Health Benefits Program (FEHBP)—program that provides health insurance to employees of the U.S. federal government. Federal employees choose from a menu of plans that include fee-for-service plans, plans with a point-of-service option and health maintenance organization plans.

Federal Employees Retirement System (FERS)—program that provides retirement benefits to U.S. government workers. The three components of FERS are a Basic Benefit Plan, Social Security and a Thrift Savings Plan (TSP). Employees make contributions to the first two programs each pay period through payroll deductions. Federal agencies automatically set up a TSP account for each employee and deposit an amount equal to 1% of the employee's pay into it each pay period. Employees have the option of making additional contributions for which the agency will make a matching contribution. Contributions are tax-deferred. FERS became effective on January 1, 1987 and covers all new Federal civilian employees who have retirement coverage. See also *Civil Service Retirement System (CSRS)*.

Federal Home Loan Mortgage Corporation (FHLMC or Freddie Mac)—created in 1970, Freddie Mac is a stockholder-owned corporation chartered by the U.S. Congress to increase the supply of funds that mortgage lenders (e.g., commercial banks, mortgage bankers, savings institutions and credit unions) can make available to home buyers and multifamily investors. Freddie Mac purchases, guarantees and securitizes mortgages to form mortgage-backed securities. The mortgage-backed securities that it issues tend to be very liquid and carry a credit rating close to that of U.S. Treasuries. On September 7, 2008, Freddie Mac was put under the conservatorship of the Federal Housing Finance Agency. See also *agency bond* and *mortgage-backed security (MBS)*.

Federal Insurance Contributions Act (FICA)—provision of the Social Security Act that requires employers and employees to pay Social Security and Medicare taxes. For decades, these payroll taxes were listed on pay stubs and W-2 forms as one deduction referred to as "FICA taxes." In 1993, Congress eliminated the wage base for Medicare taxes but kept the base for Social Security taxes. As a result, employers had to remove the "FICA" label and show separate entries for the "Social Security tax" and the "Medicare tax." See also *Social Security*.

federally qualified health center (FQHC)—designation by the U.S. government that refers to organizations offering comprehensive primary care and preventive health services—including mental health/substance abuse services—to individuals regardless of their ability to pay for care. FQHCs charge for services based on a sliding-fee scale for a patient's family income and size established by a local community board. In return for providing such care, the government provides financial support to the FQHCs in the form of cash grants, cost-based reimbursement for Medicaid patients, and free malpractice coverage. In addition to community health centers, the following programs are funded as FQHCs: migrant health centers, health care for homeless programs and public housing primary care programs.

Federal National Mortgage Association (FNMA or Fannie Mae)—organization chartered by the U.S. Congress in 1938 to provide liquidity and stability to the U.S. housing and mortgage markets. In 1970, Fannie Mae became a stockholder corporation. It is the largest of the government-initiated agencies that buy mortgages for single and small multifamily homes from mortgage bankers, brokers and other mortgage market partners. Fannie Mae groups the loans into pools that are sold as mortgage-backed securities. This repackaging of mortgages helps ensure that renters can find affordable housing and home buyers can get mortgage loans at affordable interest rates. Monthly principal and interest payments are guaranteed by FNMA but not by the U.S. government. On September 7, 2008, Fannie Mae was put under the conservatorship of the Federal Housing Finance Agency. See also *agency bond* and *mortgage-backed security (MBS)*.

Federal Open Market Committee (FOMC)—members of the board of governors of the Federal Reserve System and five Reserve Bank presidents under the leadership of the Federal Reserve chairman who hold regularly scheduled meetings during the year, and other meetings as needed, to evaluate the state of the U.S. economy and issue a risk statement indicating if a weakness or inflation poses a threat. The statement, which tends to have an impact on stock and bond markets, is generally viewed as an indication of whether the FOMC will tighten or loosen the money supply. See also *Federal Reserve System, monetary policy* and *open market operation (OMO)*.

Federal Poverty Level (FPL)—income threshold established annually by the U.S. Department of Health and Human Services (HHS) that determines individual and household eligibility for various government programs and benefits.
—income threshold set by the U.S. Census used as the basis for official poverty population statistics, such as the percentage of people living in poverty.

Federal Register—official publication of the U.S. government for rules, proposed rules and notices of federal agencies and organizations as well as executive orders and other presidential documents.

Federal Reserve System—known informally as the "Fed," the central banking system of the United States. The Fed consists of 12 district banks and 25 regional branches spread across the nation. Though structured as a corporation, the Fed functions more as a government agency than as a business. Each district bank has a president and board of directors. The entire system is supervised by the seven-member Federal Reserve board of governors. Though governors are appointed by the president and confirmed by Congress, the board operates as a monetary authority outside the control of the executive and legislative branches. The Fed is charged with setting economic policy and supervising banking operations. See also *Federal Open Market Committee (FOMC)* and *monetary policy*.

federal-state agreement—arrangement between a state and federal agency specifying terms and conditions for carrying out a federal assistance program or group of programs. See also *Section 218 agreement*.

Federal Tax Identification Number (FEIN)—see *Employer Identification Number (EIN)*.

Federal Unemployment Tax Act (FUTA)—U.S. legislation that imposes a tax on employers to fund state workforce programs and payments to workers who have lost their jobs. Employers report this tax by filing an annual Form 940 with the IRS. FUTA covers the cost of administering unemployment insurance and job service programs in every state. During periods of high unemployment, FUTA pays one-half of extended unemployment benefits and lends funds to states, if needed, to pay the benefits. See also *unemployment compensation (UC)*.

federal upper limit (FUL)—maximum payment amount that Medicaid pays for multisource generic products. FUL is published by the Centers for Medicare and Medicaid Services.

Fed funds rate—rate at which banks are willing to lend or borrow immediately available reserves on an overnight basis. The Federal Reserve System establishes this rate by buying and selling U.S. government securities through its open market operations. See also *Federal Reserve System*.

fee—charge for provision of a service or supplies.

fee-for-service (FFS) plan—traditional method for financing health care in which a provider is paid for each procedure or service rendered. Providers typically set their own charges for services, and patients are allowed to choose almost any service provider they want to use. If a service is covered by the plan, reimbursement is provided to the insured or the health care provider. Claims handling is the responsibility of the insured, although some providers may handle it as courtesy. FFS plans often have higher deductibles or copays than managed care plans; any charges in excess of policy limits are paid by the insured.

fee schedule—see *table of allowances*.

fee schedule payment structure—method used by some health maintenance organizations (HMOs) when reimbursing health care providers that places a cap (maximum limit) on the dollar amounts an HMO will pay for medical procedures or services.

fee simple—used interchangeably with fee simple absolute, an indicator that a property is owned with no conditions, limitations or restrictions. The owner has the right to use and transfer the property at will.

fidelity bond—contract with an insurance company or other issuer agreeing to reimburse an organization for losses resulting from dishonest acts (e.g., theft, fraud) by persons handling assets of the organization.

fiduciary—relationship of trust and confidence where one person (the fiduciary) holds or controls property for the benefit of another person or persons—for example, the relationship between a trustee and the beneficiaries of an employee benefit plan trust fund. Fiduciaries must discharge their duties solely in the interests of the participants and beneficiaries of an employee benefit plan. In addition, a fiduciary must act exclusively for the purpose of providing benefits to participants and beneficiaries—defraying reasonable expenses of the plan. —ERISA defines *fiduciary* as any person who (1) exercises any discretionary authority or control over the management of a benefit plan or the management or disposition of a plan's assets; (2) renders investment advice for a fee or other compensation with respect to the funds or property of a plan or has the authority to do so; or (3) has any discretionary authority or responsibility in the administration of a plan. See also *Employee Retirement Income Security Act of 1974 (ERISA)*, *fiduciary responsibility* and *prudent person rule*.

fiduciary breach—see *breach of fiduciary duty*.

fiduciary liability—see *fiduciary responsibility*.

fiduciary liability insurance—protection from losses that occur as a result of a breach in duties or responsibilities made by a fiduciary who acted in good faith. Breaches include misstatements or misleading statements, errors and omissions. See also *errors and omissions (E&O) insurance*, *fiduciary* and *fiduciary responsibility*.

fiduciary responsibility—legal responsibility of a fiduciary to safeguard assets of beneficiaries in a trust fund. Under ERISA, a fiduciary must discharge his or her duties solely in the interest of plan participants and beneficiaries and for the exclusive purpose of providing benefits while defraying reasonable expenses of the plan. Fiduciaries must keep abreast of legal developments and be able to respond to the changes necessitated by economic and demographic fluctuations. The conduct of a fiduciary is governed by the prudent man or prudent person standard. See also *Employee Retirement Income Security Act of 1974 (ERISA)*, *fiduciary* and *prudent person rule*.

fifty percent rule—each jurisdiction in Canada has some variation of this rule applying to the wind-up of a defined benefit plan. In essence, the rule compares a member's contributions (including interest) from a set date with the date of wind-up, against the total benefit credit accrued in that period. If contributions exceed 50% of the credit, the member is entitled to certain benefits based on the excess.

final average (earnings) plan—defined benefit retirement plan that bases the benefit payments on the member's average pay for a specific number of years before retirement. See also *final earnings plan*.

final earnings plan—defined benefit retirement plan that bases benefit payments on the member's annual earnings just before retirement. Also referred to as a final pay plan. See also *career pay plan* and *final average (earnings) plan*.

financial accounting—process of collecting, summarizing and reporting economic and financial information for investors, creditors and other external users. See also *management accounting*.

Financial Accounting Standard 87 (FAS 87)—guidelines intended to improve the disclosure of pension information. The standard requires that a company disclose all relevant figures concerning its pension plan on the face of the company's income statement. Previously, these figures could be placed in footnotes on the income statement. The expected liabilities of a pension plan must be recalculated annually, assuming market interest rates. FAS 87 also requires companies to report some of their unfunded pension liabilities on their balance sheets, assuming market interest rates. Issued by the Financial Accounting Standards Board, this standard is also known as employers' accounting for pensions.

Financial Accounting Standard 106 (FAS 106)—guideline issued by the Financial Accounting Standards Board for employers that are accounting for retirement, health and welfare benefits other than pensions. In contrast to the past practice of accounting for benefits on a pay-as-you-go (cash) basis, employers are required to account for actual accrual of the expected costs of benefits for each employee as well as beneficiaries and covered dependents during the years the employee is rendering service.

Financial Accounting Standard 123(R) (FAS 123(R))—also known as the share-based payment, a Financial Accounting Standards Board requirement that share-based transactions be recognized in financial statements. The cost is measured based on the fair value of the equity or liability instrument issued.

Financial Accounting Standard 158 (FAS 158)—amendment to Financial Accounting Standards Board Statements 87, 88, 106 and 132 that requires an employer to recognize the overfunded or underfunded status of a defined benefit retirement plan (other than a multiemployer plan) as an asset or liability in its statement of financial position and to recognize changes in funded status in the year in which the changes occur. With a few exceptions, employers are also required to measure the funded status of a plan as of the date of its year-end statement of financial position.

Financial Accounting Standards Board (FASB)—since 1973, the organization designated in the private sector to establish guidelines for financial accounting and reporting in the U.S. These standards are officially recognized as authoritative by the SEC and the American Institute of Certified Public Accountants. The SEC has legal authority to establish the standards for publicly held companies under the Securities Exchange Act of 1934. Throughout its history, however, the SEC has relied on the private sector for this function to the extent that the private sector demonstrates the ability to fulfill the responsibility in the public interest. The FASB is the successor to the Accounting Principles Board.

financial advisor—generic term used broadly by consumers and financial services professionals engaged in providing financial advice, services or products to a client for compensation. While some financial advisors charge a flat fee for advice, most depend on fees and commissions they receive from the purchase of securities and life insurance plans. Financial advisors who buy and sell securities for clients must have the Series 7 and 63 or Series 66 licenses. These licenses give their holders the right to act as a registered representative of a securities firm and to give financial advice. Financial advisors may also refer to themselves as financial consultants or counselors. See also *Certified Financial Planner (CFP), Chartered Financial Consultant (ChFC), financial planner, investment advisor representative, investment consultant, money manager, Personal Financial Specialist (PFS), private banker* and *securities broker.*

financial analyst—professional who assesses the economic performance of companies and industries for firms and institutions with money to invest. Also called a securities analyst or investment analyst, a financial analyst works for large institutions, helping make investment recommendations or decisions. Financial analysts read company financial statements and analyze commodity prices, sales, costs, expenses and tax rates in order to determine a company's value and to project its future earnings. They often meet with company officials to gain better insight into a firm's prospects and to determine a firm's managerial effectiveness. Financial analysts can usually be divided into two basic types: (1) those on the buy side work for mutual funds, benefit funds, hedge funds, insurance companies and charitable organizations that have substantial money to invest, while (2) those on the sell side help investment banks and other securities dealers sell their products. The business media also hire financial analysts who are supposed to be impartial and, as such, occupy a role "somewhere in the middle." Financial analysts generally focus on a specific industry, region or type of product. See also *fund manager, portfolio manager, ratings analyst* and *risk manager.*

financial asset—savings and investment holdings that are intangible in nature such as bank deposits, stocks, bonds and U.S. Treasury bills.

Financial Industry Regulatory Authority (FINRA)—largest nongovernment regulator of securities firms doing business in the United States. FINRA was created in July 2007 through the consolidation of the National Association of Securities Dealers and the member regulation, enforcement and arbitration functions of the New York Stock Exchange. FINRA touches virtually every aspect of the securities business. Among its functions are registering and educating industry participants, writing rules, enforcing rules and federal securities laws, providing information to and educating the investing public, and administering a dispute resolution forum for investors and registered firms. FINRA also performs market regulation under contract for exchanges such as the Chicago Climate Exchange, International Securities Exchange and NASDAQ.

financial literacy—ability to make informed decisions regarding the management and use of money. Financial literacy involves knowledge and skills pertaining to earning, spending, saving and investing, borrowing, paying taxes and protecting assets.

financial planner—sometimes referred to as the more generic financial advisor, a professional who assists clients with money management. Financial planners usually set up an in-person meeting with a client to obtain information concerning the client's financial situation and goals. The planner then develops a financial strategy (plan) that identifies problems, makes recommendations for improvement and selects investments that are appropriate, given the client's goals, attitude toward risk, and expectation or need for a return on investment. The strategy may be written or simply verbal advice. Some planners seek the input of attorneys or other professionals to provide specialized advice on topics such as risk management, estate planning and tax planning. See also *Certified Financial Planner (CFP), financial advisor* and *Personal Financial Specialist (PFS)*.

financial planning—process of identifying, preparing to achieve and meeting monetary goals. The process typically involves an analysis of current income, expenditures, assets and liabilities, along with a projection of future finances. Individuals and households plan in order to purchase a home, fund the education of children, achieve a secure retirement, reduce tax liabilities and provide assets to heirs, among other goals. Businesses plan to meet financial obligations and achieve strategic objectives such as providing promised worker benefits, developing new products, expanding facilities and providing a return to investors. See also *financial advisor* and *financial planner*.

financial risk—see *default risk*.

financial statement (FS)—written report that presents the monetary condition of an organization. Financial statements include balance sheets, income statements, statements of changes in financial position and statements of cash flow. Supplementary materials such as an auditor's opinion are required for publicly held companies. See also *balance sheet, cash flow, income statement* and *net worth (NW)*.

financial structure—see *capital structure*.

financing method—strategy by which an endeavor is funded.

firewall—security system comprised of hardware and software to prevent unauthorized electronic access to information.

first dollar coverage—health benefit plan that provides reimbursement for incurred health care costs starting with the first dollar of expenses; there is no deductible. See also *deductible*.

fiscal intermediary (FI)—company that contracts with an insurer to accept, evaluate for appropriateness and pay claims on behalf of an insurer. The U.S. government contracts with a fiscal intermediary (usually a private insurance company) to handle Medicare claims.

fiscal policy—government decisions concerning the amount of taxes and spending that will be made in a given year. Fiscal policy can be used in combination with, or as an alternative to, monetary policy when a government wishes to achieve goals such as increased employment and stable prices. See also *monetary policy*.

fiscal year (FY)—accounting year of a corporation. Due to the nature of their particular business, some companies do not use the calendar year for their bookkeeping, but rather any 12-month period.

five-year averaging—U.S. tax provision that allowed persons to spread the tax liability on a lump-sum distribution made from a qualified retirement plan over a five-year period. As of December 1999, this provision is no longer available. Persons receiving a lump-sum payout, however, do have the option to roll over the lump sum into an individual retirement account or another qualified retirement plan.

fixed allocation—distribution of funds in a predetermined, set manner. Retirement plans sometimes require employers to make contributions for each employee following a fixed allocation. Balanced and hybrid mutual funds have a relatively fixed allocation between different types of assets.

fixed allocation formula—see *fixed allocation*.

fixed annuity—contract in which an insurance company guarantees to pay the holder (annuitant) the principal and a minimum rate of interest for the term of the contract. The growth of the annuity's value and/or benefits paid may be fixed at a dollar amount, by an interest rate or by a specified formula established by the contract. The growth does not depend directly or entirely on the performance of the investments the insurance company makes to support the annuity. Some fixed annuities credit a higher interest rate than the minimum via a policy dividend if the company's actual investment, expense and mortality experience is more favorable than expected. Fixed annuities in the U.S. are regulated by state insurance departments. Fixed annuities are sometimes referred to as guaranteed annuities or guaranteed dollar annuities. See also *annuity, guaranteed annuity, hybrid annuity* and *variable annuity.*

fixed asset—see *capital asset.*

fixed benefit retirement plan—program providing a retirement income at a fixed amount or fixed percentage of salary. For example, the benefit might be 1% times the number of years of credited employment times the employee's average pay over the last few years prior to retirement.

fixed charge—fee assessed as a flat amount that is not a function of volume. For example, a delivery person charges $50 regardless of the number of items or the weight of the delivery.

fixed contribution formula—also referred to as a mandated contribution formula, a retirement plan arrangement in which the employer is required to make a specific contribution to the plan each year. To change this amount, the plan must be revised. The alternative to a fixed formula is a discretionary formula that gives the employer authority to change the size of the contribution (if any) from year to year. See also *discretionary contribution formula.*

fixed cost—see *fixed expense.*

fixed-coupon marketable bond—debt security issued by the government of Canada in multiples of $1,000. The bonds may only be purchased, transferred and sold—directly or indirectly—through a participant of the Debt Clearing Service. All Canadian-dollar marketable bonds are noncallable and pay a fixed rate of interest semiannually.

fixed exchange rate—official value set by the monetary authority of a country, typically its central bank, at which one nation's currency can be exchanged for another. A fixed exchange rate is sometimes referred to as pegged exchange rate. Currency may be pegged to another nation's currency, a basket of currencies or a precious metal (i.e., gold or silver). From 1945 to 1971, the major industrialized nations used a fixed exchange rate tied to gold in accordance with the Bretton Woods Agreements. Today, most of these nations use a floating exchange rate. China is one of the exceptions; it pegs its currency to the U.S. dollar. See also *Bretton Woods Conference* and *floating exchange rate.*

fixed expense—regular expense (e.g., rent, mortgage, property taxes) that does not fluctuate in the short term. A fixed expense (also referred to as a fixed cost) incurred by a business also does not fluctuate when changes in production, sales or other business activities occur. See also *variable expense.*

fixed income—money earned that remains constant and does not fluctuate (e.g., income derived from bonds, annuities and preferred stock).

fixed income fund—mutual fund that invests primarily in assets that pay a fixed dollar amount (e.g., bonds, preferred stock and certificates of deposit). These funds provide dependable current income and limit investor risk, but this may mean a lower return than is possible on a more risky fund. See also *mutual fund.*

fixed income investment—security (e.g., bonds, preferred stock) that steadily provides a regular amount of money, usually in the form of interest or dividends.

fixed period annuity—contract in which an insurance company guarantees to pay the holder (annuitant) a set amount for a predetermined period independent of how long the annuitant lives. See also *annuity, fixed annuity, guaranteed annuity, hybrid annuity* and *variable annuity.*

fixed premium—life insurance payment that does not change for any reason, including the aging of the person insured or a change in the cash value of the policy. See also *flexible premium.*

fixed rate mortgage—loan made to purchase real property that has a constant interest rate over the life of the loan. See also *adjustable rate mortgage (ARM).*

flat benefit plan—substantial differences exist in the precise formulas for determining participant benefits paid by these defined benefit retirement plans, but the most common approaches provide (1) a set dollar amount per month to every retiree or (2) a percentage of the participant's earnings. See *flat dollar benefit plan, flat percentage benefit plan* and *unit benefit formula*.

flat dollar benefit plan—defined benefit retirement plan that bases retirement benefits on a set dollar amount for each year of participant service recognized by the plan. If the employee's service is less than the required minimum, benefits are prorated. A flat dollar benefit plan is considered one variation of a *flat benefit plan* and a *unit benefit formula*.

flat dollar copay—see *copayment*.

flat fee per case—see *bundled payment*.

flat percentage benefit plan—defined benefit retirement plan that uses a percentage of employee compensation (e.g., career average earnings, final earnings, highest average earnings) and does not take into consideration the employee's years of credited service except for a minimum year requirement (e.g., 20, 25 or 30 years) by the retirement date. If the employee's service is less than the required minimum, benefits are prorated. A flat percentage benefit plan is considered one variation of a *flat benefit plan* and a *unit benefit formula*. See also *career average (earnings) plan, final average (earnings) plan* and *final earnings plan*.

flat tax—government levy that uses the same rate regardless of income.

flexible benefit plan—program that allows employees to choose the benefits they want or need from a package of benefits offered by an employer. For example, an employee who is already covered by a spouse's health benefit plan might choose vision or dental coverage or decide to set aside additional funds for retirement. A different employee might choose to use the funds for dependent care. Another employee may prefer cash instead of a benefit. The choices offered may be taxable, nontaxable or a combination of both. While technically not the same, some practitioners use the terms flexible benefit plan and cafeteria plan interchangeably. In the U.S., a flexible benefit plan may qualify as a cafeteria plan receiving tax-favored treatment if it offers at least one choice among taxable benefits and one choice among nontaxable benefits as specified under IRC Section 125. Flexible benefit plans that do not meet Section 125 criteria cannot permit cashouts or salary reductions. See also *cafeteria plan, core-plus-options plan, flexible spending arrangement (FSA), modular plan* and *Section 125*.

flexible funding—see *cost-plus arrangement*.

flexible life insurance—see *variable life insurance*.

flexible pension plan—supplement to a defined benefit pension plan in Canada that allows employees to make voluntary contributions that can be used at retirement to purchase ancillary benefits such as a better early retirement pension, bridging benefits, improved death benefits or benefits indexing. Contributions are tax-deductible and do not affect participants' RRSPs. See also *Registered Retirement Savings Plan (RRSP)*.

flexible premium—life insurance payment structure that allows the insured to decide how much to pay in any particular month. Also referred to as a variable premium. A variable life insurance policy is not the same as a policy with a flexible or variable premium.

flexible spending account (FSA)—see *flexible spending arrangement (FSA)* and *health care flexible spending account*.

flexible spending arrangement (FSA)—account that reimburses employees for expenses incurred for specific tax-qualified benefits. Established and maintained by the employer, FSAs can be funded through salary reduction, employer contributions or a combination of both. Three types of FSAs may be established: (1) medical care reimbursements not covered under an employer's insurance plan, (2) dependent care and (3) adoption assistance. Reimbursements from an FSA for qualified medical expenses are not taxed. Annual maximum contributions are set by the U.S. government for each type of account. With the exception of $500 that can be rolled over to the next year, contributions not spent by the end of the year are forfeited. See also *flexible benefit plan, health care flexible spending account* and *use-it-or-lose-it rule*.

flextime—also called flexi time, a variable work schedule in contrast to the customary work schedule of an employer. Flextime is not a reduction in workhours; it is the provision of flexibility that gives employees discretion as to how they will manage their personal and workhours.

float—idle cash balance such as checks that have been written but not paid, contributions not yet invested or outstanding distributions. Float is sometimes put into an interest-bearing account.

floating debt—short-term debt that is continuously refinanced. Using floating debt, an organization can take advantage of reductions in interest rates as well as short-term rates that may be lower than long-term rates. Of course, there is always the chance that interest rates will rise and the organization will have to refinance at a higher cost.

floating exchange rate—value of one nation's currency compared with another nation's currency as determined by supply and demand in the currency exchange market. Both the U.S. and Canadian dollars are determined by the marketplace. This has been the case for most national currencies since the collapse of the Bretton Woods Agreements of 1941. See also *Bretton Woods Conference* and *fixed exchange rate*.

floating interest rate—see *adjustable interest rate*.

floating-rate bond—see *floating debt*.

floating supply—total amount of securities it is believed security dealers and investors want to sell.

floor offset pension plan—also called a feeder plan, a hybrid arrangement that uses two separate but associated plans to provide benefits: a defined benefit plan and a defined contribution plan. Recognizing that many factors might result in a defined contribution plan providing less-than-adequate benefits, the employer maintains a defined benefit floor plan that uses a defined benefit formula to establish a minimum benefit. If the defined contribution plan provides a benefit that equals or exceeds this minimum, no benefit is payable from the floor plan. If the defined contribution benefit is less than this minimum, the floor plan makes up the difference. Thus the total benefit from both plans is equal to the minimum described in the floor plan.

fluctuation—change in the market price of a security. If a stock advances or declines three points, it is said to have experienced a three-point fluctuation.

flu shot program—provision of free or low-cost influenza vaccines. Some employers and health care plans offer flu shots in convenient locales such as worksites to encourage vaccinations and reduce the likelihood of a widespread outbreak that may result in significant absenteeism and the need for more expensive health care.

focus group—group of people brought together to discuss their attitudes, perceptions or insights on a topic.

Food and Drug Administration (FDA)—U.S. agency responsible for protecting the nation's public health by assuring the safety, efficacy and security of human and veterinary drugs, biological products, products that emit radiation, medical devices, cosmetics and the food supply. The FDA is also responsible for advancing public health by helping to speed innovations that make medicines and foods more effective, safer and more affordable, along with helping the public obtain accurate, science-based information about medicines and foods for improving health. The FDA is under the umbrella of the U.S. Department of Health and Human Services.

foreclosure—legal process initiated by a creditor to repossess and sell property used to secure a loan that has not been paid. Foreclosure is usually associated with a real estate loan.

foreign exchange rate—see *currency exchange rate*.

foreign exchange risk—chance there may be a change in the value of investment holdings in another nation as the result of a change in the value of that nation's currency.

foreign exchange transaction—buying or selling one nation's currency using the currency of another.

foreign fund—see *international fund*.

foreign national—person present in a country who is a citizen of another country.

Foreign Property Rule—limit imposed on pension fund investment in foreign assets set by Canada's Income Tax Act. The limit is 30% of total plan assets.

foreign security—financial instrument issued by a government, business or other entity from another nation.

forfeiture—loss of money, property, rights or privileges as the result of a failure to comply with a set of rules. The money a retirement plan participant loses if he or she terminates employment before being fully vested is an example of a forfeiture. In a U.S. pension plan, such amounts must be applied to reducing future employer contributions. In a U.S. profit-sharing plan, forfeitures may be allocated to the accounts of remaining participants.

Forms 1094-C and 1095-C—see "Reporting" in the *Appendix A: Affordable Care Act of 2010 (ACA)*.

Form 5500—document reporting the financial condition of a plan that must be filed annually by pension and welfare benefit plans with 100 or more participants. This joint agency form was developed by the IRS, U.S. Department of Labor and Pension Benefit Guaranty Corporation to satisfy the reporting requirements of the IRC as well as Titles I and IV of ERISA.

Form LM-10—annual report that an employer must file with the Office of Labor-Management Standards (OLMS) within the U.S. Department of Labor to disclose certain financial transactions they have with their employees, labor organization and representative of the labor organization, and labor relations consultants. Such transactions include any payment of money, loan or other thing of value (including reimbursed expenses). See also *Labor-Management Reporting and Disclosure Act of 1959 (LMRDA or Landrum-Griffin Act)*.

Form LM-30—document that labor organization officers and employees who have had certain financial dealings with employers or businesses must file with the Office of Labor-Management Standards (OLMS) within the U.S. Department of Labor to make public any actual or likely conflict between the personal financial interests of union representatives and their obligations to the union and its members. Interests and transactions involving spouses and minor children of these persons must also be reported. See also *Labor-Management Reporting and Disclosure Act of 1959 (LMRDA or Landrum-Griffin Act)*.

Form M-1—document filed annually by multiple employer welfare arrangements in the United States that provides information related to plan compliance with ERISA and health-related legislation.

Form T510—document used to register a benefit plan in Canada.

Form T920—document submitted to the Canadian government when amending a registered pension plan.

formula investing—strategy that seeks to limit the role of emotions when investing by following a strict set of rules.

formulary—see *drug formulary*.

forward contract—similar to a futures contract, an agreement between two parties to buy or sell an asset at a specified price on a future date. The purpose of such contracts is to hedge or speculate. Unlike a futures contract, however, a forward contract is traded over the counter (OTC) and can be customized to any commodity, amount and delivery date. The lack of a centralized clearinghouse for forward contracts gives rise to a higher degree of default risk. As a result, forward contracts are not as easily available to the retail investor as futures contracts. See also *futures contract*.

foul-weather fund—mutual fund that tends to do well or better than the market when the market is doing poorly. Funds are not formally given the name foul weather fund; this language is used primarily to describe the performance of a fund. See also *all-weather fund, fair-weather fund* and *mutual fund*.

Foundations of Trust Management Standards™ (FTMS™)—assessment-based certificate program for new pension and benefit plan trustees of Canadian multiemployer and public sector plans. The program is designed to provide the knowledge, framework and processes that will yield the confidence and competencies trustees need to fulfill their roles as plan fiduciaries. FTMS™ is sponsored by the International Foundation of Employee Benefit Plans. See also *Advanced Trust Management Standards™ (ATMS™)*.

fractional rule—IRS rule that an employee's accrued retirement benefit on any given date be equal to or greater than his or her projected normal benefit, with the portion based on service compared with projected total service at normal retirement age. See also *accrued benefit*.

fractional share—ownership of an asset (e.g., share of a stock) in an amount that is less than full ownership. Fractional shares are sometimes generated when stock dividends are declared or two corporations merge.

franchise insurance—insurance in which individual policies are issued to employees who have the same employer or members of an association. The employer or association agrees to collect the premiums and remit them to the insurer. The insurer usually agrees to waive its right to modify or discontinue any individual policy unless it modifies or discontinues all of the policies. Franchise insurance is also known as wholesale insurance.

fraternal insurance—insurance protection provided by a fraternal organization or society.

fraud—deception made for personal gain or to cause damage to another. See also *health care fraud*.

Freddie Mac—see *Federal Home Loan Mortgage Corporation (FHLMC or Freddie Mac)*.

free and clear—reference to ownership of property that is free of all indebtedness. Property that never had a mortgage encumbering it or that has a mortgage paid in full is considered free and clear.

freedom of choice—benefit plan provision that allows a participant to select any licensed provider for care. Participants receiving care from noncontracted providers may receive reduced benefits and/or pay a higher out-of-pocket cost.

freestanding additional voluntary contributions (FAVC)—term associated with pension plans in the United Kingdom. FAVC refers to money that can be put into a pension fund outside of the company plan in order to enhance benefits at a later date.

freestanding ambulatory facility—separate and distinct medical center where outpatient surgery and other routine services that do not require overnight admission are performed. See also *ambulatory care facility*.

fringe benefit—according to the IRS, a form of pay (including property, services, cash or cash equivalents) that is in addition to the stated pay provided to an employee or independent contractor for services rendered. Various sections of IRC determine if and how fringe benefits for employees are taxed. More than one IRC section may apply to the same benefit. A fringe benefit is taxable even if the benefit is received by someone other than the employee, such as a spouse or child. See also *employee benefit, nontaxable, partially taxable, Sections 104 and 105, Section 106, Section 117, Section 125, Section 129, Section 132* and *tax-deferred.*

front-end load—also referred to as a front-end sales load, a sales charge paid when purchasing mutual fund shares. See also *back-end load.*

fronting—use of a licensed, admitted insurance carrier to issue an insurance policy on behalf of a self-insured organization or captive insurer with no intention of transferring any of the risk. The risk of loss is retained by the self-insured or captive insurer with an indemnity or reinsurance agreement. See also *captive insurance company, indemnity insurance, reinsurance* and *self-funding.*

frozen plan—retirement benefit program to which no new contributions are being made. The plan sponsor continues to maintain the trust and pay plan benefits.

full disability—disability that is both permanent and total. Sometimes used interchangeably with total disability. See also *permanent disability* and *total disability.*

full fee—health care providers' usual, nondiscounted charge for a good or service.

full-time employee—person who works for an employer on a regular basis for a minimum number of hours (typically 40 hours per week). See "Employer shared responsibility" in the *Appendix A: Affordable Care Act of 2010 (ACA)* for an explanation of how *full-time employee* is defined as part of U.S. health care reform.

full vesting—point at which plan participants have nonforfeitable rights to 100% of their accrued benefits. In the U.S., participants are always fully vested in their salary deferral contributions as well as their SEP and SIMPLE employer contributions. The Tax Reform Act of 1986 requires that after January 1, 1989, a plan participant must be fully vested after completing five years of service with an employer, or vested at 20% after completion of three years of service with a 20% increase for each year of service thereafter until 100% vesting is achieved at the end of seven years of service. The Pension Protection Act of 2006 requires that employer nonmatching contributions to defined contribution plans for plan years after 2006 must be fully vested by the end of three years with a cliff schedule, and by the end of six years with a graded schedule. See also *cliff vesting, graded vesting, immediate vesting* and *vesting.*

fully funded—when a plan has sufficient assets to provide for all benefits at a certain date.

fully insured
—having sufficient coverage from an insurance company for all risk.
—with respect to Social Security in the U.S., when an individual has one quarter of coverage (QC) for each calendar year after the age of 21 and whichever occurs first: (1) the year before the individual turns 62, (2) the year before the individual dies or (3) the year the individual becomes disabled. Persons born before 1930 need at least one QC for each year after 1950. Other exceptions may apply. The minimum number of QCs needed is six. The maximum number needed is 40. Any year (all or part of a year) that was included in a period of disability is not included in determining the number of needed QCs. See also *disability insured* and *Social Security.*

fully insured plan—group insurance plan in which an employer contracts with the insurer to assume financial responsibility for all of the enrollees' claims and administrative costs in exchange for payment of a premium by the employer.

fund
—the assets accumulated for a purpose such as paying benefits.
—to finance or set aside dollars to cover the cost of an endeavor such as retirement benefits.

fundamental analysis—investor technique for determining the value of a stock that focuses on information such as a company's revenue, profit, debt and asset values, that affects the company's business and future prospects. On a broader scale, fundamental analysis can be performed on any security (including bonds and derivatives), industries or the economy as a whole. The term simply refers to the analysis of the economic well-being of a financial entity. Proponents of *technical analysis* and those who believe in the *efficient market hypothesis (EMH)* are critical of this approach.

fund earnings—income and other returns (e.g., interest, dividends, capital gains) on assets in a benefit plan's investment portfolio.

funded benefit plan—plan that has funds set aside in a trust to provide projected benefits. In contrast to an unfunded or pay-as-you-go plan, a funded plan is not necessarily insured.

funded debt—long-term financial obligation that matures after more than one year.

funded percentage—actuarial value of plan assets at the beginning of a retirement plan year divided by the present value of accumulated benefits in the same year.

funded ratio—retirement plan assets relative to the plan's liabilities.

fund family—group of mutual funds offered by the same company with different objectives. Typically, investors can easily move assets among funds in the family with little or no cost. One financial statement usually summarizes the investor's holdings in all the funds. Also called a *family of funds*. See also *mutual fund*.

funding—monetary support.

funding agency—government organization, insurance company or other entity that provides benefits or a means to accumulate assets to be used for the payment of benefits.

funding deficiency—see *accumulated funding deficiency*.

funding improvement plan (FIP)—under the Pension Protection Act of 2006, trustees of U.S. pension plans that are in endangered status must establish and implement a strategy that is reasonably likely to achieve a one-third reduction in the underfunded liability over a period of about ten years. For a seriously endangered plan, the goal is a one-fifth reduction in the underfunded percentage within 15 years. Generally, the strategies for achieving these goals are increasing contributions or decreasing benefits, or a combination of both. See also *critical status, endangered status* and *rehabilitation plan*.

funding instrument—legal document describing and controlling the terms of a retirement plan and the actions of the funding agent (e.g., an insurance company). With an allocated funding instrument, contributions are assigned to provide benefits for specific employees. Funds contributed by an employer are used to purchase cash value life insurance or annuities. Unallocated funding instruments, as the name suggests, do not have deposits designated for a specific employee. The accumulated funds are used to make benefit payments when an employee retires, either directly or through the purchase of annuities. Unallocated funds may also be withdrawn and otherwise invested. Most unallocated funds are set up as a group deposit administration contract, a guaranteed investment contract or an immediate participation guarantee contract. See also *group deferred annuity*.

funding policy—statement(s) clarifying the goals and objectives of a benefits plan and how to achieve them. This policy should include the amounts and timing of contributions by employers and participants.

funding rehabilitation plan—see *rehabilitation plan*.

funding standard account (FSA)—bookkeeping account required by ERISA that uses credits and debits to determine whether a benefit plan has a positive or negative balance based on actuarial valuation or actual experience for a period of time. An accumulated funding deficiency exists whenever the negative entries exceed the positive entries to the account. The FSA also acts as a reservoir in that it can store excess contributions above the minimum required. Excess contributions accumulate interest and can be used to reduce minimum required future contributions. See also *accumulated funding deficiency*.

funding waiver—see *waived funding deficiency*.

fund manager—financial analyst who manages a mutual fund or hedge fund. See also *bottom-up manager, financial analyst, growth manager, investment manager, money manager, portfolio manager, risk manager, top-down manager* and *value manager*.

fund of funds (FOF)—mutual fund that invests in other mutual funds. A fund of funds makes it possible for an investor to broadly diversify. On the other hand, if the fund of funds has operating expenses, the investor is paying double for an expense already included in the fees charged by the underlying fund. The SEC requires that these fees be disclosed as acquired fund fees and expenses. See also *mutual fund*.

funeral leave—see *bereavement leave*.

future purchase option—feature in some insurance policies (e.g., life, disability and long-term care plans) that gives the insured the right to buy additional protection. For example, some disability income policies allow the insured to increase the disability income benefit to reflect increases in the insured's earnings. Such an option is an inflation protection feature that allows the insured to periodically purchase additional coverage without proof of good health.

futures contract—agreement to buy or sell a specific amount of a commodity or financial instrument at a particular price on a specified future date. Futures contracts are used by businesses as a hedge against price changes and by speculators hoping to profit from price changes. See also *forward contract*.

future service—employment from the date a person enters a plan or from the date of benefit calculation to normal retirement date.

future service benefits—benefits accruing for service after the effective date of coverage under a benefit plan or from the date of calculation to normal retirement date.

G

gain—see *actuarial gain or loss* and *capital gain or loss*.

gainsharing—incentive plan in which employees receive awards based on increased profits, productivity or efficiency. Gainsharing is also referred to as a group incentive plan. See also *improshare*.

gaming the system—using the rules, policies and procedures of a system against itself for unintended purposes. See also *code gaming*.

garnishment—court order to an employer to withhold all or part of an employee's wages and to send this money to the court or to a person who has won a lawsuit against the employee.

GASB Statements 43 and 45—accounting and financial reporting standards that require the measurement and reporting of liabilities associated with other postemployment benefits (OPEBs) such as postretirement medical, pharmacy, dental, vision, life, long-term disability and long-term care benefits that are not associated with a pension plan. More specifically, the standards require recognition of the cost of OPEBs in the period when services are received, the provision of information about the actuarial liabilities for the promised benefits and the provision of information useful in assessing potential demands on future cash flows. Statement 45 applies to government employers, while Statement 43 applies to actual plans (i.e., trusts or equivalent arrangements) through which the benefits are funded and paid. Established in 2004, both statements were a response to growing concern over the potential magnitude of obligations for postemployment benefits. The Governmental Accounting Standards Board (GASB) is the source of generally accepted accounting principles used by state and local governments in the United States.

gatekeeper—someone who controls access. In health care plans, a primary care provider may be the gatekeeper responsible for managing medical treatment rendered to a plan participant. Alternatively, this term has been used to describe a third party who monitors care and determines what is appropriate and necessary to avoid excessive costs. See also *primary care physician (PCP)*.

gender different—see *transgender (TG)*.

gender expression—how a person communicates his or her personal sense of gender to others through behavior, clothing, hairstyle, voice or body characteristics.

gender identity—an individual's personal sense of gender. Gender identity is different from "sex," which is a person's biological status as a male or female.

General Agreement on Tariffs and Trade (GATT)—international agreement first drafted in 1947 to promote trade among nations and improve world welfare. The agreement created a framework for lowering barriers to trade and resolving trade disputes. Since then, elements of the agreement have been renegotiated a number of times. Each set of agreements is referred to as a round. The history of GATT can be divided into three phases. The first was largely concerned with commodities that would be covered by the agreement and freezing existing tariff levels. The second phase, from 1959 to 1979, focused on reducing tariffs. The third phase, from 1986 to 1994, extended the agreement to new areas such as intellectual property, services, capital and agriculture. The GATT organization established as part of the agreement was succeeded in 1995 by the World Trade Organization (WTO). Unlike its predecessor, the WTO has the power to sanction countries that don't follow its rulings.

general asset plan—also called a nontrusteed plan, a self-funding arrangement in which benefit claims are paid from current operating revenues. Supporting assets are commingled with the employer's other assets. See also *pay-as-you-go (PAYG) plan*.

general death benefit—payment under an employer-sponsored group term life insurance plan on the death of an employee, without special conditions. This type of benefit can qualify for special tax treatment under an IRC Section 79 group life insurance policy. See also *Section 79* and *Section 79 plan*.

Generally Accepted Accounting Principles (GAAP)—collection of rules and procedures established by the Financial Accounting Standards Board to ensure external financial statements are fair representations of the economic circumstances of a company.

Generally Accepted Auditing Standards (GAAS)—set of guidelines established in the United States by the American Institute of Certified Public Accountants that is used by auditors when examining a company's finances. The purpose of GAAS is to ensure the accuracy, consistency and verifiability of auditor actions and reports.

general obligation (GO) bond—municipal bond that has repayment of principal and interest guaranteed by the taxing authority of the local or state government that issued it. State law generally sets the conditions under which a local government can issue GO debt. See also *municipal bond, revenue anticipation note (RAN), revenue bond* and *special assessment bond*.

general partner—co-owner of an unincorporated business. Typically, general partners are actively engaged in operation and management, benefit from profits and tax advantages, and have unlimited personal liability for debts. See also *general partnership, limited partner* and *silent partner*.

general partnership—two or more persons who have invested in and conduct a business in which they (the partners) share business profits and losses. Each partner has full liability for the debts of the partnership. See also *general partner* and *limited partnership*.

Generation X (Gen X)—individuals born between 1965 and 1979.

Generation Y (Gen Y)—individuals born between 1980 and 1999; also referred to as Millennials.

Generation Z—individuals born after the Millennials. This population cohort is generally defined as those born from the mid- or late1990s to the 2010s, or from the early 2000s to around 2025. Generation Z is also referred to as iGen or Post-Millennials.

generic drug—also call a generic derivative, a chemically equivalent drug approved by the FDA as a substitute for a brand-name drug whose patent protection has expired. Generics have the same active ingredient(s) and are administered in the same form and dosage as brand-name drugs. They are often available from multiple sources. See also *brand-name drug, chemical equivalent* and *therapeutic equivalent*.

generic substitution—when a generic version of a brand-name drug is given to a patient instead of the brand name. In some cases, a health care plan or insurer will only pay for the generic version; the insured must pay for the brand name. With some health care networks, pharmacies automatically provide the generic version unless the patient's doctor has specified it must be the brand name. See also *drug utilization management (DUM)* and *generic drug*.

genetic counseling—service provided to individuals and families who have or are at risk of having a hereditary condition, defect or disease. Genetic counseling involves studying family history, medical records and genetics to evaluate and determine potential risk. Patients are also provided information and education to help them make informed decisions.

Genetic Information Nondiscrimination Act of 2008 (GINA)—Title II of this U.S. law prohibits the use of genetic information in employment, forbids the intentional acquisition of genetic information about applicants and employees, and imposes strict confidentiality requirements. The Equal Employment Opportunity Commission (EEOC) is charged with issuing GINA regulations.

gift tax—government levy on money or property that one living person gives to another. For the purposes of the IRS, selling something at less than its full value, or making an interest-free or reduced-interest loan, may also be considered a gift. In the United States, the donor is usually responsible for the payment of any gift tax, but arrangements can be made for the tax to be paid by the donee. See also *kiddie tax, Uniform Gifts to Minors Act (UGMA)* and *Uniform Transfers to Minors Act (UTMA)*.

Ginnie Mae—see *Government National Mortgage Association (GNMA or Ginnie Mae)*.

Ginnie Mae pass-through securities—see *Government National Mortgage Association (GNMA or Ginnie Mae)* and *mortgage-backed security (MBS)*.

glass ceiling—bias that prevents women and minorities from being promoted to leadership and executive positions.

Glass-Steagall Act of 1933—legislation passed by the U.S. Congress that prohibited commercial banks from participating in the investment banking business. In 1999, the Gramm-Leach-Bliley Act repealed the Glass-Steagall Act and removed barriers that existed between banks, insurance companies and investment firms, making it possible for one firm to function as all three.

glide path—how a target-date fund's asset mix changes as the target date approaches. Some have a very steep glide path that becomes very conservative just a few years before the target date, while others take a more gradual approach. The asset mix at the target date can be quite different as well. See also *target-date fund (TDF)*.

global budget—cash sum, usually established a year in advance, that is intended to cover the total cost of health care services. The payer of the budget lets the recipients (hospitals or other health care providers) decide how they will spend the money received. Providers do not receive any additional funding if costs exceed their budgeted payments. A nation can use a global budget as an expenditure cap for its health care expenditures rather than regulate the price of individual fee elements.

global bundled payment—see *bundled payment*.

global charge—see *global fee*.

Global Depositary Receipt (GDR)—certificate issued by a bank that represents shares in a foreign stock. The shares, referred to as Global Depositary Shares, are held by a foreign branch of an international bank. The shares trade as domestic shares but are offered for sale globally through the various bank branches. GDRs are commonly listed on European stock exchanges such as the London Stock Exchange. They are usually denominated in U.S. dollars. When denominated in euros, they may be referred to as European Depositary Receipts. GDRs, like American Depositary Receipts, eliminate the need to ship stock certificates between nations and reduce transaction costs. See also *American Depositary Receipt (ADR)* and *International Depository Receipt (IDR)*.

Global Depositary Share (GDS)—see *Global Depositary Receipt (GDR)*.

global fee—also referred to as a global charge, a set price established between a payer and a group of health care providers for a single episode of care, versus separate prices for each element of care. For example, a surgeon, hospital and rehabilitation center might agree to accept a single, flat fee for each hip surgery performed.

global fund—trust or mutual fund that invests in securities from all over the world, including the investor's home country. By contrast, an international fund invests all over the world with the exception of securities from the investor's home country. See also *mutual fund*.

globalization—trend away from distinct national economic units toward one world market. Globalization may also be used to describe the social, technological, cultural and political changes occurring as a result of increased interaction among people and businesses around the world.

global payment—see *bundled payment*.

going concern basis—assumption, when making an actuarial valuation, that a pension plan will continue in operation indefinitely.

going concern value—worth of a business if it were sold as a viable, continuing operation, rather than the proceeds upon liquidation of the assets held by the business.

going long
—buying a security such as a stock, commodity or currency with the expectation that the security will rise in value. Going long is the opposite of selling short. See also *short selling*.
—in the context of options, the buying of an options contract. See also *option*.

golden coffin—benefit package provided to the heirs of high-ranking executives who die while employed with a company. A continuation of salary, severance pay, pension benefits and accelerated unvested stock options are among the components that may comprise a golden coffin.

golden handcuffs—financial incentives designed to keep an employee from leaving a company. The handcuffs may be employee stock options that do not vest for several years, but more often are contractual obligations for the employee to give back bonuses or other compensation if the individual leaves for another company. More broadly, the term can also refer to any kind of situation in which a generous salary is used to keep an important employee from looking for a more desirable but less certain position. Some U.S. courts have held that such failures to vest benefits violate ERISA.

golden handshake—generous severance package offered to an employee, usually as an incentive to retire.

golden hello—see *sign-on bonus*.

golden parachute—see *excess parachute payment* and *parachute*.

gold plan—see "Qualified health plans" in the *Appendix A: Affordable Care Act of 2010 (ACA)*.

good faith—having honest intentions or making a sincere effort.

Goods and Services Tax (GST)—federal tax imposed on most goods and services in nations such as Australia and Canada.

goodwill—in accounting, an intangible asset on a balance sheet such as a brand name, overall corporate standing or famous association with, for example, a celebrity or an event that is carried on the books of the company at a nominal value (e.g., $1) but that is expected to generate substantial future profits.

Government Accountability Office (GAO)—investigative arm of the U.S. Congress that conducts financial studies and serves as the watchdog for government cost-efficiency. Formerly known as the General Accounting Office.

Governmental Accounting Standards Board (GASB)—organization founded by the Financial Accounting Foundation in 1984 to establish standards of financial accounting and reporting for state and local government entities in the United States. GASB is similar to the Financial Accounting Standards Board that established guidelines for the private sector.

governmental plan—benefit program established or maintained by a federal, state or other political subdivision for the employees of the government entity.

Government National Mortgage Association (GNMA or Ginnie Mae)—wholly owned government corporation within the U.S. Department of Housing and Urban Development (HUD) that primarily issues mortgage-backed securities backed by the Federal Housing Administration or guaranteed by the U.S. Department of Veterans Affairs. Other guarantors or issuers of loans eligible as collateral for Ginnie Mae securities include the U.S. Department of Agriculture's Rural Housing Service and HUD's Office of Public and Indian Housing. Most of the mortgages are for first-time and low-income home buyers. The purpose of Ginnie Mae is to ensure liquidity for government-insured loans through secondary markets, making it possible for the issuers to issue more loans. Unlike its well-known cousins Freddie Mac, Fannie Mae and Sallie Mae, Ginnie Mae is not a publicly traded company. Ginnie Mae securities are the only mortgage-backed securities guaranteed like U.S. Treasuries by the U.S. government. See also *mortgage-backed security (MBS)*.

government-sponsored retirement arrangement (GSRA)—unregistered plan in Canada that provides retirement income to individuals who are paid from public funds but are not employees of a public service organization.

grace period—period of time after a payment is due before there is a penalty or loss of protection. Insurance policies often have a grace period in which an overdue premium may be paid without penalty and the insurance policy remains in force. Credit cards and installment loans often provide for a specified period of time when payment can be made with no late fees or default. The period is commonly 28 or 30 days after a bill is issued to the debtor.

graded vesting—schedule that gives an employee nonforfeitable rights to a pension or other benefit plan in increments over a specified period of service until full vesting is achieved. For example, an employee with a defined benefit retirement plan may be 20% vested at the end of three years of employment, 40% after four years, 60% after five years, 80% after six years and 100% (fully vested) after seven years. See also *cliff vesting, full vesting, immediate vesting* and *vesting*.

gradual retirement—see *phased retirement*.

graduated vesting—see *graded vesting*.

grandfather clause—exception to a new rule that allows an old rule to continue to apply in certain circumstances or for certain entities. For an example, see the *Appendix A: Affordable Care Act of 2010 (ACA)*.

grandfathered plan—benefit plan that is exempted from provisions of a new rule. Typically, a grandfathered plan must still comply with the rules that existed prior to creation of the new rule. For an example, see the *Appendix A: Affordable Care Act of 2010 (ACA)*.

grant price—see *exercise price*.

graphic rating scale—method of performance appraisal in which the evaluator is provided points on a continuum and asked to indicate performance along the continuum. The number of points on the rating scale can vary from three upward. Research has indicated that five to nine scale points result in the highest quality of ratings.

green card—popular name for the Alien Registration Card, which identifies the bearer as a foreign national with permanent resident status in the United States. See also *resident alien*.

greenmail—purchase of enough shares in a firm to threaten a hostile takeover. Greenmail forces the target company to repurchase its stock at an inflated price to maintain control.

green zone—under the Pension Protection Act of 2006, a designation for multiemployer pension plans that (1) have a funded percentage of at least 80% at the beginning of the plan year and (2) is projected to have a positive credit balance at the end of the current year as well as the next six plan years. A plan that does not meet these requirements is certified as yellow (endangered), orange (seriously endangered) or red (critical). See also *critical status, critical and declining status, endangered status, funded percentage* and *seriously endangered status*.

grievance—complaint communicated to an employer, benefit plan, etc.

grievance procedure—process established to express complaints and seek remedies. Grievance procedures are commonly found in collective bargaining agreements and benefit plan documents. In some cases, the procedures are mandated by law.

gross charges per thousand—total benefit health care payments for a specific group of participants over a specific period divided by the average number of covered participants, which is then multiplied by 1,000. Gross charges per thousand provides an indicator useful in assessing the impact of cost-management strategies.

gross domestic product (GDP)—market value of goods and services produced within a nation in a given year. In 1991, GDP replaced gross national product (GNP) as the primary measure of U.S. production. GDP is used to distinguish economic activity within a country from that of offshore corporations. See also *gross national product (GNP)*.

grossed-up past service pension adjustment (PSPA)—amount of the provisional past service pension adjustment (PSPA) determined with respect to a past service event, before taking into account any qualifying transfers, money purchase transfers and excess money purchase transfers. Hence, the grossed-up PSPA measures the full pension adjustment value of the past service benefit being provided.

gross eligible charges—according to Financial Accounting Standard 106, a plan's cost of providing postretirement health care benefits to a plan participant before making adjustments for (1) expected reimbursements from Medicare and other providers of health care benefits and (2) the effects of the cost-sharing provisions of the plan. See also *Financial Accounting Standard 106 (FAS 106)*.

gross income—total money received before taxes and expenses are deducted. See also *adjusted gross income* and *net income*.

gross national product (GNP)—total market value of the goods and services manufactured within a country in a given year, plus income earned by residents outside the country (e.g., returns on investments abroad) minus income earned by foreigners in the domestic market (e.g., repatriated profits, migrant worker earnings). See also *gross domestic product (GDP)*.

gross revenue—income that a company receives from the sale of goods and services to customers with no deductions for expenses. A company's gross revenue may also include income from interest, dividends or royalties.

gross sales—total invoice value of sales before deducting customer discounts, returns and allowances.

gross spread—difference between the underwriting price for a stock received by an issuing company and the actual price offered to the public. By charging the public a higher price for an initial public offering of the stock than the price paid to the issuing company, the underwriters are able to make a profit.

gross-up—to make a cash payment to offset any deductions. Gross-up is used most frequently for executive salaries, with a company increasing the executive's pay to cover the payment of taxes so the full salary promised is paid.

gross yield—see *gross spread*.

group annuity—insurance contract in which an insurance company agrees to provide monthly income to a group of people for a specified period of time. Group annuities are usually purchased by an employer as a source of retirement income for employees. The individual members of the group hold certificates as evidence of their annuities. A group annuity has the same characteristics as an individual annuity, except that it is underwritten on a group basis. Group annuities tend to fall into one of three categories; see *group deferred annuity, group deposit administration contract* and *immediate participation guarantee (IPG) contract*.

Group Benefits Associate (GBA)—specialty designation focusing on health care and other group benefits. See also *Certified Employee Benefit Specialist (CEBS), Compensation Management Specialist (CMS)* and *Retirement Plans Associate (RPA)*.

group captive—stock corporation wholly owned by and used to insure a group of entities. A group captive is usually established because its participants are not large enough to form their own (single parent) captive. It makes it possible for participants to achieve a higher level of buying power with the reinsurance market or other providers by aggregating their risk or to achieve a level of true risk transfer. See also *captive insurance company*.

group contract—see *group insurance*.

group deferred annuity—contract between an insurance company and an employer in which the insurer agrees to provide retirement benefits to a group of covered workers. The employer makes periodic payments to the insurance company to purchase paid-up fixed income annuities for each employee in the group. The purchase price of the annuities is guaranteed in the group contract. At some future date, usually retirement, employees receive the sum of payments from their individual paid-up annuities. Employees know in advance that they have a certain pension income, and employers have assurance they will meet their future pension obligations in full. Some contracts promise a dividend to the employer if the mortality experience of the group or investment return proves to be more favorable than the initial contract anticipated. The employer does not pay more, however, if supplying deferred annuities turns out to be more expensive than the insurance company had originally anticipated. For retirement purposes, a group deferred annuity is considered an allocated funding instrument. See also *deferred annuity, fixed annuity* and *group annuity*.

group deposit administration contract—annuity plan in which an employer makes periodic payments to an insurance company that holds the money in an unallocated fund. The insurer promises a minimum return on this fund. When an employee retires, the insurer withdraws an amount from the fund that is sufficient to purchase an immediate fixed annuity providing the benefits promised the retiree. The insurance company does not indemnify the employer against changes in the purchase price of annuities, but the company does bear all of the risks of mortality and rate-of-return fluctuations once an employee has retired. Such a contract provides an employer with a more direct link between employer cost and the mortality or turnover experience of employees than a deferred annuity contract. See also *fixed annuity, group deferred annuity, immediate annuity* and *immediate participation guarantee (IPG) contract*.

group health plan—under ERISA, an employee welfare benefit plan providing medical care to participants and beneficiaries, directly or indirectly. Under the IRC, a plan maintained by an employer to provide medical care, directly or indirectly, to employees, ex-employees and their families.

group incentive plan—see *gainsharing*.

group insurance—insurance policy that provides coverage for many people under one contract. The group is typically employees of the same company or members of the same organization (e.g., union, trade association) who have a relationship beyond the desire for insurance. The policyholder is the organization, and the covered individuals receive a certificate of coverage. The most common group insurance policies are for life, accident, disability and health. Group insurance tends to be less costly than comparable individual policy coverage. See also *association group insurance* and *group universal life plan (GULP)*.

group permanent life insurance—see *group insurance* and *whole life insurance*.

group practice—group of medical professionals who share their premises and other resources. In some cases, income is also shared. See also *prepaid group practice*.

group practice model HMO—health maintenance organization (HMO) that contracts with a single multispecialty medical group to provide care to the HMO's membership. The group practice may work exclusively with the HMO, or it may provide services to non-HMO patients as well. The HMO pays the group a negotiated per capita rate, which the group distributes among its physicians, usually on a salaried basis. See also *health maintenance organization (HMO)* and *prepaid group practice*.

Group Registered Retirement Savings Plans (Group RRSPs)—in Canada, a collection of individual Registered Retirement Savings Plan (RRSP) contracts in a single trust. Employee contributions to Group RRSPs are deducted directly from an employee's paycheck and are not considered income. Employees have a convenient and disciplined method of saving for retirement, administrative costs are reduced and more investment opportunities are generated. See also *Registered Retirement Savings Plan (RRSP)*.

group term life insurance plan—see *group insurance* and *term life insurance*.

group universal life plan (GULP)—form of group whole life insurance that combines a death benefit with a cash value component. A GULP can be used to create nontaxable permanent insurance or to accumulate tax-deferred capital. Participation is entirely voluntary, and all premiums are paid by the employee. See also *cash value life insurance, group insurance, universal life insurance* and *whole life insurance.*

grow-in right—benefit conferred under certain circumstances upon members of plans registered in Nova Scotia and Ontario whose age plus years of service equal at least 55 when their plan winds up or they are involuntarily terminated. This right allows members to "grow into" certain benefits that they would have attained had the plan not wound up or had they continued in service and not been terminated.

growth and income fund—mutual fund that seeks both capital growth and current income. The assets of these funds may be balanced (consisting of both equities and bonds) or high-yielding common stocks. See also *balanced fund* and *mutual fund.*

growth fund—mutual fund with the primary goal of investing in stocks that will deliver returns via share price increases (capital appreciation). This type of fund is the exact opposite of an income or dividend fund; there are little or no dividend payouts. A growth fund, also referred to as a capital appreciation fund, is typically invested in companies that reinvest most of their earnings for expansion, research or development. The higher potential return of the fund usually comes with above-average risk. On the plus side, capital gains are usually taxed at a lower rate than interest income. The investor must be willing to hold shares for five to ten years to benefit from the potential higher returns. See also *aggressive growth fund, growth and income fund, income fund* and *mutual fund.*

growth manager—money managers who buy stocks they think will increase substantially in price. They typically look for stocks with relatively high price/earnings (P/E) ratios due to high earnings growth and that have the potential to provide greater returns than the market as a whole. Stocks purchased by these managers also carry greater risk because of volatile prices; hence, growth managers are viewed as more aggressive than value managers. See also *price/earnings (P/E) ratio* and *value manager.*

growth stock—ownership share in a corporation that has a record of revenue and/or earnings greater than the norm and that is expected to have considerable further expansion. Growth stocks are primarily attractive for their capital (price) appreciation potential, especially from a long-range standpoint.

guaranteed annual income—supplemental income that provides individuals or households a minimum level of income provided certain conditions are met. Eligibility may be determined by citizenship, a means test and either availability for the labor market or a willingness to perform community services. The primary goal of a guaranteed minimum income is to combat poverty. The majority of the Canadian provinces have a guaranteed annual income for low-income retirees. This money is provided in addition to what is received from other sources, up to a guaranteed level of income.

guaranteed annuity—precisely what is guaranteed varies from one annuity contract to another. Fixed annuities that promise a specific monthly payment are sometimes referred to as guaranteed annuities. A variable annuity may be labeled guaranteed because it promises a certain return on investments or protection of principal. An annuity may also guarantee payment for a specified number of years to a beneficiary or an estate if the beneficiary dies before the specified period of time has passed. Given the huge variations in the meaning of this term, a purchaser is advised to carefully read the annuity contract for how it is defined by the insurer.

guaranteed benefit policy—insurance contract that guarantees the amount of a benefit.

guaranteed dollar annuity—see *fixed annuity.*

Guaranteed Income Supplement (GIS)—nontaxable monthly benefit, on top of Canada's Old Age Security (OAS) pension, paid to low-income seniors by the federal government. To be eligible for GIS, the individual must be receiving the Old Age Security pension and meet the income requirements of the program. GIS benefits are reduced 25 cents for every dollar of non-OAS income. GIS is adjusted quarterly to reflect changes in the Consumer Price Index as protection against inflation. See also *Canada Pension Plan (CPP)/Québec Pension Plan (QPP)* and *Old Age Security (OAS)*.

guaranteed insurability—meanings vary considerably. Sometimes, guaranteed insurability is used interchangeably with guaranteed renewable and/or convertible. It can also have a separate meaning referring to an optional provision in a life insurance policy that allows the insured to purchase additional coverage without having to take a medical exam to prove insurability. Additions typically can be purchased upon the anniversary of the policy up to a maximum age (usually 45 or 50) or upon the birth of a child. See also *convertible term insurance* and *guaranteed renewable*.

Guaranteed Investment Certificate (GIC)—Canadian investment vehicle most commonly issued by a bank or trust company that offers a guaranteed rate of return over a fixed period of time (usually one to five years, although longer terms are available). The interest rate tends to be higher than on a savings account because a GIC usually does not provide for early repayment, except in special situations (financial hardship, emigration, etc.). If the money is withdrawn before the end of the term, the investor may not be paid interest or may even be required to pay a fee. Interest on a GIC may be paid periodically (e.g., monthly, quarterly, semiannually, annually) or may compound and become payable on maturity.

guaranteed investment contract (GIC)—similar to certificates of deposit that can be purchased at banks, GICs are sold by insurance companies. The value of the GIC remains stable with a fixed rate of return. The rate of return, not the principal, is guaranteed. There is a penalty for early withdrawal. See also *bank investment contract (BIC)* and *stable value fund*.

guaranteed issue—insurance coverage that must be granted regardless of health status, income or age and that guarantees coverage renewal as long as the premium is paid. Group health and life insurance plans are often described as guaranteed issue plans because the insurance company generally cannot refuse coverage to individual members of the group. As long as individuals meet certain conditions such as membership in the group, they are automatically issued a policy. Guaranteed issue provisions, however, do not limit how much an individual may have to pay for coverage. As of 2014, the Affordable Care Act of 2010 (ACA) requires insurers to offer and renew coverage to grandfathered and non-grandfathered health plans without regard to preexisting conditions. See also the *Appendix A: Affordable Care Act of 2010 (ACA)*.

guaranteed renewable—provision in an individual life or disability policy that requires the insurance company to renew the policy on the policy anniversary until the insured reaches a specified age as long as the premium payments are paid. The insurer can change the premium amount if the change applies to the entire class of insureds covered by the policy. See also *cancelable, conditionally renewable, noncancelable and guaranteed renewable* and *optionally renewable*.

guaranteed stock—common or preferred stock that has dividend payments guaranteed by an entity other than the issuing corporation. Since the dividends are guaranteed, investors are generally willing to pay a higher amount for the stock than if the stock was not backed by a guarantee. See also *common stock* and *preferred stock*.

guardian—person appointed by the court to look after the personal and property interests of another person, called a ward. Guardians are usually appointed for minors and other persons who are incapable of handling their own affairs. Guardianship can be shared among several people.

guardian ad litem—person appointed for the sole purpose of litigating and preserving the interests of persons deemed incapable of handling their own affairs. A guardian ad litem exercises no control or power over property.

GUST—acronym for the following four laws that made changes to how retirement plans are operated in the U.S.: General Agreement on Tariffs and Trade, Uniformed Services Employment and Reemployment Rights Act of 1994, Small Business Job Protection Act of 1996 and Taxpayer Relief Act of 1997.

H

habitative/habilitative services—health care that helps a person keep, learn or improve daily living skills and functioning. An example is therapy for a child who isn't walking or talking at the expected age. These services may include physical and occupational therapy, speech-language pathology and other services for people with disabilities in a variety of inpatient and/or outpatient settings.

hammer clause—provision in a liability insurance policy that restricts the amount that will be paid if the insurance company recommends a case be settled, but the insured rejects this advice and chooses to litigate.

harassment—unwanted and annoying actions of one party or a group upon another, including threats and demands. The purposes may vary, including personal malice, racial prejudice, an attempt to force someone to quit a job or grant sexual favors, illegal pressure to collect a bill or merely gaining pleasure from making someone fearful or anxious. Generally, harassment is a behavior that persists over time. However, serious one-time incidents can sometimes be considered harassment.

hard assets—physical items (land, buildings, equipment) or financial instruments (cash, credit, stock). Hard assets are tangible and are usually subjected to inventory and/or custodial safeguards. See also *soft assets*.

hard dollars—investment term that refers to the direct payment of fees for services (including research) to a brokerage firm versus payment through trade commissions, which are referred to as soft dollars.

hardship allowance/pay—compensation for the difficulty that may be experiences when workers and their families must adjust to a new location or live in challenging/unpleasant conditions. Factors that may result in hardship pay include the climate, infrastructure, civil liberties, language and culture of the locale relative to home conditions.

hardship withdrawal—removal of money from a qualified retirement plan prior to retirement to cover a pressing financial need. For the purposes of a 401(k) plan, the IRS defines hardship as the immediate and heavy financial need of an employee, including the employee's spouse, nonspouse, dependent and nondependent beneficiary. These needs include (1) certain medical expenses; (2) costs related to the purchase of a principal residence; (3) tuition and related educational fees and expenses; (4) payments necessary to prevent eviction from, or foreclosure on, a principal residence; (5) burial or funeral expenses and (6) certain expenses for the repair of damage to an employee's principal residence. A withdrawal is not considered necessary if the employee has other resources available to meet the need, including assets of the employee's spouse and minor children. The withdrawal may not exceed the amount of employee need. However, the amount required to satisfy the financial need may include amounts necessary to pay any taxes or penalties that may result from the distribution.

harmonized sales tax (HST)—consumption tax used in Canadian provinces that combines the federal goods and services tax (GST) with the regional provincial sales tax (PST).

hazardous duty pay—special compensation for employees exposed to high-risk working conditions.

health—state of physical, mental and social well-being.

health advocacy services—support offered by an employer, health plan, hospital or other entity to help patients navigate the health care arena. Examples of services include encouraging healthy behaviors, directing individuals to the best doctors and treatments, and assisting with billing and insurance coverage issues. See also "Navigators" in the *Appendix A: Affordable Care Act of 2010 (ACA)*.

Health and Human Services Department—see *U.S. Department of Health and Human Services (HHS)*.

health and productivity management—development, implementation and/or monitoring of strategies that improve employee health status and work output. Improvements in health may be measured by reductions in health risks, disability claims, health care costs, etc. Absenteeism, presenteeism and manufacturing output are among the factors that may be used to measure changes in productivity.

health and welfare benefit plan—see *employee health and welfare benefit plan*.

health and welfare fund—see *employee health and welfare fund*.

Health Care and Education Reconciliation Act of March 30, 2010—see the *Appendix A: Affordable Care Act of 2010 (ACA)*.

health care coalition—organization working on any of a broad range of health care concerns such as access, costs and quality. Participants can be businesses, health care providers, third-party payers and/or consumers. Often there is government participation as well. Health care purchasing coalitions use their collective power to obtain health care products and services with significant cost savings.

health care cooperative—nonprofit, member-owned and member-operated health insurance organization that provides coverage to individuals and small businesses. Care may be through a system of health care providers or the contracting out of medical services for members. Like other cooperatives, health care cooperatives are governed by a board of directors elected by members. See also "Consumer Operated and Oriented Plan (CO-OP) program" in the *Appendix A: Affordable Care Act of 2010 (ACA)*.

health care cost trend rate—percentage change in per capita health claim costs over time as a result of factors such as inflation, service utilization, plan design, technological developments and changes in the health status of plan participants.

Healthcare Effectiveness Data and Information Set (HEDIS)—widely used collection of 81 performance measures across five domains of health care. Developed and maintained by the National Committee for Quality Assurance (NCQA), HEDIS makes it possible to compare the performance of one health plan to another, as well as to regional and national benchmarks. A sampling of the measures include beta blocker treatment after a heart attack, controlling high blood pressure, breast cancer screening, antidepressant medication management, childhood and adolescent immunization, and advising smokers to quit.

Health Care Financing Administration (HCFA)—former name of the Centers for Medicare and Medicaid Services (CMS).

health care flexible spending account—fund established by an employer under IRC Section 125 that allows employees to use pretax dollars for qualified health care benefits. See also *flexible spending arrangement (FSA)* and *medical care expense*.

health care fraud—intentional deception or misrepresentation for the purpose of gaining an unauthorized medical benefit or benefit payment. Examples of health care fraud include billing for goods or services never provided, misrepresenting what and when treatment was provided, and performing medically unnecessary services. Health care fraud is almost always criminal, but the specific nature or degree of the criminal acts may vary from state to state.

health care provider—individual or organization (e.g., physician, nurse, hospital, laboratory) that provides medical services.

health care proxy—see *durable power of attorney*.

health care quality—degree to which health goods and services increase the likelihood of desired health outcomes and are consistent with current knowledge.

health care reform—changes in a health care delivery system, how it is structured and how it is financed. The goals of reform are typically to increase access to health care, expand health care provider options, improve the quality of care and decrease cost. See also the *Appendix A: Affordable Care Act of 2010 (ACA)*.

health care reimbursement account—see *health reimbursement arrangement (HRA)*.

health care spending account (HCSA)—individual employee account that reimburses the eligible medical and dental expenses of Canadian employees, their spouses and dependents. The sponsor of a HCSA program contributes a defined amount of funds into an account for each eligible plan member. These funds may be used to pay for health and dental expenses not otherwise covered by a group benefit or provincial health plan. Typical expenses include deductibles or coinsurance payments, expenses in excess of maximum coverage amounts and expenses that qualify for medical expense tax credits such as payments to medical practitioners and hospitals, transportation and travel expenses, medical equipment, eyeglasses, rehabilitative therapy and dentures. Accounts are governed by taxation rules and regulations developed by the Canada Revenue Agency (CRA).

health coach—person trained to help individuals address a specific health issue and, if need be, make behavioral changes. Health coaches work one-on-one to help individuals set goals, identify obstacles to achieving these goals, find solutions to challenges and remain motivated. Situations in which health coaches are used include diabetes management, weight loss and smoking cessation.

health consumerism—movement advocating that patients be partners with their physicians versus simply accepting whatever a doctor recommends. Such involvement requires patients be more informed and actively participate in the health care decision process. Patients may also be encouraged to have a better understanding of their bodies and health issues so they can take preventive measures.

health exchange—see "Public health exchanges" in the *Appendix A: Affordable Care Act of 2010 (ACA)* and *private health exchange.*

health fair—event that provides basic preventive medicine services, offers medical screenings, disseminates information on disease prevention and/or encourages healthy behavior. A health fair may also be a marketing tool for medical providers.

health flexible spending account—see *health care flexible spending account.*

health information technology (HIT)—computer systems, hardware, software, etc., used to store, update, transmit and retrieve health care information.

Health Information Technology for Economic and Clinical Health (HITECH) Act—enacted as part of the American Recovery and Reinvestment Act of 2009 (ARRA), U.S. legislation concerning health care information technology in general (e.g., creation of a national health care infrastructure) and requirements (e.g., marketing communications, restrictions and accounting) that modify the Health Insurance Portability and Accountability Act of 1996 (HIPAA). Provisions of HITECH include incentives to accelerate the adoption of electronic health record (EHR) systems among providers and a requirement that health care providers, health plans and others covered by HIPAA notify individuals when their health information is breached. See also *Health Insurance Portability and Accountability Act of 1996 (HIPAA).*

health insurance—protection against financial losses due to sickness or injury. See also *accident insurance, accidental death and dismemberment (AD&D) benefit, basic medical insurance, disability insurance, hospital-surgical expense insurance, indemnity insurance, major medical insurance* and *medical insurance.*

health insurance exchange—see "Public health exchanges" in the *Appendix A: Affordable Care Act of 2010 (ACA).*

health insurance marketplace—see "Public health exchanges" in the *Appendix A: Affordable Care Act of 2010 (ACA)* and *private exchange.*

Health Insurance Portability and Accountability Act of 1996 (HIPAA)—U.S. legislation that:
- Guarantees availability and renewability of health insurance coverage for all employers regardless of claims experience or business size
- Allows employees, their spouses and dependents to enroll for coverage outside a plan's open enrollment under special circumstances. See also *special enrollment.*
- Provides tax incentives for the purchase of long-term care insurance
- Establishes medical saving accounts (MSAs)
- Requires the U.S. Department of Health and Human Services to establish national standards for electronic health care transactions
- Addresses the security and privacy of health data. See also *Health Information Technology for Economic and Clinical Health Act (HITECH) Act, privacy office/official* and *release of information (ROI).*

health literacy—degree to which individuals are able to obtain, process and understand basic health information in order to make appropriate health decisions.

health maintenance organization (HMO)—medical system with member physicians, professional staff and facilities that provide a comprehensive benefits package including hospitalization and surgery. Supplemental services such as dental care, mental health care, eye care and prescription drugs may be part of the package as well. HMOs emphasize preventive care, early diagnosis and outpatient treatment. Both the insurer and provider of health care, HMOs are sponsored by governments, medical schools, hospitals, employers, labor unions, consumer groups and insurance companies. An HMO participant pays a fixed periodic fee that is set without regard to the amount or kind of services received. Service coverage is virtually 100%, with an occasional copay. A primary care physician authorizes and refers patients to specialists and other providers within the system. No coverage is provided outside the HMO network of providers, except for emergency treatment or when traveling outside the geographic area covered by the network. There are no claim forms to file unless a patient goes outside the network. See also *dental health maintenance organization (DHMO), exclusive provider organization (EPO), group practice model HMO, hybrid HMO, IPA model HMO, network model HMO, point-of-service (POS) plan, referral management* and *staff model HMO.*

health plan categories—see "Qualified health plans" in the *Appendix A:Affordable Care Act of 2010 (ACA).*

Health Plan Identifier (HPID)—standard identifier for health plans, which was required to be adopted under the Health Insurance Portability & Accountability Act of 1996 (HIPAA).

health promotion—education, marketing and other endeavors that help people gain greater control over their health and the factors that impact it. See also *wellness program.*

health reimbursement account—see *health reimbursement arrangement (HRA).*

health reimbursement arrangement (HRA)—employer-sponsored and employer-funded account that permits the use of pretax dollars to pay for qualified medical expenses incurred by employees, their spouses and dependents. Qualified expenses are determined by IRC Section 213(d) and plan design. Expenses may include health insurance and long-term care insurance premiums. Money remaining in the account at year-end can be carried over and used to cover future medical costs, but the account is not portable if the employee changes employers. Contributions are not included in taxable income, and reimbursements from an HRA that are used to pay qualified medical expenses are also not taxed. HRAs are a way to encourage patients to shop wisely for health care. See also *Section 213.*

health risk assessment (HRA)—also referred to as a *health risk appraisal,* the process in which lifestyle behaviors and other information specific to an individual is identified and evaluated to determine the likelihood of disease, injury or death. A health risk assessment is a common element in wellness programs. Research has shown that helping people identify threats to their health facilitates behavioral change. See also *wellness program.*

health savings account (HSA)—introduced by the U.S. Congress in the Medicare Prescription Drug, Improvement, and Modernization Act of 2003, a tax-exempt trust or custodial account created by individuals or employers for those (employees, retirees, self-employed) who are covered under a high-deductible health plan. Contributions can be made by the employer or employee. Funds contributed by the account holder are deductible for federal tax purposes. Funds can be used for qualified medical expenses qualified under Section 213(d), long-term care premiums and long-term care. The account beneficiary owns the HSA, making the plan portable. Amounts not distributed may be carried over from year to year. These accounts are designed to empower employees to take more responsibility for their own health care and help employers control health care costs. An HSA can be offered under a Section 125 cafeteria plan. See also *high-deductible health plan (HDHP)* and *medical care expenses.*

health spending account (HSA)—self-insured private health services plan (PHSP) benefit that permits an employer to allocate funds exclusively for the purpose of health and/or dental care payments by employees residing in Canada. In some cases, the employer makes advance payments including the cost of administration and taxes on behalf of employees. With other plans, payments are made on a "pay as you go" basis. The employee receives reimbursement from the account for eligible claims. Claims, administration fees and taxes are a 100% business deduction for the employer. An HSA can be used to supplement an insured private health services plan (PHSP) or to implement a standalone plan.

health stock ownership plan (HSOP)—combination of an employee stock ownership plan and 401(h) account. HSOPs allow a sponsoring employer to provide retiree medical benefits for its current employees without having to accrue future liabilities, as would be required if such benefits were provided outside the qualified plan context. The IRS is presently not issuing determination letters for new plans of this type.

health tourism—see *medical tourism.*

hearing aid coverage—benefit plan or insurance that reimburses the insured for the purchase of a hearing aid and/or offers a discount on the amount paid by the insured for a hearing aid.

hedge—strategy for reducing or eliminating financial risk; for example, taking two investment positions so that one will offset the other if prices change.

hedge fund—aggressively managed investment portfolio that uses advanced investment strategies such as leveraged, long, short and derivative positions in an effort to "hedge out" market risk and produce returns independent of overall market performance. Each fund poses a unique set of risks and investment opportunities. Most often set up as private partnerships, hedge funds are open to a limited number of investors with very large initial minimum investments. Investors generally must keep their money in the fund for at least one year. Unlike mutual funds, hedge funds are largely unregulated. U.S. law does require the majority of investors in a hedge fund to be accredited; in other words, investors must earn a minimum amount of money annually, have a net worth of more than $1 million and have significant investment knowledge.

heir—person entitled by law or the terms of a will to inherit the property of another.

high-cost excise tax—see "Fees/Taxes" in the *Appendix A: Affordable Care Act of 2010 (ACA).*

highest average indexed compensation—average of the best three non-overlapping 12-month periods of indexed compensation. For this purpose, monthly compensation is indexed to increases in the average wage from the calendar year in which the compensation was paid to the year pension payments begin. Highest average indexed compensation is used to determine the highest lifetime retirement benefit that may be paid from a defined benefit pension plan in Canada.

high-deductible health plan (HDHP)—sometimes referred to as a catastrophic health insurance plan, an HDHP is a lower-cost insurance policy that features a higher annual deductible than that of a traditional health insurance policy. As the term "catastrophic" suggests, HDHPs provide affordable coverage for health events that might wreak financial havoc on a household. With an HDHP, the insured pays for nearly all medical expenses until the annual deductible amount is reached. In the U.S., participating in a qualified HDHP is a requirement for establishing a health savings account and is used in conjunction with other tax-advantaged programs such as health reimbursement arrangements. The IRC allows HDHPs to provide some preventive care benefits without the high deductible or below the minimum annual deductible. See also *consumer-driven health care (CDHC), deductible, health reimbursement arrangement (HRA)* and *health savings account (HSA)*.

highly compensated employee (HCE)—term used when testing whether a benefit plan discriminates in favor of select workers. IRS definitions vary with the type of plan.
—for purposes of a qualified retirement plan in the U.S., an HCE is a 5% owner of the company or a person whose compensation was at least $110,000 in 2009. The income figure is indexed annually.
—for a cafeteria plan, an HCE is an officer, a shareholder who owns more than 5% of the voting power or value of all classes of the employer's stock, an employee who is highly compensated based on the facts and circumstances or a spouse or dependent of a person who meets any of those criteria.
—for purposes of a self-insured health plan, an HCE is one of the five highest paid officers, an employee who owns (directly or indirectly) more than 10% of the value of the employer's stock or an employee who is among the highest paid 25% of all employees (other than those who can be excluded from the plan).

high-risk pool—insurance plan to provide coverage to persons who find it difficult or impossible to purchase insurance. Drivers of motor vehicles who have had a number of accidents or tickets, or a serious infraction such as driving under the influence of alcohol, can be classified as "high-risk drivers." Some are able to purchase "nonstandard" insurance from a private insurance company who groups these drivers and charges higher rates that those charged to drivers with good driving records. For drivers who are rejected by private insurance carriers, insurance can be purchased through their state's "assigned risk" pool, which also has insurance premiums higher than those offered to persons with good driving records.
—prior to passage of the Affordable Care Act of 2010 (ACA), many states had private, self-funded health insurance plans for persons who had a health condition that made it impossible to get health coverage in the private individual insurance market and did not have access to group insurance. The plans were subsidized by state government with premiums up to twice as much as what an individual would pay for individual coverage if he or she were healthy. Coverage was sometimes similar to that sold by private insurers, or it might have had limited coverage for certain services (e.g., mental health or maternity care).

high self-insured deductible (HSID) plan—see *shared funding*.

high-yield bond—see *junk bond*.

hiring bonus—extra money used to entice an applicant to accept a job offer. The hiring bonus is paid upon acceptance of employment.

hiring rate—beginning wage or salary typically paid when an employee is hired.

HITECH Act—see *Health Information Technology for Economic and Clinical Health (HITECH) Act*.

holder in due course—legal doctrine that one who purchased a check or promissory note in good faith, and with no suspicion that it might not be good, claimed by another, overdue or previously dishonored, may enforce payment in court despite any borrower defense or other reason for not paying. See also *bona fide purchaser*.

hold harmless clause—contract provision in which one party promises not to hold another party liable for any damage or loss, regardless of the responsibility or negligence involved.

holding company—corporation that owns the securities of another, in most cases with voting control.

Home Buyers' Plan (HBP)—program introduced by the Canadian government in 1992 that allows individuals to borrow from their Registered Retirement Savings Plan (RRSP) to buy or build a home. The amount withdrawn must be repaid within 15 years.

home country—nation where a person was born and usually raised, regardless of his or her present country of residence and citizenship. See also *base country*.

home equity—market value of a home minus the amount still owed on the property.

home equity conversion mortgage—see *reverse mortgage*.

home health agency (HHA)—licensed entity providing skilled nursing care, home health aides and other therapeutic services in a patient's home.

home health care (HHC)—health and social services that are provided in the homes of individuals who are disabled or ill. The services range from skilled nursing care and physical therapy to personal assistance and help with household chores.

home infusion therapy—provision of vital fluids and medications outside a formal health care environment, usually to reduce the inconvenience or cost of a hospital visit.

home office—portion of a home used for business purposes. The IRS allows a business deduction for a home office if the space is used exclusively and regularly as either (1) a principal place of business or (2) a place to meet or deal with patients, clients or customers in the normal course of business. Where there is a separate structure not attached to a home, the regular and exclusive use does not need to be a principal place of business as long as the use is in connection with the worker's trade or business. A deduction is also allowed for space used on a regular basis for storage of items such as inventory or product samples.

homeopathy—treatment of disease using minute doses of natural substances that in a healthy person would produce symptoms of disease. This approach is thought to stimulate the body's natural defenses against the symptoms of the disease. Homeopathy as a formal system of medicine is no longer practiced in the United States. However, it may be informally practiced as an alternative therapy.

horizontal integration—combining of two or more similar organizations to form a larger entity. Hospitals often merge into regional systems to provide greater coverage and a fuller range of clinical services. Horizontal integration, also referred to as specialty integration, makes it possible to take advantage of economies of scale and to leverage buying power with vendors. See also *vertical integration*.

hospice—health care program providing medical care, support services and comfort to terminally ill patients and their families. The support services may include emotional, spiritual, social and financial assistance. Hospice care is available in diverse settings including an independent hospice facility, a nursing home, a unit of a hospital or as professional care in a patient's home.

hospital—facility that provides medical and surgical care to the sick and injured on a residential or inpatient basis. Hospital facilities are under the supervision of a staff of one or more licensed physicians and provide 24-hour nursing services by a registered nurse on duty or call. Facilities operated exclusively for the treatment of the aged, drug addiction or alcoholism may be operated as separate institutions by a hospital, but they are not considered hospitals. Hospitals are not convalescent, nursing, rest or extended care facilities.

hospital audit—examination of records to determine whether a patient received billed goods and services, and that the dollar amounts billed are consistent with contract agreements. A hospital audit is generally used when there is a large claim to ensure there are no billing errors.

hospital confinement insurance—see *indemnity insurance*.

hospital income insurance—see *indemnity insurance*.

hospital indemnity insurance—see *indemnity insurance*.

hospital insurance (HI)
—fee-for-service coverage for expenses incurred as the result of a stay in a hospital.
—Part A of the U.S. government's Medicare insurance that covers the cost of hospital charges for senior citizens and the disabled.

hospitalist—health care provider, usually a physician, whose practice is devoted to treating patients in a hospital setting. A hospitalist typically takes over care from a primary physician while a patient is in the hospital, keeping the primary doctor informed regarding the patient's progress. The patient returns to the care of the primary doctor when he or she leaves the hospital.

hospitalization—period of time when a person is confined to a hospital, which typically includes an overnight stay.

Hospital Quality Alliance (HQA)—national public-private partnership that includes consumer representatives, physician and nursing organizations, employers and payers, oversight organizations and government agencies committed to (1) providing public access to meaningful, relevant and easily understood information concerning hospital performance and (2) improving the quality of care provided by hospitals.

hospital referral region (HRR)—health care market defined by the Dartmouth Atlas of Health Care based on where most patients are referred for major cardiovascular surgical procedures and neurosurgery in the U.S. As of 2016, there are 306 HRRs—each contains at least one hospital performing these cardiovascular surgery and neurosurgery. Because U.S. health care is highly localized with people using doctors and hospitals close to where they live, researchers find these regions valuable in conducting health care research. See also *hospital service area (HSA)*.

hospital service area (HSA)—health care market that is a collection of ZIP codes whose residents use hospitals in a local geographic region. HSAs are defined based on where the largest proportion of Medicare residents are hospitalized. HSAs were assessed and aggregated to establish each hospital referral region (HRR).

hospital-surgical expense insurance—limited form of health insurance that reimburses the insured for expenses directly related to hospitalization such as room and board, nursing care and surgical fees. See also *indemnity insurance* and *major medical insurance*.

host country national—also called a local national, a person who is employed in a branch or plant of a company that is located in that person's country, but the company is headquartered in another country.

hour bank—method used to establish or maintain a worker's eligibility for health insurance benefits. The hours worked by an employee are credited to an individual account. At each determination date for benefits, the required hours for eligibility are drawn out. A variation of this approach is putting only the hours (or some portion of the hours) worked in excess of those required to maintain current eligibility in the hour bank account. Hour bank provisions usually specify the maximum number of hours that can be held in an account.

hours of service—measurement of time used to determine a year of service for a qualified retirement plan. Under ERISA, an hour of service is each hour for which an employee is paid (or entitled to payment) for performance of duties during the computation period. Hours of service include time when no duties were performed due to vacation, holiday, illness, incapacitation, layoff, jury duty, military duty, leave of absence and periods for which backpay is awarded. Hours of service are generally credited to the computation period in which duties are performed. However, passive hours are generally credited to the computation period during which an absence began, and hours for backpay are credited to the period for which backpay is awarded. In the U.S., plan documents must expressly set forth the U.S. Department of Labor definition of hours of service. An employer may keep records showing an employee's actual hours of service, or one of several alternative methods for crediting service may be used. Special rules govern the maritime industry and certain seasonal industries. See also *earnings equivalency method, elapsed time method, period of service equivalency method, working time equivalency method* and *year of service*.

HR 10 plan—see *Keogh plan*.

human resources information system (HRIS)—computer-based system for collecting and managing information regarding employees, volunteers and other personnel within an organization. An HRIS can be used to support a broad range of human resource management activities (e.g., recruitment, hiring, performance appraisals, training and development, and legal compliance).

hybrid annuity—annuity that combines the benefits of fixed and variable annuities. The purchase amount is allocated between the two options; a fixed portion provides a guaranteed income, while the variable portion depends on the performance of the underlying investment portfolio. See also *annuity, fixed annuity* and *variable annuity*.

hybrid fund—mutual fund that invests in a mix of stocks and bonds that may vary proportionally over time or remain fixed. A hybrid fund with a relatively fixed allocation (typically 60% stocks and 40% bonds) is sometimes referred to as a balanced fund. Other hybrid funds have a mix of stocks and bonds that is adjusted in response to market conditions. Target-date funds (TDFs) are hybrid funds that generally have a mix of assets that changes over time, moving progressively from an aggressive to a more conservative structure. See also *balanced fund, mutual fund* and *target date fund (TDF)*.

hybrid HMO—sometimes called a mixed model managed care plan, a health maintenance organization (HMO) that includes service features of indemnity insurance, such as coinsurance, deductibles, experience rating and an open panel of providers. See also *health maintenance organization (HMO)*.

hybrid pension plan—retirement benefit program that has characteristics typical of both defined benefit and defined contribution plans. Examples are cash balance plans, pension equity plans and age-weighted profit-sharing plans. Hybrids are sometimes referred to as combination plans. See also *age-weighted profit-sharing plan, cash balance plan, comparability plan, lifecycle pension plan, pension equity plan (PEP)* and *target benefit plan (TBP)*.

hybrid real estate investment trust (REIT)—type of REIT that combines features of both equity and mortgage REITs. See also *real estate investment trust (REIT)*.

hypothetical tax—amount deducted from an expatriate's salary that is equivalent to what the employee would pay for income tax if he or she had not worked away from his or her home country. This amount is only an estimate and is used by employers to satisfy tax obligations worldwide. The employee still needs to file a tax return and must settle the final liability with his or her employer for tax equalization. See also *tax equalization*.

I

ICD-10—see *International Classification of Diseases and Related Health Problems (ICD-10)*.

iGen—see *Generation Z*.

illegal alien—person who is within the boundaries of a foreign nation who does not have government authorization or papers—the person entered or stayed without permission. Undocumented alien is a term sometimes substituted for illegal alien. There is a growing preference for the use of the term undocumented or illegal immigrant.

illegal immigrant—see *illegal alien*.

illiquid—opposite of liquid; an investment that cannot quickly and easily be converted into cash. Examples of illiquid assets include real estate, collectibles and thinly traded securities. A business that does not have sufficient cash flow to cover its operational needs and debt obligations is also considered illiquid. See also *liquidity*.

immature—actuarial concept referring to newly established companies or growing organizations wherein all employees are active and no one has retired.

immediate annuity—insurance contract purchased with a lump sum of money in which an insurance company agrees to begin making income payments within a short period (e.g., one month, one year) after the purchase. This is in contrast to a deferred annuity, which begins payments at some future date. See also *annuity*.

immediate participation guarantee (IPG) contract—variation on a group deposit administration contract for providing annuitized retirement benefits. An employer makes periodic payments to an insurance company that holds the money in an unallocated fund, which is also credited with the company's share of investment income for the year. There is usually no guarantee of principal or a minimum rate of return. Actual payments to retirees are withdrawn from this fund. The employer is essentially self-insuring, participating immediately in the mortality experience gains or losses and receiving actual rather than projected investment returns. If the fund balance drops below the amount needed to pay the required guaranteed annuities, the plan becomes a standard deferred annuity contract. The insurance company uses the account balance to purchase individual annuities for all participants in the plan. If the account balance falls below the threshold, the risks are assumed by the insurer. See also *group annuity, group deferred annuity* and *group deposit administration contract*.

immediate vesting—granting an employee the full (100%) and nonforfeitable rights to a pension or other benefit plan as soon as contributions are deposited into the employee's account. In contrast, cliff and graded vesting require employees to wait a specific amount of time before the employee has full rights. Participants are granted immediate vesting in their own contributions as well as SEP and SIMPLE employer contributions. See also *cliff vesting, full vesting, graded vesting* and *vesting*.

Immigration Reform and Control Act of 1986—federal legislation that provided amnesty to certain illegal immigrants who resided in the United States and whose visa expired before January 1, 1982. Those given amnesty must demonstrate at least a minimal knowledge of the English language, U.S. history and government. See also *illegal alien* and *resident alien*.

immunization
—treatment, such as a vaccination, to help an individual resist a particular disease (e.g., measles, polio).
—passive investment strategy used to minimize the risk of investments. Immunization of bond interest rates can be accomplished by several methods including the combining of short- and long-term bonds in a portfolio to lock in a rate of return regardless of movements in interest rates over a specific time horizon. Similarly, immunization can be used to ensure that the value of a pension fund's assets will increase in exactly the opposite amount of their liabilities, thus leaving the value of the fund's surplus or firm's equity unchanged, regardless of changes in the interest rate. Other types of financial risk, such as currency risk or stock market risk, can be immunized using similar strategies. If the immunization is incomplete, these strategies are usually called hedging. If the immunization is complete, these strategies are typically called arbitrage.

impairment—as defined for purposes of the Americans with Disability Act, any physiological disorder or condition, cosmetic disfigurement or anatomical loss affecting one or more body systems, such as neurological, musculoskeletal, special sense organs, respiratory (including speech organs), cardiovascular, reproductive, digestive, genitourinary, immune, circulatory, hemic, lymphatic, skin and endocrine; or any mental or psychological disorder, such as an intellectual disability (formerly termed "mental retardation"), organic brain syndrome, emotional or mental illness and specific learning disabilities.

improshare—form of gainsharing that uses bonuses based on the overall productivity of a work team as an incentive. See also *gainsharing*.

Improving Performance in Practice (IPIP)—state-based, nationally led quality improvement initiative in the U.S. that provides small physician practices with tools, support, coaching and a collaborative learning environment in which to assess their performance and engage systematically in improvement activities. Practitioners use their own practice data and comparisons to others in their cohort group as benchmarks.

incentive—something that motivates or encourages a person or entity to do something.

incentive compensation—rewarding an employee for performance versus seniority or hours worked. Incentive compensation is usually in the form of a bonus or percentage pay above base salary. See also *incentive pay plan*.

incentive fee—see *performance-based fee*.

incentive formulary—list of medications covered by a benefit plan that is a compromise between an open- and closed formulary. Used in combination with three-tier copays, the number of medications on the list is limited, and the process for adding new drugs is very selective like a closed formulary. Generic drugs typically comprise tier one, while preferred brand drugs make up tier two. All other drugs are covered as tier three with a higher copayment. Tier three is the element that reflects the open formulary. The lower copays on tiers one and two provide an incentive for plan participants to use generics and formulary brand drugs, but there is the option to get a nonformulary or nonpreferred brand drug by paying more.

incentive pay plan—also known as pay-for-performance, compensation program that rewards the accomplishment of specific results, typically identified at the beginning of the performance cycle. See also *gainsharing, incentive compensation, incentive plan* and *profit-sharing plan*.

incentive plan—program that uses monetary or other forms of reward to motivate employees to meet specific objectives. The plan may be individual, group, companywide or a combination of these approaches. See also *gainsharing, incentive pay plan, incentive stock option (ISO)* and *long-term incentive plan (LTIP)*.

incentive stock option (ISO)—form of deferred compensation designed to influence long-term performance that gives employees the right to purchase a specified amount of company stock, usually at a predetermined price within a designated period of time. Corporate executives are often given these options as a reward for achieving certain financial goals. Increasingly, stock options are being given to rank-and-file employees as well. If the plan meets IRS requirements, employees who take advantage of the option to buy pay no tax until they sell the stock. See also *incentive plan, long-term incentive plan (LTIP), nonqualified stock option (NQSO)* and *stock option*.

incidents of ownership—any management control over a trust or insurance policy. Incidents of ownership on a life insurance policy may include the right to (1) cash in the policy, (2) receive a loan on the cash value of the policy and (3) change the beneficiary designation.

income—money received over a period of time from any source. Personal income may be earned through employment, such as wages, salaries and self-employment income. It may also be unearned, such as interest, dividends, net rental income, government benefits, retirement income, alimony and prize winnings.

income averaging—method of calculating personal income tax that allowed taxpayers with substantial differences in income from year to year to average income over a specific period of years (e.g., five or ten years). Income averaging made it possible to avoid a high marginal tax rate in the year or years that income was unusually high. The Tax Reform Act of 1986 repealed income averaging in the United States.

income bond—debt issue that promises to pay interest only when earned by the issuer; failure to pay interest does not result in default.

income fund—mutual fund that emphasizes current income in the form of stock dividends or coupon payments from bonds and/or preferred stock. Income funds are considered to be low-risk investments that provide a steady stream of cash. Of course, the size of the return is likely to be less than an investor would receive on higher risk investments. Income funds are also referred to as dividend funds. See also *fixed income fund, growth and income fund* and *mutual fund*.

income investment—purchase of a security (e.g., bonds, preferred stock) to generate income in the form of interest or dividend payments, rather than to grow principal.

income protection insurance—see *disability insurance*.

income replacement ratio—percentage of current income that will be needed each year to maintain the same lifestyle in retirement.

income statement—report that measures financial performance over a specific time period. An income statement is a valuable tool for individuals and households that want to examine their monthly or annual income and expenses in an effort to reduce spending. Companies use a similar statement to show revenue and expenses for operating and nonoperating activities. The difference between business revenue and expenses is the net profit or loss incurred for the specific accounting period, typically a quarter or a year. An income statement may also be labeled an earnings report, a profit and loss statement or a statement of revenue and expense. See also *operating activity*.

income stock—ownership share of what is typically a mature company with limited growth potential. Income stock usually pays regular dividends that steadily increase.

income supplement—payment made to an individual in addition to other income (e.g. earnings). Income supplements are usually based on need or other special circumstances.

income test—assessment of whether income fits the rules under which a person is eligible for assistance from, or participation in, a welfare program. In some cases, the test may be used to determine the extent to which benefits are provided.

increment of leave—minimum charge of leave, based on the smallest quantity supported by the employer's payroll system.

incurred but not reported (IBNR)—claims that an insurance company anticipates will be made by policyholders as the result of events that already have occurred but have not yet been filed for an accounting period.

incurred claims—estimate of the outstanding liabilities for an insurance policy in a given period. This estimate includes claims paid during the period plus a reasonable estimate of unpaid liabilities. It is calculated by adding paid claims and unpaid claims, then subtracting the estimate of unpaid claims at the end of the prior valuation period.

incurred losses—total amount of paid claims and loss reserves associated with a particular period of time, usually a policy year. Customarily, incurred losses are calculated by adding the losses incurred during the period and the outstanding losses at the end of the period, then subtracting outstanding losses at the beginning of the period. Incurred losses do not typically include incurred but not reported losses.

indemnify—to protect against loss or injury. For example, a health insurance policy indemnifies a person against the medical costs associated with illness and injury. Disability insurance indemnifies workers and their families against the wages lost as a result of these same circumstances.

indemnity—payment made by an insurer to compensate for a loss covered by an insurance policy.

indemnity insurance—contract between a purchaser and an insurance company that an individual or entity will be protected financially if a loss occurs. Indemnity plans for health and dental services typically provide a specified payment for the services rendered, regardless of the actual charges. Some hospital indemnity plans, also referred to as hospital confinement plans or hospital income protection insurance, set a specified daily amount in the contract for each day of hospitalization. An additional amount may be paid for days in an intensive care unit. This amount is paid even if the insured has other health insurance. Other plans coordinate benefits so the money received does not equal more than 100% of the hospital bill. Payment may be made to enrollees or by assignment directly to the provider. See also *fee-for-service (FFS) plan* and *managed indemnity plan*.

indemnity schedule—see *table of allowances*.

independent contractor—person who works for another, but the means and methods of work are not controlled by the employer. Only the result of the work is controlled. In contrast to employees, independent contractors pay their own taxes. Independent contractors may also be referred to as contract workers. See also *common law employee*.

independent physician association (IPA)—see *independent practice association (IPA)*.

independent practice association (IPA)—group of physicians, dentists and/or other health care providers that has a legal entity for contracting purposes. The IPA contracts to provide services to members of health maintenance organizations (HMOs) and other insurance plans, usually at a fixed fee per patient. IPA providers retain their individual practices, work in separate offices and continue to see patients outside their contracts. See also *IPA model HMO*.

index—numerical scale used to compare prices and other variables with one another. Examples of indexes include Standard & Poor's 500, Russell 1000 (large-cap U.S. companies), Russell 2500 (small- and mid-cap U.S. companies), Russell 2000 (small-cap U.S. companies), Russell 3000 (almost all of the U.S. stock market), Wilshire 5000 (total U.S. stock market), EAFE (Europe, Australasia and Far East) and Barclay's U.S. Capital Aggregate Bond Index (most of U.S. investment grade bond market). See also *price index* and *stock market index*.

index fund—mutual fund composed of securities selected to mirror a designated market index. Because the fund is passively managed to match a predetermined index, management expenses tend to be less than with an actively managed fund. Historically, passively managed index funds have also outperformed the majority of actively managed mutual funds. See also *active management, mutual fund, passive management* and *stock market index*.

indexing—periodically adjusting a benefit amount such as pension payments that recognizes a change in price or wage levels. A consumer price index is frequently used for this purpose.

index option—option based on the market value of a particular group of stocks such as the Standard & Poor's 500. Unlike stock options, index options are settled in cash when exercised. See also *stock market index* and *stock option*.

index-universal life insurance—policy in which the cash value is credited with interest based on increases in an equity index, but the cash is not directly invested in the equities market.

individual account plan—savings plan that provides a personal account for each participant with benefits based solely on (1) the amount contributed to the participant's account plus (2) any income, expenses, gains, losses and forfeitures from accounts of other participants that may be allocated to the participant's account. *Profit-sharing plans* and *self-directed defined contribution plans* are examples of individual account plans.

individual annuity—insurance contract purchased by a person (the annuitant) that provides a series of payments at regular intervals over a period of time. In some cases, employers purchase and/or hold such annuities in trust until an annuitant retires. In this case, the annuity may be referred to as a pension trust.

individual excess loss insurance—see *stop-loss insurance*.

individual health insurance market—where persons who do not have group health coverage purchase private health insurance. This market is also referred to as the non-group market. See the *Appendix A: Affordable Care Act of 2010 (ACA)* for some of the changes to the rules governing insurers in the individual market.

individual health insurance plan—medical coverage for an individual with no covered dependents. Commonly known as individual coverage.

individual insurance—contract with an insurance company that is purchased on an individual or family basis, as opposed to being offered to a group via an employer or member association.

individual life policy—in contrast to a group policy, a life insurance policy purchased through an insurance agent or directly from the insurance company. See also *group insurance* and *life insurance*.

individual mandate—see "Individual responsibility" in the *Appendix A: Affordable Care Act of 2010 (ACA)* and *mandate*.

individual pension plan—personalized, employer-sponsored, registered pension plan available in Canada that provides guaranteed payments for life. When used with a Registered Retirement Savings Plan (RRSP), an individual pension plan can boost tax-sheltered retirement savings. These plans can be structured as either defined benefit or defined contribution plans and are used primarily for executives. See also *registered pension plan (RPP)* and *Registered Retirement Savings Plan (RRSP)*.

individual practice association (IPA)—see *independent practice association (IPA)*.

individual practice HMO—see *IPA model HMO*.

individual projected benefit cost method—pension plan expense technique that allocates the actuarial cost for each employee individually, generally as a level amount or a percentage of earnings, over all or part of an employee's period of service, period of coverage under the plan or some other appropriate period uniformly applied. Costs are individually calculated for each employee or calculated using a group method in such a way as to produce essentially the same total result as though individually calculated.

individual retirement account (IRA)—personal account (or annuity) into which an individual may accumulate contributions for retirement income. An individual may set up a plan with a bank, insurance company, brokerage house or mutual fund. An employer may also agree to deduct a set amount from an employee's paycheck and send it along to a designated agent. Deemed, simplified employee pension and SIMPLE IRAs may be set up by an employer for employees. Funds in an IRA accumulate on a tax-deferred basis. See also *deemed IRA, Roth IRA, SIMPLE IRA, simplified employee pension (SEP), spousal IRA* and *traditional IRA*.

individual stop-loss insurance—see *stop-loss insurance*.

industry risk—chance of investment loss caused by uncertainties in an industry in which a business operates.

infertility benefits—insurance coverage related to the biological inability to conceive and carry a pregnancy to full term. Infertility benefits range from diagnostic tests and treatment of the underlying causes of infertility to in vitro procedures.

inflation—rise in the general level of prices for goods and services in an economy over a period of time. Essentially, inflation is a decline in the real value of money. The primary measure of inflation is the Consumer Price Index (CPI). Rising prices discourage investment and saving. In cases of extreme inflation, consumers begin hoarding goods in an effort to buy items before prices go even higher. See also *Consumer Price Index (CPI), deflation, purchasing power* and *reflation*.

inflation-indexed bond—also known as an inflation-linked bond, a debt obligation where principal and interest payments are adjusted to offset the effects of inflation. See also *real return bond (RRB)* and *Treasury Inflation-Protected Security (TIPS)*.

inflation-linked bond—see *inflation-indexed bond*.

inflation-protected—types of investments that provide protection against a rise in the prices of goods and services. Some mutual funds are created to protect investors from the negative effect of inflation. These funds focus on investing in assets that yield a real return, which is the return on the investment minus the reduction in the assets value as a result of inflation. These funds also invest in bonds backed by the U.S. government such as Treasury Inflation-Protected Securities (TIPS).

inflation risk—uncertainty that an investment or investment revenue will be worth as much in the future due to changes in the prices of goods and services. Also called purchasing power risk.

in force—when an insurance policy is active; in other words, the policy will pay if there is a claim.
—sum of the face values of all outstanding whole life insurance policies issued by an insurer plus the dividends due policyholders.

information ratio—risk-adjusted return measure that has the return on an asset (or portfolio) minus the return on the asset's benchmark in the numerator, while the denominator has the standard deviation of the excess returns of the numerator. See also *risk-adjusted return measure*.

infrastructure—basic physical and organizational systems needed for the operation of a society or enterprise. Infrastructure tends to be high-cost investments vital to economic development such as roads, bridges, water, sewers, telecommunication and electrical grids. It may be funded publicly, privately or through a public-private partnership. As an asset class, infrastructure tends to be less volatile than other equities in the long term and generally provides a higher yield.

ingredient cost—dollar value of a drug as stated on a drug claim or as calculated by multiplying the quantity of a drug dispensed by its unit cost.

inheritance tax—fee levied by government on someone who receives property or money from the estate of a person who has died. See also *estate tax*.

in-house pharmacy—store where medicinal drugs are dispensed/sold that is owned and operated by a health plan. In-house pharmacies are usually located in a plan's clinic or health care center. When an in-house pharmacy is owned and operated by a company and located at or near a worksite, it is referred to as a company pharmacy.

initial public offering (IPO)—first sale of a company's stock to the public. IPOs are often issued by smaller, younger companies seeking funds to expand, but they can also be issued by large privately owned companies that want to be publicly traded. An underwriting firm generally helps the company determine what type of stock (common or preferred) to issue, the stock price, and when to bring the stock to market. IPOs are considered risky because there is little history to predict what the stock will do on its initial day of trading and in the near future.

injection—delivery of a medication through the skin via a needle and syringe.

injunction—court order that directs a party to take or stop a specific action.

in loco parentis—Latin for "in the place of a parent" and referring to those with day-to-day responsibilities to care for and financially support a child. Under the Family and Medical Leave Act (FMLA), an employee may stand *in loco parentis* for a child and request leave to care for that child. Similarly, an employee who has a relationship with a person who was *in loco parentis* to him or her as a child (e.g., a grandparent who raised the employee) may also request leave to care for that individual.

in-network—health care providers that have agreed to accept a payment from third-party payers that is less than the amount providers accept from others with whom they do not have an agreement.

innovator—from a pharmaceutical perspective, a manufacturer whose name is listed on the application to FDA for approval of a new drug.

innovator drug—see *brand-name drug*.

inpatient—person whose treatment requires at least one night's residence in a hospital. See also *outpatient (OP)*.

inpatriate—employee of a multinational company who is from a foreign country but is transferred from a foreign subsidiary to the corporation's headquarters. See also *expatriate*.

in-service distribution—see *in-service withdrawal*.

in-service withdrawal—removal of funds from a 401(k), profit-sharing or other qualified retirement plan prior to a triggering event, such as reaching a certain age or leaving an employer. Some plans allow for a withdrawal to make house payments or to pay for the education of children. In the U.S., an employee may also elect to move assets into an individual retirement account where there are more investment options, to stretch out payments if a plan requires a lump-sum distribution upon the death of the participant, and when there is concern about the financial health of a company. In most other instances, withdrawals would be subject to the standard IRS 10% penalty for early withdrawal. No in-service withdrawals are permitted from defined benefit pension plans. In-service withdrawal is used interchangeably with in-service distribution.

insider—officer, director, major shareholder or anyone else who has access to information about a corporation that is not publicly known but which is important in valuing stock, bonds or other securities of the corporation.

insider trading—buying and/or selling corporate stock (or other securities) based on unpublished material information to make a profit. Insider trading is illegal under the Securities and Exchange Act as well as some state laws in the U.S. See also *insider* and *material information*.

installment refund annuity—see *refund annuity*.

Institute for Healthcare Improvement (IHI)—independent nonprofit organization focused on identifying and testing new models of health care and encouraging the broadest possible adoption of best practices and effective innovations.

institutional fund—mutual fund that targets pension funds, endowments and other high-net-worth entities and individuals. In the past, investors typically needed at least $1 million to invest in an institutional fund, but some discount brokers now offer access to these funds for smaller amounts. The main objective of these funds often is to reduce risk, so they invest in hundreds of different securities that make them among the most diversified funds available. Institutional funds tend not to trade securities very often, which keeps their operating costs to a minimum. See also *mutual fund*.

institutional investor—organization such as a bank, investment company, insurance company, pension fund or endowment fund with substantial professionally managed securities. Frequently, the dollar amounts of these entities are such that they qualify for preferential treatment and lower commissions.

insurability—whether a loss (risk) can be granted insurance coverage. To get life insurance, an individual may be required to have a physical examination to show that he or she is insurable.

insurance—means by which one party (the insurer) agrees to compensate another party (the insured) for any losses or damages caused by risks identified in the contract. The insured pays the insurer a lump sum or periodic amounts of money called premiums in exchange for transferring the risk. See also *accident insurance, annuity, business continuation insurance, business travel accident insurance, class rating, disability insurance, endorsement, exclusion, health insurance, high-risk pool, insurance policy, key employee insurance, life insurance, participating insurance* and *stop-loss insurance*.

insurance broker—person or business that brings together clients seeking insurance coverage with insurance companies. The broker represents the buyer rather than the company but receives a commission from the company. In general, brokers must be registered in the state where they operate. See also *broker*.

insurance carrier—see *insurer*.

insurance certificate carrier—see *certificate of insurance (COI)*.

insurance contract—see *insurance policy*.

insurance policy—legal agreement between an insurance buyer and an insurance company that establishes the rights and duties of each party. See also *insurance*.

insurance rate—cost for a specific type of insurance coverage. See also *premium*.

insured—person protected by an insurance contract.

insured event—occurrence that triggers coverage by an insurance plan. For example, the death of an insured triggers payment of life insurance benefits. Hospitalization is an event that typically triggers payment of health insurance benefits. The insolvency of a multiemployer plan is an insured event for the purposes of the Pension Benefit Guaranty Corporation. See also *plan termination*.

insured pension plan
—in the U.S., retirement benefits funded through contracts with a life insurance company that guarantees payment with annuities. The federal government also insures defined benefit plans through the Pension Benefit Guaranty Corporation. See also *Pension Benefit Guaranty Corporation (PBGC)*.
—in Canada, a retirement plan in which all benefits are purchased from and guaranteed by an insurance company as contributions are received.

insurer—company that issues a contract (insurance policy) and assumes the risk for covering a potential loss. Also referred to as an insurance carrier.

intangible asset—nonphysical resources and rights that have value to an owner. Examples would be patents, goodwill, trademarks, copyrights, computer software and financial assets such as accounts receivable, stocks, bonds and cash. For the purpose of financial reports, these items may be assigned a financial value reflecting their worth to a corporation. See also *tangible asset*.

integral service—related procedures that are necessary to perform a more comprehensive service that are included in the price of the service. For example, the cost of sterilizing instruments and providing local anesthesia when doing a dental crown is considered integral to the fee for the crown. As such, there is no separate billing for an integral service.

integrated care pathway—see *clinical pathway*.

integrated contribution limit—maximum amount that can be contributed each year in total to tax-assisted retirement savings vehicles in Canada. The limit, expressed as a percentage of annual earned income and subject to a dollar limit, applies to the total contributed to Registered Pension Plans (RPPs), Deferred Profit Sharing Plans (DPSPs) and Registered Retirement Savings Plans (RRSPs).

integrated delivery system (IDS)—group of hospitals, physicians, insurers, community agencies and/or other providers that work together to coordinate and deliver services within a locale. Also known as an integrated service network.

integrated disability management (IDM)—system that coordinates traditional occupational (workers' compensation) and nonoccupational (short-term and long-term) disability protections and treatment. Aspects of an IDM program include a common claims process, medical case management process and return-to-work program. See also *24-hour coverage*.

integrated health system—see *integrated delivery system (IDS)*.

integrated service network (IDN)—see *integrated delivery system (IDS)*.

integration
—coordination of contributions or benefits in one benefit program with those of another benefit program. In the United States, pension plans are sometimes integrated with Social Security benefits. Integration takes into consideration an employer's contributions to Social Security (FICA taxes). Pension benefits are lowered for all employees, and total retirement benefits (pensions plus Social Security) replace a more uniform percentage of final pay for all employees. Defined benefit plans may use either the offset or excess rate approach. See also *excess rate method, integration level,* and *permitted disparity*.
—in Canada, private and public pension plans are often integrated. When an individual begins to receive benefits from the Canada Pension Plan (CPP) or Québec Pension Plan (QPP), the level of other pension benefits to which an individual is entitled may be reduced. CPP/QPP benefits may also have an impact on the level of benefits received from a private sector disability insurance plan. Most workers' compensation plans take into account income from the CPP.
—from a business perspective, the combining of two or more similar organizations to form a larger entity. See also *horizontal integration* and *vertical integration*.

integration level—breakpoint in compensation specified when a defined benefit retirement plan is coordinated with Social Security benefits. IRC Section 401 does not allow the integration level to exceed the Social Security taxable wage base. The rate of employer contributions or benefits above the integration level is higher than the rate at or below the breakpoint. The rate above the breakpoint is expressed as a percentage of the employee's plan year compensation or average annual compensation above the specified dollar amount, while the rate at or below the breakpoint is expressed as a percentage of an employee's plan year compensation or average annual compensation up to the specified dollar amount. See also *base benefit percentage, base contribution percentage* and *integration*.

interactive benefits communication—use of technology for communicating employee benefits such as touch-tone phones, personal computers and public multimedia kiosks. See also *call center, employee self-service (ESS)* and *interactive voice response (IVR)*.

interactive voice response (IVR)—technology that allows a computer to detect voice and telephone keypad inputs. An IVR system can respond with prerecorded or dynamically generated audio that directs users how to proceed. Caller responses can be recorded by the computer. Such systems are increasingly being used to provide services related to employee benefits administration. See also *employee self-service (ESS)* and *interactive benefits communication*.

interchange—substituting one prescribed medication for another, usually on the basis of chemical equivalency. In some states and health plans, substitution of drugs with therapeutic equivalency may also be allowed. See also *chemical equivalent* and *therapeutic equivalent*.

interest—money paid by a borrower for the use of money and, conversely, money paid to a lender for loaning the funds. Interest is usually stated as a percentage of the amount (principal) owed. See also *compound interest* and *simple interest*.

interest rate—percentage of the money borrowed (principal) that a lender charges a borrower. The interest rate is usually expressed as a percent per year. See also *annual percentage rate (APR)* and *annual percentage yield (APY)*.

interest rate immunization—see *immunization*.

interest rate risk—potential for changes in interest rates that may adversely affect the value of a deposit or investment. When interest rates rise, the market value of fixed income contracts (e.g., bonds) declines. Similarly, when interest rates decline, the market value of fixed income contracts increases. Interest rate risk is the risk associated with these fluctuations. See also *duration*.

interest-rate-sensitive assets—investments that are strongly impacted by interest rate changes. For example, the bank stocks tend to do better in periods when interest rates are rising because the banks can raise the interest rates they charge borrowers faster than the rates they pay depositors. On the other hand, home builders are negatively impacted by rising interest rates because it is more difficult for people to purchase and finance a home.

interest rate swap—see *swap*.

interest table—value of a deposit (typically $1, $100 or $1,000) at intervals of one year assuming different simple or compound interest rates. See also *compound interest* and *simple interest*.

intermediate care facility (ICF)—state-licensed health facility that provides services to those with a variety of physical or emotional conditions (e.g., developmentally disabled persons). Patients in an ICF do not require the degree of care provided by a hospital or skilled nursing facility. The individuals must, however, require care and services above the level of room and board. An ICF is one type of extended care facility.

intermediate-term bond—definitions vary on length, but typically a debt security that matures between three and 12 years. See also *short-term bond*.

intermittent leave—separate periods of time taken off from work due to a single illness or injury, rather than one continuous period of time.

internal controls—measures put in place by an organization to help ensure financial statements are reliable, plan assets and resources are safeguarded, operations are effective and efficient, and compliance with applicable laws and regulations, etc.

internal rate of return (IRR)—see *dollar-weighted rate of return*.

Internal Revenue Code (IRC)—as amended, the basic federal tax law for the United States. See also *Section 79* through *Section 505*.

Internal Revenue Service (IRS)—part of the U.S. Department of the Treasury, the agency charged with the collection of taxes. The IRS is also responsible for administering the requirements for qualified pension plans as well as other retirement and welfare benefit plans. The agency has the authority to assess penalties for failure to comply with certain reporting and disclosure requirements.

International Classification of Diseases and Related Health Problems (ICD-10)—standard diagnostic coding system used to classify diseases and other health problems. Published by the World Health Organization, the codes are used worldwide to compile morbidity and mortality statistics and for reimbursement systems. The ICD is revised periodically and is currently in its tenth edition.

international compensation—pay practices covering employees who move across national borders, including expatriates, third-country nationals and inpatriates. The definition sometimes is extended to include domestic pay practices in foreign countries.

International Depository Receipt (IDR)—negotiable bank-issued certificate representing ownership of stock securities by an investor outside the country of origin. An IDR is the non-U.S. equivalent of an American Depositary Receipt (ADR). See also *American Depositary Receipt (ADR)* and *Global Depositary Receipt (GDR)*.

International Development Association (IDA)—see *World Bank*.

international fund—mutual fund that invests all over the world except in the investor's home country. The risk associated with international funds varies dramatically; some funds are very conservative while others are very risky. In contrast, global funds include securities from the investor's home country. See also *mutual fund*.

International Monetary Fund (IMF)—organization of 188 countries that work together to foster global monetary cooperation, secure financial stability, facilitate international trade, promote high employment and sustainable economic growth, and reduce poverty around the world. See also *Bretton Woods Conference*.

International Securities Exchange (ISE)—launched in 2000, the world's largest equity options exchange.

Internet pharmacy—see *online pharmacy*.

interrelated claims provision—fiduciary liability insurance clause that states the same insurance policy will respond to any later claim related to or arising out of an initial claim, even if the later claim happens years later. See also *claims-made policy*.

interrogatory—written questions from one party that must be answered by another party in a court action. Interrogatories are a discovery device that enables a party to learn facts that are the basis for, or support its position in, a legal case.

intervention—orchestrated attempt by an individual or group (comprised of family, friends and/or a counselor) to get someone to seek professional help. The group confronts the individual, breaks through denial and convinces him or her to enter treatment.

inter vivos trust—see *living trust*.

intestate—situation in which a person dies without a will.

intoxication exclusion—provision in an accidental death and dismemberment insurance policy that denies benefits if the accidental death or dismemberment is the result of drugs or alcohol inebriation.

inventory—list of all goods or materials in stock. Inventory value is usually stated at cost or market value, whichever is lower.

invested capital—total cash investment that shareholders and debtholders have made in a company. To calculate the value of invested capital, nonoperating cash and investments are subtracted from sum of total debt, leases, total equity and equity equivalents.

investigational drug—see *experimental drug.*

investment—process by which money is transferred from one owner to another for the purpose of making more money in the form of capital gains, additional income or a combination of both.

investment advice—personalized counsel relating to asset management. Investment advice provided by a professional may be paid for via a fee or other compensation. In the past, a fiduciary providing advice concerning a retirement plan could have violated the prohibited transaction exemption rules of ERISA. The Pension Protection Act of 2006 amended the rules to permit a broader array of acceptable investment advice in the U.S. See also *investment advisor representative, investment education* and *self-directed investment.*

Investment Advisers Act of 1940—U.S. law enforced by the SEC that governs investment advisors. The Act requires, with certain exceptions, that persons or firms engaging in the business of advising others with respect to security transactions for compensation must register with the Commission and conform their activities to statutory standards designed to protect the interests of investors. See also *Securities and Exchange Commission (SEC).*

investment advisor—see *investment advisor representative.*

investment advisor representative—individual associated with an investment advisor firm who provides investment advice to clients. In the U.S., states currently require advisors seeking a license to pass the Series 65 exam administered by the Financial Industry Regulatory Authority. See also *securities broker.*

investment analyst—see *financial analyst.*

investment bank—financial institution that performs a variety of services, including assistance in the sale of securities, helping companies raise capital, and facilitating mergers and acquisitions. Investment banks serve as an intermediary between corporations issuing new securities and the public. The banks help these companies navigate the process involved in selling new securities, including meeting securities requirements, setting prices and finding buyers. Thereafter, the market in the new security may be over the counter or on a stock exchange. Investment banks also create new investment vehicles out of existing securities, cutting them up or combining them to offer specialized products for select investors. Investment banks are also referred to as underwriters.

investment company—sometimes called an investment trust or mutual fund company, a financial institution that is engaged primarily in the business of buying, selling and holding securities. See also *mutual fund.*

Investment Company Act of 1940—legislation enforced by the SEC that defines and regulates investment companies, including mutual funds. Specifically, the Act regulates conflicts of interest in investment companies and securities exchanges and requires disclosure regarding the structure, operations and other material details concerning an investment company. See also *Securities and Exchange Commission (SEC).*

investment consultant—individual or firm that provides investment assistance for a fixed fee, a fee based upon a percentage of assets or a fee derived from brokerage commission. Such assistance may include analyzing portfolio constraints, setting performance objectives, advice on asset allocation, performance measurement, educating fiduciaries and selecting/monitoring investment managers. Consultants typically work for brokerage firms or independent advisory firms. Their clients are most often institutional investors such as pension plans but may include individuals with substantial sums to invest. On occasion, an investment consultant is also used as a generic term to describe a money manager or a financial planner.

investment earnings—return on assets including interest, dividends, rent and capital gains.

investment education—provision of educational materials and information to assist plan participants in managing assets and planning for their retirement. Topics can include specific plan information; general financial and investment information (e.g., risk, return, diversification and compound return); hypothetical asset allocation models using different time horizons and risk profiles; and interactive investment materials (e.g., questionnaires, worksheets and computer programs) for estimating retirement needs and the potential impact of asset allocation. See also *investment advice* and *investment consultant*.

investment fund—see *collective investment fund*.

investment gain or loss—realized or unrealized increase or decrease in the market value of a portfolio at the end of a time period as compared with its market value at the beginning of that period.

investment grade bond—municipal and corporate debt securities with a relatively low risk of default. See also *junk bond*.

Investment Industry Regulatory Organization of Canada (IIROC)—national self-regulatory organization that oversees all investment dealers and trading activity on debt and equity marketplaces in Canada. Created in 2008 through the consolidation of the Investment Dealers Association of Canada and Market Regulation Services Inc., IIROC sets and enforces rules regarding the proficiency and conduct of dealer firms and their registered employees.

investment manager—individual or organization responsible for making day-to-day decisions to buy, hold or sell assets. See also *bottom-up manager*, *fund manager*, *growth manager*, *money manager*, *portfolio manager*, *private banker*, *risk manager*, *top-down manager* and *value manager*.

investment objective—financial goals pursued by an investor or a mutual fund. Examples of investment objectives include income, growth, income and growth, and tax-free income.

investment policy—how contributions to an employee benefit plan are to be utilized from the time they are received until benefits are paid.

investment policy statement—document drafted between a portfolio manager and a client that outlines rules for the manager. This statement provides portfolio goals and objectives and describes the acceptable strategies that the manager may employ to meet these objectives.

investment portfolio—collection of securities (e.g., stocks, bonds) held by an individual or institution.

investment return—see *return* and *yield*.

investment risk—potential for a loss relative to the expected return on an investment. Types of investment risk include *business risk*, *currency risk*, *default risk*, *inflation risk*, *interest rate risk*, *liquidity risk*, *management risk*, *market risk*, *nonmarket risk*, *operational risk* and *prepayment risk*.

investment-sensitive life insurance—see *variable life insurance*.

investment trust—see *investment company*.

investor—someone who commits money to the purchase of property or another security in order to achieve a financial gain.

involuntary termination—see *plan termination*.

IPA model HMO—also called an open panel plan or individual practice HMO, a health maintenance organization (HMO) that contracts with individual physicians or small groups of physicians to provide services to HMO enrollees at a negotiated per capita or fee-for-service rate. Physicians maintain their own offices and can contract with other HMOs. See also *closed panel*, *health maintenance organization (HMO)* and *independent practice association (IPA)*.

IRA—see *individual retirement account (IRA)*.

irrevocable beneficiary—person or organization named in an insurance policy or pension plan to receive benefits if the insured person or plan participant dies while the policy or plan is in effect. Once irrevocable beneficiaries have been named, they cannot be removed as beneficiaries.

irrevocable trust—trust that cannot be changed or terminated. See also *revocable trust* and *trust fund*.

J

January effect—tendency for stock prices to be higher in January after tax-related selling is completed at the end of the previous year.

Jensen's alpha—risk-adjusted return measure that is an investment portfolio's return minus the return predicted by the capital asset pricing model. See also *capital asset pricing model (CAPM)* and *risk-adjusted return measure*.

job analysis—also referred to as a job audit, a systematic study of the tasks, responsibilities, knowledge, skills, work environment, etc., associated with a specific employment position. A job analysis may be used to determine the most appropriate classification, compensation or whether an individual is capable of fulfilling the responsibilities of the job.

job audit—see *job analysis*.

job classification—group of employment positions sufficiently alike with respect to duties and responsibilities to justify a common name and similar treatment in selection, compensation and other employment processes.

job cluster—series of employment positions considered together for compensation, evaluation and other administration purposes. A cluster is based on factors such as common qualifications, technology, licensing, working conditions, union jurisdictions, workplace, career paths and organizational tradition.

job conditioning—regimen of progressive physical and/or psychological training established to help a disabled employee return to work.

Job Creation and Worker Assistance Act of 2002 (JCWAA)—legislation passed by the U.S. Congress to stimulate the economy after the terrorist attacks of September 11, 2001. The act allows taxpayers to claim an education IRA exclusion and HOPE scholarship credit in the same year. It created an above-the-line deduction of up to $250 annually for the classroom expenses of elementary and secondary school teachers. JCWAA also included funding relief for defined benefit plans and technical corrections to the Economic Growth and Tax Relief Reconciliation Act of 2001 relating to qualified retirement plans.

job description—detailed summary, usually written, of the major components of an employment position. In the U.S., the typical job description consists of six major components: essential job functions, knowledge and critical skills, physical demands, environmental factors, the roles of the Americans with Disabilities Act and other federal laws such as the Occupational Safety and Health Act (OSHA), and any explanatory information that may be necessary to clarify job duties or responsibilities.

job discrimination—see *discrimination*.

job enrichment—effort to motivate employees by giving them increased responsibility and variety in their jobs.

job evaluation—systematic process for assessing a job-worth hierarchy and pay differentials within an organization. Two basic approaches are using market data or job content.

job family—jobs of the same nature but requiring different skill and responsibility levels or working conditions.

job grade—class, level or group into which jobs of the same or similar value are grouped for compensation purposes. Usually, all jobs in a grade have the same pay minimum, midpoint and maximum. However, market conditions may result in some differences.

job lock—when a worker remains in a particular job for fear of losing employee benefits (e.g., health insurance coverage). In the U.S., the Affordable Care Act of 2010 (ACA) has reduced the occurrence of job lock by prohibiting insurers from refusing to cover individuals due to preexisting conditions and providing coverage through the private health exchanges; however, high insurance rates continue to be a cause for some individuals.

job sharing—situation in which two people, typically in career-oriented professional positions, perform the tasks of one full-time position. Job sharing offers workers increased flexibility in their personal schedules, typically for child or dependent care. Salary and benefits are prorated.

job specifications—description of the worker characteristics required to competently perform a job.

job tenure—length of time an employee has worked for an employer.

job training—see *training and development program*.

job-worth hierarchy—perceived internal value of jobs in relationship to each other within an organization. A job-worth hierarchy forms the basis for grouping similar jobs together and establishing salary ranges.

joint administration—sharing of supervisory functions related to the operation of an employee benefit plan by a committee or board of trustees comprised of individuals representing both labor and management.

joint and several liability—situation in which more than one party is liable for repayment of a debt or other obligation and the creditor can obtain compensation from one or more parties, either individually or jointly.

joint and survivor (J&S) benefit—provision in annuity and pension plan contracts that provides payments for the lifetime of the holder (the annuitant) and the holder's survivor.
—In the U.S., federal law requires employers that sponsor defined benefit plans to offer joint and survivor annuities as the default payout option. Plan participants must obtain the written consent of their spouses before they may choose a single life annuity. The benefit payable when there is a joint and survivor benefit may be reduced to account for the extended life expectancy of the two persons. See also *annuity, automatic survivor coverage, contingent annuity option, pop-up option* and *qualified joint and survivor annuity (QJSA)*.
—Some Canadian jurisdictions require a joint and survivor option be provided by a pension plan if the member has a spouse at the time of retirement. A plan may provide level payments as long as one partner lives or reduce the benefit when one partner dies. In some cases, the reduction occurs only upon the death of the plan member. The reductions permitted vary by jurisdiction. See also *joint life with last survivor annuity*.

joint apprenticeship and training committee (JATC)—typically, the sponsor of an apprenticeship and training program. In the United States, the JATC is responsible for the administration of the program under the National Apprenticeship Act.

joint beneficiary—person legally entitled to share in the proceeds of an insurance policy or a retirement plan.

Joint Commission—formerly known as the Joint Commission on Accreditation of Healthcare Organizations (JCAHO), an independent nonprofit organization based in the United States that develops standards for, periodically evaluates and awards accreditation status to facilities such as hospitals, skilled nursing facilities and health maintenance organizations. Most managed care plans and some government programs such as Medicare and Medicaid require Joint Commission certification. See also *accreditation* and *Accreditation Canada*.

joint employer—company that shares control with another company over the working conditions of an employee. Joint employers commonly include temporary staffing or leasing agencies.

joint life with last survivor annuity—insurance product that provides an income to an individual and the individual's spouse until both spouses have died. The annuity also gives the individual the option to give a portion of the remaining income to a third-party beneficiary until the surviving spouse's death.

jointly sponsored pension plan—as applied in Canada, a defined benefit retirement plan in which the funding and various decisions regarding the funding of the plan is a shared responsibility of both the plan sponsor and the employees.

jointly trusteed single employer plan—employee benefit plan of one employer that is administered by a board of trustees consisting of an equal number of employee and employer representatives.

joint survivorship—see *joint and survivor benefit*.

joint tenancy—equal ownership of property by two or more persons with the rights of survivorship. See also *tenancy in common*.

joint venture (JV)—agreement between two individuals or businesses to invest in a single business property or activity. The joint venture may be a partnership or corporation.

junior security—see *subordinated debt*.

junk bond—debt security with a low credit rating that typically has a rating below "BBB" from S&P and below "Baa" from Moody's. Because of their higher risk of default, junk bonds pay a higher interest rate than that paid on investment grade bonds. Junk bonds are also referred to as high-yield bonds or speculative grade bonds.

jury duty—period of time during which a person is obliged to be available for or to serve as a member of a panel asked to render a verdict in court.

jury duty leave—time off granted to an employee called for jury duty. Most states spell out employer obligations for granting leave. See also *jury duty* and *jury duty pay*.

jury duty pay—compensation to employees by an employer that supplements the small stipend provided by local governments for jury duty. See also *jury duty*.

juvenile insurance—cash value life insurance policy written on the life of a child. See also *cash value life insurance* and *dependent life insurance*.

K

Keogh plan—qualified retirement plan for self-employed persons and their employees in the U.S. to which yearly tax-deductible contributions up to a specified limit can be made if the plan meets certain requirements of the IRC. Keogh plans, also known as HR 10 plans, include defined benefit and defined contribution plans. Withdrawals from the plan are restricted before the age of 59½.

key employee—employee who at any time during a plan year was (1) an officer with earnings of more than $130,000 (as indexed under IRC Section 416(i)), (2) a 5% owner of the employer or (3) a 1% owner of the employer who earned more than $150,000. Also known as a key person.

key employee insurance—life or disability insurance purchased by a business on the life of an employee whose continued participation in the business is necessary to the firm's success and whose death or disability would cause an adverse impact on the company. The insurance company agrees to reimburse the business for the financial loss caused by the loss of the employee. Also referred to as *key person insurance*. See also *business continuation insurance*.

key person—see *key employee*.

key person insurance—see *key employee insurance*.

kiddie tax—levy designed by the U.S. Congress to put the brakes on high-income households funneling unearned income through their kids to reduce their overall tax liability. As of 2008, a child under the age of 19 (or older, if the child is in school) has to pay the higher of the child's or parents' highest income tax rate on any investment income (i.e., interest or dividends) that the child earns above a threshold amount. Any salary or wages earned by the child through full- or part-time employment is taxed at the child's tax rate and not subject to the kiddie tax rule. See also *gift tax, Uniform Gifts to Minors Act (UGMA)* and *Uniform Transfers to Minors Act (UTMA)*.

kiosk—computer-based interactive system installed in high-traffic employee areas to perform a range of functions such as accessing general information about benefits, checking the status of savings plans, making calculations of benefits coverage and changing the mix of benefits in a flexible benefit program. Employees can access the kiosk in passing and interact through a touchscreen or mouse. See also *employee self-service (ESS)*.

knowledge-based pay—compensation system based upon an employee's attainment of skills and education. Knowledge-based pay can be an incentive for employees to acquire additional training and education, thus upgrading overall workforce skills. See also *skill-based pay*.

KSOP—qualified retirement plan available in the U.S. that combines an employee stock ownership plan (ESOP) with a 401(k) plan. The employer matches employee contributions with stock rather than cash. KSOPs benefit companies by reducing expenses that would arise by separately operating an ESOP and 401(k) retirement plan.

L

labor force—total number of people employed or looking for work. When the Bureau of Labor Statistics calculates the labor force in the United States, all persons at least 16 years of age who are employed in civilian and military jobs as well as those actively seeking employment are included. The statistic does not include people who are not looking for work, those engaged in housework in their own homes, full-time students and unpaid family workers who labor fewer than 15 hours a week (e.g., family farm workers).

labor grade—salary classification of a specific job title.

labor law—also known as employment law, the rules, regulations and court precedents that govern the relationship between workers and management. Labor law defines the rights, privileges, duties and responsibilities of each.

labor-management cooperation committee (LMCC)—authorized under the Labor-Management Cooperation Act of 1978 (LMCA), a group of individuals representing labor and management formed to address issues of mutual concern (e.g., labor-management relationships, job security, organizational effectiveness, economic development). An LMCC may be organized for a plan, an area or an industry.

Labor-Management Relations Act of 1947 (LMRA or Taft-Hartley Act)—amendment to the National Labor Relations Act of 1935 initiated to balance the bargaining power of management with that of labor in the United States. While the 1935 legislation focused on unfair labor practices by employers, the 1947 legislation defined and prohibited unfair labor practices by labor. The Taft-Hartley Act (1) outlawed closed shops, (2) prohibited labor actions such as wildcat strikes, solidarity strikes and secondary boycotts, and (3) gave the executive branch of the federal government authority to seek an injunction if an impending or current strike imperiled national health or safety. The Act also granted individual workers the right to prosecute for unfair labor practices by union or company officials and spelled out the rules under which multiemployer benefit plans must operate. See also *multiemployer plan* and *National Labor Relations Act of 1935 (NLRA or Wagner Act)*.

Labor-Management Reporting and Disclosure Act of 1959 (LMRDA or Landrum-Griffin Act)—U.S. legislation that regulates the internal affairs of labor unions and their official relationships with employers. The Act:
- Requires unions to submit annual financial reports to the U.S. Department of Labor
- Requires union officers and employees, including union trustees, to file an LM-30 report if any of these persons receive an economic benefit from service providers to a pension or welfare fund. (Some service providers under these circumstances, in addition, are required to file Form LM-10.)
- Bars members of the Communist Party and convicted felons from holding union office
- Declares that every union officer must act as a fiduciary in handling the assets and conducting the affairs of the union
- Provides certain minimum standards before a union may expel or take other disciplinary action against a member of the union
- Establishes procedures for the orderly conduct of union elections.

See also *Form LM-10* and *Form LM-30*.

lactation program—in the workplace, the provision of a private space, access to a refrigerator and sufficient break time for a nursing mother to breast-feed a child or express milk. Some states have implemented lactation accommodation laws that specify employer obligations.

ladder portfolio—investment in vehicles such as bonds or certificates of deposit with staggered maturities.

lag—period of time that occurs between one event and another. For example, the period of time between when a claim is made and the payment of the claim. With most public policy efforts to stimulate the economy, there is a lag between when action is taken and results appear.

lapsed policy—insurance contract that has been terminated due to nonpayment of the premium.

large amount pooling—placement of a plan's insurance claims over a specified limit into a pool made up of similar claims from other plans to curb fluctuations in insurance premium amounts. Providers of group life and health insurance may purchase this extra protection for a fee from an insurer, with the amount above the limit absorbed by the insurer. An industrywide pool may also be created to spread the risk of high-cost claims across all insurers.

large cap—short for large market capitalization, a reference to companies with a market value of more than $10 billion. Large caps are bigger than mid caps and smaller than mega caps. Cap classifications are only approximations that change over time. The exact definitions of these terms can also vary among brokerage houses. See also *mega cap, micro cap, mid cap, nano cap* and *small cap*.

large case management—identification and monitoring of persons at high risk of having health problems as well as those with catastrophic illnesses or injuries and/or long-term care needs. Large case management focuses on prevention, appropriate treatment and cost control. A case manager may provide information to a patient on diagnosis and treatment; provide family counseling; make a referral for complex cases such as transplant or neonatal care; assist with arrangements for services; and even negotiate discounts on services, equipment and supplies. Large case management may also be referred to as catastrophic claims management. It is a type of *case management* and *utilization management (UM)*.

lasering—underwriting practice by which a stop-loss insurer may pinpoint one individual with a high-risk condition. The insurer can eliminate coverage or assign a higher stop-loss trigger point for this person. See also *stop-loss insurance*.

late enrollee—for the purposes of group health insurance and according to HIPAA, an individual who enrolls in a group health plan at a time other than during the first period in which he or she is eligible to enroll or during a special enrollment period.

late retirement—see *deferred retirement*.

layoff—temporary suspension or permanent termination of an employee (or, more commonly, employees) for business reasons such as reduced sales or budgetary constraints. Suspension or termination due to poor performance or misconduct is not considered a layoff.

Leapfrog Group, The—voluntary organization representing many of the nation's largest corporations and public agencies that buy health benefits on behalf of their workers. Among other initiatives, Leapfrog works with its employer members to encourage transparency and easy access to health care information and rewards hospitals that have a proven record of high-quality care.

lease—legal contract by which one party (lessee) obtains the temporary use of an asset (e.g., building, copy machine, motor vehicle) from the asset owner (lessor) in exchange for making a series of periodic payments. Included in the lease are the rights and responsibilities of each party.

leaseback—arrangement whereby property is simultaneously sold and leased back to the seller. The seller is released from tax, depreciation and maintenance costs, and the buyer is guaranteed an income from the property. Also referred to as a sale and leaseback and a sale-leaseback, these arrangements are usually long-term continued use.

leased employee—full- or part-time employee of an organization that has contracted the employee's services to another business (referred to as the recipient). The employee's services are directed or controlled by the recipient. The leasing organization handles the human resources functions such as providing employees with health insurance and retirement benefits and paying wages and employment taxes using its own accounts. See also *professional employer organization (PEO)*.

least expensive alternative treatment (LEAT)—benefit plan provision that bases benefit payment on the least costly acceptable alternative treatment necessary to treat a given problem. LEAT is also referred to as the least expensive professionally acceptable alternative treatment (LEPAAT). In dental plans, this is written into the contract and known as the alternate benefit provision (ABP).

leave of absence—period of time during which an employee is not working when he or she typically would be while maintaining the status of employee. This period may be with or without pay.

legally required benefit—see *mandatory benefit*.

legal reserve—minimum amount of funds a company must keep to meet future claims and obligations. Typically, insurance companies are obligated by government to maintain a legal reserve to ensure their solvency. In Canada, minimum levels of capital and liquidity are determined by the Office of the Superintendent of Financial Institutions, while the individual states establish reserve standards in the U.S.

legal services plan—also referred to as legal aid coverage, a group benefit that provides convenient and affordable legal assistance. Examples of covered services include legal advice, drafting of wills and house closings.

legend drug—see *prescription drug*.

length of stay (LOS)—number of days that elapse between admission and discharge from a hospital or health care facility.

lessee—person, corporation or other entity to which property is leased.

lessor—person, corporation or other entity that owns and leases property.

letter bond—debt security not registered with the Securities and Exchange Commission (SEC) and, therefore, an asset that cannot be sold in the public market.

letter of credit (LOC)—agreement between a financial institution such as a bank and a sponsoring organization that provides for the security of employee benefits. The organization pays premiums to the financial institution in exchange for an agreement that the institution will pay the organization the face value of the LOC if an event specified in the agreement occurs such as a default on benefit payments or a change of control. LOCs are used in Canada to provide security of benefits without fully prefunding the benefits for supplemental executive retirement plans (SERPs) and are also permitted to meet the funding requirements for solvency deficiencies in registered retirement plans (RRPs) in some provinces.

letter ruling—private ruling issued by the IRS in response to a request from a taxpayer about the tax consequences of a proposed or completed transaction. Letter rulings are not considered precedents for use by taxpayers other than the one who requested the ruling, but they do give an indication of the current attitude of the IRS toward a particular type of transaction.

letter stock—shares of a company not registered with the Securities and Exchange Commission (SEC) and, therefore, an asset that cannot be sold in the public market.

level income option—also referred to as a notched option, the choice given a plan participant to receive an increased pension payment at retirement that will be reduced a specific amount when the retiree becomes eligible for a pension under a government program.

level load fee—see *12b-1 fee*.

level premium—payment for a life insurance policy that remains unchanged throughout the life of the policy. In a level premium plan, reserves accumulate in the early years of the policy because the actual cost of coverage is less than the premium charged. In later years, the actual cost is more than the premium charged.

level premium funding—approach to accumulating money for payment of future pension benefits where the contributions for any one employee are the same until normal retirement age, at which time the benefit is fully funded.

level term life insurance—death benefit policy with a premium that remains unchanged versus a policy with a premium that increases with the increased risk as a person ages.

leverage—strategy that uses borrowed money to purchase financial assets with the objective of increasing returns. Leverage can be created through options, futures, margins and other financial instruments. For example, instead of investing $1,000 in ten shares of stock, an investor might decide to invest the same money in options contracts that would make it possible to control 500 shares. Companies also use leverage to increase equity. A business may borrow money to invest in business operations and create more opportunity to increase value for shareholders. Leveraging has the potential to magnify a positive investment outcome, but there is also the risk of magnifying a negative outcome.

leveraged buyout (LBO)—purchase of another company by using a substantial amount of borrowed funds (e.g., loans, bonds) with very little or no equity. A ratio of 90% debt to 10% equity is common. Because of this high debt/equity ratio, bonds used in an LBO are generally referred to as junk bonds. Assets of the company being purchased and those of the acquiring company are typically used as collateral. A leveraged buyout makes it possible to make a large acquisition without having to commit a lot of capital.

leveraged ESOP—employee stock ownership plan (ESOP) in which money is borrowed by the ESOP trust for the purpose of buying the stock of the employer. The stock is normally held as security by the lender and released for allocation to participant accounts as the loan is paid off.

liability—legal obligation, responsibility or potential loss. Bonds, mortgages, accrued taxes and unpaid bills are all examples of financial liabilities. Individuals and plans also face the possibility that they will be held legally liable for injury or harm caused to another; liability insurance offers a means to reduce the size of a legal liability that might occur. See also *actuarial accrued liability, current liability, fiduciary responsibility, joint and several liability* and *liability insurance.*

liability-driven investment (LDI)—see *asset liability matching.*

liability insurance—promise by an insurance company that it will provide a benefit payable on behalf of a covered party who is held legally responsible (liable) for harming others or the property of others. See also *fiduciary liability insurance* and *stop-loss insurance.*

liability matching—see *asset liability matching.*

liability risk—potential losses that arise when an individual or organization is sued for bodily injury or other damages.

licensure—process by which an agency of government grants permission to an individual or organization to engage in a given occupation or business. Licensure usually requires an applicant to provide evidence of competency. Accountants, attorneys, brokers, insurance agents, doctors and nurses are examples of professionals who must be licensed. See also *accreditation* and *certification.*

lien—right of one person, usually a creditor, to keep possession or control of the property of another for the purpose of satisfying a debt. See also *mechanic's lien.*

life annuity—promise under an insurance contract or defined benefit pension plan to make periodic payments (usually monthly) for the lifetime of an individual (the annuitant). Payments stop upon the death of the annuitant.

life care—see *continuing care retirement community (CCRC).*

lifecycle benefits—benefits designed to meet the needs of employees throughout the stages of life: when they are single, married, with the birth or adoption of a child, as the child grows, when they are responsible for elderly parents, before they retire, after they retire and at death.

lifecycle fund—see *target-date fund.*

lifecycle pension plan—defined benefit retirement plan that expresses benefits as a lump sum rather than as an annuity. There are no account balances for the plan participants. Under the lifecycle plan, a participant earns credits for each year of service. Age is not directly a factor, except as it pertains to how much service an individual could accrue. The total of these credits is considered as a percentage, which is multiplied by the final average salary of the participant to determine what lump sum will be paid at retirement. Also referred to as a retirement bonus or lump-sum plan.

life-enhancing drug—see *lifestyle drug.*

life expectancy—length of time a person of a given age is expected to live. The period is a statistical average, based on mortality tables showing the rate of death given specific demographics such as age and gender. See also *mortality rate.*

Life Income Fund (LIF)—registered retirement account offered by Canadian financial institutions that is used to hold and pay out pension money upon retirement. An LIF is an alternative to the traditional life annuity and gives the account owner the opportunity to maintain control over pension capital, its investment and the flow of income. Retiring individuals with money purchase plans, defined benefit plans (if permitted by the plan), locked-in retirement accounts and locked-in retirement income funds may transfer funds to an LIF. Legislation restricts the minimum and maximum that can be withdrawn. Any funds that remain at the time an account owner reaches the age of 90 must be used to purchase a life annuity.

life insurance—insurance contract that provides a sum of money if the person who is insured dies while the policy is in effect. See also *cash value life insurance, corporate-owned life insurance (COLI), dependent life insurance, group insurance, insurance, juvenile insurance, participating insurance, retired lives reserve (RLR), split dollar life insurance* and *term life insurance*.

Lifelong Learning Plan (LLP)—program established by the Government of Canada that permits the withdrawal of some funds from a Registered Retirement Savings Plan (RRSP) for the training or education of a plan participant as well as the participant's spouse, common-law partner and children. LLP withdrawals are considered loans that must be repaid to the plan.

life partners—see *domestic partnership*.

lifestyle drugs—prescription drugs, such as those used to treat obesity, erectile dysfunction, male pattern baldness, infertility, smoking cessation or cosmetic problems (e.g., Botox), which are not considered medically necessary. Lifestyle drugs are frequently excluded from the list of drugs covered by a formulary. They are also referred to as *life-enhancing drugs*.

lifestyle fund—see *target-risk fund*.

lifetime annuity—insurance contract that provides income for the remaining life of a person (the annuitant). A variation of lifetime annuities continues income until the second one of two annuitants dies (joint and survivor option). The amount that is paid depends on the age of the annuitant (or ages, if a two-life annuity), the amount paid into the annuity and, if a fixed annuity, the interest rate the insurance company believes it can support for the length of the expected payout period. With a pure lifetime annuity, the payments stop when the annuitant dies, regardless of when the payments began. The purchaser may have an option added to the lifetime annuity contract that guarantees payments for a fixed period of time or a refund of principal. See also *annuity, fixed annuity, fixed period annuity, joint and survivor benefit, refund annuity* and *reversionary annuity*.

lifetime limit—maximum benefits a person may get from a health benefit plan in a lifetime. After a lifetime limit is reached, a plan no longer pays for covered services. The Affordable Care Act of 2010 (ACA) prohibits health plans from putting a lifetime dollar limit on most benefits received.

lifetime maximum benefit—see *lifetime limit*.

light duty—work that is less demanding (physically, mentally or because it requires fewer hours of work) than an employee's usual position.

limited benefit health plan—see *bare bones health plan*.

limited formulary—preferred drug list with a restricted number of medications permitted in each therapeutic class covered by a benefit plan. The addition of a new drug requires the deletion of a medication already on the list. See also *closed formulary, drug formulary, formulary, incentive formulary, open formulary, partially closed formulary, therapeutic class* and *unlimited formulary*.

limited liability—financial obligation limited to a fixed sum, most commonly the value of a person's investment in a limited liability company or partnership.

limited liability company (LLC)—legal structure for businesses that is designed to combine attributes of corporate and partnership structures. An LLC is an incorporated business owned by a limited number of shareholders with limited financial obligations. They are taxed like a partnership, preventing double taxation.

limited partner—investor who has no management authority and no responsibility for debts beyond his or her initial investment. Return on investment may also be limited by the partnership agreement. See also *general partner, limited partnership* and *silent partner*.

limited partnership—unincorporated business with two or more investors that has at least one general partner and one or more "limited" partners. While general partners have unlimited liability for the financial obligations of the business, the liability of the limited partners is no more than their investment in the firm. The general partners pay the limited partners a return on their investment (similar to a dividend) that is usually defined in the partnership agreement. See also *general partnership* and *limited partner.*

limited payment life insurance—variation of whole life insurance with premium payments for a shorter, predetermined number of years (e.g., 10, 15 or 20 years). The death benefit remains available for the lifetime of the insured or until the insured reaches a specific age (e.g., 100 or 120 years). Premiums may be paid monthly, quarterly, semiannually or annually. The policy's guaranteed cash value grows tax-deferred. Because there are fewer payments, premiums for limited payment life insurance tend to be higher than those paid for other whole life policies. See also *whole life insurance.*

limited-scope audit—investigation of procedures, financial accounts, etc., in which the investigator (auditor) is allowed to rely on the certification of an institutional trustee or custodian, hence, reducing the scope of testing of the information. In the U.S., a limited-scope audit of a benefit plan is allowed under circumstances specified by ERISA and usually applies to information prepared and certified by a bank or similar institution or by an insurance carrier that is regulated and subject to periodic examination by a state or federal agency.

limiting charge—maximum amount a nonparticipating health care provider can bill a Medicare patient for covered services. Also called a charge limit.

limit order—instruction from an investor to a broker to buy or sell a security at a set price.

line manager—individual who has direct responsibility for other employees, including their work and duties.

liquid asset—also called a quick asset, a resource that can quickly be converted to cash with no significant loss in value. In addition to cash, examples of highly liquid assets include money in savings and checking accounts, U.S. Treasury notes and money market funds. At the other extreme are relatively illiquid assets such as real estate and collectibles.

liquidated claim—dollar amount established by contract or court judgment that one party owes another for a breach of contract.

liquidation—process of converting securities or other property into cash. The liquidation of a company involves the sale of all company assets followed by the payment of all debts, with any remaining funds distributed to the owners/shareholders.

liquidity—ease with which an asset can be converted into cash without a significant loss in value. Assets vary greatly in their level of liquidity. Cash and money market funds are examples of very liquid assets. At the other extreme are illiquid assets such as real estate and collectibles. Liquidity also refers to the ability of a business to generate cash in order to meet its financial obligations. See also *illiquid* and *liquid asset.*

liquidity risk—risk that an asset cannot be quickly converted into cash without a significant loss in value. Liquidity risk occurs when a seller is unable to find an interested buyer. Emerging markets and low-volume markets frequently have higher liquidity risk. See also *illiquid, liquid asset* and *liquidity.*

liquid market—exchange where selling and buying can be accomplished quickly and easily without great fluctuations in price. Liquid markets are characterized by a large number of interested buyers and sellers who are willing and able to trade. In a liquid market, price volatility is minimal.

listed stock—ownership shares of a company traded on an organized stock exchange.

list price—published dollar amount that is not the actual price paid for a drug. Calculating the price of drugs in certain pharmaceutical transactions is based on list prices. The *average wholesale price (AWP)* and the *wholesale acquisition cost (WAC)* are examples of list prices.

living benefit—see *viatical settlement.*

living trust—also known as an inter vivos trust, a trust that becomes effective during the life of the individuals who own the trust. Property placed in the trust is managed by a trustee for the benefit of the owners. Living trusts are not included in probate when the owner of the trust dies.

living wage—hourly rate of pay that is high enough for an employee and his or her family to maintain a given level of living. Generally, this level is described as meeting basic needs and maintaining health.

living will—legal document that conveys a person's desires concerning health care if the person is unable to communicate his or her wishes at some future date. This special type of will is designed to avoid confusion and potential disputes among family, friends and health care professionals. Referred to as an advance directive by some, the living will tells how a person feels about care intended to sustain life. A person can accept or refuse medical care and address specific issues such as the use of dialysis, breathing machines, feeding tubes, resuscitation and organ donation. See also *durable power of attorney*.

load—fee or commission charged at the time a mutual fund share is bought or sold. The two general types of sales loads are front-end loads and back-end loads. See also *12b-1 fee, back-end load, front-end load, load fund* and *no-load fund*.
—amount added to the estimated cost of a pension plan to provide for expenses of a variable or minor nature (e.g., special retirement pensions, trustee fees).

load fund—mutual fund that charges a fee when shares are bought or sold. See also *12b-1 fee, back-end load, front-end load, load* and *no-load fund*.

loan broker—see *mortgage broker*.

local national—employee who lives in the place where a subsidiary or branch of a multinational company operates. Local nationals are usually, but not always, a citizen of the country where they reside and work.

lockbox—service provided by a bank or other third party in which payments are collected at a postal or local drop box, then deposited into a bank account with transaction receipts sent to the business that has arranged for the service. This procedure is used to speed up the processing of insurance premiums and other payments instead of having payments sent to a central office.

lockdown—see *blackout period*.

locked in
—when investors are unwilling or unable to sell a stock because they will incur taxes or other financial penalties.
—when transfer or withdrawal of funds from a retirement plan is restricted by law and/or would result in an early withdrawal penalty.
—when members of a health plan are restricted to certain doctors, hospitals or other health care providers.

locked-in account—under Canadian pension legislation, an individual retirement savings plan with money that cannot be removed until the individual either retires or reaches a specific age—though a few exceptions do exist, such as a member's shortened life expectancy and financial hardship grounds. Money earned in the account is also considered to be locked in.

Locked-In Retirement Account (LIRA)—see *locked-in account*.

Locked-In Retirement Savings Plan (LRSP)—see *locked-in account*.

lock-in—minimum period of time that a plan member, once enrolled, must stay enrolled in an insurance program. Lock-ins are most common for small group, voluntary and individual insurance policies to prevent adverse selection. While a true lock-in is difficult to enforce, some plans require members to pay the first year's premium in advance to achieve a similar result.

lockout—work stoppage in which an employer prevents employees from working, usually in an effort to force workers to come to an agreement with management on a labor issue.

lock-out period—time after a participant exits an insurance plan before he or she is allowed to reenroll. Lock-out periods, like lock-ins, are common with small group, voluntary and individual insurance plans to prevent or reduce adverse selection.

London Stock Exchange (LSE)—originating in 1773, the primary stock exchange in the United Kingdom and the largest in Europe. The LSE is the most international stock exchange, attracting companies from more than 60 nations.

longevity risk—chance that a person will live longer than his or her retirement income can support.

long-term care (LTC)—variety of medical and nonmedical services needed by the elderly, the disabled, and persons with chronic health issues who need assistance with the activities of daily living (e.g., feeding themselves, dressing and bathing). Long-term care can be provided at home, in the community, in an assisted living facility or in a nursing home. See also *extended care facility (ECF)*.

long-term care insurance—insurance that covers costs associated with the long-term care provided at home or in a residential facility (e.g., nursing home) for persons who are unable to care for themselves as the result of a chronic illness, disability or mental impairment (e.g., dementia, Alzheimer's disease). Long-term care insurance is available to some workers as an employee benefit; it is most frequently purchased as an individual policy.

long-term debt-to-equity ratio—see *debt-to-equity ratio*.

long-term disability (LTD)—injury or illness that prevents a person from continuing in the occupation for which he or she was trained. For most purposes, an LTD is defined as lasting more than three to six months.

long-term disability (LTD) insurance—insurance that offers income payments for long-term injuries, illnesses and disabilities. Generally, monthly payments commence after a specified waiting period and continue while the employee remains disabled or up to the age of 65. Payments are a percentage of the earned income lost by the employee as a result of the disability. Long-term disability insurance is available to some workers as an employee benefit; it may also be purchased as an individual policy. See also *disability* and *short-term disability (STD) insurance*.

long-term gain/loss—for U.S. tax purposes, an increase or decrease in the value of a capital asset that has been held for more than one year. Long-term gains are presently taxed at a lower rate than the gains on assets held one year or less. See also *capital gain/loss* and *short-term gain/loss*.

long-term incentive plan (LTIP)—reward system created to improve an employee's long-term (multiyear) performance that provides financial incentives tied to specific goals such as an increase in a company's stock price. Executives, high-level managers and professionals are those most often provided such an incentive. A common approach is to use company shares as the incentive, with half the shares provided upon achievement of the goals and the remaining shares given only if the employee stays with the company for a predefined number of years. See also *incentive plan* and *incentive stock option (ISO)*.

look-back period—period of time preceding a specific date or event that is used by government agencies, insurers and other entities for eligibility and regulatory purposes. For example, the U.S. government has look-back periods of five years for the transfer of assets to certain trusts when determining a person's eligibility for Medicaid.

loss—from a financial perspective, a reduction in an amount or value. See also *actuarial gain/loss* and *capital gain/loss*.

loss-of-income benefit—payments made to an insured person or beneficiary to help replace income lost as the result of death or disability. See also *disability, disability insurance* and *life insurance*.

loss ratio—ratio of incurred claims to premiums received by an insurance company. See also *medical loss ratio (MLR)*.

loss reserve—estimate of the value of a claim or group of claims not yet paid by an insurance company.

lost participants—plan participants who have vested benefits but whose whereabouts are unknown.

loyalty program—provision of a reward to participants who remain continuously enrolled in a benefit plan or are insured with the same company for an extended period of time. Examples of rewards include higher benefits to the participant or reduced premiums with each year of participation.

lump-sum compensation—money paid at one time to a beneficiary, in contrast to a series of smaller payments made over a period of time.

lump-sum distribution—payment to a plan participant or beneficiary for the entire amount in a retirement account as a single cash payment versus a series of payments over time.

lump-sum plan—see *lifecycle pension plan*.

lump-sum refund annuity—see *refund annuity*.

M

macroeconomics—see *economics*.

magnetic resonance imaging (MRI)—noninvasive diagnostic procedure that takes photos of the internal structures of the body using a powerful magnet and radio waves linked to a computer. See also *computerized axial tomography (CAT or CT) scan* and *positron emission tomography (PET)*.

mail-order drug program—method of dispensing medication directly to a patient through the mail or other shipping service. Such programs often reduce the cost for prescriptions, especially long-term drug therapies.

mail-order pharmacy—also referred to as a mail-service pharmacy, an organization that provides pharmacy services via telephone, mail or the Internet and delivers medications using the mail or another shipping service. See also *online pharmacy*.

mail-service pharmacy—see *mail-order pharmacy*.

maintenance drug—prescription medication taken for the treatment of a chronic condition such as high blood pressure or high cholesterol for an extended period of time.

maintenance drug list—also referred to as an additional drug benefit list, medications approved for dispensing in larger quantities for long-term use and chronic conditions.

maintenance-of-benefits (MOB) plan—health insurance that covers persons eligible for Medicare. The benefit paid by the MOB plan is calculated on the plan's eligible expenses once those paid by Medicare are subtracted along with deductibles, coinsurance and any other benefit limitations.

major diagnostic categories (MDC)—organization of all possible principal diagnoses into 25 mutually exclusive groups. The diagnoses in each category correspond to a single organ system or etiology and, in general, are associated with a particular medical specialty.

major life activity—actions that include, but are not limited to, caring for oneself, performing manual tasks, seeing, hearing, eating, sleeping, walking, standing, lifting, bending, speaking, breathing, learning, reading, concentrating, thinking, communicating and working; the operation of a major bodily function; and the operation of an individual organ within a body system.

major medical insurance—form of health care coverage that pays for many of the medical expenses not covered by basic medical coverage. Major medical usually covers hospital stays, surgeries, intensive care, x-rays and other hospital fees after any deductibles have been met. Coinsurance is a common element of this coverage; a 20% payment by the insured is typical. Major medical plans tend to fall into one of two groups: comprehensive major medical insurance and supplemental major medical insurance. Comprehensive coverage combines basic and major medical coverage in one plan. Supplemental coverage is a separate major medical plan that picks up the expenses not covered by the basic policy. The term *catastrophic health insurance* is used interchangeably with *major medical insurance*. See also *basic medical insurance, comprehensive major medical insurance* and *supplemental major medical insurance*.
—for Canada, see *extended medical expense*.

malfunction of the body—medical condition that results from the failure of one or more of the body's systems (e.g., respiration, digestion) versus those conditions caused by an accident.

malingering—intentional fabrication or exaggeration of a mental or physical disorder in order to obtain drugs or financial compensation, avoid work or evade criminal prosecution or for another external motivation.

malpractice—substandard or wrongful actions on the part of a professional that result in injury or loss to another. Malpractice is usually associated with medical professionals, but it can also be the result of a failure on the part of a lawyer, accountant or other professional.

managed account—arrangement in which an individual client's investment portfolio is managed by a broker or other professional. The allocation of assets is tailored to the specific needs of the account holder. See also *discretionary account*.

managed behavioral healthcare organization (MBHO)—organization that diagnoses and treats mental health and/or substance abuse disorders using managed care techniques. MBHOs are now moving beyond these traditional services to address other behaviors that also affect health and wellness. See also *behavioral health* and *managed care*.

managed behavioral health program—traditionally, the diagnosis and treatment of mental health and/or substance abuse disorders using managed care techniques. Programs now are addressing a broader range of behaviors (e.g., diet, smoking) that also affect health and wellness. Services in such a program are usually "carved out" from a health benefit or insurance plan. See also *behavioral health, carve-out* and *managed care*.

managed care (MC)—approach to health care in which an organization (e.g., HMO, service provider network, insurance company) monitors and recommends service utilization. A primary goal of managed care is to deliver cost-effective care without sacrificing quality or access. Techniques commonly used by managed care programs include provider networks, case management, primary care physicians and components of utilization review. See also *exclusive provider organization (EPO), health maintenance organization (HMO), managed indemnity plan, point-of-service (POS) plan, preferred provider organization (PPO), provider-sponsored organization (PSO)* and *utilization review (UR)*.

managed care organization (MCO)—national or regional network of health care providers offered to employers as an alternative to (or total replacement for) traditional indemnity insurance. Examples of MCOs include a *health maintenance organization (HMO), preferred provider organization (PPO)* and *point-of-service (POS) plan.* See also *managed care.*

managed competition—health care reform strategy in which purchasers of health goods and services, acting on behalf of a large group of consumers, require health care providers to compete through price and quality. The purchasers establish rules of equity, select participating plans, and manage the enrollment process.

managed fund—see *collective investment fund* and *mutual fund.*

managed indemnity plan—almost the same as a standard indemnity plan, but some basic utilization management programs are used, such as precertification, second opinions, concurrent review and case management. Unlike a preferred provider organization (PPO), where fees are deeply discounted and expressed as a fee schedule, managed indemnity plans often base reimbursement on a targeted percentile (e.g., 80th percentile). As a result, managed indemnity plans have reimbursement levels closer to what might be paid under an indemnity (nonmanaged) plan. See also *indemnity insurance* and *utilization management (UM).*

managed payout funds—mutual fund that aims to provide a sustainable retirement income over a fixed time horizon or the lifetime of the investor. Strategies for achieving this goal vary. A fund might provide inflation-protected income using TIPS ladders with end dates, so the funds don't offer longevity protection. Another might issue target-liquidation dates. A third strategy is to attempt to balance income and growth with a targeted distribution rate (e.g., 4%) of principal each year. With this last approach, the actual monthly payments for a year are set in January and may be more or less than the target depending on fund performance. Payment amounts can also change if the investor makes additional investments or withdraws funds from the account. Managed payout funds are designed to be an alternative to an annuity. See also *ladder portfolio, mutual fund* and *Treasury Inflation-Protected Security (TIPS).*

management
—act of getting people together to accomplish desired goals.
—officers of a business responsible for the management process.

management accounting—analysis and manipulation of financial and other data that provide a foundation for business planning and decision making. See also *financial accounting.*

management by objective (MBO)—performance appraisal based on the establishment of specific goals agreed upon by a manager and subordinates. Short-term targets are established, with periodic meetings to discuss progress toward achieving the goals and to provide other feedback. Characteristics of MBO include involving subordinates in the planning process, focusing on quantitative targets and the allocation of rewards tied to the meeting of targets. See also *performance appraisal.*

management fee—money paid by investors for the management of a portfolio. The management fee compensates investment professionals and their firms for selecting which securities to buy and sell, doing the related paperwork, providing investors information about their fund's holdings and performance, etc. See also *12b-1 fee.*

management risk—possibility that an investment professional's decisions to buy and sell assets will negatively affect a portfolio's value. There is no guarantee an investment manager will provide the return investors might expect to achieve.

management services organization (MSO)—organization that sells administrative and other business support services to individual physicians or small group practices. In some cases, the MSO simply provides services for a fee. In other situations, the MSO purchases tangible assets (e.g., buildings, equipment and supplies) and leases them to clients. An MSO can relieve physicians of nonmedical business functions so they can concentrate on the clinical aspects of their practice. The organizations are typically owned by a group of physicians or investors in conjunction with physicians.

manager—in very broad terms, someone who controls resources and expenditures. See also *administrative manager, financial analyst, fund manager, investment manager, line manager, money manager, portfolio manager, private banker* and *risk manager.*

mandate—requirement, often by legislation. For example, a state may mandate that a health plan cover a specific type of service such as chiropractic care or the treatment of autism. Mandates can also place requirements on individuals; the Affordable Care Act of 2010 (ACA) mandates U.S. citizens and legal residents have a minimum amount of health benefits coverage or pay a penalty. See "Benefit mandates" in the *Appendix A: Affordable Care Act of 2010 (ACA).*

mandate-free plan—see *bare-bones health plan.*

mandate-light plan—see *bare-bones health plan.*

mandatory benefit—benefit that is required by statutory law. In the United States, Social Security, Medicare, unemployment insurance and leave under the Family and Medical Leave Act of 1993 are all federally mandated. Workers' compensation is state-mandated. Benefit mandates vary from nation to nation, and companies operating in foreign countries must comply with host-country mandates. Mandates may also be referred to as a statutory or legally required benefit.

mandatory employee contribution—amount that must be paid by a worker in order to participate in a benefit plan or to in some way receive more favorable treatment than those not contributing.

mandatory retirement—see *compulsory retirement*.

manipulation—effort to influence or control another person or thing to one's advantage. See also *stock manipulation*.

manual rate—insurance fee that is applied on a generic basis to similar risks within the same market. Manual rates, also referred to as table rates, used to be published in a ratings manual by an insurance rating organization to assist insurance companies in establishing premiums. Today, insurance companies and rate service organizations in the U.S. are required to file these rates in a manual or as standardized tables with state departments of insurance. See also *class rating*, *community rating* and *experience rating*.

manual rating—see *manual rate*.

margin
—in a general business context, the difference between a sales price and the cost of production.
—for investment purposes, the borrowed money used to purchase securities. Margin may also refer to the amount of equity contributed by an investor as a percentage of the current market value of the securities held in a margin account. See also *buying on margin*.
—also, the portion of the interest rate on an adjustable rate mortgage that is over and above the adjustment index rate. This portion is retained as profit by the lender.

margin account—credit account by a brokerage firm that helps an investor purchase securities. The loan in a margin account is collateralized by the cash or other securities owned by the investor. This collateral must equal a portion of the price of the security being purchased. See also *buying on margin*, *margin* and *margin call*.

marginal cost—increase or decrease in total cost as a result of one more or one less unit of output.

marginal job functions—duties that are not considered essential to a job. In the U.S., employers must consider removing marginal job functions as an accommodation under the Americans with Disabilities Act but do not have to remove essential functions. See also *essential job functions*.

margin call—demand by a broker that an investor deposit enough cash or other collateral to bring the investor's margin up to a minimum requirement. See also *buying on margin*, *margin* and *margin account*.

margin of profit—measure of the financial benefit resulting from a business activity after costs, expressed as a percentage or dollar amount. The percentage is calculated by dividing income by sales. The dollar amount is simply income minus expenses.

marital deduction—tax provision that allows a married person to transfer an unlimited amount of assets to his or her spouse with no tax imposed upon the transfer. The transfer may occur while both persons are still living or as part of the estate process after one spouse dies.

marketability—speed and ease with which something can be sold. The potential for a product or service to be commercially viable. The marketability of assets is also referred to as *liquidity*.

marketable bond—see *fixed-coupon marketable bond*.

marketable securities—stocks, bonds and other financial assets that can be easily sold and converted into cash.

market capitalization—value of a company based on its current share price and the total number of outstanding stocks.

market correction—reverse movement, usually at least 10% decline in the value of a stock, bond, commodity or market index to adjust for an overvaluation. A correction is typically a temporary interruption to an upward trend in the value of an asset or market.

market excess return—rate of return (percent of monetary gain) on a security (e.g., stock, bond) that exceeds a relatively risk-free rate of return.

market exchange—see "Public health exchanges" in the *Appendix A: Affordable Care Act of 2010 (ACA)* and *private health exchange*.

market index—see *index*.

market index ratio—for compensation purposes, a comparison of an individual's salary to the market average for the position. Assume an individual earns $60,000 and a review of external salary information indicates the average for the job externally is $70,000. The market index ratio for the person would be .86, or 86%. See also *compa-ratio*.

market letter—any publication that comments on securities and is prepared for distribution to clients or the public.

market neutral fund—mutual fund with an aggressive investment approach that attempts to deliver superior returns by balancing bullish stock picks with bearish ones. Alternatively, the fund's income may be generated from the interest proceeds of the sales of short securities. These funds attempt to offer a type of investing strategy that has been found chiefly in hedge funds and separately managed accounts. They tend to have fairly high fees as well as turnover.

market order—instructions to a broker to buy or sell a security at the most advantageous price available after the order reaches the trading floor. A buy order is executed at the lowest price available, and a sell order is executed at the highest price available.

market price—also called market value, the dollar amount for which a seller is willing to sell and a buyer is willing (and able) to purchase a good or service in the marketplace.

market pricing—establishing the worth of a good or service based on current market values.

market rate—interest rate or exchange rate at which a transaction occurs in the current market.

market risk—also called systematic risk, the chance that an investment's value will decline as the result of macroeconomic forces that affect all assets in a market. Such risk cannot be eliminated through diversification. See also *nonmarket risk*.

market timing—making decisions to buy and sell securities based on market predictions. The goal is to sell when prices are high and buy when prices are low.

market value—see *market price*.

market value adjusted annuity—annuity that allows the holder to select and fix the time period and interest rate over which the annuity will grow and offers the holder the flexibility to withdraw money before the end of the time period selected. The withdrawal flexibility is achieved by adjusting the annuity's value up or down to reflect the change in the market interest rates from the start of the selected time period to the time of withdrawal. See also *annuity* and *fixed period annuity*.

market value per share—current price at which a single share of stock is trading in the open market.

mark-to-market accounting—see *fair value accounting*.

mass withdrawal—in the context of multiemployer benefit plans, the exit of all the employers from a plan that results in plan termination. Under ERISA, liability for employers that withdraw in the plan year that the mass withdrawal occurs is calculated under the normal rules, except no relief provisions apply. Certain benefit reductions and suspensions also apply. Employers that withdrew during the three years prior to the mass withdrawal are treated as if they were part of the mass withdrawal. The Pension Benefit Guaranty Corporation has issued regulations concerning the various administrative steps a plan must go through if a mass withdrawal occurs. See also *complete withdrawal* and *partial withdrawal*.

master contract—agreement between an employer or plan sponsor and an insurance company that provides coverage for a large group of employees. The individuals covered are not considered parties to the contract.

master limited partnership—investment that combines the tax benefits of a limited partnership with the liquidity of publicly traded securities.

master plan
—in broad terms, an outline of the process to be followed to achieve a goal.
—in the benefits field, a standardized retirement plan that has been approved and qualified by the IRS and made available by an insurance company, bank, mutual fund or other financial institution for the use of employers. Employers simply sign a participating agreement. Contributions from the multiple employers that sign up for the plan are placed in a single trust account. See also *model plan, nonstandardized plan, prototype plan* and *standardized plan*.

master trust—pooling of assets or trusts for multiple plans under one trust agreement.

matching contribution—funds an employer puts in a retirement plan on behalf of an employee. The amount is typically a preestablished percent of a contribution made by the employee, up to a set maximum.

matching gift—employer's match (usually dollar for dollar) for an employee's contribution to a qualified charity.

material information—knowledge that is relevant to a decision. Material information can affect a stock transaction, sale of real estate or an insurer's willingness to provide insurance. See also *insider*.

materiality concept—principle that accountants focus on items of significance in reports and ignore insignificant details; otherwise, accounting would be burdened with minutiae.

material misrepresentation—misstatement, hiding of a fact or falsification that, if known to another party, would significantly change a contract, transaction, etc. For example, a plan participant might have made a different decision regarding receipt of benefits or an insurance company might have chosen to not issue a policy if they had been provided additional information.

material modification—significant or substantial change to a benefit plan. See also *summary of material modifications (SMM)* and *summary plan description (SPD)*.

maternity benefit—employer-provided benefit for a new mother that may include paid or unpaid leave, flexible work opportunities, health insurance provisions, and information resources. See also *Employment Insurance (EI)* and *Pregnancy Discrimination Act of 1978 (PDA)*.

maternity leave—paid or unpaid time off work provided a mother with the arrival of a new child. See also *Employment Insurance (EI), Family and Medical Leave Act of 1993 (FMLA), parental leave* and *Pregnancy Discrimination Act of 1978 (PDA)*.

mature—when the age distribution of participants (including retirees) in a defined benefit retirement plan is stable and expected to be the same in future years despite new entries and dropouts (i.e., deaths and withdrawals). Companies with a pension plan that has long been in effect and a workforce that is neither increasing nor decreasing typically have mature groups of participants. Newly established companies and growing companies ordinarily have immature employee groups. Employee groups covered by pension plans that have just recently been adopted also tend to be immature.

maturity—date on which a loan, bond, mortgage or other debt security becomes due and is to be paid.

maturity value—amount an issuer of a bond or other debt instrument will pay the holder on the instrument's due (maturity) date. Maturity value is the par (face) value of the instrument plus interest. See also *par value*.

maximum age—for the purposes of ERISA, being within five years of a plan's normal retirement age. A company that maintains a defined benefit retirement plan may be discouraged from hiring older employees because of the cost of funding benefits for them. Consequently, ERISA permits these plans to exclude employees within this age window at the time service begins. The plan must still comply with coverage and antidiscrimination rules.

maximum allowable—see *allowed amount*.

maximum allowable cost (MAC)—highest unit price that a health plan or insurer will pay for a medication.

maximum allowable reimbursement—see *fee schedule*.

maximum benefit limit—highest amount of money a benefit plan or insurance company will pay for a specific procedure or event or during the lifetime of the insured.

maximum fee schedule—see *fee schedule*.

maximum out-of-pocket payment—see *out-of-pocket maximum/limit*.

maximum pension adjustment rule—in Canada, benefits accruing and contributions being made under a hybrid plan during one year cannot exceed the contribution limit that may be made to a defined contribution pension plan. This maximum is the less of the 18% of the year's compensation and the money purchase limit.

maximum pension rule—limit on the yearly benefit accrual for individuals under a defined benefit retirement plan in Canada. The rule dictates the maximum benefit provided be the lower of (1) 2% $\times$ a member's years of service $\times$ a member's highest average compensation and (2) the defined benefit limit set by the Canada Revenue Agency.

mean—average of a set of numbers that is calculated by dividing the sum of the numbers by how many numbers were in the set. A mean is a measure of central tendency; it is always between the extreme values in the set of numbers. See also *median*.

means test—assessment of whether income, assets and/or expenses fit the rules under which a person is eligible for assistance from, or participation in, a welfare program. In some cases, the test may be used to determine the extent to which benefits are provided. A means test may also be referred to as a needs test.

mechanic's lien—legal claim against property. Persons who provide work or materials for the erection, improvement or repair of property may place a claim against the property if they do not receive payment. State and provincial laws vary as to the procedures and degree of protection accorded. See also *lien*.

median—measure of central tendency; the middle value in an ordered set of values. The median divides the distribution of numbers in half. See also *mean*.

mediation—process to resolve a dispute between two parties that uses an impartial third party (a mediator) to help the adversaries reach an agreement. Mediation is usually voluntary, although participation is sometimes mandated by contract or the court. The two parties in the dispute usually select the mediator, whose role is to meet with the two sides (jointly and/or separately) to help narrow the areas of disagreement and make proposals for settlement. With "facilitative mediation," the mediator does not make a decision who wins or loses or have the authority to force a settlement. In an alternative process, "evaluative mediation," the mediator does make a decision on the value of the arguments presented and suggests a settlement. The mediation process may be terminated at any time without cause by the mediator or either party. Mediation is common in both labor and insurance claim disputes. See also *alternative dispute resolution (ADR)* and *arbitration*.

Medicaid—as implemented by Title XIX of the Social Security Act, a medical benefit program administered by the states and subsidized by the U.S. government that pays certain medical expenses for persons with low income and limited resources. See also *categorically needy* and *medically needy*.

medical cannabis—see *medical marijuana*.

medical care—prevention, treatment and management of illness, and the preservation of mental health, through the services offered by health professionals.

medical care expense—for tax purposes, IRC Section 213(d) identifies a medical care expense as a cost for (1) the diagnosis, cure, mitigation, treatment or prevention of disease or for the purpose of affecting any structure or function of the body; (2) transportation primarily for, and essential to, medical care; (3) qualified long-term care services; and (4) insurance (including amounts paid as premiums under Part B of Title XVIII of the Social Security Act, relating to supplementary medical insurance for the aged).

medical certification—written document prepared by a health care provider that verifies an employee's need to take leave for a serious health condition.

medical child support order—see *qualified medical child support order (QMCSO)*.

medical error—mistake by a health care provider regardless of whether it harms a patient. Such mistakes might be an incomplete or inaccurate diagnosis, the provision of an inappropriate dosage of medication or wrong-site surgery.

medical examination—procedure or test that seeks information about an individual's physical or mental health or impairments.

medical expense budgeting—effort to control health benefit cost increases that allocates a set dollar amount each employee can use to purchase health benefits. Employees are typically allowed to choose from a variety of insurance options. If an employee selects a benefit-rich plan with a cost that exceeds the amount set aside, the employee makes up the difference.

medical expense insurance—see *medical insurance*.

medical home—approach to providing comprehensive patient care that facilitates a partnership between the individual patient, the patient's personal physician and, when appropriate, the patient's family. In 2007, the American Academy of Family Physicians, American Academy of Pediatrics, American College of Physicians and American Osteopathic Association released joint principles for a medical home. Among these principles, it is stated that each patient should have an ongoing relationship with a personal physician who provides first contact and continuous and comprehensive care. This physician leads a team that collectively takes responsibility for the patient's care. The physician provides all the patient's health care needs or arranges care with other professionals across all elements of the health care system as appropriate. Quality and safety are considered hallmarks of this model, with the medical home serving as a patient advocate guided by evidence-based medicine. Access to care is emphasized through systems such as expanded hours and communication options.

Medical Information Bureau (MIB)—cooperative organization formed by life insurers to exchange information about the physical condition of prior applicants.

medical insurance—often used interchangeably with health insurance, an insurance plan that pays for medical, surgical and hospital expenses. See also *insurance*.

medical loss ratio (MLR)—insurance company's cost of delivering health care benefits as a percentage of premiums received. See also "Medical loss ratio" in the *Appendix A: Affordable Care Act of 2010 (ACA)*.

medically indigent (MI)—person who is unable to pay, directly or through an insurance program, the full cost of his or her own health care. Such persons generally earn too much to be eligible for Medicaid but not enough to purchase insurance.

medically necessary—health care services and supplies that are deemed appropriate and essential for the diagnosis or treatment of a medical condition. Such treatment is to be in accordance with generally accepted standards of medical practice.

medically needy—persons who may have too much income to qualify under the mandatory or optional categorically needy groups established by Medicaid. In some states, a medically needy program allows people to spend down to Medicaid eligibility by incurring medical and/or remedial care expenses to offset their excess income, thereby reducing resources to a level below the maximum allowed by that state's Medicaid plan. States may also allow families to establish eligibility as medically needy by paying monthly premiums to the state in an amount equal to the difference between family income (reduced by unpaid expenses, if any, incurred for medical care in previous months) and the income eligibility standard. See also *categorically needy* and *Medicaid*.

medical marijuana—use of cannabis (marijuana) and its cannabinoids to treat disease or improve symptoms. A limited amount of evidence suggests cannabis may be useful for reducing nausea and vomiting during chemotherapy, improving the appetite in people with HIV/AIDS, and treating chronic pain and muscle spasms.

medical practice guideline—see *practice guideline*.

medical reimbursement plan—employer benefit program that directly reimburses employees for health care expenses from employer funds versus an insurance policy.

medical savings account (MSA)—see *Archer medical savings account (MSA)*.

medical self-care—the prevention, detection and treatment of illness and disease by a patient. This care may be performed by a patient (1) based on personal knowledge, (2) with the assistance of laypersons (e.g., family, friends) outside the professional health care system, or (3) in collaboration with and after instruction by a health care professional.

medical spending account—see *health care flexible spending account, health savings account (HSA)* and *health reimbursement arrangement (HRA)*.

medical tourism—also called medical travel or health tourism, traveling across an international border to obtain health care. Medical tourism is being used by some health plans as a cost-management technique for nonemergency surgeries.

Medicare
—administered by the Centers for Medicare and Medicaid Services, a U.S. government plan that pays hospital and medical expenses for persons primarily over the age of 65. Benefits are provided regardless of income level. The program is government-subsidized and government-operated.
- Part A, hospital insurance, provides for inpatient hospital services and posthospital care.
- Part B, supplementary medical insurance, pays for medically necessary physician services, outpatient hospital services, and a number of other medical services and supplies not covered under Part A. Enrollment in Part B is voluntary and available for a small premium.
- Part C, also known as Medicare Advantage, consists of coverage provided by private companies (e.g., HMOs and PPOs).
- Part D covers prescription drugs. Medicare was established through Title XVIII of the Social Security Act. See also *Medicare Advantage, Medicare Part D, Medicare Prescription Drug, Improvement, and Modernization Act of 2003 (MMA), Medicare secondary payer program* and *qualified Medicare beneficiary (QMB)*.

—unofficial name for Canada's universal publicly funded health insurance plan. See also *Canada Health Act*.

Medicare Advantage—also known as Medicare Part C, a Medicare option that provides health coverage under Medicare Parts A and B, as well as preventive and prescription drug coverage, through private companies that have contracted with Medicare. Often the coverage is provided through a health maintenance organization, preferred provider organization or private fee-for-service plan. Medicare provides a fixed dollar amount per month to these plans for an individual's coverage; the additional cost to the individual varies depending on the extent of services and options chosen. Formerly called Medicare+Choice. See also *Medicare* and *special needs plan (SNP)*.

Medicare Advantage MSA—Archer medical savings account designated by Medicare to be used solely to pay the qualified medical expenses of an accountholder who is enrolled in Medicare. Contributions are made only by Medicare. Contributions are not reported as taxable income. Distributions used to pay for qualified medical expenses are also not taxed. See also *Archer medical savings account (MSA)*.

Medicare carve-out—coordination of Medicare with an employer's retiree health plan. Medicare is the primary insurer and the employer plan serves as a secondary payer. The result is usually a lower cost for the employer's plan.

Medicare Part A—see *Medicare*.

Medicare Part B—see *Medicare*.

Medicare Part C—see *Medicare Advantage*.

Medicare Part D—created by the Medicare Prescription Drug, Improvement, and Modernization Act of 2003, this voluntary Medicare option provides prescription drug coverage for those who qualify, primarily those over the age of 65. Plans are run by insurance or other private companies and must provide at least a standard level of coverage as set by Medicare. Options and the extent of coverage vary. The premiums, copayments, deductibles, etc., vary accordingly.

Medicare Prescription Drug, Improvement, and Modernization Act of 2003 (MMA)—U.S. legislation that (1) creates a prescription drug benefit for retirees (Part D), (2) increases Medicare payments to the Medicare Advantage program, (3) provides a means-tested Part B premium that increases costs to high-income beneficiaries, (4) creates health savings accounts (HSAs) as a new tax-favored vehicle for individuals who want to prefund health care costs, and (5) makes significant changes in Medicare fee-for-service and managed care administration. See also *health savings account (HSA)*, *Medicare*, *Medicare Advantage* and *Medicare Part D*.

Medicare Savings Programs—Medicaid program that helps eligible low-income persons in the U.S. pay their Medicare Part A and B premiums, deductibles, coinsurance and copayments.

Medicare secondary payer program—U.S. law has established Medicare as the secondary payer to other health insurance plans under certain circumstances. Among the beneficiaries most likely to be affected by the Medicare secondary payer rules are (1) those over the age of 65 who have current group coverage from an employer or the employer of their spouse, (2) those who are disabled and their disabled dependents, and (3) individuals with end-stage renal disease (up to the first 30 months). Factors such as the size of the employer providing the group coverage, an individual's COBRA eligibility, and whether there is other coverage such as liability insurance or workers' compensation are also considered in determining when Medicare is secondary payer.

Medicare supplement policy—see *medigap*.

medication management—see *medication therapy management (MTM)*.

medication possession ratio (MPR)—mathematical formula used to measure a patient's compliance with drug therapy instructions. The number of drug doses a patient obtains is compared with the number of doses the patient should have obtained. A value of one means all refills were obtained while a value less than one indicates less than perfect compliance. MPR does not measure how many medications a patient has actually taken, but it has been shown to be a valid substitute measure for medication *compliance*.

medication therapy management (MTM)—patient-centered service provided by a pharmacist that is outside the normal scope of practice by the profession. For each patient, the pharmacist evaluates medications (including alternative medications and nutritional supplements) to determine appropriateness and effectiveness given the patient's medical condition(s). The process also focuses on preventing, identifying and resolving drug therapy problems that may be responsible for a patient's decision not to take a medication as recommended. MTM was formerly known as cognitive services.

medigap—voluntary private insurance plan that Medicare beneficiaries may purchase to cover the costs of deductibles, coinsurance and health care services not covered by Medicare. Also referred to as a Medicare supplement policy.

mega cap—short for mega market capitalization, a reference to companies with a market value of more than $200 billion. These are the very largest companies, such as General Electric, Microsoft and Wal-Mart. Cap classifications are only approximations that change over time. The exact definitions of these terms can also vary among brokerage houses. See also *large cap*, *micro cap*, *mid cap*, *nano cap* and *small cap*.

member—see *plan member* or *participant*.

member-funded pension plan—defined benefit retirement program permitted by Quebec's minimum standards legislation. Employer contributions are fixed at a predetermined rate, while member contributions may vary, depending on the rate of return the plan's fund receives on investments. Such a plan essentially reverses the funding roles of the employer and the plan members from those in a traditional defined benefit plan.

mental health—a person's emotional, psychological and social well-being, which affects how the individual thinks, feels and acts. Mental health also helps determine how a person handles stress, relates to others and makes choices. The World Health Organization defines mental health as a state of well-being in which every individual realizes his or her own potential, can cope with the normal stresses of life, can work productively and fruitfully, and is able to make a contribution to his or her community. See also *behavioral health*.

mental health care—treatment of cognitive and emotional issues that range from stress and depression to losing touch with reality. Many mental health conditions can interfere with a person's ability to function or cope on a day-to-day basis. See also *behavioral health* and *Mental Health Parity and Addiction Equity Act of 2008*.

Mental Health Parity Act of 1996 (MHPA)—see *Mental Health Parity and Addiction Equity Act of 2008*.

Mental Health Parity and Addiction Equity Act of 2008—legislation that requires a group health plan that provides mental health and substance abuse benefits to (1) have financial requirements (e.g., deductibles and copayments) and limitations no more restrictive than those applied to the plan's medical and surgical benefits, and (2) have no separate cost-sharing requirements or limitations applicable only to mental health or substance abuse benefits. The act does not require group health plans to offer mental health and/or substance abuse benefits. This act replaces and expands the Mental Health Parity Act of 1996. Under the Affordable Care Act of 2010 (ACA), parity standards are extended to health insurance sold through the public health exchanges. See also *mental health care* and *substance abuse treatment*.

mentor—individual who serves as an advisor, counselor or guide to a less-experienced worker. Some companies establish a formal mentoring system under which senior or more experienced individual employees are asked to serve as mentors to junior employees or trainees. The mentor is responsible for providing support and feedback to the individual in his or her charge.

merger—combining of two or more companies or corporations. In Canada, a merger is called an amalgamation. See also *swap*.

merger of plans—consolidation of benefit plans. In the U.S., federal law requires that each plan participant receive a benefit after the merger at least equal to the value of the benefit he or she would have been entitled to receive before the merger. If a multiemployer plan is involved, this rule applies only to the extent that the Pension Benefit Guaranty Corporation determines this provision is necessary for the protection of participants.

merit bonus—payment in addition to normal salary and wages typically given at a manager's discretion to recognize work performance. A merit bonus is usually made as one lump sum. Unlike a merit increase, a merit bonus is not a permanent increase in compensation.

merit increase—permanent increase in salary based on performance.

merit matrix—two-factored table using performance and pay within a salary range that helps managers make decisions concerning raises across an employee population.

merit pool—total amount of dollars available for salary increases.

merit progression—process by which an employee progresses through a wage range due to performance or other measurable criteria.

merit shop—see *open shop*.

mezzanine financing—intermediate stage in the venture capital process that comes after the initial stage of venture capital funding and, generally, just prior to the business going public.

Michelle's Law—named in memory of college student Michelle Morse, a U.S. law passed in October 2008 that prohibits group health plans from terminating dependent coverage for a college student taking a leave of absence from school or changing to a part-time status while the student is suffering from a serious illness or injury. Coverage must be extended for at least one year; however, coverage may end earlier for certain reasons such as the student aging out of the plan (e.g., exceeding the plan's normal dependent eligibility age). Plans are also required to provide notice of the requirements of the law along with any notice regarding a requirement for certifying student status for coverage under the plan. The law applies to almost all insured and self-insured group plans. A number of states have passed similar laws with slight variations in provisions. Now that the Affordable Care Act requires group health plans to provide coverage for participants' adult children up to the age of 26, this law is of primary concern to students who are aged 26 years and older.

micro cap—short for market capitalization, a reference to companies with a market value between $50 million and $300 million. A micro cap is larger than a nano cap but smaller than a small cap. Cap classifications are only approximations, changing over time. The exact definitions of these terms can vary among brokerage houses. See also *large cap, mega cap, mid cap, nano cap* and *small cap*.

microeconomics—see *economics*.

mid cap—short for market capitalization, a reference to companies with a market value of $2 billion to $10 billion. As the name suggests, a mid cap is in between a small cap and a large cap. Cap classifications are only approximations, changing over time. The exact definitions of these terms can vary among brokerage houses. See also *large cap, mega cap, micro cap, nano cap* and *small cap*.

military caregiver leave—the National Defense Authorization Act for Fiscal Year 2008 amends the Family and Medical Leave Act of 1993 to permit a spouse, parent, child or next of kin in the U.S. to take up to 26 weeks of leave from work to care for a member of the armed forces (including a member of the National Guard or Reserves) who has a serious injury or illness. See also *Family and Medical Leave Act of 1993 (FMLA)*.

military leave—time away from work that employees who are members of the National Guard or Reserves take when they must report for military duty. Employers are generally not required to provide compensation while employees are on leave; however, some elect to voluntarily pay employees the difference between military pay and what they would have received if their employment had not been interrupted by military service. Some companies even pay full salary up to a certain number of days. See also *Uniformed Services Employment and Reemployment Rights Act of 1994 (USERRA)*.

Millennial—individual born between 1980 and 1999. Also referred to as Generation Y.

mini med coverage or plan—see *bare-bones health plan*.

mini medical plan—see *bare-bones health plan*.

minimum benefit—feature in a defined benefit retirement plan that establishes a lower limit for benefit payment amounts. This minimum is usually payable only if certain service requirements are met at retirement.

minimum benefit plan—see *bare-bones health plan*.

minimum compensation level—amount of salary or wages an employee must earn before being eligible to participate in a benefit plan.

minimum contribution requirement—amount that a plan sponsor or plan participant is required to put into a benefit plan. In the U.S., federal government rules determine the contributions that must be made by plan sponsors when a plan is underfunded.

minimum distribution rules—see *required minimum distribution (RMD)*.

minimum essential coverage—see "Employer shared responsibility" and "Individual responsibility" in the *Appendix A: Affordable Care Act of 2010 (ACA)*.

minimum funding—least amount that must be contributed by an employer to a benefit plan. See also *accumulated funding deficiency* and *funding standard account (FSA)*.

minimum group—least number of employees required under law to comprise a group for insurance purposes. The purpose of this standard is to minimize risk and maintain a distinction between individual and group forms of insurance.

minimum participation requirement
—provision of small group and voluntary health and dental insurance plans that mandates at least a certain number or percentage of eligible individuals must be enrolled in the plan to reduce adverse selection. If the minimum is not reached, the insurer may refuse to provide coverage or charge a higher premium than originally quoted.
—IRS rule that a qualified benefit plan must cover at least 50 employees or, if fewer, 40% of the workforce.

minimum participation standard—government mandates regarding eligibility for participation in a benefit plan. For example, the IRC mandates that no qualified retirement plan can require the date for employee eligibility for participation be later than (1) the date on which the employee attains the age of 21 or (2) when the employee completes one year of service—whichever is later. There are exceptions to this rule for government and church plans, plans maintained by tax-exempt educational institutions and plans that have an immediate-vesting-upon-participation feature.

minimum premium plan (MPP)—agreement between the sponsor of a self-insured benefit plan and an insurance company that the sponsor will be responsible for paying all claims up to a predetermined aggregate level, with the insurance carrier responsible for the excess. The aggregate level is usually based on the amount of claims paid in the past two or three years, adjusted for projected increases in claims due to inflation and greater utilization. The carrier usually processes claims and provides other administrative services. See also *self-funding* and *shared funding*.

minimum standards legislation—collective reference to the pension legislation issued by the Canadian provinces (and the federal government for employees subject to federal employment standards). The legislation sets out the rules for individual employee rights under registered retirement plans (RRPs) as well as the administration and financing of these plans.

minimum wage—lowest rate of pay that employers may legally give to workers. In the United States, the minimum wage is administered by the U.S. Department of Labor. A national minimum hourly wage was established in 1938 under the Fair Labor Standards Act; the Fair Minimum Wage Act of 2007 is the current law. In Canada, the responsibility for enacting and enforcing labor laws rests with the provinces and territories; each has the authority to set a minimum wage for work performed in its jurisdiction.

mirror plan—nonqualified plan with the same features as a qualified plan, except that the features of the former begin where the latter ends. For example, a nonqualified pension plan might establish a mirror plan to give benefits to highly compensated employees that are not possible as the result of qualified pension plan limitations.

mitigating measures—medical treatment or devices that lessen the effects of an impairment, such as medication, a prosthesis or a hearing aid. When determining whether a person has a disability in the U.S. under the Americans with Disabilities Act, the effect of mitigating measures is not to be considered.

model plan—qualified retirement plan developed by the IRS for employers. Model plans are easy and inexpensive to implement due to the simple IRS procedures required for qualification. See also *master plan* and *prototype plan*.

modern portfolio theory (MPT)—belief that a risk-averse investor can use diversification in the creation of a portfolio to maximize expected return for a given level of market risk. MPT is also referred to as modern investment theory, portfolio theory and portfolio management theory.

modification—revision to a benefit plan or legal agreement.

modified adjusted gross income (MAGI)—measure used by the IRS to determine if a taxpayer is eligible to use certain deductions, credits, retirement plans and government social programs. The MAGI is used under the Affordable Care Act of 2010 (ACA) to determine eligibility for Medicaid and for tax credits available to people buying insurance in the public exchanges. Calculating the MAGI takes into account family size and income from all family members. Generally, MAGI is a person's or household's adjusted gross income plus any tax-exempt Social Security, interest and foreign income. See also *adjusted gross income (AGI)*.

Modigliani Risk-Adjusted Performance (M^2, M2 or RAP)—measure of how well the return on an investment portfolio rewards an investor for the amount of risk taken, relative to a market index (or other benchmark) and the risk-free rate of return. Derived from the Sharpe ratio, M^2 is easier to interpret. If two investment portfolios have M^2 values of 4.3% and 4.8%., the portfolio with the M^2 of 4.8% provides 0.5 percentage points more return per year for the same risk. See also *Sharpe ratio*.

modular plan—flexible benefit plan that offers a choice of benefit packages rather than a selection of individual benefits. The packages may have different levels or types of coverage. Packages might be structured to meet employee lifecycle needs, such as a plan for single employees with no dependents, another for single parents, one for married workers with dependents and another for employees approaching retirement. An employee may select only one bundle, and coverage level substitutions are not usually allowed. See also *flexible benefit plan*.

monetary policy—process by which a nation's central bank or monetary authority controls the supply of money, the availability of money and interest rates in order to attain economic objectives such as price stability and economic growth. In the United States, monetary policy is a function of the Federal Open Market Committee headed by the Chairman of the Federal Reserve System. The principal tools of monetary policy are the discount rate, open market operations and reserve requirements. See also *Federal Open Market Committee (FOMC), Federal Reserve System* and *fiscal policy*.

money follows the man—see *reciprocity*.

money management—process of managing money, including investments, budgeting, banking and taxes; also called investment management.

money manager—individual who typically designs a portfolio for clients (or works with a design developed by a financial planner) comprising individual securities, bonds, real estate or other financial assets and investments and who manages the portfolio on a discretionary basis. Manager compensation is usually a small percentage of the value of the assets under management. Money managers may range from an independent advisory firm to a bank trust department, pension fund, mutual fund or insurance company. See also *bottom-up manager, fund manager, growth manager, investment manager, portfolio manager, private banker, risk manager, top-down manager* and *value manager*.

money market—where short-term debt securities with a maturity of one year or less are bought and sold.

money market deposit account—also called a money market account, this savings account has some of the characteristics of a money market fund; it is a safe and highly liquid investment but offers a lower interest rate than most other investments. The accounts offer many of the same services as checking accounts, although transactions may be somewhat more limited. Managed by banks or brokerages, money market deposit accounts are insured by the federal government. See also *money market fund*.

money market fund—mutual fund that invests in highly liquid low-risk securities, such as government securities, certificates of deposit or commercial paper. Fund managers attempt to keep the net asset value or purchase price at a constant $1 per share; only the yield goes up and down, generally reflecting short-term interest rates. Investor losses in a money market fund are possible but rare. Unlike a money market deposit account, money market funds have not traditionally been federally insured. Investors are allowed to write checks against their accounts. See also *money market deposit account* and *mutual fund*.

money market hedge—borrowing and lending in multiple currencies; for example, to eliminate currency risk, an investor might lock in the value of a foreign currency transaction using the currency of the investor's own country.

money market instrument—short-term (less than one year) debt security such as a Treasury bill, bankers' acceptance, certificate of deposit, commercial paper and repurchase agreement. Money market instruments are also called *cash equivalents* because they are easy to buy and sell.

money purchase plan
—in Canada, the terms money purchase plan and defined contribution plan are used interchangeably. Both are retirement savings vehicles that define payments to be made by employer and possibly employees but not the benefit formula. Accumulated contributions and interest determine the retirement benefit amount that can be provided or purchased as an annuity for the member when the employee retires.
—in the U.S., a type of defined contribution plan in which the employer's contribution to an employee's retirement account is fixed, usually as a percentage of compensation. The benefits for each employee are based on the sums contributed to his or her account.

money supply—measure of the amount of money in circulation.

monograph—summary of the research and clinical literature available on a drug.

monopoly—sometimes referred to as an exclusive market, a market in which there are many buyers but only one seller.

Monte Carlo simulation—named for the city known for casinos and games of chance, a problem-solving technique used to approximate the probability of certain outcomes by running multiple trial runs, called simulations, using random variables. The simulation is used in retirement planning to evaluate whether retirement income will last as long as needed. Computer software can simulate thousands of market condition scenarios to estimate the probability of funds lasting a lifetime.

moonlighting—working at an additional job after one's regular, full-time job.

morbidity—relative incidence (number of cases) of a disease, illness or injury within a particular population at a particular period of time.

morbidity table—chart that shows the rates of sickness or injury among given groups of people.

mortality—how often death occurs among a given group of people. Some of the ways that people may be grouped include by age, locale and specific type of illness or disease.

mortality charge—portion of a life insurance premium that is the actual cost to the insurance company for protecting an individual against the risk of death.

mortality experience—rate at which participants in a pension or insurance plan die. Also the financial effect of such deaths on the plan.

mortality rate—percentage of deaths for a group of people in a given period of time. See also *life expectancy*.

mortality table—chart that indicates life expectancy or death as a function of age, gender, occupation, nation, etc. A mortality table is useful to insurance companies and retirement plans when estimating expected future benefits to be paid.

mortgage—loan by which a borrower (mortgagor) gives a lender (mortgagee) a lien on property (typically real property) as security for the payment of the debt obligation. The borrower continues to use the property while loan payments are being made. When the loan has been paid in full, the lien on the property is removed. Mortgage loans are used in connection with the purchase of single family structures, condominiums, multifamily structures, office buildings, large commercial centers, industrial plants and even undeveloped land.

mortgage-backed security (MBS)—bond or other financial obligation backed by a pool of mortgage loans. Investor returns are periodic payments that pass through the interest and principal from the underlying mortgages. In some cases, the security is issued and guaranteed by a federal agency such as Fannie Mae, Freddie Mac or Ginnie Mae. A mortgage-backed security may also be referred to as a mortgage-related security or a mortgage pass-through security. See also *agency bond, asset-backed security, collateralized mortgage obligation (CMO), commercial mortgage-backed security (CMBS), Federal Agricultural Mortgage Corporation (FAMC or Farmer Mac), Federal Home Loan Mortgage Corporation (FHLMC or Freddie Mac), Federal National Mortgage Association (FNMA or Fannie Mae), Government National Mortgage Association (GNMA or Ginnie Mae), pass-through security* and *real estate mortgage investment conduit (REMIC).*

mortgage banker—firm that furnishes its own funds for mortgage loans, which are typically sold later to permanent investors. Most mortgage bankers continue to service the loans for a specified fee.

mortgage bond—debt obligation secured by a property pledge. A mortgage bond, in effect, is a lien or mortgage against the issuing corporation's properties and real estate assets.

mortgage broker—individual or company that obtains mortgage loans for others by finding insurance companies, lending institutions or private sources that will lend the money.

mortgage correspondent—agent of a lending institution authorized to handle and process loans.

mortgagee—one who provides a loan secured with the borrower's property; in other words, the lender in a mortgage agreement.

mortgage pass-through security—see *mortgage-backed security (MBS).*

mortgage redemption insurance—insurance plan that provides for the payment of the amount remaining on a mortgage loan in the event of death or disability. A decreasing term life insurance policy is used to provide the death benefit. See also *term life insurance.*

mortgage REIT—real estate investment trust formed for the purpose of purchasing mortgages and lending money on real estate. See also *hybrid real estate investment trust (REIT)* and *real estate investment trust (REIT).*

mortgagor—borrower (debtor) who conveys property as security for a mortgage loan.

most favored nation (MFN) status—arrangement between a vendor and purchaser that assures the lowest price or best terms available will be given to the purchaser.

MSCI World—index that measures the total return (with dividends reinvested) on stocks from the developed nations around the world, including the United States and Canada. The index serves as a common investment benchmark for global stock funds. See also *stock market index.*

Multiemployer Pension Plan Amendments Act of 1980 (MPPAA)—legislation that amended ERISA to strengthen the funding requirements for multiemployer pension plans. The act removes multiemployer plans from ERISA's plan termination insurance system and substitutes a system that imposes liability for certain unfunded vested benefits when an employer partially or totally withdraws from a multiemployer plan. See also *plan termination.*

Multiemployer Pension Reform Act of 2014 (MPRA)—U.S. law that makes a number of changes to the funding and Pension Benefit Guaranty Corporation (PBGC) rules for multiemployer pension plans, including making permanent the funding rules affecting these plans under the Pension Protection Act of 2006. The changes include a PBGC premium hike for multiemployer plans, new rules that allow certain financially distressed plans to suspend accrued benefits, new rules on plan mergers and partitions, changes to the rules for determining employer withdrawal liability, and technical modifications to various ERISA and Tax Code rules for multiemployer plans. See also *critical status* and *critical and declining status.*

multi-employer plan—benefit plan in Canada that covers employees of two or more financially unrelated employers. The plan may be established through collective bargaining or statute. A common fund is used to accumulate contributions and pay benefits. An employee's service with any of the contributing employers counts toward benefit eligibility unless a break in service (as defined by the plan) cancels credits earned before the break.

multiemployer plan—collectively bargained benefit plan in the U.S. that is maintained by more than one employer, usually within the same or related industries. Multiemployer plans, also known as jointly administered or Taft-Hartley plans, are governed by a board of trustees with labor and management equally represented. Members of the board of trustees are either elected or appointed to their positions. The board typically makes decisions about the types of benefits to be offered in the plan. Bargaining parties negotiate a contribution rate, and the trustees translate that rate into a benefit. Decisions to increase benefits or change the plan are also typically made by the board. In some industries (especially mining and segments of trucking), employers and unions set the benefit levels through collective bargaining. Multiemployer plans are subject to many of the same vesting, accrual and minimum participation rules that apply to single employer plans. The costs of administering a plan are paid from plan assets. See also *contribution base unit (CBU), employee health and welfare fund, Labor-Management Relations Act of 1947 (LMRA or Taft-Hartley Act)* and *pension fund*.

multi-jurisdictional pension plan (MJPP)—defined benefit retirement plan that has members in more than one Canadian jurisdiction. Where MJPPs are in effect, the Agreement Respecting Multi-Jurisdictional Pension Plans facilitates the application and administration of the various Canadian pension laws that regulate these plans.

Multilateral Investment Guarantee Agency—see *World Bank*.

multinational corporation (MC)—firm with independent business units operating in multiple countries.

multinational pooling—arrangement in which a corporation brings the benefit plans of local subsidiaries and/or divisions in various countries together into a single unit or pool for the purpose of reducing the risk to an insurer and, hence, the cost of the plan to the corporation. This is accomplished by experience rating the pool versus the individual units for underwriting purposes.

multiple coverage—see *duplication of benefits*.

multiple employer group—group of two or more employers that are not financially related.

multiple employer plan—benefit plan maintained by more than one employer allowing the pooling of plan assets for investment purposes and a reduction in the cost of plan administration. A multiple employer plan maintains separate accounts for each employer so that contributions provide benefits only for employees of the contributing employer. There are no collective bargaining agreements requiring contributions in a multiple employer plan, as there are in a multiemployer plan. See also *multiemployer plan, multiple employer trust (MET)* and *multiple employer welfare arrangement (MEWA)*.

multiple employer trust (MET)—trust formed by a health benefit plan sponsor to combine a number of small employers for the purpose of providing medical coverage on an insured or self-insured basis. The claims experiences of the individual employers are usually pooled. See also *multiple employer plan* and *multiple employer welfare arrangement (MEWA)*.

multiple employer welfare arrangement (MEWA)—defined in ERISA Section 3(40), a vehicle that can be used to provide health and welfare benefits other than retirement benefits to the employees of two or more employers (including one or more self-employed individuals). A MEWA must be established and maintained by a group of employers, an employee organization or both. Arrangements that are established by a single employer, rural electric cooperative or rural telephone cooperative or are pursuant to a collective bargaining agreement are excluded from this type of plan. MEWAs that meet the definition of an employee welfare benefit plan in ERISA Section 3(1) are required to comply with all obligations of the Act. States are free to regulate non-ERISA MEWAs.

multiple-source brand—brand version of a drug when it is available in both brand-name and generic versions from more than one manufacturer.

multiple-source drug—medication available in both brand-name and generic versions from more than one manufacturer.

multi-state plan—private health insurance plan sold through a public health exchange under a contract between the U.S. Office of Personnel Management (OPM) and an insurance company. Multi-state plans must include essential health benefits and, generally, must cover any additional benefits required by state law. Enrollees in these plans are eligible for the same income-based savings as enrollees in other marketplace plans. Some, but not all, multi-state plan options offer in-network care out of state. For additional information, see "Benefit mandates," "Premium tax credit" and "Public health exchanges" in the *Appendix A: Affordable Care Act of 2010 (ACA)*.

multi-tiered drug formulary—see *drug formulary*.

municipal bond—debt obligation issued by a state, state agency or local government. In general, interest paid on municipal bonds in the United States is exempt from federal income tax as well as state and local income tax within the state of issue. Gains or losses that result from the sale of a bond, however, are subject to federal income tax. See also *general obligation (GO) bond, revenue anticipation note (RAN), revenue bond, special assessment bond, tax-equivalent (TE) yield* and *tax-exempt*.

municipal bond fund—mutual fund that invests in municipal bonds issued by state and local governments. The tax-exempt status of municipal bonds is passed on to fundholders. See also *bond fund, municipal bond* and *mutual fund*.

mutual fund
—inside the U.S., an investment portfolio managed by an investment company that raises money from investors (shareholders) and uses this money to purchase a variety of assets for the portfolio. The stocks, bonds and other securities purchased are in accordance with the stated objectives of the fund. In return for the money they give to the fund, investors receive an equity position in the fund and, effectively, in each of its underlying securities. Thousands of shareholders may participate in one mutual fund. Advantages of such a fund include reduced transaction costs and the ability to diversify assets far beyond what might be possible if small individual investors bought securities on their own. In addition, a professional team of managers makes the decisions regarding which securities to buy and sell. A mutual fund may be an open-end or closed-end fund. Some are load funds while others are no-load funds. Funds are also categorized by their investment objectives, for example, an income fund or a growth fund. See also *asset allocation fund, balanced fund, bond fund, closed-end fund, emerging market fund, exchange fund, fund family, fund of funds, global fund, growth and income fund, growth fund, hybrid fund, income fund, index fund, international fund, load fund, market neutral fund, money market fund, municipal bond fund, no-load fund, open-end fund, regional fund, sector fund, specialty fund, stable value fund* and *stock fund*.
—outside the U.S., mutual fund may have a broader meaning. See also *collective investment fund*.

mutual fund custodian—commercial bank or trust company that physically holds the securities owned by a mutual fund company. It may also act as a transfer agent. It does not, however, act in a managerial capacity.

mutual insurance company—insurance company owned by its policyholders rather than stockholders. The policyholders are members who contribute premiums to a common fund on which they are entitled to make a claim if they experience a covered loss. The policyholders elect a board of directors or trustees through whom business is conducted. Premiums and other earnings in excess of paid claims and other expenses are distributed to the policyholders as dividends. In years when the loss experience is unfavorable, assessments, in addition to normal premiums, may be made against policyholders.

N

named fiduciary—person who is named in a plan instrument or who is identified through a procedure set forth in the plan as having express authority to control plan operations.

nano cap—short for market capitalization, a reference to companies with a market value under $50 million. This is the smallest of the cap classifications, and investment in these companies is generally considered high risk. Cap classifications are only approximations, changing over time. The exact definitions of these terms can also vary among brokerage houses. See also *large cap, mega cap, micro cap, mid cap* and *small cap*.

narrow therapeutic index (NTI)—any pharmaceutical that has less than a twofold difference between the minimum toxic concentration and minimum effective concentration in blood. See also *therapeutic index*.

NASD—see *Financial Industry Regulatory Authority (FINRA)*.

NASDAQ—created in 1971, the largest electronic screen-based stock market in the United States. NASDAQ is the acronym for the National Association of Securities Dealers Automated Quotations. The market consists primarily of technology and growth stocks. It contains both U.S. and international stocks.

NASDAQ Composite Index—value of all companies traded on the NASDAQ, which is used as an indicator of the performance of U.S. technology and growth stocks. See also *composite index, NASDAQ* and *stock market index*.

National Association of Insurance Commissioners (NAIC)—organization comprised of insurance regulators from the 50 states, the District of Columbia and U.S. territories that addresses the need to coordinate regulation of multistate insurers. A major function of NAIC is the drafting of model laws that promote regulatory consistency across the nation.

National Committee for Quality Assurance (NCQA)—independent, private sector group that reviews care quality and the procedures of health plans and providers to render an accreditation. NCQA is responsible for the development of HEDIS and health plan quality report cards. See also *Healthcare Effectiveness Data and Information Set (HEDIS)*.

National Drug Code (NDC)—unique numerical code for a drug that is assigned by the drug's manufacturer under guidelines set by the U.S. Food, Drug and Cosmetic Act. The NDC identifies the specific drug's (1) labeler (i.e., manufacturer, repackager or distributor), (2) strength, dosage form (i.e., capsule, tablet, liquid) and formulation, and (3) package size/type.

National Futures Association (NFA)—self-regulatory organization for the U.S. futures industry that develops rules, programs and services to ensure market integrity, protect investors and help members meet their regulatory responsibilities. For those conducting business in the U.S. futures exchanges, membership in NFA is a requirement.

National Health Information Center (NHIC)—health information referral service of the U.S. government that links consumers and health professionals with the organizations best able to provide answers to health-related questions.

national health insurance—system of health insurance that covers all (or nearly all) citizens within a country. The insurance may be administered by the public sector, private sector or a combination of both. Funding mechanisms vary with the particular program and country.

National Health Plan Collaborative (NHPC)—project bringing together 11 major health insurance companies with other organizations from the public and private sectors in the U.S. to identify ways to improve the quality of health care for racially and ethnically diverse populations.

National Institute of Mental Health (NIMH)—U.S. agency that conducts and supports research seeking to understand, treat and prevent mental illness.

National Institutes of Health (NIH)—primary federal agency for conducting and supporting medical research in the U.S.

National Labor Relations Act of 1935 (NLRA or Wagner Act)—U.S. law giving employees of private employers (with some exceptions) the right to (1) form, join or assist labor organizations; (2) bargain collectively through representatives of their own choosing; and (3) take part in strikes and other activities in support of labor demands. The act also identifies five unfair labor practices on the part of employers:
1. Interference, restraint or coercion directed against union or collective activity
2. Domination of unions
3. Discrimination against employees who take part in union or collective activities
4. Retaliation for filing unfair labor practice charges or cooperating with the National Labor Relations Board
5. Refusal to bargain in good faith with union representatives.

NLRA created the National Labor Relations Board to enforce these employee rights and to take action against unfair labor practices that might discourage organizing or prevent workers from negotiating a union contract. See also *Labor-Management Relations Act of 1947 (LMRA or Taft-Hartley Act)*, *Labor-Management Reporting and Disclosure Act of 1959 (LMRDA or Landrum-Griffin Act)* and *National Labor Relations Board (NLRB)*.

National Labor Relations Board (NLRB)—independent U.S. government agency charged with enforcing the National Labor Relations Act of 1935 (also called the Wagner Act) and its amendments. The NLRB is charged with mediating disputes between management and labor unions. It conducts elections to determine bargaining agents and adjudicates unfair labor practice charges. The board seeks enforcement of its orders through the court system. See also *Labor-Management Relations Act of 1947 (LMRA or Taft-Hartley Act)*, *Labor-Management Reporting and Disclosure Act of 1959 (LMRDA or Landrum-Griffin Act)* and *National Labor Relations Act of 1935 (NLRA or Wagner Act)*.

national provider identifier (NPI)—nonproprietary (in the public domain) national identifier code consisting of eight alphanumeric characters intended for universal use by all health care providers. For the purposes of the NPI, a provider is an individual, group or organization that provides medical or other health services or supplies. It includes individual physicians and other practitioners; physician/practitioner groups; institutions such as hospitals, laboratories and nursing homes; organizations such as health maintenance organizations; and suppliers such as pharmacies and medical supply companies.

National Quality Forum (NQF)—nonprofit partnership comprised of U.S. health care stakeholders that includes consumer organizations, public and private health care purchasers, health care providers, accrediting and certifying bodies, supporting industries, and research and quality improvement organizations. NQF is committed to building consensus on national health priorities and goals for performance improvement, standards for measuring and publicly reporting performance, and promoting attainment of goals through education and outreach.

naturopathy—also known as naturopathic medicine or natural medicine, a complementary and alternative method of treatment that emphasizes the body's intrinsic ability to maintain and heal itself. Naturopaths prefer to use natural remedies such as manual manipulation, light, heat, sunshine, herbs and foods rather than surgery or synthetic drugs. Some naturopaths use no medications, either pharmaceutical or herbal.

navigator—see "Navigators" in the *Appendix A: Affordable Care Act of 2010 (ACA)*.

needs test—see *means test*.

negative election—see *automatic enrollment*.

negative enrollment—see *automatic enrollment*.

negative selection—see *adverse selection*.

negotiable certificate of deposit (NCD)—large denomination ($100,000 or more) unsecured promissory note that is guaranteed by a bank. An NCD can be sold but cannot be cashed in before maturity. Due to their large denominations, NCDs are most often purchased by large institutional investors. See also *certificate of deposit (CD)* and *Yankee certificate of deposit (Yankee CD)*.

negotiable instrument—written promise or order signed by the issuer to transfer a specified sum of money on demand or at a fixed future time to the person named on the instrument or to the bearer. Negotiable instruments can easily be transferred from one party to another; they include checks, drafts, certificates of deposit, bills of exchange and promissory notes.

negotiated plan—see *collectively bargained plan*.

negotiated rate—see *allowed amount*.

negotiation—dialogue between two parties that is intended to resolve disputes, produce an agreement on a course of action or develop a solution that satisfies various interests. Labor unions and management negotiate to reach agreement on a wide range of issues concerning compensation, benefits, work environment, etc. Negotiation is normally the first step in collective bargaining.

net assets available for benefits—difference between a plan's assets and liabilities not including participants' accumulated plan benefits.

net asset value (NAV)—price of a mutual fund share calculated by dividing the current price of the fund (minus any fees or expenses) by the number of outstanding shares. A fund's NAV is calculated once a day based on the closing market price for each security in the fund's portfolio. The NAV increases when the prices of the individual securities held by the fund increase.

net income (NI)—also called net earnings, the total money received minus taxes and expenses. See also *adjusted gross income (AGI)* and *gross income*.

net incurred claims cost—as defined by Financial Accounting Standard 106, the employer's share of the cost of providing postretirement health benefits after adjusting for retiree contributions, reimbursements from Medicare and other providers of health care benefits and for the effects of cost-sharing provisions such as deductibles and coinsurance. See also *Financial Accounting Standard 106 (FAS 106)*.

net price—dollar amount paid for a prescription drug after discounts and other reductions have been deducted.

net replacement rate or ratio—income after retirement compared with income immediately before retirement. In some cases, adjustments are made to take into account changes in tax rates, retirement savings contributions, etc.

net return—see *net income (NI)*.

network—health care providers that have contracted with a health plan or insurer to provide care. Network providers are usually reimbursed at a reduced rate negotiated in advance.

network model HMO—health maintenance organization that contracts with multiple physician groups to provide services to HMO members. A large number of single and multispecialty groups may be in the network. See also *health maintenance organization (HMO)*.

network provider—see *preferred provider*.

net worth (NW)—amount by which assets are greater than liabilities.

never-events—medical errors that should never occur, such as: performing the wrong procedure, dispensing the wrong medication, leaving objects in the body after surgery and allowing bed sores.

Newborns' and Mothers' Health Protection Act of 1996—U.S. law requiring health plans offering maternity coverage to pay for at least a 48-hour hospital stay following childbirth (a 96-hour stay in the case of a cesarean section). Plans may not offer incentives to mothers to accept less time, nor may they penalize providers for adherence to the law. Group health plans that provide maternity or newborn infant coverage must include a statement in their summary plan description advising individuals of the Act's requirements.

New York Stock Exchange (NYSE)—market where the majority of the world's largest and best-known companies are traded. Foreign-based corporations can list their shares on the NYSE if they adhere to the rules of the U.S. Securities and Exchange Commission. Also known as the Big Board, NYSE relied for many years on floor trading with members buying and selling in an auctionlike setting. While floor trading is still used, NYSE is increasingly moving to electronic trades. See also *stock market*.

New York Stock Exchange Composite Index—capitalization-weighted index of all common stocks listed on the New York Stock Exchange. The value of the index varies with the aggregate value of the common equity. See also *composite index* and *stock market index*.

Nikkei 225—now more commonly called the Nikkei, the Nikkei index or the Nikkei Stock Average, the leading index of Japanese stocks. Calculated since 1949, it is a price-weighted index comprised of Japan's top 225 blue-chip companies on the Tokyo Stock Exchange. The Nikkei is equivalent to the Dow Jones Industrial Average in the United States. In fact, it was called the Nikkei Dow Jones Stock Average from 1975 to 1985.

no balance billing—contract provision with a health care provider that states the provider will accept the amount the plan pays for a good or service. The provider agrees not to bill the patient for any additional amount with the exception of cost-sharing elements in the plan (e.g., deductibles, copays and coinsurance). See also *balance billing*.

no-fault insurance—system of automobile insurance where a person who is injured in an automobile accident recovers damages up to a specific amount against his or her own insurance company, regardless of who was responsible for the accident. The purpose of this system is to eliminate the need for litigation, particularly with respect to minor accidents.

no-load fund—mutual fund that does not charge the investor a sales load (broker fee) when shares are bought or sold. A no-load fund is permitted, however, to cover annual operating expenses and to charge other fees that are not considered sales loads. See also *account fee, exchange fee, load fund* and *purchase fee*.

nominal interest rate—see *interest rate*.

nominal rate of return—see *rate of return (ROR)*.

nominal yield—see *coupon yield*.

nonaccumulation provision—clause in a liability insurance policy that states what happens if a series of claims are made during the policy period that result from a single wrongful act, error or omission. The clause establishes the limit on coverage that applies. For example, assume a pension plan has terminated and plan trustees are sued separately for denial of benefits by three different beneficiaries in the three years that follow. One claim is filed in each of these years. Under a nonaccumulation clause, the policy limits that apply in the year of the first claim represent the total limit available to pay and defend all three claims—regardless of the fact that claims were made in the two years that follow.

nonadherence—see *noncompliance*.

nonadmitted carrier—insurance company that does not operate under a particular state's insurance laws. Such carriers do not have to submit their rates to the state for review and thus have more pricing flexibility than admitted carriers. Nonadmitted carriers can insure higher risk events, such as earthquakes, and specialty risks (e.g., professional liability insurance) that admitted carriers often can't afford to cover.

nonbargaining unit (NBU) employee—worker who is not covered under a multiemployer plan pursuant to the terms of a collective bargaining agreement. Employees of a union, multiemployer fund office or employer association are examples of NBU employees. Multiemployer plans often choose to provide benefits to NBU employees.

noncancelable—see *noncancelable* and *guaranteed renewable*.

noncancelable and guaranteed renewable—sometimes simply referred to as noncancelable, a feature in an individual insurance policy that states the insurance company cannot terminate the policy once it is in force as long as the premiums are paid. In addition, the company cannot change the premium amount or monthly benefit. See also *cancelable, conditionally renewable, guaranteed renewable* and *optionally renewable.*

noncompete agreement—provision in a contract under which one party (usually an employee) agrees not to pursue a similar profession or trade in competition with another party (usually an employer). Typically, the contract specifies a period of time and other limitations.

noncompliance
—from a health care perspective, a failure to follow instructions or practice guidelines. Patients are noncompliant when they do not follow the directions for taking a medicine or fail to show up for clinic visits. A prescriber who does not follow a plan's list of preferred drugs may also be described as being noncompliant. Noncompliance is often used interchangeably with nonadherence.
—more generally, when an organization does not follow government rules.

noncompliance period—under COBRA, the period beginning on the date a violation first occurs. The period is used to calculate the penalty excise tax imposed on employers that violate COBRA rules. See also *Consolidated Omnibus Budget Reconciliation Act of 1985 (COBRA).*

noncontributory—when an employer bears the full cost of a benefit for employees; employees are not required to share the cost of the benefit.

noncore coverage—dental, vision and other types of benefits, as opposed to what are considered essential benefits (e.g., health care).

noncovered service (NCS)—activity for which a benefit plan or insurance carrier does not provide payment.

noncumulative preferred stock—ownership share in a company (stock) that does not pay the holder any dividends in arrears. This is in contrast to cumulative preferred stock that must pay accumulated dividends in arrears. See also *convertible preferred stock, cumulative preferred stock, participating preferred stock* and *preferred stock.*

nondisabling injury—injury that may require medical care but does not result in a loss of work time or income that might qualify an insured person for disability benefits.

nondiscrimination rule—requirement in Section 105(h) of the IRC that limits the extent to which employers can target tax-favored retirement benefits toward higher paid versus lower paid employees. Compliance with the nondiscrimination rule is required for a plan to be considered qualified under ERISA. A company may, however, offer a nonqualified plan that is discriminatory or selective in nature in addition to standard qualified plans. See also *nondiscrimination test* and *qualified separate line of business (QSLOB).*

nondiscrimination test—calculations used to determine whether a plan satisfies a nondiscrimination rule. See also *actual contribution percentage (ACP) test, actual deferral percentage (ADP) test, alternative limitation* and *nondiscrimination rule.*

non-duplication-of-benefits provision—see *coordination-of-benefits (COB) provision.*

nonelective contribution—any employer payment to a retirement plan (other than a matching contribution) for which (1) the employee may not choose to receive cash in lieu of the payment, (2) the payment is vested when made, and (3) the payment cannot be withdrawn prior to the attainment of certain conditions.

nonexempt employee—worker in the U.S. who is subject to the minimum wage and overtime pay provisions of the Fair Labor Standards Act. Most nonexempt employees are paid on an hourly basis.

nonforfeitable—condition under which an employee cannot lose the right to contributions the employee or the employee's employer makes to a retirement plan for the benefit of the employee. Typically, benefit plans have a time schedule for service that specifies how an employee gains rights to employer contributions. Under ERISA, all employee contributions are nonforfeitable. See also *vesting* and *vesting schedule.*

nonforfeiture options—provision available with a life insurance policy that allows the payment of a reduced cash value, reduced paid-up coverage or another alternative if premiums on a policy with a cash value component are no longer being paid.

nonformulary drug—medication not on a benefit plan list of preferred drugs. Health and drug benefit plans often require higher copays for nonformulary medications to encourage patients to use medications that are on the list. See also *copayment* and *drug formulary.*

non-group market—see *individual health insurance market.*

non-highly compensated employee (NHCE)—employees eligible to participate in a benefit plan who do not meet the definition of *highly compensated employee (HCE)*.

noninsured plan—see *self-funding*.

nonmarket risk—chance that events specific to a company or its industry will adversely affect a stock's price. For instance, the ouster of a company's management team would affect only the one company. A nonmarket risk is also referred to as specific risk, unsystematic risk or diversifiable risk. An investor can reduce nonmarket risk within an investment portfolio through diversification. See also *market risk*.

nonoccupational death benefit—life insurance or pension money payable upon the death of an employee whose death resulted from any cause other than the employee's work. See also *death benefit* and *occupational death benefit*.

nonoccupational disability benefit—periodic payments (typically through an insurance company) when an employee is unable to perform the duties of his or her regular job because of an injury or illness that is not associated with the person's work activities. See also *disability benefit* and *occupational disability benefit*.

nonoccupational policy—insurance contract that insures a person against an off-the-job injury or illness. It does not cover a disability resulting from an injury or illness covered by workers' compensation.

nonpreferred provider—also referred to as out-of-network providers, a health care provider that does not have a contract with a patient's health plan or insurance company. The cost to the individual for using a nonpreferred provider is typically higher than if the person had chosen a preferred provider that had contracted with the plan or insurer to provide services at a discounted rate. See also *preferred provider*.

nonprofit insurer—business organized under special state laws to provide hospital, medical and/or dental insurance on a nonprofit basis (e.g., Blue Cross and Blue Shield). Such plans are usually exempt from some taxes imposed on regular insurers. See also *Blue Cross and Blue Shield plan*.

nonprofit organization (NPO)—association, club or other entity that supports or engages in activities for a social welfare, civic improvement, education, recreation, religious or similar purpose. NPOs do not provide a profit to their owners, directors or members, but they can generate income to pay for their activities, salaries and overhead. In the U.S., NPOs are exempt from federal and state income taxes. See also *not-for-profit organization (NFPO)*.

nonqualified annuity—annuity that has been funded with money taxed by the U.S. government in the year in which the funds were deposited. See also *annuity*.

nonqualified deferred compensation (NQDC) plan—executive benefit program in which participants defer income in exchange for an unsecured promise from the company to pay future benefits. In the U.S., tax-deferred savings of this nature are subject to creditors in the event the business enters bankruptcy. Popular among small businesses, the two main types of NDCPs are supplemental executive retirement plans and deferred savings plans.

nonqualified employee plan—employer-sponsored benefit plan that does not meet the requirements of IRC Section 401(a). Such plans are not given the tax advantages available to qualified plans. See also *excess benefit plan, nonqualified deferred compensation plan (NDCP), nonqualified stock option (NQSO)* and *qualified employee benefit plan*.

nonqualified stock option (NQSO)—employee's right to buy corporate stock at a stated price within a set period of time. An NQSO does not meet IRS criteria for incentive stock options. As a result, if an employee exercises the option to purchase stock, the company is required to withhold state and federal income tax, Medicare and FICA on the difference between the fair market value and option price on the exercise date. When the stock is sold, the employee must report the capital gain or loss. An NQSO is also referred to as a nonstatutory stock option. See also *incentive stock option (ISO)*.

nonresident alien—noncitizen who is in a country on a visa or temporary basis. In the U.S., nonresident aliens include lawful permanent residents with green cards and those who meet the test for substantial days of physical presence. See also *resident alien*.

nonstandardized plan—master or prototype retirement plan generally designed to satisfy the coverage and nondiscrimination requirements of the IRC. Nonstandardized plans have more flexibility than standardized plans; they permit the exclusion of any class of employees provided the plan satisfies IRC requirements. See also *master plan, nonstandardized safe harbor plan, prototype plan* and *standardized plan*.

nonstandardized safe harbor plan—master or prototype retirement plan with the same features as a nonstandardized plan except that the allocation or benefits formula must satisfy safe harbor rules under IRC Section 401(a)(4). See also *nonstandardized plan* and *safe harbor plan*.

nonstatutory stock option (NSO)—see *nonqualified stock option (NQSO)*.

nontaxable—excluded from wages by a specific IRC section; for example, qualified health plan benefits are excluded from income for federal tax purposes under IRC Section 105. See also *partially taxable* and *tax-deferred*.

nontrusteed plan—see *general asset plan*.

normal form of benefit—default distribution option for a retirement plan. For single participants, the normal form of benefit is typically a monthly income payable for life. A joint and survivor annuity is most common for married persons. See also *qualified joint and survivor annuity (QJSA)*.

normal pension—retirement benefit to which an employee is or would be entitled on reaching normal retirement age based on the person's earnings and/or service. See also *normal retirement age (NRA)*.

normal pension cost—present value of pension benefits gained as a result of employee service in the current year. Also called service cost, normal pension cost is funded dollar for dollar and usually assumes a plan's "normal" retirement age for participants.

normal retirement—termination of an employee that involves the payment of retirement benefits with no reduction as the result of age or service or with special qualifications such as disability.

normal retirement age (NRA)—age established by a plan when retirement normally occurs and an employee will receive full benefits. If a person retires prior to this age, there may be a reduction in retirement benefits.
—When the IRS refers to normal retirement age, it may be referring to when an employee becomes vested in a retirement plan or the fifth anniversary of commencement of plan participation. It may also be referring to the age at which a person is eligible for full Social Security retirement, which varies from the age of 65 to 67 depending on the employee's year of birth. See also *Social Security full retirement age*.

normal retirement date (NRD)—earliest date at which a participant qualifies for retirement with full benefits under a retirement plan.

North American Free Trade Agreement (NAFTA)—signed in 1994, an agreement by the United States, Canada and Mexico that established a schedule for phasing out tariffs and other hindrances to encourage freer trade among the three nations. NAFTA also promotes investment among these countries.

notary—person legally empowered by government to verify signatures and certify the validity of documents.

notched option—see *level income option*.

note—debt security issued by a bank, government or other entity, usually maturing in one to ten years, whereas bonds mature in more than ten years. See also *bond*.

notice of intent to terminate—as defined by the Pension Benefit Guaranty Corporation (PBGC), 60-day advance notice to affected parties advising them of a proposed termination of a defined benefit plan covered by the PBGC.

not-for-profit organization (NFPO)—broad-based term encompassing all organizations known variously as charities, nonprofit organizations (NPOs), nongovernmental organizations, private voluntary organizations, etc. While the terms "nonprofit" and "not-for-profit" are often used interchangeably for any organization that does not operate for commercial gain, some differences exist. In contrast to a nonprofit, a not-for-profit pays taxes on income and may make a profit. A not-for-profit organization may also have a membership roster that directly benefits from the income of the organization. For example, an organization that has fund drives to send children to a destination would likely be a not-for-profit if the children were the ones that took part in the fundraising efforts (e.g., selling candy to raise funds).

not yet accredited health plan—benefit program that has not yet been given a "seal of approval" by an independent company indicating it meets national quality standards for health plans. There are many reasons why a health plan may not be accredited. For example, some plans have never gone through the accreditation process or have gone through the process with a different accrediting organization. Other plans are too new to be accredited or have started but not finished the accreditation process. Not being accredited doesn't mean that a plan is lower quality than a plan that is accredited.

nurse advice line—utilization management strategy that employs a registered nurse to answer health care questions via the telephone. The service may include counseling and patient education, guidance in obtaining services, and referrals to service providers. See also *utilization management (UM)*.

nurse practitioner (NP)—registered nurse who has completed advanced education (generally a master's degree) and training in the diagnosis and management of common as well as complex medical conditions. Nurse practitioners provide a broad range of health care services, including many of the duties of a physician.

nursing home—place of residence licensed under state law that provides health care and related services to the chronically ill and those unable to take care of daily living needs who do not require the degree of care provided by a hospital or skilled nursing facility. Nursing homes do not qualify as a skilled nursing facility under the definition established for Medicare reimbursement. Under limited circumstances, however, Medicare will pay for some nursing home costs. Private medigap insurance plans also reimburse only a small portion of the costs incurred in a nursing home. In contrast, Medicaid covers the entire cost for persons with limited income and assets. See also *extended care facility (ECF)* and *skilled nursing facility (SNF)*.

Nursing Home Compare—website sponsored by the Centers for Medicare and Medicaid Services designed to provide nursing home quality information to consumers.

NYSE MKT LLC—initially, the American Stock Exchange (AMEX), a mutual organization owned by its members. NYSE MKT LLC is located in New York.

O

obesity—condition characterized by the excessive accumulation of fat in the body that may have an adverse effect on health and life expectancy. An adult with a *body mass index (BMI)* of 30 or greater is generally considered obese.

occupational death benefit—life insurance or pension money payable upon the death of an employee whose death resulted from his or her employment. See also *death benefit* and *nonoccupational death benefit*.

occupational differentials—comparably stable differences in wage rates among occupations.

occupational disability benefit—periodic payments (typically through an insurance company) when a worker is unable to perform the duties of his or her regular job due to an injury or illness associated with work activities. See also *disability benefit* and *nonoccupational disability benefit*.

occupational disease (OD)—see *occupational illness*.

occupational hazard—condition on a job that can cause an accident, illness or death.

occupational health services—activities performed to protect the physical health and safety of employees at work.

occupational illness—disease or health impairment resulting from employment or conditions inherent in a work environment. In most states, occupational illnesses are now covered under workers' compensation.

occupational pension plan—retirement benefit program sponsored by an employer, labor union or professional organization for workers. Other names for these plans are private pension plans, company pension plans, registered pension plans and employer-sponsored pension plans.

Occupational Safety and Health Act (OSHA)—U.S. statute establishing national standards for health and safety conditions in the workplace, which are enforced by the Occupational Safety and Health Administration. The act also provides for the reporting and compiling of statistics pertaining to occupational illnesses and injuries.

Occupational Safety and Health Administration (OSHA)—agency within the U.S. Department of Labor charged with setting standards for promoting and enforcing a safe and healthy work environment for employees.

occupational therapy (OT)—treatment by means of productive and creative activities that helps a disabled person perform the tasks of daily living (e.g., bathing, dressing, eating, working). OT often involves helping a patient develop skills and find new ways of accomplishing tasks that allow the person to have an independent, productive and satisfying life. Treatment may address psychological, social and environmental factors as well as physical factors that impede successful functioning. See also *physical therapy (PT)*.

occurrence policy—insurance coverage for claims that result from events during a specific period of time. Coverage is based on the date of the event leading to the loss versus when the claim is presented to the insurance company. Hence, a claim may arise years after the policy has expired. See also *claims-made policy*.

OCONUS—acronym used to reference places "outside the continental United States."

odd lot—amount of a security that is less than the normal unit traded. For stocks, any transaction of less than 100 shares is considered an odd lot. See also *round lot*.

offer—price at which a person is willing to buy or sell.

offering price—see *asking price*.

Office of Federal Contract Compliance Programs (OFCCP)—part of the U.S. Department of Labor's Employment Standards Administration, the unit responsible for ensuring that contractors doing business with the government do not discriminate.

Office of Labor-Management Standards (OLMS)—within the U.S. Department of Labor's Employment Standards Administration, OLMS administers and enforces most provisions of the Labor-Management Reporting and Disclosure Act of 1959, which helps to ensure basic standards of democracy and fiscal responsibility in labor organizations representing employees.

Office of Management and Budget (OMB)—organization within the executive branch of the U.S. government that is responsible for providing fiscal accounting and budgeting services.

Office of the Comptroller of the Currency (OCC)—agency that charters, regulates and supervises the activities of U.S. banks, their international branches, and U.S. branches of non-U.S. banks. The goals of the OCC are to keep the banking system secure and honest as well as to ensure banking services are widely available.

Office of the Superintendent of Financial Institutions (OSFI)—federal agency that regulates and supervises Canadian financial institutions, including banks, insurance companies, trust and loan companies, and co-operative credit associations. OSFI is charged with protecting the rights and interests of depositors and policyholders of financial institutions and ensuring public confidence in Canada's financial system. The Office also makes sure pension plans comply with the requirements of the Pension Benefits Standards Act. See also *Pension Benefits Standards Act (PBSA) of 1985*.

Office of Thrift Supervision (OTS)—unit within the U.S. Treasury that supervises savings associations and their holding companies in order to maintain their fiscal soundness and compliance with consumer laws.

Office of Workers' Compensation Programs (OWCP)—government office that administers four major disability compensation programs providing wage replacement benefits, medical treatment, vocational rehabilitation and other benefits to certain workers or their dependents who experience work-related injury or occupational disease. OWCP is housed within the Employment Standards Administration of the U.S. Department of Labor.

officer—key appointed position of authority within a business (e.g., president, vice president or director).

office visit—face-to-face contact between a physician and patient in an office, clinic or other health facility.

official check—see *bank draft*.

off-label drug—medication used for a purpose other than that for which it was originally approved by the FDA for marketing in the United States. Also referred to as an unapproved drug.

offset—amount used to compensate or counterbalance another amount. For example, a person's earnings may result in the reduction of another benefit payable to a person. In some cases, the benefit received from one program is offset by the amount a person receives through another benefit program.

Old Age Security (OAS)—monthly payment from the federal government funded from general tax revenue that is available to Canadian citizens and other qualified persons aged 65 and over regardless of past earnings or current income. OAS provides a floor of income support below which most Canadians will not fall. Indexed to the Consumer Price Index, this benefit is taxed back wholly or partially for those with incomes over a certain level. OAS is one of Canada's Social Security programs. See also *Canada Pension Plan (CPP)/Québec Pension Plan (QPP)* and *Guaranteed Income Supplement (GIS)*.

Old-Age, Survivors, Disability and Health Insurance (OASDHI)—see *Social Security*.

Older Workers Benefit Protection Act of 1990 (OWBPA)—amendment to the Age Discrimination in Employment Act of 1967 that requires equal benefits or equal cost in employee benefit plans that treat participants differently based on age. This U.S. law also makes it illegal for an employer to use an employee's age to discriminate in benefits or to target older workers for layoffs.

Omnibus Budget Reconciliation Act (OBRA)—annual tax and budget reconciliation act of the U.S. Congress that often impacts employee benefits, pension plans and Medicare.

Omnibus Budget Reconciliation Act of 1986 (OBRA '86)—U.S. legislation that:
- Changed Medicare reimbursement to physicians and hospitals
- Amended COBRA to make the loss of retiree health coverage as the result of a firm's Chapter 11 bankruptcy filing a qualifying event for continuation of health insurance coverage for retirees and their dependents
- Required employers with pension plans to provide pension accruals or allocations for newly hired employees who are within five years of normal retirement age and employees working beyond the age of 64.

Omnibus Budget Reconciliation Act of 1987 (OBRA '87)—U.S. legislation that (1) allowed states to extend Medicaid coverage to pregnant women and infants in families with incomes up to 185% of poverty level and (2) contained provisions affecting the minimum funding standards. OBRA '87 also requires *drug regimen review (DRR)* by a pharmacist in all federally reimbursed long-term care facilities.

Omnibus Budget Reconciliation Act of 1989 (OBRA '89)—federal legislation that:
- Allowed COBRA continuees who become covered under another plan to continue their former employer coverage for a health problem considered to be a preexisting condition under the new plan
- Extended the continuation period for individuals who are disabled at termination of employment and raised the premium for the extended period
- Partially repealed the interest exclusion on employee stock ownership plan loans
- Imposed mandatory civil penalties on violations by qualified plan fiduciaries
- Created a tax penalty for substantial overstatement of pension liabilities in determining deductibility
- Required various forms of deferred compensation be included in determination of average compensation and, in turn, the Social Security taxable wage base. See also *Omnibus Budget Reconciliation Act (OBRA)*.

Omnibus Budget Reconciliation Act of 1990 (OBRA '90)—U.S. legislation that requires *drug utilization review (DUR)* activities by state Medicaid programs and mandates basic community pharmacy counseling requirements to be done by pharmacists when dispensing a medication.

Omnibus Budget Reconciliation Act of 1993 (OBRA '93)—U.S. legislation that:
- Impacted many direct and indirect components of pay (such as qualified retirement plan limits)
- Increased the Medicare tax base
- Eliminated the deduction for executive pay in excess of $1 million under most circumstances
- Extended the tuition reimbursement exclusion.

on-call employees—workers who are called to work as needed, often on short notice, although they may be scheduled to work for several days or weeks in a row.

online pharmacy—also referred to as an Internet pharmacy, an organization providing pharmacy services via a networked computer. Mail or another shipping service delivers medications to consumers. See also *Verified Internet Pharmacy Practice Sites (VIPPS)*.

open access—managed care plan that allows a beneficiary to go directly to a health care specialist without going through a gatekeeper.

open access network—health or dental plan with providers in various locations. Beneficiaries are not required to use providers who have contracted with the plan to receive full benefits. See also *closed plan* and *open panel*.

open-end fund—type of mutual fund that places no restrictions on the amount of shares that can be issued. Shares are continuously bought and sold directly from the mutual fund company and/or a brokerage house. The price of a share in an open-end fund fluctuates daily depending on the performance of the securities held by the fund. Open-end funds offer choice, liquidity and convenience but charge fees and often require a minimum investment. If a fund's investment manager determines that total assets have become too large to effectively execute its stated objective, a fund can be closed to new investors. In an extreme situation, the fund may be closed to new investment by existing fund investors. See also *closed-end fund* and *mutual fund*.

open-end mortgage—loan on real property that permits the borrower to borrow more funds at a later date on the same loan, typically up to a preset maximum. Such a provision is common in construction loans.

open enrollment—period that employees are allowed to enroll in a benefit program. Open enrollment most typically is used to refer to the period when health plan participants are allowed to select an alternate health plan offered by the program. Uninsured employees and their dependents may also be allowed to obtain coverage without presenting evidence of insurability.

open formulary—also referred to as a voluntary formulary, a relatively unrestricted list of drug choices available to participants through a benefit plan. Open formularies, however, may have a list of preferred medications that are generally less expensive. Patients are encouraged but not required to choose drugs from the preferred list. If a medication is not on the preferred list, the patient may have to pay an additional out-of-pocket expense. See also *closed formulary, drug formulary, incentive formulary, limited formulary, partially closed formulary* and *unlimited formulary*.

open market operation (OMO)—principal tool used by the Federal Reserve System to expand or contract the amount of money in the nation's banking system. The purchase of government securities injects money into the system and is used to stimulate growth, while the sale of securities does the opposite. See also *Federal Open Market Committee (FOMC), Federal Reserve System* and *monetary policy*.

open mortgage—mortgage that can be paid off in part or in full at any time before maturity without penalty.

open network—group of pharmacies in which any pharmacy may join if it agrees to the group's contract and reimbursement parameters. See also *closed network* and *pharmacy network*.

open panel—managed care plan that directly or indirectly contracts with health care providers to deliver care. In contrast to a closed panel, an open panel reimburses members for health services obtained from outside of its provider network. See also *closed panel* and *IPA model HMO*.

open shop—sometimes called a nonunion or merit shop, a company or place of business where joining a labor union is not a condition of being hired or continued employment. Open shops are required by law in right-to-work jurisdictions and by employers such as the federal government. See also *closed shop* and *right-to-work law*.

operating activity—regular function of a business, such as manufacturing or the provision of a service. Other functions, such as the sale of land or used equipment, are classified as nonoperating activities.

operational audit—evaluation of how an organization's management and operating procedures are functioning with respect to effectiveness, efficiency and economy.

operational risk—potential for loss as a result of failed or inadequate processes, systems, people or external events.

opinion letter—written statement issued by a government agency to approve an action. For example, the IRS issues an opinion letter when ruling on the acceptability of a prototype retirement plan.

opportunistic real estate—all types of investment property including niche sectors such as health care facilities and senior housing. These properties are those most likely to have lower quality buildings that require extensive redevelopment or land needing development. Of the three broad categories of real estate, opportunistic real estate has the greatest fluctuations in price but the most return potential. Return is primarily (although not exclusively) price appreciation. See also *core real estate*, *real property* and *value-added real estate*.

optimal portfolio—see *efficient portfolio*.

option—see *option agreement*.

option agreement
—contract between a client and a brokerage firm used to verify the client's level of investment experience and to ensure the client understands the risk involved before the client is allowed to trade options. It is also known as an option.
—agreement between two parties that provides one of the parties the right but not the obligation to buy, sell or obtain a specific asset at an agreed-upon price at some time in the future. A "call option" gives the party holding the agreement the right to purchase an asset under the terms stated. In contrast, a "put option" gives the holder the right to sell. See also *exercise price*, *index option*, *International Securities Exchange (ISE)*, *stock option*, *straddle*, *strangle* and *underwater*.

optionally renewable—term in an individual insurance policy that indicates the policy is renewable only if the insurance company chooses to renew it. See also *cancelable*, *conditionally renewable*, *guaranteed renewable and noncancelable* and *guaranteed renewable*.

optionee—person (buyer) who receives an option for the purchase of an asset.

optioner—person (seller) who gives an option to another party for the purchase of an asset.

opt-out incentive—financial motivation, such as a lump-sum or monthly payout, offered by an employer to employees who decline participation in a health care plan.

oral and maxillofacial surgeon—dental specialty dealing with the diagnosis and treatment of diseases, defects, deformities and injuries involving the head, neck, face, jaws, and the hard and soft tissues of the oral (mouth) and maxillofacial (jaws and face) regions.

oral health—as defined by the World Health Organization (WHO), freedom from chronic mouth and facial pain, oral and throat cancer, oral sores, birth defects such as cleft lip and palate, periodontal (gum) disease, tooth decay and tooth loss, and other diseases and disorders that affect the oral cavity.

orange zone—see *endangered status*.

ordinary care—care that a reasonable person would exercise under a given set of circumstances. Ordinary care is a standard used for determining legal duty. See also *prudent person rule*.

ordinary life insurance—see *whole life insurance*.

ordinary life pension trust—trust-funded pension plan that provides death benefits through the purchase of whole life insurance contracts for covered employees. The trust pays premiums on the insurance coverage until the employee reaches retirement age. The trust also accumulates, in an auxiliary fund, the additional money needed to purchase retirement benefits for plan participants, using the paid-up cash value of the life insurance policy for each employee as part of the purchase price of the annuity.

organizational chart—hierarchical diagram depicting an organization's structure, which may include the names of units, titles and names of individuals, relative ranks and interrelationships.

orphan's benefits—one of the children's benefits available under the Canada Pension Plan and Québec Pension Plan. A child of a deceased contributor to either of these plans is eligible to receive a fixed monthly payment from the plan if the child is:
- Under the age of 18 or between the ages of 18 and 25 and in full-time attendance at a recognized school or university
- A natural or an adopted child or a child that is/was in the care and control of the contributor who is disabled/diseased.

orthodontic benefits—insurance coverage for the repositioning of teeth and jaws. Orthodontic benefits are not included in all dental plans. When provided, the coverage may be restricted to persons under a certain age and to yearly or lifetime dollar limits.

orthodontics—branch of dentistry dealing with the proper positioning of teeth and jaws, usually through the use of braces.

orthotics—brace, splint or other device used to support, align, prevent or correct the function of a body when moving. For example, shoe inserts are orthotics intended to correct an abnormal or irregular walking pattern; the devices alter the angle at which the foot strikes a walking or running surface.

osteopathic medicine—form of conventional medicine that gives particular attention to the muscles, joints, bones and nerves of the body. There is an underlying belief that all of the body's systems work together and disturbances in one system may affect function elsewhere in the body. Osteopathic physicians are granted a doctor of osteopathy, or D.O., degree.

other diagnosis—coding terminology used by health care providers when noting conditions that exist at the time of admission or care, as well as conditions that subsequently develop, which affect the treatment received and/or the length of stay in a hospital. Diagnoses relating to an earlier episode that have no bearing on the present hospital stay are excluded.

other postemployment benefits (OPEB) plan—program for retired employees covering benefits other than a pension. OPEBs include postretirement medical, pharmacy, dental, vision, life, long-term disability and long-term care benefits that are not associated with a pension plan. See also *GASB Statements 43 and 45* and *substantive plan.*

outcome—clinical result achieved through a health care service and/or medication that may be positive, negative or neutral in terms of success.

outcomes management—collection of data regarding the results of health care treatments to better understand which treatments are the most successful. Outcomes management may lead to the development of clinical protocols.

outcomes measurement—collection and use of data to show how well a given medical intervention is meeting the health and cost goals of plan sponsors, patients and other stakeholders.

outlier
—one who does not fit the typical or overall pattern of distribution. For example, a physician who prescribes a medication much more frequently than is normal for other physicians is considered an outlier. See also *clinical outlier.*
—one whose residence is an appreciable distance from his or her place of work.

out-of-area benefit—coverage that a health care plan supplies when participants are outside the plan's geographical limits. These benefits usually include emergency care plus low-indemnity payments for nonemergency benefits. Most plans stipulate that out-of-area services for emergency care will be provided until the participant can be returned to the plan for medical management of the case.

out-of-network provider—service provider that has not directly contracted with a benefit plan, provider system or insurance company to provide a service at a predetermined fee. For example, health care providers not affiliated with a preferred provider organization are labeled "out of network." This term is also used to refer to a service not available within a health care plan or network. See also *preferred provider organization (PPO).*

out-of-pocket expense
—cost incurred and paid for by an individual. Some out-of-pocket expenses incurred while on the job such as supplies, cab fare, gasoline or a business lunch may be reimbursed by an employer. In addition, the federal government allows some out-of-pocket expense categories to be deducted when calculating personal income taxes.
—from an insurance perspective, out-of-pocket expenses are the deductibles, copays and coinsurance not covered by the insurance policy. See also *out-of-pocket maximum/limit*.

out-of-pocket maximum/limit—highest amount a health plan specifies a plan participant must pay for deductibles, copayments, coinsurance payments and similar charges. For details regarding the out-of-pocket maximums established by the ACA, see "Benefit Mandates" in the *Appendix A: Affordable Care Act of 2010 (ACA)*.

outpatient (OP)—person who receives health care services from a hospital, clinic or other medical unit without being admitted as an overnight patient.

outpatient care—see *outpatient service*.

outpatient service—health care service including prevention, diagnosis, observation, treatment and rehabilitation that is provided to a patient who has not been admitted to a hospital for an overnight stay. The services may be provided by a freestanding or hospital-based center, a clinic or even a mobile unit. Outpatient services are also commonly referred to as ambulatory or outpatient care.

outpatient surgery—treatment of an injury or disorder of the body by incision or manipulation—especially with instruments—that does not require an overnight hospital stay. Also referred to as ambulatory surgery, same-day surgery or day surgery.

outplacement assistance—employment counseling and other aid for employees who have been dismissed when an organization downsizes or changes its business strategy.

outsourcing—transfer of a business function to an external provider.

overbilling—charging a plan or insurer more than what has been agreed upon; for example, a health care provider might not disclose a waiver of a patient copayment.

overcoding—see *upcoding*.

overfunded plan—defined benefit retirement plan that has projected benefit obligations smaller than the fair value of the plan's assets. If a plan is overfunded, plan sponsors may be able to skip contributions. A sponsor of a single-employer plan may also have the option, within limits, to reclaim the overfunding as profit. Other options that may be available to plan sponsors include electing to increase benefits, transferirng some assets to a new plan or merging the overfunded plan with an underfunded plan. See also *projected benefit* and *projected benefit obligation (PBO)*.

overinsurance—when the amount of insurance payments to an insured on a loss is greater than the actual loss incurred.

over the counter (OTC)
—pharmaceutical products legally available without a prescription.
—in the financial world, OTC refers to the direct trade of stocks and other financial instruments between two parties versus through an exchange. Securities traded in this manner are usually not able to meet exchange listing requirements.

over the counter (OTC) market—trading of securities and financial instruments (e.g., stocks, bonds, futures, derivatives) via a broker-dealer network over the telephone or electronically versus on a physical trading floor such as the New York Stock Exchange. Most OTC stocks represent small companies that are unable to meet the listing requirements of the other exchanges. For this reason, they are referred to as unlisted stocks. Although NASDAQ operates as a dealer network, NASDAQ stocks are generally not classified as OTC because the NASDAQ is considered a stock exchange. Some (not all) OTC stocks are penny stocks or offered by companies with bad credit records. See also *over the counter (OTC)* and *stock market*.

overtime—time worked by an employee in addition to regularly scheduled hours and in excess of the legal maximum hours of work.

overtreatment—provision of more services than are consistent with, or justified by, a diagnosis and treatment plan; the care provided is neither necessary nor appropriate. Overtreatment is often used as synonymous with overutilization. See also *undertreatment*.

owner-employee—for IRS purposes, a self-employed individual who owns the entire interest in an unincorporated business or a partner who owns more than 10% of the capital or profit interest of the partnership. If the owner-employee establishes a benefit plan just for his or her employees but does not cover himself or herself, the rules for qualification and tax treatment of contributions and benefits are the same as those plans established by corporate employers.

owners' equity—difference between a property's fair market value and current indebtedness.

P

package pricing—see *bundled payment*.

paid claims—in the financial reporting by benefit plans and insurers, the dollar value of all claims paid during a specific time period with no adjustment for anticipated or known liabilities that have not yet been paid.

paid-time-off (PTO) program—arrangement that gives an employee a set amount of days away from work to be used at the employee's discretion. These days can be used for sick time, personal time, vacation or any other reason the employee chooses. Like other forms of time off, the number of days in a PTO program generally accumulate with increasing years of service.

paid-up life insurance—death benefit coverage purchased from an insurance company that requires no further premium payments be made.

paired comparison—technique that compares each job individually to every other job to determine which one has a higher value. The job rankings created can be pegged to the market via benchmark jobs.

panic selling—wide-scale selling of an investment or investments, causing a sharp decline in prices. When panic selling, investors typically want to get out of the investment with little regard for the price at which they sell. The reaction is emotional rather than based on asset fundamentals. Almost every market crash has been the result of panic selling. Most major stock exchanges use trading curbs and halts to limit panic selling, to allow people to digest any information on why the selling is occurring and to restore some degree of normalcy to the market. See also *circuit breaker, stock market crash* and *trading curb*.

paper profit/loss—unrealized gain or loss on an investment calculated by subtracting the investor's cost from the current market price. Paper profits and losses are realized when a security is sold. See also *capital gain/loss* and *realized profit/loss*.

parachute—contractual agreement that provides payments or benefits to employees if there is a change in corporate control (e.g., merger, acquisition). Some parachutes are triggered when a change in control occurs regardless of whether an employee keeps his or her job. Others are triggered only if the employee is terminated. Agreements that provide benefits for top executives are referred to as golden parachutes. Such an agreement allows an executive to dispassionately consider the future of a company, confident that his or her financial well-being is secure. Similar agreements that generally have less generous packages for managers and nonmanagers are respectively called silver and tin parachutes. Any and all of these agreements discourage hostile takeovers because the parachutes are one of the costs of the takeover. Parachutes are also referred to as change-of-control or change-in-control agreements. See also *excess parachute payment*.

paramedical exams—medical assessment conducted by a medical professional (usually a non-M.D.) for the purpose of evaluating an individual's health risk. Paramedical exams are paid for by the insurer and can be conducted at an applicant's home or work. The applicant may also choose to go to the office of the paramedical firm. The exam is specific to each person's circumstances. The examiner may ask questions, take blood pressure, check height and weight, check pulse, obtain a blood and/or urine specimen or perform an EKG.

paramedical services—in Canada, services provided by professionals who aren't covered by the public health system (e.g., chiropractic care, physiotherapy, massage therapy, naturopathy, acupuncture and osteopathy.
—in the U.S., services that require authorization and training by a medical professional before they can be provided.

parental leave—paid or unpaid time off work provided by an employer to a mother or father in order to care for a child or to make arrangements for a child's welfare. Parental leave often includes maternity, paternity and adoption leave. See also *Family and Medical Leave Act of 1993 (FMLA)* and *Pregnancy Discrimination Act of 1978 (PDA)*.

partial disability—illness or injury that renders a person incapable of performing one or more but not all of the duties of a job. Substantial variations exist in definitions for this term, including whether the job is a person's current occupation or any job. See also *permanent disability, temporary disability* and *total disability*.

partially closed formulary—list of drug choices available through a benefit plan that is relatively unrestricted; however, the list does not cover a few specific drugs or classes of medications (e.g., weight-loss or cosmetic medications). There may also be restrictions on the amount of a medication that is covered (e.g., a single course of treatment of nicotine patches). Clinical necessity and the cost of a medication are important factors in whether a medication is covered. As with an open formulary, a partially closed formulary may also have a preferred list of drugs. Patients prescribed a medication not on the preferred list may have to pay an additional out-of-pocket expense. See also *closed formulary, drug formulary, incentive formulary, limited formulary, open formulary* and *unlimited formulary.*

partially taxable—portion of income or a benefit that is taxable, while the remainder is excluded from taxation. Under IRC Section 132, benefits such as a life insurance, a public transportation subsidy or parking may be excludable as income within specific dollar limits. See also *nontaxable,* and *tax-deferred.*

partial termination—reducing benefits or making participation requirements less liberal, although not to the extent that the benefit plan ceases to exist. See also *plan termination.*

partial vesting—employee entitlement to a specified portion of accrued pension benefits. The Tax Reform Act of 1986 established minimum levels of vesting for the U.S. After three years of service, an employee must be vested at 20%. Each year of service thereafter, vesting must increase by 20% until 100% vesting is achieved at the end of seven years of service. See also *cliff vesting* and *vesting.*

partial withdrawal—for the purposes of multiemployer benefit plans, a decline of 70% or more in an employer's contribution base units or a partial cessation of the employer's obligation to contribute. To ensure U.S. employers who gradually reduce their contributions do not escape withdrawal liability, ERISA has rules under which a partial cessation of an employer's obligation to contribute would trigger liability. See also *complete withdrawal, contribution base unit (CBU)* and *mass withdrawal.*

participant—see *plan member/participant.*

participant audit—typically, a voluntary program in which participants are asked to review their hospital and physician bills prior to payment by their heath plan to identify any billing errors. A financial incentive such as a fixed dollar reward or a percentage of any error the participants find may be used to encourage participants to conduct such a review.

participant bonus program—sharing a portion of the difference between a plan's total health costs for a period and the amount the plan was expected to spend in order to encourage the wise use of medical services.

participant-directed plan—see *consumer-driven health care (CDHC), self-directed investment* and *self-directed retirement plan.*

participant engagement—see *employee engagement.*

participating annuity—see *variable annuity.*

participating employer—employer that is making a contribution to a benefit plan.

participating group annuity—contract purchased from an insurance company in which the company agrees to provide a group of people with payments at some future date. The policyholder (typically an employer) and the insurance company share the mortality and investment risk. See also *annuity* and *immediate participation guarantee (IPG) contract.*

participating insurance—insurance (usually life insurance) in which policyholders share in surplus earnings of the insurance company. Payment is made as a dividend. Policyholders are usually given a choice as to how they wish to receive this dividend: (1) cash, (2) premium reduction, (3) additional paid-up insurance, (4) on deposit with interest or (5) additional term insurance. See also *life insurance.*

participating preferred stock—preferred stock that, under certain conditions, gives holders a share of the earnings over and above the fixed dividend rate. Dividends are frequently cumulative. See also *convertible preferred stock, cumulative preferred stock, noncumulative preferred stock* and *preferred stock.*

participating provider—see *preferred provider.*

participation—to join or take part in, such as participation in a benefit plan.

participation agreement—written contract between the trustees of a benefit plan and each participating employer that establishes the employer's contractual obligation to contribute to the plan.

participation requirement—condition that must be met before an employee may become part of a benefit plan. See also *minimum participation standard.*

partition—segregation of a portion of multiemployer plan assets and liabilities ordered by the Pension Benefit Guaranty Corporation to reduce the chance of plan insolvency. The segregated portion is treated as a separate plan after the partition.

partnership—cooperative relationship between people or groups sharing responsibility for achieving a goal. Co-ownership of a business by two or more people is considered a partnership. Each owner is equally and personally responsible for the debts of the whole business, not just a share.

Partnership for Prescription Assistance (PPA)—effort to connect uninsured and underinsured persons to public and private programs that provide medications for free or nearly free.

part-time employee—generally, any person who works fewer hours in a day or during a workweek than the 35 to 40 hours per week that an employer considers full-time employment. Those who work only during certain parts of the year are also considered part time. When compiling employment statistics, the U.S. Bureau of Labor Statistics classifies any person who works less than 34 hours a week (regardless of the number of hours worked in a given week) as a part-time employee. Protections under the Fair Labor Standards Act of 1938 are the same for part-time as for full-time workers. Under ERISA, part-time employees may be eligible for an employer's qualified retirement plan if they work at least 1,000 hours per year, which is about 20 hours per week. The employer has the choice of whether to provide benefits for part-time employees. See also *full-time employee*.

party in interest—ERISA term used to describe individuals who have a close relationship to a plan and who are prohibited from certain transactions with the plan. Examples of parties in interest include plan fiduciaries, service providers, sponsors, employees and any relative of the same. See also *prohibited transaction (PT)* and *Qualified Professional Asset Manager (QPAM)*.

par value—dollar amount assigned to a security by an issuer. For stocks, the very small amount (e.g., $0.01) bears no relationship to its market price. The par value of preferred stock is used to calculate dividend payments. For a bond, par value is the amount stated on the face of the bond and repaid to the investor when the bond matures. In the secondary market, a bond's price fluctuates with interest rates. If interest rates are higher than the coupon rate on a bond, the bond will be sold below par value (at a discount). If interest rates have fallen, the price will be sold above par value. Par value is also referred to as face value. See also *coupon rate* and *maturity value*.

passive management—style of investing that tries to match the average return and risk of a market or index by attempting to mirror its makeup. Adjustments are longer term and automatic versus the shorter-term approach dependent on personal judgment used in active management. Index mutual funds are passively managed. Since the fund manager's strategy is to make as few portfolio transactions as possible, transaction costs and capital gains taxes tend to be lower than with actively managed funds. In addition, passively managed funds have historically outperformed most actively managed funds. Passive management is also referred to as passive strategy, passive investing and index investing. See also *active management* and *index fund*.

pass-through pricing—invoicing a client for every drug dispensed based on the actual cost paid by a drug's manufacturer or other vendor. When a pharmacy benefits manager (PBM) says it uses pass-through pricing, the amount charged the client should reflect the cost of a drug after adjustments are made for any discounts, dispensing fees, rebates, credits, etc., that are paid or received by the PBM. See also *price transparency*.

pass-through security—fixed-income investment vehicle (e.g., bond, certificate) backed by a pool of assets (e.g., bonds, mortgages). An intermediary collects the monthly payments from issuers of the underlying assets, deducts a management fee, then passes the remaining funds to the holders of the pass-through security. The most common type of pass-through is a mortgage-backed certificate, where mortgage principal and interest are passed from mortgage lenders through a government agency or investment bank to investors. Pass-through securities are also known as pass-through certificates and pay-through securities. See also *mortgage-backed security (MBS)*.

past service benefit/credit—value received toward a pension benefit plan, provided by an employer, for a participant's years of service that occurred before the initiation of a pension plan or an amendment to a plan. For Canada, see also *grossed-up past service pension adjustment (PSPA), pension adjustment (PA)* and *provisional past service pension adjustment (PSPA)*.

past service pension adjustment (PSPA)—retroactive change in pension service credits, pension benefits or how benefits are determined. A PSPA is equal to the additional pension credits that would have been included in the member's pension adjustment if the upgraded benefits or additional service had actually been provided in those previous years. See also *pension adjustment (PA)*.

paternity benefit—employer-provided benefit for a new father that may include paid or unpaid leave, flexible work opportunities and information resources. See also *Employment Insurance (EI), paternity leave* and *Pregnancy Discrimination Act of 1978 (PDA)*.

paternity leave—paid or unpaid time off work benefit provided to a father upon the arrival of a new child. See also *Family and Medical Leave Act of 1993 (FMLA)*.

patient advocate—one who is charged with helping a person receiving health care. A patient advocate often serves as liaison between the patient and the care provider, addressing patient complaints and concerns. Other functions of an advocate may include protecting patient rights and helping find support services the patient needs upon discharge from a health care facility.

patient assistance program (PAP)—program administered by a pharmaceutical company or its agent that offers free or reduced-price drugs to persons who meet the program's qualification criteria, for example, low-income individuals. See also *Partnership for Prescription Assistance (PPA)*.

patient-centered care—in contrast to disease-centered care, a health care model that involves patients as active participants in their own care with services rendered on the basis of individual needs and preferences, in addition to the advice of health professionals. See also *disease-centered care*.

patient-centered medical home (PCMH)—see *medical home*.

Patient-Centered Outcomes Research Institute (PCORI)—federal authority created under the Affordable Care Act of 2010 operating as a nonprofit corporation to advance the quality and relevance of evidence that can be used by patients, clinicians, purchasers and policy makers to make informed health care decisions. PCORI replaces the Federal Coordinating Council, which was created to make recommendations on comparative effectiveness initiatives. PCORI has a Board of Governors consisting of the Director of the Agency for Healthcare Research and Quality, the Director of the National Institutes of Health and 17 members appointed by the Comptroller General of the United States, and representing patients, providers, drug and device manufacturers, health service researchers, experts in quality improvement and federal and state government officials.

Patient-Centered Outcomes Research Institute (PCORI) Fee—see "Fees/Taxes" in the *Appendix A: Affordable Care Act of 2010 (ACA)*.

patient day—unit used for accounting purposes by health care facilities and planners that represents the amount of time during which the services of the institution or facility are used by a patient. If 100 patients use hospital beds for five days each, patient days would equal 500.

patient experience—divergent views exist as to the meaning of this term. Among the various factors that may be considered in measuring the patient experience are the timeliness of care, accommodating the emotional and spiritual aspects of care, customer service and even the physical setting in which care is provided.

Patient Protection and Affordable Care Act (PPACA) of 2010—see the Appendix A for a short summary of key provisions and terms from this landmark health care reform legislation.

patient registry—database maintained by a hospital, doctors' practice or health plan that allows caregivers to identify persons being provided care according to disease, demographic characteristics and other factors. Patient registries can help providers better coordinate care for patients, monitor treatment and progress, and improve overall quality of care.

patient satisfaction—degree to which an individual regards a health care service or product as useful, effective or beneficial.

pay-as-you-go (PAYG) plan—paying benefits or liabilities as they are incurred using current revenue. The U.S. government's Social Security program is essentially a PAYG system in that contributions from current workers are used to pay the benefits to retirees. In Canada and the United Kingdom, PAYG is sometimes referred to as pay go. A modified pay-as-you-go plan is partially funded. See also *general asset plan*.

pay compression—only a small difference in pay exists between employees, regardless of their skills or experience. As a result, an inexperienced new employee could earn the same or even more than an experienced worker doing the same job.

pay differential—factor used in determining differences in compensation. Pay differentials may or may not be performance-based. Other reasons for differentials include overtime hours, night shift work, education attained, level of responsibility, geography and hazardous working conditions.

pay-direct drug card plan—see *prescription drug card program*.

payee—person or entity paid with money.

payer—person or entity that pays money for something. In health care, the payer generally refers to entities, other than the patient, that finance or reimburse the cost of health services. In most cases, these are insurance carriers, health plan sponsors (employers or unions) and/or other third-party payers. Persons who do not have a benefit plan or insurance are the payers if there is no government or nonprofit entity willing to pick up or absorb the costs.

pay for knowledge (PFK)—see *knowledge-based pay*.

pay-for-performance—see *incentive pay plan*.

pay go plan—see *pay-as-you-go (PAYG) plan*.

payment allowance—see *allowable amount*.

payment reform—effort to improve current mechanisms for reimbursing providers such as including incentives for quality and efficiency.

pay-out ratio—percentage of earnings a stock pays out in the form of dividends.

pay range—minimum to maximum compensation established for a pay grade or class. The most common use of pay ranges is to set individual employee salaries or wages.

pay-related plan—benefit program that uses a formula based on compensation to determine benefits. Life insurance provided by an employer is often determined by an employee's compensation. Most defined benefit retirement plans also use a formula based on compensation during some time frame in an employee's service to calculate monthly retirement payments. See also *career pay plan* and *final earnings plan*.

payroll audit—examination of an employer's payroll records to determine the accuracy of the employer's figures and/or compliance with a legal agreement. For example, an insurance company that provides workers' compensation may audit a policyholder's payroll to determine the accuracy of the figures being used to establish the insurance premium being paid. In the context of multiemployer benefit plans, the payroll records of a contributing employer may be audited to ensure sufficient contributions are being made in accordance with the provisions of the collective bargaining agreement.

pay-through security—see *pass-through security*.

PBGC termination—see *plan termination*.

pecuniary—consisting of or measured in money.

pediatric—branch of medicine that deals with the care of infants, children and adolescents. The age limit for patients usually ranges from birth to 18 or 21 years of age. In some places, it is the completion of secondary education.

peer comparison—looking at how data in a similar situation are the same or different. Peer comparison is useful when establishing salaries that will attract qualified employees in a particular field of expertise, industry or locale. Some employee incentive plans establish goals based on how a business compares to its peers.

peer review—subjecting research or other work to the scrutiny of others who are equals or experts in the same field. See also *quality review committee*.

penny stock—share in the equity of a company that trades at a relatively low price and usually outside the major stock exchanges. Some consider a penny stock to be any stock trading under $5. In general, penny stocks are considered high risk because they have relatively low liquidity, large bid-ask spreads, small capitalization, fewer investors following them and fewer regulatory standards regarding disclosure. They often trade over the counter. See also *speculative stock*.

pension—steady income given to a person as the result of service (e.g., employee, military) that begins when a specific event (e.g., disability, retirement) occurs. Pensions are typically paid monthly and based on factors such as years of service and prior compensation. The payment may be made by a government, employer, pension fund or life insurance company. See also *annuity, employee retirement plan, multi-employer plan, multiemployer plan, multiple employer plan* and *pension fund*.

pensionable earnings/salary—income used to calculate a pension; generally, the average of a number of years' pay prior to retirement or the last year's pay. A term more often used outside the U.S. it is comparable to a *final earnings plan* in the U.S.

pensionable service—see *creditable service*.

pension adjustment (PA)—amount that reduces the Registered Retirement Savings Plan (RRSP) deduction limit of a person who is a member of a company-sponsored registered pension plan. Persons who are not in a pension plan do not have a pension adjustment. The RRSP/PA system has a single maximum for tax-assisted retirement savings of 18% of earned income (up to a yearly dollar limit) that applies to total contributions and benefits earned under all registered retirement plans. The PA is an attempt to equalize the various tax-deferred savings programs in Canada and to ensure that persons who participate in a company plan do not have the same level of RRSP contributions as those who do not. The adjustment also ensures all employees at comparable income levels have access to comparable tax assistance, regardless of the type of registered pension plan to which they belong.

pension adjustment reversal (PAR)—restoration of lost registered retirement savings plan contribution room to an individual. This occurs when a person receives a termination benefit that is less than the individual's total pension adjustments and past service pension adjustments. Under a deferred profit-sharing plan or a money purchase provision, an individual's PAR is the amount included in his or her pension credits but to which the individual ceases to have any rights at termination. See also *pension adjustment (PA)*.

pension administrator—see *administrator*.

Pension and Welfare Benefits Administration (PWBA)—see *Employee Benefits Security Administration (EBSA)*.

pension benefit formula—see *benefit formula*.

Pension Benefit Guaranty Corporation (PBGC)—nonprofit corporation created by ERISA and charged with protecting the pensions of workers and retirees. Sponsors of defined benefit plans in the U.S. pay premiums to the PBGC, which help guarantee benefits up to a specified maximum for participants and beneficiaries if their defined benefit plan terminates. The PBGC administers the plan termination provisions of ERISA Title IV and the Multiemployer Pension Plan Amendments Act of 1980. See also *plan termination* and *reportable event*.

Pension Benefits Standards Act (PBSA) of 1985—law enacted by the Canadian federal and provincial governments to govern the terms and operation of private pension plans set up for employees working in businesses under federal jurisdiction in Canada.

pension committee—persons other than the trustees who have been designated by pension plan management and/or a union to determine the eligibility of employees to receive a pension, select providers and/or address other plan issues.

pension equity plan (PEP)—defined benefit plan that provides a guaranteed lump-sum amount upon retirement that is based on a participant's years of service, age at which service was rendered and final average pay during a specified period (commonly three or five years when the participant's pay is usually the highest). A pension equity plan functions similar to a cash balance plan except the participant accumulates percentage points versus dollars for years worked. Guaranteed benefits are expressed in terms of a current lump sum. If a participant does not begin to receive benefits immediately after terminating employment, the lump-sum amount is credited with interest until benefit payments begin. Cited advantages of a PEP over traditional defined benefit plans include the ability to (1) provide portable benefits upon employment termination or retirement and (2) accommodate early retirement. See also *cash balance plan* and *hybrid pension plan*.

pension freeze—when some or all of the employees in a defined benefit retirement plan stop earning some or all of their benefits after a set date. Benefits accrued by these employees at the time of the freeze are not reduced. Generally, when a freeze occurs, new hires are not permitted to join the plan.

pension fund—pool of assets set aside by an employer or group of employers to provide a steady income for retired workers and their beneficiaries. Some pension funds also provide disability and health care benefits. See also *pension*.

Pension Funding Equity Act of 2004 (PFEA)—U.S. legislation providing interim relief to pension plans that were experiencing significant asset losses as the result of a downturn in the stock market. The act (1) changed quarterly contribution requirements for defined benefit pension plans and (2) updated the interest rate used for determining a plan's current liability for funding purposes. The act also provided additional funding relief primarily to companies in the automotive, steel and airline industries facing stiff competition, as well as a very limited number of severely underfunded multiemployer plans. The Pension Protection Act of 2006 modified and extended key provisions of PFEA. See also *Pension Protection Act of 2006 (PPA)*.

pension plan—a plan organized and administered to provide a regular income for the lifetime of retired members; other benefits that may be provided include payments on permanent disability, death, etc. See also *defined benefit (DB) plan, defined contribution (DC) plan* and *money purchase plan*.

Pension Protection Act of 2006 (PPA)—most sweeping U.S. pension legislation since ERISA, the Pension Protection Act of 2006 included significant changes for enhancing and protecting retirement savings. Key provisions of the legislation:
- Established new minimum funding standards for pension plans
- Set forth rules governing the valuation of plan assets and liabilities; set forth special rules for at-risk plans, including certification and notice requirements
- Established additional requirements for annual reports to the secretary of labor
- Allowed the secretary of the Treasury to waive minimum funding standards in the event of a temporary hardship or if the standard would be adverse to the interests of plan participants in the aggregate
- Required the secretary of the Treasury to prescribe mortality tables to be used for determining any present value based on the actual experience of pension plans and projected trends in such experience
- Permanently extended the defined contribution provisions of the Economic Growth and Tax Relief Reconciliation Act of 2001
- Created a new safe harbor for automatic enrollment of participants in 401(k) cash or deferred arrangements
- Made it easier for defined contribution sponsors to offer investment advice to plan participants
- Provided multiple exemptions to the prohibited transaction rules.

pension trust—see *pension fund*.

pension wear-away—approach for transitioning between a defined benefit retirement plan formula (e.g., a final-average-pay formula) to a cash balance formula. Each participant's benefits under the old plan are frozen and calculated as a lump sum used to offset the participant's balance in the new cash balance plan. The net effect is benefit growth of zero until the new benefit "catches up" with the old benefit. The period of zero net growth during the catch-up period gives "wear-away" its name. Under U.S. law, a wear-away period during which a participant does not accrue additional benefits is not permitted. Participants must receive the sum of the pre-amendment benefit plus benefits under the new cash balance formula.

P/E ratio—see *price/earnings (P/E) ratio*.

percentage participation clause—see *coinsurance*.

percentage test—one of three standards that can be used to determine whether a qualified retirement plan satisfies the IRS minimum coverage requirement. The qualified plan must benefit at least 70% of employees who are not highly compensated employees.

percent copay—see *coinsurance*.

percentile—value on a scale of zero to 100 that indicates the percent of distribution that is equal to or below it. One method a third-party payer of health care services may use to determine what it will pay is to identify the range of fees charged for a specific service, then state it will pay no more for a service than the charge at the 90th percentile. Percentiles are also commonly used to analyze the distribution of income and income trends within a nation. When looking at aggregate income in a nation, one might examine whether the proportion of income received by the top 10% of the population is increasing or decreasing—relative to the remaining 90%, over time. See also *quartile*.

per diem rate—charge per day. A per diem rate is used by some employers as the maximum allowable reimbursement to an employee for lodging and meal expenses. A per diem rate also refers to a flat charge established in advance to cover the daily cost of patient care at a hospital or other health care facility. This fee covers room and board charges; it may or may not cover ancillary service charges

performance appraisal—also referred to as an employee appraisal, an assessment of an employee's work. A performance appraisal is typically done at regular intervals (e.g., annually) and involves setting work standards, determining the employee's actual performance relative to those standards and providing feedback to the employee. A performance appraisal is used to determine training needs, merit increases, promotions, demotions and terminations. See also *alternate ranking method, graphic rating scale, management by objective* and *straight ranking method*.

performance-based fee—payment to providers such as investment managers or third-party administrators based, at least in part, on investment results or achievement of goals. Also known as an incentive fee.

performance guarantee—contractual provision between a care provider and benefit plan sponsor that certain services will be performed at a specified, measurable level. If the provider fails to meet a guarantee, a financial penalty may result. Common guarantees pertain to claims processing (e.g., turnaround time, coding accuracy, payment accuracy) and customer service (e.g., average response time, average time on hold).

performance guarantee audit—measuring the extent to which a vendor has complied with contractual guarantees to a client. For example, a pharmacy benefits manager might be audited to determine ID card production turnaround time, accurate dispensing, customer response time and participant satisfaction. See also *audit*.

performance improvement (PI)—see *quality improvement (QI)*.

performance measure—quantitative indicators used to report an outcome (e.g., productivity, health care quality).

performance sharing—assessment process in which goals are established for a group of individuals, a department or at a company level. Incentive awards are for persons within the defined group and are contingent upon the group meeting its goals.

performance standard—quantitative measure against which results are compared. Performance standards are often used in assessing worker productivity and program success. See also *performance measure*.

period certain annuity—see *annuity certain*.

period-of-service equivalency method—one of three approaches permitted by ERISA when tracking an employee's hours-of-service credit for a qualified retirement plan. With this particular method, the number of hours an employee is credited with is based on a specific period of employment during which the employee is paid. The equivalencies are 10 hours of service for a day, 45 hours for a week, 95 hours for semimonthly periods and 190 hours for a month. This method may also be based on work shifts if an employee who has at least one hour of service in a shift receives full credit for the full number of hours in the shift. See also *hours of service* and *year of service*.

periodontics—dental specialty that involves the diagnosis, prevention and treatment of diseases involving the supporting structures of teeth.

perks—see *perquisite*.

permanent disability—illness or injury that renders a person incapable of performing one or more duties of his or her occupation, typically for a lifetime. Substantial variations exist in definitions for this term. Some consider a disability permanent only if a person is incapable of doing any job. See also *partial disability, temporary disability* and *total disability*.

permanent life insurance—see *whole life insurance*.

permanent resident—noncitizen who has been given permission to permanently reside and work in a foreign nation. See also *green card* and *resident alien*.

per member per month (PMPM)—unit of measure by which comparisons can be made across groups or different health care organizations. Also used by health care providers when discussing the fee paid for health services. In a capitated health plan, PMPM is the amount prepaid to a provider for each plan member, regardless of the services actually used.

permissible withdrawal—in situations where there is a qualified automatic contribution arrangement for a defined contribution plan (i.e., 401(k) cash or deferred arrangement, 403(b) tax-sheltered annuity or 457(b) government plan), the ability of the participant to withdraw default elective deferrals within 90 days of the first deferral. See also *qualified automatic contribution arrangement (QACA)*.

permitted disparity—ability to skew pension contributions or benefits in favor of more highly compensated employees as granted by IRC Section 401(l) when a qualified retirement plan is integrated with Social Security. The rationale for this disparity in treatment is the fact that the employer and employee pay FICA taxes on all employee compensation up to the taxable wage base established for Social Security. For an employee with compensation less than the taxable wage base, the employer's contribution is based on all of the employee's pay. For employees who earn more than the taxable wage base, the employer makes no contribution to Social Security, and replacement of earnings above this maximum by Social Security is zero. Permitted disparity allows the employer to make up for some of this difference. See also *excess rate method, highly compensated employee (HCE)* and *integration*.

perquisite—sometimes referenced as perqs or perks, special privileges typically given executives such as a company car, credit card, club membership or meal allowance. Perquisites may also be given as recognition of outstanding performance or seniority; for example, a reserved parking space near the building or first choice on vacation scheduling.

person—from a legal perspective, an individual, partnership, joint venture, corporation, mutual company, joint stock company, trust, estate, unincorporated organization, association or employee organization.

Personal Earnings and Benefit Estimate Statement (PEBES)—document prepared annually by the Social Security Administration for each U.S. worker that shows the earnings reported to the agency for the employee over the employee's lifetime and that provides estimates of the different types of Social Security benefits for which the employee and his or her beneficiaries may qualify.

personal financial advisor—see *financial advisor* and *financial planner*.

personal financial planner—see *financial advisor* and *financial planner*.

personal financial planning—see *financial planning*.

Personal Financial Specialist (PFS)—Certified Public Accountant (CPA) specializing in personal financial planning. To earn a PFS designation, the accountant must meet the learning and experience requirements established by the American Institute of Certified Public Accountants (AICPA). The CPA must pass the PFS exam conducted by the AICPA and be an organizational member in good standing. See also *Certified Public Accountant (CPA)* and *financial planner*.

personal health record (PHR)—medical history maintained by an individual. A PHR may be kept on paper, a computer, the Internet, a portable device such as a flash drive or mobile phone, or a combination of these. New services are allowing persons to use an interactive system on the Internet for storing, updating and sharing health information with care providers.

Personal Information Protection and Electronic Documents Act (PIPEDA)—Canadian legislation that requires private sector organizations to get a person's consent before collecting, using or disclosing personal information in the course of commercial business. The information can be used only for purposes for which the person has given consent. In addition, the act contains various provisions for facilitating the use of electronic documents. PIPEDA incorporates and makes mandatory provisions of the Canadian Standards Association's Model Code for the Protection of Personal Information, which was developed in 1995.

personal leave—days provided to an employee to use for undefined personal business that may be paid or unpaid. Depending on its policy, an employer may allow a set number of days to be used each year, or the days may be granted on a case-by-case basis. The purpose and time limits can be specified or unspecified in the policy. Leave can be granted for reasons such as volunteer work, educational or political activities, family commitments, travel, etc.

personal risk—potential losses that directly affect an individual; for example, the possibility of a reduction in income, extra expenses and the elimination of financial assets. Hazards that may result in these losses include unemployment, poor health, premature death, liability, old age and property damage/theft risk. See also *liability risk, longevity risk* and *property risk*.

personal tax exemption—see *tax exemption*.

per thousand members per year (PTMPY)—number used to report health care utilization (e.g., days in the hospital PTMPY).

pet insurance—financial protection that can be purchased from an insurance company that will pay veterinary costs for a pet if it becomes ill or is injured in an accident. Some policies will also pay out if a pet is lost, stolen and/or dies. Pet insurance is offered by some employers as a voluntary employee-pay-all benefit.

phantom stock plan—nonqualified deferred compensation plan that gives select upper-level or key employees many of the benefits of stock ownership, without actually giving them any corporate stock. The pretend stock, sometimes referred to as shadow stock, follows the price movement of the company's actual stock. A full-value phantom stock plan gives the employee a payment in cash equal to the stock price on a date specified in the plan or award. In contrast, an incremental-value plan gives the employee an amount in stock or cash that equals the increase in value of the stock from the time the phantom stock was granted to the date of payment.

pharmaceutical assistance program—see *drug assistance program*.

pharmaceutical care—design, implementation and monitoring of a drug plan to produce a specific therapeutic outcome.

pharmacoeconomics—field of study that compares the value of different drug therapies with respect to both financial and quality-of-life outcomes. The three most common types of analysis are cost-benefit, cost-effectiveness and cost-minimization. Other forms of analysis include cost-utility, cost-avoidance analysis (CAA) and cost-consequence analysis (CCA).

pharmacoepidemiology—scientific study to determine the use and effects of pharmaceutical intervention on individual patients and patient populations.

pharmacogenetics—study of how genes affect a person's response to drugs, which combines pharmacology and genomics to develop safe and effective medication dosages specific to an individual's DNA.

pharmacology—chemical and physiologic study of drugs including drug preparation, properties, uses and effects on humans.

pharmacy
—establishment where medicinal drugs are dispensed and sold.
—science or practice of the preparation and dispensing of medicines.

pharmacy and therapeutics (P&T) committee—group of pharmacists and physicians from different specialties who design a formulary. For this reason, a P&T is sometimes referred to as a formulary committee. Most P&T committees evaluate drugs to determine which products are most medically appropriate and cost-effective. Typically, P&T committees also establish policies on the use of drug products and therapies. As part of the decision process, members examine therapeutic class reviews and drug monographs compiled from various public and private sources.

pharmacy benefits management/manager (PBM)—organization that manages pharmacy benefits on behalf of a health plan, insurer or plan sponsor. A PBM conducts activities that go beyond those of a third-party administrator in that it is designed to influence the behaviors of providers and patients that can affect the outcomes and cost of a drug benefit program. A PBM typically develops formularies and conducts drug utilization reviews to help contain costs.

pharmacy card program—use of a drug benefit identification card that, when presented to a participating pharmacy, entitles the recipient to receive the medication at a discount or for a minimal copay.

pharmacy network—pharmacies and pharmacy service providers that have contracted to provide pharmaceutical goods and services to health plan enrollees under specific terms and conditions. A common element of the arrangement is a negotiated reduction in reimbursement rates and dispensing fees paid to the pharmacies. See also *closed network* and *open network*.

pharmacy services administrative organization (PSAO)—individual pharmacies that negotiate and contract as a group with health plans, insurers or employers to provide pharmaceutical services to beneficiaries. The PSAO offers individual pharmacies negotiating power they would not have if they tried to negotiate on their own.

phased retirement—formal or informal employment arrangement that allows an employee at or near retirement to gradually move from full-time work to full-time retirement. The transition may take many forms, including part-time or temporary work, an extended leave of absence or a deferred retirement option plan. Phased retirement is sometimes referred to as gradual retirement.

physical safeguards—as prescribed by HIPAA privacy regulation, physical measures, policies and procedures that protect electronic health information systems, related buildings and equipment from natural and environmental hazards and unauthorized intrusion. See also *administrative safeguards* and *technical safeguards*.

physical therapy (PT)—treatment of a disease or injury by physical means, including exercise, massage, electricity, heat, cold and water. Physical therapy does not include the use of chemicals or radiation. The primary purpose of PT is to maintain and restore maximum movement and functional ability of bones, muscles, joints and nerves. See also *occupational therapy (OT)*.

physician guidelines—see *practice guideline*.

physician-hospital organization (PHO)—alliance between physicians and hospitals to further mutual interests such as negotiating with third-party payers, achieving a larger market share and reducing costs. These entities sell their services to managed care organizations or directly to employers.

physician profiling—looking at individual doctors to determine how their practices compare to those of their peers. Practices that may be analyzed include the frequency of basic diagnostic tests, forms of preventive care, specific medications prescribed, referrals made, etc. Results may be sent to each physician to create an awareness of how his or her practice differs from that of others and may provide the basis for corrective action or removal of a doctor or facility as a care provider.

physician's assistant (PA)—licensed health professional who is trained to perform certain medical procedures (e.g., physical exams) previously reserved for a physician. The work of a PA is done with the supervision of the physician.

physician services—health care provided by or coordinated by a licensed medical physician. Such physicians include medical doctors (MDs) and doctors of osteopathic medicine (DOs).

piecework—employment in which a worker is paid a fixed rate for each unit produced or action performed.

piercing the corporate veil—legal concept whereby corporate officers, directors or shareholders may be held responsible for the liabilities of a corporation despite the general principle that shareholders are immune from corporate liability. This doctrine essentially disregards the corporate entity when it appears incorporation was a veil of protection and the formalities of a corporation had been disregarded at will.

plaintiff—individual, company or other entity that brings a case against another in a court of law. See also *defendant*.

plan administrator—see *administrator*.

plan amendment—see *amendment*.

plan assets—stocks, bonds and other securities that have been segregated and restricted (usually in a trust) for use in the provision of employee benefits. Plan assets include any money contributed by an employer or plan participants plus amounts earned as a result of investing those contributions, less benefits paid, income taxes and other expenses incurred.

plan document—written description of an employee benefit plan maintained by a plan sponsor that sets forth the benefits available and eligibility requirements. The plan document is often separate from the trust agreement in order to allow plan modifications without frequent trust agreement amendments.

plan loan—feature of some retirement plans that permits a participant to borrow against accumulated assets. In the U.S., the federal government has established limits as to when loans are allowed from qualified plans such as profit-sharing plans, money purchase pension plans, defined benefit plans, target benefit plans, 401(k) plans and 403(b) plans if an employer elected the loan provision when completing the adoption agreement for the plan. Individual retirement accounts (IRAs) and IRA-based employer plans do not allow loans.

plan member or participant—any person who is or may become eligible to receive a benefit from an employee benefit plan or whose beneficiaries may be eligible to receive a benefit. See also *active participant*.

plan sponsor—entity that establishes and maintains a benefit plan. The sponsor may be (1) a single employer, (2) an employee organization or (3) an association, committee, joint board of trustees or other similar group of representatives of the entities involved.

Plant Closing Act of 1988—see *Worker Adjustment and Retraining Notification Act (WARN)*.

plan termination—when a benefit plan ceases to exist and benefits are settled. Replacement with another plan is not a termination. Also referred to as a wind up. See also *partial termination and Pension Benefit Guaranty Corporation (PBGC)*.

plan termination date—date a benefit plan ceases to exist. When a plan is terminated by a plan administrator, the date is established by the administrator and must be agreed to by the Pension Benefit Guaranty Corporation (PBGC). If the plan is terminated by the PBGC, the date is established by the PBGC and agreed to by the plan administrator. In either case, if the administrator and PBGC cannot agree, the date is set by a court. See also *Pension Benefit Guaranty Corporation (PBGC)*.

plan termination insurance—insurance protecting defined benefit pension plan participants from loss of benefits if a plan has not been properly funded. The U.S. has a federal insurance program set forth under Title IV of ERISA that is administered by the Pension Benefit Guaranty Corporation. See also *Pension Benefit Guaranty Corporation (PBGC)* and *plan termination*.

plan year—calendar, policy or fiscal year on which records of a benefit plan are kept.

platinum plan—see *health plan categories*.

play-or-pay provision—see "Individual responsibility" under the *Appendix A: Affordable Care Act of 2010 (ACA)*.

point
—$1 change in the value of a stock or stock market index. For example, if shares of a company rise three points, the price of each share has risen $3.
—in the mortgage industry, a point is equal to 1% of the total amount mortgaged. Hence, one point on a $300,000 home is $3,000. The purchase of each point generally lowers the homebuyer's interest rate on a mortgage by 0.25%. The dollar value of points is deductible as an interest expense on federal income tax Schedule A.

point-of-sale (POS) network—computerized system that processes transactions at the time they occur. Also called a point-of-service network, a POS network makes it possible for pharmacists to view and enter data as a prescription is being prepared for and dispensed to a consumer.

point-of-service (POS) network—see *point-of-sale (POS) network*.

point-of-service (POS) plan—managed care plan that blends key features of a preferred provider organization (PPO) and health maintenance organization (HMO). Like PPOs, POS plans use a network of contracted caregivers to provide services to members. Like an HMO, the plans require the patient to select a primary care physician, who serves as a gatekeeper for care within the network. The primary care physician selects the specific physicians and other providers the patient will see. A POS plan can be offered in conjunction with an HMO, PPO or other plan. See also *health maintenance organization (HMO)* and *preferred provider organization (PPO)*.

poison pill—strategy used by corporations to discourage a hostile takeover by another company. The target company attempts to make its stock less attractive to the acquirer by allowing existing shareholders (1) to buy more shares at a discount (referred to as a flip-in) to dilute the shares of those attempting the takeover or (2) to purchase the acquirer's shares at a discounted price after the merger (called a flip-over).

policy—rule or rules governing the acceptable use of resources, practices, procedures, etc. See also *insurance policy*.

policy dividend—see *dividend*.

policyholder—owner of an insurance policy. With a group insurance plan, the policyholder is the employer, labor union or other entity to which the group contract is issued. Individual insurance policies are contracted directly with the individual or family to whom the contract is issued.

Ponzi scheme—illegal investment scam that uses funds from new investors to provide returns to prior investors. Such schemes typically involve promises of low risk and guaranteed high returns. In the beginning, this promise is fulfilled. Eventually, however, it becomes difficult to get sufficient new investors and new investment dollars to continue paying the high returns. In reality, there is no return on a real investment with the scheme, only the funds from the most recent investors. A Ponzi scheme is a variation on a pyramid scheme with the pyramid of investors eventually collapsing. See also *affinity fraud* and *pyramid scheme*.

pooled fund—see *commingled fund*.

Pooled Registered Pension Plan (PRPP)—retirement savings program available to individuals who (1) are employed or self-employed in the Northwest Territories, Nunavut or Yukon (2) work in a federally regulated business or industry for an employer who chooses to participate in a PRPP or (3) live in a province that has the required PRPP legislative provisions in place. A PRPP is similar to a defined contribution plan in that employees make voluntary contributions. Employer contributions are permitted, but not mandatory. Contributions are combined and placed in one fund to achieve lower investment and plan administration costs. Employer and employee contributions are combined and tax-deductible to the extent total contributions do not exceed 18% of earned incomes up to the federal maximum per annum. Interest and other returns accumulated on the funds in a plan are also not taxed, but withdrawals are subject to income tax.

pooled trust—common trust fund generally established and maintained by one employer to accumulate the assets of the multiple benefit plans sponsored by the employer and its subsidiaries.

population health management—strategies to improve the health outcomes for a specific group of individuals. The group may be adolescents, the working poor, persons in a particular geographical locale or individuals who are at risk of a particular disease. Strategies for managing care are as diverse as the populations identified.

pop-up option—variation on the joint and survivor benefit that allows a pension plan participant who is predeceased by his or her contingent beneficiary (usually a spouse) to revert to the benefit payable if there had been no spouse. In other words, a one-life-only benefit pops up. There may be a charge associated with taking advantage of this option.

portability—ability to retain benefits or the right to benefits when changing employers. For example, the ability of an employee to take health insurance or pension credits from one employer to another. See also *job lock* and *reciprocity*.

portable alpha—investment strategy in which a portfolio manager separates two aspects of portfolio return—the alpha and the beta. The beta is the extent to which an investment moves with the overall market and an increase can be said to result from an overall market increase. Alpha is the measure of a manager's ability to pick investments that outperform the market in a given period. If an investment manager is able to improve alpha by investing in securities that are not correlated with the beta of the existing portfolio, the manager has created a portable alpha.

portfolio
—in finance, a collection of investments held by an individual or other entity.
—insurance companies sometimes use portfolio to refer to all the products the company offers or all the insurance policies held by a policyholder.

portfolio manager—financial analyst who supervises a team of analysts and helps guide a mutual fund, private institutional fund or company in selecting the right mix of products, industries and regions for the company's investment portfolio. See also *financial analyst* and *money manager*.

portfolio mix—how different types of investments held by an individual or other entity are allocated. The mix considers the variety of assets (e.g., stocks, bonds, real estate) and their potential risk and return.

positron emission tomography (PET)—radioactive imaging technique that produces a three-dimensional image of blood flow used for a variety of purposes including assessment of brain activity and heart function. A PET may also be used to identify cancerous tissue that may not be visible with other medical imaging techniques. See also *computerized axial tomography (CAT or CT) scan* and *magnetic resonance imaging (MRI)*.

Post-Millennials—see *Generation Z*.

postponed retirement—see *deferred retirement*.

postretirement adjustment—change in the amount of payments by a pension plan after payments have begun. The most common adjustment is an increase to reflect changes in the cost of living. See also *cost-of-living adjustment (COLA)*.

postretirement benefits—all forms of benefits, other than retirement income, provided by an employer to its retirees.

power of attorney (P/A)—written document authorizing another to act as one's agent or attorney in fact. Power of attorney may be granted to allow an agent to take care of a variety of transactions such as executing a stock power, handling a tax audit or maintaining a safe-deposit box. Powers of attorney can be written to be either general (full) or limited to special circumstances. A power of attorney generally is terminated when the principal dies. The traditional power of attorney takes effect as soon as it is executed, while a durable power of attorney is executed only when a specific event occurs, such as the disability of the principal. See also *durable power of attorney*.

practice guideline—evidence-based recommendation for medical intervention designed to improve, maintain or at least slow the deterioration of a patient's health status. Also referred to as treatment protocols or critical pathways, practice guidelines are systematically developed by health experts to assist practitioners, patients and others to make health care decisions. See also *protocol*.

practice policy—see *practice guideline*.

practitioner—within the field of medicine, person who has trained and been given the authority to diagnose, initiate, alter or terminate health care treatment regimens. Physicians, chiropractors, dentists, podiatrists and physician assistants are all examples of practitioners.

preadmission certification—see *precertification*.

preadmission review—see *precertification*.

preadmission testing (PAT)—process in which a patient is asked to answer questions and obtain diagnostic services prior to a nonemergency hospital admission in order to reduce the length of stay.

preauthorization—see *precertification*.

precertification—process of obtaining authorization from a health plan or insurer for care prior to provision of the care. Notifying the payer allows the payer to authorize payment, as well as to recommend alternative courses of treatment. Failure to obtain precertification may result in a financial penalty to either the provider or plan member. Precertification is also referred to as preauthorization, prior approval and preadmission review. See also *prospective review* and *utilization review (UR)*.

predetermination—see *precertification*.

predictive modeling—analysis of data to forecast trends and the likelihood that an event will occur.

preemption—judicial doctrine that federal legislation supersedes state legislation on the same subject. ERISA is an example of a federal law that supersedes all state law pertaining to employee benefit plans. However, the preemptive effect of ERISA does not relieve any person from state law regulating insurance, banking or securities; nor does it preempt any generally applicable state criminal law.

preexisting condition—medical condition that exists prior to a person's admission to a hospital, issuance of a health insurance policy or enrollment in a health care plan. See also "Preexisting condition exclusions" in the *Appendix A: Affordable Care Act of 2010 (ACA)*.

preference-sensitive care—when making health care decisions that involve significant trade-offs affecting a patient's quality and or/length of life, taking into consideration the patient's personal values and desires. An example of such a decision is a woman's choice to have a mastectomy rather than a lumpectomy for treating early stage breast cancer. Preference-sensitive care requires communication with the patient regarding the risks and benefits of various treatment options.

preferred drug list (PDL)—see *drug formulary*.

preferred provider—supplier of dental or health care who agrees to render services under the terms of a legal agreement with a benefit plan. The preferred provider accepts predetermined plan fees as payment in full for covered services. Patients may be given incentives (e.g., smaller deductibles and cost sharing, higher annual maximums) for using these providers, who may also be referred to as contracted providers, network providers or participating providers. See also *preferred provider organization (PPO)*.

preferred provider organization (PPO)—group of health care providers (i.e., hospitals, physicians and pharmacists) or dental professionals who discount their services to plan participants. A PPO may be organized by a group of care providers, an insurance company, third-party administrators or an employer with a self-insurance plan. PPOs agree to accept a discounted fee as payment in full and handle claims for participants, which means there is no balance billing. Providers are usually required to refer care to others within the PPO network, but they do not have to get preauthorization to make the referral. If participants want to go outside of the network for care, they usually have more out-of-pocket costs and must submit their own claims to the plan. There are some exceptions for emergency and out-of-area services. See also *exclusive provider organization (EPO)*, *point-of-service (POS) plan* and *out-of-network provider*.

preferred risk class—group of insurance applicants who have the probability of lower-than-usual losses. A person whose physical condition, occupation, mode of living and other characteristics suggest a long and healthy life might be placed in a preferred risk group paying reduced life insurance premiums. See also *class rating*, *declined risk class*, *qualified impairment insurance*, *rated policy*, *standard risk class* and *substandard risk class*.

preferred stock—fractional ownership in a public corporation represented by a certificate or book entry. Preferred stockholders have preferential rights over common stockholders with regard to the payment of dividends as well as the distribution of assets if the company is liquidated. Preferred dividends are normally fixed, whereas common stock dividends may fluctuate depending on company earnings. Claims of both common and preferred stockholders are secondary to claims of bondholders and other creditors of the company. Preferred stock usually does not carry voting rights. See also *capital stock*, *common stock*, *convertible preferred stock*, *cumulative preferred stock*, *guaranteed stock*, *noncumulative preferred stock* and *participating preferred stock*.

pregnancy disability—period of time when a female employee is unable to perform the duties of her job because of pregnancy, childbirth or related medical conditions. Under Title VII of the Civil Rights Act of 1964, employers in the U.S. must treat such disabilities on parity with other non-pregnancy-related conditions. See also *Pregnancy Discrimination Act of 1978 (PDA)*.

Pregnancy Discrimination Act of 1978 (PDA)—amendment to Title VII of the Civil Rights Act of 1964 that categorizes discrimination on the basis of pregnancy, childbirth and related medical conditions as unlawful sex discrimination. As a result of this legislation, women in the U.S. who are pregnant or are affected by pregnancy-related conditions must be treated in the same manner as other applicants or employees with similar abilities or limitations. The PDA amendments require that:
- Employers permit pregnant employees to work as long as they are able to perform their jobs
- Employers treat pregnancy the same as any other disability in providing employee benefits, providing alternative work assignments and granting leaves of absence
- Employer-sponsored health insurance cover expenses for pregnancy-related conditions on the same basis (e.g., fixed, reasonable and customary charges) as costs for other medical conditions
- The same level of employer-sponsored health benefits provided for spouses of female employees be provided for spouses of male employees
- Pregnancy-related benefits not be limited to married employees.

premature distribution—in general, an individual's removal of funds from a retirement plan before reaching a specific age or meeting other plan criteria. In the U.S., a withdrawal from a qualified retirement plans prior to the age of 59½ years may result in a 10% penalty tax. There are some exceptions such as disability, death, separation from service after the age of 55, an IRS levy and corrective distributions.

premium
—higher price or bonus. See also *premium pay*.
—for insurance purposes, the fee a policyholder agrees to pay an insurance company for an insurance policy. The premium may be a single sum or a series of periodic payments. The size of the premium is influenced by risk factors that help determine the likelihood an insured will file claims and the size of the claims (if any). Among the factors that an insurer may consider when setting health or life insurance premiums are the age, health history, lifestyle and occupation of the insured. With passage of the Affordable Care Act of 2010, U.S. insurers can no longer consider preexisting conditions when establishing the premium for a health policy issued to an individual or family.
—in the investment world, the difference between a fixed security's (e.g., bond's) face amount and a higher price paid for the security by an investor. In this case, the premium is essentially the opposite of a discount. When the price of a stock during an initial public offering (IPO) is lower that what it sells for in the after market, the difference is also referred to as a premium.

premium conversion plan—see *premium-only plan (POP)*.

premium-delay arrangement—see *deferred premium arrangement*.

premium drag—insurance provision that allows a group to pay its premiums late, typically within 30 days after the due date. While the insurer charges interest on the late payment, some groups find the cost of interest is less than the income from holding the funds for an extended period.

premium-only plan (POP)—type of Section 125 plan that allows for certain employee-paid group insurance premiums (e.g., health, dental, vision, term life) to be paid with pretax dollars. Also called a premium conversion plan. See also *Section 125*.

premium pay—extra compensation for work performed outside of a regular work schedule (e.g., Sundays, holidays, nights). Premium pay is also used as an incentive for an employee who undertakes a foreign assignment.

premium payment plan—benefit program in which employees purchase insurance on a pretax basis via salary reduction. The most common use of this plan is employee payment of a share of health insurance premiums, but this type of plan can also be used for other types of coverage, including life, disability, dental and vision insurance. See also *cafeteria plan* and *flexible benefit plan*.

Premium Reimbursement Account (PRA)—defined contribution plan that can be funded by an employer and/or employee that provides tax-free dollars an employee can use to purchase a qualified insurance policy for the employee, a spouse and any tax dependents. The policy may provide protection for medical, hospital, surgical, dental and vision care; long- and short-term disability; vision loss and dismemberment; wage continuation and disability income; and accidental death. It cannot be used to purchase life insurance, long-term care coverage, COBRA continuation coverage or Medicare B premiums. Any group insurance also cannot be sponsored by another employer.

premium subsidy—see "Premium tax credit" and "Small business health care tax credit" in the *Appendix A: Affordable Care Act of 2010 (ACA)*.

premium tax—assessment paid by an insurance company to a state or provincial government based on premiums collected in the jurisdiction by the insurer.

premium tax credit or subsidy—see "Premium tax credit" and "Small business health care tax credit" in the *Appendix A: Affordable Care Act of 2010 (ACA)*.

premium waiver—provision that can be added to a life insurance policy that allows a policyholder to stop making payments in the event of a disability that leads to loss of income.

prenatal care—information, testing, monitoring and other services provided by a physician, midwife or other health care professional to a pregnant woman in an effort to keep her healthy and to maximize the likelihood of a full-term pregnancy and a healthy infant.

prepaid care plan—see *health maintenance organization (HMO)* and *prepaid group practice*.

prepaid group practice—group of multispecialty physicians or other health professionals who contract to provide services on a continuous basis to a group of enrollees. Members of the practice are paid on a salary or per capita basis. See also *health maintenance organization (HMO)*.

prepaid pension cost—assets in a pension fund that exceed the accrued pension costs. See also *unfunded accrued pension cost*.

prepaid program—financing of a good or service prior to receipt. For example, many states offer prepaid college tuition programs. See also *529 plan*.

prepayment clause—element in a loan contract spelling out how and when the borrower is permitted to pay some or all of an unpaid balance before it becomes due. Some creditors charge a penalty for prepayments. See also *prepayment penalty*.

prepayment penalty—fee imposed by a lender when some or all of a loan is paid off before it becomes due.

prepayment risk—chance that a debt instrument such as a mortgage or callable bonds will be paid before the end of the expected payment period and that the investor will not be able to find another investment that provides a similar return for the prepaid dollars. See also *callable*.

preretirement counseling—advice and guidance offered to employees as they prepare for retirement. Topics that may be addressed include emotional and social as well as financial and legal issues.

preretirement death benefit—payments made to beneficiaries when a participant dies before reaching retirement age.

preretirement survivor benefit—see *qualified preretirement survivor annuity (QPSA)*.

prescriber—health professional permitted by law or regulation to order the dispensing and use of a medication that can be obtained only by prescription. Prescribers are typically medical doctors (MDs), dentists (DDSs), nurse practitioners (NPs), physician assistants (PAs) and pharmacists (RPhs).

prescribing criteria—practice guidelines that focus on the appropriate use of a particular drug or drug class. The criteria indicate for whom and how a drug or drug class should be prescribed. See also *practice guideline* and *protocol*.

prescription assistance program—see *drug assistance program*.

prescription benefits management/manager—see *pharmacy benefits management/manager (PBM)*.

prescription drug—also known as a legend drug, a medication that may be obtained only with an order from an individual legally permitted to order its dispensing and use. See also *prescriber*.

prescription drug card program—use of a benefit identification "card" that entitles a patient to receive medications as a covered benefit through a participating pharmacy.

prescription drug formulary—see *drug formulary*.

prescription drug plan—insurance or benefit program that helps pay for the costs of medications prescribed by a health professional. Most, but not all, prescription drug plans are a component of health care coverage. See also *Medicare Part D*.

prescription drug reimportation—when a medication is manufactured in one country, sent to another country, then shipped back to a buyer in the originating nation. At present, the U.S. government prohibits the reimporting of prescription drugs from Canada and other nations; however, various groups are lobbying Congress to eliminate some of the restrictions as a cost-saving measure.

presenteeism—presence of an employee at work even if he or she is too sick or too engaged in work/life issues to be productive. The term is also used by some to refer to an employee working beyond his or her expected hours.

present value—given a specific interest rate, the amount of money needed today to provide (1) a sum of money at a specific future date or (2) a series of payments over a set period of time. See also *actuarial present value (APV)*.

preservice review—see *prospective review*.

presumptive method—approach established by ERISA for calculating and allocating an employer's withdrawal liability from a multiemployer pension plan.

pretax contribution—money placed in an account (e.g., cafeteria plan, deferred compensation plan) for which income taxes have not yet been paid. Pretax contributions often are more advantageous than after-tax contributions. See also *after-tax contribution*.

pretreatment estimate—see *precertification*.

prevailing fee—amount customarily charged for a service. The prevailing fee typically falls within a range of fees most frequently charged by service providers in a given locality; it may be defined as a specific percentile of all charges in the community. See also *percentile*.

prevailing wage rate—average hourly payment that employers give employees in a labor market for similar work. The average may be either the mean or the median.

prevention—stopping something from occurring. See also *preventive care*.

preventive care—health services focused on reducing the likelihood of illness and the risk of a condition getting worse or returning. Elements of preventive care include immunizations and routine physical examinations for early diagnosis and treatment.

preventive services—see *preventive care.*

price/book (P/B) ratio—current share price of a stock divided by its most recent quarter's book value (net worth) per share. A lower P/B ratio suggests the stock is undervalued, but it could also mean that something is fundamentally wrong with the company.

price/earnings (P/E) ratio—current share price of a stock divided by its current or estimated future earnings per share (EPS). The EPS used in this calculation may be the last four quarters (trailing P/E), but sometimes it is taken from the estimates of earnings expected in the next four quarters (projected or forward P/E). A third variation uses the sum of the last two quarters and the estimates of the next two quarters. A high P/E ratio generally suggests investors are expecting higher earnings growth in the future compared to companies with a low P/E ratio. The ratio is most useful when comparing one company to others in the same industry, to the market in general or against the company's historical P/E ratio. Also known as the price or earnings multiple. See also *earnings per share (EPS).*

price/equity ratio—see *price/book (P/B) ratio.*

price index—relative measure of the general price level of goods and services over time. It is obtained by calculating the ratio of the prices of a collection of goods and services during one period with the prices of the same goods and services during a selected base period. See also *Consumer Price Index (CPI)* and *Employment Cost Index (ECI).*

price multiple—see *price/earnings (P/E) ratio.*

price transparency—disclosure of cost-related information by an organization to those outside the organization. An increasing demand for transparency has developed as a result of concern that too much revenue may be flowing from pharmaceutical companies to PBMs and too little flowing down to plan sponsors. In a transparent model, the actual discounts, rebates, incentives and other benefits earned on behalf of the sponsor are "passed through" to the plan sponsor and members. See also *pass-through pricing.*

primary beneficiary—person or entity designated as the first in line to benefit from a will, trust or insurance policy. See also *contingent beneficiary.*

primary care—basic or general health care as opposed to care provided by a specialist or subspecialist. Primary care providers serve as a first point of contact with the medical system in nonemergency situations. They provide routine care for individuals with common health problems and chronic illnesses that can be managed on an outpatient basis. Primary care is provided by primary care physicians (PCPs), nurse practitioners (NPs), physician assistants (PAs) and other mid-level practitioners. See also *primary care physician (PCP).*

primary care case management—see *gatekeeper.*

primary care network (PCN)—group of primary care physicians who have agreed to share the risk of providing services to enrollees in a prepaid plan. See also *primary care physician (PCP).*

primary care physician (PCP)—doctor trained to give basic health care. A primary care physician provides preventive care and is the first doctor seen for nonemergency health problems. The PCP coordinates a patient's care with other health care professionals. Physicians specializing in family practice, general practice, obstetrics/gynecology and pediatrics are all PCPs. See also *gatekeeper.*

primary insurance amount (PIA)—benefit (before rounding down to the nearest whole dollar) that a person would receive if he or she elects to begin receiving Social Security retirement benefits at normal retirement age. At this age, the benefit is neither reduced for early retirement nor increased for delayed retirement. The PIA is the sum of three different portions of an individual's average indexed monthly earnings (AIME) multiplied by three separate and declining percentages. By reducing the percentage multipliers as the AIME increases, persons with a lower AIME receive a higher percentage of their earnings than persons with higher AIMEs. Generally, the more a person pays into the program during work years, the higher the PIA will be. However, specific rules in its calculation may result in exceptions. See also *average indexed monthly earnings (AIME).*

primary market—exchange where businesses and governments raise capital by selling stocks and bonds to investors.

primary offering—see *initial public offering (IPO).*

primary payer—insurance carrier that has first responsibility for payment of benefits when the insured has duplicate coverage. See also *coordination-of-benefits (COB) provision, duplication of benefits, Medicare secondary payer program* and *secondary payer.*

prime rate—lowest interest rate that a financial institution (e.g., bank) charges its most creditworthy customers for short-term loans. This rate is influenced by the rate the Federal Reserve sets for banks to borrow from each other. The higher the Federal Reserve rate, the higher a bank's prime rate will generally be. Many home equity loans and lines of credit, as well as adjustable rate mortgages, are tied to the prime rate.

principal
—in finance, the amount of a debt owed and on which interest is calculated.
—from a legal perspective, one of the main parties in a contract or court case.

principal sum
—from an investment perspective, capital versus the income derived from the capital.
—in an insurance policy, the principal sum is the lump-sum payment made in the event of a covered loss such as death or injury.

prior acts coverage—type of claims-made liability insurance that covers claims arising from acts that took place before the policy's start date; claims are covered regardless of how far in the past they occurred. Such coverage is sometimes purchased when there is a change in insurance carriers. See also *claims-made policy*.

prior approval (PA)—see *precertification*.

prior authorization (PA)—see *precertification*.

priorities—set of rules established by an employment pension plan or via legislation that specifies how plan assets will be allocated to beneficiaries if the plan is terminated.

prior service cost—expense associated with a retroactive benefit granted for periods of service that occurred before the initiation of a pension plan or an amendment to a plan.

prior service credit—see *past service benefit/credit*.

privacy office/official—person or unit of an organization that HIPAA requires be designated by each covered entity. The privacy office or official is responsible for the development and implementation of the policies and procedures necessary for compliance. See also *covered entity* and *Health Insurance Portability and Accountability Act of 1996 (HIPAA)*.

private banker—also called a wealth manager, a personal financial planner who works for people with more money to invest than the general public. Private bankers generally manage portfolios for a small number of clients using the resources of the bank, including teams of financial analysts, accountants, lawyers and other professionals. Unlike most personal financial planners, private bankers meet with their clients regularly to keep them abreast of financial matters; they often have the responsibility of directly managing customers' finances. See also *financial planner*.

private equity—money invested in companies that are not publicly traded on a stock exchange. Private equity is highly illiquid because sellers must locate willing buyers. Investors in private equity are generally compensated when a firm (1) goes public, (2) is sold or merges with another firm or (3) is recapitalized.

private health exchange—marketplace, typically operated by brokers or insurers, that sells insurance products (e.g., medical, prescription drug, disease, disability, dental and vision coverage) via the Internet. The policies offered through private health exchanges can range from high-cost down to low- or no-cost-sharing plans. Private exchanges also provide information to help consumers make choices among the products offered and collect the information required for enrollment. Employers can give their employees a set amount of money and then direct employees to a specific exchange where they can shop for a health plan and other benefits based on what the employer has selected as options. Employees make up any difference between the cost of the insurance and the amount provided by the employer. In some cases, an employer funds all of an employee's coverage. Individuals can also purchase coverage through a private health exchange. Unlike public health exchanges (a.k.a. the health insurance marketplace), U.S. government subsidies to low-income persons are not available via these private exchanges. See also "Public health exchanges" in the *Appendix A: Affordable Care Act of 2010 (ACA)*.

private health services plan—vehicle providing coverage for any combination of hospital, medical and dental expenses. An arrangement where an employer reimburses its employees for the cost of such care may also come within the definition of private health services plan. Such plans in Canada are more specifically defined under Subsection 248(1) of the Income Tax Act.

private letter ruling (PLR)—see *letter ruling*.

private mortgage insurance (PMI)—financial protection for a mortgage lender if a borrower defaults on a loan. Most lenders require PMI for loans that exceed 80% of the home's value. The borrower pays the premium for the coverage as a monthly charge added to the mortgage payment. Once the borrower's equity in a home reaches 20%, this coverage can be terminated.

private pension plan—retirement program established by an employer, labor organization, nonprofit organization or other nongovernment entity.

private placement—sale of securities (e.g., stocks, bonds) to one or a few investors (usually banks, life insurance companies, pension funds and other financial institutions) versus the general public. Securities sold in this manner do not have to be registered with the U.S. Securities and Exchange Commission. When debt instruments are involved, private placement may provide an opportunity for an investor to get a higher interest rate and a tailor-made maturity that is difficult to obtain in a public offering.

privatization—transfer of ownership or management from the public sector (government) to the private (nongovernment) sector.

probate—legal process of settling the estate of a deceased person, which includes verifying the legality of the will, resolving all claims against the decedent and distributing the decedent's assets. The executor (if there is a will) or a court-appointed administrator (if there is not a will) is responsible for the probate process. See also *executor*.

probationary period
—for health insurance purposes, the days between the effective date of a policy and the date coverage begins for all or certain physical conditions. See also *preexisting condition*.
—in the workplace, the days after an individual is hired until permanent employment is established. Typically 30 to 90 days, this period gives management an opportunity to closely evaluate the progress and skills of the newly hired worker and to determine whether a successful employment relationship can be established. The employer may reserve the right to terminate the new hire if it is concluded the person is not suitable for the position. Some companies place other employees on probationary status if their performance is not up to the standard expected or for disciplinary reasons. In this instance, the probationary period is an opportunity for the employee to improve performance or change behavior before the employer takes more severe action such as termination.

producer-owned insurance company (POIC)—separate business owned by one or more insurance producers (i.e., insurance companies, brokers and other intermediaries) whose insurance business is reinsured into the producer owned reinsurance company (PORC). Unlike with PORC, there is no independent fronting insurer. See also *captive insurance company* and *fronting*.

producer-owned reinsurance company (PORC)—separate business owned by one or more insurance producers (i.e., insurance companies, brokers and other intermediaries) whose insurance business is reinsured into the PORC through an independent fronting insurer. See also *captive insurance company* and *fronting*.

productivity—relationship between output (quantity of goods and services produced) and inputs (labor, material and capital) needed to produce the output. Productivity is usually measured in terms of output per worker, per hour. It is affected by factors such as the availability of technology, production organization, worker skill and corporate morale.

professional employer organization (PEO)—company that provides payroll, workers' compensation, human resources and employee benefits administration for business clients. In a coemployment contract, the PEO becomes the employer of record for tax and insurance purposes, filing paperwork under its own identification numbers. The client company continues to direct the employees' day-to-day activities. PEOs charge a service fee for taking over functions of the client company, such as a percentage of payroll in addition to the normal expenses of employees, which include taxes, benefits and unemployment insurance. The aggregation of employees from multiple clients through a PEO can yield lower health insurance premiums. Another substantial benefit to a client is the reduction in staff time required for the administration of payroll and benefits plans. For these reasons, the PEO model is especially attractive to small and midsize organizations. See also *administrative services organization (ASO)* and *leased employee*.

profit—money remaining after all costs of operating a business are paid.

profit and expense charge—see *risk charge*.

profit and loss (P&L) statement—see *income statement*.

profit commission—profit-sharing provision found in some reinsurance agreements. The insurer and the group policy holder agree to a formula for calculating profit, an allowance for the reinsurer's expenses and the policyholder's share of such profit after expenses.

profit-sharing plan—program established and maintained by an employer that allows employees and their beneficiaries to benefit from the money remaining after all costs of operating a business are paid. Profit sharing is a form of incentive pay plan. See also *incentive pay plan.*
—Canada has four types of profit-sharing plans; see *current distribution profit-sharing plan, employee's profit-sharing plan, deferred profit-sharing plan (DPSP)* and *registered profit-sharing plan.*

profit taking—sale of stock or other securities to convert a paper gain into cash. Profit taking is sometimes used to explain a market decline after a noticeable run-up in prices.

program trading—computerized buying and selling of stocks used primarily by institutional investors and typically for large-volume trades. Orders from the trader's computer are entered directly into the market's computer system and automatically executed. The transactions occur if an index price rises or falls to a certain level. Program trading can result in very volatile market conditions. As a result, a market may have restrictions as to when program trading may be used. See also *Black Monday, trading curb* and *trading halt.*

progressive tax—government levy in which individuals with higher incomes pay higher tax rates than individuals with lower incomes. The marginal tax rates in the U.S. federal income tax structure are an effort to establish a progressive tax system. See also *proportional tax* and *regressive tax.*

prohibited group—employees who are officers, shareholders or highly compensated. Discrimination in favor of a prohibited group may cause disqualification of a plan for tax advantages. See also *discrimination* and *discrimination testing.*

prohibited transaction (PT)—specific action by a benefit plan or plan fiduciaries that is forbidden by law. Prohibited transactions in the U.S. generally include:
- Transfer of plan income or assets to, or use of them by or for the benefit of, a disqualified person
- Any act of a fiduciary by which plan income or assets are used for his or her own interest
- The receipt of consideration by a fiduciary for his or her own account from any party dealing with the plan in a transaction that involves plan income or assets
- The sale, exchange or lease of property between a plan and a disqualified person
- Lending money or extending credit between a plan and a disqualified person
- Furnishing goods, services or facilities between a plan and a disqualified person.

A prohibited transaction can also occur with respect to an individual retirement account (IRA) if the owner or the beneficiary of the IRA engages in any of the actions just described. See also *prohibited transaction exemption (PTE)* and *Qualified Professional Asset Manager (QPAM).*

prohibited transaction exemption (PTE)—statutory or administrative exception that permits a benefit plan or its fiduciaries to take an action that is usually forbidden by law. The U.S. Department of Labor (DOL) has granted class exemptions for certain types of investments under conditions that protect the safety and security of the plan assets. In addition, a plan sponsor may apply to DOL to obtain an administrative exemption for a particular proposed transaction that would otherwise be prohibited.

projected benefit—amount that it is expected a defined benefit pension plan will pay to a beneficiary given a set of actuarial assumptions such as past and anticipated future compensation, service credits and the predicted life span of the recipient. See also *overfunded plan, projected benefit obligation (PBO)* and *unfunded projected benefit obligation.*

projected benefit obligation (PBO)—present value of accrued liability for a defined benefit plan that takes into consideration anticipated future salary increases. See also *accumulated benefit obligation (ABO).*

promissory note—legal document signed by a lender and borrower acknowledging a loan has been made and stating the terms under which it is to be repaid.

prompt-pay (cash) discount—reduction in price granted a purchaser if payment is made within a designated time, often ten, 30 or 60 days after delivery of a good or service.

proof of insurability—evidence that an individual is in good health when applying for life insurance. Usually an individual must submit to a physical examination or some type of medical screening to show evidence of good health. Group insurance plans generally do not require individuals to show proof of insurability.

proof of loss—documents required by an insurer to prove a valid claim exists. In group life insurance, the proof is usually a completed claim form and proof of death (i.e., death certificate or acceptable substitute). Proof of loss for a health claim is typically a completed claim form and itemized medical bill.

property risk—possibility of financial loss as the result of owning real estate, for example, a legal suit, fire, theft, loss of rental income and purchasing property with an imperfect title. See also *liability insurance*.

proportional tax—government levy on income that has the same rate regardless of a person's income. Low-income persons have the same tax rate on their income as high-income persons. See also *progressive tax* and *regressive tax*.

proprietorship—see *sole proprietor*.

proprietary formula—see *closed formulary*.

pro rata (PR)—in proportion to some factor that can be exactly calculated. For example, an equal share in a debtor's assets after liquidation. See also *reciprocity*.

proration of coverage—division of insurance payments on a loss when there is more than one policy covering the same loss.

prosthetics—device, either external or implanted, that substitutes for or supplements a missing or defective part of the body.

prospective experience rating—method used to establish the insurance premium for a policy period based on the loss experience of a prior period. The insurer compares the actual claims (experience) of an insured group to what is normally expected from others with similar characteristics (a rating class). If the experience rating is better than that of the group's rating class, the result may be a lower premium. If the opposite is the case, the premium may be higher. The amount the insurer charges may be partially or fully based on the plan's past claim experience. See also *rating class* and *retrospective experience rating*.

prospective future service benefit—portion of a participant's retirement benefit that relates to his or her period of credited service to be rendered after a specified current date.

prospective payment schedule/system (PPS)—reimbursement based on a predetermined, fixed amount for a particular service. A classification of services is used such as the diagnosis-related group (DRG) for inpatient hospital services. See also *diagnosis-related group (DRG)*.

prospective pricing—establishment of an all-inclusive price for a health care service based on a diagnosis or procedure prior to the delivery of the service. The price is established by the health care plan or payer; in some cases, it may be the result of negotiation required by the SEC with the provider. See also *retrospective payment*.

prospective rating—see *prospective experience rating*.

prospective review—assessment to determine whether proposed health care is appropriate for a particular patient or that the care to be provided is covered by a benefits plan. See also *concurrent review, precertification, retrospective review, second opinion* and *utilization review (UR)*.

prospectus—legal document that provides information about an investment (e.g., stock, bond, mutual fund) that is being offered for sale to the public. The document contains such details as the security's objectives, policies, risks, fees and expenses, and past performance. The prospectus for an initial offering of a security is also known as an offer document. There are two types: preliminary and final. The preliminary prospectus (also known as a first offering document) is distributed by the security's issuer. The final prospectus is printed after a deal has been made and the security can be offered for sale; it supersedes the preliminary prospectus and contains final information as to the exact number of shares/certificates issued and the precise offering price. Provision of a prospectus to potential investors is a legal mandate for many security transactions in the U.S. and Canada. The prospectus required by the U.S. Securities and Exchange Commission that is used to promote mutual funds continuously offered for sale is referred to as a final prospectus. See also *Securities and Exchange Commission (SEC)*.

protected class—any group of persons protected by anti-discrimination laws. Examples of protected classes in the U.S. are the disabled, women, persons over the age of 40 and racial minorities. See also *Age Discrimination in Employment Act of 1967 (ADEA), Americans with Disabilities Act of 1990 (ADA), disparate impact, Equal Pay Act of 1963 (EPA), Rehabilitation Act of 1973, Title VII of the Civil Rights Act of 1964* and *Title IX of the Education Amendments of 1972*.

protected health information (PHI)—under HIPAA, medical records and other individually identifiable medical data that are maintained or transmitted in any form or medium (including orally). See also *electronic protected health information (EPHI or ePHI)*.

protocol—treatment guideline designed to yield the best overall outcome for the majority of cases once a diagnosis is made. See also *practice guideline*.

prototype plan—standardized retirement plan approved and qualified by the IRS that is made available by an insurance company, bank, mutual fund or other financial institution for the use of employers. Employers simply sign a participating agreement. In contrast to a master plan in which contributions from all employers are placed in a single trust account, contributions from each employer in a prototype plan are placed in a separate trust account. See also *master plan, model plan* and *volume submitter plan*.

provident fund—savings plan in nations such as India, Malaysia, Singapore and Thailand that is established to provide income upon retirement and sometimes support for health expenses after retirement. Plan features vary by country. India has a voluntary tax-favored plan that can be set up by an individual at a local post office. In Singapore, the fund is compulsory with both employees and employers making contributions that vary with the employee's age. Malaysia's plan also provides financial assistance during periods of unemployment or disability.

provider—supplier of a good or service.

provider choice—ability of an individual to choose the supplier of a good or services.

provider-sponsored organization (PSO)—health care delivery network owned and operated by a group of physicians, hospitals and others that provides services under contract to employers, plan sponsors and/or insurers.

provisionally funded—when a pension plan is not fully funded but solvent. While current annual costs are being met, special payments are being made to amortize the unfunded liabilities.

provisional past service pension adjustment (PSPA)—sum of the pension credits for a past service event, offset by any transfers of tax-sheltered assets that will be used to reduce the PSPA. The provisional PSPA is the PSPA reported to the Canada Revenue Agency. It is either deducted automatically from the plan member's Registered Retirement Savings Plan (RRSP) contribution room (if the PSPA is exempt) or certified prior to being deducted from the member's RRSP (if the PSPA is nonexempt).

provision for adverse deviation (PfAD)—setting a reserve greater than the amount projected to be needed by a plan to pay for benefits to enhance benefit security and the stability of contributions over time. A PfAD may be fixed (e.g., based on a percentage of actuarial liabilities) or variable (e.g., one that increases or decreases depending on plan experience).

proxy—person authorized to act for another; for example, a person empowered by a shareholder to vote on his or her behalf at a shareholder meeting. Proxy is also used to refer to the written document a shareholder uses to authorize the other person to vote on his or her behalf at a shareholder meeting. See also *proxy statement*.

proxy statement—document providing information about matters that will be voted on at an annual (or any special) meeting of a publicly traded corporation. The SEC requires proxy statements explaining the issues to be voted on, along with ballots for voting, to be sent to all shareholders prior to these meetings. See also *Securities Exchange Act of 1934*.

prudent expert rule—evolution of the common law prudent man rule applied to fiduciaries of pension and profit-sharing plans governed by ERISA. This higher standard expects fiduciaries to be familiar with and knowledgeable about the management of money, not just prudent. ERISA states that fiduciaries must manage a portfolio "with the care, skill, prudence, and diligence, under the circumstances then prevailing, that a prudent man acting in a like capacity and familiar with such matters would use in the conduct of an enterprise of a like character and with like aims." See also *Employee Retirement Income Security Act of 1974 (ERISA), fiduciary, prudent investor rule* and *prudent person rule*.

prudent investor rule—officially named the Uniform Prudent Investment Act, this U.S. model legislation was drafted by the National Conference of Commissioners on Uniform State Laws in 1994 and has been adopted in most states. The rule, where adopted, updates trust investment law with respect to the prudent person rule by stating no investment is automatically imprudent. Trustees must consider an investment as part of a plan's total portfolio, rather than as an individual investment. The central consideration of fiduciary investing should be the trade-off between risk and return. Categorical restrictions on types of investments have been eliminated, allowing trustees the ability to invest in anything that plays an appropriate role in achieving the risk/return objectives of the trust and the other requirements of prudent investing. A former rule that forbid trustees from delegating investment and management functions is also reversed by the model rule, though it is subject to safeguards. ERISA Section 404(a)(1)(C) generally follows the prudent investor rule. See also *Employee Retirement Income Security Act of 1974 (ERISA), fiduciary* and *prudent person rule.*

prudent layperson standard—medical symptoms that would lead a person who possesses an average knowledge of health and medicine to decide an emergency medical condition exists. Several states have established, and others (including the U.S. Congress) are considering, mandates that require insurance companies to cover emergency services when some form of this standard is met. See also *emergency medical condition.*

prudent man rule—see *prudent person rule.*

prudent person rule—standard that requires those responsible for the money of others to exercise sound discretion in the administration, supervision and management of assets. Decisions are to be made in the same manner in which these persons would manage their personal affairs, seeking a reasonable return and preserving capital. The prudent person rule is derived from the prudent man rule stated by Judge Samuel Putnum in 1830: "Those with responsibility to invest money for others should act with prudence, discretion, intelligence, and regard for the safety of capital as well as income." See also *fiduciary, prudent expert rule* and *prudent investor rule.*

PS 58 costs—see *table 2001 rates.*

public accommodation—under Title III of the Americans with Disabilities Act of 1990 (ADA), U.S. facilities whose operations affect commerce and fall within at least one of the following categories:
- Places of lodging (e.g., inns, hotels, motels) except for owner-occupied establishments renting fewer than six rooms
- Establishments serving food or drink (e.g., restaurants and bars)
- Places of exhibition or entertainment (e.g., motion picture houses, theaters, concert halls, stadiums)
- Places of public gathering (e.g., auditoriums, convention centers, lecture halls)
- Sales or rental establishments (e.g., bakeries, grocery stores, hardware stores, shopping centers)
- Service establishments (e.g., laundromats, dry-cleaners, banks, barber shops, beauty shops, travel services, shoe repair services, funeral parlors, gas stations, offices of accountants or lawyers, pharmacies, insurance offices, professional offices of health care providers, hospitals)
- Public transportation terminals, depots or stations (not including facilities relating to air transportation)
- Places of public display or collection (e.g., museums, libraries, galleries)
- Places of recreation (e.g., parks, zoos, amusement parks)
- Places of education (e.g., nursery schools, elementary, secondary, undergraduate or postgraduate private schools)
- Social service center establishments (e.g., day care centers, senior citizen centers, homeless shelters, food banks, adoption agencies).

Under Title III, public accommodations must remove barriers in existing facilities if it is readily achievable to do so. See also *readily achievable.*

Public Company Accounting Reform and Investor Protection Act of 2002—see *Sarbanes-Oxley Act of 2002 (SOX).*

public employee—person employed by a government entity including persons who work for hospitals, schools, colleges and universities funded by government. Public employees are also referred to as public sector employees and civil servants.

public employee retirement system (PERS)—organization providing retirement benefits for employees of a government and/or its political subdivisions. Some systems also provide health and welfare benefits. See, for example, *CalPERS (California Public Employees' Retirement System).*

public health exchange—see "Public health exchanges" in the *Appendix A: Affordable Care Act of 2010 (ACA).*

public offering—new securities for sale to the public at a price that has been agreed upon by the issuer and the investment banker handling the sale. The purpose of a public offering is to raise funds for business expansion and investment. In the U.S., public offerings must be registered with the Securities and Exchange Commission. See also *initial public offering (IPO)* and *prospectus*.

public sector plan—benefit program established for civil service employees. Workers covered by such a plan may be employed by a federal, state, provincial and/or local government. Persons who work for publicly funded organizations such as hospitals, school systems and universities may also be covered by public sector plans.

published price—see *list price*.

punitive damages—compensation in excess of actual losses incurred by a plaintiff as a form of punishment in a legal case. Punitive damages are typically awarded in situations where a loss is the result of wanton, reckless or malicious behavior on the part of the other party.

purchase fee—amount that some mutual funds charge investors at the time shares are bought. A purchase fee differs from, and is not considered to be, a front-end sales load because a purchase fee is paid to the fund (not to a broker) and is typically imposed to defray some of the fund's costs associated with the purchase.

purchase security—insurance offered by credit card companies that provides a warranty on purchases made with a credit card.

purchasing coalition/pool—individuals or organizations that join together to capitalize on their collective strength and buying power to negotiate for goods or services. Prescription drug benefits are an increasingly popular service provided by purchasing coalitions. Purchasing pool is another term used when referring to purchasing coalitions.

purchasing power—quantity of goods and services that can be purchased with a given amount of money. Over time, rising prices result in a loss of purchasing power if salaries and wages do not increase at a comparable rate. See also *Consumer Price Index (CPI)*, *deflation* and *inflation*.

purchasing power risk—chance that an investment will lose its buying power due to price increases (inflation).

pure captive—see *single parent captive*.

put option—see *option*.

pyramiding
—increasing the size of an investment position by using unrealized paper profits to make additional purchases on margin.
—strategy used by some conglomerates that have a highly leveraged capital structure and relatively small amount of stock to control one or more other companies. The focus becomes extracting profit from the companies being controlled versus the production of goods and services.

pyramid scheme—unsustainable model that involves the payment of money for enrolling other people into an endeavor. One of the simplest types of pyramid schemes is a chain letter that encourages people to recruit friends and families to put their name at the bottom of a list and to send money to the person at the top of the list. Another common scheme is inviting new recruits to pay a sum of money to become a distributor of a product or service. Recruits make money based on the number of new recruits they bring in versus actual sales. The higher up on the pyramid a participant is, the more money that person makes. In most cases, the originators of the scheme make money and the rest lose their money when the pyramid scheme collapses as a result of the last of the recruits being unable to convince additional persons to join. Pyramid schemes are generally illegal. See also *affinity fraud* and *Ponzi scheme*.

Q

qualification period—time before a person has the right to receive or do something. For example, the time between the onset of a disability and the start of disability benefits.

qualification requirement—criteria, rules and regulations that must be met before an entity may be granted or acquire a right or privilege. A very common qualification requirement for participating in an employer-sponsored benefit plan is that a person be employed for a minimum number of hours by the employer sponsoring the plan. In both Canada and the U.S., multiple qualification requirements exist that employee benefit plans must meet in order to be given favorable tax treatment. See also *qualified annuity, qualified retirement plan* and *Section 125*.

qualified annuity—tax-deferred investment product typically purchased through an insurance company with employer contributions in lieu of a company pension plan. In the U.S., the qualified annuity may be an individual retirement account, a Keogh plan, or a plan governed by IRC Sections 401(k), 403(b) or 457. Annual contribution limits are set by the IRS. The contributions are not included in taxable income for the year in which they are paid. Earnings are tax-deferred until withdrawn, at which point they are treated as taxable income. See also *annuity, automatic survivor coverage* and *group annuity.*

qualified asset account—fund assets set aside for future payment of disability, medical, severance pay or life insurance claims. The IRC sets limits on the size of the account in any taxable year as the amount reasonably and actuarially necessary to fund (1) claims incurred but unpaid (as of the close of such taxable year) and (2) administrative costs with respect to such claims.

qualified automatic contribution arrangement (QACA)—automatic contribution arrangement for retirement plans encouraged by the Pension Protection Act of 2006 (PPA). QACAs meeting safe harbor criteria established by the PPA are exempt from nondiscrimination testing. Plan fiduciaries are given liability protection with the use of a qualified default investment alternative as the default investment. See also *automatic contribution arrangement* and *qualified default investment alternative (QDIA).*

qualified beneficiary—person who meets the criteria to receive funds or other benefits. For the purposes of COBRA, a qualified beneficiary is generally an individual covered by a group health plan on the day before a qualifying event occurs. In addition, any child born to, or placed for adoption with, a covered employee during the period of COBRA coverage is considered a qualified beneficiary. See also *Consolidated Omnibus Budget Reconciliation Act of 1985 (COBRA)* and *qualifying event.*

qualified benefit—employer-provided benefit that is not considered income for federal tax purposes.

qualified cash or deferred arrangement—see *cash or deferred arrangement (CODA).*

qualified cost—limit on a contribution to a Section 419 welfare benefit fund that an employer may deduct from income for federal tax purposes. This amount equals the fund's qualified direct cost and permitted additions to a qualified asset account, minus the fund's after-tax income for the taxable year. See also *Section 419.*

qualified default investment alternative (QDIA)—fund used for automatic enrollment programs and in other situations where a participant has the opportunity to direct the investment of assets in his or her account but chooses not to. The U.S. Department of Labor requires that a QDIA:
- Be managed by an investment manager or an investment company registered under the Investment Company Act of 1940
- Be diversified so as to minimize the risk of large losses
- Not invest participant contributions directly in employer securities
- Be a lifecycle or targeted-retirement-date fund, a balanced fund or a professionally managed account.

QDIAs that meet these criteria are relieved from liability for losses resulting from the investment of the participant's account in a QDIA. The sponsor does, however, remain responsible for the prudent selection and monitoring of plan funds generally and of the QDIA in particular. While this relief is generally similar to the relief provided under ERISA Section 404(c), a plan does not have to comply with Section 404(c) in all respects to qualify for the default investment safe harbor. See also *automatic contribution arrangement.*

qualified defined benefit plan—see *defined benefit (DB) plan* and *qualified retirement plan.*

qualified defined contribution plan—see *defined contribution (DC) plan* and *qualified retirement plan.*

qualified direct cost—aggregate benefit and administrative expenses of a welfare benefit fund that a cash basis employer would be entitled to deduct if it paid the expenses directly. See also *qualified cost* and *Section 419.*

qualified distribution—payments from a Roth IRA that are tax- and penalty-free. To be qualified, the distribution must occur at least five years after the Roth IRA owner established and funded his or her first Roth IRA. In addition, one of the following conditions must be met:
- The owner must be at least aged 59½ when the distribution occurs.
- The distribution is no more than $10,000 and it is used toward the purchase or rebuilding of a first home for the Roth IRA owner or a qualified family member.
- The distribution occurs after the Roth IRA holder becomes disabled.
- The distribution is to a beneficiary of the Roth IRA.

See also *Roth IRA.*

qualified domestic relations order (QDRO)—judgment or decree (including an approval of property settlement agreement) that relates to the provision of child support, alimony payments or marital property rights to a spouse, former spouse, child or other dependent. A QDRO is made pursuant to a state domestic relations law (including community property law). Such an order is considered a QDRO if (1) it creates or recognizes the existence of an alternate payee's right, or assigns to an alternate payee the right, to receive all or a portion of the benefits payable to a plan participant; and (2) it fulfills other requirements specified in ERISA Section 206(d)(3). The plan administrator that provides the benefits affected by the order is responsible for determining whether the order is qualified. A QDRO is an exception to the antialienation rule that governs ERISA-qualified retirement plans. See also *alternate payee, antialienation rule* and *assignment of benefits*.

qualified employee annuity—retirement annuity purchased by an employer for employees and their beneficiaries that meets IRC requirements for income-tax advantages.

qualified employee benefit plan—program established by an employer to provide retirement, health and/or welfare benefits for employees and their beneficiaries. Qualified plans allow the employer a tax deduction for contributing to the plan, and employees typically do not pay taxes on plan assets until the assets are distributed; furthermore, any earnings on qualified plans are tax-deferred. In order for a plan to maintain its qualified status, it must operate in accordance with requirements as provided by the IRC, U.S. Department of Labor and ERISA. See also *nonqualified employee plan*.

qualified health plan—see "Qualified health plans" in the *Appendix A: Affordable Care Act of 2010 (ACA)*.

qualified impairment insurance—form of substandard or special class health insurance that waives an applicant's preexisting medical condition by attaching an endorsement to the policy stating that no benefits will be paid in connection with the condition. The waiver enables an applicant, who otherwise would not qualify, to be insured. Such plans are no longer sold in the U.S. due to the passage of the Affordable Care Act of 2010 (ACA) and its ban on preexisting condition exclusions. See also *class rating, declined risk class, endorsement, preferred risk class, rated policy* and *standard risk class*.

qualified joint and survivor annuity (QJSA)—series of equal periodic retirement benefit payments over the lifetime of a participant, with the payment continuing to the participant's spouse for the rest of the spouse's life if the spouse survives the participant. In the U.S., the payment to the surviving spouse must be at least 50%, and not more than 100%, of the periodic payment received during the couple's joint lives. The Pension Protection Act of 2006 requires defined benefit plans and money purchase plans to provide benefits in this form unless a plan participant and spouse (if any) choose otherwise. See also *joint and survivor benefit, qualified annuity, qualified optional survivor annuity (QOSA)* and *qualified preretirement survivor annuity (QPSA)*.

qualified matching contributions (QMACs)—funds placed in an employee 401(k) plan by an employer that matches employee contributions. QMACs are 100% vested at all times and are subject to distribution restrictions by the federal government.

qualified medical child support order (QMCSO)—judgment, decree or order issued pursuant to a state domestic relations law or community property law that creates or recognizes the right of a child to receive benefits under a noncustodial parent's group health plan. To be qualified, the order must meet the requirements of ERISA Section 609. See also *alternate recipient*.

qualified medical expense—see *medical care expense*.

qualified Medicare beneficiary (QMB)—person eligible for Medicare Part A insurance whose income falls below 100% of federal poverty guidelines. The state where the person resides must pay the Medicare Part B premiums, deductibles and copayments.

qualified nonelective contributions (QNEC or QNC)—employer contribution to an employee's 401(k) plan for which the employee does not have a choice between receiving cash compensation or having the employer make a contribution to the plan on his or her behalf. Nonelective contributions are 100% vested at all times and are subject to the same distribution restrictions as elective contributions. See also *cash or deferred arrangement (CODA)*.

qualified nonguaranteed contract—insurance contract that is excluded from the IRC definition of a welfare benefit fund. All insurance contracts are treated as qualified nonguaranteed contracts unless they provide (1) a guarantee of renewal at set rates and (2) benefits beyond insurance protection and nonguaranteed policy dividends or experience-related refunds determined by factors other than the level of welfare benefits paid.

qualified opinion—conclusion by a professional auditor that the financial information provided by a corporation or benefit plan was limited in scope and/or the organization being audited has not maintained Generally Accepted Accounting Principles. See also *adverse opinion, disclaimer of opinion, Generally Accepted Accounting Principles (GAAP), unmodified opinion* and *unqualified opinion.*

qualified optional survivor annuity (QOSA)—retirement payments for the life of a plan participant, with payment continuing to the participant's spouse if the spouse survives the employee. The payments must equal either 50% or 75% of the amount payable that would be payable during the joint lives of the participant and the spouse and that would be the actuarial equivalent of a single life annuity for the life of the participant. The Pension Protection Act of 2006 requires defined benefit and defined contribution plans that are subject to the funding standards of IRC Section 412 or that do not satisfy the requirements exemption from IRC Section 401(a)(11) to offer this alternative to participants who waive a qualified joint and survivor annuity (QJSA). The plan must offer a 75% annuity option if it currently offers a QJSA with less than 75% continuation. Plans offering a QJSA with a survivor continuation percentage equal to or greater than 75% must offer a 50% survivor annuity. See also *qualified annuity, qualified joint and survivor annuity (QJSA)* and *qualified preretirement survivor annuity (QPSA).*

qualified preretirement survivor annuity (QPSA)—if a vested pension plan participant is married and dies before he or she begins to receive pension benefits, the surviving spouse must be offered this type of annuity. ERISA specifies how the QPSA is calculated. The dollar amount depends on the type of plan and the age of the participant at death. See also *qualified annuity, qualified joint and survivor annuity (QJSA)* and *qualified optional survivor annuity (QOSA).*

Qualified Professional Asset Manager (QPAM)—bank, insurance company or other registered investment advisor that meets ERISA requirements. The use of a QPAM by a qualified plan helps ensure that trustees do not inadvertently violate ERISA's party-in-interest guidelines and allows the plan to engage in certain transactions that would otherwise be prohibited under ERISA. See also *party in interest* and *prohibited transaction (PT).*

qualified retirement plan—employee program established to provide retirement benefits for employees and their beneficiaries on a tax-advantaged basis. A qualified plan may be a defined benefit or a defined contribution plan. More specifically, it may be:
- A qualified employee plan such as a 401(k) plan
- A qualified employee annuity plan under Section 403(a)
- A tax-sheltered annuity plan under Section 403(b) for employees of public schools or tax-exempt organizations
- An eligible state or local government Section 457 deferred compensation plan (to the extent that any distribution is attributable to amounts the plan received in a direct transfer or rollover from one of the other plans listed here or an individual retirement account).

Unlike simplified employee pension plans and SIMPLE IRAs, a qualified retirement plan is not IRA-based or subject to the same rules concerning contributions and distributions. The same types of business may choose either a qualified or IRA-based plan, but the decision usually depends on the contribution limits (and how much the business wants or can afford to contribute) and the employer's desire or ability to handle the administration of the plan. See also *defined benefit (DB) plan, defined contribution (DC) plan, qualified employee annuity* and *qualified employee benefit plan.*

qualified separate line of business (QSLOB)—line of business that meets IRS requirements for treatment as a distinct unit for purposes of applying nondiscrimination requirements.

qualified start-up costs—limited U.S. tax credit that can be taken by employers for the expenses incurred to establish and administer a qualified employee benefit plan for the first three years of its existence.

qualified total distribution (QTD)—payment representing an employee's interest in a qualified retirement plan. The payment must be prompted by retirement (or other separation from service), death, disability or attainment of the age of 59½. Payment can be in installments as long as the complete distribution is made within a single tax year. See also *qualified retirement plan.*

qualified tuition program—see *529 plan.*

qualifying event—occurrence that entitles a person to a benefit. Qualifying events for the purposes of continuing health coverage under COBRA include termination of employment (or a reduction in hours); the death, divorce or legal separation of a covered employee; a covered employee's eligibility for Medicare; a dependent's loss of dependent status; or the loss of coverage due to the employer's filing of a bankruptcy proceeding. See also *Consolidated Omnibus Budget Reconciliation Act of 1985 (COBRA)* and *qualified beneficiary.*

qualifying period—see *waiting period*.

quality
—in general, a measure of excellence; being free from defects, deficiencies and variation.
—for health care, the degree to which the care provided increases the likelihood of a desired outcome and is consistent with current medical knowledge.

Quality Alliance Steering Committee (QASC)—coalition comprised of health care alliances as well as leaders among physicians, nurses, hospitals, health insurers, consumers, accrediting agencies and the public sector. Members of QASC are working together to ensure quality measures are constructed and reported in a clear, consistent and person-focused way to inform both consumer and employer decision making, in addition to improving care.

quality assessment (QA)—systematic process to improve the quality of health care within an organization by monitoring quality, finding what is not working and fixing problems.

quality assurance (QA)—planned or systematic actions that provide confidence a product or service meets specific standards. A hospital may have a system of processes and controls to make sure the care provided its patients is of the highest quality and to identify where problems need to be addressed.

quality improvement (QI)—also referred to as *performance improvement (PI)*, a management technique for improving a product and/or operations on a continuing basis. QI involves setting goals, implementing change, measuring outcomes and following up as necessary. In health care, the end result of QI ranges from simply making a recommendation but leaving the decision making primarily in the hands of physicians (e.g., a *practice guideline*) to prescribing patterns of care (e.g., a *clinical pathway*).

Quality Improvement Organization (QIO)—group of professionals, mostly doctors and health care experts, that the U.S. government contracts with to check on and improve the care given to Medicare patients. QIOs are private, mostly not-for-profit organizations that work under the direction of the Centers for Medicare & Medicaid Services, an agency of the U.S. Department of Health and Human Services. Among the core functions of QIOs are ensuring Medicare pays only for reasonable and necessary goods and services and addressing beneficiary complaints. There are 53 QIOs responsible for each state, U.S. territories and the District of Columbia.

quality indicator—data that provides evidence regarding the level of quality achieved. The number of complications, patient mortality rates and return admissions are all common indicators of the quality of hospital care.

quality management—see *quality assurance (QA)*.

quality of care—degree of success to which health care increases the probability of desired patient outcomes and is consistent with standards of care.

quality of life
—term used in a wide range of contexts that refers to the general well-being of individuals and societies.
—for health care purposes, a patient's ability to enjoy normal life activities. Some medical treatments can impair the quality of a person's life with no appreciable benefit.

quality review committee—group of persons established by a professional organization or institution to assess and/or assure quality. Unlike a peer review committee, a quality review committee can function on its own initiative on a broad range of topics. See also *peer review*.

quantitative job analysis (QJA)—reliance on scaled questionnaires and inventories to produce job-related data that is documentable, can be statistically analyzed and may be more objective than other analyses.

quarters of coverage (QC)—basic unit of measurement for determining Social Security coverage in the U.S. A QC is one-fourth of a year, or three months. The number of QCs during which an individual must earn enough money to receive credit toward Social Security eligibility depends on the individual's age; 40 is the maximum number required.

quartile—measurement used to divide a population into four equal parts. The first quartile represents the lowest fourth of the data (1% to 25%), the second represents 26% to 50%, the third represents 51% to 75% and the fourth quartile is 76% to 100%.

Québec Pension Plan—see *Canada Pension Plan (CPP)/Québec Pension Plan (QPP)*.

quick asset—see *liquid asset*.

quick ratio—see *acid test ratio*.

quintile—measurement used to divide a population into five equal parts. The first quintile represents the lowest fifth of the data (1% to 20%), the second represents 21% to 40%, the third represents 41% to 60%, the fourth represents 61% to 80% and the fifth is the highest with 81% to 100%.

quitclaim deed—document transferring ownership of property with no warranty of ownership. Often used to remove a cloud on a title.

quorum—minimum number of persons that must be present to make the proceedings of a meeting valid.

quotation/quote—in the financial world, the current price of a security, be it either the highest bid price for the security or the lowest ask price.

R

rabbi trust—type of trust used by a business or other entity to defer taxes until the beneficiary receives payments from the trust. Employers most often use a rabbi trust to set aside money for payment of excess pensions or deferred pay to an executive or key employee. Since it is a nonqualified arrangement, the employer takes no tax deduction. Beneficiaries pay no tax on contributions to the trust until they start receiving their money. Although funds are subject to an employer's creditors, they are inaccessible to present and future management.

radiation therapy—use of high-energy, penetrating waves or particles of radiation in the treatment of cancer patients. Radiation therapy is provided by a therapist or physician qualified in therapeutic radiology.

Railroad Retirement Act of 1935—federal legislation that created a social security program for railroad workers in the United States. Benefits are provided for:
- Workers who retired because of age or disability
- Eligible spouses and divorced spouses of retired employees
- Surviving widows, widowers, divorced spouses, children and dependent parents of deceased employees
- Unemployed workers
- Workers who are sick or injured.

Among other requirements, the eligible employee must have ten or more years of railroad service.

random walk theory—loosely based on the efficient market hypothesis, the idea that even uninformed investors buying a diversified portfolio will obtain a rate of return as generous as that achieved by the experts. Burton G. Malkiel, originator of the theory, proposed in 1973 that a "blindfolded chimpanzee throwing darts at the *Wall Street Journal* could select a portfolio that would do as well as the experts." See also *efficient market hypothesis (EMH)*.

range—extent or scope. The range of pay grades is the extent to which maximum pay exceeds minimum pay. In the investment world, it might refer to the difference between the highest and lowest prices recorded for a stock during a given trading period.

range penetration—an individual's pay compared with the total pay range (rather than compared with the midpoint, as in compa-ratio). Range penetration is calculated by subtracting the range minimum from the person's salary, then dividing by the range maximum less the range minimum. For example, if the range is $50,000 to $75,000 and the salary is $60,000, the range penetration is 0.4, or 40%. See also *compa-ratio* and *market index ratio*.

ranking format—appraisal technique in which employees are compared with each other on a performance measure to determine their relative order.

ranking method—in job evaluation, the listing of jobs according to their relative value without attempting an exact numerical rating.

rapid cycle change/improvement—use of standard quality tools to improve performance in a short time period. The rapid cycle change model includes the identification, implementation and measurement of changes made to improve a process or a system. At the onset, a team sets a global outcome measure based on the system's goals. Improvement occurs through small, rapid PDSA (Plan, Do, Study, Act) cycles of change. When applied to health care processes, the idea is that there should be a constant cycle of innovation or improvement.

rate—measure, quantity, or frequency; also the process of assessing a value. See also *class rating, insurance rate, interest rate* and *wage rate*.

rated policy—sometimes referred to as an extra risk policy, an insurance contract covering an entity classified as a substandard risk. The policy's premium rate is higher than the rate for a standard policy, or the policy is issued with special limitations, exclusions or both. See also *class rating* and *substandard risk class*.

rate of exchange—see *currency exchange rate*.

rate of return (ROR)—money gained or lost (both realized and unrealized) as a percentage of money invested. The money gained or lost may be interest or an increase or a decrease in the value of the investment. The ROR may be based on a security's purchase price (yield to maturity) or its current market price (current income return). It is also referred to as return on investment, nominal rate of return and, sometimes, just return. When adjusted for inflation, the ROR is known as the real rate of return. See also *fair rate of return* and *yield to maturity (YTM)*.

rating
—process that estimates the standing of a person or object; for example, rating an employee's performance.
—for insurance and investment purposes, rating is an assessment of risk and the process used to assess risk. See also *class rating, community rating, default risk, experience rating, rating service* and *retrospective rating.*

ratings analyst—financial specialist that evaluates the ability of bond issuers to repay their debts. On the basis of the evaluation, a management team assigns a rating to a bond that helps the team decide whether to include the bond in a portfolio. See also *credit rating* and *rating service.*

rating service—organization that evaluates securities and credit risk such as Fitch Ratings, Moody's Investors Services, Morningstar and Value Line.

ratio test—one of three standards that can be used to determine whether a qualified retirement plan satisfies the IRS minimum coverage requirements. The percentage of non-highly compensated employees covered by a plan must be at least 70% of highly compensated employees covered. The other two tests are the *average benefit test* and *percentage test.*

readily achievable—for purposes of the Americans with Disabilities Act (ADA), something that can be accomplished and carried out with little difficulty or expense. Under Title III of the ADA, public accommodations must remove barriers in existing facilities if it is readily achievable to do so. In determining whether an action is readily achievable, factors considered include the nature and cost of the action, available resources to achieve accommodation, legitimate safety requirements, impact on the operation of a site and, when applicable, overall financial resources, size and type of operation of the entity. See also *public accommodation* and *reasonable accommodation.*

readmission—a patient return to a hospital after a previous stay that may or may not be related to the previous stay. Readmission within 30 days of discharge is often used as a marker of poor quality care and a lack of focus on transitioning the patient.

real estate—see *real property.*

real estate agent—individual who works for a real estate broker. The agent may hold an individual real estate broker's license. See also *real estate broker.*

real estate broker—person who arranges the purchase or sale of property for a buyer or seller in return for a commission. The broker may help buyers finance a real estate purchase through their contacts with banks, savings and loans, and mortgage bankers. A broker must be licensed by the state in which he or she operates. See also *real estate agent.*

real estate fund—mutual fund, investment trust or other investment vehicle that owns real estate (usually commercial) and/or invests in the stocks of companies that participate in the real estate industry.

real estate investment trust (REIT)—corporation or trust that uses pooled funds to purchase and manage real estate assets and/or mortgage loans. REITs are usually publicly traded. In the U.S., they are required to distribute (or pass through) 95% of their income to shareholders to qualify for special tax treatment. See also *hybrid real estate investment trust (REIT)* and *mortgage REIT.*

real estate mortgage investment conduit (REMIC)—pass-through vehicle authorized in the U.S. by the Tax Reform Act of 1986 that holds commercial and residential mortgages in trust. The REMIC issues certificates, multiclass bonds or other securities representing an undivided interest in these mortgages to individual investors in the secondary mortgage market. A REMIC may be organized as a corporation, a partnership or a trust that pools mortgages and issues certificates. REMICs have some similarities with collateralized mortgage obligations (CMOs), but REMICs are more flexible, allowing the issuers the ability to separate mortgage pools not only into different maturity classes but into different risk classes as well. A REMIC is exempt from federal taxes, although income earned by investors is fully taxable. REMICs also tend to be more risky than CMOs. See also *collateralized mortgage obligation (CMO), mortgage-backed security (MBS)* and *tranche.*

real estate operating company (REOC)—corporation that invests in real estate and whose shares trade on a public exchange. An REOC is similar to a real estate investment trust (REIT), except an REOC reinvests its earnings into the business while an REIT distributes its earnings to its unit holders. In addition, REOCs are more flexible than REITs in terms of what types of real estate investments they can make. See also *real estate investment trust (REIT).*

Real Estate Settlement Procedures Act (RESPA)—federal consumer protection statute, passed in 1974, that requires lenders to give written disclosures to those applying for a mortgage loan to purchase a one- to four-family residential property in the U.S. The disclosures, which spell out the costs and practices associated with settlement, must be provided at various points of time throughout the purchasing process. RESPA also prohibits kickbacks and referral fees that unnecessarily increase the costs of certain settlement services. See also *closing cost*.

real income—income that has been adjusted for inflation so that it reflects actual purchasing power. See also *inflation*.

realized profit/loss—actualized gain or loss from the sale or surrender of a security. See also *paper profit/loss*.

real property—land and anything permanently affixed to the land (e.g., buildings, fences) and those things attached to the buildings (e.g., light fixtures, plumbing, heating fixtures), as opposed to personal property that is not attached. See also *core real estate, employer real property, opportunistic real estate* and *value-added real estate*.

real rate of return—see *rate of return (ROR)*.

real return bond (RRB)—bond issued by the Canadian government that offers protection against inflation. Coupon payments and the principal are automatically adjusted to compensate for inflation. RRBs pay interest semiannually based on an inflation-adjusted principal and, at maturity, repay the principal in inflation-adjusted dollars. RRBs must be purchased, transferred or sold—directly or indirectly—through a participant of the Debt Clearing Service. They are available only in integral multiples of $1,000. See also *Treasury Inflation-Protected Security (TIPS)*.

real wages—see *real income*.

reasonable accommodation—adjustments that do not cause undue hardship. For example, the Americans with Disabilities Act of 1990 requires employers with 15 or more employees to make the following accommodations for disabled persons unless the adjustments cause undue hardship to an employer: (1) changes to the job application process, (2) changes to the work environment or the way a job is usually done, and (3) changes that enable an employee with a disability to enjoy equal benefits and privileges of employment (such as access to training). See also *Americans with Disabilities Act of 1990 (ADA)* and *readily achievable*.

reasonable and customary (R&C) charge—amount billed for a specific procedure by a particular type of health care provider practicing within a defined geographic area. Insurance companies often use R&C to define the amount they will cover for a particular procedure. If a provider charges more, the plan participant may be responsible for paying the additional amount. See also *usual, customary and reasonable (UCR) fee*.

reasonable care—acting in the same manner as a prudent and intelligent person would act in similar circumstances. Failure to use reasonable care is negligence.

reasonable compensation—as defined by the IRS, the amount that would ordinarily be paid to an employee for like services by like organizations in like circumstances. Two tests are used to determine reasonable compensation: (1) an amount test focuses on the reasonableness of the total amount paid while (2) a purpose test examines the services for which the compensation was paid. The term *compensation* includes at least the following: (1) salary or wages; (2) contributions to pension and profit-sharing plans; (3) unpaid deferred compensation; (4) payment of personal expenses; (5) rents, royalties or fees; and (6) personal use of an organization's property or facilities. IRC Section 162 imposes a reasonableness requirement for deductibility of compensation as a business expense.

rebalancing—adjusting the proportion of assets in an investment portfolio through the buying and selling of securities so the proportion is consistent with a target allocation. The decision to rebalance a portfolio can be made on a calendar basis or a contingency basis.

rebate—money returned from a prescription drug manufacturer or other supplier based upon purchases made to a payer.

rebate audit—analysis of the ability of a pharmacy benefits manager (PBM) to obtain and recover rebate amounts as well as passing the appropriate portion back to a client according to the contract terms established between the PBM and client. See also *audit* and *pharmacy benefits management/manager (PBM)*.

receivership—form of bankruptcy in which a person (receiver) is appointed to manage a company and recoup as many debts as possible. The receiver manages the company under the direction of a court until a more permanent resolution is agreed upon by all parties in interest. See also *bankruptcy*.

recertification—reconfirmation of certain characteristics of an object, person or organization. For example, (1) reconfirmation of the need for medical leave from work due to a serious health condition or (2) designating a person or organization as still qualified to perform a job or task. Additional training, education, testing or a peer review may be required to assure that the standards of the organization granting certification are being maintained. See also *certification* and *concurrent review*.

recession—phase of the business cycle when there is a downturn in economic activity characterized by sluggish market demand, the failure of real output to rise and an increase in unemployment. Two or more consecutive quarters with a decline in gross national product is generally considered to be a recession. See also *business cycle, depression* and *gross national product (GNP)*.

recidivism—relapse. In medicine, the recurrence of a behavior or illness requiring readmission to a health care facility.

reciprocal agreement—see *reciprocity*.

reciprocal transfer arrangement—also referred to as a reciprocal portability arrangement, agreement that permits a plan member to accept service or benefits previously credited under another registered pension plan (RPP) in his or her current employer's plan in return for the member giving up rights to such service or benefits under the former plan.

reciprocity—understanding that two entities will exchange favors or privileges. For example, a group health plan participant, temporarily away from home, may be allowed to receive necessary medical care from a group health plan in the area the member is visiting. Two multiemployer retirement plans may have an agreement that allows participants to fulfill service requirements and accumulate benefit credits with either plan. Under a pro-rata agreement, each retirement plan pays its proportionate share of benefits. The alternative is a money-follows-the-man agreement in which the employer contributions are made to the participant's home or terminal fund, which then pays the full retirement benefit. See also *pro rata*.

recognition program—acknowledgment of employee contributions and service. Examples include giving employees spot awards, gifts on milestone anniversaries, granting an extra personal day for perfect attendance, or paying a one-time cash bonus for making a cost-saving suggestion. See also *reward system* and *service award*.

recordkeeping—systematic collection and maintenance of documents and data that can take on a variety of forms and mediums.

recourse—ability to demand compensation or take action. For example, if a consumer has a warranty on a defective product, he or she has recourse to change the situation.

recurring clause—also referred to as a recurrence clause, a provision in some health insurance policies that specifies a period of time during which the return of a condition is considered a continuation of a prior period of disability or hospital confinement.

red circle rate—individual pay rate above the established range maximum assigned to the job grade. When this occurs, the employee may not be eligible for further base pay increases until the range maximum surpasses the individual's pay rate.

redeemable—see *callable*.

redemption fee—see *back-end load*.

redemption price—see *call price*.

reduction in force (RIF)—temporary or permanent termination of employees for business reasons (e.g., certain positions are no longer necessary or there is a business slowdown). RIFs do not involve delinquency, misconduct or inability of an employee to perform a job.

red zone—see *critical status*.

referee—person given the authority to make a decision or settlement. Referees are commonly used to professionally evaluate the research of colleagues for publication. In the judicial system, an attorney may be appointed to serve as a referee to investigate and make recommendations on a case.

reference-based pricing (RBP)—strategy for controlling the cost of prescription medications that aggregates drugs into generic groups, related drug groups (e.g., ACE inhibitors) or drugs grouped by therapeutic indication (e.g., antihypertensives). For each drug group, a single reimbursement level or reference price is set. Drugs above the reference price require partial or total payment by the patient. If a patient chooses a brand-name drug when a generic drug is available, the patient may be required to pay the difference between the two.

reference price—lowest price available for a drug within a group of drugs that have similar therapeutic application but different active ingredients. Plan beneficiaries may be allowed to purchase drugs other than the reference product, but they might be required to pay the difference between the retail and the reference price.

referral—recommendation of a person or business to another. In health care, a referral is a recommendation by a physician and/or health plan for a patient to receive care from a different provider. See also *gatekeeper* and *primary care physician (PCP)*.

referral management—process by which a primary care physician (PCP) determines whether a patient needs to see a specialist or have a service performed outside of the PCP's office (e.g., diagnostic tests, outpatient surgery, home health care). When a referral is required, the PCP decides to whom the referral is made, for how long and for what services. See also *gatekeeper, health maintenance organization (HMO)* and *primary care physician (PCP)*.

refinance—replacing a loan with a new one. Refinancing is typically used to save interest costs, consolidate debt, lengthen loan maturities or some combination of the three.

reflation—restoration of prices to a desirable level after a period of deflation; a form of inflation. Reflation is generally achieved through specific acts of government such as increasing the money supply or reducing taxes. See also *deflation* and *inflation*.

refund annuity—if an annuitant dies before receiving annuity income at least equal to the premiums paid, the beneficiary designated by the annuitant is paid the difference. When payment is to the beneficiary as a lump sum at the time of death, the policy is referred to as a cash or lump-sum refund annuity. A second type of policy is an installment refund annuity that makes monthly payments to the beneficiary until the full cost of the annuity has been received. See also *annuity, fixed period annuity* and *guaranteed annuity*.

refunding—retiring an outstanding bond on or before maturity by using money from the sale of a new bond. Refunding is used by a bond issuer to reduce interest payments or to postpone payment.

regional fund—mutual fund that invests in securities from a specific locale. This might be a state (e.g., New York, California), a nation (e.g., Japan, Germany) or a group of nations (e.g., Southeast Asia, Latin America, Europe). A regional mutual fund generally seeks to own a diversified investment portfolio representing companies based in and operating out of its specified geographical area. However, some regional funds invest in a specific type of asset (e.g., municipal bonds, venture capital) or a sector (e.g., energy, chemicals). See also *mutual fund* and *sector fund*.

regionalization—sharing resources and coordinating services within a geographical area.

registered bond—debt obligation that is registered on the books of the issuer in the owner's name. The issuer keeps records and automatically makes payments to the owner. A registered bond can be transferred to another owner only when endorsed by the registered owner. Most securities issued today are in registered form versus the other option, unregistered bearer bonds. See also *bearer bond* and *coupon bond*.

Registered Disability Savings Plan (RDSP)—savings account set up to help parents and others save for the long-term financial security of a person who is eligible for Canada's disability tax credit (DTC). Contributions are tax-deductible and can be made until a beneficiary turns the age of 59. Within limits set by the federal government, the withdrawal of contributions is not taxable as income. Investment income earned in the plan, however, is taxable.

Registered Education Savings Plan (RESP)—Canadian tax-deferred account for the accumulation of assets to be used to pay a child's postsecondary education. RESPs are offered by most financial institutions in Canada. Savings grow tax-deferred until the student withdraws them for educational purposes. Withdrawals are taxed in the student's hands, which is typically at a lower rate.

Registered Investment Advisor (RIA)—individual or organization that manages the assets of high-net-worth individuals and institutional investors. Most RIAs are partnerships or corporations. In the U.S., RIAs must register with the Securities and Exchange Commission as well as any state in which they operate.

registered pension plan (RPP)—employer-sponsored defined benefit (DB), defined contribution (DC) or hybrid plan that provides retirement benefits to Canadian employees upon retirement. The latter includes target benefit, cash balance and combination plans, etc. RPPs must be registered with the Canada Revenue Agency and meet criteria under the nation's Income Tax Act.

Employer contributions are required for a DB plan—the amount is whatever is necessary to provide the benefits promised members. With plans that are not a DB plan, the plan's design determines whether an employee may contribute and whether an employee is required to contribute. One exception is a money purchase plan, for which an employer must contribute a minimum of 1% of a worker's income. Contributions and gains are tax-deferred. Funds are taxed when they are withdrawn from the plan.

While employed by the employer sponsoring their RPP, members cannot withdraw required employer contributions. Members may, however, withdraw amounts accumulated through their own voluntary contributions. At termination of employment, a member is entitled to his or her own contributions and plan sponsor vested contributions unless the assets are locked-in. Members also have the option to transfer accumulated amounts to another RPP or a locked-in RRSP.

Generally, funds in a locked-in plan cannot be withdrawn, but there are some exceptions such as small entitlements and a member's shortened life expectancy. Members can also apply to the minimum standards regulator to withdraw funds on hardship grounds. See also *cash balance plan, defined benefit (DB) plan, locked-in account, money purchase plan* and *target benefit plan*.

registered profit-sharing pension plan—money purchase pension plan with employer contributions related in some way to corporate profits. Registered under Section 147.1 of Canada's Income Tax Act, these plans operate in the same manner as other pension plans. Tax-deductible employee and employer contributions can be made within the maximum contribution amounts established for other plans. Money in a fund must remain there until retirement or termination of employment. The interest income on contributions deposited accumulates tax-free. Benefits are taxable when paid out and, normally, must be paid in the form of an annuity upon retirement. Lump-sum payments are available only in exceptional circumstances. See also *current distribution profit-sharing plan, deferred profit-sharing plan (DPSP), employee's profit-sharing plan (EPSP), money purchase plan, profit-sharing plan* and *registered pension plan*.

registered representative—see *securities broker*.

Registered Retirement Income Fund (RRIF)—retirement fund registered with the Canada Revenue Agency and governed by Section 146.3 of the Income Tax Act. An individual establishes an RRIF with a carrier (e.g., bank, trust or insurance company) that accepts the money from a Registered Retirement Savings Plan, a registered pension plan or another RRIF. Starting the year after the RRIF is established, a minimum amount must be withdrawn annually using a predetermined formula designed to fully pay out all assets in the fund by the year the annuitant reaches 90 years of age. The amount withdrawn is taxed. A participant in an RRIF plan has the option of managing the investment portfolio using a self-directed RRIF.

Registered Retirement Savings Plan (RRSP)—voluntary defined contribution (DC) plan that an individual or a group of individuals who do not have a registered pension plan (RPP) can use to accumulate money for retirement. Set up at a financial institution such as a bank, credit union, trust company, mutual fund company, insurance company or brokerage firm, the plan may be a regular RRSP or a self-directed one. A self-directed RRSP allows the plan participant to build and manage his or her own investment portfolio. The RRSP must be registered with the Canada Revenue Agency and subject to Section 146(1)(j) of the Income Tax Act.

Plan rules determine whether the RRSP is voluntary or compulsory for members. Contributions are tax-deductible and investment income is tax-free until withdrawn, when it is treated as income for tax purposes. Upon retirement, the holder of the RRSP may purchase a prescribed form of annuity or transfer plan assets to a Registered Retirement Income Fund (RRIF). Although contributions are not locked-in, an employer may place limits on withdrawals from an RRSP as long as an employee remains employed. Employers cannot, however, restrict employee access once the worker retires or the worker's employment is terminated. See also *money purchase plan, pension adjustment (PA)* and *Registered Retirement Income Fund (RRIF)*.

Registered Retirement Savings Plan (RRSP) contribution room/deduction limit—amount an individual may contribute in any one year to an RRSP on a fully tax-deductible basis. Alternatively, it is the amount an individual may deduct from taxable income in the year that relates to an RRSP contribution made by an individual in the previous year that6 the person could not deduct, or chose not to deduct, from taxable income in the previous year.

Registered Retirement Savings Plan (RRSP) dollar limit—typically, the defined contribution (money purchase) limit for the preceding year.

regressive tax—government levy that takes a larger percentage of income from low-income people than from high-income people. The Social Security tax system in the U.S. is considered a regressive tax because there is a maximum level at which incomes are taxed. See also *progressive tax* and *proportional tax*.

regulation—system of rules established by government or members of an industry to achieve goals believed to be in the public interest. Regulation of banking, insurance and securities in the United States is a mixture of rules and laws at the federal and state levels. The securities industry also regulates itself. See also *Commodity Futures Trading Commission (CFTC)*, *Securities and Exchange Commission (SEC)* and *self-regulatory organization (SRO)*.

rehabilitation—process of restoring a person or part of the body to near normal function after an injury or a disease.

Rehabilitation Act of 1973—U.S. law that prohibits discrimination on the basis of disability in programs conducted by federal agencies, in programs receiving federal financial assistance, in federal employment and in the employment practices of federal contractors. The standards for determining employment discrimination under the Rehabilitation Act are the same as those used in the Americans with Disabilities Act.

rehabilitation plan—under the Pension Protection Act of 2006, trustees of pension plans in the U.S. that are certified as being in critical status must establish and implement a scheme that will remove the plan from critical status within ten years. Generally, the strategies for achieving this goal are increasing contributions, decreasing benefits or a combination of both. If it is determined the plan cannot reasonably be expected to emerge from critical status within a decade, trustees are expected to take reasonable measures to emerge from critical status at a later time and to forestall possible insolvency. See also *critical status* and *endangered status*.

reimportation—see *drug reimportation*.

reinstatement—resumption of coverage under an insurance policy that has lapsed. The insurer usually requires evidence of insurability and payment of past-due premiums plus interest before a policy can be reinstated.

reinsurance—insurance for insurance companies; a contract that an insurance company makes with another insurer to protect against a major payout of claims in excess of a designated limit. Essentially, the insurance protects the insurance company when there are catastrophic losses such as those incurred with a major hurricane or flood. See also *retrocession*.

reinsurance fee—see "Fees/Taxes" in the *Appendix A: Affordable Care Act of 2010 (ACA)*.

reinvestment—using dividends, interest and capital gains earned from an investment to purchase additional shares or units, rather than receiving the distributions in cash.

reinvestment risk—typically used in reference to bonds, the chance that future proceeds will have to be reinvested at a lower potential interest rate.

relative return—difference in the money gained or lost on an investment over a period of time compared with another investment (usually a stock or mutual fund). Because relative return compares the return on one investment with another, it is more helpful than absolute return—especially when reviewing the performance of an investment manager who is expected to achieve a return higher than a benchmark investment. See also *absolute return*.

relative value fund—see *arbitrage fund*.

relative value strategy—attempt to generate investment returns by taking advantage of price differences between securities in the same sector, industry or market. A relative value manager trades on gaps, rather than the price of a specific security alone. The manager determines what he or she considers normal differences in prices or rates by examining historical movements and takes positions that exploit gaps until the normal state is reached. Long positions are taken on securities considered undervalued, while short positions are taken on securities considered overvalued. See also *arbitrage*.

release of information (ROI)—also referred to as disclosure, sharing of knowledge concerning an individual. In general, no information about a patient may be released without his or her authorization unless it's immediately necessary for care (as in a medical emergency in which he or she is incapacitated). HIPAA and state privacy rules protect the release of health care information. See also *Health Insurance Portability and Accountability Act of 1996 (HIPAA)*.

relief—sought by a plaintiff in a lawsuit; usually, whatever it is that would make the plaintiff "whole" or at least compensated for an injury.

relocation services—benefits offered by an employer to a current employee accepting an assignment in a new location. Examples include reimbursement for house-hunting expenses household moving costs or interim travel expenses or help in orienting to a new culture or learning a new language.

remedial amendment period—frame of time during which a retirement plan must be amended to conform to new legislation or other regulations in order to retain its qualified status. This period is usually stated in the regulation. If a plan terminates prior to the date amendments must be adopted, the plan must be amended to conform to the applicable new rules in connection with the termination.

remediation—process of correcting a situation.

remedy—judicial means or court procedures by which legal and equitable rights are enforced.

renegotiable rate mortgage (RRM)—also called a *rollover mortgage*, a variation on an adjustable rate mortgage that typically has a renewable short-term balloon payment due at the end of three to five years. Interest on the loan is generally fixed until the balloon payment is due, then the interest rate is renegotiated or rolled over to the current rate. Increases and decreases are based on an index linked to average mortgage rates. See also *adjustable rate mortgage (ARM)*.

renewal—continuance of coverage under an insurance policy beyond its original term by the insurer's acceptance of a premium for a new policy term.

rent-a-captive—typically, a stock company owned by an insurance company that allows third parties to pay a fee to insure their risk via the captive company. The upfront capital and surplus needed for risk underwriting and program administration are provided by the owner of the captive. The entity renting the captive must relinquish a large part of the management control. Rent-a-captives are used to insure entities that are too small to create their own insurance captives and firms undecided about forming their own captive program. See also *captive insurance company*.

rental risk—chance that the owner of a property will not be able to find tenants. In addition, the chance a tenant will damage the property or not pay the rent.

repackaged—prescription drug taken from its original manufacturer's container and placed into another labeled container for dispensing.

repatriation—making the transition from an overseas work assignment to the home country.

repetitive stress injury—see *cumulative trauma disorder (CTD)*.

replacement ratio—proportion of preretirement earnings received as retirement benefits.

reportable event—for the purpose of benefit plans in the U.S. and Pension Benefit Guaranty Corporation (PBGC) notification, any of the following:
- Disqualification for tax purposes
- A benefit decrease by amendment
- A decrease in participation to less than 80% of that at the start of the plan year
- An IRS determination letter indicating partial or complete plan termination
- Failure to meet minimum funding standards
- Inability to pay benefits when due
- Distribution to a substantial owner
- Filing an actuarial statement with the IRS before a plan merger, consolidation or the transfer of assets, or the granting of an alternative method of ERISA compliance by the U.S. Department of Labor
- Any other occurrence determined by the PBGC, including bankruptcy, insolvency, liquidation, dissolution or a change in the plan sponsor of a single employer plan.

Such events usually must be reported to the PBGC within 30 days unless expressly waived. Notice is required to allow the PBGC adequate time to protect the benefits of participants and beneficiaries. See also *Pension Benefit Guaranty Corporation (PBGC)*.

report card—written assessment of work or progress. Report cards are commonly used to provide information on the quality of service provided by health plans and health care providers; they make it possible to compare providers using standardized measures. Report cards are published by a variety of entities including states, private health organizations, consumer groups and health plans. The *National Committee for Quality Assurance (NCQA)* provides health plan quality report cards that can be used by consumers.

repricing audit—examining the adherence of a pharmacy benefit manager to a contract's financial terms with a client such as discounts, dispensing fees and copayments. Compliance with plan design may also be included in the scope of a repricing audit. See also *audit* and *pharmacy benefits management/manager (PBM)*.

repurchase agreement (RP or repo)—promise of one party to sell securities at a specified price to a second party with a simultaneous agreement of the first party to repurchase the securities at a specified price or at a specified later date.

request for admission—invitation from one party to another party in a legal case to admit or deny that a statement is true under oath. Through admission, a fact becomes undisputed and does not require further proof later in the case. Eliminating issues where there is agreement can save money and time.

request for information (RFI)—instrument used to collect written data about the capabilities of vendors regarding the provision of goods and/or services. Normally, an RFI follows a format that can be used for comparative purposes. An RFI is sometimes used as a preliminary step by an organization before preparing an RFP. See also *request for proposal (RFP)*.

request for proposal (RFP)—invitation to vendors to submit information and a bid for the provision of a good or service.

required minimum distribution (RMD)—U.S. law requires that withdrawals from a tax-qualified plan must generally begin by April 1 of the year that is the later of the following: (1) the calendar year in which the employee reaches the age of 70½ or (2) when the employee actually retires. Withdrawals usually must be paid over a period not to exceed the life expectancy of the retiree. Amounts are determined by the amount in the employee's account and the employee's life expectancy.

rescission of coverage—revocation or cancellation of protection from risk under a benefit plan or insurance policy. The Affordable Care Act of 2010 restricts when an insurance company may cancel health plan coverage to situations such as consumer fraud and misrepresentation. See also "Rescission" in the *Appendix A: Affordable Care Act of 2010 (ACA)*.

reserve—fund set aside to assure the fulfillment of future claims.

reserve requirements—funds that banks and other depository institutions must keep as cash in their vaults or on deposit with a Federal Reserve Bank. The requirement set by the board of governors of the Federal Reserve System is expressed as a percentage of the depository institution's deposit liabilities. The Federal Reserve stipulates what these ratios must be. See also *Federal Reserve System* and *monetary policy*.

resident alien—individual who has legally established temporary or permanent residence in a nation for which he or she does not have citizenship. Those who have a tourist visa are not considered resident aliens. See also *green card, illegal alien, nonresident alien* and *permanent resident*.

residential care facility—see *assisted living facility*.

residential treatment center (RTC)—facility that specializes in 24-hour mental health and substance abuse care and treatment.

residual—that which remains after the subtraction of one amount from another.

residual disability benefit—provision in an insurance policy that pays a partial benefit for a partial disability. Persons are considered residually disabled if they are not totally disabled and are able to work but, as a result of the injury or illness, they suffer a loss of income.

resource-based relative value scale (RBRVS)—classification system used to pay health care providers that is based on the time, training, skill and other factors required to deliver various services. RBRVS was initially mandated for use for Medicare and Medicaid reimbursements; it is now used by nearly all health maintenance organizations.

respite care—services provided to a sick or elderly person in order to allow the person's primary caregiver a temporary period of relief or rest. Respite care may be provided by a home health agency or another state-licensed facility and is reimbursable under a long-term care policy.

respondeat superior—literally, "let the master respond." Refers to the legal doctrine of vicarious liability that holds an employer, manager and others superior to an employee liable for that employee's negligent actions while on the job.

restoration of benefits—allowing an insured person who has used a portion of his or her benefits to regain full benefits after a stated period of time. A restoration-of-benefits clause is sometimes a provision of a long-term care policy.

restorative care—in dentistry, the repair of teeth.

restricted formulary—see *closed formulary*.

restricted stock—equity shares that have restrictions (e.g., a certain amount of time must pass, a specific goal must be achieved, the holder must be employed by the company for a specific amount of time) on sales and that must be traded in compliance with SEC regulations outlined under IRC Section 1244. Restricted stock is usually given to officers and key employees, but it can be used more broadly. See also *restricted stock plan*.

restricted stock plan—when an employee is given equity shares or allowed to purchase shares at a discount. The employee is not permitted to sell or transfer the shares until restrictions on the shares lapse. If the employee leaves the organization before the end of the restriction period, the stock is usually forfeited. Employees can choose whether to be taxed when the restrictions lapse, in which case they will pay ordinary income tax on the difference between the current price and anything they may have paid for the shares, or they can pay when the right is first granted by filing an 83(b) election. In that case, the employee pays ordinary income tax on the difference (if any) between the current price and the purchase price and capital gains tax when he or she actually sells the shares. While the employee holds the restricted stock, it may or may not provide dividends or voting rights at the option of the company. See also *equity compensation*.

restructuring—reorganizing the legal, ownership, operational, financial or other configurations of a company to reduce debt, increase profits or better address present and future needs.

retail network audit—examination by a pharmacy benefits manager, managed care organization or other external party to ensure the validity of prescription claims. Typically, this type of audit is conducted to curb fraud and abuse at the pharmacy level. See also *pharmacy benefits management/manager (PBM)*.

retained asset account (RAA)—temporary repository for proceeds of a life insurance policy that gives a beneficiary time to consider the policy's payout options while earning interest on the funds. An RAA essentially operates like a checking account with the payment of the total proceeds accomplished through delivery of a "checkbook."

retained earnings—after-tax corporate income not paid out as dividends that is reinvested in the business or used to pay off debt. Other terms for retained earnings are accumulated earnings and earned surplus.

retired lives reserve (RLR)—group life insurance product for employees that is composed of two basic parts: (1) annually renewable term life insurance until the employee reaches a specified age such as 100 and (2) the accumulation of a reserve element while the employee is working from which premium payments are made after the employee retires. Premium payments that the employer makes on behalf of the employee are a tax-deductible expense; they are not considered taxable income to the employee. Should an employee terminate service prior to retirement, funds remaining in the employee's account are used to fund the benefits of the remaining employees. See also *group insurance, life insurance* and *term life insurance*.

retiree—person who has withdrawn from active employment and is eligible for retirement benefits. See also *deferred retirement, early retirement, mandatory retirement, normal retirement age (NRA)* and *phased retirement*.

retiree medical account (RMA)—funds in a pension or annuity plan that may be used to provide health care benefits for retired employees, their spouses and their dependents, as specified in IRC Section 401(h). RMA benefits must be subordinate to pension benefits and must be established and maintained in a separate account. See also *401(h) account*.

retiree medical plan—generally, a group health care program for retired employees that is integrated with Medicare. These plans are not Medicare supplemental policies.

retirement—withdrawal from a career or active participation in the workforce that most commonly occurs later in life. Retirement may be a choice at a specific age or the result of life events that make it difficult to continue in one's chosen occupation.

retirement age—see *deferred retirement, early retirement, mandatory retirement, normal retirement age (NRA)* and *phased retirement*.

retirement benefits—income and other benefits (e.g., health care, life insurance) to which retirees, their spouses and their dependents are eligible. See also *annuity, employee retirement plan, life insurance, Medicare, retiree medical plan* and *retirement income*.

retirement bonus plan—see *lifecycle pension plan*.

Retirement Compensation Arrangement (RCA)—Canadian benefit plan set up by an employer, former employer or, in some cases, an employee. A custodian holds the funds in a trust with the intent of eventually distributing them to the person for whom the account was established when the employee retires, loses his or her employment, or has another substantial change in services to an employer. An RCA is not a registered pension plan; however, contributions to such a plan must comply with generally accepted guidelines. In addition, an RCA Account Number must be obtained from the Canada Revenue Agency before any contributions can be made to the custodian. An employer that sets up an RCA must deduct and remit a 50% refundable tax on any contributions it makes to the custodian. The recipient pays no taxes until benefits are received. See also *specified retirement arrangement*.

Retirement Equity Act of 1984 (REA)—U.S. law that amended ERISA with the purpose of providing greater pension equity for female workers and surviving spouses. Key provisions of REA:
- Liberalized ERISA participation, vesting and break-in-service requirements
- Established qualified domestic relations orders. See also *qualified domestic relations order (QDRO)*.

retirement income—payments from pensions and other sources to which a retired person is entitled. These sources may include both private and public pension payments, income from personal savings and investments, government income supplements, etc.

retirement plan—from an individual's perspective, a strategy to provide for all aspects (e.g., financial, social, emotional, medical) of a person's retirement.

Retirement Plans Associate (RPA)—designation granted jointly by the International Foundation of Employee Benefit Plans and the Wharton School of the University of Pennsylvania to individuals who complete three college-level courses and examinations focused on all aspects of retirement plans. In Canada, the program is presented jointly by the International Foundation of Employee Benefit Plans and Dalhousie University. See also *Certified Employee Benefit Specialist (CEBS), Compensation Management Specialist (CMA)* and *Group Benefits Associate (GBA)*.

Retirement Protection Act of 1994 (RPA)—federal legislation amending ERISA and the IRC that:
- Strengthens pension funding for underfunded plans
- Increases the termination insurance premiums that underfunded plans pay to the *Pension Benefit Guaranty Corporation (PBGC)*
- Requires additional reporting by companies with large underfunded plans
- Gives PBGC concurrent authority to go to court to enforce certain missed funding contributions in PBGC-covered plans
- Keeps workers and retirees better informed about their pensions
- Establishes a missing participant program.

Specific elements of the RPA raised the minimum funding and liquidity of retirement plans, modified interest assumption limitations for lump-sum calculations, and rounded down cost-of-living adjustments. RPA was passed and signed as part of the 1994 General Agreement on Tariffs and Trade.

retiring allowance—also referred to as severance pay, money paid by a Canadian employer to an employee who is losing his or her employment due to termination or retirement. A retiring allowance includes payments for unused sick leave and other dollar amounts that individuals receive when terminated. A retiring allowance does not include payments for accumulated vacation leave. Subject to certain restrictions, a retiring allowance may be paid directly into an employee's *Registered Retirement Savings Plan (RRSP)* without being taxed.

retroactive—effective on a date earlier than the date enacted. For example, when an employer applies a percentage increase in compensation to pay periods prior to the date when the increase was announced, the pay raise is said to be retroactive to an earlier date.

retrocession—practice of one reinsurance company insuring another reinsurance company by accepting business that the other company had agreed to underwrite.

retrospective experience rating—insurance arrangement that adjusts the premium for an insured group at the end of the coverage period based on the group's actual claims (experience) for the period. The amount ultimately charged is subject to a minimum and maximum and also must be sufficient to cover the insurer's administrative and other expenses. With this arrangement, a surplus is created if the group's claims experience during the insured period is lower than what was predicted and paid by the group at the start of the period. Of course, there could also be a deficit that requires an additional payment to the insurer if claims are more than what was paid. How surpluses and deficits are calculated and handled is determined by the insurance contract. Surpluses may be returned to the purchaser of the contract or be placed in a "stabilization reserve" fund to cover future deficits. See also *class rating, community rating, experience rating, prospective experience rating* and *retrospective premium*.

retrospective payment—most common method of payment to health facilities. Payment is made after the services are rendered on the basis of costs incurred by the facility; also known as retrospective reimbursement. See also *prospective pricing*.

retrospective premium—additional payment that must be made by an insured benefit plan at the end of the contract year if the claims submitted to and expenses incurred by the insurer exceed the amount initially paid for protection at the beginning of the coverage period. See also *retrospective experience rating*.

retrospective rating—see *retrospective experience rating*.

retrospective reimbursement—see *retrospective payment*.

retrospective review—determining an individual's benefit plan coverage after treatment by confirming member eligibility and the availability of benefits. Patient care data is also analyzed to support the coverage determination process. See also *concurrent review, prospective review* and *utilization review*.
—alternatively, a process similar to an audit looking for errors and inappropriate services that require correction and/or a bill adjustment. The review may also involve the monitoring of physician practice patterns and hospital length-of-stay averages to identify providers that are outside the norm.

return—money gained or lost (both realized and unrealized) on an investment. The return may be interest, dividends, rent, an increase in the value of the investment or a decrease in the investment's value. Also referred to as total return, it is typically calculated for a year. See also *rate of return (ROR)* and *yield*.

return-of-premium life insurance—policy that returns the premiums paid for coverage if the insured party outlives the policy's term.

return on equity (ROE)—also known as return on net worth, an indicator of a company's profitability relative to shareholder investment, expressed as a percentage. To calculate ROE, the expenses of the company and dividends paid to preferred stock shareholders (but not the dividends of common stock shareholders) for the year are subtracted from the corporation's annual income, then divided by shareholder equity. ROE is useful for comparing the profitability of a company with that of other firms in the same industry. Several variations of this formula exist depending on the purpose for which its use is intended.

return on investment (ROI)—money gained or lost as the result of resources invested. For example, the ROI on an employee wellness program may be the dollars that result from reduced absenteeism, increased productivity and the reduction in total health claims. See also *rate of return (ROR)* and *return*.

return on net worth (RONW)—see *return on equity (ROE)*.

return-to-work program—employer-sponsored program of rehabilitation, job modification and monitoring to get disabled employees back to work as soon as possible.

revenue—income, usually from the sales of a company's products and services, before any costs or expenses are subtracted.

revenue anticipation note (RAN)—short-term debt obligation sold by a public entity that will be repaid using future nontaxable income. See also *general obligation (GO) bond, municipal bond, revenue bond* and *special assessment bond*.

revenue bond—debt obligation typically sold by a public entity with a promise that the principal and interest will be paid back using earnings from the project it is being used to fund. For example, tolls might be used to repay a bond that funded a bridge or highway. See also *general obligation (GO) bond, municipal bond, revenue anticipation note (RAN)* and *special assessment bond*.

revenue procedure—process to be followed when dealing with the IRS. Revenue procedures may also set forth guidelines for the IRS to follow when handling certain tax matters.

revenue ruling—statement issued by the IRS expressing its view with respect to a specific tax issue.

reverse copay—see *reverse copayment*.

reverse copayment—method used by some health plans for sharing the cost of prescription drugs with plan participants. The plan pays a fixed amount of a medication's cost and the participant pays the remainder. Reverse copays protect insurers and sponsors from price inflation and increase participant awareness of drug prices. The participant is given the responsibility to work with the physician and pharmacist to find drugs that are the best value. See also *copayment* and *cost sharing*.

reverse mortgage—special type of loan that enables older homeowners to convert the equity they have in their homes into cash. The lender disburses money to the homeowner (borrower) in monthly checks or lump sums, and the borrower keeps the home. When the borrower dies or vacates the home, he or she, or the heirs, pay off the debt by selling the property. Also known as a home equity conversion mortgage.

reverse stock split—reduction in the number of outstanding equity shares of a corporation by exchanging one new share of stock for two or more old shares. Shareholders maintain the same percentage of equity as before the split. Reverse stock splits usually occur when a corporation's stock is trading at a very low price and it wants to increase the market value per share.

reversionary annuity—guaranteed lifetime income to a beneficiary only if the beneficiary survives the annuitant. The beneficiary, not the annuitant, is the recipient of the payments. A reversionary annuity blends some of the features of an annuity and a life insurance plan. See also *annuity* and *lifetime annuity*.

reversion of employer contributions—in the U.S., qualified benefit plans are prohibited from diverting assets or income for purposes other than the exclusive benefit of employees. However, this prohibition does not preclude the return of a contribution made by an employer if the contribution was made, for example, by reason of a mistake of fact or conditioned on the qualification of the plan or the deductibility of the contribution.

review of systems (ROS)—series of questions used by a health care provider to identify clinical symptoms a patient may have overlooked or forgotten with respect to his or her health status.

revocable trust—trust that can be changed or terminated during the grantor's lifetime, which permits the grantor to recover the property. See also *irrevocable trust* and *trust fund*.

reward system—formal or informal program using cash or something else of value to recognize employee achievement (e.g., meeting goals or completing a project). See also *recognition program*.

reward-to-variability ratio—see *Sharpe ratio*.

reward-to-volatility ratio—see *Treynor ratio*.

rider—see *endorsement*.

right of conscience—from a health benefits perspective, a law that prohibits discrimination against health care professionals, health insurers and other entities that refuse to furnish or cover certain types of treatment because of religious or personal beliefs.

right of recourse—being entitled to collect on a debt or seek help from the courts. In fiduciary liability policies, a right-of-recourse provision gives an insurer the right to collect against an insured. As an example, assume a fiduciary's negligence in administering a benefit plan caused a loss covered by a fiduciary liability policy. After paying the loss, the insurer has the right to seek reimbursement from the fiduciary whose negligence caused that loss. See also *waiver of recourse*.

right-to-work law—legislation that prohibits agreements between unions and employers that make union membership or payment of union dues a condition of employment.

risk—hazard or chance of loss. Insurance companies are a means by which individuals, businesses and others reduce the financial loss associated with various risks. When investing, there are many risk factors that may result in an investment not achieving a desired return. See also *currency risk, default risk, health risk assessment (HRA), insurance, interest rate risk, liquidity risk, management risk, market risk, nonmarket risk, operational risk, prepayment risk, purchasing power risk, reinvestment risk, risk manager* and *volatility*.

risk-adjusted return measure—way to gauge how much return an investor is getting per unit of risk. Four popular measures include the Sharpe ratio, Treynor ratio, information ratio and Jensen's alpha.

risk adjustment—statistical process used to identify and make changes when differences exist in the likelihood an event will occur. To increase fairness when comparing patient outcomes among health care providers, risk adjustments are made for differences in patient age, gender and preexisting conditions. Insurance companies adjust health insurance premiums to reflect the variance in risk (potential dollar losses) created by the same factors. For example, persons who are older with preexisting conditions are likely to have more claims; hence, the insurer makes a risk adjustment that yields a higher premium for these individuals. See also *risk classification*.

risk administration—implementing a risk management plan and monitoring the results. See also *risk management*.

risk analysis—examining the chance a risk will occur and the potential impact on the organization. Risk exposures and their potential impacts are weighted or ranked to determine where risk control or risk reduction is needed.

risk and expense charge—see *risk charge*.

risk and profit charge—see *risk charge*.

risk assessment—determination of the likelihood that something will happen and the extent to which it will happen. A health care provider may assess the chance that a particular medication will yield a dangerous side effect when making a treatment decision. A health insurer must estimate risk in terms of the anticipated number of claims it will receive and the dollar amount of these claims when setting a policy premium.

risk averse—description of an investor who dislikes securities with a relatively high chance of loss. Risk-averse investors generally stick to securities such as index funds and government bonds, which have lower returns. See also *risk tolerance*.

risk avoidance—choosing not to become involved in a hazardous situation such as mountain climbing, driving at a high rate of speed or smoking cigarettes. See also *risk management*.

risk budgeting—process focused on how risk is distributed throughout an investment portfolio. The goal is to identify, quantify and spend investment risk in the most efficient manner possible. The investor calculates how much different assets in a portfolio contribute to the total risk of a portfolio. If the investor is uncomfortable with the amount of risk an asset in the portfolio represents, some of the money invested in the asset is moved to another investment option. The risk exposure of a portfolio can come from various factors including inflation, economic growth, steepness of the yield curve and changes in short-term interest rates.

risk charge—payment to an insurer as compensation for the potential loss assumed. Also referred to as profit and expense charge, risk and profit charge, or risk and expense charge. See also *experience refund* and *profit commission*.

risk classification—process by which a company decides how its premium rates for insurance should differ according to the risk characteristics of individuals (e.g., age, occupation, sex, state of health), and then applies the resulting rules to individual applications. See also *underwriting*.

risk control—stage in risk management where options for minimizing the probability, severity, frequency and/or unpredictability of a loss are examined. A balance is chosen between affordability and effectiveness to support management objectives. It is in this step that a risk management plan is developed.

risk factor—characteristic that is capable of provoking ill health, injury or loss. For example, smoking is considered a risk factor for poor health.

risk financing—acquisition of funds to pay for retained losses and risk. An organization might use internal funds, loans from external sources or secure letters of credit for this purpose. See also *risk retention*.

risk-free asset—security with a certain rate of return and no chance of failure. U.S. Treasury securities (especially T-bills) are considered risk-free because they are backed by the federal government.

risk-free rate of return—theoretical guaranteed return on an investment. The three-month interest rate of a U.S. Treasury bill is often used to approximate risk-free return.

risk identification—finding and examining an organization's exposures (e.g., geographic, natural, operational and industry). Numerous techniques are used to identify risk. One of the most common is a checklist or survey.

risk management—process seeking cost-effective ways to prevent or reduce uncertainty and loss and other techniques for minimizing exposure to loss or injury. See also *risk administration, risk analysis, risk avoidance, risk control, risk financing, risk identification* and *risk reduction*.

risk manager—professional who analyzes investment portfolio decisions and determines how to maximize profits through diversification and hedging. See also *financial analyst*.

risk mitigation—see *risk reduction*.

risk pool—population of insured persons or entities across which claims, administrative expenses and other costs are spread via a premium or other mechanism.

risk prevention—implementation of initiative(s) to reduce the frequency of losses from activities that cannot be avoided. For example, a benefit plan sponsor might introduce education programs and promote practices to improve participant health and reduce the chance participants will have to file a claim for care.

risk reduction—adoption of practices that reduce the possible occurrence of a harmful event or the extent of a loss resulting from an event. Installing smoke detectors throughout a building and using a seat belt while driving are both practices that reduce risk. See also *risk management*.

risk retention—risk management option where an individual or organization decides to accept the consequences of a particular risk. A reserve fund may be established to cover losses associated with the risk; for example, a household may have an emergency fund to cover health insurance deductibles and coinsurance. Self-funding of health benefits by an employer or benefit plan is also risk retention.

risk retention group (RRG)—insurance company under the auspices of the Risk Retention Act (RRA) of 1981 and 1986 amendments to the Act that permit the underwriting of all types of liability risks (except workers' compensation) to avoid multistate licensing laws. An RRG must be owned by its insureds and be domiciled in the U.S., except for those grandfathered under the 1981 Act. Most RRGs are captives subject to the laws of the state where they were chartered or domiciled. See also *captive insurance company*.

risk-return tradeoff—when investing, the higher chance of a loss associated with a greater chance of money gained. See also *risk* and *return.*

risk-reward spectrum—construct used to illustrate that (in a rational marketplace) higher and higher anticipated rewards are always accompanied by incremental increases in risk (measured as the deviations between expected and actual results). The left end of the spectrum represents the lowest risk investment, typically short-term government obligations. Moving to the right on the spectrum, through a continuum of common stock investments, each incremental increase in expected return is accompanied by an incremental increase in risk.

risk sharing
—distributing the financial responsibility for losses. Deductibles, copayments and coinsurance are techniques used by benefit plans to share risk with plan participants. Risk sharing also occurs when a health care provider agrees to adhere to fixed fee schedules in exchange for services. Common risk-sharing methods are *prospective payment schedules (PPS), capitation,* a fee based on a *diagnosis-related group (DRG)* and prenegotiated fees.
—more generally, spreading risk over a group of insureds. In these situations, risk sharing may also be referred to as risk pooling.

risk transfer—shifting the responsibility for a potential loss to another party. Purchasing insurance is a very common means to transfer a risk.

risk tolerance—extent to which an investor is willing to accept uncertain returns. Comfort with risk reflects emotional as well as rational factors. See also *risk averse.*

rollover—reinvestment of funds from one vehicle to a similar vehicle. Retirement funds are sometimes moved from one plan to another to avoid taxation or to achieve a higher return on investment. See also *Unemployment Compensation Amendments of 1992.*

rollover IRA—individual retirement account (IRA) that holds assets distributed (rolled over) from a qualified retirement plan. Assets in a rollover IRA continue to be tax-deferred until they are withdrawn. If the assets are mixed with other assets, they lose the favorable tax treatment. A rollover IRA can be used to store assets until they can be rolled into the qualified plan of a new employer. Hence, a rollover IRA is sometimes called a conduit IRA.

rollover mortgage—see *renegotiable rate mortgage (RRM)*

Rollovers for Business Start-Ups (ROBS)—U.S. government program that permits the use of funds from an eligible retirement account (e.g., a 401(k) plan, IRA) to purchase a new business or refinance an existing business without taking a taxable distribution or loan.

Roth 401(k) plan—type of retirement savings plan authorized by IRC Section 402A that combines features of a Roth IRA and a traditional 401(k) plan. Employers may amend their 401(k) plan document to allow employees to elect Roth IRA-type tax treatment for a portion or all of their retirement plan contributions. The same option is also allowed for 403(b) and 457 retirement plans. See also *Roth IRA.*

Roth IRA—created by the Taxpayer Relief Act of 1997, an individual retirement account (IRA) or annuity set up by an individual. Contributions can be made to a Roth IRA by an account holder at any age and can be left there (along with any earnings) as long as the account holder lives. Annual contribution limits are set by the IRS and depend on the holder's income, filing status and other IRAs. Many of the rules that apply to traditional IRAs apply to Roth IRAs. However, a Roth IRA is funded by after-tax versus pretax contributions. If the IRS requirements for qualified distributions are met, Roth IRA earnings and withdrawals are tax-free. While a deemed IRA can be a Roth IRA, neither a simplified employee pension nor a SIMPLE IRA can be designated as such. See also *deemed IRA, designated Roth account, individual retirement account (IRA), qualified distribution* and *traditional IRA.*

round lot—usual quantity of securities that is traded. A round lot of stocks is generally 100 shares; anything less is considered an *odd lot.*

R-squared—statistical measure that represents the percentage of a fund or security's movements that can be explained by movements in a benchmark index. For fixed income securities, the benchmark is the T-bill.

rule of 69, 70 or 72—convenient technique for estimating approximately how long it will take an investment to double in value given a specific compound interest rate. Either 69, 70 or 72 is divided by the interest percentage per period (usually a year). Which number to use is a matter of personal preference; 69 is more accurate for continuous compounding, while 70 and 72 work well in common interest situations and are more easily divisible. Assuming the growth rate to be positive, the rule of 70 is more accurate up to 4%, while the rule of 72 is more accurate for 5% to 10%. For an example that uses the number 70, assume there is $1,000 in a savings account drawing 4% interest compounded annually; the account will double to $2,000 in 17.5 years (70 divided by 4). Note that none of these rules work if the investor continues to deposit money into the account beyond the initial investment.

rule of parity—ERISA rule that states for eligibility and vesting purposes, a qualified pension plan may ignore a participant service credit prior to a break in service if the nonvested employee has at least five consecutive one-year breaks in service and the consecutive breaks in service exceed his or her prebreak service. See also *break in service (BIS)*.

Russell 1000 Index—market-weighted index measuring the performance of the largest 1,000 stocks in the Russell 3000 Index. The Russell 1000 serves as a benchmark for large cap stocks in the United States. See also *large cap* and *Russell 3000 Index*.

Russell 2000 Index—market-weighted index measuring the performance of about 2,000 small cap companies in the Russell 3000 Index. The Russell 2000 serves as a benchmark for small cap stocks in the United States. Unlike the S&P 500, the components of the Russell 2000 Index are selected by a formula—the bottom 2000 of the Russell 3000—and not by a committee. See also *Russell 3000 Index* and *small cap*.

Russell 2500 Index—market-weighted index measuring the performance of about 2,500 mid cap and small cap companies in the Russell 3000 Index. See also *mid cap, Russell 3000 Index* and *small cap*.

Russell 3000 Index—market-weighted index that measures the performance of the largest 3,000 U.S. companies representing approximately 98% of the investable U.S. equity market. Companies excluded from the Russell 3000 and other Russell indexes include OTC stocks, stocks priced less than $1 and all companies not incorporated in the United States. The Russell 1000 Index, Russell 2000 Index and Russell 2500 Index are three of the indexes derived from the Russell 3000 Index. See also *large cap*.

S

sabbatical—leave of absence of six months or longer. Most commonly, sabbaticals have been offered to university faculty for professional development activities such as professional certification, curriculum development or research every seven years. Sabbaticals are increasingly a means for private sector employees to pursue personal endeavors or just rejuvenate. A sabbatical usually provides the recipient with benefits and some or all of his or her pay during the period of leave.

safe harbor plan—401(k) or 403(b) plan exempt from nondiscrimination testing of elective and/or matching contributions in exchange for providing certain minimum levels of matching or nonelective contributions.

safe harbor rule—legal or regulatory provision that reduces or eliminates a party's liability on the condition the party complies with specific guidelines or acts in good faith.

salaried administrator—person employed full-time to manage a business, trust fund or other entity.

salary—compensation given to an employee and paid weekly, monthly or yearly as opposed to hourly. Salaried positions are usually exempt from Fair Labor Standards Act provisions and do not receive overtime pay.

salary continuation plan
—benefit option designed to provide some form of protection during a disability. See also *sick leave* and *workers' compensation*.
—also, a retirement plan for key employees when there is no qualified plan. See also *key employee* and *supplemental executive retirement plan (SERP)*.

salary deferral plan—see *salary reduction plan*.

salary reduction plan—retirement benefit program that lets participants have a portion of their compensation (otherwise payable in cash) contributed to a retirement account on their behalf. An employer may contribute to the plan as well. Some plans allow contributions to be made on a pretax versus after-tax basis. The best-known salary deferral plans are 401(k) plans. Until the Tax Reform Act of 1986, salary reduction plan was synonymous with 401(k) plan, but the act prohibited employees of state and local governments and tax-exempt organizations from establishing new 401(k) plans and added restrictions to existing arrangements that have created, in effect, a broadened definition of salary reduction plan. See also *401(k) plan, 403(b) plan, 457 plan, cafeteria plan, cash or deferred arrangement (CODA), flexible benefit plan* and *premium payment plan*.

Salary Reduction Simplified Employee Pension Plan (SARSEP)—retirement savings program available to companies with 25 or fewer employees. The Small Business Protection Act of 1996 eliminated this retirement savings option, though existing SARSEPs may be continued. See also *simplified employee pension (SEP) plan*.

salary structure—hierarchy of job grades and pay ranges established within a company. Salary structure may be expressed as job grades, job evaluation points or policy lines.

sale and leaseback—see *leaseback*.

sale-leaseback—see *leaseback*.

sales commission—see *commission*.

sales load—fee or commission charged on an investment product at the time a share is bought or sold. The two general types of sales loads are front-end loads and back-end loads. Also referred to simply as a load. See also *back-end load, front-end load, load fund* and *no-load fund*.

same-day surgery—see *outpatient surgery*.

sandwich generation—persons, typically middle-aged, who must simultaneously provide care for their children and their elderly parents.

Sarbanes-Oxley Act of 2002 (SOX)—also known as the Public Company Accounting Reform and Investor Protection Act of 2002, this U.S. law was enacted in response to a number of major corporate and accounting scandals, including those affecting Enron, Tyco International and WorldCom, which cost investors billions of dollars when the share prices of the affected companies collapsed and shook public confidence in the nation's securities markets. The Act contains 11 sections that mandate reforms in corporate governance, internal financial controls and record-management rules for publicly traded companies. Reforms included increasing ERISA criminal penalties, prohibiting public companies from providing loans to company executives, requiring executives to forfeit compensation in cases of certain misconduct, and prohibiting registered public accounting firms from performing certain nonaudit services. The act also created the Public Company Accounting Oversight Board to oversee the activities of accounting firms in their roles as auditors of public companies. See also *blackout period*.

saver's tax credit—U.S. income tax credit available to low- and middle-income taxpayers over the age of 18 who are not full-time students and cannot be claimed as a dependent on another person's tax return. Taxpayers are allowed to take a credit of up to $1,000 ($2,000 if filing jointly) if they make a voluntary contribution to an employer-sponsored retirement plan or an individual retirement account. The credit is a percentage of the qualifying contribution amount, with the highest rate for those with the least income.

Savings Are Vital to Everyone's Retirement Act of 1997 (SAVER Act)—legislation that required the U.S. Department of Labor to (1) conduct bipartisan national summits on retirement and (2) establish an ongoing public outreach program to promote retirement savings. The first summit took place in 1998; additional summits were held in 2001 and 2005.

savings bond
—nontransferable, registered security issued by the U.S. government that offers a fixed income return with minimal risk. Savings bonds are sold at a discount in denominations of $50 to $10,000. The interest earned on a savings bond is exempt from state and local taxation; it is also exempt from federal taxation until it is redeemed or reaches maturity. Savings bonds must be held at least one year before they can be redeemed. A penalty of three months' interest is assessed if a bond is held for less than five years. See also *Series E/EE savings bond, Series H/HH savings bond* and *Series I savings bond*.
—for Canada, see *Canada Premium Bond (CPB)* and *Canada Savings Bond (CSB)*.

Savings Incentive Match Plan for Employees (SIMPLE)—tax-favored retirement account that small employers (including self-employed individuals) can establish for the benefit of the employer and employees. The plan may be set up in the form of a 401(k) plan or a SIMPLE IRA. Employers match salary reduction contributions that employees choose to make. Instead of making matching contributions, an employer may also be able to make nonelective contributions on behalf of each eligible employee, whether or not the employee chooses salary reductions. Contributions to these plans must be within IRS guidelines. The employer can deduct contributions made for employees. Earnings on contributions are generally tax-free until distributions are received. In most situations, these plans cannot be set up for employees who have another active retirement plan. See also *401(k) plan* and *SIMPLE IRA*.

say on pay—shareholders' right to vote on a corporation's executive compensation. The Dodd-Frank Wall Street Reform and Consumer Protection Act of 2010 requires companies have a say-on-pay vote at least once every three years beginning with the first annual shareholders' meeting taking place on or after Jan. 21, 2011. Companies also are required to hold a "frequency" vote at least once every six years that allows shareholders to decide how often they would like to be presented with a say-on-pay vote.

schedule of allowances—see *table of allowances*.

schedule of benefits—list of amounts that an insurance company will pay for specific goods and services claimed under an insurance policy.

Schedule SSA—IRS form that must be filed by all benefit plans subject to ERISA Section 203 minimum vesting requirements. The schedule, attached to Form 5500, provides data on participants who separated from service with a vested benefit but were not paid benefits.

S corporation—corporation in which shareholders elect tax status under Subchapter S of the IRC. Also referred to as an S corp., an S corporation is taxed like a partnership with profits and losses passing directly through to the shareholders. Income is not taxed at the corporate level. The maximum number of shareholders in an S corp. is 75. S corporations have a similar legal status to C corporations with respect to liability and the continuity of business in succession transfers. See also *C corporation* and *corporation*.

screening—diagnostic testing of a large number of people to detect a disease or other health concern in persons who do not necessarily have symptoms. Screening may be examinations of blood and urine, height and weight, vision and hearing, blood pressure; x-rays and/or questionnaires.

secondary beneficiary—next person or entity in line to receive benefits from a will, trust or insurance policy if the first person named to receive benefits (the primary beneficiary) is deceased. The secondary beneficiary may also be referred to as a contingent beneficiary.

secondary care—services provided by a medical specialist to whom a patient has been referred, usually by a primary care provider. Cardiologists, dermatologists and urologists are examples of secondary care providers that typically do not have first contact with a patient.

secondary market—exchange where investors buy and sell stocks, bonds, etc., among themselves. The initial issuance of these securities is through a primary market.

secondary offering—issuance of additional stock shares by a company to raise more capital. A secondary offering follows an initial public offering. Corporations are often wary of issuing more shares as the larger supply dilutes the value of the shares previously issued.

secondary payer—benefit plan or insurance company that has a responsibility for paying a claim after another entity (the primary payer) when duplicate coverage exists. Medicare is a secondary payer to certain primary plans. See also *coordination-of-benefits (COB) provision, duplication of benefits* and *primary payer*.

second injury fund—insurance pool set up by most states to reimburse an employer or its insurance carrier for the part of an employee's workers' compensation that resulted from a previous work-related injury with another employer. The second employer is responsible only for the portion of the workers' compensation benefit that resulted from a second injury or disease. The fund makes up the difference. Second injury funds are financed through general state revenues or assessments on workers' compensation insurers.

second opinion—review of a recommended surgical procedure or other medical treatment by another health care professional prior to the performance of the procedure.

second surgical opinion program (SSOP)—cost-management strategy that encourages or requires participants to obtain the opinion of another doctor when nonemergency or elective surgery has been recommended. Some health benefit plans reduce or deny reimbursement if the participant does not obtain the second opinion in certain situations.

Section 79—IRC section governing the income tax treatment of employer-sponsored group life insurance. Section 79 also prohibits group life insurance plans from favoring key employees by establishing nondiscrimination rules. If an employer-sponsored group plan meets the requirements of Section 79, all employees may be provided life insurance coverage of up to $50,000 without tax consequences. Amounts in excess of $50,000 generate taxable income to the insured employee. If a plan favors key employees, the cost of the entire amount of the insurance to the key employees is taxable. See also *group insurance, key employee, life insurance* and *Section 79 plan*.

Section 79 plan—group whole life insurance policy designed to reduce an employee's exposure to income tax on the value of life insurance provided by the employer. The policy separates the term life insurance element from the cash value element and apportions part of the premium to each. The plan takes advantage of the tax-exemption to employees on $50,000 of coverage. The imputed cost of coverage in excess of $50,000 must be included in income, using the IRS Premium Table, and is subject to Social Security and Medicare taxes. See also *group insurance, life insurance, term life insurance* and *whole life insurance*.

Section 104 and Section 105—provisions in the IRC that specify tax treatment of health insurance, disability insurance and workers' compensation benefits paid to an employee due to sickness and injury.

Section 106—IRC detailing tax treatment of employer contributions to accident and health plans.

Section 117—one of the most common IRC provisions used by employers to provide educational assistance programs. Employers are also allowed to offer education benefits to employees under IRC Sections 127 and 132(d).

Section 120—IRC concerning the tax treatment of qualified group legal services plans.

Section 125—IRC allowing an employer to offer employees the choice between a taxable benefit (such as cash) and one or more nontaxable benefits. See also *cafeteria plan, constructive receipt, dependent care reimbursement account (DCRA), flexible benefit plan* and *premium-only plan (POP)*.

Section 127—guidelines from the IRS concerning the tax treatment of educational assistance programs.

Section 129—IRC concerning the treatment of employer-provided dependent care assistance.

Section 132—identification of nontaxable fringe benefits not mentioned in other sections of the IRC, including employee discounts, transportation benefits and moving expense reimbursements.

Section 162—IRC imposing a reasonableness requirement for the deductibility of business expenses. See also *reasonable compensation*.

Section 204—ERISA requirement that plan administrators provide participants with written notification of any plan amendment that will result in a significant reduction in the rate of future benefit accrual, including any elimination or significant reduction of an early retirement benefit or retirement-type subsidy. The notice must be given in a manner calculated to be understood by the average plan participant and must contain sufficient information to allow participants to understand the effect of the amendment.

Section 213—IRC listing the expenses that are considered tax-qualified for the purposes of health savings accounts, health reimbursement arrangements and flexible spending arrangements. This same section grants taxpayers the opportunity to deduct uncompensated household expenses for medical care and health insurance during a taxable year that exceeds 7.5% or 10% of adjusted gross income depending on the age of the taxpayer and the taxpayer's spouse (if any).

Section 218 agreement—voluntary agreement between a state and the Social Security Administration (SSA) to provide Social Security and Medicare hospital insurance or only Medicare hospital insurance coverage for state and local government employees. These agreements are called Section 218 agreements because they are authorized by Section 218 of the Social Security Act. All 50 states and some interstate agencies have such an agreement with the SSA.

Section 219—IRC concerning the extent to which retirement savings are tax-deductible and provisions for catch-up contributions.

Section 401—IRC requirements for qualified retirement, profit-sharing and stock bonus plans. See also *401(k) plan, profit-sharing plan, qualified retirement plan* and *stock bonus plan*.

Section 401(k)—IRC rule that makes it possible for employees to avoid immediate taxation on a portion of income they elect to receive as deferred compensation. As a result, many employers replaced older, after-tax thrift plans with 401(k) plans and added 401(k) options to profit-sharing and stock bonus plans. IRC Section 401(k) was originally the Revenue Act of 1978. See also *401(k) plan*.

Section 403(b)—portion of the IRC established in 1958 that makes it possible for certain tax-exempt organizations such as schools, hospitals, charities and churches to establish tax-deferred retirement savings programs for employees. Initially, the only permissible investment was an annuity; investments such as mutual funds are now allowed. See also *403(b) plan*.

Section 404(c)—provided an employer offering a participant-directed defined contribution plan meets certain requirements, this section of ERISA protects an employer from liability for losses incurred by employees who make bad investment choices. To be protected, employers must offer at least three investment options with different levels of risk and return, allow transfers among investments at least quarterly, provide basic investment information to help participants make investment decisions, and provide additional specific information on the various investment options. See also *404(c) plan*.

Section 409—IRC minimum participation standards for qualified retirement plans. See also *qualified retirement plan*.

Section 409A—see *American Jobs Creation Act of 2004 (AJCA)*.

Section 411—IRC establishing the minimum vesting standards for qualified retirement plans. See also *qualified retirement plan*.

Section 412—minimum funding standards for qualified plans under IRC Section 401(a) and those plans satisfying the requirements of IRC Section 403(a). See also *qualified retirement plan*.

Section 415—IRC limiting the contribution and/or benefit amount that a retirement plan may provide to individual participants on a tax-deductible basis.

Section 416—vesting requirements and minimum benefit requirements for top-heavy benefit plans.

Section 417—IRC definitions and minimum survivor requirements for qualified retirement plans. See also *qualified joint and survivor annuity (QJSA)*, *qualified preretirement survivor annuity (QPSA)* and *qualified retirement plan*.

Section 419—IRC detailing the requirements for qualifying as a welfare benefit trust. See also *qualified cost*.

Section 423—IRC regulating employee stock purchase plans. See also *employee stock purchase plan (ESPP)*.

Section 457—IRC allowing employees of state and local governments, as well as those employed by 501(c)(3) organizations, to establish tax-deferred retirement accounts. See also *457 plan*.

Section 501—circumstances under which the income of 501(c) nonprofit organizations and trusts, including 501(c)(9) voluntary employees' beneficiary associations, are exempt from federal taxation. See also *nonprofit organization (NPO)* and *voluntary employees' beneficiary association (VEBA)*.

Section 503 through Section 505—additional requirements for 501(c) organizations. See also *501(c) organization* and *Section 501*.

Section 529 plan—see *529 plan*.

sector fund—mutual or exchange-traded fund that confines investments to one economic or industrial sector (e.g., utilities, technology). Because the holdings of this type of fund are in the same industry, there is less diversification. See also *exchange-traded fund (ETF)* and *mutual fund*.

secular trust—irrevocable trust, usually established by an employer, for the exclusive purpose of paying nonqualified benefits to select high-level employees. A secular trust has a design similar to that of a rabbi trust, but the assets contained within the trust are not subject to claims of the company's general creditors if a bankruptcy occurs. Typically, the after-tax value of a benefit is funded within a secular trust and the participating employee is provided additional bonus money to satisfy the income tax consequences of the security.

Securities Act of 1933—first major federal legislation to regulate the offer and sale of securities. This law, also known as the Truth in Securities Act, required that investors be provided financial and other significant information concerning securities offered for public sale. Prior to this act, securities regulation was chiefly governed by state laws (commonly referred to as blue-sky laws). See also *prospectus* and *Securities and Exchange Commission (SEC)*.

securities analyst—see *financial analyst*.

Securities and Exchange Commission (SEC)—independent, quasi-judicial government agency that oversees the securities industry in the United States. The purpose of the commission is to protect investors and create a fair playing field for sellers. The SEC requires the registration of new securities and the disclosure of important financial information that may influence the value of the security. There are some securities given an exemption to the registration requirement: private offerings to a limited number of persons or institutions, offerings of limited size, intrastate offerings, and securities of municipal, state and federal governments. See also *Investment Advisers Act of 1940*, *Investment Company Act of 1940*, *prospectus*, *Securities Act of 1933*, *Securities Exchange Act of 1934* and *Trust Indenture Act of 1939*.

securities broker—agent who handles orders to buy and sell stocks, commodities and other assets. Securities brokers recommend securities to clients and earn a commission on all trades as compensation. Brokers must be affiliated with a stock exchange member broker/dealer firm and register as a representative of the firm with the Financial Industry Regulatory Authority (FINRA). To register, brokers must pass a FINRA licensing exam (Series 6 or Series 7), which covers federal securities law. The Series 6 license limits a broker to the sales of mutual funds, variable annuities and variable life insurance products. The Series 7 license is broader and allows a broker to sell all types of securities. Generally, brokers must also pass the Series 63 exam, covering state-specific securities regulations, and be registered in the state in which they operate. Brokers with a Series 65 license are allowed to serve in the capacity of an investment advisor. Those with a Series 66 license have passed a combined state law exam.

Securities Exchange Act of 1934—U.S. legislation governing the secondary trading of stocks, bonds and other investments. Commonly referred to as the Exchange Act or Act of '34, this sweeping legislation provided the foundation for regulation of the nation's financial markets and their participants. The Act:
- Created the Securities and Exchange Commission (SEC) to register, regulate and oversee market participants, including brokers, dealers, transfer agents, clearing agencies, self-regulatory organizations and the various stock exchanges. See also *Securities and Exchange Commission (SEC)*.
- Empowers the SEC to require periodic reporting of information by companies with publicly traded securities
- Requires disclosure of important information by anyone seeking to acquire more than 5% of a company's securities by direct purchase or tender offer
- Governs information disclosure in materials used to solicit shareholders' votes in annual or special meetings held for the election of directors and the approval of other corporate action. See also *proxy* and *proxy statement*.
- Identifies and prohibits certain types of conduct in the markets and provides the SEC with disciplinary powers over regulated entities and persons associated with this conduct
- Broadly prohibits fraudulent activities of any kind in connection with the offer, purchase or sale of securities. See also *fraud*.

securities lending—when one broker borrows a security (e.g., stock) from another. Eventually the same security must be returned. The broker lending the security earns an increased return through finance charges. The borrower hopes to gain additional revenue through short selling. See also *going long* and *short selling*.

security—in finance, a negotiable instrument representing financial value. Securities are broadly categorized into debt securities (e.g., bank notes, bonds) and equity securities (e.g., stocks). The company, government or other entity issuing the security is called the issuer. Securities may be represented by a certificate or, more typically, by an electronic book entry.

security incident—for the purposes of HIPAA privacy rules, the attempted or successful unauthorized access, use, disclosure, modification or destruction of health information or interference with operations in an information system.

security measure—administrative, physical or technical safeguard required by HIPAA to ensure the confidentiality, integrity and availability of protected health information. See also *protected health information (PHI)*.

security valuation—use of analytical methods to estimate the intrinsic value (as opposed to the market price) of a security. The intrinsic value is then compared with the market price to determine whether the security appears to be attractively priced.

segregated fund—assets of a Canadian pension plan held by an insurance company for investment management only. Assets in a segregated fund are kept separate from assets of the insurance company. Principal and interest are not guaranteed.

self-administered plan—benefit plan administered by an employer or fund trustee(s) rather than through an insurance carrier or third-party administrator.

self-care—personal efforts to improve, maintain or restore health. Elements of self-care include exercise, eating properly, good hygiene, self-medicating and avoiding health hazards such as smoking. Self-care is also taking care of minor ailments, long-term conditions or one's own health after discharge from secondary and tertiary health care. See also *demand management*.

Self-Correction Program (SCP)—one of three IRS-sponsored programs comprising the Employee Plans Compliance Resolution System that allow sponsors to correct operational and plan document errors affecting their tax-qualified plans. SCP allows a plan sponsor that has established compliance practices and procedures to, at any time without fee or sanction, correct insignificant operational failures, provided the plan is established and maintained by an approved document. In certain cases, the plan sponsor may correct even significant errors without penalty. See also *Audit Closing Agreement Program (Audit CAP)*, *Employee Plans Compliance Resolution System (EPCRS)* and *Voluntary Correction Program (VCP)*.

self-dealing—situation in which a director or trustee derives personal benefit from the organization or trust he or she administers. Under ERISA, self-dealing is prohibited. Such actions include using plan assets for personal profit, taking bribes or kickbacks from someone who deals with the plan, and acting on behalf of a party whose interests are adverse to those of the plan.

self-directed health care—see *consumer-driven health care (CDHC)*.

self-directed investment—option in some employee benefit plans (typically a retirement plan and occasionally a health savings account) that allows plan participants to make investment choices for their individual accounts. See also *self-directed retirement plan*.

self-directed plan—see *consumer-driven health care (CDHC), self-directed investment* and *self-directed retirement plan.*

self-directed retirement plan—retirement plan that allows plan participants to make investment choices for their individual accounts. See also *404(c) plan* and *Section 404(c).*

self-employed retirement plan—see *Keogh plan, Savings Incentive Match Plan for Employees (SIMPLE), Simplified Employee Pension (SEP),* and *solo 401(k) plan.*

self-funding—arrangement in which an individual or organization assumes the responsibility for some or all of the losses caused by a risk. With a self-funded benefit plan, the plan sponsor essentially acts as its own insurer, determining what will be covered by the plan and paying claims directly. The plan may contract with an insurance company or other third party to administer the plan. The sponsor of a fully self-funded plan (also called a fully self-insured or noninsured plan) assumes all the risk and associated losses. An alternative approach used by many sponsors is to purchase an insurance policy to cover catastrophic losses above a specific dollar amount using stop-loss coverage. Such plans are considered partially self-funded. For regulatory purposes, both self-funding and self-insured are used. Plans in the U.S. that meet the ERISA definition of *self-insured* are exempt from state laws and regulations that mandate benefits, control financial management and assess taxes on insured benefits. See also *administrative services only (ASO), disbursed self-funded plan, minimum premium plan (MPP), shared funding, stop-loss insurance* and *voluntary employees' beneficiary association (VEBA).*

self-insurance—see *self-funding.*

self-pay option—under some multiemployer health care plans, an opportunity offered to laid-off workers, or those with insufficient hours worked, to maintain eligibility for health benefits through the individual's payment of a premium, thus avoiding lapses in coverage. The self-pay premium frequently does not cover the costs of carrying such individuals; there is a partial subsidy by the plan.

self-referral
—process whereby a patient seeks care directly from a specialist, without seeking advice or authorization from a primary care physician.
—practice of referring patients to clinics, laboratories or other medical facilities in which the referring physician is an investor. Section 1877 of the Social Security Act prohibits physicians from referring Medicare patients for certain health services to an entity with which the physician or a member of the physician's immediate family has a financial relationship.

self-regulatory organization (SRO)—association in which members of an industry govern themselves. SROs have the power to create and enforce industry regulations and standards. The Financial Industry Regulatory Authority is the largest industry self-regulator in the United States. Other major SROs include markets and exchanges where trading occurs, such as the National Futures Association. See also *Financial Industry Regulatory Authority (FINRA), Investment Industry Regulatory Organization of Canada (IIROC), National Futures Association (NFA)* and *regulation.*

semivariance—measure of downside risk; in other words, the risk of a return below what is anticipated. Semivariance is similar to variance except no consideration is given to the chance the return will be greater than the expected return.

sensitivity—degree to which a security (e.g., stock, bond) reacts to changes in underlying factors. Sensitivity accounts for all factors that impact a security. See also *risk.*

sentinel event—unexpected event in a health care setting that causes death or serious injury to a patient and is not related to the natural course of the patient's illness. Providers are required to report such events to the Joint Commission and, often, a state licensing agency. See also *Joint Commission.*

separate account—fund administered by an insurance company in the form of an insurance contract that offers certain guarantees (e.g., reimbursement of capital upon death) to the policyholder. As required by law, these funds are kept totally separate from the insurance company's general investment funds.

separate line of business (SLOB)—IRC Section 414(r) provides guidance on qualifying for separate-line-of-business treatment: (1) there must be "bona fide business reasons" for operating separate lines of business, and (2) all property and services provided to customers must be available exclusively through the line of business with no operations existing outside the separate line. A separate-line-of-business exception permits electing businesses that are part of a controlled group to ignore affiliates when testing retirement plans for nondiscrimination, thereby treating each business as a standalone company for this purpose. See also *discrimination testing.*

separately managed account (SMA)—portfolio of assets owned by a relatively large investor under the management of a professional investment firm. One or more portfolio managers are responsible for day-to-day investment decisions, supported by a team of analysts, operations and administrative staff. The client maintains direct ownership and control over the securities that comprise the account. SMAs are typically used by wealthier individual investors who want professional management but with the additional control that is not available with a mutual fund. An SMA may also be an option for a trust fund that does not have the minimum $25 million often required of institutional investors. See also *commingled fund*.

SEP IRA—see *simplified employee pension (SEP) plan*.

serial bond—bond issue with maturity dates scheduled at regular intervals over a period of years. Serial bonds are also used to finance projects with regular level debt payments, such as residential developments.

serial maturity—see *balloon maturity*.

Series E/EE savings bond—nonmarketable U.S. government debt security that pays interest for up to 30 years. Series EE bonds issued after May 2005 are assigned a fixed coupon rate; rates are set twice per year, in May and November, and apply to all issuances for the ensuing six months. Bonds issued after this date increase in value monthly, but interest payments are semiannual. Paper EE bonds are issued at one-half of face value; however, electronic EE bonds are purchased at face value. The latter are guaranteed to be worth twice their original value after 20 years. E bonds are the predecessor to EE bonds and are no longer issued. See also *savings bond*.

Series H/HH savings bond—nonmarketable U.S. government debt security with a maturity of 20 years that pays semiannual interest based on a coupon rate. The coupon is a fixed rate for the first ten years, after which it is reset by the U.S. Treasury for the rest of the bond's life. Series H and HH bonds are no longer available for purchase or exchange. Denominations were available in amounts ranging from $500 to $10,000. See also *savings bond*.

Series I savings bond—nonmarketable U.S. government debt security that combines two separate interest rates: a fixed rate providing a guaranteed minimum return plus a variable inflation rate (adjusted semiannually) to provide protection on the investor's purchasing power. Paper I bonds are sold at face value in $50, $75, $100, $200, $500, $1,000 and $5,000 denominations. Electronic bonds can be bought to the penny; for example, a bond may be purchased for $100.10. Series I bonds increase in value monthly for up to 30 years, with interest paid when the bond is redeemed. See also *savings bond*.

seriously endangered status—designation specified by the Pension Protection Act (PPA) of 2006 for multiemployer pension plans when a plan is not in critical status but:
- The plan's funded percentage is less than 80%
- The plan has an accumulated funding deficiency in the current year or projected in the next six years, taking into account PPA amortization extensions.

Upon receiving certification of seriously endangered status (a.k.a. the orange zone), plan trustees must notify the U.S. Department of Labor, Pension Benefit Guaranty Corporation, beneficiaries, unions and employers of the designation. A funding improvement plan must be prepared and implemented. See also *accumulated funding deficiency, critical and declining status, critical status, endangered status, funding improvement plan (FIP)* and *green zone*.

serious mental illness (SMI)—per the National Advisory Mental Health Council, a serious mental illness that includes the following:
- Twelve-month prevalence of nonaffective psychosis or mania
- Lifetime prevalence of nonaffective psychosis or mania accompanied by evidence that the respondent would have been symptomatic if it were not for treatment (i.e., use of medication or any professional treatment in the past 12 months)
- Twelve-month prevalence of either major depression or panic disorder with evidence of severity indicated either by hospitalization or use of major psychotropic medications.

Specific disorders include those with psychotic symptoms such as schizophrenia, manic-depressive disorder and autism as well as severe forms of other disorders such as major depression, panic disorder and obsessive-compulsive disorder. States frequently have their own definition of SMI for the purposes of state mental health parity laws.

service area
—approved area of operation for a managed care organization under federal or state regulations. See also *catchment area*.
—geographic area from which a particular health care plan draws the majority of its members.
—geographic area in which a health insurance plan's benefits are made available. Some health insurance plans will not provide coverage outside of the plan's service area.

service award—something (e.g., trophy, medal, certificate, plaque, money) given to a person or group to recognize an accomplishment. See also *recognition program*.

service provider—contractors, subcontractors, professional service contractors, consultants, suppliers, agents and employers who provide goods, assets, facilities or services to a client. Examples of service providers for benefit plans include accountants, attorneys, actuaries, investment managers, third-party administrators and insurance carriers.

settlement
—with respect to a pension plan, an irrevocable action that relieves the employer (or the plan) of the primary responsibility and risk associated with benefit obligations. Examples of transactions that constitute a settlement include (1) making lump-sum cash payments to plan participants in exchange for their rights to receive specified pension benefits and (2) purchasing nonparticipating annuity contracts to cover vested benefits. See also *curtailment* and *plan termination*.
—process in which contractual obligations concerning a property transaction occur. The settlement of a securities transaction is an arrangement between brokerage houses for the payment and receipt of securities. Similarly, during a real estate transaction, settlement is the final step when the buyer pays the seller the purchase price in exchange for the property deed. If a mortgage is involved, a representative of the mortgage lender may also be involved. See also *Real Estate Settlement Procedures Act (RESPA)*.
—in a legal dispute, when the opposing parties reach an agreement prior to a court decision. Settlement may occur before the case goes to court or while it is being presented to the court.

settlement conference—meeting between opposing sides of a lawsuit at which the parties attempt to reach a mutually agreeable resolution of their dispute without having to go to trial. The parties and their attorneys meet with a settlement judge who hears both sides and tries to help them reach a compromise. Usually the judge cannot make any decisions regarding the outcome but will listen to each side, giving his/her critique and advising what s/he would be likely to decide in court.

settlement costs—see *closing cost* and *Real Estate Settlement Procedures Act (RESPA)*.

settlor—see *trustor*.

settlor functions—under ERISA, the following functions concerning a benefit plan:
- Choosing the type of plan or options in the plan
- Amending a plan, including changing or eliminating plan options
- Requiring employee contributions or changing the level of employee contributions
- Terminating a plan or part of a plan, including terminating or amending as part of a bankruptcy process.

severance package—pay and benefits an employee receives when he or she leaves an employer. In addition to the employee's remaining regular pay, the package may include an additional payment based on months of service; payment for unused vacation or sick leave; payment in lieu of a required notice period; medical, dental or life insurance; retirement benefits; stock options; and assistance in searching for new employment. See also *severance pay* and *termination benefit*.

severance pay—money paid as compensation to someone whose employment has ended.

sex discrimination—treating someone (an applicant or employee) unfavorably because of that person's gender. In Canada, persons discriminated against as a result of their gender are protected under the Canadian Human Rights Act. Several pieces of U.S. legislation also forbid discrimination on the basis of gender. Under Title VII of the Civil Rights Act of 1964, gender may not be used, by and of itself, in any decision regarding employees. The Equal Pay Act of 1963, an amendment to the Fair Labor Standards Act, specifically requires men and women be given equal pay for equal work in the same establishment. Title IX of the Education Amendments of 1972 prohibits discrimination on the basis of gender in educational programs or activities that receive federal assistance. See also *comparable worth*.

sexual harassment—as defined by the Equal Employment Opportunity Commission, unwelcome sexual advances, requests for sexual favors, and other verbal or physical conduct of a sexual nature when (1) submission to the conduct is made either explicitly or implicitly a term or condition of an individual's employment; (2) submission to or rejection of the conduct by an individual is used as a basis for employment decisions affecting such individual; or (3) the conduct has the purpose or effect of unreasonably interfering with an individual's work performance or creating an intimidating, hostile or offensive working environment. See also *Canadian Human Rights Act* and *harassment*.

share—one of the equal parts into which the capital stock of a corporation is divided. A share represents an owner's proportion of interest in the company and is issued to the shareholder in the form of a stock certificate.

shared employee—someone who works for more than one business at the same time. Frequently, a shared employee works for professionals who share an office. See also *leased employee*.

shared funding—variation on self-funding used to fund employee health benefits. The benefit plan combines basic health insurance for major medical expenses with employer-sponsored funding for routine outpatient care. The employer selects a deductible level and pays expenses for plan participants who incur claims, up to this maximum. An insurance company processes claims and assumes the risk over the deductible. Shared funding offers an employer a means of providing an affordable health plan that competes with more costly, benefit-rich plans. The routine services can be funded with the insurance premium savings and usually cost less than if they were provided through the insurance company. Sometimes called a high self-insured deductible plan, a shared funding plan is essentially a minimum premium plan for small employers. Most carriers do not offer a minimum premium plan to employers under a certain size due to underwriting or state filing limitations. See also *self-funding*.

shared savings—payment mechanism in which a health plan shares with a health care provider a percentage of savings accrued as a result of more efficient, coordinated care being delivered. See also *risk sharing*.

shareholder—see *stockholder*.

shareholder-employee—with regard to a Subchapter S corporation, an employee who is more than a 5% shareholder in the business.

shareholder equity—total assets minus total liabilities of a corporation; essentially the same as a company's net worth.

Sharpe ratio—risk-adjusted measure of an investment's performance; in other words, whether the return on a portfolio is the result of smart investment decisions or excess risk. The greater the Sharpe ratio, the better the return for the same risk. A negative ratio indicates a portfolio with less risk will perform better than the one analyzed. The Sharpe ratio is also referred to as the Sharpe index, Sharpe measure and reward-to-variability ratio. See also *Modigliani Risk-Adjusted Performance*.

shift differential—extra pay given on top of regular pay for employees who work an undesirable shift (e.g., late nights).

shoe box effect—propensity of plan beneficiaries to save reimbursable expense receipts to claim at a later date, then never making a claim. This effect is common with indemnity health insurance plans.

short selling—selling a security that the seller has borrowed. Short sellers assume they will be able to buy the stock at a lower amount than the price at which they sold short before it must be returned to the lender. See also *going long*.

short-term bond—debt security with a holding period that is usually less than three years to maturity. See also *intermediate-term bond*.

short-term disability (STD) insurance—insurance that provides a percentage of a person's salary if he or she is unable to work for a short period of time due to sickness or injury (excluding on-the-job injuries, which are covered by workers' compensation insurance). Short-term disability policies typically have a limit on the amount that will be paid per month, and another limit on the amount of time benefits will be paid. A typical STD policy provides one-half to two-thirds of the insured person's salary for no more than two years. The provisions of the STD are usually coordinated with the features of a long-term disability insurance plan. See also *long-term disability (LTD) insurance*.

short-term gain/loss—for U.S. tax purposes, an increase or decrease in the value of a capital asset that has been held for one year or less. Short-term gains are taxed using a taxpayer's ordinary income rates whereas, gains on assets held more than one year have a special reduced tax rate. See also *capital gain/loss* and *long-term gain/loss*.

short-term incentive (STI)—financial or other inducement offered to employees for achieving specific goals within one year or less.

short-term income protection—see *short-term disability (STD) insurance* and *unemployment compensation (UC)*.

short-term investment fund (STIF)—collective investment fund consisting of highly liquid and readily marketable interest-bearing securities. Investments are usually of high quality and low risk. See also *collective investment fund*.

short-time compensation—prorated unemployment benefits for workers whose hours are reduced through work sharing, often in lieu of layoff.

sick leave—benefit program, typically with full pay for a maximum number of days per year, that an employer provides to employees before short-term or long-term disability benefits are initiated. Sick leave is usually for a minor illness or injury.

sidecar IRA—see *deemed IRA*.

side effect—unintended consequences of a drug or other medical treatment. The effect may or may not be clinically significant. In general, side effects are undesirable but there are some exceptions. For example, an antihistamine may be used for its side effect which causes drowsiness and induces sleep.

side fund—see *conversion fund*.

significant break in coverage—under HIPAA, generally a period of 63 consecutive days or longer during which an individual has no creditable health care coverage. Prior to the passage of the Affordable Care Act of 2010 (ACA) and its prohibition of preexisting conditions in health plans, a person with a significant break in coverage was unable to get a credit against the exclusion for preexisting conditions with a health plan provided by a new employer.

sign-on bonus—lump sum of cash or stock granted at the time an employee joins a company. Also referred to as a golden hello.

silent partner—nonlegal term for an investor who puts money into a business but takes no part in the management and whose association is not public knowledge. Silent partners participate in profits and tax benefits of the company. They are also liable for any losses up to the amount of their invested capital. See also *general partner* and *limited partner*.

silver parachute—see *parachute*.

silver plan—see "Qualified health plans" in the *Appendix A: Affordable Care Act of 2010 (ACA)*.

SIMPLE 401(k) plan—cross between a SIMPLE IRA and traditional 401(k) plan for a small employer that is easier to set up than a qualified retirement plan. These plans are also exempt from actual contribution percentage, actual deferral percentage and top-heavy testing. Contributions are immediately vested, and participants are able to borrow funds from their own accounts. Contribution limits are lower than the limits for a traditional 401(k) plan. A SIMPLE 401(k) plan cannot be used in conjunction with any other active qualified plan covering the same employees. See also *actual contribution percentage (ACP) test, actual deferral percentage (ADP) test, discrimination testing, qualified retirement plan, SIMPLE IRA, top-heavy test* and *traditional IRA*.

simple interest—amount a lender pays a borrower for the use of money that is calculated only on the principal. For example, a $100 deposit in a savings account earning 5% simple interest would pay out $5 each year and would be worth $115 at the end of three years. In contrast, compound interest pays interest on the principal and interest accrued. See also *compound interest* and *interest*.

SIMPLE IRA—known by its acronym and rarely by its full name, an individual retirement account (IRA) (or annuity) that small employers (including self-employed individuals) can set up for the benefit of themselves and employees. A SIMPLE IRA cannot be used in conjunction with any other active qualified plan. See also *individual retirement account (IRA)* and *Savings Incentive Match Plan for Employees (SIMPLE)*.

SIMPLE plan—see *Savings Incentive Match Plan for Employees (SIMPLE)*.

simplified employee pension (SEP) plan—as the name suggests, an arrangement that provides an easier method for an employer to set up a retirement plan for employees than a qualified retirement plan. Employer contributions are made to traditional IRAs created for employees and referred to as SEP IRAs. Employer contributions must be the same percentage of each employee's salary. As long as the amount contributed does not exceed the indexed annual maximum, contributions are not included in the taxable income of the employee and are tax-deductible for the employer. Self-employed individuals may set up and contribute to a SEP plan. See also *individual retirement account (IRA)* and *traditional IRA*.

single employer plan—pension or other benefit plan maintained by one employer. Single employer plan is also used to describe a plan maintained by related parties such as a parent company and its subsidiaries.

single life annuity—insurance contract in which an insurance company agrees to provide income payments to one person for as long as he or she lives. See also *annuity, joint and survivor benefit* and *lifetime annuity*.

single parent captive—stock corporation wholly owned by its insured "parent" organization. The sole purpose of a single parent captive (also referred to as a pure captive) is to insure the risk of the parent, affiliates and/or subsidiaries. See also *captive insurance company*.

single payer system—approach to health care financing with only one source used to pay health care providers. The scope may be national (e.g., Canada's medicare), statewide or community-based. The payer may be a governmental unit or other entity such as an insurance company. Health care providers are in private practice and are paid on a fee-for-service basis. The government does not own or manage these medical practices or hospitals. See also *socialized medicine*.

single premium annuity—contract with an insurance company that agrees to provide a stream of income for a specified period of time that is funded by a single (lump-sum) payment. The payment might be invested for a long period of time before payments begin (single premium deferred annuity) or invested for a short time, after which payout begins (single premium immediate annuity). Single premium annuities are often funded by retirement plan rollovers or the sale of an appreciated asset. See also *annuity* and *single premium deferred annuity (SPDA)*.

single premium deferred annuity (SPDA)—contract with an insurance company that agrees to provide a stream of income for a specified period of time that is purchased with a single (lump-sum) payment. The payment is typically invested for a long period of time before payout begins. See also *annuity, deferred annuity* and *single premium annuity*.

single-source brand—medication with patent protection that is sold under a brand name and can be purchased only from one manufacturer or from manufacturers under license from the patent holder.

single tier drug formulary—see *drug formulary*.

sinking fund—money set aside to cover future debt, an anticipated major expense or potential losses.

six sigma—first developed by Motorola in 1986, a statistics-driven business management strategy to improve efficiency and eliminate defects in the manufacturing process. The goal is driving toward six standard deviations between the mean and the nearest specification limit—a failure rate of no more than 3.4 parts per million.

skill-based pay—compensation system based on the number of specified competencies or tasks mastered by an employee. See also *knowledge-based pay*.

skilled nursing care—higher level of nursing and rehabilitative care prescribed by a physician that is performed under the supervision of a registered nurse or licensed practical nurse.

skilled nursing facility (SNF)—institution or part of an institution that meets criteria for accreditation established by the sections of the Social Security Act that determine the basis for Medicaid and Medicare reimbursement of skilled nursing and rehabilitation care. Among the law's requirements are that the care of every patient be under the supervision of a physician, that a physician be available on an emergency basis, that records of the condition and care of every patient be maintained, that nursing service be available 24 hours a day and that at least one full-time registered nurse be employed. While the terms skilled nursing facility and nursing home are frequently used interchangeably, only an SNF meets the requirements for reimbursement. A nursing home may, however, have a skilled nursing unit for which services will be reimbursed. Also called a long-term care facility.

sliding fee scale—payment schedule under which the amount charged a patient for services varies with the patient's ability to pay.

small business health care tax credit—see "Small business health care tax credit" in the *Appendix A: Affordable Care Act of 2010 (ACA)*.

Small Business Health Options Program (SHOP)—see "Small Business Health Options Program (SHOP)" in the *Appendix A: Affordable Care Act of 2010 (ACA)*.

Small Business Job Protection Act of 1996 (SBJPA)—U.S. legislation containing a number of provisions aimed at simplifying retirement plan administration and expanding access to these plans. Major provisions affecting plans include:
- Establishment of the Savings Incentive Match Plan for Employees (SIMPLE)
- Creation of a new nondiscrimination safe harbor to encourage employers to allow participation by young, short-tenured employees
- Provision of a new definition of highly compensated employees
- Requirement that 457 plans be held in trust
- Allowing nonworking spouses to contribute up to $2,000 to an individual retirement account (IRA) if the working spouse is eligible
- Temporary reinstatement of the exclusion for employer-provided educational assistance, but elimination of the exclusion for graduate-level education.

small cap—short for market capitalization, a reference to companies with a market value of $300 million to $2 billion. A small cap is larger than a micro cap, but smaller than a mid cap. Cap classifications are only approximations that change over time. The exact definitions of these terms can also vary among brokerage houses. See also *large cap, mega cap, micro cap, mid cap, nano cap* and *Russell 2000 Index*.

small employer—generally, in the U.S., an entity that has fewer than 50 employees. Definitions vary with the context in which the term is used, such as a particular statute or regulation.

small group market—with respect to U.S. health insurance, an exchange offering coverage to small businesses—those with between two and 50 employees in most states. The Affordable Care Act of 2010 (ACA) broadens the market to those with between one and 100 employees.

small welfare plan—typically, an employee welfare plan that covers fewer than 100 participants at the beginning of a plan year.

smart card—plastic card coded with patient information that may be accessed by authorized health care providers for routine or emergency services.

smoking-cessation program—type of wellness program designed to help employees quit smoking tobacco products.

social insurance—government-sponsored program that has benefits, eligibility requirements and other aspects of the program defined by statute. The purpose is generally to provide economic protection or security to a large group of persons. Social Security is an example of a social insurance program in the United States, while the Employment Insurance (EI) program is an example in Canada.

socialized medicine—health care system in which the government owns and operates health care facilities and employs health care professionals, thus paying for all health care services. The British National Health Service and the national health systems in Finland and Spain are examples of socialized medicine. Canada's publicly funded medicare system is not considered a socialized system because it does not own all of the health facilities.

socially responsible investing (SRI)—also known as sustainable investing or ethical investing, socially responsible investing is an investment strategy that takes into consideration social, political, economic and/or environmental issues as well as financial gain. In general, socially responsible investors favor stock in corporations that promote environmental stewardship, consumer protection, human rights and diversity. Some (but not all) avoid corporations involved in alcohol, tobacco, gambling, weapons and/or the military. See also *economically targeted investment (ETI)*.

socially responsible investment—taking into consideration social, political, economic and/or environmental issues when selecting securities. See also *economically targeted investment (ETI)*.

Social Security
—federal program that provides monthly payments to workers, their spouses and dependents when workers retire, become disabled or die. Also known as *Old-Age, Survivors, Disability, and Health Insurance (OASDHI)*, Social Security was established under the Social Security Act of 1935. The program is funded by payroll taxes paid by employers and employees. Employees typically see the deductions on their pay stubs denoted as Social Security and Medicare. See also *disability insured, Federal Insurance Contributions Act (FICA), fully insured, Medicare, quarters of coverage (QC)* and *Social Security Act of 1935*.
—benefits arising from the Old Age Security plan (which provides income for essentially all senior Canadians), the Canada and Québec pension plans (which provide income to workers and their families in cases of retirement, disability and death) and other income support programs. See also *Canada Pension Plan (CPP)/Québec Pension Plan (QPP)* and *Old Age Security (OAS)*.

Social Security Act of 1935—U.S. legislation that established:
- Old-age assistance
- Unemployment insurance
- Aid to dependent children
- Grants to states to provide various forms of medical care.

Assistance was in the form of Title I Grants to States for Old-Age Assistance supporting state welfare programs for the aged, and Title II Federal Old-Age Benefits, which promised to pay a continuing income to retired workers aged 65 and older. Title II is known today as Social Security. Certain features of the latter program, notably disability coverage and medical benefits, were not part of the original program and were added in later years.

Social Security Administration (SSA)—established by the Social Security Act of 1935 to manage the Social Security program. SSA delivers a broad range of services online at www.ssa.gov and through a nationwide network of over 1,400 offices that include regional offices, field offices, card centers, teleservice centers, processing centers, hearing offices, the Appeals Council and Disability Determination Services. SSA also has a presence in U.S. embassies around the globe.

Social Security disability freeze—when calculating retirement or survivor benefits, the Social Security Administration ignores periods of disability. The logic behind the freeze is to avoid penalizing workers for periods when they are unable to work and have little or no earnings, which has the potential for reducing and, in some cases, entirely eliminating future retirement and survivor benefits. The future benefits are based on a minimum number of years of covered employment and the average indexed earnings of a worker over his or her lifetime.

Social Security Disability Insurance (SSDI)—see *Social Security*.

Social Security full retirement age—age at which full Social Security retirement benefits are payable. For persons born prior to 1938, full retirement age is 65. The 1983 Social Security amendments raised the full retirement age for those born after 1938 and before 1960 to between 65 and 67. Full retirement age for those born in 1960 and later was raised to 67. The earliest a person can start receiving Social Security reduced retirement benefits remains at age 62. See also *normal retirement age (NRA)*.

Society of Actuaries (SOA)—association dedicated to education, research and furthering the actuarial profession. SOA members are typically involved in health, pension and life insurance practices. Fellows of the Society of Actuaries (FSA) is the designation given to SOA members who complete a series of examinations in mathematics, statistics, insurance, actuarial science, accounting, finance and employee benefits.

soft assets—human resources (e.g., people, skills, knowledge) and intangible assets (e.g., information, brands, reputation). See also *hard assets*.

soft dollars—arrangement in which an investment manager directs the commission generated by a financial transaction with a client toward a third party (or in-house party) in exchange for services that are for the benefit of the client but are not client-directed. In contrast to hard dollars (actual cash), soft dollars are incorporated into other brokerage fees and expenses, not reported directly. Soft dollars may also refer to a situation in which payment is made in kind or by passing business to another party versus hard cash.

sole proprietor—form of business organization in which a single owner has total control over his or her own business and makes all management decisions. The business is unincorporated with the owner entitled to all of its profits and responsible for all of its liabilities. Sometimes called a *proprietorship*.

solo 401(k) plan—retirement plan similar to a 401(k) plan that is available only to an individual business owner and his or her spouse.

solvency—capacity of a benefit fund, corporation or other entity to meet its present and future financial obligations as they become due.

special assessment bond—municipal bonds issued to cover the cost of public improvements or development projects. A tax is levied on the community benefiting from the particular project to repay the debt obligation. See also *general obligation (GO) bond, municipal bond, revenue anticipation note (RAN)* and *revenue bond*.

special enrollment—HIPAA provision that permits employees, their spouses and dependents who previously declined health coverage to enroll for coverage outside a plan's open enrollment period under specific circumstances. One scenario is when a person declines coverage due to other health coverage, then loses eligibility or employer contributions to the other plan. Special enrollment is also allowed as the result of a marriage, birth, adoption or placement for adoption. In those situations, the employee must request enrollment within 30 days of the loss of coverage or life event triggering the special enrollment.

special enrollment period—time outside of a benefit plan's open enrollment period during which persons have a right to sign up for coverage.

specialist—health care professional who focuses on a particular area of medical care or patients. A specialist usually has advanced clinical training and postgraduate education in his or her area of care. Some health plans require participants to have a referral from a primary care provider before they can see a specialist in order to have the cost of that care covered by the plan.

specialized fund—see *specialty fund*.

special needs plan (SNP)—type of Medicare Advantage plan for a defined group of beneficiaries such as long-term care patients, those eligible for both Medicare and Medicaid (dual eligibles) and those with certain chronic or disabling conditions (e.g., diabetes). Established by the Medicare Prescription Drug, Improvement, and Modernization Act of 2003 (MMA) and introduced in 2005, these plans are not available in all areas. SNP is often pronounced as "snip." See also *Medicaid* and *Medicare Advantage*.

special risk class—see *substandard risk class*.

specialty drug—high-cost medication used to treat certain complex and rare medical conditions. Specialty drugs are often self-injected or, otherwise, self-administered. Many grow out of biotech research and may require refrigeration or special handling. As a result, they may not be available at the typical retail pharmacy. See also *biotech drug*.

specialty fund—mutual fund that concentrates holdings in a specific industry (e.g., technology, natural resources, health care) or geographical location. See also *mutual fund, regional fund* and *sector fund*.

specialty network—group of physicians focused on one type of health care (e.g., cardiology, oncology or pediatrics).

specialty pharmacy—facility that dispenses specialty drugs.

specific risk—see *nonmarket risk*.

specific stop-loss coverage—see *stop-loss insurance*.

specified beneficiary—spouse of a member of a defined contribution (DC) plan who has been so designated by the member for the purpose of determining the minimum payment required from the DC account if the benefits are payable after retirement.

specified distribution—lump sum commuted value of a benefit paid to an individual upon his or her exit from a defined benefit provision in a pension plan. The sum may be paid in cash or transferred to a tax-sheltered retirement savings vehicle such as a Registered Retirement Savings Plan (RRSP).

specified employee—see *key employee*.

specified individual—person connected with a participating employer at any time during a calendar year or whose total compensation during the year from participating employers exceeds 2½ times the year's maximum pensionable earnings for the year. See also *connected person* and *year's maximum pensionable earnings (YMPE)*.

specified multi-employer pension plan (SMEPP)—pension plan that has collectively bargained contributions, covers employees of two or more employers and has been designated in writing as a SMEPP by the applicable Canadian regulatory authority (where permitted).

specified retirement arrangement—partially funded or unfunded retirement compensation arrangement maintained by a tax-exempt employer. See also *Retirement Compensation Arrangement (RCA)*.

specimen plan—in Canada, registered retirement plan text, funding document or both that been pre-approved by the Registered Plans Directorate with limited specified variables. When a plan administrator elects to use a specimen plan, there is no need to submit copies of the pre-approved documents, just a list of the chosen variables and a completed Form T510. See also *prototype plan, registered pension plan (RPP)* and *standardized plan*.

speculative grade bond—see *junk bonds*.

speculative stock—share in the equity of a company that has high risk relative to any potential positive returns. Penny stocks are an example of speculative stock.

spell of illness—period of time an insured is sick and entitled to receive health insurance benefits. For the purposes of Medicare benefits, a spell of illness begins when a patient receives inpatient hospital services and ends at the conclusion of a 60-consecutive-day period during which the patient has not been an inpatient of any hospital or skilled nursing facility.

spending phase—period in life following retirement when earning income (e.g., salary, wages) has ended and funds saved for retirement and government benefits are used to cover living expenses.

spin-off—new entity formed by a split from another larger entity. See also *divestiture*.

split dollar life insurance—insurance policy in which an employer and employee share in the expenses, equity and death benefits. Such policies typically involve life insurance with a savings component. See also *cash value insurance, corporate-owned life insurance (COLI), life insurance* and *Table 2001 rates*.

split funding—when applied to retirement plans, the use of two or more funding sources. For example, a portion of a plan may be funded by a life insurance company while the remainder is invested in stocks through a corporate trustee.

spot award—see *spot bonus*.

spot bonus—relatively small, one-time gift to an employee in recognition of exceptional performance. Also called a spot award.

spousal carve-out—provision in an employer-provided health plan that denies or reduces the coverage available to an employee's spouse if the spouse has coverage (or the ability to get coverage) through the spouse's own employer. The features of carve-out provisions can vary substantially. Some employers allow an employee to purchase insurance for the spouse if the cost through the spouse's employer is over a certain dollar limit. If the cost of insurance is below this limit, the employee may also be permitted to purchase secondary coverage for the spouse. Also referred to as a working spouse provision.

spousal equivalent—see *domestic partnership*.

spousal IRA—individual retirement account (IRA) created by an employee for the exclusive benefit of a spouse who has little or no employment compensation. Allowable annual contributions to the employee's IRA and the spousal IRA combined is double the dollar limit in effect for the taxable year (or 100% of the employee's earnings, if less). The contributions to both IRAs need not be split equally between the spouses. See also *individual retirement account (IRA)*.

spousal surcharge—additional fee charged by an employer-sponsored health insurance plan for coverage of an employee's spouse if the spouse chooses to decline the health insurance provided by the spouse's own employer.

spouse's benefit—payment or series of payments to the surviving spouse of a deceased worker that typically terminates with the survivor's remarriage or death. See also *qualified joint and survivor annuity (QJSA)*.

spread—difference between what a dealer pays for a security and the price at which he or she offers to sell it.

stable value fund—mutual fund typically providing a return that is a few percentage points higher than the average money market fund, with just marginally more risk. Stable value funds are invested heavily in guaranteed investment contracts and wrapped bonds. See also *bank investment contract (BIC), guaranteed investment contract (GIC), mutual fund* and *wrapped bond*.

staff model HMO—health maintenance organization (HMO) in which physicians and other staff are employees of the HMO and compensated through salary, bonus plans, etc., versus a fee-for-service arrangement. Medical services that cannot be provided internally are referred to outside providers with the HMO picking up the costs. See also *health maintenance organization (HMO)*.

stagflation—coined during the 1970s, a period in which there is slow to no growth in real output (stagnation) and higher-than-normal unemployment, in combination with inflation. See also *inflation* and *recession*.

stakeholder—person or entity with a financial or other interest in an organization. Stakeholders may include executives, employees, shareholders, suppliers, customers and communities.

standalone plan—see *carve-out*.

Standard & Poor's 500 (S&P 500)—as the name implies, an index representing the price of 500 companies, mostly large and mid caps listed on the New York Stock Exchange. Covering about 75% of the U.S. equity market by capitalization, the S&P 500 is considered by many to be more representative of the market as a whole than some of the other indexes. The S&P 500 is one of the indexes frequently referenced when analysts are assessing financial or economic performance. See also *large cap, mid cap* and *stock market index*.

standard deduction—amount set by the Internal Revenue Code that may be deducted (along with personal exemptions) by a taxpayer who does not itemize deductions when filing an annual federal income tax return. See also *tax deduction* and *tax exemption*.

standard deviation—statistical measure of the dispersion of a set of numbers around an average (the mean) that is calculated as the square root of variance. When used in reference to an asset or investment portfolio, the standard deviation reflects historical price volatility. The broader the range of prices, the higher the deviation. See also *volatility*.

standard indemnity plan—see *indemnity insurance*.

standardized plan—master or prototype retirement plan generally designed to satisfy the coverage and nondiscrimination requirements of the IRC. Standardized plans have less flexibility than nonstandardized plans, but an employer may be able to avoid filing with the IRS for a determination letter to obtain assurance that the plan document satisfies qualification. See also *master plan, nonstandardized plan, nonstandardized safe harbor plan, prototype plan* and *specimen plan*.

standard of care—expected level and type of health services provided by the average, prudent provider given the circumstances.

standard risk class—group of insurance applicants who represent average risk within the context of an insurer's underwriting practices. See also *class rating, declined risk class, preferred risk class, qualified impairment insurance, rated policy* and *substandard risk class*.

standard termination—see *plan termination*.

state disability insurance (SDI)—see *state disability plan*.

state disability plan—disability insurance required by state legislation of employers doing business in that particular state. See also *disability, disability insurance* and *temporary disability insurance (TDI)*.

State Health Insurance Assistance Program (SHIP)—state program that gets funding from the U.S. government to provide free local health coverage counseling to people with Medicare. A SHIP can also help individuals with Medicare complaints and appeals.

statement of investment policies and procedures (SIP&P)—guidelines that the administrator of a federally regulated pension plan in Canada must establish, implement and monitor concerning the obligations of the plan, fund objectives and other factors that may affect the ongoing funding and solvency of the plan including the plan's ability to meet its financial obligations. More specifically, some of the issues an SIP&P must address are:
- The plan's investment philosophy, objectives and risk tolerance
- How investment managers will be chosen, compensated and replaced
- The role of those involved in the investment process and what is expected of them
- Retention or delegation of voting rights attached to investments
- Valuation of investments not regularly traded at a public exchange
- Related party transactions.

A SIP&P is mandated under Canada's Pension Benefits Standards Act of 1985 and Pension Benefits Standards Regulations.

statement of revenue and expense—see *income statement*.

statutory benefit—see *mandatory benefit*.

steerage—use of strategies such as financial incentives to direct health plan participants to use specific care providers. Establishing higher copays for out-of-network providers and more expensive brand-name drugs are examples of how a health plan can steer plan participants to lower cost choices.

step-rate integration—application of lower rate to earnings up to the year's maximum pensionable earnings (YMPE) under the Canada Pension Plans (CPP)/Québec Pension Plan (QPP) and a higher rate above the YMPE. See also *year's maximum pensionable earnings (YMPE)*.

step rate method—see *excess rate method*.

step rates—standard progression of pay established within a pay range. Step rates generally are a function of time in grade and are often automatic increases. In some cases, they are used with merit programs.

step therapy—requiring a beneficiary to use the most cost-efficient treatment before proceeding to something more expensive or difficult to use. A benefit plan may require evidence of a side effect or other therapeutic failure before coverage is granted for an alternative treatment. See also *drug utilization management (DUM)*.

STIF account—see *short-term investment fund (STIF)*.

stock—ownership share in a public corporation. Stock is a means of raising the capital a company needs to cover start-up costs and expansion. Ownership is usually indicated via a stock certificate or book entry. Depending on the type of stock owned, the holder may be given the right to vote on major corporate issues and benefit from stock dividends, capital gains, and—if the corporation is dissolved—a claim upon assets remaining after all creditors have been paid. Stocks are also referred to as equity securities and equities. See also *capital stock, common stock, penny stock, preferred stock* and *speculative stock*.

stock appreciation right (SAR)—opportunity given to an employee to receive a bonus equal to the difference between a stock option price and the current market price of a company's stock without actually buying any of the stock. A SAR functions much like an employee stock option plan, with the employee benefiting only if the value of the stock at the time the employee exercises his or her right is greater than the option price. See also *employee stock option plan (ESOP)* and *stock bonus plan*.

stock bonus plan—program established and maintained by a corporate employer that is used to motivate and reward employees in the form of stock instead of cash. In contrast to a profit-sharing plan, a stock bonus plan is not dependent on the company earning a profit to provide benefits. See also *equity compensation, profit-sharing plan* and *stock appreciation right (SAR)*.

stock broker—see *securities broker*.

stock certificate—document that provides evidence of stock ownership in a corporation.

stock dividend—share of profits paid to corporate shareholders. Corporations that want to conserve cash for expansion or another purpose may provide stockholders with a dividend in the form of more stock.

stock exchange—see *stock market*.

stock fund—mutual fund comprised mostly of stocks. Investing in stock funds usually results in higher returns than bond funds in the long run, but they also have higher risk. See also *common stock fund, growth fund* and *mutual fund.*

stockholder—one who owns shares of stock in a company or shares of a mutual fund. Also known as a shareholder, a stockholder is eligible to share in profits and losses.

stockholder of record—name of an individual or entity that an issuer carries in its records as the registered holder (not necessarily the owner) of the issuer's securities. Dividends and other distributions are paid only to shareholders of record.

stockholders' equity—see *shareholder equity.*

stock manipulation—actions by owners of a company or others to artificially increase or decrease the value of a stock so they can buy or sell shares at a profit. Stock manipulation is typically illegal.

stock market—also referred to as an equity market or stock exchange, where equity shares in public corporations are issued and traded. The trading place may be a physical location such as the New York Stock Exchange or simply a network of broker-dealers that trade electronically such as an over the counter (OTC) market. See also *London Stock Exchange (LSE), NASDAQ, New York Stock Exchange (NYSE), NYSE MKT LLC, over the counter (OTC) market, primary market, secondary market* and *Toronto Stock Exchange (TSX).*

stock market crash—sudden dramatic decline in stock prices across a significant cross section of companies in a market. There is no numerically specific definition of a stock market crash, but the term commonly applies to steep, double-digit percentage losses in a stock market index over a period of several days. Crashes tend to be driven by investor panic as much as any underlying economic factors. They often follow speculative stock market bubbles. The most recent crash in the U.S. was in 2008-2009. There were two crashes in the 20th century, in 1929 and 1987.

stock market index—compilation of the prices of a group of stocks representing a specific market, market sector or industry. Indexes are often used as an indicator of financial or economic performance. See also *Dow Jones Industrial Average (DJIA), Dow Jones Transportation Average (DJTA), Europe, Australasia and Far East (EAFE) Index, MSCI World, NASDAQ Composite Index, New York Stock Exchange Composite Index, Nikkei 225, Russell 2000 Index, Standard & Poor's 500 (S&P 500), Toronto Stock Exchange (TSX)* and *Wilshire 5000 Total Market Index (TMWX).*

stock option—right to buy corporate stock at a stated price within a set period of time. The price (called the exercise price) is usually the market price of the stock at the time an option is granted. The hope is that the price of the shares will go up, so that selling them later at a higher market price will yield a profit. See also *employee stock option plan (ESOP), incentive stock option (ISO), International Securities Exchange (ISE), nonqualified stock option agreement (NQSO), option agreement* and *underwater.*

stock purchase plan—see *employee stock purchase plan (ESPP).*

stock split—bookkeeping increase in the number of outstanding shares of a corporation without changing shareholder equity. Stock splits, sometimes called stock divides, are usually made on a two-for-one basis, with shareholders receiving two new shares in exchange for one old share. The purpose of a split is typically to reduce the price of shares and heighten market interest.

stock swap—see *swap.*

stock warrant—see *warrant.*

stock yield—see *yield.*

stop-loss insurance—also called excess-loss insurance, an insurance contract or provision in a contract between a self-funded benefits plan and an insurance carrier that provides financial protection if claims to the plan exceed a specified dollar amount over a set period of time. There are two types of stop-loss coverage. Individual or specific stop-loss insurance covers claims incurred and/or paid by an individual during a specific period of time (usually 12 months) that exceed a threshold set for employees. The threshold is established by the plan sponsor. In contrast, aggregate stop-loss insurance protects the plan and plan sponsor from total claim costs that exceed a specific limit during a specific time period. See also *reinsurance.*

stop-loss order—instructions to sell a security when it reaches a certain price. The purpose of a stop-loss order is to limit an investor's loss to a specific amount if prices fall.

straddle—purchase of a call and put option with the same strike price (long straddle) or a sale of a call and put option with the same strike price (short straddle). See also *option* and *strangle*.

straddle rule—U.S. regulation that considers a life insurance policy as "carried" by an employer if the employer arranges for the premium payments and the premiums paid by at least one employee subsidize those paid by at least one other employee. See also *Section 79*.

straight bond—debt issue that pays a predetermined amount of interest on specific dates and the principal on its maturity date. A straight bond does not carry the opportunity to convert it to stock or other special features. See also *bond*.

straight life annuity—promise by a pension plan or an insurance company to make regular payments for the lifetime of an individual. There is no guarantee payments will be made for a minimum period, and no part of it is payable to another person after the annuitant's death.

straight life insurance—see *whole life insurance*.

straight ranking method—simple strategy for performance appraisal that involves listing employees from best to poorest on the basis of their overall performance. See also *alternate ranking method* and *performance appraisal*.

strangle—options strategy where an investor holds a position in both a call and put with different strike prices but with the same maturity and underlying asset. This is a good strategy only if an investor thinks there will be a large price movement in the near future but is unsure as to the direction the price will move. Strangling is profitable only if there are large movements in the price of the underlying asset. A strangle is a variation of a *straddle*.

strategic planning—process of determining or reassessing the vision, mission and goals of an organization and then identifying actions for accomplishing the identified goals. Strategic planning is medium to long range in nature and is intended to lay out the major goals of an organization.

stress management—techniques for coping with and reducing the impact of stressors at work and in other facets of life.

strike price—see *exercise price*.

strip—see *coupon stripping*.

structured products—financial assets that consist of various elements combined to generate a risk-return profile specific to an investor's needs.

Student Loan Marketing Association (Sallie Mae)—largest provider of educational loans in the United States. In addition to providing student loans, Sallie Mae purchases student loans from other lenders and provides financing to state student loan agencies. Formed in 1972 as a government enterprise, Sallie Mae became a publicly traded, independent corporation in 2004.

subordinated debt—loan (or security) that ranks below other loans (or securities) with regard to claims on assets or earnings. If a default occurs, creditors with subordinated debt do not get paid until senior debtholders are paid in full. Hence, subordinated debt is more risky than unsubordinated debt. Also known as a junior security or subordinated loan.

subordinated loan—see *subordinated debt*.

subpoena—written command for a person to appear in court or else be punished. Subpoenas may also be issued that require the submission of documents or other information.

subrogation—legal process by which an insurance company (or benefit plan), after paying a loss, has the right to recover that loss from another legally liable party. For example, an insurance company might attempt to recoup benefits paid to an insured through a lawsuit against a third party that caused an accident.

subscriber—person who contracts for a good or service. Persons who elect coverage under a benefit plan are sometimes referred to as subscribers.

subsidiary—company owned and/or controlled by a larger company referred to as the parent company.

substance abuse—use of alcohol or drugs for purposes other than those for which they are indicated or in a manner that is hazardous.

substance abuse treatment—activities carried out by professionals to intervene in and support the reduction or elimination of an individual's abusive use of alcohol and/or other chemical substances. See also *Mental Health Parity and Addiction Equity Act of 2008*.

substandard risk class—also known as special class risk, a group of insurance applicants who have the potential for claims greater in number and size than what is considered typical (standard). Those with poor driving records (auto insurance) or poor physical health (life insurance) may not qualify for standard insurance rates due to the extra risk the insurer would incur. Such persons may be able to purchase a substandard insurance policy with a higher premium and/or special contract provisions. In a substandard life insurance policy, the insurer might state it will not pay benefits for death caused by a specific illness or medical condition, or will provide only partial benefits. See also *class rating, declined risk class, preferred risk class, qualified impairment insurance, rated policy* and *standard risk class*.

substantive plan—for the purposes of auditing an "other post-employment benefits plan" under Financial Accounting Standard 106, the terms of the plan as understood by the employer-sponsor and plan members. This interpretation includes both historical practices and employer practices. See also *other postemployment benefits (OPEB) plan*.

succession planning—identifying (and preparing) candidates to replace key persons should they leave the company. See also *key employee*.

successor plan—benefit program established after the termination of a group health plan.

successor plan rule—U.S. regulation that an employer may not terminate a 401(k) plan and then start a new one (a successor plan) for at least 12 months after the original plan is terminated. The 12-month waiting period begins on the date that all elective deferrals have been distributed from the terminated 401(k) plan, not the date of the resolution terminating it. The purpose of this rule is primarily to prevent employers from avoiding the restriction on elective deferrals before attainment of age 59½ by terminating a plan, making distributions and then immediately restarting another plan.

suggested wholesale price (SWP)—dollar amount that manufacturers recommend wholesalers charge when selling a drug to customers. Wholesalers are not obligated to sell a medication at this price. See also *wholesaler*.

suicide provision—element of a life insurance policy that states the insurer will not pay a death benefit if the insured commits suicide within a specific period of time after opening the policy.

summary annual report (SAR)—document containing financial and other information on an employee benefit plan that ERISA requires must be given to participants automatically at the end of each financial year.

summary judgment—decision entered by a court for one party and against another party on the basis of statements and evidence presented in the legal pleadings and documents filed, without a full trial.

Summary of Benefits and Coverage (SBC)—see "Summary of Benefits and Coverage (SBC)" in the *Appendix A: Affordable Care Act of 2010 (ACA)*.

summary of material modifications (SMM)—plain language document that describes changes to a summary plan description. ERISA requires that plan administrators send out an SMM to plan participants and beneficiaries no later than 210 days after the close of a plan year in which a material modification was made. See also *material modification* and *summary plan description (SPD)*.

summary plan description (SPD)—easy-to-read written statement describing the provisions and features of a qualified benefit plan, including eligibility, coverage, employee rights and appeals procedures. The SPD must be provided to participants, beneficiaries and, upon request, to the U.S. Department of Labor.

sunset clause or provision
—element of a statute or regulation that says a rule will cease to have effect after a specific date, unless further legislative action is taken to extend it.
—in the corporate arena, intentionally stopping something such as a project or aspects of a job.

superimposed major medical insurance—see *supplemental major medical insurance*.

supplemental benefit—see *ancillary benefit* and *supplemental unemployment benefit (SUB)*.

supplemental employee retirement plan (SERP)—see *supplemental executive retirement plan (SERP)*.

supplemental executive retirement plan (SERP)—nonqualified retirement plan that allows an employer to give deferred compensation to a select group of employees above and beyond what is possible in other retirement plans, such as an individual retirement account (IRA), 401(k) plan or nonqualified deferred compensation plan (NDCP). SERPs are also known as top-hat plans.

supplemental executive retirement plan (SERP) swap—exchange of all or a portion of a SERP for a split dollar insurance policy, with the company paying all or a portion of the premium. See also *supplemental executive retirement plan (SERP)* and *split dollar life insurance*.

supplemental life insurance—coverage over and above the basic coverage available via an employee benefit package. Each employee has the option to purchase a rider providing the additional coverage in an amount chosen by the individual employee. Depending on the age of the employee and amount of coverage purchased, the insurance company may allow the purchase without a statement of good health or completion of a medical exam. See also *voluntary life insurance.*

supplemental major medical insurance—health care coverage designed to pay for expenses not covered by a basic medical plan. Besides limiting the types of expenses covered, the basic plan usually has a maximum dollar amount that it will pay. Covered persons are first reimbursed for medical expenses under the basic plan. Expenses not covered by this plan are reimbursed under the supplemental major medical plan. A corridor-type deductible between the two plans is often required before the supplemental coverage begins. See also *basic medical insurance, corridor deductible* and *major medical insurance.*

Supplemental Security Income (SSI)—federal income support program for U.S. citizens and some noncitizens over the age of 65, blind or disabled who fall below specified income and resource thresholds.

supplemental unemployment benefit (SUB)—payment from an employer-financed fund provided under a labor contract to an employee who has been temporarily laid off or terminated. The SUB is in addition to unemployment compensation provided by law. The payments are taxable as wages and subject to income tax withholding, but not subject to Social Security, Medicare or federal unemployment taxes. See also *unemployment compensation (UC).*

supplementary medical insurance (SMI)—see *Medicare.*

surety bond—promise by a third party (surety) to assume liability for damages or losses caused when someone fails to fulfill a contractual obligation. Surety bonds are used to guarantee the payment of debts and to provide a guarantee that work will be performed according to the terms of a contract. See also *bonding.*

surplus—more than what is needed; for example, when plan assets exceed liabilities.

surrender charge—fee charged for the exchange of an annuity or life insurance or annuity policy for its cash value.

surrender value—money a policyholder receives if an annuity or life insurance policy is cashed in or canceled before maturity.

surviving spouse benefit—annuity or retirement payments to the spouse of a deceased participant. Sometimes, this term refers only to payments other than those provided by a joint and survivor annuity. See also *automatic survivor coverage, qualified joint and survivor annuity (QJSA)* and *reversionary annuity.*

survivor annuity—annuity payments to a spouse or designated beneficiary. See also *automatic survivor coverage, qualified joint and survivor annuity (QJSA)* and *reversionary annuity.*

survivor benefit—payment or other benefit provided to a family member (or other named beneficiary) upon the death of an individual.

suspension—temporary interruption; for example, an insurance company may allow the suspension of premium payments under certain circumstances. Some pension plans suspend payments when a retiree returns to work for the same employer or under a multiemployer plan.

swap
—contract in which two parties agree to exchange certain benefits (often cash flows) of two related financial instruments. One cash flow is generally fixed, while the other is variable (i.e., based on a benchmark interest rate, floating currency exchange rate or index price). Typically, the actual instruments do not change hands. The swap agreement defines the dates when the cash flows are to be paid and the way they are calculated. Swaps can be used to hedge certain risks or to speculate on changes in underlying factors. Common swaps are interest rate swaps, credit default swaps, commodity swaps and equity swaps.
—in the context of mergers and acquisitions, an exchange where an acquiring company's stock is swapped for the stock of the company being acquired at a predetermined rate. Typically, only a portion of a merger is completed with a stock-for-stock transaction, with the rest of the expenses being covered with cash or another method of payment.
—also a method for satisfying the option price or increasing one's ownership position in an employee stock option plan without a cash outlay. See also *employee stock option plan (ESOP).*

swap fund—see *exchange fund.*

SWOT analysis—approach to strategic planning that assesses the strengths, weaknesses, opportunities and threats associated with a project or change.

syndicate—group of individuals or companies formed to transact a specific business or to promote a common interest. Investment bankers form syndicates to underwrite and distribute a new issue of securities or a large block of an outstanding issue.

synthetic security—combination of investments that mimics the properties of another security.

systematic risk—see *market risk*.

systematic withdrawal—draw down of funds from a retirement account in preset amounts for a specified payment frequency. A common withdrawal approach is to withdraw a fixed dollar amount (with or without adjustments for inflation) or a fixed percentage of assets.

systemic health—condition or disease (e.g., diabetes) that can affect the whole body.

T

table of allowances—list of dollar amounts that a dental or health insurance plan will pay providers for specific services rendered. The patient pays the difference between the allowance and the actual cost of service. Also referred to as a fee schedule, indemnity schedule or schedule of allowances.

table rate—see *manual rate*.

table 2001 rates—values issued by the IRS and used to calculate the cost of pure insurance protection from a split dollar life insurance plan or qualified retirement plan. The cost is taxable employee income. These rates must be used with split dollar life insurance plans entered into, or materially modified, on or after September 18, 2003. If a plan was entered into and not materially modified prior to this date, the insurance company's most frequently used published renewable one-year term rates may be substituted if they are lower than the rates found in Table 2001. Table 2001 replaced IRS Table PS 58 in 2001. See also *split dollar life insurance*.

Taft-Hartley Act—see *Labor-Management Relations Act of 1947 (LMRA or Taft-Hartley Act)*.

Taft-Hartley plan—multiemployer benefit plan providing retirement, health and welfare, apprenticeship, vacation or other benefits through a trust fund that is managed by a board of trustees who equally represent labor and management. All trustees are charged with the fiduciary responsibility of discharging their duties with respect to the plan "solely in the interests of participants and beneficiaries." Mobile employees can change employers without losing coverage, provided their new job is with an employer who participates in the same Taft-Hartley fund. See also *trustee* and *trust fund*.

takeover deterrent—see *poison pill*.

tangible asset—physical resources that have value. Tangible assets include land, buildings, equipment, natural resources, etc. See also *capital asset, current asset* and *intangible asset*.

target benefit plan (TBP)—hybrid retirement plan in Canada that includes features of a defined benefit (DB) plan and defined contribution (DC) plan. A TBP is similar to a DB plan in that there is a pooling of funds, and employer contributions are based on the amount needed to accumulate sufficient funds (at an assumed interest rate) to pay a projected future benefit—the target benefit—to plan members upon retirement. Unlike a DB plan, however, a TBP does not guarantee the benefit amount to be paid. The obligation of the plan is only to pay whatever benefit can be provided given plan funding. Depending on the financial status of the plan and plan policies, actions can be taken to:
- Increase or decrease contributions
- Decrease benefits for all members
- Grant indexing for all members
- Enhance other base or ancillary benefits.

While the potential for such actions introduces a degree of uncertainty for plan members, it is not near the level of uncertainty that exists with a DC arrangement, and it provides a steady stream of income like a DB plan. Because members share the risks associated with the plan through the possible reduction of their benefits, TBPs are also referred to as shared-risk plans. See also *hybrid pension plan*.

target compensation—expected pay for a job or position, including base pay, incentives and bonuses.

target-date fund (TDF)—hybrid mutual fund that invests in a mix of assets (i.e., stocks, bonds and cash) that is automatically reset at specific times as the " target date" approaches. Investors typically choose a fund with a date that is near their planned retirement year. The asset mix becomes less risky so shareholders have more stable values and returns when they are ready to begin withdrawals. While proponents cite the convenience of using these funds to put retirement investing on autopilot, critics are wary of the one-size fits-all approach and express concern as to whether the risk associated with the mix of assets is appropriate. Target-date funds are also referred to as target-retirement-date funds and age-based funds.

target-retirement-date fund—see *target-date fund.*

target-risk fund—also known as a lifestyle fund, a mutual fund that invests in an asset mix determined by the level of risk and return that is appropriate for investors. Factors that determine the appropriate mix include the investor's age, risk aversion, investment purpose and time until the principal will be withdrawn. A target-risk fund can have conservative, moderate or aggressive growth strategies. Typically, aggressive growth funds are more appropriate for young investors, while conservative growth funds are more suited to investors nearing retirement and the withdrawal of their funds. Target-risk funds are designed to be the main investment in a person's portfolio. The purpose of the fund may be defeated if other funds are chosen at the same time, because the asset allocation mix may be distorted. See also *mutual fund.*

taxable wage base (TWB)—for the purpose of Social Security taxes, the maximum annual earnings that may be considered wages and taxed.

taxable year—12-month period used for reporting income for tax purposes. An employer's taxable year does not have to coincide with the year used by a benefit plan sponsored by the employer.

tax anticipation bill (TAB)—U.S. Treasury bill sold on an irregular basis and scheduled to mature in periods of heavy tax receipts. No tax anticipation bills have been issued since 1974. See also *Treasury bill.*

tax basis—see *basis.*

tax credit—amount a person or business can subtract from the income tax they owe. If a tax credit is refundable, the taxpayer can receive a payment from the government to the extent that the credit is greater than the amount of tax he or she would otherwise owe. One example of a tax credit is the saver's tax credit. For other examples, see the "Premium tax credit" and "Small business health care tax credit" in the *Appendix A: Affordable Care Act of 2010 (ACA).*

tax deduction—amount a person or business can subtract from income before calculating taxes owed.

tax deferral—postponing the payment of taxes for income earned in the current year to a time in the future. Taxes on contributions and earnings associated with qualified retirement plans are generally deferred until participants receive retirement benefits.

tax-deferred—income that is not taxed until a later date. For example, contributions to various retirement plans are not taxable until paid out as plan distributions.

tax equalization—arrangement in which an employee working outside his or her home country pays no more (and no less) tax than if he or she had stayed at home. See also *hypothetical tax.*

Tax Equity and Fiscal Responsibility Act of 1982 (TEFRA)—legislation that:
- Established new top-heavy retirement plans
- Repealed special Keogh plan and Subchapter S restrictions
- Imposed more stringent Section 415 funding and benefit limits
- Allowed certain loans from retirement plans to be treated as distributions
- Reduced the estate tax exclusion for retirement plan death benefits to a maximum of $100,000
- Restricted medical expenses for federal tax purposes to amounts in excess of 5% of adjusted gross income (AGI)
- Allowed health insurance premiums to be treated as a medical expense
- Changed the rules for calculating the share of employer-paid life insurance that must be reported as employee income
- Set age limits for retirement plan distributions.

tax-equivalent (TE) yield—formula used by investors to determine whether a tax-exempt security (e.g., a municipal bond) will provide a better return than a taxable fund. The formula shows the tax-free yield an investor needs to earn on a taxable fund to have the same return after taxes. The tax-equivalent yield = the tax-free yield /(1- the federal tax bracket), with the tax bracket representing the federal income tax bracket of the investor. The TE yield is higher for investors in higher tax brackets. See also *municipal bond, tax-exempt* and *yield*.

tax-exempt—not subject to tax. For example, earnings on bonds issued by state and local governments (i.e., municipal bonds, revenue bonds or special assessment bonds) as well as certain investment accounts such as Roth IRAs and 529 college savings plans are exempt from federal income tax.

tax exemption—reduction in taxes granted for special classes of people. The IRS gives taxpayers a personal tax exemption for themselves and their dependents when filing federal income taxes. Additional exemptions may be claimed for taxpayers who are blind, disabled or over the age of 65. For each exemption, the taxpayer receives a standard reduction in taxable income.

Tax-Free Savings Account (TFSA)—introduced in 2009, an account that may be set up by an individual or group of employees through a bank or other financial institutions that allows Canadians, aged 18 and over, to set aside money for retirement. In contrast to a Registered Retirement Savings Plan (RRSP), any money withdrawn from a TFSA in past years may also be put into the account. Contributions are not tax-deductible, but no tax is paid on the principal, capital gains or investment income upon withdrawal. Earnings from a TFSA don't affect income-tested government benefits such as Old Age Security (OAS) and the Guaranteed Income Supplement (GIS).

Taxpayer Relief Act of 1997 (TRA '97)—U.S. legislation that provided tax relief in the form of reduced tax rates on capital gains, new exclusions for gains on the sale of a primary residence and a child credit for children under the age of 17. With respect to benefits, the legislation:
- Simplified retirement plan administration
- Created new retirement planning options, such as the Roth IRA. See also *Roth IRA*.
- Permitted individual retirement account (IRA) withdrawals for education and home purchases prior to the age of 70½ without penalty. See also *individual retirement account (IRA)*.
- Extended employer-provided educational assistance.

tax-qualified plan—see *qualified employee benefit plan*.

Tax Reform Act of 1984—see *Deficit Reduction Act of 1984 (DEFRA)*.

Tax Reform Act of 1986—U.S. legislation with extensive changes governing the income tax code. Referred to as the second of the two Reagan tax cuts, the act simplified the tax code, reduced the number of tax brackets, repealed income averaging, eliminated many tax shelters and did away with the deductibility of nonmortgage consumer interest. Some of the changes were nullified in later legislation. With respect to benefits, the act:
- Ended the full deductibility of individual retirement accounts (IRAs) for employees at higher income levels
- Imposed a penalty on withdrawals from IRAs before the age of 59½
- Established minimum levels of pension plan vesting for employees. See also *partial vesting* and *vesting*.
- Prohibited employees of state and local governments and tax-exempt organizations from establishing new 401(k) plans and added restrictions to existing arrangements
- Imposed the comprehensive nondiscrimination rules of IRC Section 89. See also *nondiscrimination rule*.

Tax Relief and Health Care Improvement Act of 2006—U.S. legislation that, among other things:
- Raised the contribution limit for health savings accounts (HSAs)
- Required the establishment of quality measures for hospital outpatient services
- Provided incentives for physicians and service providers to report on specified performance measures.

tax shelter—method used by investors to legally avoid or reduce tax liabilities. One of the most common legal tax shelters used to offset taxable income is the depreciation of real estate or equipment. Depletion allowances for oil and gas exploration provide another means for creating losses to offset taxable income.

tax-sheltered annuity (TSA)—also referred to as a 403(b) plan, a special type of tax-qualified deferred compensation arrangement for employees of nonprofit 501(c)(3) organizations and public education systems. See also *403(b) plan* and *Section 403(b)*.

technical analysis—tracking the historical price and volume movements of security trades to predict future (usually short-term) market trends and investment choices. In contrast to fundamental analysis, technical analysis ignores the actual nature of the company, market, currency or commodity and is based solely on charts of price and volume data. See also *efficient market hypothesis (EMH)* and *fundamental analysis*.

Technical and Miscellaneous Revenue Act of 1988 (TAMRA)—U.S. legislation that:
- Limited the annual tax-free benefit for legal services offered by group plans to $70 per employee
- Revised Section 89 nondiscrimination rules
- Amended the penalties for noncompliance with COBRA
- Provided technical definitions and rules concerning required distributions, excess distributions, individual retirement account (IRAs) rollovers and vesting schedules for all pension and profit-sharing plans
- Increased the excise tax on excess pension assets upon termination of qualified plans.

technical safeguards—in the HIPAA privacy context, the technology, policies and procedures that protect electronic health information and control access to it. See also *administrative safeguards* and *physical safeguards*.

telecommuting—arrangement whereby an employee performs full- or part-time work at home, usually with a computer, while maintaining communication with the office.

telemedicine—use of video links, e-mail, telephone or another interactive telecommunications system to deliver medical services over a geographical distance.

temporary disability—illness or injury that renders a person incapable of performing one or more duties of a job for some limited period of time. Substantial variations exist in the length of time such a condition exists before it is considered a disability and when it is considered a permanent disability. Differences also exist in whether the job is a person's current occupation or any job. See also *partial disability, permanent disability* and *total disability*.

temporary disability insurance (TDI)—insurance in a limited number of states that covers off-the-job injury or sickness. Benefits, eligibility and financing vary by state. Also called unemployment compensation disability insurance or state disability insurance.

tenancy in common—when property is owned by two or more persons with the terms of a joint tenancy, but, in the event one of the owners dies, his or her share of the property would automatically go to the decedent's heirs and not the surviving owner. See also *joint tenancy*.

tender offer—offer to buy securities for cash, other securities or both.

term certain annuity—see *annuity certain*.

terminal illness (TI)—medical condition that, in the opinion of medical experts, cannot be cured and will lead to death. For purposes of viatical settlements, HIPAA defines *terminally ill* as being diagnosed by a certified physician to have a life expectancy of less than 24 months.

termination—end of an employee's duration with an employer or benefit plan. See also *plan termination*.

termination benefit—amount paid an employee who ceases to work for an employer. The amount of the benefit may be in the form of an annuity or lump-sum payment. See also *severance package* and *severance pay*.

termination indemnity—payment commitment to an employee when the employment is terminated by the employer. See also *parachute* and *termination benefit*.

termination insurance—see *plan termination insurance*.

termination rate—proportion of workers whose employment or participation has ended for reasons other than death or retirement.

term life insurance—financial protection if an insured dies within a specified period. The person or persons named by the insured as beneficiaries are provided the amount (face value) specified when the policy was written. If the insured survives the insurance contract term specified, the policy expires. Unlike cash value life insurance, term life insurance has no cash value buildup. The cost of a term life insurance policy (called the premium) increases with the age of the insured. The premium may also vary with factors such the health of the insured. If the term policy is guaranteed renewable, the policy can be renewed without a medical exam. With other types of term insurance, the insured must undergo a medical exam to again prove insurability. See also *cash value life insurance, convertible term insurance, decreasing term life, guaranteed renewable, level term life insurance* and *life insurance*.

tertiary beneficiary—third person or entity in line to receive benefits from a will, trust or insurance policy if the first and second beneficiaries are deceased. The tertiary beneficiary may also be referred to as a contingent beneficiary.

tertiary care—highly technical or specialized care provided for patients with severe, complicated or unusual medical problems. Neurosurgeons, burn centers and intensive care units are examples of tertiary care providers.

therapeutic alternative—see *therapeutic equivalent*.

therapeutic class—group of drugs that are similar in the diseases they are used to treat or the effect they can produce in the human body. Therapeutic classes are often used to categorize drugs on a formulary list. See also *formulary*.

therapeutic drug class review—evaluation of clinical evidence to identify preferred drugs within a therapeutic class. See also *therapeutic class*.

therapeutic equivalent—medication that contains an active ingredient that is different from that used in another drug but that provides similar treatment outcomes. Therapeutic equivalents, also referred to as therapeutic alternatives, are usually within the same pharmacologic class. See also *chemical equivalent*.

therapeutic index—used in assessing the safety of a drug, the ratio of the median lethal dose to the median effective dose. See also *median* and *narrow therapeutic index (NTI)*.

therapeutic interchange—dispensing a medication different from the one prescribed that is thought to produce the same patient outcome. The alternative drug is clinically similar to, but chemically different from, the medication initially prescribed. The terms therapeutic interchange and therapeutic substitution are used interchangeably. See also *therapeutic equivalent*.

therapeutic substitution—see *therapeutic interchange*.

therapy management—process of defining and implementing a regimen for the management of a particular illness, typically done in the context of an integrated health system.

third-country national (TCN)—citizens of one country who are employed by a company headquartered in a second country to work in a third country.

third opinion (3O)—for purposes of the Family and Medical Leave Act of 1993 (FMLA), an outside judgment when a second opinion differs from the opinion in the initial medical certification. The source of this opinion is designated or approved jointly by the employer and the employee and obtained at the expense of the employer.

third-party administrator (TPA)—organization external to a benefit plan that provides the plan with administrative services such as collecting premiums, handling claims and negotiating for stop-loss protection. A TPA may also be referred to as an administrative agent or contract administrator. See also *administrative services only (ASO)* and *self-funding*.

third-party payer—entity that pays for health care services provided to a patient. The payer may be an insurance company, government, self-insured employer or managed care organization.

thirteenth check—additional benefit payment made to plan retirees as a result of investment earnings in excess of those needed by the plan.

three hundred sixty degree review—performance appraisal system that reviews and measures employee performance from the perspective of the employee's supervisor, peers, subordinates, customers and others with whom the employee has interaction. Self-assessment is also part of the process.

three-legged stool—theory that a combination of individual savings, private pension payments and Social Security benefits will provide secure retirement income in the U.S.

three-tier copayment—system where a beneficiary typically pays one price for generic drugs, a higher price for preferred brand-name drugs and an even higher price for nonpreferred brand-name drugs.

thrift plan—see *thrift savings plan (TSP)*.

thrift savings plan (TSP)—also known as a thrift plan, a defined contribution retirement plan to which employees make deposits, usually on a pretax basis as a percentage of income. Employers are also permitted to make matching contributions on behalf of participating employees. See also *Federal Employee Retirement System (FERS)*.

tiered benefit plan—health plan with two or more levels (tiers) of benefits that allows subscribers to choose their level of coverage. Higher levels of benefits generally have higher premiums.

tiered provider network—system that classifies hospitals or physicians into groups (typically two or three groups) using cost per episode, service or stay or some combination of cost and quality metrics. Participants pay a higher price to use the higher cost or less efficient providers in the plan network. While not requiring the use of providers in the lower cost or more efficient tier, this type of plan design provides an incentive for participants to choose the most efficient and/or higher quality providers. Providers are also motivated to become more efficient and/or improve the quality of their care.

time horizon—amount of time available to meet objectives.

time-off bank—paid leave program that combines different types of leave (e.g., vacation, sick, personal, floating holidays, bereavement) into one pool of paid time off.

time off in lieu—see *comp time.*

time value of money—idea that a dollar now is worth more than a dollar in the future, even after adjusting for inflation. The logic is that a dollar now can be invested and earn interest or other appreciation until the time the dollar in the future would be received.

time-weighted rate of return—measure of the compound rate of growth in a portfolio used to compare different investment alternatives and managers. Unlike the dollar-weighted rate of return, this approach eliminates distortions created by cash inflows and outflows. The method assumes a single investment at the beginning of a period and measures the growth or loss of market value to the end of that period. The portfolio is evaluated each time there is a cash transaction (i.e., new purchases and sales, dividend and income payments, deposits or withdrawals). The performances of periods between cash flows are linked together to reflect a return for the whole period. See also *dollar-weighted rate of return.*

timing risk—chance that an investor will purchase securities when prices hit their peak. There is also the chance an investor will need to sell investments for a loss during a market setback to fund a planned or unplanned expense.

tin parachute—see *parachute.*

title insurance—insurance that protects the owner of real estate from financial loss resulting from property rights issues not discovered by a title search.

Title VII of the Civil Rights Act of 1964—U.S. legislation and amendments that prohibit discrimination in the employer-employee relationship on the basis of race, color, sex/gender (including pregnancy and sexual harassment), national origin, age, religion, creed, disability and Vietnam War veteran status. The law applies to employers with 15 or more employees that are engaged in interstate commerce, as well as employment agencies and unions. Enforced by the Equal Employment Opportunity Commission, Title VII also applies to state and local governments as well as the federal government. See also *discrimination, disparate impact* and *Pregnancy Discrimination Act of 1978 (PDA).*

Title IX of the Education Amendments of 1972—U.S. legislation that prohibits discrimination on the basis of gender in educational programs, employment and activities that receive federal assistance.

top-down manager—investor who takes a broad look at the economy and tries to select industries and then stocks that tend to benefit from major trends. See also *bottom-up manager.*

top-hat plan—see *supplemental executive retirement plan (SERP).*

top-heavy plan—qualified plan in which the share of benefits allocable to key employees is more than 60%. When a plan is deemed top-heavy, it may be subject to special accelerated vesting provisions and minimum contribution rates for non-key employees. See also *1% owner, 5% owner* and *key employee.*

top-heavy test—test performed each year on a qualified retirement plan to determine whether the total account value of key employees exceeds 60% of the total account value of all employees in the plan. See also *top-heavy plan.*

Toronto Stock Exchange (TSX)—largest stock exchange in Canada. Formerly the TSE, the TSX is home to a large number of natural resources companies.

tort—any wrongful act or omission (other than a breach of contract) for which the law permits compensation for damages to the person, property or reputation of another. A tort is commonly referred to as a private wrong, as opposed to a public wrong, which is labeled a crime. A very common tort is negligent operation of a motor vehicle that results in property damage or personal injury from an automobile accident.

total compensation—see *compensation.*

total compensation statement—see *annual benefits statement.*

total debt-to-equity ratio—see *debt-to-equity ratio.*

total disability—sometimes referred to as full disability, an illness or injury that renders a person incapable of performing most duties of a job. Substantial variations exist in definitions for this term. Some definitions specify a person is unable to perform his or her current occupation, while others state a disability occurs only if the person is unable to perform any job. In some cases, total disability is considered immediate subsequent to the loss of sight or limbs. See also *partial disability, permanent disability* and *temporary disability.*

totalization agreement—arrangements intended to protect the social security benefits of employees who move between countries and to ensure single country social security coverage for employees on assignment in other countries.

total quality management (TQM)—comprehensive management process designed to control quality and improve all aspects of an organization's activities using statistical techniques, employee teamwork, employee training, joint problem solving and open communication on a continuous basis.

total return—see *return*.

total reward system—all of the tools used by an employer to attract, motivate and retain employees. These rewards include everything an employee may perceive to be of value as a result of the employment relationship, such as financial compensation, benefits, opportunities for social interaction, security, recognition, status, work variety, workload, autonomy, feedback, safe working conditions, personal and professional development and the likelihood of advancement.

Trade Act of 2002—also called the U.S. Trade Promotion Authority Act, federal legislation that granted the president of the United States the authority to negotiate trade deals with other countries and to force Congress to vote only yes or no on the agreement, without amendment or filibuster. This authority is sometimes called fast-track authority, since it is thought to streamline the approval of trade agreements.

Trade Adjustment Assistance (TAA) program—federal program established under the Trade Act of 1974 that provides aid to workers who lose their jobs or whose hours of work and wages are reduced as a result of increased imports. The TAA program offers a variety of benefits and reemployment services to help unemployed workers prepare for and obtain suitable employment. Workers may be eligible for training, job search and relocation allowances, income support and other services.

Trade Adjustment Assistance Reform Act of 2002—U.S. legislation that amended and added provisions to the Trade Adjustment Assistance (TAA) program. Among the changes, the act:
- Expanded eligibility to more worker groups
- Increased benefits
- Established tax credits for health insurance coverage assistance
- Increased timeliness for benefit receipt, training and rapid-response assistance.

See also *Trade Adjustment Assistance (TAA) program*.

trading curb—temporary restriction on program buying and selling in a particular security or market, usually to reduce dramatic price movements. A trading curb may be either a halt on all trading or a restriction that certain sales can be executed only when the trading price is higher than the price on the previous transaction. See also *circuit breaker* and *trading halt*.

trading halt—temporary suspension in the trading of a particular security on one or more exchanges, usually in anticipation of a news announcement, to give all investors an equal opportunity for evaluation before making a decision to trade. Trading halts are also used to correct an order imbalance and for regulatory purposes. See also *trading curb*.

traditional broker—person or business that provides trading advice and other guidance in selecting securities that best fit an investor's needs, in addition to making the actual buy and sell transactions. Traditional brokers collect information from many sources and frequently share it with clients in an effort to help them make the best choices. Because they provide more assistance, traditional brokers almost always charge higher fees than discount brokers, who simply make transactions for investors.

traditional IRA—individual retirement account (IRA) (or annuity) set up by an individual. Persons up to the age of 70½ may set up and make contributions to a traditional IRA. The amount that can be contributed per year is set by the IRS. Whether contributions can be made on a pretax basis depends on the accountholder's income, tax filing status, coverage by a retirement plan at work and whether Social Security benefits are being received. An owner must begin making minimum distributions in the year following the year he or she reaches the age of 70½. Distributions are taxed as ordinary income but, if some nondeductible contributions were made, not all distributions are taxable. A 10% penalty (in addition to regular taxes) applies to any money withdrawn before the owner reaches the age of 59½. An exception is if the owner becomes disabled. Exceptions are also made if withdrawals are used to pay for medical insurance during unemployment, qualified higher education expenses or first-home expenses. Upon the death of an owner, funds in a traditional IRA can be inherited by a spouse or other designated beneficiary. See also *deemed IRA, individual retirement account (IRA), Roth IRA, simplified employee pension (SEP) plan* and *SIMPLE IRA*.

training—systematic process for achieving proficiency in a specialized area. Whereas education may focus on broad principles and the acquisition of knowledge, training focuses on action, skills and the direct application of principles learned.

training and development program—endeavor that has experts working with learners to transfer knowledge and skills for performing a job, or to improve job performance.

training and education fund—multiemployer trust fund established to support apprenticeship programs and/or instructional opportunities for plan participants.

tranche—specific class of debt securities within a larger pool of debt securities. A tranche is often used to describe a group of bonds offering a different degree of risk to an investor. For example, a collateralized mortgage obligation may have tranches with one-, two-, five- and 20-year maturities. A tranche can also refer to segments that are offered domestically and internationally. See also *collateralized mortgage obligation (CMO)* and *real estate mortgage investment conduit (REMIC)*.

transaction
—all the activity of an investment portfolio: contributions and disbursements, the purchase and sale of securities, transfers, income receipts from dividends and bond interest, and payment of any administrative expenses.
—for the purposes of HIPAA, an activity involving the electronic transfer of health care information for a specific reason. HIPAA requires that if a provider engages in a transaction, it must comply with the electronic data interchange standards for that transaction.

transexual—medical term for persons whose gender identity and sex do not align. Such persons often seek medical treatment to bring their body and gender identity into alignment. See also *gender identity* and *transgender (TG)*.

transitioning—process by which a person goes from male to female or female to male. The process may include changes in dress, name and gender identity, as well as hormonal and surgical therapy. See also *gender identity*.

transgender (TG)—sometimes called gender different, persons whose gender identity or gender expression is different from that typically associated with the sex they were assigned at birth. A transgender person may be a transsexual, crossdresser or one who is otherwise gender nonconforming. See also *gender expression* and *gender identity*.

transitional care—actions of health care providers designed to ensure the coordination and continuity of care before a patient returns home following treatment for an acute illness or surgery.

transition management—systematic, controlled process utilizing multiple sources of liquidity to minimize the cost and risk associated with investment changes. The transitions may be as simple as moving funds from one bank account to another, or more complex such as a multicountry, multicurrency transition that spans asset classes and time zones.

transparency—see *price transparency*.

transportation benefits—bus tokens, van pools, parking reimbursement and other benefits provided by employers to reduce the cost to employees of commuting to work.

trauma
—severe, life-threatening physical injury that requires emergency care and possibly extensive lifesaving measures.
—emotional wound or shock often having long-lasting effects.

Treasury bill—short-term government-backed bond that is offered with a maturity of a few days to one year. Also known as T-bills, common maturities for these bonds are one month, three months and six months.
—In the U.S., these debt securities are sold in denominations of $1,000 and purchased at a discount determined by auction. A Treasury bill grows to full face value by maturity. It can be held until it matures or sold at auction prior to maturity. Rather than paying fixed interest payments as with conventional bonds, the appreciation of U.S. Treasury bills provides the return to the holder. The yield is exempt from state and local taxes. See also *savings bond, tax anticipation bill (TAB), Treasury bond, Treasury Inflation-Protected Security (TIPS)* and *Treasury note*.
—Treasury bills issued by the Government of Canada are available in multiples of $1,000. They must be purchased, transferred or sold—directly or indirectly—through a participant of the Debt Clearing Service. Periodically, Canada also issues cash management bills (CMBs) with maturities of less than three months; they may have a maturity as short as one day. CMB auctions take place on any business day.

Treasury bond
—In the U.S., a long-term government-backed debt security issued with a maturity of 30 years that pays a fixed rate of interest every six months. A U.S. Treasury bond is commonly referred to as T-bond. The purchase price is determined at auction, which means the price may be greater than, less than or equal to its face value. When a U.S. Treasury bond matures, the holder is paid its face value. The yield is exempt from state and local taxes. See also *savings bond, Treasury bill, Treasury Inflation-Protected Security (TIPS)* and *Treasury note*.
—Canada has two types of Treasury bond, see *real return bond (RBB)* and *fixed-coupon marketable bond*.

Treasury Inflation-Protected Security (TIPS)—marketable U.S. government-backed debt security with a maturity of five, ten or 20 years that offers protection against inflation. The principal on a TIPS is automatically adjusted when there is a change in the Consumer Price Index (CPI). Because the rate is applied to the adjusted principal, however, interest payments can vary from one period to the next. Inflation (an increase in the CPI) increases the principal and thus the amount of interest paid. Deflation (a decline in the CPI) has the opposite effect. Taxes must be paid yearly on the increased value of a TIPS. At maturity, the holder receives the adjusted principal or the original principal, whichever is greater. See also *real return bond (RRB), savings bond, Treasury bill, Treasury bond* and *Treasury note*.

Treasury note—intermediate-term U.S. government-backed bond (also called a T-note) that matures in two to ten years and pays a fixed rate of interest twice a year. To purchase a U.S. Treasury note, an investor can submit a competitive or noncompetitive bid. With a competitive bid, the buyer specifies the desired yield; however, this does not mean the bid will be accepted. With a noncompetitive bid, the buyer accepts whatever yield is determined at auction. The purchase price may be greater than, less than or equal to the face value of the note. When a Treasury note matures, the holder is paid face value. There is a large secondary market for the purchase and sale of Treasury notes. The yield is exempt from state and local taxes. See also *savings bond, Treasury bill, Treasury bond* and *Treasury Inflation-Protected Security (TIPS)*.
—for Canada, see *Canada Note*.

Treasury regulation—rules promulgated by the U.S. Department of the Treasury. Because the IRS is part of the Treasury Department, the IRC is technically a Treasury regulation.

treasury stock—ownership share in a company that has been issued, then bought back, by the issuing corporation. While held by the corporation, treasury stock is nonvoting and no dividends are paid.

treatment episode—period of care occurring between admission and discharge from a health care facility (e.g., hospital, outpatient clinic). If the care is on an outpatient basis, a treatment episode begins with the first procedure and ends with the last procedure given for a diagnosis.

treatment guideline or protocol—see *practice guideline*.

trend rate—see *health care cost trend rate*.

Treynor ratio—also known as the reward-to-volatility ratio, a measure of returns earned in excess of that which could have been earned on a riskless investment per unit of market risk. The ratio equals the average return of the portfolio minus the average return of the risk-free rate, which is then divided by the portfolio's beta. Similar to the Sharpe ratio, the difference is that the Treynor ratio uses beta as the measurement of volatility. See also *information ratio, Jensen's alpha, risk-adjusted return measure* and *Sharpe ratio*.

TRICARE—health care program for active duty service members, National Guard and Reserve members, retired service members, their dependents, survivors and certain former spouses. TRICARE brings together the health care resources of the uniformed services and supplements them with networks of civilian health care professionals, institutions, pharmacies and suppliers. TRICARE offers several health plan options and several additional special programs. This managed care system replaced the Civilian Health and Medical Program of the Uniformed Services (CHAMPUS).

trust—see *trust fund*.

trust agreement—legal document that spells out the methods of receipt, investment and disbursement of assets in a benefit plan trust fund. The agreement contains provisions concerning the investment powers of trustees; irrevocability and nondiversion of trust assets; payment of legal, trustee and other fees relative to the plan; liability of the trustees; periodic reports to be made by the trustees; maintenance of records and accounts; conditions for removal, resignation or replacement of trustees; benefit payments under the plan; and the rights and duties of the trustees in case of amendment or termination of the plan. In Canada, a trust agreement is known as a trust deed. See also *trust fund*.

trust deed—see *deed of trust* and *trust agreement*.

trustee—person, bank or trust company that has responsibility over the receipt, disbursement and investment of property or funds for the benefit of another party. When this responsibility is not exercised by a bank or trust company, it is usually exercised by a board of trustees, with each trustee given one vote.

trusteed pension plan—employee retirement plan in which an employer's contributions are placed in a trust for investment, as distinguished from a plan in which the benefits are secured by life insurance. Plan sponsors are responsible for making sufficient contributions to maintain plan solvency. Benefits are not insured, except to the extent annuities are purchased. See also *Taft-Hartley plan*.

trust fund—assets managed by an individual, a group of individuals or an organization for the benefit of another party or parties. Trusts are established for a wide range of purposes. For example, a trust may be set up for a child and managed by an adult until the child reaches a specified age. In relation to benefits, trusts are set up to provide pension, health and welfare benefits to employees and retirees. A trust agreement in combination with state and federal laws may restrict what trustees may do with assets. In the case of employee benefit plans in the U.S., ERISA sets minimum standards for most voluntarily established plans in private industry. See also *fiduciary, irrevocable trust, prudent person rule* and *revocable trust.*

Trust Indenture Act of 1939—U.S. legislation that requires the creation of a formal agreement between an issuer and an investor when bonds, debentures and notes are offered for sale.

trustor—person who establishes a trust for the benefit of another. Trustor is used interchangeably with creator, grantor and settlor.

tuition reimbursement plan—see *educational assistance plan.*

turnover rate
—ratio of workers who have to be replaced by an employer in a given time period to the average number of workers.
—for benefit plans, the proportion of persons leaving or dropping out of a plan.
—in investment circles, the frequency with which securities within a portfolio are exchanged for other securities.

two-tier copayment—system where a beneficiary pays one price for generic drugs and a higher price for brand-name drugs.

two-tier pay plan—dual compensation structure that attempts to control labor costs by keeping the current structure for existing employees but starting new employees under a second, lower-level pay structure.

U

ultrasound—diagnostic technique that uses high-frequency sound waves to provide structural information on parts of the human anatomy that cannot be obtained by traditional x-ray and radioisotopic methods. Ultrasound permits visualization of both the surface and internal structures of many body organs; it is often used for fetal monitoring.

unallocated funding instrument—see *funding instrument.*

unapproved drug—see *off-label drug.*

unbundling—selling and pricing of service components separately, rather than as a package with a single price. In benefit plan administration, a plan sponsor may elect to use different service providers for various aspects of administration. Under Part B of Medicare, billing for nonphysician services provided to hospital inpatients by a source other than the hospital is labeled "unbundling." See also *bundled payment.*

uncompensated care—measure of the costs of health care services provided but not paid for by the patient or health plan. Health care providers, along with governments, incur some of these costs.

unconditional vesting—when there is no limitation in a contributory pension plan to an employee's right to withdraw vested benefits. See also *conditional vesting* and *vesting.*

underdistribution—see *excess accumulation.*

underfunded benefit plan—employee benefit plan in which the sponsor's past contributions are insufficient to cover current and future liabilities.

underinsured—not having sufficient insurance to cover a loss or damage.

undertreatment—failure to recommend or provide timely health care consistent with diagnosis and treatment. See also *overtreatment.*

underuse—failure to take advantage of or provide a health care service when it would have produced a favorable outcome for a patient. Patients might underuse a free flu shot program. From the provider perspective, a physician might not recommend preventive services or proven therapies for a diagnosis.

underwater—condition when the strike price of a call option is higher than the market price of the underlying stock. The condition also exists when the strike price for a put option is lower than the market price of the underlying stock. See also *option agreement, stock option* and *exercise price.*

underwriter
—individual who has the responsibility for making decisions regarding the acceptability of a particular insurance contract and in determining the amount, price and conditions under which the contract is acceptable.
—with respect to investments, a broker or bank that arranges the sale of new issues of securities on behalf of a client. See also *investment bank.*

underwriting—process used by a financial services provider (e.g., bank, insurance company, investment house) to assess the risk associated with providing a product (e.g., insurance, mortgage, credit). If the risk is acceptable, the underwriting process includes determining what level of risk will be acceptable and the cost of the risk (e.g., insurance rate, interest rate). See also *underwriter.*

undocumented alien/resident—see *illegal alien.*

unemployed person
—as defined by the U.S. government, a civilian aged 16 or over who, during a given week, had no hours of employment. The person must (1) have been available for work and sought a job during the prior four weeks or (2) have been waiting to be called back to work or to a new position within 30 days.
—in Canada, persons aged 15 and over who, during a week, met one of these criteria:
- Were on temporary layoff with an expectation of recall and were available for work
- Were without work, had looked for work in the past four weeks and were available for work
- Had a new job to start within four weeks and were available for work.

unemployment compensation (UC)—payments made by government to persons who have become unemployed through no fault of their own.
—The unemployment compensation program in the United States was created by the Social Security Act of 1935 and is administered through the states. Eligibility usually requires that:
- The worker has previously worked in employment that is covered by the law
- The unemployment is involuntary
- The worker is willing and able to take an employment offer
- An initial waiting period has elapsed before compensation begins.

In almost every state, programs are entirely employer-financed. See also *Federal Unemployment Tax Act (FUTA)* and *supplemental unemployment benefit (SUB).*
—Canada's Employment Insurance (EI) program provides temporary income support to those who are between jobs. The program is financed by employees and employers. Claimants are not entitled for benefits if they:
- Were suspended from their employment because of misconduct
- Have voluntarily taken employment leave without just cause authorized by their employer with an agreed upon date of return.

Unemployment Compensation Amendments of 1992—U.S. legislation that directs plan administrators of qualified plans and payers of Section 403(b) annuities to:
- Provide a direct rollover option into an individual retirement account (IRA) or other qualified plan
- Withhold 20% of federal income tax on eligible rollover distributions (ERDs) not directly rolled over into an eligible retirement plan
- Give written notice to recipients before ERDs are made.

unemployment compensation disability insurance—see *temporary disability insurance (TDI).*

unfunded accrued pension cost—pension costs accrued in excess of plan assets. See also *prepaid pension cost.*

unfunded accumulated benefit obligation—excess accumulated benefit obligation over plan assets. See also *accumulated benefit obligation (ABO).*

unfunded actuarial accrued liability (UAAL)—actuarial accrued liability that exceeds the actuarial value of fund assets. If the value is negative, it is referred to as a negative unfunded actuarial accrued liability, or a funding excess. Also referred to as unfunded actuarial liability.

unfunded actuarial liability—see *unfunded actuarial accrued liability (UAAL)*.

unfunded benefit plan—plan that is not insured or funded through a trust; benefits are paid for by the plan sponsor as needed. See also *pay-as-you-go (PAYG) plan*.

unfunded deferred compensation agreement—contract between an employer and employee to pay certain sums of money at any later date, usually upon retirement, without payment by the employer into a funding vehicle.

unfunded past service cost—see *unfunded actuarial accrued liability (UAAL)*.

unfunded plan—retirement plan funded by an employer out of current income. See also *pay-as-you-go (PAYG) plan*.

unfunded projected benefit obligation—projected benefit obligations that exceed plan assets. See also *projected benefit* and *projected benefit obligation (PBO)*.

unfunded vested benefits—difference between assets and the value of benefits that are vested.

unified benefits or program—see *carve-in*.

Uniformed Services Employment and Reemployment Rights Act of 1994 (USERRA)—U.S. law that provides protection of jobs and benefits for employees who take a leave of absence for military service. Under USERRA, it is unlawful for an employer to deny initial employment, reemployment, promotion or any benefit of employment to a person who is obligated to perform in a uniformed service. If a person is called to duty, an employer does not have a right of refusal for the military leave, except in extreme cases. Employees are not responsible for finding a replacement. USERRA also forbids an employer from requiring an employee to use his or her vacation or similar leave during a period of military service. In some cases, employees may ask to use vacation time and/or personal days for military duty; in such a case, the time off would be paid at the regular base pay rate. Individuals re-employed after military service are entitled to the seniority and other rights and benefits they would have had by remaining continuously employed.

Uniform Gifts to Minors Act (UGMA)—legislation in some states that makes it possible for a person to give money or securities to a child without having to set up a trust account. The assets are the legal property of the child and are taxed at the child's tax rate. Like a trust, the donor must appoint a custodian (trustee) to look after the account, and the donor may be the custodian. Should a donor acting as the custodian die before the custodial property is transferred to the minor, the entire custodial property is included in the donor's taxable estate. Access to the gift must be given to the minor when he or she reaches the age of majority, generally either 18 or 21 (sometimes even 25), depending on the state. Putting money into an UGMA account can harm the chances for student financial aid, since financial aid officers weigh children's assets much more heavily than parents' assets. See also *gift tax, kiddie tax* and *Uniform Transfers to Minors Act (UTMA)*.

Uniform Prudent Investors Act (UPIA)—legislation prepared in 1992 by the American Law Institute and now adopted in most states that removes many of the common law restrictions placed on trust fiduciaries:
- The standard of prudence is applied to any investment as part of the total portfolio, rather than to individual investments.
- The term *portfolio* embraces all of a trust's assets.
- The trade-off in all investing between risk and return is identified as the fiduciary's central consideration.
- Restrictions on types of investments have been abrogated; the trustee can invest in anything that plays an appropriate role in achieving the risk/return objectives of the trust and that meets the other requirements of prudent investing.
- The long familiar requirement that fiduciaries diversify investments has been integrated into the definition of prudent investing.

A much-criticized rule forbidding a trustee from delegating investment and management functions has been reversed. Delegation is now permitted, subject to safeguards.

Uniform Transfers to Minors Act (UTMA)—statute in a majority of states that supersedes the Uniform Gifts to Minors Act (UGMA) but is still referenced as UGMA. The replacement statute allows items other than cash or securities to be considered gifts, such as real estate, art, patents and royalties. See also *gift tax, kiddie tax* and *Uniform Gifts to Minors Act (UGMA)*.

unilateral plan—benefit plan that does not result from collective bargaining. See also *collectively bargained plan*.

uninsured class—see *declined risk class.*

union shop—see *closed shop.*

union-sponsored plan—benefit program developed by a union. The union may contract for the benefits or operate the program directly. Benefits are usually paid out of a fund, which receives its income from (1) employer contributions, (2) union member contributions or (3) a combination of both.

unique user identification—assignment of a name and number/password that identifies and tracks user identity.

unit benefit formula—method of determining benefit payments from a defined benefit (DB) pension plan that multiplies an employee's years of credited service by (1) a percentage of the employee's final or highest average pay, (2) a percentage of career average pay or (3) some dollar amount. The percentage may increase as the number of years of service increases. For example, 1% might be used for years of service up to 15 years, and 1.5% for 16 years through 30 years. Today, most defined benefit plans use some form of unit benefit formula. These plans often have a limit on the years of service taken into account. If the employee's service is less than the required minimum, benefits are prorated. See also *flat benefit plan.*

universal health coverage—as defined by the World Health Organization (WHO), a system ensuring all people can use the promotive, preventive, curative, rehabilitative and palliative health services they need and that the services are of sufficient quality to be effective, while also ensuring the use of these services does not expose the user to financial hardship.

universal health care—see *universal health coverage.*

universal life insurance—also known as adjustable life insurance, a type of whole life insurance that pays a death benefit and accumulated cash value. After an initial payment, the insured is allowed to vary the death benefit, the premium payment and the protection periods to suit changing family needs. To increase the death benefit, an insurance company usually requires the policyholder to furnish satisfactory evidence of continued good health. See also *cash value life insurance, group universal life plan (GULP), index-universal life insurance, variable universal life insurance (VULI)* and *whole life insurance.*

universe bond index—collection of bonds providing a broad measure of a fixed income market in Canada.

unlimited formulary—list of preferred drugs that, unlike a limited formulary, does not restrict the number of drugs permitted in each therapeutic class. See also *closed formulary, drug formulary, incentive formulary, limited formulary, open formulary, partially closed formulary* and *therapeutic class.*

unlisted securities—investment vehicles not listed on a stock exchange, such as those traded over the counter. See also *over the counter (OTC) market* and *security.*

unmodified opinion—conclusion by an independent auditor that a company's or benefit plan's financial statements are fairly presented and in accordance with Generally Accepted Accounting Principles (GAAP). See also *adverse opinion, disclaimer of opinion, Generally Accepted Accounting Principles (GAAP), qualified opinion* and *unqualified opinion.*

unqualified opinion—an unmodified opinion that has an emphasis of matter paragraph attached. See also *unmodified opinion* and *emphasis of matter.*

unrealized profit or loss—see *paper profit or loss.*

unsecured debt—loan not secured by an underlying asset or collateral. Government bonds and most corporate bonds are in this category. Unsecured loans to individuals generally carry a higher interest rate than secured debt, due to the higher risk incurred by the lender.

unsystematic risk—see *nonmarket risk.*

upcoding—also referred to as overcoding, a deceptive practice of health care providers in which service codes reported are for a higher cost or more complex service than what was actually performed. See also *downcoding.*

urgent care—care for an illness or injury serious enough that a reasonable person would seek care right away, but not severe enough to require emergency room care.

urgent care center—ambulatory care facility that provides extended or 24-hour service for minor health issues that are not serious enough to require emergency room treatment.

U.S. Department of Education (ED)—agency that focuses on and promotes key educational issues. ED establishes policies on federal financial aid for education, distributes financial aid funds, collects data and disseminates research on schools, and is responsible for ensuring equal access to education.

U.S. Department of Health and Human Services (HHS)—primary agency responsible for protecting the health of the nation's citizens and providing essential human services, especially for those who are least able to help themselves. Organizations within HHS include the Centers for Medicare and Medicaid Services, Administration on Aging, National Institutes of Health, Centers for Disease Control and Prevention, and the Food and Drug Administration, among others.

U.S. Department of Labor (DOL)—agency that oversees employment and labor issues including compensation, worker conditions and employee benefits. The nontax (regulatory and administrative) provisions of ERISA are administered by DOL.

U.S. Department of Veterans Affairs (VA)—agency that provides services to veterans and their families. The agency serves as the principal advocate for ensuring the receipt of medical care, benefits and social support. The VA is also charged with helping veterans make a smooth transition from active military service to civilian life.

use-it-or-lose-it rule—flexible spending arrangement requirement that participants must spend their total annual election amount by the end of the plan year; otherwise, the remaining funds become employer assets.

usual and customary (U&C) fee or price—dollar amount that a health care provider charges when a consumer does not have coverage through insurance or another third-party payer. See also *usual, customary and reasonable (UCR) fee.*

usual, customary and reasonable (UCR) fee—base amount that third-party payers generally use to determine how much they will be paid for health care services provided under a benefit plan or insurance policy. The amount typically paid to the provider is a percentage (e.g., 70%, 80%, 90%) of what is determined to be the UCR fee. The plan participant may be responsible for the rest, unless the provider is willing to accept a reduced payment. The method used to determine a UCR fee varies by insurer, but usually it is established by using the data collected or purchased by the payer concerning what is usual and customary. "Usual" is what the provider most frequently charges, while "customary" is a range of charges for a similar good or service by similar providers within a geographical area. "Reasonable" is the charge that, in the opinion of a review committee, is usual and customary considering the situation and any special circumstances. See also *reasonable and customary (R&C) charge.*

usury—practice of lending money at an exorbitant interest rate. Usury is illegal in some locales.

utilization—extent to which a given group uses a particular service in a specific period. Usually expressed as the number of services used per year per 100 or 1,000 eligible persons. Utilization rates are established to help in comprehensive health planning, budget review and cost containment.

utilization management (UM)—wide range of techniques used to control costs and eliminate both the overuse and underuse of health care services. UM seeks to ensure the efficiency and appropriateness of services provided to patients by integrating case management and utilization review. Care is considered prospectively, concurrently and retrospectively. See also *case management, centers of excellence, certified length of stay, discharge planning, drug utilization management (DUM), large case management, nurse advice line, precertification, prenatal care, prospective review* and *utilization review (UR).*

utilization review (UR)—evaluation of the necessity, appropriateness and efficiency of medical goods, procedures and facilities. Before the expansion of managed care, utilization reviews tended to be done retrospectively. Today, they may be done before, during or after care is provided. The focus tends to be on the physician's diagnosis, treatment and billing amount. A utilization review can be of value to an employer sponsoring a health care plan, a plan itself, an insurer and health care providers. UR is one element of utilization management (UM). See also *concurrent review, drug utilization review (DUR), precertification, prospective review, utilization management (UM)* and *utilization review organization (URO).*

utilization review organization (URO)—independent entity, insurance company or in-house group providing utilization review (UR) services. See also *utilization review (UR).*

V

vacation—time off from work for which employees typically are paid. The amount of time granted is typically based on years of service. While private employers are not required by law to provide vacation leave or benefits to employees on leave, most do. Also referred to as *annual leave.*

vacation pay plan—benefit plan, typically established through collective bargaining, that provides paid employee time off. The employer generally makes a contribution to a trust that pays the benefits. Vacation pay plans are covered by ERISA.

vacation trading—program that allows employees to buy or sell vacation time. Unused vacation days can be cashed out or sold back to the plan. Employees who wish to take more vacation time may opt to purchase extra vacation days. A vacation trading program may be one of the options in a flexible benefit plan. Under such an arrangement, employees may use pretax contributions to purchase extra leave. When a trading plan is part of a cafeteria plan, elective days must be used within the plan year when the election was made to comply with the requirement that cafeteria plans may not defer income. In applying this rule, it is assumed regular vacation days are taken before elective days. Also known as vacation buy-sell.

Valdez principles—see *CERES Principles*.

valuation—determination of the worth of an investment or investment portfolio on a given date. See also *actuarial valuation*.

valuation assets (AVA)—see *actuarial value of assets (AVA)*.

valuation reserves—funds set aside in anticipation of the decreased value of an asset (i.e., depreciation or depletion reserves).

value added—products or services provided without charge to a recipient for the purpose of promoting goodwill or enhancing the overall worth of a contract.

value-added real estate—broad category of real property that includes core real estate (i.e., existing office, retail, residential, industrial and hotel properties) plus some additions such as self-storage facilities. Redevelopment, releasing or repositioning of the properties is required to maximize the investment return relative to the risk. Value-added real estate has moderate levels of price volatility with both income and appreciation components into overall expected return. See also *core real estate, opportunistic real estate* and *real property*.

value-based benefit design—planning and administration of health benefits based on the specific needs of an organization and the individuals who are part of the organization, as well as the potential value the benefits offer. The total value and total return (e.g., improved clinical outcomes, improved productivity and lower total health-related costs) are weighed against the cost of a specific design element (e.g., lowering copays for a specific drug class).

value-based health care (VBHC)—holistic, system-level approach to creating a culture of health for an organization and its employee population across the health care continuum. VBHC strives to remove barriers and align both financial and nonfinancial incentives and rewards for living healthy and productive lifestyles and using high-value prevention, health enhancement and health care services. VBHC extends beyond health care benefits to include the design, implementation and continuous evaluation of high-value approaches for improving employee health, well-being and productivity while reducing the need for high-cost medical services.

value-based health management (VBHM)—approach to health care design that tailors cost-sharing to the evidence-based value of specific services for targeted groups of patients. VBHM helps control an organization's health care costs by:
- Removing barriers to care such as high out-of-pocket costs (e.g., copays, coinsurance) and coverage limits/exclusions that keep people from getting the care they need. Incentives such as waiving or reducing out-of-pocket costs may be used to encourage people to get the treatment they need and stay with it.
- Creating care provider teams to support patients through wellness programs, medical decision making and care management.
- Focusing on prevention through programs such as smoking-cessation, weight management, nutrition classes, vaccination programs and screenings to help prevent/detect chronic health problems.

value-based insurance design—see *value-based benefit design*.

value-based purchasing—buying practices aimed at improving the value of health care services, where value is a function of both quality and cost. Value may be calculated as quality divided by cost. Value-based purchasing brings together information on the quality of health care, including patient outcomes and health status, with data on the dollar outlays going toward health. It focuses on reducing inappropriate care and rewarding the best-performing providers.

value manager—investment manager who looks for securities that are selling for less than what the manager believes they are worth; for example, stocks with low price/earnings (P/E) ratios. Value managers take a more conservative approach to investing than growth managers. See also *growth manager* and *price/earnings (P/E) ratio*.

value stock—equity in a company that is trading at a lower price than that of peers based on its fundamentals (e.g., dividends, earnings and sales). See also *deep value stock* and *arbitrage fund*.

variability—measure of the fluctuations in rates of return. These measurements are used frequently as proxies for risk management.

variable annuity—also known as a participating annuity, an insurance contract in which an insurance company promises payments to a holder (the annuitant). The amount of the payments depends on the performance of the investments placed in the fund associated with the annuity. Variable annuities offer greater potential rewards and greater risk than fixed annuities. In the U.S., most variable annuities are structured to offer investors different fund alternatives. The annuities are regulated by state insurance departments and the SEC. See also *annuity, fixed annuity* and *hybrid annuity.*

variable benefit—an option, available to pension plans with a money purchase component, that allows retired members to receive income directly from the plan. The income, payable from a variable benefit account, mirrors payments from a *Life Income Fund (LIF).*

variable benefit plan—defined benefit retirement plan in which payments may change given economic circumstances specified by the plan. To protect the purchasing power of the recipients, plan benefit may be tied an index, typically the Consumer Price Index (CPI). In other cases, the change is connected to the plan's investment portfolio at the time of retirement or payment of actual benefits. With an equity annuity plan, the benefit may be influenced in part by the investment experience of the stocks used to fund the plan. See also *flat benefit plan* and *unit benefit formula.*

variable compensation—additional payment for work, such as profit sharing, bonuses and stock options, that is typically based on the performance of the employee, the employee's team or the organization as a whole. Also referred to as *variable incentive pay.*

variable cost—see *variable expense.*

variable expense—cost (e.g., utilities, food, clothing) that changes from period to period. When applied to business, variable expenses (also referred to as variable costs) fluctuate with changes in production, sales and other business activities. Variable costs are the sum of the marginal costs. See also *fixed expense* and *marginal cost.*

variable hour employee—see "Employer shared responsibility" in the *Appendix A: Affordable Care Act of 2010 (ACA).*

variable incentive pay—see *variable compensation.*

variable interest rate—see *adjustable interest rate.*

variable life insurance—insurance with a fixed premium and a minimum guaranteed death benefit. Above the promised minimum, benefits reflect the value of assets behind the contract at the time benefits are paid. Sometimes referred to as investment-sensitive or nonguaranteed life insurance. See also *cash value life insurance, life insurance* and *variable universal life insurance (VULI).*

variable pay—see *variable compensation.*

variable premium—see *flexible premium.*

variable rate mortgage (VRM)—see *adjustable rate mortgage (ARM).*

variable universal life insurance (VULI)—also called flexible life, insurance with a guaranteed death benefit that combines the flexible premium features of universal life with the investment component of variable life. See also *universal life insurance* and *variable life insurance.*

variance—measure of variability based on squared deviations of individual observations from the mean value of the distribution. Its square root is the standard deviation. See also *standard deviation.*

vendor—supplier of goods or services.

venture capital—money provided by investors to start-up firms and small businesses with perceived long-term growth potential. Venture capital generally has higher risks for the investor, but it also has the potential for above-average returns.

Verified Internet Pharmacy Practice Sites (VIPPS)—program developed by the National Association of Boards of Pharmacy (NABP) that certifies online pharmacies that comply with state licensing and inspection requirements, as well as criteria such as patient privacy, authentication and the security of prescription orders, quality assurance and meaningful consultation.

vertical integration—grouping together of different yet related organizations in order to offer a continuum of services. For example, a health maintenance organization may acquire a hospital to handle a portion of its inpatient care, or a hospital may link up with a physician network to better operate as a full-service managed care organization.

vested benefit obligation (VBO)—present value of retirement benefits for which an employer or plan sponsor has liability. Calculation of the VBO takes into consideration liability for benefits that are nonforfeitable (vested). Also referred to as vested liabilities.

vested benefits—accrued benefits of a participant that have become nonforfeitable under the schedule adopted by a pension plan.

vested liabilities—see *vested benefit obligation (VBO)*.

vesting
—process by which a participant obtains nonforfeitable rights to benefits, such as those of an employee retirement plan. Typically, these rights accrue based on an employee's years of service to an employer. Vested benefits cannot be taken from a participant, even if the participant's employment is terminated. See also *cliff vesting, deferred vesting, full vesting, graded vesting, immediate vesting* and *partial vesting*.
—vesting can also refer to a set period of time (such as 60 days) before an heir specified in a will can inherit. This is generally done to avoid disputes over the time of death, and avoid the payment of taxes twice in a short period of time should multiple family members die as a result of the same event.

vesting schedule—time frame that determines a participant's right to employer contributions to an accrued benefit such as a pension plan. The precise schedule varies from employer to employer. See also *cliff vesting, full vesting, graded vesting, immediate vesting* and *partial vesting*.

viatical settlement—also known as a living benefit or accelerated death benefit, a feature of life insurance policies that allows a policyholder to receive a payout before death. Typically, this benefit is allowed in cases of terminal illness or long-term severe health problems. The policy owner can sell his or her policy to a viatical settlement company or other such investor that pays out a percentage of the policy's face value to the policyholder, assumes responsibility for future premium payments and becomes the policy's beneficiary. In the U.S. under HIPAA, the proceeds of a settlement are tax-free at the federal level for individuals who are terminally or chronically ill. Many states, but not all, have also declared such payments exempt from state taxes. See also *chronic condition* and *terminal illness (TI)*.

vision coverage—benefit program providing treatment relating to the eye. Coverage typically includes eyeglasses, contact lenses, preventive screening and other care provided by optometrists, opticians and ophthalmologists. Coverage may be subject to deductibles, coinsurance, per visit copayments, maximum dollar reimbursement levels or annual maximums. Coverage may be separate or part of a broader health benefit plan.

visits per thousand—number of appointments with a specific type of care provider in a year or other period per thousand plan participants. Visits per thousand is a standard measure used to assess the impact of managed care strategies.

vocational rehabilitation—evaluation and training to return to work following personal injury.

volatility—statistical measure of price fluctuations for a given asset or portfolio. If the price moves up and down rapidly in a short period of time, volatility is high. If the price almost never changes or changes at a steady pace over time, volatility is low. Higher volatility usually indicates higher risk. One method for measuring volatility is to use the standard deviation or variance between returns on the investment being analyzed. A second method is to use beta. See also *beta* and *standard deviation*.

volume—from an investment perspective, the total number of shares of stock traded in a market during a given period.

volume purchase agreement—provider promise to sell pharmaceuticals with discounts or rebates that is conditional on the buyer purchasing a preestablished quantity during a defined time period.

volume submitter plan—IRS program that allows a practitioner to request an advisory letter regarding a specimen plan that contains provisions identical or substantially similar to the provisions in plans that the practitioner's clients have adopted or are expected to adopt. The specimen plan can be structured like a prototype (with a basic plan document and an adoption agreement) or as a self-contained single document that reflects only the provisions selected by an adopting employer. See also *master plan, model plan, prototype plan* and *specimen plan*.

voluntary additional contribution—see *additional voluntary contribution*.

voluntary benefit—ancillary benefit made available by an employer often at a group rate or discount to employees. Examples include dental coverage, vision coverage, prescription drug coverage, life insurance, long-term care insurance, financial planning, legal services and college savings plans. The voluntary benefit is administered by the employer but paid for by employees. Traditional group benefits require high levels of participation, typically 75%, but voluntary programs generally require only 20% of the eligible employees to enroll, and plans from some carriers have no participation requirement at all.

voluntary compliance resolution program—see *Employee Plans Compliance Resolution System (EPCRS)*.

voluntary contribution—salary, wages or other monetary compensation that an employee elects to pay into an employer-sponsored benefit plan. Participation by the employee in such a plan is not required, and the voluntary contributions do not affect the level of employer contributions. See also *contributory plan*.

Voluntary Correction Program (VCP)—one of three Employee Plans Compliance Resolution System (EPCRS) programs that allows a plan sponsor to correct operational and plan document errors affecting a tax-qualified plan. VCP allows a plan sponsor, at any time before audit, to pay a limited fee and receive approval for the correction of a qualified plan. There are special procedures for anonymous submissions. See also *Audit Closing Agreement Program (Audit CAP), Employee Plans Compliance Resolution System (EPCRS)* and *Self-Correction Program (SCP)*.

voluntary employees' beneficiary association (VEBA)—tax-exempt entity organized under IRC Section 501(c)(9) to provide medical, dental, life insurance, vacation, severance, unemployment compensation or other qualified benefits to members, dependents or beneficiaries. Members are employees who have an employment-related common bond such as the same employer, coverage under the same bargaining agreement or membership in the same union. Either employers or employees may contribute to the plan, which is usually financed through a self-funded trust or commercial insurance. If the plan is properly structured, the employer's contributions are immediately tax-deductible, the trust's investment income is tax-exempt and employee contributions are not currently taxed. A benefit paid from a VEBA can be distributed tax-free if it is a death benefit from life insurance under IRC Section 101(a) or a health benefit under IRC Section 105(h). See also *419A trust* and *self-funding*.

Voluntary Fiduciary Correction Program (VFCP)—U.S. Department of Labor program designed to encourage employee benefit plan sponsors, officials and parties in interest to correct fiduciary breaches on a voluntary basis. Fiduciaries who comply with program criteria and procedures can avoid potential ERISA civil actions and penalties.

voluntary formulary—see *open formulary*.

voluntary life insurance—death benefit coverage that can be purchased above and beyond any basic coverage provided in an employee benefits package. The employee selects the coverage amount and typically pays the entire cost. Unlike supplemental life insurance, voluntary life insurance typically uses a separate policy and, generally, the carrier is not the insurance company providing the basic life insurance. See also *supplemental life insurance*.

Voluntary Retirement Savings Plan (VRSP)—available only in Québec, group retirement savings plans offered by employers through authorized administrators. VRSPs, which are similar to pooled registered pension plans, are mainly intended for employees aged 18 and over who do not have access to a group retirement savings plan with source deductions through their employers. See also *Pooled Registered Pension Plan (PRPP)*.

volunteerism—giving time to support a meaningful cause. An increasing number of companies are providing employees with paid time off to contribute to causes of their choice.

voting right—right of a stockholder to vote in person or by proxy in the affairs of a company. See also *proxy*.

voucher program—distribution of a document giving the holder access to a service such as education or child care. For example, an employee may submit a monthly voucher for dependent care expenses to a provider, with the employer covering all or a part of the cost of the services.

W

wage—amount of money paid to a worker for a specified quantity of work, usually expressed on an hourly basis.

Wage and Hour Division (WHD)—unit within the Employment Standards Administration of the U.S. Department of Labor responsible for enforcing federal labor laws concerning minimum wage, overtime pay, recordkeeping, youth employment and special employment, family and medical leave, migrant workers, lie detector tests, protections in certain temporary worker programs and the prevailing wages for government service and construction contracts.

wage loss insurance—see *disability insurance*.

wage measure—monthly average of the weekly salaries and wages of the industrial aggregate in Canada published by Statistics Canada. The wage measure includes overtime pay.

wage rate—hourly payment that an employer gives an employee. See also *prevailing wage rate*.

Wagner Act—see *National Labor Relations Act of 1935 (NLRA or Wagner Act)*.

waiting period—time frame before a person is eligible for participation in a plan or to receive plan benefits. Many employee benefit plans require new employees to wait a specified length of time before they are eligible for participation. Disability plans generally have a waiting period between the onset of the disability and when benefits begin to be paid. Elimination period or qualification period are other terms sometimes used to refer to a waiting period. See also *minimum participation standard*.

waive—see *waiver*.

waived funding deficiency—part of the minimum funding standard for a retirement plan that the IRS determines a business may leave unpaid in a given plan year if it is determined that meeting the standard would result in substantial business hardship for the employer and be adverse to the interests of plan participants in the aggregate. The waived funding deficiency does not include previously waived amounts that have not been satisfied by employer contributions.

waiver—intentional or voluntary surrender of a right or privilege. A waiver may be given expressly through words or by failure to take action on a claim when required.

waiver of premium—provision in some insurance policies that allows a policyholder to stop making premium payments under specific circumstances (e.g., the insured suffers a permanent disability or dies).

waiver of recourse—provision in a fiduciary liability insurance policy that states the insurance company will not try to recover from an insured fiduciary any payments made for the fiduciary's liability. See also *right of recourse*.

Wall Street—financial district in lower Manhattan, New York. It is also the street where the New York Stock Exchange as well as many banks and brokerage firms are located. Wall Street, also called The Street, is also used to refer to the investment community in general.

warrant
—court authorization to police officers to perform specified acts (e.g., a search or arrest)
—in finance, type of security issued by a corporation (usually with a bond or preferred stock) that gives the holder the right to purchase securities (usually stock) from the issuer at a preset price within a specified time frame. Warrants are often included with a new debt issue to enhance the return on a bond and to entice new investors for a stock.

warranty statement—declaration used when a liability insurance policy is first issued that says no person covered by the policy is aware of any matter that may give rise to a future claim.

wasting trust—fund in which plan participants no longer accrue benefits; however, the fund remains in existence as long as necessary to pay already-accrued benefits.

wealth manager—see *private banker*.

wear-away—see *pension wear-away*.

weekly benefit amount (WBA)—dollar amount a claimant receives from an unemployment program during a claim week. See also *unemployment compensation (UC)*.

weekly indemnity insurance—see *disability insurance*.

weighted average life—see *average life*.

weighted mean—average of a set of numbers that have been "weighted" (i.e., multiplied by their number of occurrences).

weighting—emphasizing some aspects of a set of data by giving them more value in the final result; for example, giving the most important elements in a performance evaluation more points than those elements deemed less important.

Welfare and Pension Plans Disclosure Act (WPPDA)—federal law passed in 1958 that requires administrators of benefit plans with more than 25 participants to file a plan description with the U.S. Department of Labor. This description must include a schedule of benefits, the type of administration and a copy of the plan. If the plan has more than 100 participants, the administrator must also file an annual financial report. This information must be made available to plan participants upon request, and the person responsible for handling the funds must be bonded.

welfare benefits plan—see *employee welfare benefit plan*.

welfare fund—see *employee health and welfare fund*.

Wellness Councils of America (WELCOA)—national, nonprofit organization providing information and training concerning wellness in the workplace.

wellness program—broad range of employer- and union-sponsored facilities/activities designed to promote safety and good health among employees. Other goals include increasing worker morale and reducing the costs associated with accidents and ill health leading to absenteeism, lower productivity and health care expenses. Examples of wellness programs include physical fitness programs, smoking-cessation efforts, health risk appraisals, dissemination of information on a healthy diet and weight loss, stress management tips and blood pressure screening. Wellness programs are divided into two categories. The first, participatory programs, are generally available without regard to an individual's health status. These include, for example, programs that reimburse the cost of membership in a fitness center; reward employees with cash for attending a monthly, no-cost health education seminar or provide a discount on the employee's share of a health insurance premium to employees who complete a health risk assessment. Rewards are based simply on joining the program. In contrast, a health-contingent program provides a reward for a health-specific outcome such as walking a minimum of five miles per week. See also *preventive care* and "Wellness programs" in the *Appendix A: Affordable Care Act of 2010 (ACA)*.

whistle-blower—person who exposes wrongdoing to authorities or the public. Whistle-blowers are usually employees of the company or government agency charged with misconduct.

whistle-blowers protection—legal protection for those calling attention to wrongdoing that varies with circumstances including where the case arises. The United States has a patchwork of federal and state laws protecting employees who call attention to violations, help with enforcement proceedings or refuse to obey unlawful directions. When retaliation occurs against an employee, the process for making a proper complaint differs greatly, with some reporting deadlines as short as ten days.

white knight—individual or company, friendly to management, that makes an offer to take over a company that is facing a hostile takeover. See also *black knight*.

whole life insurance—insurance policy that provides a benefit upon the death of an insured or when the insured reaches 120 years. With older policies, the age was typically 100 years. In addition to the death benefit, a whole-life policy accumulates a cash value that may be borrowed or otherwise used by the insured prior to his or her death. Premiums may be paid for a specified number of years (limited payment life) or for life (ordinary or straight life). The premiums may remain level or decrease. With both approaches, there is an overpayment of premiums for the death benefit in the early years of the policy and an underpayment in the latter years, which averages out over the life of the policy. Sometimes called ordinary, permanent or straight-life insurance, whole life insurance is a form of cash value insurance. See also *cash value life insurance, endowment insurance, life insurance, limited payment life insurance, universal life insurance, variable life insurance* and *variable universal life insurance (VULI)*.

wholesale acquisition cost (WAC)—dollar value that wholesalers report they pay to a manufacturer for a drug product. WAC does not represent the actual price paid by wholesalers because wholesalers may obtain discounts through special purchases or discount deals.

wholesale insurance—see *franchise insurance*.

wholesaler—business participating in pharmaceutical distribution channels that handles logistics such as assembling, sorting and redistributing. Wholesalers purchase drugs from manufacturers in bulk and redistribute them to pharmacies, physicians and other drug retailers.

widely available market price (WAMP)—dollar amount a prudent physician or supplier would pay for a medication, taking into account the discounts, rebates and other price concessions routinely available for the product.

Wilshire 5000 Total Market Index (TMWX)—market capitalization-weighted stock index that tracks U.S. companies with stock actively traded on a U.S. stock exchange with stock pricing information that is widely available to the public. Originally comprised of 5,000 stocks as the name suggests, the index now consists of more than 6,700. High-value companies are weighted more heavily than those with lower values. The TMWX is one of the broadest stock market indexes and is designed to track the overall performance of U.S. stocks. See also *stock market index*.

wind-up—see *plan termination*.

withdrawal—see *complete withdrawal, mass withdrawal* and *partial withdrawal*.

withdrawal liability—financial responsibility of a contributing employer to make contributions necessary to fund vested employee benefits when the employer withdraws in part or completely from a qualified multiemployer defined benefit plan. The Multiemployer Pension Plan Amendments Act of 1980 removed multiemployer plans from the termination insurance system that governs single and multiple employer plans, and substituted this liability for certain unfunded vested benefits. Calculation of the liability may be based on one of four statutory methods or on an alternative method approved by the *Pension Benefit Guaranty Corporation (PBGC)*.

withdrawal of employee contributions—removal of funds a participant previously put into a benefit plan. If the participant withdraws any part of his or her mandatory contributions to a benefit plan in which employer contributions are less than 50% vested, ERISA permits forfeiture of the benefit attributable to employer contributions. If the benefit attributable to employer contributions is 50% vested or more, no forfeiture is permitted. When an employee withdraws mandatory contributions, he or she must be permitted to repay the full amount plus interest.

withdrawal of vested benefits—right of an employee to withdraw money credited to him or her in an employer's profit-sharing plan. Special regulations apply. Typically, the IRS does not allow accumulations to be distributed in less than two years. After this time, the employee can withdraw an amount equal to the first year's contributions and the investment income credited that year only. The withdrawn amount is taxable as ordinary income in the year received.

withhold arrangement—payment agreement between a health care provider and plan sponsor used to control health care costs. A portion of the health care provider's payment is set aside by the sponsor until the end of a predetermined financial period. Participant claims that exceed the budgeted costs for care are charged against the funds that were withheld. After excess claims are paid, the providers receive any money set aside that is left. If costs exceed the amount withheld, the plan sponsor or managed care organization (MCO) must take responsibility for the rest. Withholds are a form of risk sharing. See also *managed care (MC)*.

withholding—amount of an employee's income that an employer sends directly to the federal, state or local tax authority as partial payment of that individual's tax liability for the year. When a person starts a new job in the U.S., he or she is required to fill out a W-4 form on which he or she can indicate his/her filing status and the number of allowances he or she is claiming.

Women's Health and Cancer Rights Act of 1998 (WHCRA)
—U.S. legislation that requires insurance and health plans covering mastectomies to also cover breast reconstruction, prostheses and treatment of mastectomy complications.

Worker Adjustment and Retraining Notification Act (WARN)
—U.S. statute requiring employers to provide employees with at least a 60-day advance notice of plant closures and mass layoffs. Failure to comply with this requirement entitles employees to recover pay and benefits for the period for which notice was not given, typically up to a maximum of 60 days.

Worker Economic Opportunity Act of 2000
—amendment to the Fair Labor Standards Act of 1938 that states stock options and bonuses need not be included in calculating overtime pay. Employee stock purchase plans also qualify for the exemption if they are tax-qualified or substantially similar to a tax-qualified plan. The act limits to 15% the discount that employees may be given on stock options and stock appreciation rights. Employees must hold the option or right for at least six months before exercising.

worker engagement—see *employee engagement*.

Worker, Retiree, and Employer Recovery Act of 2008 (WRERA)
—U.S. legislation providing emergency relief to pension funds and technical corrections to the Pension Protection Act of 2006. Elements of the law include suspending the required minimum distributions from retirement accounts in 2009 and the easing of funding rules for single and multiemployer plans.

workers' compensation (WC)—also termed workmen's compensation and employers' liability, an insurance program found in some form in every state that provides weekly payments and covers the cost of medical care for employees who suffer job-related illnesses or injuries. Dependents of those who suffer a job-related death are also eligible for benefits. While the laws and benefits vary from state to state, most workers' compensation statutes in the U.S. hold the employer strictly liable and bar the employee from suing for damages. See also *24-hour coverage*.

workforce—generally used to describe those working for a single company or industry but can also apply to a geographical region like a city, state or nation. Workforce may also mean all those who are available for work. Workforce generally excludes employers and management. See also *labor force*.

Workgroup for Electronic Data Interchange (WEDI)
—task force formed in 1991 by the U.S. secretary of health and human services to develop recommendations for the use and transmission of electronic data in health care.

working capital—money used for day-to-day operations of a business. For accounting purposes, working capital is the total current assets minus the total current liabilities. Also called current capital.

working capital ratio—see *current ratio*.

Working Families Tax Relief Act of 2004—U.S. legislation that extends various personal income tax reductions that had been scheduled to expire for middle-class taxpayers and businesses. A notable change was the creation of a uniform definition for a dependent child for tax purposes. The Gulf Opportunity Zone Act of 2005 revised the rules of the 2004 legislation relating to claims of divorced parents for the tax exemption for dependent children.

working spouse provision—see *spousal carve-out*.

working time equivalency method—one of three equivalency approaches that employers may use when tracking an employee's hours of service credit for a qualified retirement plan. The working time equivalency method ignores passive hours (other than backpay hours) when crediting service. The hours-worked option treats 870 hours worked as equivalent to 1,000 hours or one year of service. The regular-time option treats 750 time hours as equivalent to 1,000 hours or one year of service. See also *hours of service* and *year of service*.

work/life benefits—broad range of programs and services designed to improve the balance between work and personal life. These benefits tend to result in healthier, more productive employees and are seen as a retention tool for employers. Work reorganization initiatives such as job sharing, flextime and telecommuting are examples of work/life benefits. Others include on-site child care and/or elder care, emergency/sick child care, tuition assistance, concierge services and financial and career counseling.

Work Opportunity Credit—amount an employer can subtract for the first-year wages of a new employee with a disability from federal income tax. The disabled individual must be referred by state or local vocational rehabilitation agencies, a state commission for the blind, or the U.S. Department of Veterans Affairs and must be certified by a state employment service.

works council—most common in Western Europe, an organization of employers and employees within a benefit plan or business that meets to discuss working conditions, wages and other work-related issues.

work sharing—practice of spreading a firm's available work hours among its employees during a cutback as an alternative to layoffs.

work team—cross-functional, multiskilled and self-directed group of employees responsible for its own goals, assignments, cost control, quality control, work orders, work scheduling, and other such duties and tasks.

World Bank—part of the United Nations system, an international financial institution that provides loans to the governments of developing nations at affordable interest rates to help finance capital programs and economic reforms. Long-term loans through the bank's International Development Association are interest-free. The World Bank raises money by issuing bonds guaranteed by the nearly 200 countries that own the bank. Its official goal is the reduction of poverty.

World Trade Organization (WTO)—international organization that supervises all agreements and arrangements concluded under the auspices of the Uruguay Round of multilateral trade negotiations. The WTO agreement was signed by nearly 100 nations in 1995; it is the successor to the General Agreement on Tariffs and Trade (GATT) and the court of final settlement in trade disputes. WTO objectives include (1) removal of all barriers to international trade in goods, services and intellectual property; (2) equitable and speedy resolution of disputes between trading partners and (3) identification of noncompliance with trade agreements. See also *General Agreement on Tariffs and Trade (GATT)*.

wraparound mortgage—loan that includes the remaining balance on an existing property loan, plus a new amount. The borrower makes one monthly payment (shared between the first lender and the new lender, if different). In this arrangement, the borrower saves penalties associated with a new mortgage, and the lender gets to charge a new (usually higher) interest rate on the entire loan amount. Also called an inclusive mortgage.

wraparound plan
—insurance or health care coverage that pays the copays and deductibles for a basic medical plan. Wraparound plans are often used with Medicare.
—see also *401(k) wraparound plan*.

wrapped bond—bond that is insured by a third party. Wrapped bonds, also called synthetic GICs, are common in the municipal bond market. If the rate of return drops below the guarantee set by the wrapper, the insurer pays the difference. On the other hand, if the rate of return is higher than the set return, the fund pays the insurer the difference. See also *guaranteed investment contract (GIC)* and *stable value fund*.

wrongful discharge—termination of an employee that violate terms of the employee's contract or is illegal. Also referred to as wrongful termination or wrongful dismissal. See also *constructive discharge*.

wrongful dismissal—see *wrongful discharge*.

wrongful termination—see *wrongful discharge*.

Y

Yankee bond—debt security issued in the United Sates by a foreign bank or corporation. The bond is denominated in U.S. dollars and can be as large as $1 billion. Foreign issuers tend to prefer issuing Yankee bonds during times when U.S. interest rates are low, as this enables the foreign issuer to pay out less money in interest payments.

Yankee certificate of deposit (Yankee CD)—certificate evidencing a time deposit issued in the United States by a U.S. branch of a foreign bank. Yankee CDs must have a minimum face value of $100,000. They cannot be cashed in before maturity, but they can be sold in a secondary market. A Yankee CD is an example of a negotiable certificate of deposit. See also *certificate of deposit (CD)* and *negotiable certificate of deposit (NCD)*.

year of service—under ERISA and for the purposes of participating or vesting in a qualified retirement plan, a plan year or other service computation period in which an employee is credited with 1,000 or more hours of service (although some plans may require fewer hours). If an employee fails to work 1,000 hours during the initial 12 months of his or her employment, he or she must begin meeting the 1,000-hour requirement in the next 12-month period. See also *hours of service*.

year's basic exemption (YBE)—portion of earnings upon which no contributions to the Canada Pension Plan (CPP)/Québec Pension Plan (QPP) are required.

years certain annuity—see *annuity certain*.

year's maximum pensionable earnings (YMPE)—highest annual earnings, prior to reduction of the amount of the year's basic exemption, upon which benefits and contributions to the Canada Pension Plan (CPP)/Québec Pension Plan (QPP) are based. The YMPE has been subject to yearly adjustments; and, since 1989, increases have been determined by changes in the Industrial Aggregate as reported by Statistics Canada. The figure is rounded down to a multiple of $100.

yield
—income earned or projected on an investment expressed as a percentage of an investment's cost, current value or face value. There are various ways to calculate yield depending on whether the security is a bond, stock or mutual fund. With the exception of a bond's yield to maturity, yield generally takes into account only interest earned on an investment and not changes in value. For investments with stable values such as certificates of deposit and money market funds, yield and return may be used interchangeably. Such is not the case for stocks, bonds and mutual funds, which may have capital gains and losses. Unlike yield, return takes into consideration the changes in value. See also *annual percentage yield (APY)*, *annual yield*, *rate of return (ROR)* and *return*.
—bonds yields are calculated using the security's interest earned relative to the bond's cost. See also *bond basis book*, *coupon yield*, *current yield*, *tax-equivalent (TE) yield*, *yield to call* and *yield to maturity (YTM)*.
—for stocks, yield is calculated by dividing the total of the annual dividends by the current market price.
—yield on a mutual fund is a fund's income (interest and dividends minus fund expenses) as a percentage of its net asset value. See also *net asset value (NAV)*.

yield curve—bond interest rates available for each maturity from one day out to 30 years. The curve is positive when long-term debt instruments have higher yields than short-term debt instruments. This is the usual condition and happens because investors demand a higher return for taking on the additional risk of the longer-term investment. Also called normal yield curve.

yield to call—internal rate of return from holding a bond, assuming the bond is called by the issuer at the earliest time possible.

yield to maturity (YTM)—approximate return on a bond if it is held to its maturity date. YTM takes into consideration, on a percentage basis, all of the bond's earnings from a given point in time until the bond matures. It includes any gain or loss on the price paid for the bond, the interest the bond will pay and what would have been earned if the holder had reinvested the bond interest payments at the same coupon rate paid by the bond. The YTM formula is useful when comparing two bonds with different interest rates and maturities. See also *yield*.

yellow zone—see *endangered status*.

Z

zero-balance reimbursement account (ZEBRA)—pre-January 1985-type of flexible spending arrangement (FSA) under which amounts were allocated to the account only when an expense was incurred. The employee was then reimbursed by the employer by subtracting the amount of the covered expenses from his or her taxable income at the end of the year. Such arrangements are specifically forbidden in a *cafeteria plan*.

zero-based budget (ZBB)—financial plan that disregards the expenses of the prior year. A manager starts with a clean slate, considering objectives, exploring alternatives and justifying each expenditure.

zero-based forecasting—predicting the future of a company free from historical information. The past is not relevant for firms undergoing rapid change, such as most rapid growth firms and distressed organizations in turnarounds.

zero-coupon bond—bond that has no interest payments. A zero-coupon bond is sold at a deep discount from its value at maturity, with the discount reflecting an interest rate. The issuer pays the bondholder the face value of the bond at the date of the bond's maturity. See also *discount bond*.

zones—in compensation, pay ranges within pay bands used to keep the system more structurally intact. Maximums, midpoints and minimums provide guides for appropriate pay for certain levels of work. Without zones, employees might float to the maximum pay, which, for many jobs in the band, is higher than market value.

APPENDIX A: AFFORDABLE CARE ACT OF 2010 (ACA)

Affordable Care Act of 2010 (ACA)—name used to refer to the Patient Protection and Affordable Care Act (PPACA) signed into law on March 23, 2010 and amended via the Health Care and Education Reconciliation Act on March 30, 2010. ACA is intended to increase access to health care and improve the quality of health care in the United States. ACA changes impact workplace health benefit plans, the commercial health insurance market, Medicare and Medicaid.

With respect to group health plans, some ACA rules and regulations apply to all plans while others apply only when a plan is no longer grandfathered under ACA. Group health plans in existence as of March 23, 2010 are grandfathered and do not have to comply with many of the law's benefit mandates as long as they remain grandfathered. A plan loses its grandfathered status if certain types of changes are made to a plan's design. There are also exceptions for retiree-only group health plans—They are not subject to all the rules concerning benefit plan mandates, care providers, claims and appeals. Among the key provisions of the ACA are:

Preexisting condition exclusions. No preexisting condition exclusions are permitted with either grandfathered or nongrandfathered group plans.

Benefit mandates. Nongrandfathered plans sold via the individual and small group markets (both inside and outside of the public health exchanges) must offer a comprehensive package of items and services known as essential health benefits. These benefits must include items and services within at least the following ten categories:
1. Ambulatory patient services
2. Emergency medical services
3. Hospitalization
4. Maternity and newborn care
5. Mental health and substance use disorder services, including behavioral health treatment
6. Prescription drugs
7. Rehabilitative and habilitative services and devices
8. Laboratory services
9. Preventive and wellness services, and chronic disease management
10. Pediatric services, including oral and vision care.

States expanding their Medicaid programs must also provide these benefits to people newly eligible for Medicaid.

Lifetime and annual dollar limits on essential health benefits are generally prohibited when they are provided by group health plans and health insurance policies—regardless of whether the plan/policy is grandfathered or nongrandfathered. Grandfathered individual health insurance plans are not required to follow the rules on annual limits. Any plan can put an annual or lifetime dollar limit on spending for health care services that are not considered essential health benefits.

Large employer and self-funded group plans do not have to provide a full list of essential health benefits. However, if they do provide any of these benefits, annual and lifetime caps cannot be imposed on the benefits category.

Nongrandfathered group plans have these additional benefit rules:
- In-network coverage for certain preventive-care services (e.g., well-child care, immunizations and screenings for colorectal cancer, cervical cancer, osteoporosis, cholesterol abnormalities, high blood pressure, diabetes, sexually transmitted diseases, depression, obesity and tobacco use).
- Plans must provide services to women including well-woman visits, contraceptives and breastfeeding support.
- If a plan provides emergency room services, the plan must cover these services without prior authorization—regardless of whether the provider is in or out of network.
- Plans must cover routine patient costs for items and services furnished in connection with participation in approved clinical trials for life-threatening diseases.
- Plans must limit the amount participants (and their families) pay out of pocket for in-network essential health benefits. The amount of the limit is indexed annually.

Excepted benefits. Limited-scope health benefits that supplement comprehensive medical coverage are exempt from the insurance market reform provisions of ACA (as well as the health insurance requirements of the Health Insurance Portability and Accountability Act of 1986). Hospital indemnity insurance, accidental death and dismemberment insurance, specified disease and illness coverage, workers' compensation, long-term care insurance, dental care, vision care and on-site medical clinics are examples of benefits that commonly are excepted. For some of these benefits to be excepted, they must be offered independently from comprehensive medical coverage.

Affordable Care Act of 2010 (ACA)

Care providers. Nongrandfathered group plans:
- May not discriminate against a health care provider acting within the scope of his/her license with respect to participating in plan network coverage
- Must permit participants to select their own primary care physicians and pediatricians. Direct access obstetric and gynecological services must also be provided—In other words, plans cannot require prior authorization or referral to an OB-GYN.

Medical loss ratio (MLR). An insurance company must spend a minimum percentage of premium dollars on the care of patients and to improve health care quality.

Eligibility. As of 2014, both grandfathered and nongrandfathered group health plans:
- Must cover a participant's adult children up to the age of 26. Coverage of these older children must be provided regardless of whether the child has his or her own health coverage through a job or spouse. Coverage tiers based on family size are still permitted, but a plan cannot charge more because the family member is an adult child.
- Cannot have a waiting period of more than 90 days before a full-time participant or the participant's dependent may enroll. Special rules apply if a worker is part-time, variable hour, seasonal or part of a multiemployer plan.

Discrimination. When the regulations are published, fully insured nongrandfathered plans will have to comply with nondiscrimination rules to prevent favoring highly compensated participants.

Rescission. Nongrandfathered plans are not permitted rescind coverage retroactively, except for certain limited reasons (e.g., fraud and misrepresentation). Plans must give prior notice of such termination.

Claims and appeals. Nongrandfathered group health plans and health insurance companies must make a number of changes to their internal claims and appeals procedures, for example:
- Notice of an adverse determination (denial) must be written in a "manner calculated to be understood by the claimant."
- The notice must state the specific reason(s) for the denial and refer to the specific plan provisions on which the denial is based.
- If a claim is incomplete, the notice must include a description of the information needed to "perfect" the claim and an explanation of why the information is needed.
- The notice must describe the appeal procedures.
- In some circumstances where 10% or more of a population is literate only in the same non-English language, the notice may have to be provided in that language.

Furthermore, consumers have the right to appeal a plan decision with an external review process performed by a party not under the direct control of the entity being evaluated. A beneficiary may request an external review when a health plan denies an appeal that involves medical judgment including but not limited to:
- Treatment based on a plan's or issuer's requirements for medical necessity, appropriateness, health care setting, level of care or effectiveness of a covered benefit
- Treatment that is experimental or investigational
- Rescissions of coverage.

The external review either upholds the plan decision or overturns some or all of the decision. The plan must accept the decision. In urgent situations, this review may be requested even if a plan's internal appeals process isn't completed.

Reporting. Employers with 50 or more full-time employees (including full-time equivalent employees) in the previous year must use Forms 1094-C and 1095-C to report information to the IRS about offers of and enrollment in health coverage for their employees. Form 1094-C must be used to report summary information for each employer. Form 1095-C is used to report information about each employee. Forms 1094-C and 1095-C are used to determine whether an employer owes a payment under the employer shared responsibility provisions of ACA. Form 1095-C is also used to determine the eligibility of employees for the premium tax credit. Employers that offer employer-sponsored self-insured coverage also use Form 1095-C to report information to the IRS and to employees about individuals who have minimum essential coverage under the employer plan and therefore are not liable for the individual shared responsibility payment for the months that they are covered under the plan.

When the regulations are published, nongrandfathered plans will have to report information relating to enrollment and disenrollment, quality of care, claim payment policies and practices, claims denied, cost-sharing features, out-of-network coverage and finances.

Summary of Benefits and Coverage (SBC). All group health plans/insurance companies must provide plan participants and potential participants/consumers a short, plain-language "Summary of Benefits and Coverage," or "SBC," using terms and format that are standardized to help individuals compare plans. For benefit plans in the workplace, the SBC must be delivered to an employee the first day the employee is eligible to enroll for plan coverage. If a person doesn't speak English, the SBC must be provided in the individual's native language upon request.

Employer shared responsibility. This ACA rule—also referred to as the *play-or-pay provision*—requires large employers to offer full-time employees and their dependent children the opportunity to enroll in an employer-sponsored health plan providing a health package with essential health benefits. Employers that do not do so must pay a penalty referred to as the *Employer Shared Responsibility Payment (ESRP)*. The plans offered must also provide:

- **Minimum value**—coverage for at least 60% of the total cost of all employee health benefits. The minimum value percentage is calculated by using the cost of benefits a plan pays for a standard population divided by the total costs of benefits. The standard population is based on state and national health claims data.
- **Affordable coverage**—protection that is reasonably priced considering the financial resources of those buying it. ACA considers health care coverage affordable if a person's cost for the lowest-priced self-only coverage is no greater than 9.5% of the person's household income.

Whether an employer is considered large is generally based on hours worked by all employees of the employer in the previous year. As of January 1, 2016, any employer with more than 50 full-time equivalent employees is considered a large employer. An employee is typically any person for which the company issues a W-2, regardless of full-time, part-time or seasonal status and whether or not the employee has medical coverage. *Full-time employee* is defined as a worker providing on average 30 or more hours of service per week (or 130 hours in a calendar month). Hours of service include hours for which an employee is paid but does not actually work (e.g., vacation, jury duty, military duty, disability and leaves of absence). Since an employer may hire a new employee and not be reasonably certain of the number of hours they may work, a new "variable hour employee" category has been created for employers that have "part-time" employees.

Affordable Care Act of 2010 (ACA)

Individual responsibility. An individual mandate requires all U.S. citizens and legal residents to have coverage that qualifies as "minimum essential health benefits coverage" or pay a penalty. Examples of this coverage are:
- Any job-based plan, including retiree plans and the Federal Employees Health Benefit Program
- Any plan purchased through a public health exchange
- Individual plans purchased outside the public health exchange that are certified as meeting ACA standards such as the provision of essential health benefits and limits on cost-sharing
- Any grandfathered individual insurance plan that an individual has had since March 23, 2010 or earlier
- Medicare Parts A and C, but not Part B
- Most Medicaid plans, except limited-coverage plans
- Most TRICARE plans
- The Children's Health Insurance Program (CHIP)
- Most student health plans
- Health coverage for Peace Corps and AmeriCorps volunteers
- Certain types of veterans coverage through the Department of Veterans Affairs.

There are some exceptions for the individual mandate. For persons up to the age of 30, the purchase of a catastrophic plan is an acceptable substitute to avoid the penalty. Individuals who can show a "hardship" prevented them from becoming insured also do not have to pay the penalty. Other circumstances that may qualify a person for an exemption include:
- Being homeless
- Facing eviction or foreclosure
- Receiving a shut-off notice from a utility company
- Recently experiencing domestic violence
- Recently experiencing the death of a close family member
- Experiencing a fire, flood or other natural or human-caused disaster that caused substantial damage to an individual's property
- Filing bankruptcy in the last six months
- Medical expenses that couldn't be paid in the last 24 months that resulted in substantial debt
- Unexpected increases in necessary expenses resulting from the care of an ill, disabled or aging family member.

Public health exchanges. All states must establish and operate a health insurance marketplace or use the marketplace created by the federal government to offer a place where consumers in the United States can:
- Learn about their medical and prescription drug coverage options
- Learn about the premium tax credit
- Compare health insurance plans based on costs, benefits and other features
- Choose a health insurance plan
- Enroll for coverage.

Accessible via websites, call centers and in-person assistance, the public health exchanges serve persons without employer-sponsored plans, those who have employer coverage offered that does not meet the ACA minimum value and affordability requirements, and some small businesses. ACA also provides guidelines for states to enter into interstate compact agreements that permit health plans to be sold in multiple states.

Qualified health plans. Any plan offered through a public health exchange must be certified as a "qualified health plan," which indicates it meets the minimum federal insurance market rules and any state benchmarks (i.e., essential health benefits) established by the state where the plan is sold. Plans offered by a public exchange fit into one of four categories or are separate catastrophic plans:
- **Bronze plans** provide the minimum essential coverage and cover 60% of benefit plan costs.
- **Silver plans** provide the minimum essential health benefits and cover 70% of benefit plan costs.
- **Gold plans** provide the minimum essential health benefits and cover 80% of benefit plan costs.
- **Platinum plans** provide the minimum essential health benefits and cover 90% of benefit plan costs.
- **Catastrophic plans** are available to those up to the age of 30 and those who are exempt from the mandate to purchase coverage. These plans protect consumers from financial disaster in the case of a major medical event. The out-of-pocket limits are set at the federal health savings account (HSA) level except that prevention benefits and coverage for three primary care visits are exempt from the deductible. These plans are only available in the individual market. An example of a catastrophic health plan is a high-deductible health plan associated with an HSA.

Private exchanges selling group insurance do not need to meet the qualified health plan guidelines. However, some do for competitive purposes.

Premium tax credit. This reduction in federal income taxes was instituted to help low-income persons purchase coverage through the public health exchanges. Those who qualify can choose to have the credit applied in advance to each monthly premium as an "advanced premium tax credit (APTC)." If the amount advanced is less than the credit calculated at the end of the year, the difference is claimed on a person's federal income tax return. On the other hand, if the advance is greater than the end-of-year credit calculation, the difference must be repaid with the person's tax return. People offered employer-sponsored coverage that is deemed affordable and provides minimum value aren't eligible for this tax credit.

Small Business Health Options Program (SHOP). This health insurance marketplace has been set up for small employers (less than 50 employees) that want to provide health and dental coverage to their employees. While the federal government defines small employers as those with 50 or fewer full-time equivalent employees (FTEs), some states may use different employee maximums.

Small business health care tax credit. Employers that have fewer than 25 full-time workers with average wages of less than $50,000 are offered this federal income tax reduction as an incentive to provide their employees with health insurance and pay for a portion of the coverage. Varying with the contribution, size and tax status of the employer, the credit enables employers to deduct an amount—usually a percentage of the contribution they make toward their employees' premiums—from the federal income taxes they owe. The tax credit is available to nonprofit organizations that do not pay federal taxes.

Basic health program. States have the option to cover low-income persons directly, rather than through a health insurance exchange. States choosing to do so receive 95% of what the federal government would have spent on subsidies for adults between 133% and 200% of the federal poverty level and legal resident immigrants with incomes below 133% who have been in the U.S. for fewer than five years (and, therefore, do not qualify for Medicaid).

State innovation waivers. States can ask the Secretary of the U.S. Department of Health and Human Services for permission to replace the public health exchange system with another approach to coverage. The Secretary can exempt states from provisions of ACA related to qualified health plans, consumer choices, cost-sharing protections, and individual and small employer tax credits. Waivers of ACA provisions can be combined with Medicare and Medicaid waivers so states can create an entirely different form of health insurance coverage (e.g., a single payer plan).

Consumer Operated and Oriented Plan (CO-OP) program. This program has been established to foster the creation of qualified health plans sold through the health exchanges by nonprofit organizations that are customer-owned and -governed. Formed at a national, state or local level, these cooperatives can include doctors, hospitals and businesses as member-owners. Grants and loans are to be made available to help co-op plans enter the marketplace.

Navigators. Special programs are to be established that employ individuals specialized in helping consumers and small businesses purchase health coverage through the health insurance marketplace. The role of the navigator includes helping buyers determine whether they qualify for federal or state insurance programs, completing eligibility and enrollment forms, and outreach to raise awareness of the marketplace. Navigators must complete comprehensive training and provide free, unbiased services. They may not work for insurers or be paid by insurers for plan enrollment.

Center for Consumer Information and Insurance Oversight (CCIIO)—within the Department of Health and Human Services, the entity created to develop policies and help implement many of the ACA reforms. More specifically, CCIIO is charged with oversight of provisions related to private health insurance and establishing the Health Insurance Marketplaces (a.k.a. public health exchanges).

Affordable Care Act of 2010 (ACA)

Wellness programs. ACA regulations place restrictions on employment-based wellness programs and consolidate nondiscrimination rules contained in the Health Insurance Portability and Accountability Act (HIPAA).
- Wellness programs that provide a reward for a health-specific outcome must provide an employee an alternative means to achieve the goal if the employee has a health condition preventing him or her from achieving the goal. For example, if a program requires employees to walk a minimum of five miles per week to obtain a reward and an employee has a walking restriction due to an injury, the sponsor must provide an alternative method to achieve the same reward. The alternative might be using exercise equipment to produce the same cardiac benefits as walking a mile per day. Plan sponsors can also choose to waive the penalty or grant a reward if no alternative is feasible.
- Wellness incentives in group health plans can be increased from 20% to 30% of plan costs and up to 50% for programs designed to prevent or reduce tobacco use.

FSAs, HRAs and HSAs. With respect to these health savings accounts, ACA:
- Removes nonprescription medications as eligible for reimbursement in flexible spending accounts (FSAs), health reimbursement arrangements (HRAs) and health savings accounts (HSAs)
- Increases the HSA penalty on nonmedical withdrawals to 20%.

Fees/Taxes. Three new fees have been created to fund specific elements of ACA:
- **Patient-Centered Outcomes Research Institute (PCORI) Fee**—formerly known as the Comparative Effectiveness Research Fee, a tax that health plan sponsors and insurance companies pay through 2018 to fund the Patient-Centered Outcomes Research Institute (PCORI) established under the Affordable Care Act.
- **Reinsurance fee**—temporary 2014 through 2016 annual tax charged to any plan that provides medical coverage with the exception of (1) retiree plans that pay secondary to Medicare and (2) self-funded and self-administered plans in 2015 and 2016. Determined by the number of covered lives enrolled in a health plan (excluding retirees), the fee creates a pool of funds to help evenly spread the risk of persons with costly conditions that the ACA requires marketplace insurers to cover.
- **Excise tax on high-cost health plans (a.k.a. Cadillac tax)**—starting in 2020, 40% tax imposed on health plan coverage that exceeds a specific threshold indexed to the Urban Consumer Price Index.

Medicare Hospital Insurance. The Medicare Part A tax rate on wages is increased by 0.9% (from 1.45% to 2.35%) on earnings of *high-income taxpayers*, defined as individuals with earnings over $200,000 and married couples earning more than $250,000. These thresholds are not indexed. In an effort to achieve fairness, a 3.8% tax is also assessed on high-income taxpayers with unearned income (e.g., interest, dividends, annuities, royalties and rents.) The percentage is equal to the combined employer and employee share of the existing Medicare Hospital Insurance Tax paid by those whose earnings are below the high-income thresholds.

Medicare Part D. ACA improves prescription drug coverage in Medicare including a phase-out of the Part D "donut hole." It also eliminates the tax deduction for employers that were receiving Medicare Part D retiree drug subsidy payments.

Amendment to the Fair Labor Standards Act (FLSA). Employers must provide reasonable unpaid break time for up to one year after the birth of a child and provide a private place other than a bathroom for nursing mothers to express breast milk. Employers with fewer than 50 employees do not have to comply if doing so would cause undue hardship.

APPENDIX B: ACRONYMS AND ABBREVIATIONS

The employee benefits and compensation field encompasses many subjects: accounting, business, government regulations, health care, human resources, finance, insurance, law, real estate and so forth. Each has a collection of acronyms and other abbreviations. This list brings together many of these shorter references that are used by benefits and compensation professionals.

Entries are alphabetized as if they were single words. Commas, slashes and spaces are ignored in alphabetization. Letters combined with numbers appear before letters combined with letters. If an entry has more than one definition, those definitions appear in alphabetical order within the entry.

3O	third opinion
AAA	(1) American Academy of Actuaries
	(2) American Accounting Association
	(3) American Arbitration Association
	(4) Area Agency on Aging
AABD	Aid to the Aged, Blind and Disabled
AAC	(1) actual acquisition cost
	(2) affirmative action clause
	(3) affirmative action committee
AAFP	American Academy of Family Physicians
AAHP	American Association of Health Plans
AALL	American Association for Labor Legislation
AAP	affirmative action program
AAPPO	American Association of Preferred Provider Organizations
AARP	American Association of Retired Persons
ABA	(1) American Bankers Association
	(2) American Bar Association
ABCD	Actuarial Board for Counseling and Discipline
ABCP	asset-backed commercial paper
ABO	accumulated benefit obligation
ABP	(1) account balance pension
	(2) alternate benefit provision
	(3) average benefit percentage
ABS	asset-backed security
ACA	(1) Affordable Care Act
	(2) American Chiropractic Association
	(3) American Compensation Association (merged with CCA to form World at Work)
	(4) American Counseling Association
ACC	ambulatory care center
ACLI	American Council of Life Insurers
ACLU	American Civil Liberties Union
ACOPA	American Society of Pension Professionals and Actuaries College of Pension Actuaries
ACP	(1) actual contribution percentage
	(2) average contribution percentage
ACPM	(1) American College of Preventive Medicine
	(2) Association of Canadian Pension Management
ACR	(1) accelerated cost recovery
	(2) accounts receivable
	(3) actual contribution ratio
	(4) adjusted community rating
	(5) average cost ratio
AcSB	Accounting Standards Board
ADA	(1) American Dental Association
	(2) American Diabetes Association
	(3) Americans with Disabilities Act
AD&D	accidental death and dismemberment
ADB	accidental death benefit
ADEA	Age Discrimination in Employment Act of 1967
ADL	activities of daily living
ADP	actual deferral percentage
ADR	(1) actual deferral ratio
	(2) adverse drug reaction
	(3) alternative dispute resolution
	(4) American Depositary Receipt
ADS	(1) alternative delivery system
	(2) American Depositary Share
AF4Q	Aligning Forces for Quality
AFFE	acquired fund fees and expenses

AFL	American Federation of Labor (merged with CIO to form AFL-CIO)	**AMP**	(1) Administrators Masters Program (2) average manufacturer price
AFL-CIO	American Federation of Labor-Congress of Industrial Organizations	**AMT**	alternative minimum tax
		AMW	average monthly wage
AFSCME	American Federation of State, County and Municipal Employees	**ANA**	American Nurses Association
		ANSI	American National Standards Institute
AGI	adjusted gross income	**AOPA**	American Orthotic & Prosthetic Association
AHA	(1) American Heart Association (2) American Hospital Association	**APA**	(1) American Psychiatric Association (2) American Psychological Association
AHCPR	Agency for Health Care Policy and Research	**APB**	(1) Accounting Principles Board (2) all-points bulletin
AHIP	America's Health Insurance Plans		
AHP	(1) affinity health plan (2) allied health professional (3) association health plan	**APBO**	(1) actuarial present value of accumulated benefits (2) actuarial present value of future benefits
AHQA	American Health Quality Association	**APhA**	American Pharmaceutical Association
AHRQ	Agency for Healthcare and Research Quality	**APHA**	American Public Health Association
AI	(1) aggregate income (2) artificial intelligence	**APPWP**	Association of Private Pension and Welfare Plans
AICPA	American Institute of Certified Public Accountants	**APR**	annual percentage rate
		APRSC	Administrative Policy Regarding Self-Correction
AIDS	acquired immune deficiency syndrome	**APTC**	advanced premium tax credit
AIME	average indexed monthly earnings	**APV**	actuarial present value
AIMR	Association for Investment Management and Research	**APY**	annual percentage yield
		AQA	Ambulatory Care Quality Alliance
AIR	annual information return	**AQL**	acceptable quality level
AIRE	American Institute of Retirement Education	**AR**	accounts receivable
AJCA	American Jobs Creation Act of 2004	**ARC**	(1) AIDS-related complex (2) American Red Cross
a.k.a.	also known as		
ALI-ABA	American Law Institute-American Bar Association	**ARM**	adjustable rate mortgage
		ARTLI	annual renewable term life insurance
ALOS	average length of stay	**ASA**	(1) Associate of the Society of Actuaries (2) Fellow of the Society of Actuaries
AMA	(1) American Management Association (2) American Medical Association		
AMB	accrued monthly benefit	**ASB**	Actuarial Standards Board
AMC	academic medical center	**ASC**	(1) administrative services contract (2) ambulatory surgery center
AMEX	American Stock Exchange		
AML	adjustable mortgage loan		

ASCII	American Standard Code for Information Interchange
ASHP	American Society of Healthcare Pharmacists
ASM	Alliance of Specialty Medicine
ASO	(1) administrative services only (2) administrative services organization
ASOP	(1) Actuarial Standards of Practice (2) American Society of Orthopedic Professionals
ASP	(1) application service provider (2) average sales price
ASPA	(1) American Society for Personnel Administration (former name for Society of Human Resource Management) (2) American Society of Pension Actuaries (3) American Society for Public Administration
ASTD	American Society for Training and Development
ASU	Accounting Standards Update
ATMS®	Advanced Trust Management Standards®
AV	audiovisual
AVA	actuarial value of assets
AVC	additional voluntary contribution
AWI	average weekly income
AWP	(1) any willing provider (2) average wholesale price
BA	(1) bankers acceptance (2) business agent
BAPCPA	Bankruptcy Abuse Prevention and Consumer Protection Act of 2005
BBA	Balanced Budget Act of 1997
BCBSA	Blue Cross and Blue Shield Association
BFOQ	bona fide occupational qualification
BIA	Bankruptcy and Insolvency Act
BIC	bank investment contract
BIS	break in service
BLS	Bureau of Labor Statistics
BMI	body mass index
BNA	Bureau of National Affairs
BP or bp	basis point
BPO	business process outsourcing
BR	business representative
BRIC	Brazil, Russia, India and China
C of C	Chamber of Commerce
CA	chartered accountant
CAA	cost-avoidance analysis
CAD	computer-aided design
CAI	computer-assisted instruction
CAGR	compound annual growth rate
CAHPS	Consumer Assessment of Healthcare Providers and Systems
CalPERS	California Public Employees' Retirement System
CAM	(1) complementary and alternative medicine (2) computer-assisted manufacturing
CANSIM	Canadian Socio-Economic Information Management Database
CAP	(1) capital accumulation plan (2) Closing Agreement Program
CAPM	capital asset pricing model
CAPP	cash account pension plan
CAPPP®	Certificate of Achievement in Public Plan Policy®
CAPSA	Canadian Association of Pension Supervisory Authorities
CAS	Casualty Actuarial Society
CAT	computerized axial tomography
CB	Cumulative Bulletin
CBA	(1) collective bargaining agreement (2) cost-benefit analysis
CBO	Congressional Budget Office
CBOE	Chicago Board Options Exchange

CBP	(1) Bureau of Customs and Border Protection (2) cash balance plan (3) Certified Benefits Professional		**CFA**	(1) Chartered Financial Analyst (2) Consumer Federation of America
CBU	contribution base unit		**CFO**	chief financial officer
CCA	(1) Canadian Compensation Association (merged with ACA to form World at Work) (2) Conference of Consulting Actuaries (3) cost-consequence analysis		**CFP**	Certified Financial Planner
			CFPB	Consumer Financial Protection Bureau
			CFR	Code of Federal Regulations
			CFTC	Commodities Futures Trading Commission
CCAA	Companies' Creditors Arrangement Act		**CHAMPUS**	Civilian Health and Medical Program of the Uniformed Services
CCIIO	Center for Consumer Information and Insurance Oversight		**CHC**	community health center
CCIR	Canadian Council of Insurance Regulations		**CHCS**	Center for Health Care Strategies
CCP	Certified Compensation Professional		**ChFC**	Chartered Financial Consultant
CCRA	Canada Customs and Revenue Agency (formerly the Canada Revenue Agency)		**CHI**	Center for Health Improvement
			CHIN	community health information network
CCRC	continuing care retirement community		**CHIP**	Children's Health Insurance Program
CCU	coronary care unit		**CHIPRA**	Children's Health Insurance Program Reauthorization Act of 2009
CD	(1) certificate of deposit (2) compact disc		**CHPA**	community health purchasing alliance
CDC	(1) Centers for Disease Control and Prevention (2) Community Development Corporation		**CHRP**	Certified Human Resources Professional
			CIA	(1) Canadian Institute of Actuaries (2) certified internal auditor
CDHC	consumer-driven health care		**CIC**	(1) Certified Insurance Counselor (2) change-in-control agreement
CDIC	Canada Deposit Insurance Corporation			
CDO	collateralized debt obligations		**CICA**	Canadian Institute of Chartered Accountants
CD-ROM	compact disc read-only memory		**CIMA**	Certified Investment Management Analyst
CDT	Current Dental Terminology		**CIO**	(1) chief information officer (2) chief investment officer (3) Congress of Industrial Organizations (merged with AFL to form AFL-CIO)
CE	continuing education			
CEA	cost-effectiveness analysis			
CEAP	Certified Employee Assistance Professional			
CEB	Council on Employee Benefits		**CIPM**	Certificate in Investment Performance Measurement
CEBS	Certified Employee Benefit Specialist			
CEIC	Canada Employment Insurance Commission		**CIRB**	Canada Industrial Relations Board
			CLHIA	Canadian Life and Health Insurance Association
CEO	chief executive officer			
CERES	Coalition for Environmentally Responsible Economies		**CLO**	collateralized loan obligation

CLRAM	Construction Labour Relations Association of Manitoba	**CPI**	Consumer Price Index
CLU	Chartered Life Underwriter	**CPP**	Canada Pension Plan
CLUW	Coalition of Labor Union Women (AFL-CIO)	**CPP/QPP**	Canada Pension Plan/Québec Pension Plan
CM	case management	**CPR**	(1) cardiopulmonary resuscitation (2) customary, prevailing and reasonable
CMA	cost-minimization analysis	**CPT**	Current Procedural Terminology
CMB	cash management bill	**CPU**	central processing unit
CMBS	commercial mortgage-backed securities	**CQI**	continuous quality improvement
CMO	collateralized mortgage obligation	**CRA**	Canada Revenue Agency (formerly Canada Customs and Revenue Agency)
CMS	(1) Centers for Medicare and Medicaid Services (2) Compensation Management Specialist	**CRPC**	Chartered Retirement Planning Counselor
		CRPS	Chartered Retirement Plans Specialist
CMV	current market value	**CRT**	(1) cathode ray tube (2) charitable remainder trust
CNM	certified nurse midwife		
COA	cost of illness analysis	**CS**	credited service
COB	coordination of benefits	**CSA**	Canadian Securities Administrators
COBRA	Consolidated Omnibus Budget Reconciliation Act of 1985	**CSO**	(1) chief security officer (2) claims services only
CODA	cash or deferred arrangement	**CSR**	continued stay revenue
COE	center of excellence	**CSRS**	Civil Service Retirement System
COI	(1) certificate of insurance (2) cost of illness analysis	**CT**	computerized axial tomography
		CTD	cumulative trauma disorder
COLA	cost-of-living adjustment	**CTF**	collective trust fund
COLI	corporate-owned life insurance	**CV**	convertible
CON	certificate of need	**DALYs**	disability adjusted life years
CONUS	continental United States	**D&O**	director and officer
COO	chief operating officer	**DAW**	dispense as written
COPD	chronic obstructive pulmonary disease	**DB**	defined benefit
COPE	Committee on Political Education (AFL-CIO)	**d/b/a**	doing business as
CP	commercial paper	**DBP**	defined benefit plan
CPA	Certified Public Accountant	**DC**	(1) deferred compensation (2) defined contribution (3) Doctor of Chiropractic
CPC	Certified Pension Consultant		
CPCU	Chartered Property Casualty Underwriter		
CPDP	Consumer-Purchaser Disclosure Project	**DCA**	(1) dependent care account (2) dependent care assistance
CPE	continuing professional education		

DCAP	(1) dependent care assistance plan (2) dependent care assistance program	**DRO**	domestic relations order
DCFSA	dependent care flexible spending account	**DROP**	deferred retirement option plan
DCI	duplicate coverage inquiry	**DRR**	drug regimen review
DCP	defined contribution plan	**DSM**	disease state management
DCPP	defined contribution pension plan	**DSOs**	dental service organizations
DCRA	dependent care reimbursement account	**DSPP**	direct stock purchase plan
DEFRA	Deficit Reduction Act of 1984	**DTC**	(1) Depository Trust Company (2) direct-to-consumer
DESI	Drug Efficacy Study Implementation	**DUE**	drug use evaluation
DFVCP	Delinquent Filer Voluntary Compliance Program	**DUM**	drug utilization management
DHHS	Department of Health and Human Services	**DUR**	drug utilization review
DHMO	dental health maintenance organization	**DVD**	(1) digital versatile disc (2) digital video disc
DI	(1) disability income (2) disability insurance	**DXL**	diagnostic x-ray and lab
DJIA	Dow Jones Industrial Average	**EA**	Enrolled Actuary
DJTA	Dow Jones Transportation Average	**EAC**	estimated acquisition cost
DM	disease management	**EACA**	eligible automatic contribution arrangement
DME	durable medical equipment	**EAFE**	Europe, AustralAsia, Far East Index
DNA	deoxyribonucleic acid	**E&O**	errors and omissions
DNR	(1) Department of Natural Resources (2) do not renew (3) do not resuscitate	**EAP**	employee assistance program
		EAPA	Employee Assistance Professionals Association
DO	(1) Doctor of Optometry (2) Doctor of Osteopathy	**EBC**	equity-based compensation
		EBIT	earnings before interest and taxes
DOB	date of birth	**EBITDA**	earnings before interest, taxes, depreciation and amortization
DOL	Department of Labor		
DOT	(1) Department of Transportation (2) Dictionary of Occupational Titles	**EBRI**	Employee Benefit Research Institute
		EBSA	Employee Benefits Security Administration (formerly Pension and Welfare Benefits Administration)
DP	direct price		
DPO	dental plan organization	**EC**	European Community (formerly the European Economic Community)
DPSP	deferred profit-sharing plan		
DR	direct reimbursement	**ECA**	eligible automatic contribution arrangement
DRG	diagnosis related grouping	**ECF**	extended care facility
DRIP	dividend reinvestment plan	**e-CFR**	Electronic Code of Federal Regulations
		ECI	employment cost index

ED	(Department of) Education	EPEO	employee plans and exempt organizations
EDGAR	Electronic Data Gathering, Analysis, and Retrieval system	ePHI	electronic protected health information
EDI	electronic data interchange	EPO	exclusive provider organization
EDP	electronic data processing	EPR	electronic patient record
EDR	European Depositary Receipt	EPS	earnings per share
EEC	European Economic Community (former name for European Community)	EPSDT	early and periodic screening, diagnosis and treatment
EEG	electroencephalogram	EPSP	employee profit-sharing plan
EEO	equal employment opportunity	EPTA	Employee Plans Team Audit
EEOC	Equal Employment Opportunity Commission	ERA	Equal Rights Amendment
EFAP	(1) Emergency Food Assistance Program (2) employee and family assistance program	ERIC	ERISA Industry Committee
		ERIP	early retirement incentive program
EFAST	ERISA Filing Acceptance System	ERISA	Employee Retirement Income Security Act of 1974
EGTRRA	Economic Growth and Tax Relief Reconciliation Act of 2001	ERPA	Enrolled Retirement Plan Agent
EGWP	employer group waiver plan	ERR	expected rate of return
EHC	extended health care	ERTA	Economic Recovery Tax Act of 1981
EI	Employment Insurance	ESA	(1) Coverdell Education Savings Account (2) Employment Standards Administration
EIN	Employer Identification Number		
EITC	earned income tax credit	ESG	environmental, social and governance
EITF	Emerging Issues Task Force	ESOP	(1) employee stock option plan (2) employee stock ownership plan
EKG	electrocardiogram		
ELOS	estimated length of stay	ESOT	employee stock ownership trust
EMH	efficient market hypothesis	ESPP	employee stock purchase plan
EMS	emergency medical device	ESS	employee self-service
EMU	European Monetary Union	ESRD	end-stage renal disease
ENT	ear, nose and throat	ESRP	Employer Shared Responsibility Payment
EOB	explanation of benefits	ETA	Employment and Training Administration
EOE	equal opportunity employer	ETF	exchange-traded fund
EP	earned premium	ETI	economically targeted investment
EPA	(1) Environmental Protection Agency (2) Equal Pay Act of 1963	EU	European Union
		EVA	economic value added
EPCRS	Employee Plans Compliance Resolution System	EWL	employer withdrawal liability
		FAF	Financial Accounting Foundation

FAMC	Federal Agricultural Mortgage Corporation (Farmer Mac)	**FOMC**	Federal Open Market Committee
FAQ	frequently asked questions	**FQHC**	federally qualified health center
FAS	Financial Accounting Standard	**FR**	Federal Register
FASB	Financial Accounting Standards Board	**FS**	financial statement
FAVC	freestanding additional voluntary contributions	**FSA**	(1) Fellow of the Society of Actuaries (2) flexible spending account (3) flexible spending arrangement (4) funding standard account
FCIC	Federal Citizen Information Center		
FCRA	Fair Credit Reporting Act	**FSCO**	Financial Service Commission of Ontario
FDA	Food and Drug Administration	**FSLIC**	Federal Savings and Loan Insurance Corporation (abolished in 1989)
FDIC	Federal Deposit Insurance Corporation		
FEDVIP	Federal Employees Dental and Vision Insurance Program	**FSPA**	Fellow, Society of Pension Actuaries
		FTC	Federal Trade Commission
FEGLI	Federal Employees' Group Life Insurance	**FTE**	full-time equivalent
FEHB	Federal Employees Health Benefits Program	**FTMS**	Foundations of Trust Management Standards (FTMS™)
FEIN	Federal Employer Identification Number	**FUL**	federal upper limit
FERS	Federal Employees Retirement System	**FUTA**	Federal Unemployment Tax Act
FFS	fee for service	**FY**	fiscal year
FHA	Federal Housing Administration	**FYB**	fiscal year budget
FHLB	Federal Home Loan Bank	**GAAP**	Generally Accepted Accounting Principles
FHLBB	Federal Home Loan Bank Board	**GAAS**	Generally Accepted Auditing Standards
FHLMC	Federal Home Loan Mortgage Corporation (Freddie Mac)	**GAINS**	Guaranteed Annual Income System
FI	fiscal intermediary	**GAO**	Government Accountability Office
FICA	Federal Insurance Contributions Act	**GASB**	Governmental Accounting Standards Board
FINRA	Financial Industry Regulatory Authority	**GATT**	General Agreement on Tariffs and Trade
FIP	funding improvement plan	**GAW**	guaranteed annual wage
FLMI	Fellow, Life Management Institute	**GBA**	Group Benefits Associate
FLSA	Fair Labor Standards Act	**GDP**	gross domestic product
FMLA	Family and Medical Leave Act of 1993	**GDR**	Global Depositary Receipt
FMV	fair market value	**GDS**	Global Depositary Share
FNMA	Federal National Mortgage Association (Fannie Mae)	**GFOA**	Government Finance Officers Association
FOF	fund of funds	**GIC**	(1) Guaranteed Investment Certificate (2) guaranteed investment contract
FOIA	Freedom of Information Act		

GINA	Genetic Information Nondiscrimination Act of 2008	**HEW**	(Department of) Health, Education, and Welfare (now split into HHS and ED)
GIS	Guaranteed Income Supplement	**HHA**	home health agency
GLS	group legal services	**HHC**	home health care
GLSO	group legal services organization	**HHS**	(Department of) Health and Human Services
GNMA	Government National Mortgage Association (Ginnie Mae)	**HI**	(1) health insurance (2) hospital insurance
GNP	gross national product	**HIAA**	Health Insurance Association of America
GO	general obligation	**HIP**	health incentive plan
GOCO	government-owned contractor-operated	**HIPAA**	Health Insurance Portability and Accountability Act of 1996
GPM	graduated payment mortgage	**HIPC**	(1) health insurance purchasing coalition (2) health insurance purchasing cooperative
GPO	(1) Government Printing Office (2) guaranteed purchase option	**HIT**	health information technology
GRP	Global Remuneration Professional	**HITECH**	Health Information Technology for Economic and Clinical Health Act of 2009
GSRA	Government-Sponsored Retirement Arrangement	**HIV**	human immunodeficiency virus
GST	Goods and Services Tax	**HMO**	health maintenance organization
GULP	group universal life plan	**HPA**	Hospital-Physician Alliance
GUST	GATT, USERRA, SBJPA and TRA	**HPID**	Health Plan Identifier
HBP	Home Buyers' Plan	**HPO**	hospital-physician organization
HCA	health care account	**HPPC**	health plan purchasing cooperative
HCE	highly compensated employee	**HQA**	Hospital Quality Alliance
HCFA	Health Care Financing Administration	**HR**	human resources
HCO	health care organization	**HRA**	(1) health reimbursement arrangement (2) health risk appraisal (3) health risk assessment
HCPA	health care power of attorney		
HCPCS	HCFA Common Procedural Coding System		
HCSA	health care spending account	**HRD**	human resources development
HCTC	health coverage tax credit	**HRIS**	human resource information system
HDHP	high-deductible health plan	**HRR**	hospital referral region
HEART	Heroes Earnings Assistance and Relief Tax Act of 2008	**HRSDC**	human resources and skills development
		HSA	(1) health savings account (2) health spending account (3) hospital service area
HEDIS	Healthcare Effectiveness Data and Information Set		
HERO	Heroes Earned Retirement Opportunities Act	**HSC**	Center for Studying Health System Change
		HSID	high self-insurance deductible

HSOP	health stock ownership plan	**IPG**	immediate participation guarantee
HST	harmonized sales tax	**IPIP**	Improving Performance in Practice
HUD	(Department of) Housing and Urban Development	**IPO**	initial public offering
		IPP	individual pension plan
IB	interpretive bulletin	**IRA**	individual retirement account
IBA	International Bar Association	**IRB**	Internal Revenue Bulletin
IBNR	incurred but not reported	**IRC**	Internal Revenue Code
ICD-10	International Classification of Diseases and Related Health Problems	**IRR**	internal rate of return
		IRRA	IRS Restructuring and Reform Act of 1998
ICF	intermediate care facility	**IRS**	Internal Revenue Service
ICIC	Improving Chronic Illness Care	**ISCEBS**	International Society of Certified Employee Benefit Specialists
ICM	individual case management		
ICU	intensive care unit	**ISE**	International Securities Exchange
IDM	integrated disability management	**ISO**	(1) incentive stock option (2) Insurance Services Office, Inc. (3) International Organization for Standardization
IDN	integrated delivery network		
IDR	International Depositary Receipt		
IDS	integrated delivery system	**ISOP**	investment stock option plan
IFEBP	International Foundation of Employee Benefit Plans	**ITC**	investment tax credit
		IUC	incurred but unreported claims
IFIC	Investment Funds Institute of Canada	**IVR**	interactive voice response (system)
IHI	Institute for Healthcare Improvement	**J&S**	joint and survivor (annuity)
IHM	integrated health management	**JATC**	joint apprenticeship and training committee
IIROC	Investment Industry Regulatory Organization of Canada	**JCWAA**	Job Creation and Workers Assistance Act of 2002
ILP	independent living program	**JIT**	just-in-time (system)
IME	independent medical examination	**JOBS**	Job Opportunities and Basic Skills Training
IMF	International Monetary Fund	**JSOA**	joint and survivor option annuity
IO	investment only	**JSPP**	Jointly Sponsored Pension Plans
IOM	Institute of Medicine	**JV**	joint venture
IOMA	Institute of Management Administration	**KBS**	knowledge-based system
IP	(1) inpatient (2) integrated provider	**KLN**	key local national
		KMS	knowledge management system
IPA	(1) independent physician association (2) independent practice association (3) individual practice association	**KSOP**	401(k) employee stock option plan
		LAN	local area network

LBO	leveraged buyout	**MC**	managed care
LCN	local country national	**MCC**	Minimum Creditable Coverage
LDI	liability-driven investment	**MCCA**	Medicare Catastrophic Coverage Act
LEAT	least expensive alternative treatment	**MCM**	medical case management
LEPAAT	least expensive professionally acceptable alternative treatment	**MCO**	managed care organization
LESOP	leveraged employee stock ownership plan	**MCP**	managed care plan
		MD	Doctor of Medicine
LIF	Life Income Fund	**MDC**	major diagnostic categories
LIHEAP	Low-Income Home Energy Assistance Program	**MDIB**	minimum distribution incidental benefit
LIRA	Locked-In Retirement Account	**MEPP**	multi-employer pension plan
LLC	limited liability corporation	**MET**	multiple employer trust
LLP	lifelong learning plan	**MEWA**	multiple employer welfare arrangement
LMCC	Labor-Management Cooperation Committee	**MFB**	maximum family benefit
LMRA	Labor-Management Relations Act of 1947 (Taft-Hartley Act)	**MFN**	most favored nation
		MGIC	Mortgage Guaranty Insurance Corporation
LMRDA	Labor-Management Reporting and Disclosure Act of 1959 (Landrum-Griffin Act)	**MH/CD**	mental health/chemical dependency
		MHPA	Mental Health Parity Act of 1995
LMS	learning management system	**MH/SA**	mental health/substance abuse
LOC	letter of credit	**MI**	medically indigent
LOS	length of stay	**MIA**	medically indigent adult
LRSP	Locked-In Retirement Savings Plan	**MIB**	Medical Information Bureau
LSE	London Stock Exchange	**MIS**	management information system
LTC	long-term care	**MIT**	modern investment theory
LTD	long-term disability	**MLR**	(1) medical loss ratio (2) multiple location risk
LTIP	long-term incentive plan		
LWO	living wage ordinance	**MMA**	Medicare Prescription Drug, Improvement, and Modernization Act of 2003
M&A	mergers and acquisitions		
MAAC	maximum allowable actual charge	**MNC**	(1) multinational company (2) multinational corporation
MAC	maximum allowable cost		
MAGI	modified adjusted gross income	**MOB**	maintenance of benefits
MBHO	managed behavioral healthcare organization	**MOE**	maintenance of effort
		MPP	minimum premium plan
MBO	management by objectives	**MPPAA**	Multiemployer Pension Plan Amendments Act of 1980
MBS	mortgage-backed security		

MPT	modern portfolio theory	NFA	National Futures Association
MRI	magnetic resonance imaging	NFPO	not-for-profit organization
MSA	medical savings account	NGO	non-governmental organization
MSDS	Material Safety Data Sheets	NHCAA	National Health Care Anti-Fraud Association
MSO	management services organization	NHCE	non-highly compensated employee
MSP	Medicare secondary payer	NHIC	National Health Information Center
MSPA	Member, Society of Pension Actuaries	NHPC	National Health Plan Collaborative
MTM	medication therapy management	NI	net income
MJPP	multi-jurisdictional pension plan	NIH	National Institutes of Health
NA	not applicable	NIMH	National Institute of Mental Health
NABP	National Association of Boards of Pharmacy	NIOSH	National Institute for Occupational Safety and Health
NAFTA	North American Free Trade Agreement	NLRA	National Labor Relations Act of 1935 (Wagner Act)
NAIC	National Association of Insurance Commissioners	NLRB	National Labor Relations Board
NAICS	North American Industry Classification System	NMB	National Mediation Board
NASDAQ	National Association of Securities Dealers Automatic Quotations	NOC	National Occupation Classification
NASRA	National Association of State Retirement Administrators	NOW	negotiable order of withdrawal
		NP	nurse practitioner
NAV	net asset value	NPI	national provider identifier
NBER	National Bureau of Economic Research	NPO	nonprofit organization
NBU	nonbargaining unit	NPV	net present value
NCCI	National Council on Compensation Insurance	NQA	National Quality Award
NCD	negotiable certificate of deposit	NQDC	nonqualified deferred compensation
NCPDP	National Council on Prescription Drug Programs	NQF	National Quality Forum
NCQA	National Committee for Quality Assurance	NQSO	nonqualified stock option
NCREIF	National Council of Real Estate Investment Fiduciaries	NRA	normal retirement age
		NRD	normal retirement date
NCS	(1) National Compensation Survey (2) noncovered service	NSF	non-sufficient funds
		NTI	narrow therapeutic index
NDAA	National Defense Authorization Act for Fiscal Year 2008	NW	net worth
		NYSE	New York Stock Exchange
NDC	National Drug Code	OAA	old age assistance
NDCP	nonqualified deferred compensation plan		

OAS	Old Age Security	**PA**	(1) pension adjustment
OASDHI	Old-Age, Survivors, Disability and Health Insurance		(2) performance appraisal
			(3) physician's assistant
			(4) prior approval
OBRA	Omnibus Budget Reconciliation Act		(5) prior authorization
OCC	(1) Office of the Comptroller of Currency	**P/A**	power of attorney
	(2) Options Clearing Corporation	**PADRO**	plan-approved domestic relations order
OCONUS	outside the continental United States	**P&L**	profit and loss statement
OD	(1) occupational disease	**PAP**	patient assistance program
	(2) organizational development	**PAR**	pension adjustment reversal
OECD	Organisation for Economic Co-operation and Development	**PARC**	Program for Assessment of Regulatory Compliance
OEM	original equipment manufacturer	**PARCA**	Patient Access to Responsible Care Act of 1997
OEO	Office of Economic Opportunity	**P&T**	pharmacy and therapeutics
OFCCP	Office of Federal Contract Compliance Programs	**PAT**	preadmission testing
		PAYG	pay as you go
OJT	on-the-job training	**PAYSOP**	(1) payroll-based stock option plan
OLMS	Office of Labor-Management Standards		(2) payroll-based stock ownership plan
OMB	Office of Management and Budget	**P/B**	price to book
OMO	open market operations	**PBA**	principal business activities
OOA	out of area	**PBGC**	Pension Benefit Guaranty Corporation
OP	outpatient	**PBM**	(1) pharmacy benefits management
OPEB	other postemployment benefits		(2) pharmacy benefits manager
OPM	Office of Personnel Management	**PBO**	projected benefit obligation
OR	(1) operating room	**PBSA**	Pension Benefits Standards Act
	(2) operations research	**PC**	(1) participation certificate
OSFI	Office of the Superintendent of Financial Institutions		(2) personal computer
			(3) politically correct
			(4) professional corporation
OSHA	(1) Occupational Safety and Health Act	**PCMA**	Pharmaceutical Care Management Association
	(2) Occupational Safety and Health Administration	**PCMH**	patient-centered medical home
OT	occupational therapy	**PCN**	(1) primary care network
OTC	over the counter		(2) primary care nurse
OTS	Office of Thrift Supervision	**PCO**	Pension Commission of Ontario
OWBPA	Older Workers Benefit Protection Act of 1990	**PCORI**	Patient-Centered Outcomes Research Institute
OWCP	Office of Workers' Compensation Programs	**PCP**	primary care physician
		PDA	Pregnancy Discrimination Act of 1978

PDL	preferred drug list	**PMPM**	per member per month
PDP	prescription drug plan	**POP**	premium-only plan
P/E	price/earnings	**PORC**	producer-owned reinsurance company
PEBES	Personal Earnings and Benefit Estimate Statement	**POS**	(1) point of sale (2) point of service
PEO	professional employer organization	**PPA**	Pension Protection Act of 2006
PEP	pension equity plan	**PPACA**	Patient Protection and Affordable Care Act of 2010
PEPPRA	Public Employee Pension Plan Reporting and Accountability Act of 1984	**PPD**	permanent partial disability
PERS	public employee retirement system	**PPO**	preferred provider organization
PET	positron emission tomography	**PPP**	personal pension plan
PFEA	Pension Funding Equity Act of 2004	**PPS**	(1) personal pension scheme (UK) (2) prospective payment schedule/system
PFK	pay for knowledge	**PR**	pro rata
PFS	Personal Financial Specialist	**PRD**	pro-rata distribution
PHD	Doctor of Philosophy	**PRI**	Principles for Responsible Investment
PHI	protected health information	**PRO**	peer review organization
PHO	physician-hospital organization	**PSAO**	pharmacy services administrative organization
PHR	(1) personal health record (2) Professional in Human Resources	**PSC**	personal service corporation
PhRMA	Pharmaceutical Research and Manufacturers of America	**PSO**	provider-sponsored organization
PHS	public health service	**PSP**	performance share plan
PHSP	private health services plan	**PSPA**	past service pension adjustment
PI	personal injury	**PSRO**	professional standards review organization
PIA	primary insurance amount	**PST**	provincial sales tax
PIAC	Pension Investment Association of Canada	**PT**	(1) physical therapy (2) prohibited transaction
PIH	Public and Indian Housing	**PTCE**	prohibited transaction class exemption
PIN	personal identification number	**PTD**	permanent and total disability
PIPEDA	Personal Information Protection and Electronic Documents Act	**PTE**	prohibited transaction exemption
PL	(1) public law (2) public liability	**PTO**	paid time off
		PTMPY	per thousand members per year
PLI	professional liability insurance	**PWA**	person with AIDS
PLR	private letter ruling	**PWBA**	Pension and Welfare Benefits Administration (former name for Employee Benefits Security Administration)
PMI	private mortgage insurance		

Acronyms and Abbreviations

QA	(1) quality assessment (2) quality assurance		**RBD**	required beginning date
QACA	qualified automatic contribution arrangement		**RBRVS**	resource-based relative value scale
QALY	quality adjusted life year		**RCA**	retirement compensation arrangement
QASC	Quality Alliance Steering Committee		**RDSP**	registered disability savings plan
QBU	qualified business unit		**REA**	Retirement Equity Act of 1984
QC	(1) quality control (2) quarters of coverage		**REIT**	real estate investment trust
			REMIC	real estate mortgage investment conduits
QDEC	qualified deductible employee contribution		**REOC**	real estate operating company
QDIA	qualified default investment alternative		**RESP**	Registered Education Savings Plan
QDOT	qualified domestic trust		**RESPA**	Real Estate Settlement Procedures Act of 1974
QDRO	qualified domestic relations order		**RFI**	request for information
QJA	quantitative job analysis		**RFP**	(1) Registered Financial Planner (2) request for proposal
QJSA	qualified joint and survivor annuity			
QKA	Qualified 401(k) Administrator		**RHOSP**	Registered Home Ownership Savings Plan
QMAC	qualified matching contribution		**RHS**	Rural Housing Service
QMB	qualified Medicare beneficiary		**RIA**	registered investment advisor
QMCSO	qualified medical child support order		**RICO**	Racketeer Influenced Corrupt Organizations Act of 1971
QNC	qualified nonelective contribution		**RIF**	reduction in force
QNEC	qualified nonelective contribution		**RIPA**	Retirement Income Policy Act of 1985
QOSA	qualified optional survivor annuity		**RLR**	retired lives reserves
QPA	Qualified Pension Administrator		**RMA**	retiree medical account
QPAM	Qualified Professional Asset Manager		**RMBS**	reverse mortgage-backed securities
QPFC	Qualified Plan Financial Consultant		**RMD**	required minimum distribution
QPP	Québec Pension Plan		**ROBS**	Rollovers for Business Start-Ups
QPSA	qualified preretirement survivor annuity		**ROE**	return on equity
QSLOB	qualified separate line of business		**ROI**	(1) release of information (2) return on investment
QTD	qualified total distribution		**ROM**	range of motion
QTIP	Qualified Terminable Interest Property (Trust)		**RONW**	return on net worth
RAA	retained asset account		**ROR**	rate of return
RAN	revenue anticipation note		**ROS**	review of systems
R&C	reasonable and customary		**RP**	repurchase agreement
RBP	reference-based pricing			

RPA	(1) Retirement Protection Act of 1994 (2) Retirement Plans Associate	SERP	(1) supplemental employee retirement plan (2) supplemental executive retirement plan
RPh	Registered Pharmacist	SERPS	state earnings-related pension scheme
RPP	Registered Pension Plan	SFAS	Statement of Financial Accounting Standards
RRB	real return bond	SHARE	Shareholder Association for Research and Education
RRG	risk retention group		
RRIF	Registered Retirement Income Fund	S/HMO	social/health maintenance organization
RRM	renegotiable rate mortgage	SHOP	Small Business Health Options Program
RRSP	Registered Retirement Savings Plan	SHRM	Society of Human Resource Management (now the American Society for Personnel Administration)
RSI	(1) repetitive strain injury (2) repetitive stress injury		
RTC	residential treatment center	SIIA	Self-Insurance Institute of America
RTK	right to know	SIMPLE	Savings Incentive Match Plan for Employees
RVS	relative value scale	SIP&P	statement of investment policies and procedures
R/W	returned to work		
S&P	Standard & Poor's	SIPC	Securities Investor Protection Corporation
SAR	(1) stock appreciation right (2) summary annual report	SLFI	selected listed financial institution
		SLMA	Student Loan Marketing Association (Sallie Mae)
SARSEP	Salary Reduction Simplified Employee Pension Plan		
		SLOB	separate line of business
SAVER	Savings Are Vital to Everyone's Retirement Act of 1997	SMA	separately managed account
		SME	subject matter expert
SBA	Small Business Administration	SMEPP	specified Ontario multi-employer pension plans
SBC	summary of benefits and coverage		
SBJPA	Small Business Job Protection Act of 1996	SMI	(1) serious mental illness (2) supplementary medical insurance
SCHIP	State Children's Health Insurance Program	SMM	summary of material modifications
SCP	Self-Correction Program	SNF	skilled nursing facility
SDA	salary deferral arrangement	SNP	special needs plan
SDBA	self-directed brokerage account	SOA	Society of Actuaries
SDI	state disability insurance	SOP	standard operating procedure
SEC	Securities and Exchange Commission	SOX	Sarbanes-Oxley Act of 2002
SEP	simplified employee pension (plan)	SPD	summary plan description
SEPPAA	Single Employer Pension Plan Amendments Act of 1986	SPDA	single premium deferred annuity
		SPHR	Senior Professional in Human Resources
		SRI	socially responsible investing

SRO	self-regulatory organization	**TMP**	Trustees Masters Program
SSA	(1) Social Security Act of 1935 (2) Social Security Administration	**TMWX**	Wilshire 5000 Total Market Index
		TPA	third-party administrator
SSDI	Social Security Disability Insurance	**TQM**	total quality management
SSI	Supplemental Security Income	**TRA**	(1) Tax Reform Acts 1984, 1986 (2) Taxpayer Relief Act of 1997
SSN	Social Security Number		
SSOP	second surgical opinion program	**TRASOP**	Tax Reduction Act Stock Ownership Plan
SSRA	Social Security retirement age	**TRS**	teacher retirement system
STD	(1) sexually transmitted disease (2) short-term disability	**TSA**	tax-sheltered annuity
		TSP	thrift savings plan
STI	short-term incentive	**TSX**	Toronto Stock Exchange
STIF	short-term investment fund	**TWB**	taxable wage base
SUB	supplemental unemployment benefit	**UAAL**	unfunded actuarial accrued liability
SUTA	State Unemployment Tax Act	**U&C**	usual and customary
TAA	trade adjustment assistant	**UAW**	United Automobile Workers
TAB	tax anticipation bill	**UBTI**	unrelated business taxable income
TAMRA	Technical and Miscellaneous Revenue Act of 1988	**UC**	unemployment compensation
		UCC	Uniform Commercial Code
TBP	target benefit plan	**UCCC**	Uniform Consumer Credit Code
TCN	third-country national	**UCD**	unemployment compensation disability
TDA	tax-deferred annuity	**UCFE**	Unemployment Compensation for Federal Employees
TDB	temporary disability benefits		
TDD/TTY	telecommunications device for the deaf/teletypewriter	**UCI**	unemployment compensation insurance
		UCR	usual, customary and reasonable
TDF	target-date fund	**UCX**	Unemployment Compensation for Ex-service members
TDI	temporary disability insurance		
TE	tax equivalent	**UGMA**	Uniform Gifts to Minors Act
TEFRA	Tax Equity and Fiscal Responsibility Act	**UI**	unemployment insurance
TFSA	tax-free savings account	**UIT**	unit investment trust
TG	transgender	**UM**	utilization management
TI	terminal illness	**UMPERSA**	Uniform Management of Public Employee Retirement Systems Act
TIN	Taxpayer Identification Number		
TIPRA	Tax Increase Prevention and Reconciliation Act of 2005	**UPIA**	Uniform Prudent Investors Act
		UPIN	unique physician identifier number
TIPS	Treasury inflation-protected securities		

Acronym	Definition
UPP	uniform pension plan
UR	utilization review
URAC	Utilization Review Accreditation Commission
URL	uniform resource locator
URO	utilization review organization
U.S.C.	United States Code
USERRA	Uniformed Services Employment and Reemployment Rights Act of 1994
USWA	United Steelworkers of America
UTMA	Uniform Transfers to Minors Act
UTU	United Transportation Union
UVB	unfunded vested benefits
UVL	unfunded vested liability
VA	(Department of) Veterans Affairs
VAT	value-added tax
VBO	vested benefit obligation
VCP	Voluntary Correction Program
VCR	(1) variable coupon renewable note (2) voluntary compliance resolution program
VEBA	voluntary employees' beneficiary association
VFCP	Voluntary Fiduciary Compliance Program
VIPPS	Verified Internet Pharmacy Provider Sites™
VNA	Visiting Nurse Association
VRM	variable rate mortgage
VUL	variable universal life insurance
W-2	Wage and Tax Statement
WAC	wholesale acquisition cost
WARN	Worker Adjustment and Retraining Notification Act
WBA	weekly benefit amount
WC	workers' compensation
WEDI	Workgroup for Electronic Data Interchange
WELCOA	Wellness Councils of America
WFTRA	Working Families Tax Relief Act of 2004
WHCRA	Women's Health and Cancer Rights Act of 1998
WHD	Wage and Hour Division
WHEA	Women's Health Equity Act of 1990
WHO	World Health Organization
WPM	words per minute
WPPDA	Welfare and Pension Plans Disclosure Act
WRERA	Worker, Retiree, and Employer Recovery Act of 2008
WSIA	Workplace Safety and Insurance Act
WSIB	Workplace Safety and Insurance Board
WSJ	Wall Street Journal
WTO	World Trade Organization
WWW	world wide web
XRA	expected retirement age
YBE	year's basic exemption
YMPE	year's maximum pensionable earnings
YTM	yield to maturity
YRT	yearly renewable term
YTD	year to date
YTM	yield to maturity
ZBB	zero-based budget
ZEBRA	zero-balance reimbursement account
ZPG	zero-population growth